WORLD HISTORY Early Ages

INTERACTIVE

SAVVAS
LEARNING COMPANY

To start, download the free **BouncePages** app on your smartphone or tablet. Simply search for the BouncePages app in your mobile app store. The app is available for Android and IOS (iPhone®/iPad®).

Activate your digital course videos directly from the page.

To launch the videos look for this icon.

1. **AIM** the camera so that the page is easily viewable on your screen.
2. **TAP** the screen to scan the page.
3. **BOUNCE** the page to life by clicking the Bounce icon.

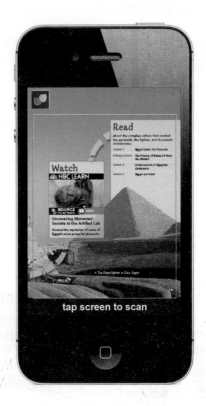

ISBN-13: 978-0-32-896460-4
ISBN-10:   0-32-896460-3
11 20

AUTHORS AND CONSULTANTS

Program Authors

Frank Karpiel

teaches at the Citadel Military College in South Carolina and earned his Ph.D. degree in history from the University of Hawaii. His focus of study is world history and how cross-cultural interactions shape present-day human society.

George F. Sabato

is a Past President of the California Council for the Social Studies.

Michael Yell

is a Past President of the National Council for the Social Studies.

Program Consultants

ELL Consultant
Jim Cummins Ph.D.

Professor Emeritus, Department of Curriculum, Teaching, and Learning
University of Toronto
Toronto, Canada

Differentiated Instruction Consultant
Marianne Sender

In-Class Resource Teacher
Renaissance @ Rand Middle School
Montclair, New Jersey

Reading Consultant
Elfrieda H. Hiebert Ph.D.

Founder, President and CEO of TextProject, Inc.
University of California, Santa Cruz

Inquiry and C3 Consultant
Dr. Kathy Swan

Professor of Curriculum and Instruction
University of Kentucky
Lexington, Kentucky

REVIEWERS

Savvas would like to extend a special thank you to all of the teachers who helped guide the development of this program. We gratefully acknowledge your efforts to realize Next Generation Social Studies teaching and learning that will prepare American students for college, careers, and active citizenship.

Program Reviewers

Warren J. Blumenfeld, Ed.D.
Former Associate Professor, Iowa State University,
    School of Education
South Hadley, Massachusetts

J.P. Dessel
Department of History
University of Tennessee
Knoxville, Tennessee

J. Michael Francis
Department of History
University of North Florida
Jacksonville, Florida

Judy E. Gaughan
Department of History
Colorado State University
Fort Collins, Colorado

Huping Ling
Department of History
Truman State University
Kirksville, Missouri

Gordon Newby
Department of Middle Eastern and South Asian Studies
Emory University
Atlanta, Georgia

Thomas J. Sanders
Department of History
United States Naval Academy
Annapolis, Maryland

David Webster
Department of Anthropology
Pennsylvania State University
University Park, Pennsylvania

Teacher Reviewers

Ruth Castro
Inglewood USD
Inglewood, California

Colleen Eccles
Instructional Coach and PDLT
Samuel Ogle Middle School
Bowie, Maryland

Piper Hudmon
Content Specialist/Secondary Social Studies
Muscogee County School District
Columbus, Georgia

Dana L. Roberts, Ed. S
Academic Coach and Gifted Lead Coordinator
Lindley Middle School
Mableton, Georgia

Anthony Zambelli
San Diego Center for Economic Education
San Diego, California

PROGRAM PARTNERS

NBC Learn, the educational arm of NBC News, develops original stories for use in the classroom and makes archival NBC news stories, images, and primary source documents available on demand to teachers, students, and parents. NBC Learn partnered with Savvas to produce the topic opening videos that support this program.

Campaign for the Civic Mission of Schools is a coalition of over 70 national civic learning, education, civic engagement, and business groups committed to improving the quality and quantity of civic learning in American schools.

Constitutional Rights Foundation is a nonprofit, nonpartisan, community-based organization focused on educating students about the importance of civic participation in a democratic society. The Constitutional Rights Foundation is the lead contributor to the development of the Civic Discussion Quests for this program.

CONTENTS

TOPIC 3
Ancient Egypt and Kush
(3000 BCE–600 BCE)

TOPIC 4
Early Civilizations of India
(3100 BCE–540 CE)

CONTENTS

TOPIC 5
Early Civilizations of China
(1700 BCE–220 CE)

TOPIC 6
Ancient Greece (2000 BCE–300 BCE)

TOPIC 7
The Roman Republic (800 BCE–30 BCE)

CONTENTS

TOPIC 8
The Roman and Byzantine Empires
(30 BCE–1453 CE)

ACCESS MORE ONLINE
videos, audio, etext, interactivities, games, worksheets, and more!

TOPIC 9
Life in Medieval Christendom
(486–1300)

TOPIC 10
Struggle in Medieval Europe
(962–1492)

CONTENTS

TOPIC 11
The Islamic World and South Asia
(610–1550)

TOPIC 12
Civilizations of East Asia and Southeast Asia (250 BCE–1644 CE)

TOPIC 13
Civilizations of the Americas
(Prehistory–1533 CE)

CONTENTS

ACCESS MORE ONLINE
videos, audio, etext, interactivities, games, worksheets, and more!

TOPIC 16
Global Convergence (1415–1763)

DIGITAL RESOURCES

Core Concepts

These digital lessons introduce key concepts for all of the social sciences and personal finance.

Culture
Economics

Geography
Government and Civics

History
Personal Finance

Topic Videos NBC LEARN

Begin each topic with a front seat view of history.

TOPIC 1
Çatalhöyük: Life in an Ancient Settlement

TOPIC 2
The Code of Hammurabi

TOPIC 3
In the Artifact Lab

TOPIC 4
Indian Classical Dance in the Modern World

TOPIC 5
Shi Huangdi, First Emperor of Unified China

TOPIC 6
Pericles and The Golden Age of Athens

TOPIC 7
Cicero and the Roman Republic

TOPIC 8
Augustus and the Pax Romana

TOPIC 9
Women in Medieval Times

TOPIC 10
The Black Death

TOPIC 11
Advances in Medicine

TOPIC 12
Elements of a Culture

TOPIC 13
Farming in Ancient Empires

TOPIC 14
A Keeper of History

TOPIC 15
The Endurance of the Human Character

TOPIC 16
The Conquest of a Golden City

Lesson Videos

Preview key ideas from the lesson in these videos.

TOPIC 1
Lesson 1 How Hunter-Gatherers Lived
Lesson 2 Learning to Live in New Environments
Lesson 3 The Agricultural Revolution
Lesson 4 Effects of the Agricultural Revolution
Lesson 5 What Makes a Civilization?

TOPIC 2
Lesson 1 Adapting to Life in Mesopotamia
Lesson 2 Hammurabi's Code
Lesson 3 The Assyrian and Persian Empires
Lesson 4 The Alphabet
Lesson 5 The Origins of Judaism
Lesson 6 The Central Beliefs of Judaism
Lesson 7 Israel and the Jewish Diaspora

TOPIC 3
Lesson 1 Pharaohs of Ancient Egypt
Lesson 2 The Legacy of Ancient Egypt
Lesson 3 Trade Between Egypt and Kush

TOPIC 4
Lesson 1 Indus Valley Achievements
Lesson 2 The Vedic Age
Lesson 3 Hindu Traditions and Practices
Lesson 4 Teachings and Spread of Buddhism
Lesson 5 Chandraputra Maurya's Rule
Lesson 6 The Life of Asoka
Lesson 7 The Golden Age of the Gupta

TOPIC 5
Lesson 1 The Influence of Geography on China
Lesson 2 The Dynastic Cycle and the Mandate of Heaven

DIGITAL RESOURCES

Interactive Primary Sources

Go to the original sources to hear voices from the time.

TOPIC 2
Lesson 2 Code of Hammurabi
Lesson 7 Psalm 23

TOPIC 4
Lesson 3 *The Bhagavad-Gita*
Lesson 6 Asoka, Edicts

TOPIC 5
Lesson 3 Confucius, *Analects*
Lesson 3 Laozi, *The Dao de Jing*

TOPIC 6
Lesson 5 Herodotus, *The Persian Wars*
Lesson 6 Euripides, *Medea*
Lesson 7 Aristotle, *Politics*
Lesson 7 Plato, *The Republic*

TOPIC 8
Lesson 3 Paul, First Letter to the Corinthians

TOPIC 10
Lesson 2 Magna Carta

TOPIC 11
Lesson 6 Guru Granth Sahib

TOPIC 12
Lesson 6 Murasaki Shikibu, *The Tale of Genji*

TOPIC 13
Lesson 4 The Iroquois Constitution

TOPIC 14
Lesson 3 Ibn Battuta, *Travels*

TOPIC 15
Lesson 1 Machiavelli, *The Prince*
Lesson 2 Dante Alighieri, excerpt from *The Inferno*
Lesson 5 John Calvin, *Institutes of the Christian Religion*
Lesson 6 Francis Bacon, *The New Method*

TOPIC 16
Lesson 2 las Casas, *Destruction of the Indies*
Lesson 6 Mayflower Compact
Lesson 7 Olaudah Equiano, *The Interesting Narrative of the Life of Olaudah Equiano*

Interactive Biographies

Read about the people who made history.

TOPIC 2
Lesson 2 Hammurabi
Lesson 7 David
Lesson 7 Yohan ben Zaccai

TOPIC 4
Lesson 6 Asoka

TOPIC 5
Lesson 3 Confucius
Lesson 4 Shi Huangdi

TOPIC 6
Lesson 7 Hypatia
Lesson 8 Alexander the Great

TOPIC 7
Lesson 4 Julius Caesar

TOPIC 8
Lesson 1 Augustus
Lesson 5 Constantine
Lesson 6 Justinian I

TOPIC 9
Lesson 1 Charlemagne

TOPIC 12
Lesson 2 Ghengis Khan
Lesson 4 Prince Shotoku

TOPIC 15
Lesson 1 Desiderius Erasmus
Lesson 2 Leonardo da Vinci
Lesson 2 Michelangelo
Lesson 2 William Shakespeare
Lesson 4 Martin Luther
Lesson 4 St. Ignatius of Loyola
Lesson 6 Nicholas Copernicus
Lesson 6 Galileo
Lesson 6 Isaac Newton
Lesson 6 Rene Descartes

21st Century Skills

Learn, practice, and apply important skills using these online tutorials.

Analyze Cause and Effect
Analyze Data and Models
Analyze Images
Analyze Media Content
Analyze Political Cartoons
Analyze Primary and Secondary
  Sources
Ask Questions
Avoid Plagiarism
Being an Informed Citizen
Categorize
Compare and Contrast
Compare Viewpoints
Compromise
Consider and Counter Opposing
  Arguments
Create Charts and Maps
Create Databases
Create a Research Hypothesis
Develop a Clear Thesis
Develop Cultural Awareness
Distinguish Between Fact and
  Opinion

Draw Conclusions
Draw Inferences
Evaluate Existing Arguments
Evaluate Web Sites
Generalize
Generate New Ideas
Give an Effective Presentation
Identify Bias
Identify Evidence
Identify Main Ideas and Details
Identify Trends
Innovate
Interpret Sources
Make Decisions
Make a Difference
Make Predictions
Organize Your Ideas
Participate in a Discussion or
  Debate
Paying Taxes
Political Participation
Publish Your Work
Read Charts, Graphs, and Tables

Read Physical Maps
Read Special Purpose Maps
Search for Information on the
  Internet
Sequence
Serving on a Jury
Set a Purpose for Reading
Share Responsibility
Solve Problems
Summarize
Support Ideas With Evidence
Synthesize
Take Effective Notes
Use Content Clues
Use Parts of a Map
Voting
Work in Teams
Write an Essay
Write a Journal Entry

Interactivities

**Explore maps one layer at a time to see how events unfolded over time, go on
a gallery walk to examine artifacts and primary sources, analyze data, and explore
key historical sites and objects in 3-D!**

INTERACTIVE MAPS

Fossil Finds in Africa Topic 1 Topic Map
Migrations of *Homo sapiens* Topic 1 Lesson 2
River Valley Civilizations Topic 1 Lesson 5
Early Civilizations of the Fertile Crescent Topic 2
  Topic Map
Sumer and the Fertile Crescent Topic 2 Lesson 1
Assyrian and Persian Empires Topic 2 Lesson 3
The Exodus in Jewish Tradition Topic 2 Lesson 5
The Ancient Nile Valley Topic 3 Topic Map
Indian Subcontinent: Physical Features Topic 4
  Topic Map
The Origins and Spread of Buddhism Topic 4 Lesson 4
Geography of China Topic 5 Topic Map
Ancient Chinese Dynasties Topic 5 Lesson 5
Geography of Ancient Greece Topic 6 Topic Map
The Journey of Odysseus Topic 6 Lesson 1

Expansion and Trade in the Greek World Topic 6
  Lesson 4
Persian Wars, 490 BCE–479 BCE Topic 6 Lesson 5
The Developing Roman Republic Topic 7 Topic Map
Growth of the Roman Republic, 500 BCE to 44 BCE
  Topic 7 Lesson 1
The Roman World Topic 8 Topic Map
Invasions of the Roman Empire Topic 8 Lesson 5
The Byzantine Empire Topic 8 Lesson 6
Medieval Christendom Topic 9 Topic Map
Europe Before and After the Fall of Rome Topic 9
  Lesson 1
Invasions of Europe, 700–1000 Topic 9 Lesson 3
Cities of Medieval Christendom Topic 10 Topic Map
The Black Death Topic 10 Lesson 5
Locations of Muslim Empires and Dynasties Topic 11
  Topic Map

Interactivities (continued)

Spread of Islam Topic 11 Lesson 3
Dynasties and Empires in South Asia Topic 11
Lesson 5
Geography of East Asia Topic 12 Topic Map
The Mongol Empire Topic 12 Lesson 2
Geography of Japan Topic 12 Lesson 4
Mesoamerican and South American Geography and
Empires Topic 13 Topic Map
Growth of the Inca Empire Topic 13 Lesson 3
Native American Architecture Topic 13 Lesson 4
Trans-Saharan Trade Topic 14 Topic Map
Africa's Vegetation Regions Topic 14 Lesson 1
Europe During the Renaissance and the Reformation
Topic 15 Topic Map
Renaissance Italy's City-States Topic 15 Lesson 1
Major European Religions About 1600 Topic 15
Lesson 5
European Powers and Their Colonial Claims,
1500s–1700 Topic 16 Topic Map
Trade Among Europe, Africa, and Asia Topic 16
Lesson 5
Triangular Trade Routes Topic 16 Lesson 7

INTERACTIVE CHARTS

Akkadian and Babylonian Empires Topic 2 Lesson 2
Technology of the Indus Civilization Topic 4 Lesson 1
Confucianism and Daoism Topic 5 Lesson 3
Greek Philosophers Topic 6 Lesson 7
Comparing Characteristics of Manor Life and Town
Life Topic 9 Lesson 4
Feudal Society in Japan Topic 12 Lesson 5
Comparing Ghana, Mali, Songhai Topic 14 Lesson 2
Causes and Effects of Spanish Colonization Topic 16
Lesson 3

INTERACTIVE GALLERIES

Piecing the Past Together Topic 1 Lesson 1
Paleolithic Cave Art Topic 1 Lesson 3
Otzi, the Neolithic Ice Man Topic 1 Lesson 4
Significance of Major Jewish Holidays Topic 2
Lesson 6
Origins of Judaism Topic 2 Lesson 7
Egyptian Religion Topic 3 Lesson 1
Village Life in India Topic 4 Lesson 5
The Gupta Empire Topic 4 Lesson 7
Chinese Writing Topic 5 Lesson 1
Terra Cotta Army of Shi Huangdi Topic 5 Lesson 4
Silk Making in Ancient China Topic 5 Lesson 6
Athenian Democracy Topic 6 Lesson 2
Art and Architecture of Ancient Greece Topic 6
Lesson 6

Alexander the Great's Conquests and Contributions
Topic 6 Lesson 8
Who Was Julius Caesar? Topic 7 Lesson 4
Early Christian Symbols Topic 8 Lesson 2
Christianity Today Topic 8 Lesson 3
Hagia Sophia Topic 8 Lesson 7
The Gothic Cathedral Topic 9 Lesson 5
The Papacy in the Middle Ages Topic 10 Lesson 1
Muslim Spain Topic 10 Lesson 4
Geography of the Arabian Peninsula Topic 11 Lesson 1
The Five Pillars of Islam Topic 11 Lesson 2
Arts of Tang China Topic 12 Lesson 3
Japanese Art and Theater Topic 12 Lesson 6
Mayan Learning Topic 13 Lesson 1
Architecture of the African Kingdoms Topic 14
Lesson 3
Religious Traditions of Africa Topic 14 Lesson 4
Realism in Northern European Renaissance Art
Topic 15 Lesson 2
The Printing Press Topic 15 Lesson 3
Brazil: Portuguese Exploration and Colonization
Topic 16 Lesson 4

INTERACTIVE TIMELINES

Development of the Modern Latin Alphabet Topic 2
Lesson 4
Asoka's Life Topic 4 Lesson 6
Roman Rulers Who Made History Topic 8 Lesson 1
Key Events in Medieval English History Topic 10
Lesson 2
The Reformation and Counter-Reformation Topic 15
Lesson 4
Spanish Exploration and Conquest of the Americas
Topic 16 Lesson 2

INTERACTIVE ILLUSTRATIONS

Vedic Era Gods Topic 4 Lesson 2
The Dynastic Cycle Topic 5 Lesson 2
Comparing Sparta and Athens Topic 6 Lesson 3

INTERACTIVE 3D MODELS

Egyptian Pyramids Topic 3 Lesson 2
Hindu Temple Topic 4 Lesson 3
Roman Villa Topic 7 Lesson 3
Pantheon Topic 8 Lesson 4
Medieval Monastery Topic 9 Lesson 2
The Dome of the Rock Topic 11 Lesson 4
Angkor Wat Topic 12 Lesson 7
Aztec Temple Topic 13 Lesson 3
The Heliocentric Universe Topic 15 Lesson 6
Explorer's Ship Topic 16 Lesson 1

INTERACTIVE SIMULATIONS
Ancient Egypt and Kush Topic 3 Lesson 3
The Roman Republic Topic 7 Lesson 2
Conflicts and Crusades Topic 10 Lesson 3
China in the Middle Ages Topic 12 Lesson 1
Building a Colony Topic 16 Lesson 6

Maps

SPECIAL FEATURES

All of these resources are found right here in your student textbook.

Ask questions, explore sources, and cite evidence to support your view!

Primary Sources

Excerpts from original sources allow you to witness history.

Primary Source Quotations

Quotations in the text bring history to life.

SPECIAL FEATURES

All of these resources are found right here in your student textbook.

Primary Source Quotations (continued)

Analysis Skills

Practice key skills.

SPECIAL FEATURES

All of these resources are found right here in your student textbook.

Biographies

Read about the people who made history.

Charts, Graphs, Tables, and Infographics

Find these charts, graphs, and tables in your text. It's all about the data!

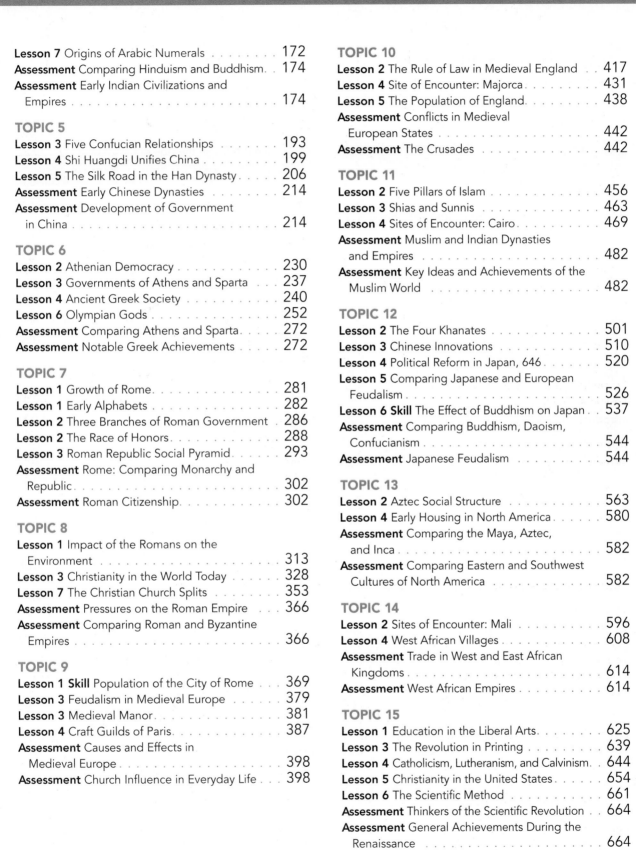

SPECIAL FEATURES

Charts, Graphs, Tables, and Infographics (continued)

Timelines

When did this happen? Find out with these timelines.

Maps

Where did this happen? Find out with these maps.

Maps (continued)

ENGLISH-LANGUAGE ARTS HANDBOOK

As you explore world history in this course, you will read informational texts and primary sources. For this course and in other courses and beyond, you will need to think critically about the texts you read to absorb information and be able to express your thoughts about world events, past and present. You will need to communicate your ideas through writing (summaries, arguments, informative essays, and narratives), speaking (debates and one-on-one and small group discussions), and by giving presentations.

This Handbook will give you some tools for reading critically and expressing your ideas. The Quests and other activities in this program give you opportunities to write and speak about your ideas and create projects that will help you practice these skills.

▶ INTERACTIVE

The 21st Century Skills Tutorials, found on Realize, support many of the skills discussed here. Go online to find a Quick Reference, video of the skill being modeled, and more.

READING

Analyze Informational Text

Reading nonfiction texts, like a magazine article or your textbook, is not the same as reading a fictional story or novel. The purpose of reading nonfiction is to acquire new information. It's something that you, and the adults around you, do all the time.

Process What You Read When you read informational text, it helps to know what to look for and what questions to ask yourself as you read. Use the chart below as a guide when you read.

	Look for	Questions to Ask	For More Help
Central Ideas and Details	• Central ideas or claims • Supporting details or evidence	• What is the subject or main point of this text? • What details support the main point? • What inferences do you need to make? • How does the author develop a few central ideas throughout a text?	▶ **Skills Tutorial** • Identify Main Ideas and Details • Draw Inferences • Summarize **Analysis Skill** Identify Central Issues and Problems
Word Choice	• Unfamiliar words and phrases • Words and phrases that produce a certain effect on a reader	• What inferences about word meaning can you make from the context? • What tone and mood are created by word choice? • What alternate word choices might the author have made?	▶ **Skills Tutorial** • Draw Inferences
Text Structure	• Ways the author has organized the text • Ways sentences and paragraphs work together to build ideas • Clue words signaling a particular structure	• Does the text have a specific structure? • For instance, is it structured by sequence or chronology? By comparisons and contrasts? By causes and effects?	▶ **Skills Tutorial** • Identify Evidence • Analyze Cause and Effect • Sequence • Compare and Contrast

Evaluate Arguments

One important reason to read and understand informational text is so you can recognize and evaluate written arguments. An argument is a logical way of presenting a belief, conclusion, or stance. A good argument is supported with reasoning and evidence and will often address opposing claims. Study the model below to see how the writer developed an argument about the impact of writing on the world.

Writing Has Changed the World

Here the writer clearly states the claim.

At one time, knowledge was shared by word of mouth. By 3000 BCE, however, ancient peoples had created systems of writing. Over time, writing has grown in importance.

The writer uses this example to support one of the claims.

At first, writing was a practical way to record information. The Sumerians began writing to keep track of grain production. In time, people found additional uses for writing. Scholars began to write about mathematics and science. They created calendars and wrote about their history. Much of what we know about the Sumerians, Egyptians, and Mayans comes from their writings.

The claim is supported by an example from the Babylonian empire.

Perhaps most importantly, writing has been used to unite people. For example, Hammurabi had his law code written in stone. It was displayed throughout the Babylonian empire. All the people knew the laws. For the first time, an entire empire was united by the written word.

The writer finishes by summarizing the impact of writing on our lives today.

People today find it hard to imagine a world without writing. Print and online sources provide a steady stream of written words. It began as a way to count bushels of grain, but now it's our greatest source of knowledge.

> **INTERACTIVE**
>
> Go online for these interactive skills tutorials:
> - Evaluate Arguments
> - Consider and Counter Opposing Arguments
> - Support Ideas with Evidence

Analyze Visuals

Another key component of understanding informational texts is being able to understand any visuals that go with written text, like the maps, graphs, charts, and photos. Study the chart and the example to help you analyze some common types of visuals in your social studies text.

	Look for	For More Help
Maps	• Read the title. • Read the key. • Study the locator globe, scale bar, and compass rose. • Apply the key and labels to the map.	▶ **Skills Tutorial** • Use Parts of a Map • Read Physical Maps • Read Political Maps • Read Special-Purpose Maps
Graphs and Tables	• Read the title. • Use labels and key. • Look for patterns or changes over time.	▶ **Skills Tutorial** • Read Charts, Graphs, and Tables • Create Charts and Maps
Photographs	• Identify the content. • Note emotions. • Read captions or credits. • Study the image's purpose. • Consider context. • Respond.	▶ **Skills Tutorial** • Analyze Images • Analyze Political Cartoons

Origins of Arabic Numerals

Late Gupta (India, 500s)	Gwalior (India, 800s)	Western Arabic (North Africa and Spain, 900s)	Western Arabic (Worldwide, Today)
o	o	o	0
—	1	1	1
=	2	2	2
≡	3	3	3
4	8	ع	4
h	4	5	5
૬	6	6	6
7	7	7	7
S	૮	8	8
2	9	9	9

❶ What is the title of the chart?

❷ Read the labels. What does the first column on the left show?

❸ Which numbers seem to be the most consistent through all four written languages?

❹ What evidence supports your conclusion?

Analyze Primary and Secondary Sources

A primary source is information from someone who saw or was part of what is being described. A secondary source is information recorded later by someone who was not part of the event. You will encounter many primary and secondary sources throughout your textbook and in Quests and other activities. Study these questions and the model primary sources that follows to help you unlock the meaning of these sources.

	Questions to Ask	For More Help
Determine the Author's Purpose	• Is the source written mainly to convey information, like a textbook? • Or, is its purpose to persuade you to think a certain way, like an opinion piece in a newspaper?	▶ **Skills Tutorial** • Analyze Primary and Secondary Sources • Analyze Media Content • Draw Inferences
Determine the Author's Point of View	• What is the author's point of view? • Is the author's point of view shaped by subjective influences such as feelings, prejudices, experiences? • Is the author's point of view shaped by his or her field of study?	▶ **Skills Tutorial** • Analyze Primary and Secondary Sources • Compare Viewpoints
Compare Viewpoints	• How is the author's point of view different from that of other authors' writing on the same subject? • Does the author avoid including certain facts that would change his or her point of view?	▶ **Skills Tutorial** • Compare Viewpoints
Analyze Word Choice	• Does the author use words in a neutral, factual way? • Does the author use loaded words that try to persuade the reader to think a certain way?	▶ **Skills Tutorial** • Identify Bias
Analyze Interactions	• How have individuals, events, and ideas influenced each other? • What connecting words signal these interactions (*next, for example, consequently, however,* etc.)?	▶ **Skills Tutorial** • Analyze Cause and Effect

Primary Sources Model Shi Huangdi founded the Qin dynasty. His rule was marked by great accomplishments as well as strict and sometimes cruel actions. This excerpt describes Shi Huangdi's rule. Study the excerpt and call-outs to help you better understand the author's purpose, word choices, and point of view.

The adjectives are all positive and suggest that Emperor Shi Huangdi was a good emperor.

This inscription was ordered by Shi Huangdi, so the writer probably needed to make the descriptions positive.

The author only refers to Shi Huangdi's positive actions and not his more controversial ones.

Sima Qian lived about 100 years after the life of Shi Huangdi. He is quoting from a marker put up during Shi Huangdi's time.

Shi Huangdi Memorial Inscription

A new age is inaugurated by the Emperor;
Rules and measures are rectified, . . .
Human affairs are made clear
And there is harmony between fathers and sons.
The Emperor in his [wise ways], [kindness], and justice
Has made all laws and principles [understandable].

He set forth to pacify the east,
To inspect officers and men;
This great task accomplished
He visited the coast.
Great are the Emperor's achievements,
Men attend diligently to basic tasks,
Farming is encouraged, . . .

All the common people prosper;
All men under the sky
Toil with a single purpose;
Tools and measures are made uniform,
The written script is standardized,
Wherever the sun and moon shine. . . .

—*The Records of the Grand Historian*, Sima Qian.

Support Your Analyses with Evidence

Historians and other writers make assertions, or claims, about events.
Before accepting a claim as fact, however, look carefully at the evidence
the author provides. Study the chart and the model secondary source to
learn more about how to use evidence to support your ideas.

	Look for	Questions to Ask	For More Help
Support Your Analyses With Evidence	• The subject of the passage • Any assertion or claim that something is true • Appropriate evidence to support the claim • How well the evidence supports the claim, either explicitly or by inference	• What is the passage about? • Are there claims that something is true? • If so, what language supports the claim? • Does the evidence support the claim? • Did the author convince you that the claim was correct?	▶ **Skills Tutorial** • Identify Evidence • Support Ideas with Evidence

Model Secondary Source Look for evidence in this model passage.
Do you think the main point is supported by the evidence?

The subject of a passage is usually stated toward the beginning of the passage. This passage's subject is about how Jericho was a busy town.

These sentences show how Jericho's food surplus allowed Jericho to support many people.

This sentence provides evidence that trade made Jericho busy.

The ancient town of Jericho lies near the Dead Sea. In 8000 BCE, Jericho was a hub of activity. The surrounding fields yielded huge crops of wheat and barley. The nearby wilderness provided a good supply of meat. Gazelles and ibexes were plentiful. With this agricultural surplus, Jericho was able to support a population of up to three thousand people.

Traders did a brisk business in Jericho. People came from near and far to trade salt, obsidian, and semiprecious stones.

Jericho was well protected against attack. There was a high stone wall around the town. There was also a broad ditch and watchtower almost 30 feet high.

WRITING

Using the Writing Process

Writing is one of the most powerful communication tools you will use for the rest of your life. Follow these steps to strengthen your writing.

Prewriting: Plan Your Essay

1. **Choose a topic.** Often your teacher will provide you with a topic. Sometimes, you will be able to choose your own. In that case, select a topic that you care about and that you think will interest others.

2. **Narrow your focus.** Most writers begin with too broad a topic and need to narrow their focus. For example, you might decide to write about the Renaissance. You will need to narrow your focus to a single artist or discovery in order to write a meaningful essay.

3. **Gather information.** Collect facts and details you'll need to write your essay. Research any points that you are unsure about.

4. **Organize your ideas.** Writers often find it useful to create an outline to help them plan their essay. You need not create a formal outline, but you'll at least want to jot down your main ideas, the details that support them, and the order in which you will present your ideas. A graphic organizer can help you organize your ideas. Here is a graphic organizer for a paper on Leonardo da Vinci:

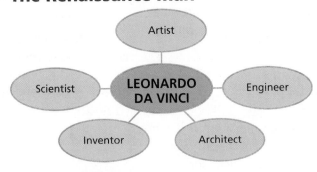

The Renaissance Man

5. **Write a thesis statement.** A thesis statement focuses your ideas into a single sentence or two and tells readers what the essay is about.

Drafting

1. **Maintain a clear focus.** If you find that your writing is starting to get off track, go back to your thesis statement.

2. **Elaborate for interest and emphasis.** Give details and specific examples about each point in your essay.

3. **Provide evidence.** Evidence is key to convincing an audience. Provide factual, concrete evidence to back up your ideas and assertions.

Revising, Editing, and Rewriting

1. **Add transition words.** Make cause-and-effect relationships clear with words such as *because*, *as a result*, and so on. To compare or contrast ideas, use linking words, such as *similarly*, *both*, and *equally* or *in contrast*, *instead*, and *yet*. Use words such as *first*, *second*, *next*, and *finally* to help readers follow steps in a sequence. Look at the following examples. In the revised version, a reader knows the correct order in which to perform the steps.

First Draft	Revision
Historians form an educated guess called a hypothesis. They test that hypothesis with further research.	<u>Next</u>, historians form an educated guess called a hypothesis. <u>Then</u>, they test that hypothesis with further research.

2. **Focus on how well you have addressed your purpose.** Be sure that your essay addresses your purpose for writing. For a problem-solution essay, that means anticipating opposing arguments and responding to them. For a cause-and-effect essay, stress the way one event leads to the next.

3. **Focus on your audience.** Check that you have not left out any steps in your essay and that your audience can follow your thinking. Make sure that your writing will hold your audience's interest.

4. **Review organization.** Confirm that your ideas flow in a logical order. Write your main points on sticky notes. Reorganize these until you are satisfied that the order best strengthens your essay.

5. **Revise sentences and words.** Use both short and long sentences. Scan for vague words, such as *good* or *nice*. Replace them with specific and vibrant words, such as *helpful* or *friendly*.

6. **Peer review.** Ask a peer—a friend or classmate—to read your draft. Is it clear? Can your reader follow your ideas? Revise confusing sections.

> ▶ **INTERACTIVE**
>
> Go online for these interactive skills tutorials:
> - Identify Main Ideas and Details
> - Organize Your Ideas
> - Write an Essay

Proofread Always proofread for spelling and grammar errors. Do not simply rely on spellchecking apps or programs. A spellchecker won't catch the difference between *see* and *sea* or between *deer* and *dear*.

Use Technology
Here are a few ideas:
☑ Use a word processing program to plan and write your essay.
☑ Use the Internet for research (see guidelines later in this Handbook).
☑ Use email and other online tools to collaborate with classmates.
☑ Create informative charts, graphs, and diagrams for presentations.
☑ Share your writing with others through a blog or website.

Write an Argument

In addition to evaluating other writers' arguments, you also need to be able to express arguments of your own, in writing and speaking. An argumentative, or persuasive, essay sets forth a belief or stand on an issue. A well-written argument may convince the reader, change the reader's mind, or motivate the reader to take a certain action.

In this program, you'll practice writing arguments in some Document-Based Inquiry Quests and Writing Workshops, with support in your 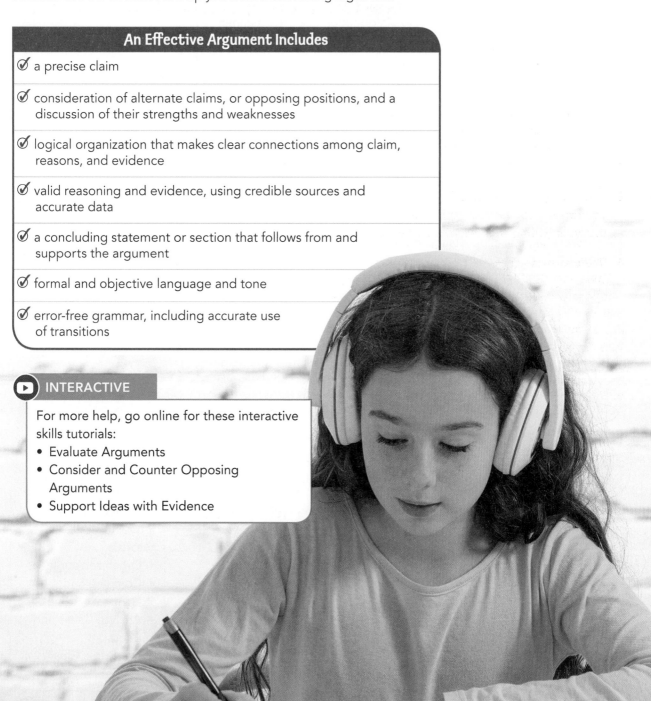 **Active Journal**. Use the checklist to help you write a convincing argument.

An Effective Argument Includes

- ☑ a precise claim

- ☑ consideration of alternate claims, or opposing positions, and a discussion of their strengths and weaknesses

- ☑ logical organization that makes clear connections among claim, reasons, and evidence

- ☑ valid reasoning and evidence, using credible sources and accurate data

- ☑ a concluding statement or section that follows from and supports the argument

- ☑ formal and objective language and tone

- ☑ error-free grammar, including accurate use of transitions

▶ INTERACTIVE

For more help, go online for these interactive skills tutorials:
- Evaluate Arguments
- Consider and Counter Opposing Arguments
- Support Ideas with Evidence

Write Informative or Explanatory Essays

Informative or explanatory texts present facts, data, and other evidence to give information about a topic. Readers turn to informational and explanatory texts when they wish to learn about a specific idea, concept, or subject area, or if they want to learn how to do something.

An Effective Informative/Explanatory Essay Includes

- ✓ a thesis statement that introduces the concept or subject
- ✓ an organization (such as definition, classification, comparison/contrast, cause/effect) that presents information in a clear manner
- ✓ headings (if desired) to separate sections of the essay
- ✓ definitions, quotations, and/or graphics that support the thesis
- ✓ relevant facts, examples, and details that expand upon a topic
- ✓ clear transitions that link sections of the essay
- ✓ precise words and technical vocabulary where appropriate
- ✓ formal and objective language and tone
- ✓ a conclusion that supports the information given and provides fresh insights

Suppose you are writing an essay comparing and contrasting city and village life in West African societies.

Your thesis statement might be "West African cities and villages both valued family and trade. However, the languages they spoke, the religions they practiced, and the goods they produced differed greatly."

Your organization might be:

I City life	OR	I Family
A. Family		A. City Life
B. Language		B. Village Life
C. Religion		II Language
D. Economy		A. City Life
II Village Life		B. Village Life
A. Family		III Religion
B. Language		A. City Life
C. Religion		B. Village Life
D. Economy		IV Economy
		A. City Life
		B. Village Life

▶ INTERACTIVE

Go online for these interactive skills tutorials:
- Organize Your Ideas
- Compare and Contrast
- Analyze Cause and Effect
- Develop a Clear Thesis

Write Narrative Essays

A narrative is any type of writing that tells a story. Narrative writing conveys an experience, either real or imaginary, and uses time order to provide structure. Usually its purpose is to entertain, but it can also instruct, persuade, or inform.

An Effective Narrative Includes
☑ an engaging beginning in which characters and setting are established
☑ a well-structured, logical sequence of events
☑ narrative techniques, such as dialogue and description
☑ a variety of transition words and phrases to convey sequence and signal shifts from one time frame or setting to another
☑ precise words and phrases, relevant descriptive details, and sensory language that brings the characters and setting to life
☑ a conclusion that follows naturally from the story's experiences or events

Model Narrative This passage is the beginning of a West African folk tale. Notice how it begins in an engaging way that introduces the characters—a man, a yam, and a cow—and the setting, a garden. Note too how it uses dialogue to move the story along and tells the story in the sequence in which it occurred.

> Once . . . a country man went out to his garden to dig up some yams to take to market. While he was digging, one of the yams said to him, "Well, at last you're here. You never weeded me, now you come around with your digging stick. Go away and leave me alone!"
>
> The farmer turned around and looked at his cow in amazement. . . .
>
> "Did you say something?" he asked.
>
> —*The Cow-Tail Switch and other West African Stories,*
> Harold Courlander and George Herzog

▶ INTERACTIVE

For more help, go online for these interactive skills tutorials:
- Sequence
- Draw Conclusions
- Write an Essay
- Write a Journal Entry

Find and Use Credible Sources

You will often need to conduct research using library and media sources to gain more knowledge about a topic. Not all of the information that you find, however, will be useful—or reliable. Strong research skills will help you find accurate information about your topic.

Using Print and Digital Sources An effective research project combines information from multiple sources. Plan to include a variety of these resources:

☑ **Primary and Secondary Sources:** Use both primary sources (such as interviews or newspaper articles) and secondary sources (such as encyclopedia entries or historians' accounts).

☑ **Print and Digital Resources:** The Internet allows fast access to data, but print resources are often edited more carefully. Plan to include both print and digital resources in order to guarantee that your work is accurate.

☑ **Media Resources:** You can find valuable information in media resources such as documentaries, television programs, podcasts, and museum exhibitions.

☑ **Original Research:** Depending on your topic, you may wish to conduct original research, such as interviews or surveys of people in your community.

Evaluating Sources It is important to evaluate the credibility and accuracy of any information you find. Ask yourself questions such as these to evaluate sources:

☑ **Authority:** Is the author well known? What are the author's credentials? Does the source include references to other reliable sources? Does the author's tone win your confidence? Why or why not?

☑ **Bias:** Does the author have any obvious biases? What is the author's purpose for writing? Who is the target audience?

☑ **Currency:** When was the work created? Has it been revised? Is there more current information available?

Using Search Terms Finding information on the Internet is easy, but it can be a challenge to find facts that are useful and trustworthy. If you type a word or phrase into a search engine, you will probably get hundreds of results.

Did you know?

Beware of online encyclopedias. They can be a good starting place for information, but their contributors are not required to fact-check their submissions.

However, those results are not guaranteed to be relevant or accurate. These strategies can help:

- ☑ Create a list of keywords before you begin using a search engine.

- ☑ Enter six to eight keywords.

- ☑ Choose unique nouns. Most search engines ignore articles and prepositions.

- ☑ Use adjectives to specify a category. For example, you might enter "ancient Rome" instead of "Rome."

- ☑ Use quotation marks to focus a search. Place a phrase in quotation marks to find pages that include exactly that phrase.

- ☑ Spell carefully. Many search engines correct spelling automatically, but they cannot catch every spelling error.

- ☑ Scan search results before you click them. The first result isn't always the most useful. Read the text before you make a choice

Avoiding Plagiarism Whenever you conduct research, you must be careful to give credit for any ideas or opinions that are not your own. Presenting someone else's ideas, research, or opinion as your own—even if you have phrased it in different words—is plagiarism. Plagiarism is the equivalent of stealing. Be sure to record your sources accurately so you can identify them later. When photocopying from a source, include the copyright information. Include the web addresses from online sources.

Quoting and Paraphrasing When including ideas from research into your writing, you will need to decide whether to quote directly or paraphrase. You must cite your sources for both quotations and paraphrases. **A direct quotation** uses the author's exact words when they are particularly well-chosen. Include complete quotations, without deleting or changing words. Enclose direct quotations in quotation marks. **A paraphrase** restates an author's ideas in your own words. Be careful to paraphrase accurately. A good paraphrase does more than simply rearrange an author's phrases, or replace a few words with synonyms.

Formats for Citing Sources When you cite a source, you acknowledge where you found your information and give readers the details necessary for locating the source. Always prepare a reference list, called a bibliography, at the end of a research paper to provide full information on your sources.

▶ INTERACTIVE

Go online for these interactive skills tutorials:
- Search for Information on the Internet
- Evaluate Web Sites
- Take Effective Notes
- Avoid Plagiarism

Did you know?

A citation for a book should look like this: Pyles, Thomas. *The Origins and Development of the English Language*. 2nd ed. New York: Harcourt, 1971. Print.
A citation for a website should include this information:
Romey, Kristin. "Face of 9,500-Year-Old Man Revealed for First Time." Rothbart, Davy. "How I Caught up with Dad." *National Geographic*, Jan. 2017. *news. nationalgeographic.com* Web. 20 Jan. 2017.

Write Research Papers

You will often need to conduct research in the library or on the Internet for a project or essay. In this program, you will conduct research for Quest projects and some Writing Workshop assignments. Before you begin, review the information in Using the Writing Process as well as in Find and Use Credible Sources. Then follow these additional tips to help you make the most of your research.

1. Narrow or Broaden Your Topic Choose a topic that is narrow enough to cover completely. If you can name your topic in just one or two words, it is probably too broad. For example, a topics such as The Middle Ages would be too broad. When you begin to research, pay attention to the amount of information available. If there is way too much information when you begin your research on your topic, narrow your focus.

On the other hand, you might need to broaden a topic if there is not enough information available. A topic is too narrow when it can be thoroughly presented in less space than the required size of your assignment. It might also be too narrow if you can find little or no information in library and media sources. Broaden your topic by including other related ideas.

2. Generate Research Questions Use research questions to focus your inquiry. For example, instead of simply hunting for information about Augustus, you might ask, "Why are people still interested in Augustus?" or "How might the history of Rome have been different if Augustus had not ruled?" As you research your topic, continue to ask yourself questions. Follow your new questions in order to explore your topic further. Refocus your research questions as you learn more about your topic.

3. Synthesize Your Sources Effective research writing is more than just a list of facts and details. Good research synthesizes—gathers, orders, and interprets—those elements. These strategies will help you synthesize effectively:

- ✓ Review your notes. Look for connections and patterns among the details you have collected.

- ✓ Organize notes or notecards to help you plan how you will combine details.

- ✓ Pay close attention to details that emphasize the same main idea.

- ✓ Also look for details that challenge each other. For many topics, there is no single correct opinion. You might decide to conduct additional research to help you decide which side of the issue has more support.

> ▶ **INTERACTIVE**
>
> For more help, go online for these interactive skills tutorials:
> - Ask Questions
> - Create a Research Hypothesis
> - Synthesize

SPEAKING AND LISTENING

Discuss Your Ideas

A group discussion is an informal meeting of people that is used to openly discuss ideas, readings, and issues. You can express your views and hear those of others. In this program, you'll participate in Discussion Inquiry Quests and many one-to-one, group, and teacher-led discussions. You'll work with different partners on many topics and issues. Use the Keys to Effective Discussions to help you be an active participant in lively discussions.

Keys to Effective Discussions

☑ Come to discussions prepared, having studied the required material and/or read relevant background information.

☑ Build on others' ideas and express your own ideas clearly.

☑ Be sure that your comments directly contribute to the topic, text, or issue under discussion.

☑ Give specific evidence for the points you wish to make.

☑ Follow rules for civic discussions, including letting everyone have a chance to speak and listening carefully to others' points of view.

☑ Pose and respond to specific questions and issues with elaboration and details.

☑ Be prepared to demonstrate your understanding of the different perspectives people have put forth during the discussion.

☑ Acknowledge the views of others respectfully, but ask questions that challenge the accuracy, logic, or relevance of those views.

▶ **INTERACTIVE**

Go online for these interactive skills tutorials:
- Participate in a Discussion or Debate
- Support Ideas With Evidence
- Work in Teams

Give an Effective Presentation

Many of the Quests in this program will require you to give a presentation to your teacher and classmates, and sometimes even to a wider audience. These presentations will be good practice for the presentations you will need to give in school and in professional settings. You can speak confidently if you prepare carefully and follow this checklist.

Keys to Effective Presentations

- ☑ Prepare your presentation in advance and practice it in order to gain comfort and confidence.

- ☑ Present your claims and findings in a logical sequence so that your audience can easily follow your train of thought.

- ☑ Use relevant descriptions, facts, and specific details.

- ☑ Consider using nonverbal elements like hand gestures and pauses to emphasize main ideas or themes.

- ☑ Use appropriate eye contact, adequate volume, and clear pronunciation.

- ☑ Use appropriate transitions (*for example, first, second, third*) to clarify relationships.

- ☑ Use precise language and vocabulary that is specific to your topic.

- ☑ Provide a strong conclusion.

- ☑ Adapt your wording to your purpose and audience. Use formal English for most presentations, but try to sound natural and relaxed.

- ☑ Include multimedia components such as you see in the chart to clarify information.

Maps	Graphs/Charts/Diagrams	Illustrations/Photos	Audio/Video
Clarify historical or geographical information	Show complex information and data in an easy-to-understand format	Illustrate objects, scenes, or other details	Bring the subject to life and engage audiences

▶ INTERACTIVE

Go online for these interactive skills tutorials:
- Give an Effective Presentation
- Create Charts and Maps
- Support Ideas With Evidence

Effective Listening

Active listening is a key component of the communication process. Like all communication, it requires your engaged participation. Follow the Keys to Effective Listening to get the most out of discussions, presentations by others, lectures by your teacher, and any time you engage in listening.

Keys to Effective Listening

☑ Look at and listen to the speaker. Think about what you hear and see. Which ideas are emphasized or repeated? What gestures or expressions suggest strong feelings?

☑ Listen carefully to information presented in different media and formats—including videos, lectures, speeches, and discussions—so you can explain how the information you learn contributes to the topic or issue you are studying.

☑ Listen for the speaker's argument and specific claims so that you can distinguish claims that are supported by reasons and evidence from claims that are not.

☑ Listen to fit the situation. Active listening involves matching your listening to the situation. Listen critically to a speech given by a candidate for office. Listen with kindness to the feelings of a friend. Listen appreciatively to a musical performance.

▶ **INTERACTIVE**

For more help, go online for these interactive skills tutorials:
- Identify Bias
- Identify Evidence
- Distinguish Between Fact and Opinion
- Evaluate Existing Arguments

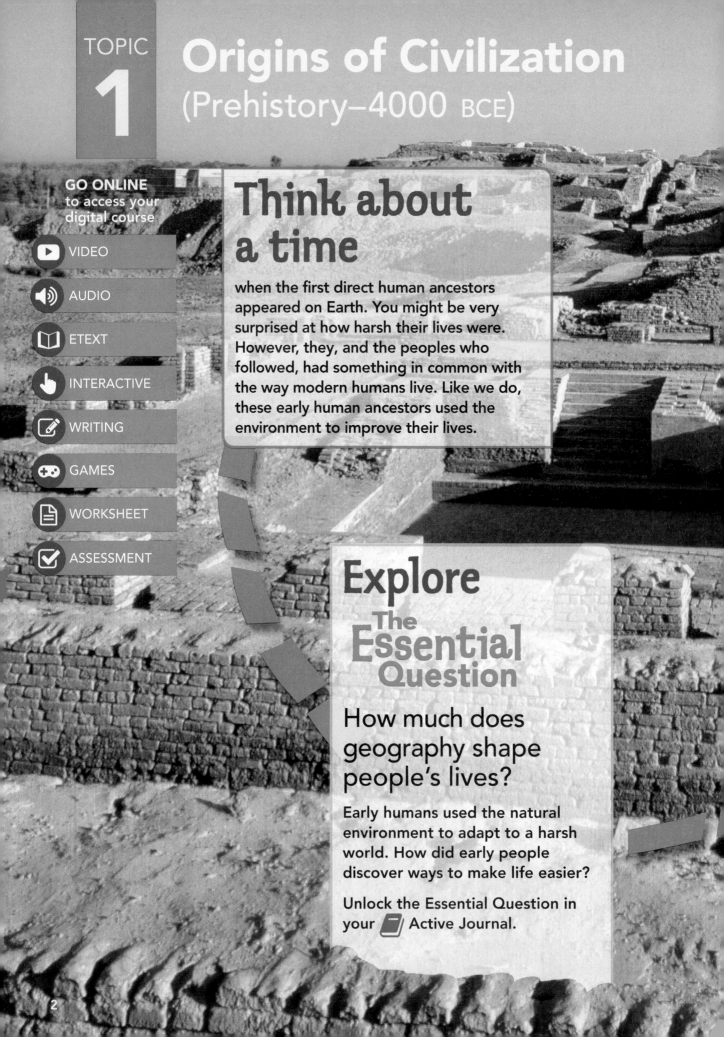

Origins of Civilization
(Prehistory–4000 BCE)

GO ONLINE
to access your
digital course

▶ VIDEO

🔊 AUDIO

📖 ETEXT

👆 INTERACTIVE

✏️ WRITING

🎮 GAMES

📄 WORKSHEET

✅ ASSESSMENT

Think about a time

when the first direct human ancestors appeared on Earth. You might be very surprised at how harsh their lives were. However, they, and the peoples who followed, had something in common with the way modern humans live. Like we do, these early human ancestors used the environment to improve their lives.

Explore
The Essential Question

How much does geography shape people's lives?

Early humans used the natural environment to adapt to a harsh world. How did early people discover ways to make life easier?

Unlock the Essential Question in your 📓 Active Journal.

Read

about early people and the ways they lived.

Watch

BOUNCE TO ACTIVATE ▶ VIDEO

Çatalhöyük: Life in an Ancient Settlement

Find out about how scientists work to uncover the secrets of the distant past.

Ruins of ancient baths, Mohenjo-Daro, Indus Valley, Pakistan

Origins of Civilization
(Prehistory–4000 BCE)

Learn more about human beginnings and the world's first civilizations by making your own map and timeline in your 📓 Active Journal.

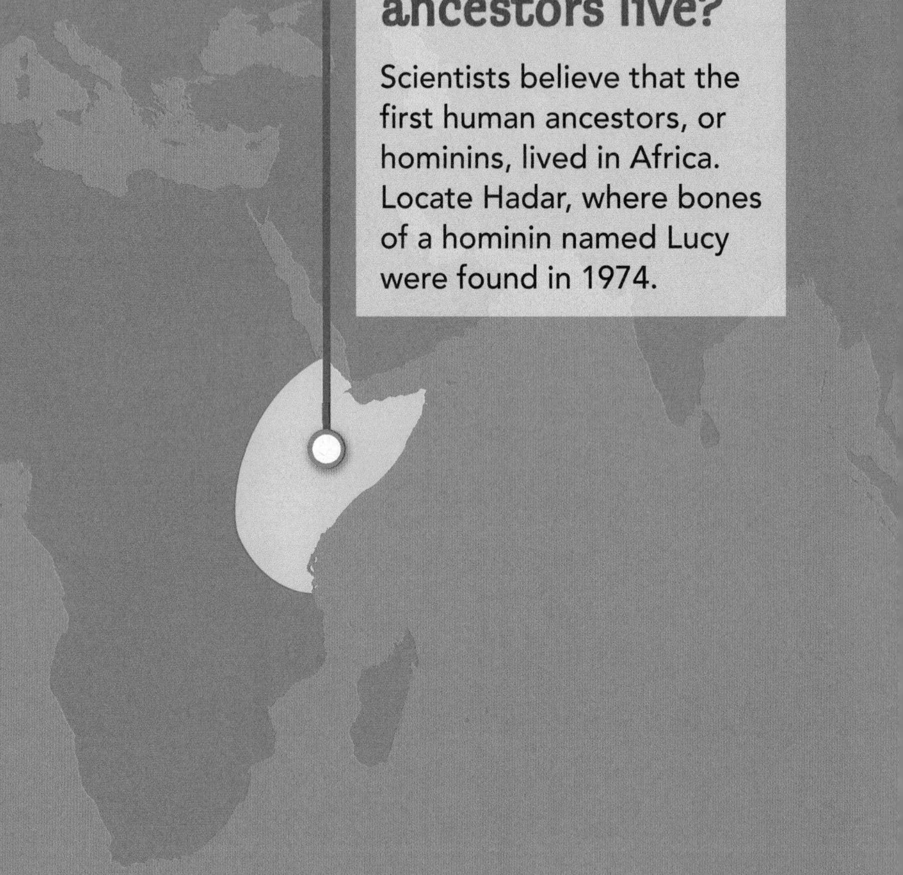

INTERACTIVE

Topic Map

Where did the first human ancestors live?

Scientists believe that the first human ancestors, or hominins, lived in Africa. Locate Hadar, where bones of a hominin named Lucy were found in 1974.

INTERACTIVE

Topic Timeline

What happened and when?

Basic stone tools...hunting and gathering for food... farming...the birth of villages and cities. Explore the timeline to see what was happening during our earliest history.

2.5 million years ago Hominins in Africa make stone tools.

230,000 years ago Neanderthals appear in Europe.

70,000 years ago Last ice age begins.

TOPIC EVENTS

| 2 million years ago | 300,000 years ago | 200,000 years ago | 100,000 years ago |

1.9 million years ago hominins migrate to Eurasia.

200,000 years ago *Homo sapiens* appear in Africa.

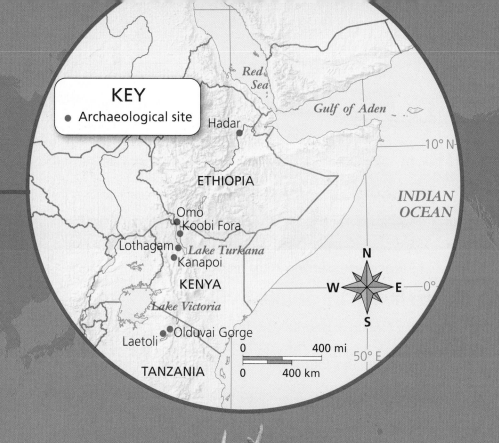

KEY
• Archaeological site

Red Sea

Gulf of Aden

Hadar

ETHIOPIA

Omo
Koobi Fora

Lothagam
Kanapoi

Lake Turkana

KENYA

Lake Victoria

Laetoli

Olduvai Gorge

TANZANIA

INDIAN OCEAN

10° N

0°

50° E

N
W   E
S

| 0 | 400 mi |
| 0 | 400 km |

Who will you meet?

Mary Leakey, an archaeologist who made an important discovery

Child from a Stone Age burial

The people of Uruk, the world's first city

6,000-7,000 years ago
Uruk, the world's first city, in Southwest Asia, is established.

8,500 years ago
Oldest known farming village in Turkey appears.

12,000 years ago
Last ice age ends.

| 20,000 years ago | 15,000 years ago | 10,000 years ago | 5,000 years ago |

10,000 years ago
People begin to grow food; Neolithic agricultural revolution begins.

5

Quest
Project-Based Learning Inquiry

Design a Village

Quest KICK OFF

About 8,000 years ago, people were living in a time of great change. Humans were beginning to farm and were settling in the first villages.

What was it like to live in an ancient village?

How did early humans and the Neolithic people who followed them live? Explore the Essential Question "How much does geography shape people's lives?" in this Quest.

1 Ask Questions

Thousands of years ago, human societies were very different from those that followed. Get started on your Quest by making a list of questions you want to ask about how people lived in the distant past. Write the questions in your 📖 Active Journal.

2 Investigate

As you read the lessons in this topic, look for **Quest CONNECTIONS** that provide information about the way people lived long ago. Capture notes in your 📖 Active Journal.

3 Conduct Research

Next, find valid primary sources of information about life during the Neolithic Era on your own. Capture notes in your 📖 Active Journal.

Quest FINDINGS

4 Design Your Village

As society became more complex, Neolithic people formed villages. At the end of the topic you'll design a Neolithic village and create a drawing of how your village will look. When you complete your drawing, you will present it to the class in an oral presentation. Get help for creating your village in your 📖 Active Journal.

▲ Remains of Skara Brae, a Neolithic village in Scotland

The Distant Past

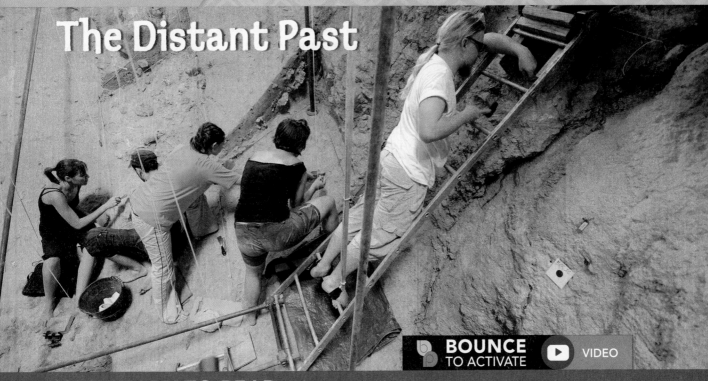

BOUNCE TO ACTIVATE ▶ VIDEO

GET READY TO READ

START UP
What does this photo tell you about how people gather information from the distant past?

GUIDING QUESTIONS
- How do scientists use fossils and artifacts to draw conclusions about early humans?
- How does archaeological evidence indicate that human life began in Africa?
- How did people live by the gathering and hunting way of life?

TAKE NOTES
Literacy Skills: Identify Main Ideas
Use the graphic organizer in your 📓 Active Journal to take notes as you read the lesson.

PRACTICE VOCABULARY
Use the vocabulary activity in your 📓 Active Journal to practice the vocabulary words.

Vocabulary		Academic Vocabulary
anthropology	artifact	evidence
archaeologist	hunter-gatherer	conclude
prehistory		
fossil	culture	
geologist		

We are all interested in people. But certain people, called anthropologists, have made a science out of studying people. **Anthropology** is the study of how human beings behave, how they act together, where they came from, and what makes one group of people different from another.

In this lesson, we will look at the work of a particular group of anthropologists known as archaeologists. **Archaeologists** study human life in the past by examining the things that people left behind.

Studying Early Humans
Until about 5,000 years ago, people had no way to write things down. To study **prehistory**, or the time before written records, archaeologists look for the places where people may have lived.

What Are Fossils? To learn about the earliest humans, archaeologists depend mainly on fossils. **Fossils** are hardened remains or imprints of living things that existed long ago. These remains may include plants, feathers, bones, and even footprints.

INTERACTIVE

Piecing the Past
Together

Fossils form in several ways. For example, after a living thing dies, it may quickly become covered by sand or mud. Once covered, the soft parts of the plant or animal rot away. The harder parts, such as bones, teeth, or woody stems, last much longer. Over many years, minerals from the soil slowly replace this once-living material. What remains is a rocklike copy of the original.

How Are Ancient Remains Dated? Archaeologists use several methods for determining the ages of fossils and other prehistoric objects. In this work, they get valuable information from **geologists**, scientists who study the physical materials of Earth itself, such as soil and rocks.

One dating method is to compare objects found in similar layers of rock or soil. Objects found in lower layers are generally older than those found in upper layers. Archaeologists may also compare an object with a similar fossil or artifact whose age is already known.

Radioactive dating is another method for determining the age of objects up to about 50,000 years old. Living things contain radioactive elements that decay, or break down, over time. By measuring the radioactive material in bones and other materials that were once alive, scientists can tell when an object was formed.

In recent years, scientists have developed other methods to study fossils. They use DNA to compare human remains from the past with people living today. Genetic evidence has uncovered new information about how people changed and how they moved from place to place.

Why Do Scientists Look for Artifacts? Human ancestors, called hominins, lived millions of years ago. To study prehistoric people who lived more recently, archaeologists look for old settlements, such as villages or campsites. Such sites often lie buried beneath layers of soil.

GEOGRAPHY **SKILLS**

Archaeologists have made major archaeological discoveries in Africa.

1. **Region** In what part of Africa did most fossil finds occur?

2. **Human-Environment Interaction** What environmental factors may have led to the development of early humans in East Africa?

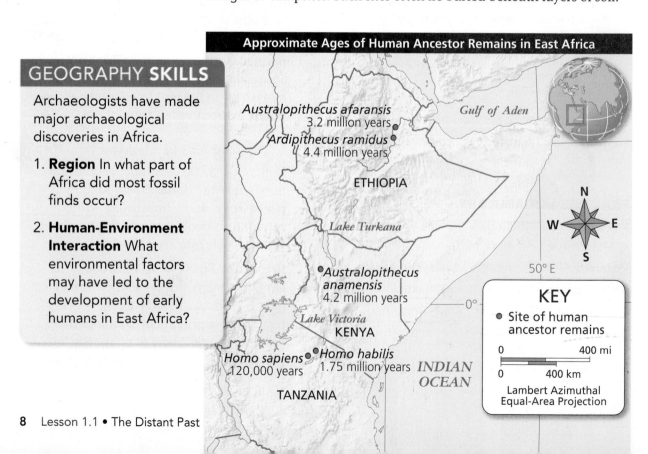

Approximate Ages of Human Ancestor Remains in East Africa

Australopithecus afaransis
3.2 million years

Ardipithecus ramidus
4.4 million years

Gulf of Aden

ETHIOPIA

Lake Turkana

Australopithecus anamensis
4.2 million years

50° E

Lake Victoria
KENYA

Homo sapiens
120,000 years

Homo habilis
1.75 million years

INDIAN OCEAN

TANZANIA

KEY
• Site of human ancestor remains

0 — 400 mi
0 — 400 km
Lambert Azimuthal Equal-Area Projection

Archaeologists must carefully excavate, or uncover, these sites to learn about the people who once lived there.

As archaeologists dig up a site, they look for artifacts such as tools, pottery, or weapons. **Artifacts** are anything made and used by humans. These scientists then try to identify patterns, examining what artifacts are found together in the same spot. Artifacts found in an ancient campsite can help archaeologists understand how the people who once camped there hunted for food or what they ate.

☑ READING CHECK **Use Evidence** What types of objects do archaeologists study to learn about the past?

Where Did Human Ancestors Live?

Where did human ancestors first appear on Earth? For a long time, scientists could not agree on an answer.

Then, in 1960, British archaeologists Mary and Louis Leakey discovered a piece of a human-like skull at Olduvai Gorge in East Africa. The Leakeys called their find *Homo habilis* ("handy man") because **evidence** showed that these early human ancestors made and used tools. Tests showed that the *Homo habilis* fossils were at least 1.75 million years old. From that point on, the search for the origins of humankind has largely focused on Africa.

African Beginnings On November 30, 1974, American anthropologist Donald Johanson made a discovery that helped shape how scientists view early human history. For three years, Johanson had been searching for evidence of human ancestors in Ethiopia, a country in East Africa. Johanson later recalled,

▲ Mary Leakey at work in Tanzania, Africa

Primary Source

On this November morning, it was about noon, I was heading back to my Land Rover to drive back to camp. And I happened to look over my right shoulder. And as I did so, I saw a fragment of a bone which I recognized as coming from the elbow region in a skeleton. . . . There was a piece of a leg, there was a piece of a pelvis, there was a piece of a jaw, there was a piece of a skull. And I realized almost instantaneously that we had part of a skeleton.

—Donald C. Johanson, Academy of Achievement interview, 1991

Academic Vocabulary
evidence • *n.*, something that can be used as proof

After two weeks of careful searching, Johanson and his team had uncovered hundreds of pieces of bone. They decided that all the bones belonged to one individual because they did not find two examples of any one type of bone. They determined that she was a 3.5-foot-tall female. Johanson named her "Lucy" after a song by the Beatles.

Johanson's team found some 40 percent of Lucy's skeleton. The bones of her legs, pelvis, ankle, and spine suggest that, like us, she walked upright on two legs. However, she lived 3.2 million years ago.

Since then, even older fossils have been found in Africa. In 1992, American anthropologist Tim White found remains of hominins who lived in Ethiopia at least 4.4 million years ago. Beginning with a single tooth, White's team uncovered more fragments. Finally, in 2009, White unveiled a nearly complete skeleton of a female that he named "Ardi." More than a million years older than Lucy, Ardi was taller and heavier. She probably walked upright, but slowly and awkwardly.

What Is the "Oldest One"?

Academic Vocabulary

conclude • v., to decide as a result of thinking or reasoning

Many scientists believe that the oldest humans began to develop, or evolve, from their great ape cousins about 5-7 million years ago. This process is what's known as evolution. Discoveries such as Lucy and Ardi have also led most scientists to **conclude** that humankind began in East Africa about 4.5 million years ago.

French scientist Michel Brunet is one of a group of scientists that believes that human life started elsewhere in Africa. In 2001, Brunet found a humanlike skull in the country of Chad. Tests showed the skull to be nearly 7 million years old. That makes it, says Brunet, "the oldest one."

Brunet's discovery has raised questions. Chad is in central Africa. Did humankind begin there rather than in East Africa? The skull Brunet found is older than other human fossils discovered so far. Is humankind older than scientists once thought?

Scientists will continue to look for answers to questions like these. Meanwhile, the search continues. "This is the beginning of the story," says Brunet of his work in Chad, "just the beginning."

✓ **READING CHECK** Identify Main Ideas Why do most scientists believe that human life began in Africa?

Analyze Images A scientist cleans the rib of a long extinct elephant. **Infer** Why is it easier to find ancient animal bones than the bones of human ancestors?

Analyze Images This painting of a bull was found in a cave in Lascaux, France, and dates from the Paleolithic Era. **Draw Conclusions** How do you think ancient artists chose which subjects to paint?

How Did Hunter-Gatherers Live?

Early humans were **hunter-gatherers**, which means that they lived by hunting small animals and gathering plants. They also probably scavenged for food left by predators. They formed societies and developed ways to improve their chances for survival.

Archaeologists know very little about how early hunter-gatherers such as Lucy lived. But they do know that their lives were often harsh. Many groups appeared for a time and died out. To survive and grow, early humans developed technology, tools, and skills to meet their needs.

How Were the First Tools Made? About 2.5 million years ago, early humans learned how to make tools out of stone. This technology was so important to human survival that archaeologists call this period the Paleolithic Era, or the Old Stone Age. The Paleolithic Era ended about 2,500 to 10,000 years ago.

Over time, toolmakers become more skillful, making thinner and sharper stone blades. Some blades were used to tip spears and arrows. Toolmakers also began making weapons from bones and antlers. As their skills and weapons improved, Paleolithic hunters were able to turn from hunting small animals to hunting larger animals such as deer.

How Did Fire Affect Human Development? Around 800,000 years ago, people also learned how to use fire. With fire, people could have light on dark nights, cook meat and plants, and use flames to aid in hunting and to scare off dangerous animals. Making fire also had important long-term effects such as enabling people to live in places where it otherwise would have been too cold for people to survive.

Did you know?

Many of the artifacts found in North America are cutting tools and arrowheads made of flint.

Here, a British archaeologist explains why learning to control fire was an important step in human development.

Primary Source

The control of fire was presumably the first great step in man's [freedom] from the bondage of his environment . . . . [Mankind] is no longer restricted in his movement to a limited range of climates, and his activities need not be entirely determined by the sun's light. But in mastery of fire man was controlling a mighty physical force.

—V. Gordon Childe, *Man Makes Himself*

What Was Life Like for Hunter-Gatherers? **Culture** includes the many different elements that make up the way of life of a people. These include social and family organization, beliefs and values, technology, shelter and clothing, common activities, storytelling, rituals, and art.

Stone age hunter-gatherers lived in small groups, or bands. After gathering as much food as they could in one area, they moved on. They built temporary huts out of branches or made tents of animal skins. Bands stayed small so they could move easily. A typical band included ten or twelve adults and their children.

Men generally did the hunting, but they also gathered other food. Women usually gathered fruit, grains, seeds, nuts, eggs, and honey. They caught small animals and may have picked herbs for medicine.

☑ READING CHECK **Identify Cause and Effect** How did people survive during the Paleolithic Era?

☑ Lesson Check

Practice Vocabulary

1. How do scientists date **fossils** and **artifacts**?

2. What **technology** was used during the Paleolithic Era?

Critical Thinking and Writing

3. **Summarize** How do archaeologists look for evidence about early people?

4. **Infer** Why do you think scientists are trying to find out more about how and where early humans lived?

5. **Identify Cause and Effect** Why was the ability to control fire a significant advancement for humans?

6. **Writing Workshop: Introduce Characters** Imagine you are traveling through different periods of human history. Your first stop is the Paleolithic Era. Write a few sentences in your 📔 Active Journal about how a member of a hunter-gatherer group lived and the person's role in the wandering band.

The Epic of Gilgamesh

Nearly 3,000 years ago, a writer inscribed clay tablets like the one shown here with a legend about Gilgamesh, the legendary king of Uruk—here called *Erech*. As you've learned, Uruk was the world's first city. The Epic of Gilgamesh tells the story of Gilgamesh—Gish, in this reading—and his friend Enkidu, who work together to defeat a monster named Huwawa. Here Gish announces his daring plan. ▶ text on a clay tablet

I will lure him to the cedar forest,
Like a strong offspring of Erech.
I will let the land hear [that]
I am determined to lure (him) in the cedar [forest].
A name I will establish. ①

The underlined elders ② of Erech of the plazas brought word to Gish:
"Though art young, O Gish, and thy heart carries thee away. ③
Thou dost not know what thou proposes to do.
We hear that Huwawa is enraged.

*   *   *

"Huwawa, whose roar is a deluge, ④
whose mouth is fire, whose breath is death.
Why does thou desire to do this?"

*   *   *

Gish heard the report of his counselors. ⑤
He saw and cried out to [his] friend:
"Now, my friend, thus [I speak]
I fear him, but [I will go to the cedar forest]."

—*The Epic of Gilgamesh*, translated by Morris Jastrow, Jr. and Albert T. Clay

Analyzing Primary Sources

Cite specific evidence from the document to support your answers.

1. **Draw Conclusions** What kind of name do you think Gilgamesh believes he will establish for himself by carrying out his plan?

2. **Generate Explanations** Gilgamesh says that he fears Huwawa. Why do you think he admits this fact?

3. **Summarize** Write a brief summary that explores the central ideas of this excerpt.

Reading and Vocabulary Support

① What do you think it means when Gilgamesh says "A name I will establish"?

② An *elder* is an older and wiser person.

③ What do you think the elders mean when they say to Gilgamesh "your heart carries you away"?

④ A *deluge* in this sense means something that overwhelms and overpowers a person.

⑤ A *counselor* is a person who provides advice.

Distinguish Essential from Incidental Information

Use the secondary source and these steps to distinguish essential from incidental information.

1 Identify a focus or topic. Set a purpose for your research.

  a. What exactly are you trying to find out?

  b. What key question are you trying to answer?

  c. What idea or event are you trying to understand?

2 Locate your sources. The sources you choose will depend on your focus and topic. What sources might you use if you were researching the domestication of grains during the Neolithic Age?

3 Identify information that is essential to your topic. Based on your focus:

  a. What information will help you achieve your goal?

  b. What kinds of data will answer questions or increase your understanding?

4 Identify information that is incidental to your topic. Remember the focus you have set for your research. Information that is not related to this focus is incidental. Take a look at the excerpt from the text below. If you were conducting research on only the plants that were domesticated by early humans, what information in the excerpt would be incidental to your focus?

Secondary Source

Domesticated crops, such as wheat, rice, or maize, became a nutritious and reliable source of food. These grains were chief food sources for entire societies. Animals were a source of food. People ate their meat, but also the eggs, milk, and honey they produced. Horses and oxen helped them work the fields. The fur of sheep and llamas was used to make clothing.

Domesticated animals, such as horses, sheep, and cattle, were easier to control than their wild counterparts. Some people lived in places where growing food was difficult. They traveled to different places with their animals so that they would have grasslands to eat from. The people herding the animals would use them for food and clothing. This way of life was called pastoral nomadism.

At first, wild and domesticated breeds were similar. But over time, people selected the seeds of the plants that produced the best crops. Domesticated plants began to produce more abundant food that was larger, easier to cook, and tastier. A domesticated tomato is the size of an orange, but a wild tomato is the size of a cherry. By contrast, some breeds of domesticated goats, pigs, and cattle are smaller than their wild ancestors. Smaller animals may have been easier to manage.

LESSON 2

Humans Spread Out

GET READY TO READ

START UP

What questions would you ask the people who once lived in this settlement located on the French coast?

GUIDING QUESTIONS

- How and why did modern humans succeed and populate most regions of the world?
- How did the environment influence the migrations of early humans?
- How did early humans adapt to new environments and climate changes?

TAKE NOTES

Literacy Skills: Analyze Cause and Effect
Use the graphic organizer in your 📓 Active Journal to take notes as you read the lesson.

PRACTICE VOCABULARY

Use the vocabulary activity in your 📓 Active Journal to practice the vocabulary words.

Vocabulary	Academic Vocabulary
migration	complex
environment	network
adapt	

Over time, new species of hominins arose. In this lesson, you will read about these human ancestors and the ways they were different from those who came before them.

What Were Later Stone Age Peoples Like?

Toward the end of the Paleolithic Era, two groups of larger-brained hominins appeared. Both groups had more developed technologies than earlier peoples. However, only one of these groups would survive past the Stone Age.

Who Were the Neanderthals? A group known as Neanderthals appeared in Europe and parts of Asia about 230,000 years ago. Their name comes from the Neander Valley in present-day Germany, where their fossil remains were first found. Fossils of a close relative of the Neanderthals, called the Denisovans, have been found in Asia.

Some archaeologists believe that the Neanderthals were the first hominins to bury their dead. Remains of flowers and other objects in burial sites may be evidence that Neanderthals carefully buried bodies and may have believed in life after death. Other archaeologists, however, disagree. Even if Neanderthals did bury their dead, their burial practices were much simpler than those of later people.

When Did Modern Humans Appear? About 200,000 years ago, the last new group of humans appeared. The scientific name of this group is *Homo sapiens*, which means "wise people." *Homo sapiens* were the first modern humans—or people like us.

These people were like Neanderthals in some ways. Both groups made tools, used fire, and hunted animals. But modern humans were taller, lighter, and less muscular.

Although at one time it was thought that Neanderthals could only make noises resembling a frog's croak, we know from fossil finds that Neanderthals could speak and form words. About 70,000 years ago, however, *Homo sapiens* developed a powerful new skill—**complex language**. Having a shared language gave *Homo sapiens* a great advantage in the struggle to survive. They could organize a hunt, warn of danger, and pass knowledge and skills on to their young.

The ability to use complex language, think, and cooperate with other people helped *Homo sapiens* develop new skills and teach them to each other. As a result, they could survive harsh conditions and live in new places. These traits also made it possible for them to defend against threats.

For thousands of years, Neanderthals and modern humans lived near each other, but the Neanderthals eventually disappeared. Although the two groups intermingled, some archaeologists believe they fought with the newcomers and lost. Whatever the cause, there is no fossil evidence of Neanderthals in Europe after about 28,000 years ago.

READING CHECK **Identify Supporting Details** What skill gave modern humans an advantage over Neanderthals?

Academic Vocabulary

complex • *adj.*, having many related parts; not simple

Analyze Visuals This photograph shows a Neanderthal skull on the left and a Homo sapiens skull on the right. **Compare** What differences do you notice between the two skulls?

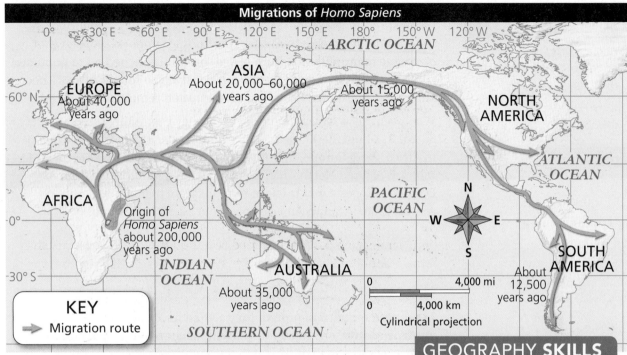

Migrations of *Homo Sapiens*

ARCTIC OCEAN

EUROPE
About 40,000 years ago

ASIA
About 20,000–60,000 years ago

About 15,000 years ago

NORTH AMERICA

ATLANTIC OCEAN

AFRICA

Origin of *Homo Sapiens* about 200,000 years ago

PACIFIC OCEAN

SOUTH AMERICA

About 12,500 years ago

INDIAN OCEAN

AUSTRALIA
About 35,000 years ago

0   4,000 mi
0   4,000 km
Cylindrical projection

KEY
Migration route

SOUTHERN OCEAN

What Do We Know About Early Human Migration?

Most archaeologists agree that *Homo sapiens* have walked on Earth for only about 200,000 years. But they do not agree on where modern humans came from or how they spread. Scientists have studied both fossils and genetic information, or the physical qualities that living things pass from one generation to the next. They have developed two main theories, or possible explanations, about the movement of early humans.

Migration from Africa Most scientists think that *Homo sapiens*, like other early humans, originated in Africa. From there, *Homo sapiens* began a long **migration** to other regions of the world. A migration occurs when people leave their homeland to live somewhere else. Scientists who support the "out of Africa" theory suggest that as modern humans migrated from Africa to new places, they gradually replaced the older groups who were already living there.

Some scientists argue that large-brained humans developed separately in many different parts of the world and they eventually mixed together. However, most scientists disagree with this theory.

New Evidence For years, there was little fossil evidence to support either theory. Then in 2007, scientists analyzed a fossil skull that had been found in South Africa. Tests showed that it was about 36,000 years old, the same as skulls found in Europe from the same period. This similarity suggests that humans were already in their modern form when they migrated from Africa.

GEOGRAPHY SKILLS

Early humans are thought to have migrated throughout the world roughly according to the routes shown on this map.

1. **Region** At what point on this map did human migration begin?

2. **Movement** Based on this map, describe the movement of early people from their starting point in Africa.

 INTERACTIVE

Migrations of *Homo sapiens*

In 2008, scientists completed a genetic study of nearly a thousand people around the globe. Scientists found the greatest genetic variety in communities closest to Africa. This finding supports the idea that, as people migrated away from Africa, groups branched off to populate new areas. The new evidence gives a boost to the "out of Africa" theory. Still, many questions about human migration remain unanswered.

Wherever *Homo sapiens* first appeared, they eventually spread across Earth. By about 30,000 years ago, these modern humans were living in Africa, Asia, Europe, and Australia. About 15,000-18,000 years ago, humans entered North America by crossing a land bridge from Asia. Evidence suggests that modern humans were living as far south as central Chile in South America by about 12,500 years ago.

READING CHECK Ask Questions What questions do you think still remain about human migration?

How Did Humans Adapt to Varied Environments?

As modern humans migrated, they settled in a variety of **environments**, or surroundings. With each move, people had to **adapt**, or change their way of life, to suit their new environment. They had to find out which plants could be eaten, hunt different animals and find new materials for tools and shelters.

How Did the Climate Change?
Over time, people also had to adapt to changes in the world's climate. During the past two million years the Earth has experienced four long ice ages. The last great Ice Age began about 70,000 years ago, soon after modern humans appeared.

Analyze Diagrams Many factors helped early humans to survive. **Demonstrate Reasoned Judgment** Which of the key factors for human survival shown do you think was the most important? Choose one and explain your reasoning.

EARLY HUMAN SURVIVAL

EARLY HUMANS LIVED IN A HARSH ENVIRONMENT. THEY DEVELOPED DIFFERENT WAYS TO **SURVIVE**.

They **hunted** for meat and **gathered** plants and nuts to eat.

They **avoided** dangerous predators.

They were **social**, working together to survive.

They made stone **tools** such as hand axes.

They used **fire** for heat, cooking, and protection.

They found **shelter** to protect themselves from the weather.

During the last Ice Age, thick sheets of ice, called glaciers, spread across large regions of Earth. Glaciers covered the northern parts of Europe, Asia, and North America. Parts of the Southern Hemisphere were also under ice. Moving glaciers created many of the world's mountains, lakes, and rivers.

With so much of Earth's water frozen in the glaciers, rainfall decreased. Areas that had once been grasslands became deserts. Sea levels dropped, exposing "land bridges" where ocean waters had once been. Because of these changes, many animals had to migrate to find food. The people who depended on those animals had to follow the herds.

How Did Humans Stay Warm? As winters grew longer, people learned to use whatever materials they could find to build warm shelters. In Eastern Europe, for example, people built huts out of mammoth bones. Mammoths were huge furry animals, related to elephants, that lived during the Ice Age. Hunters covered these huts with animal skins and kept fires burning in their hearths day and night.

▲ Woolly mammoth skull

Why Did People Form Larger Communities? Some groups adapted to change by forming larger communities. In larger groups, hunters could work together to kill animals such as mammoths. They could also better defend their communities from attack by other nomadic groups.

Growing communities might be organized into groups of families with a common ancestor. A group would be made up of perhaps 25 to 50 people. Group leaders took on decision-making roles, such as organizing hunts. Everywhere human society developed, **networks** of groups or families played a vital role in creating strong communities.

In time, Stone Age communities began to trade with one another for special stones or shells. They likely also traded information about finding food during hard times.

✓ READING CHECK Identify Supporting Details What did humans do to survive in different environments?

Academic Vocabulary
network • *n.* a closely interconnected group of people or things

---

✓ Lesson Check

Practice Vocabulary

1. What are some of the things that make up a person's **environment**?

2. What did humans do to **adapt** after moving to new environments?

Critical Thinking and Writing

3. **Compare and Contrast** How did Neanderthals and *Homo sapiens* differ from earlier people?

4. **Understand Effects** How did the development of language help humans survive harsh conditions and live in new places?

5. **Draw Conclusions** Why did early humans migrate?

6. **Understand Effects** How did forming larger communities help people survive?

7. **Writing Workshop: Establish Setting** In your 📓 Active Journal, explain how the hunter-gatherer in your story is adapting to a changing climate.

Relate Events in Time

Use the sources and these steps to relate events in time.

INTERACTIVE

Sequence

1 **Identify key events and topics.** Set a purpose for your research by listing the time period, people, or events you are focusing on. For example, the excerpt from the text covers a time period that stretches from two million years ago to 70,000 years ago. What period does the timeline cover?

2 **Look for clues about time.** Important clues include information about dates and times of key events. For example, the excerpt uses the phrase "over time," which suggests that a long period of time is going to be discussed. What other words or phrases indicate that events are happening in sequence?

3 **Look for clues about relationships.** Besides dates and times, a variety of words can signal how key events are related in time. Examples include words such as *before*, *after*, *during*, or *while*. The excerpt says many creatures that lived *during* the last Ice Age have gone extinct.

a. What are two other words that suggest how events are related in time?

b. Use those words to summarize the information in the timeline.

Secondary Source

Many of the creatures who roamed the planet during the Ice Age have become extinct. Large mammals, such as mastodons, ground sloths, and sabercats, died off and disappeared from the earth. Some animals, however, managed to adapt over time. For example, the first jaguars hunted and ate very large prey. As time passed and the number of large prey animals dwindled, jaguars began to eat smaller animals. Making this change enabled jaguars to survive as a species when the large prey animals they had once depended on went extinct. As a result, jaguars are still found in the wild today.

Ice Age Events in Years Ago

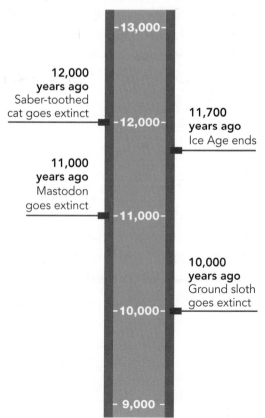

- 13,000 -

12,000 years ago
Saber-toothed cat goes extinct

- 12,000 -

11,700 years ago
Ice Age ends

11,000 years ago
Mastodon goes extinct

- 11,000 -

10,000 years ago
Ground sloth goes extinct

- 10,000 -

- 9,000 -

LESSON 3

Developing Complex Cultures

BOUNCE TO ACTIVATE

▶ VIDEO

GET READY TO READ

START UP

This image shows a reproduction of a cave painting from about 20,000 years ago. Why are people today interested in these ancient paintings?

GUIDING QUESTIONS

- What evidence reveals how human societies became more complex?
- How did humans learn to modify their environment?
- Why did some people develop agriculture while others lived as herders?

TAKE NOTES

Literacy Skills: Sequence
Use the graphic organizer in your 📔 Active Journal to take notes as you read the lesson.

PRACTICE VOCABULARY

Use the vocabulary activity in your 📔 Active Journal to practice the vocabulary words.

Vocabulary	Academic Vocabulary
populate	potential
animism	reliable
domesticate	
revolution	
nomad	

Over millions of years, many groups of early humans appeared and then died out. *Homo sapiens*, or modern humans, were the last of these groups to appear. As you will read, scientists still have much to learn about the development of the first modern humans. But one fact is clear: These large-brained "wise people" were often on the move. Over many thousands of years, they spread out to **populate**, or become inhabitants of, almost every land area of the world.

When Did People Start to Create Art?

Over the course of the Ice Age, the culture of Paleolithic communities became more and more complex. One of the most important signs of a complex culture is the existence of artwork such as paintings and statues.

What Can We Learn from Ancient Cave Paintings? In 1940, four French teenagers and their dog made a remarkable discovery. The boys were exploring a cave near Lascaux in southern France. By the dim light of their lamps, they were amazed

Analyze Images This Neolithic cave painting of animals was found in Laas Geel, Somalia. **Draw Conclusions** What can you conclude about the skill of early artists from this painting?

Academic Vocabulary

potential • *n.,* possibility to grow and change in the future

to see that the walls were covered with paintings of horses, bison, bulls, and other prehistoric animals. Other paintings in the cave showed human figures or abstract designs.

Scientists later determined that the Lascaux cave paintings dated back about 16,000 years, to the time of the last Ice Age. Some images were carved into the stone, but most were painted. The artists made pigments by grinding up minerals of various colors.

Even older cave paintings have been found elsewhere in France, as well as in Spain. Examples of cave and rock art have also been discovered in many other parts of the world where early people lived. For example, the rock paintings shown at the beginning of this chapter are from the Sahara, a vast desert in North Africa.

Stone Age artists also carved small statues. Like the cave paintings, many of these carvings represent animals. Others depict pregnant women.

What Does Stone Age Art Tell Us? Early works of art such as these show that Stone Age people were capable of complex thoughts and actions. After visiting one French cave, an archaeologist commented,

Primary Source

The mark of human genius is here, full-blown, with its immense and eternal mystery, and with all its potential for hope in the success of the adventure of modern man. We become modest in these surroundings; a great feeling of timelessness [comes] from them. When we return to the surface, we can't help but question the motivations that lie behind the creation of all those frescoes. To imagine the unimaginable. In any case, in contemplating them we feel the presence ... of an intense, enormous will to create.

—Robert Begouën, *The Cave of Chauvet-Pont-d'Arc*

We do not know the exact reasons Stone Age people created these works of art. Perhaps hunter-gatherers believed that creating an image of an animal would give them power over that animal during the hunt. Statues of pregnant women may have been intended to bring good luck to women about to give birth.

INTERACTIVE

Paleolithic
Cave Art

✓ READING CHECK **Draw Inferences** What subjects did Stone Age people show in their art? Why might Stone Age artists have chosen to show animals, human figures, and abstract designs?

What Do We Know About Stone Age Religion?

Cave paintings and other art provide strong evidence that the cultures of Stone Age people became more complex over time. Another sign of a more complex culture is the development of religious beliefs and practices. Many of these practices involve death and burial.

Quick Activity

Explore ancient cave paintings in your ▧ Active Journal.

How Did Early People Bury Their Dead? Scientists have found much evidence to show that Ice Age people buried their dead. One grave found in present-day Russia contained the bodies of two children, a boy about 13 years old and a girl about 8 years old. Both children were covered with thousands of ivory beads. On his chest, the boy wore an ivory pendant carved in the shape of an animal. The girl wore a bead cap and an ivory pin at her throat.

What Were Some Early Religious Practices? Discoveries such as cave paintings, statues, and burial sites may suggest how early humans reacted to what they thought were mysterious and powerful forces. These rituals and symbols were an important part of early culture. They go beyond survival, and express deeper meanings of the natural and social world.

The evidence suggests that these early people believed that the natural world was filled with spirits, a belief known as **animism**. To early humans, there were spirits in the animals they hunted. There were also spirits in the trees, rocks, water, and weather around them. Prehistoric people may have painted pictures of animals, such as bison or deer, to honor the spirits of those animals and to ask forgiveness for having to kill them.

✓ READING CHECK **Identify Implied Main Ideas** What did the development of religious practices suggest about the relationship early humans had with the natural and social world?

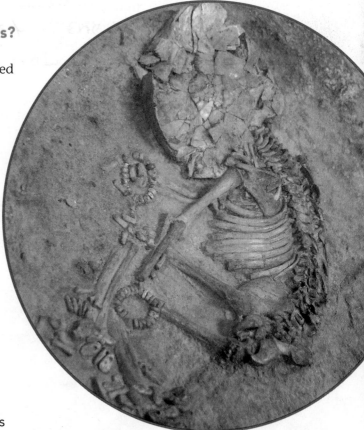

Analyze Images This child was carefully buried with jewelry made of bones and precious stones. **Infer** What does this burial suggest about the culture of the people who buried him?

When Did People Start to Farm?

By the end of the Paleolithic Era, human beings occupied many regions of the world. They had developed complex spoken language, learned to make a variety of tools and weapons, and adapted to different environments. Yet, in many important ways, their lives had not changed. They still lived in relatively small groups as hunter-gatherers, following the herds of animals that they depended on for survival.

Then, beginning as much as 18,000 years ago, humans gradually began to learn a new skill that over time changed how they would live. By around 10,000-9,000 years ago, some communities were relying on farming for food. This development marked the end of the Paleolithic Era and the beginning of what we call the Neolithic Era, or New Stone Age. (The prefix neo- means "new".) Around this time, temperatures increased and rainfall patterns changed. Glaciers that had covered so much of Earth began to shrink. As the ice from the glaciers melted, ocean levels rose.

Most plants and animals adapted to these changes. Fir trees, which could survive cold weather, spread north into once-icy regions.

Quest CONNECTIONS

Study the photo. What does it suggest about what makes a good location for a village? Record your answer in your ▱ Active Journal.

Some large Ice Age animals, however, did not adapt to a warmer world, and many species died out. People who had hunted some of these animals for food had to find something else to eat. Some people adapted to these changes by searching for new sources of food. They found smaller animals to hunt. People living near rivers or lakes began to depend more on fishing.

▲ Céide Fields, Ireland, is the site of a Neolithic settlement. It is about six and a half thousand years old and one of the oldest known system of fields used for farming in the world.

How Did People First Modify the Environment?

Others learned to modify or change their environment so that it would provide more food. For example, people cleared trees and bushes by setting them on fire. The grasses that grew back attracted grazing animals such as deer. People may also have noticed that, if seeds were scattered on the ground, new plants grew there the next year. This discovery led them to find ways to encourage the growth of wild food plants.

How Did Domesticated Plants and Animals Change People's Lives?

Over time, people learned to domesticate plants and animals, especially those that they used for food. To **domesticate** means to change the growth of plants or behavior of animals in ways that are useful for humans. Widespread domestication marked the birth of farming. The shift from hunting to farming was so important that historians call it the Neolithic Agricultural Revolution. A **revolution** is a complete change in ways of thinking, working, or living.

Even before the Agricultural Revolution, wild wolves developed into dogs, which humans then domesticated. Dogs provided help in the hunt, as well as companionship and protection.

Domesticated plants, or crops, became a **reliable** source of food. Grains such as wheat, rice, or maize became chief food sources for entire societies. Many animals also provided food—not only meat, but eggs, milk, and even honey. Horses and oxen became work animals. Sheep and llamas had coats of hair that were used to make clothing.

Domesticated animals, such as horses, sheep, and cattle, were easier to control. People who lived in places where growing food was difficult traveled to different places with their animals. By moving to new areas, the animals would find new grasslands to eat from. The people herding, or guiding, the animals would use them for food and clothing. This way of life was called pastoral nomadism. **Nomads** are people who move from place to place with their herds.

▲ These Neolithic stone farm tools are about 10,000 years old. On the left is a hoe. On the right is a plow blade.

At first, there was little difference between wild and domesticated breeds. But over time, people selected the seeds of the plants that produced the best crops to sow again. As a result, domesticated plants began to produce more abundant food that tasted better, were larger, and easier to cook. A wild tomato, for example, is the size of a cherry, but a domesticated tomato is the size of an orange. By contrast, some breeds of domesticated goats, pigs, and cattle are smaller than their wild ancestors. Smaller animals may have been easier to manage.

What New Tools Did People Make? Farmers invented new tools. They used axes to cut down trees for farmland and sickles to harvest grain. The grain was then ground into flour with grinding stones or hand mills.

All of these tools were at first made out of stone. Later people mined for bronze and iron and learned how to smelt, or use heat, to remove metals from a mineral. They used these metals to create more efficient tools. That is why historians refer to different stages of early history as the Stone Age, the Bronze Age, and the Iron Age.

☑ READING CHECK **Analyze Cause and Effect** Why might learning to farm have led early farmers to create new tools?

☑ Lesson Check

Practice Vocabulary

1. What is a belief in **animism**?

2. Why do historians say the ability to **domesticate** plants and animals was a **revolution**?

Critical Thinking and Writing

3. **Understand Effects** What are two signs that people who lived during the Ice Age developed more complex cultures?

4. **Draw Inferences** What skills and tools would be needed to make cave paintings? What does this suggest about the people who created them?

5. **Identify Supporting Details** What did animals do to improve life for humans?

6. **Identify Cause and Effect** Why did some people choose pastoral nomadism as a way of life?

7. **Writing Workshop: Introduce Characters** You're now visiting the Neolithic Era. Write one or two sentences in your ▢ Active Journal about an early man or woman who worked with domesticated plants and animals. Write another sentence or two about a herder (pastoral nomad).

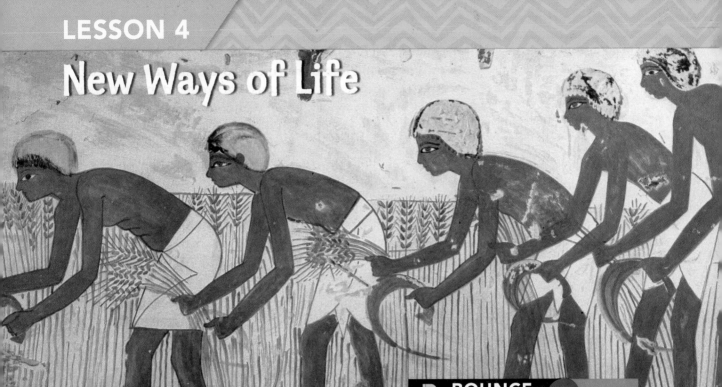

LESSON 4
New Ways of Life

GET READY TO READ

START UP
What are these ancient Egyptians doing? What does this activity suggest about their way of life?

GUIDING QUESTIONS
- How did farming enable people to settle in one place and develop specialized skills?
- How did farming villages develop into cities?
- What were the effects of these new ways of life?

TAKE NOTES
Literacy Skills: Analyze Cause and Effect
Use the graphic organizer in your 📕 Active Journal to take notes as you read the lesson.

PRACTICE VOCABULARY
Use the vocabulary activity in your 📕 Active Journal to take practice the vocabulary.

Vocabulary	Academic Vocabulary
surplus	benefit
specialization	accumulate
economy	

People of the Paleolithic Era, or Old Stone Age, lived as hunter-gatherers. They could not have imagined many of the things that we now take for granted. People often had to follow herds of animals, so they were unable to settle for long in one place. People could own few possessions—only what they could easily carry. Food supplies were uncertain. Life for many was short and dangerous.

In time, most hunter-gatherers stopped wandering in search of food and settled in one place. Life was still difficult, and survival was still the main concern. But with people staying in one place, the world began to take on many features we recognize today.

Where Did Farming Begin and How Did It Spread?

No one knows for sure where people first began to plant seeds for food. Still, archaeologists have found evidence to suggest where farming began and how it spread. They have also learned something about the way people lived in early farming communities.

Where Were the First Centers of Agriculture?

Most historians believe that about 10,000 years ago southwestern Asia became the first center of agriculture. There, scientists have unearthed seeds from domesticated wheat plants that were buried long ago. The seeds are similar to wild varieties of wheat that still grow in the area.

Farming may then have spread from southwestern Asia westward into Africa. It may also have spread northward into Europe and eastward into the Indus River valley of South Asia.

Other centers of agriculture appeared independently in different areas of the world. In southwestern Asia, for example, farming began when people started to plant wheat and barley. In the southern part of present-day China, farming began with the domestication of rice. Farther to the north, a grain called millet was the first crop to be domesticated.

In Central and South America, people learned to grow potatoes, beans, and squash. In Africa, farming began with crops such as sorghum and yams.

What Were the Costs and Benefits of Farming?

In every place that agriculture developed, the transition from hunting and gathering to farming took place gradually, over a long period of time. Each way of life had costs as well as **benefits**.

Some of the costs of shifting to agriculture were clear. First, planting crops and herding, or bringing together, animals took a great deal of time and energy. Second, farming was uncertain. If a year's crop failed due to bad weather or disease, a family might starve. Third, farming could be dangerous. Evidence suggests that bands of nomads sometimes attacked farmers and stole their food.

Analyze Diagrams
Domestication started with dogs. Other animals and fruits, vegetables, and grains followed. **Sequence** How many years did it take before horses and cats were domesticated?

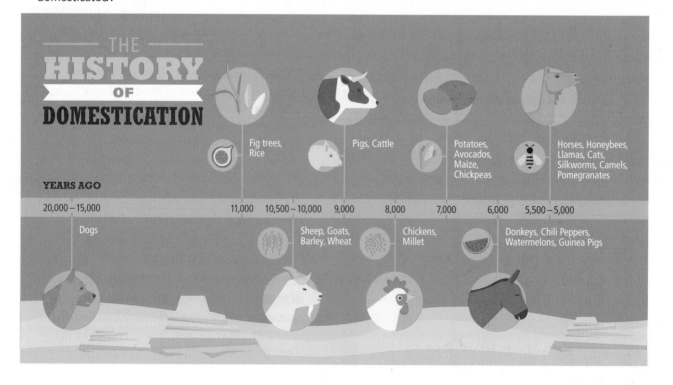

THE

HISTORY

OF

DOMESTICATION

Fig trees, Rice — Pigs, Cattle — Potatoes, Avocados, Maize, Chickpeas — Horses, Honeybees, Llamas, Cats, Silkworms, Camels, Pomegranates

YEARS AGO

| 20,000–15,000 | 11,000 | 10,500–10,000 | 9,000 | 8,000 | 7,000 | 6,000 | 5,500–5,000 |

Dogs — Sheep, Goats, Barley, Wheat — Chickens, Millet — Donkeys, Chili Peppers, Watermelons, Guinea Pigs

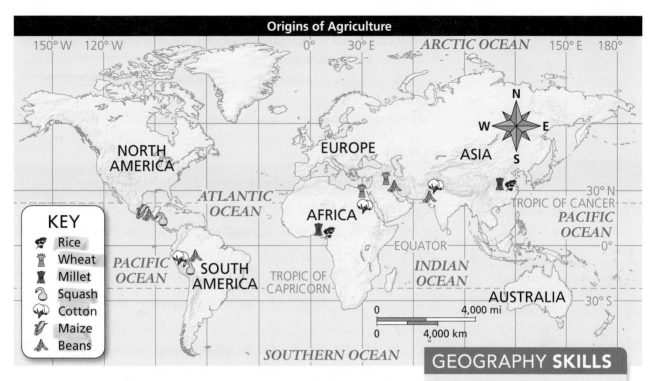

Origins of Agriculture

KEY
- 🦅 Rice
- 🌾 Wheat
- 🌿 Millet
- 🎃 Squash
- 🌸 Cotton
- 🌽 Maize
- 🍌 Beans

GEOGRAPHY SKILLS

Agriculture most likely originated in many regions.

1. **Interaction** What were some early crops grown in South America? In West Africa?

2. **Region** Identify a crop that was grown in more than one part of the world.

Agriculture also offered many benefits. Farming produced more food and required less land than hunting and gathering. An early farm family might need only six to seven acres of land to raise enough wheat or maize to feed themselves for a year. In contrast, a hunter-gatherer family needed about 20,000 acres on which to find enough food for a year.

As a result of agriculture, more people were able to build permanent homes and farming villages. Farming also provided new sources of material for clothing. (Later in this section, you will read more about the new types of shelter and clothing that were invented during the Neolithic Era.)

Some groups tried farming for a time and then returned to hunting and gathering. But in the end, most people chose to remain farmers.

✅ **READING CHECK** **Summarize** Where did farming begin and how did it spread?

How Did Farming Change Human Culture?

The first effect of farming was on people's food supply. But over time, the Neolithic Agricultural Revolution transformed every part of human culture.

What New Kinds of Shelter Did People Build? Farmers found ways to build permanent shelters. People used a mixture of mud and straw to form walls. The sun baked and hardened the mixture. People made roofs by placing poles and branches across the tops of walls and covering them with mud.

👆 **INTERACTIVE**

Otzi the Neolithic Ice Man

Quick Activity

Explore ancient innovations, including farming, in your 📖 Active Journal.

One of the oldest known farming settlements in the world is a village called Çatalhöyük (chah tahl hyoo yook). It stood in present-day Turkey more than 8,000 years ago.

At its height, up to six thousand people may have lived in Çatalhöyük. The environment provided sources of water and building materials. A British archaeologist described the two-story homes that made up the settlement:

Primary Source

The houses of Çatalhöyük were so tightly packed together that there were few or no streets. Access to interior spaces was across roofs—which had been made of wood and reeds plastered with mud— and down stairs. People buried their dead beneath the floors. Above all, the interiors were rich with artwork—mural paintings, reliefs, and sculptures, including images of women that some interpreted as evidence for a cult of a mother goddess.

—Ian Hodder, "This Old House"

Quest CONNECTIONS

Based on the primary source, what was life like in a Neolithic village? Record your findings in your 📖 Active Journal.

Each home had its own kitchen and food storage area. The people grew grains and raised flocks of sheep and goats.

How Did Farming Change Clothing?

Agriculture also changed the way that people dressed. For hunter-gatherers, the most important materials for clothing were animal hides and furs. Farming provided new materials that were lighter and easier to work with. From Egypt and India to the Americas, farmers domesticated the cotton plant. They learned to weave cloth from the plant fibers. Another plant, flax, became a source of linen.

Domesticated animals such as sheep and yaks also provided clothing materials. People used wool and other animal hair to form yarn or thread. In China, people later learned to breed silkworms.

What Were the Effects of Food Surpluses?

As crops and herds improved, the amount of food that farmers could produce each year increased. Some families were able to raise a **surplus**, or more than they needed to feed themselves. Surplus food could support a growing population. The size of farming villages thus increased.

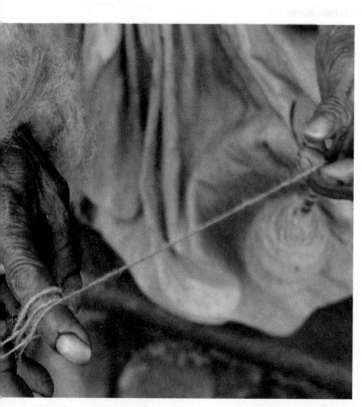

▲ Spinning yarn from wool the way it would have been done in ancient times

When there was a surplus of food, not everyone in a village needed to farm. Some people could specialize. **Specialization** occurs when people spend most of their time working at a single job or craft. They could then trade the goods they made for the surplus food grown by farmers. Skilled toolmakers turned stone into polished axes and knives. Potters shaped clay into bowls. Weavers wove sheep's wool into cloth. A few people also became skilled at metalworking. Early metalworkers heated ore to extract, or remove, such metals as copper and tin.

How Did Farming Change Social Organization?

Early farming communities remained small. Like hunting, farming required close cooperation among members of the community. Heads of families consulted to make important decisions. They might discuss when to plant and harvest crops, what to do with food surpluses, or how to protect the community from outside dangers.

Archaeologists have uncovered the remains of several Neolithic villages, such as Skara Brae in Scotland. In these villages, all homes were more or less the same size. Some historians believe this means that great differences in social standing did not yet exist.

Still, having a permanent place to live meant that people could own more possessions. Early farmers filled their homes with furniture, tools, clay pots, and other goods. These items would have been too heavy to move from one campsite to another. Over time, some families **accumulated** more food and possessions than others. Food surplus sometimes led to conflict, however, as some groups wanted to expand their supplies at the expense of others. Some people hired guards to protect their wealth.

As surpluses increased and people began to specialize, greater social differences emerged. As evidence of this inequality, scientists have unearthed graves with jewelry and other fine materials while other graves have none of these things.

☑ READING CHECK Identify Cause and Effect How did farming lead to specialization?

How Did the First Cities Begin?

The world's first cities began as farming villages in the Middle East. As the villages grew, they began to trade with one another. Trade, like farming, became an important source of wealth.

The City of Uruk Many historians consider Uruk to be the world's first city. It is thought to have been founded 6,000 to 7,000 years ago. Uruk was different from Çatalhöyük and older farming villages. One difference was Uruk's size. Çatalhöyük covered about 32 acres and was home to no more than 6,000 people. When Uruk was at its height, more than 40,000 people lived there. Uruk covered an area of nearly 1,000 acres and had houses, gardens, and large public buildings such as temples.

Analyze Images This gold stag was crafted by an artist in Çatalhöyük. **Infer** What does it suggest about the skills of ancient craftspeople?

Academic Vocabulary

accumulate • v., collect or attain a large amount of something

▲ A reconstructed Neolithic settlement in the eastern Mediterranean

Another difference was Uruk's form of government. Villages such as Çatalhöyük had little need for complex government. People acted and made decisions according to ancient village customs. A village council settled most disputes. A city such as Uruk was too large to manage that way. Uruk had a strong, well-organized government. The city's first rulers were probably temple priests. Later, powerful military leaders ruled Uruk as kings. These rulers had far more power than a village council did.

How Did Cities Become Centers of Wealth? A city such as Uruk also had a more complex economy than did early farming villages. An **economy** is the system that a community uses to produce and distribute goods and services.

In the earliest human communities, each group produced those goods and services that were necessary for its survival. The group produced these goods and services by hunting and gathering. The goods and services were then shared by the members of the community.

Çatalhöyük's economy was based mainly on farming. By contrast, Uruk's more complex economy was based on both farming and trade. Workshops that produced all kinds of goods lined the city's streets. Traders from Uruk traveled widely. Archaeologists have found pottery and other trade goods from Uruk in many places in the Middle East.

The wealth of Uruk and other early cities attracted many newcomers. People began to move from the countryside into the cities. Many early cities built walls to protect themselves from raiders. Uruk, for example, was surrounded by a thick wall that stretched for 6 miles around the city. This wall was a sign that Uruk was a wealthy city worth protecting.

☑ READING CHECK **Compare and Contrast** How did the government of Uruk differ from that in villages such as Çatalhöyük?

Quest CONNECTIONS

Based on the photo, what conclusions can you draw about life in a Neolithic village? Record your findings in your 📓 Active Journal.

☑ Lesson Check

Practice Vocabulary

1. How did a **surplus** of food affect the size of the population?

2. How was Uruk's **economy** different from the economy of Çatalhöyük?

Critical Thinking and Writing

3. **Identify Implied Main Ideas** How did farming change the kinds of communities people lived in?

4. **Draw Conclusions** What are some of the benefits and drawbacks of job specialization?

5. **Infer** Why do you think people in early cities began to trade with other cities?

6. **Writing Workshop: Organize Sequence of Events** Make an ordered list in your 📓 Active Journal to show what happens to your characters in your narrative essay. You will use this sequence of events when you write your narrative essay at the end of the Topic.

LESSON 5

The Rise of Civilizations

BOUNCE TO ACTIVATE   ▶ **VIDEO**

GET READY TO READ

START UP

Examine the photo of the ruins of the ancient city of Uruk. What does it tell you about the society that was centered there?

GUIDING QUESTIONS

- What environmental factors helped civilizations grow?
- What impact did civilizations and complex urban societies have on the surrounding environment?
- How and why did cities give rise to the world's first civilizations?
- What features did all early civilizations have in common?

TAKE NOTES

Literacy Skills: Summarize

Use the graphic organizer in your 🗐 Active Journal to take notes as you read the lesson.

PRACTICE VOCABULARY

Use the vocabulary activity in your 🗐 Active Journal to practice the vocabulary words.

Vocabulary		Academic Vocabulary
civilization	religion	manage
resource	social class	specialization

As farming spread, many small settlements appeared. In time, some villages grew into cities. In this lesson, you will read about the rise of early civilizations.

How Did Cities Lead to Civilizations?

— Evolved /evolution

As early cities grew in size and power, some of them became centers of civilizations. A **civilization** is a complex society that has cities, a well-organized government, and workers with specialized job skills. The word *civilization* comes from the Latin word *civis*, meaning "resident of a city."

8 aspects of Civilization

What Resources Were Important? The rise of early civilizations depended on the creation of a food surplus. Creating that surplus, in turn, depended on the ability of people to manage their resources well. A **resource** is a supply of something that can be used as needed.

depend

The most important resources that people needed were fertile soil, fresh water, and seeds. However, these resources were worth

reason

need of little if people could not provide the labor and
Surplus tools needed to produce enough food. Managing
these resources well required a level of planning
and organization that marked a new stage in
Planing human society.

Where Were Early Civilizations? Like the
earliest villages, the earliest civilization also
appeared in southwestern Asia, in the city-state
of Sumer. In time, other civilizations appeared in
different parts of the world.

depend Four of these early civilizations developed in the
on fertile valleys surrounding major rivers: the Nile in
rivers northeastern Africa; the Tigris and Euphrates in the
southwest Asian area of Mesopotamia; the Indus in
South Asia; and the Huang River in China.

River valleys provided a good setting for permanent
settlements. Each year, the rivers rose and flooded
the nearby land. When the floodwaters went down, a
fresh layer of fertile soil remained that farmers could
use to grow crops.

Not all early civilizations began in river valleys.
Greek civilization, for example, emerged on a
rocky peninsula in southeastern Europe and a
series of islands in the eastern Mediterranean
Sea. Civilizations also changed their surrounding
environment. Farmers near rivers built irrigation
systems. Civilizations in the Americas cut down
trees and burned them to create farmland.
People cleared land to build houses, temples,
and markets.

▲ Statue of a man from
about 3500-3300 BCE found
in Uruk, Iraq

✓ READING CHECK **Understand Effects** Why did many early
civilizations arise in river valleys?

What Are the Features of Civilizations?

The civilizations that arose in different parts of the world differed in
many ways. Still, all of them had certain things in common. Most early
civilizations shared eight basic features: cities; organized governments;
established religion; job specialization; social classes; public works; arts
and architecture; and a system of writing.

Cities The first of these features was cities. Early cities emerged near
farming centers. As food surpluses led to rapid population growth,
villages grew into cities and cities grew into civilizations. They served as
centers of religion, government, and culture. A few ancient population
centers, such as Damascus, Syria, are still major cities today.

👆 INTERACTIVE

River Valley
Civilizations

Organized Government The second feature of early civilizations was a well-organized government. One role of government is **managing** society's resources so that people get those things they need to survive. A strong government can also form and train an army to defend a society from attack or to expand its borders.

[handwritten: definition]

As populations grew, government became more difficult. Powerful rulers called warlords took control of tribes in larger areas and formed governments headed by kings or queens. They relied on large numbers of public officials who handled different duties.

Established Religion A third common feature of a civilization was an established **religion**, or a set of shared spiritual beliefs. Everyone generally followed the same beliefs and practices. Religion was often linked to government. Rulers of early civilizations usually claimed that their right to rule came from the gods. In China, for example, emperors were called "Sons of Heaven."

[handwritten: definition]

In most early civilizations, people believed in many gods and goddesses that controlled most events in their lives. People feared their gods, but also hoped that the gods would protect them from harm.

[handwritten: important aspect of religion]

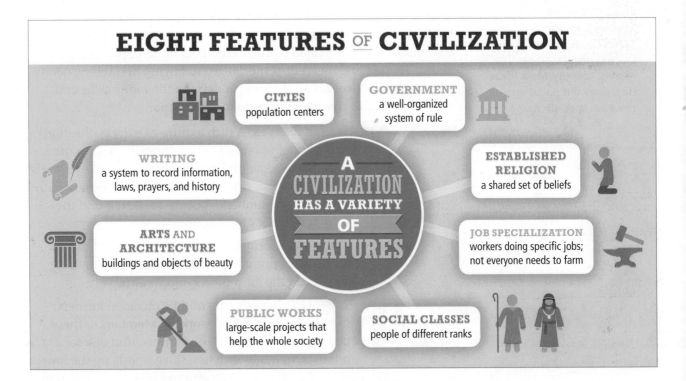

EIGHT FEATURES OF CIVILIZATION

CITIES population centers

GOVERNMENT a well-organized system of rule

WRITING a system to record information, laws, prayers, and history

A CIVILIZATION HAS A VARIETY OF FEATURES

ESTABLISHED RELIGION a shared set of beliefs

ARTS AND ARCHITECTURE buildings and objects of beauty

JOB SPECIALIZATION workers doing specific jobs; not everyone needs to farm

PUBLIC WORKS large-scale projects that help the whole society

SOCIAL CLASSES people of different ranks

Analyze Diagrams Although civilizations arose in different parts of the world, they shared these eight characteristics. **Demonstrate Reasoned Judgment** What feature do you think was the most important to a successful civilization? Why?

To keep their gods and goddesses happy, priests offered sacrifices and led prayers. This prayer is from the civilization of ancient Sumer:

Primary Source

May the known and unknown god be pacified!

May the known and unknown goddess be pacified!

The sin which I have committed I know not. . . .

My god, my sins are seven times seven; forgive my sins!

My goddess, my sins are seven times seven; forgive my sins!

—"Penitential Psalms," translated by Robert F. Harper

Academic Vocabulary

specialization • *n.*, act of concentrating on a limited number of goods or activities

From earliest times, religion included beliefs about life after death. People also looked to their religion for rules about how to treat one another and how to live moral lives.

Job Specialization Job specialization was a fourth feature that was common to civilizations. Most people in early civilizations were farmers. They produced enough food to support many kinds of specialized workers. Skilled craftworkers specialized in producing goods. Traders and merchants specialized in buying and selling goods. Job **specialization** allowed people to develop the many skills and talents needed to create and maintain a civilization.

Analyze Images In this painting from about 1425 BCE, Egyptians are shaping metal storage vessels. **Identify Main Ideas** How does this painting show job specialization?

Social Classes A fifth feature of early civilizations was a system of social classes. **Social classes** are groups of people that occupy different ranks or levels in society. Class structures resembled pyramids, with the smallest number of people at the top and the largest number at the bottom.

The highest social class in most early societies was made up of priests and rulers. The people at these ranks had the most power and wealth.

The social classes in the middle included farmers, merchants, and skilled workers. Members of these classes varied in wealth and status from one society to another. In many societies, slaves made up the lowest class. Slaves were often prisoners captured in war or poor people who sold themselves to pay their debts.

Public Works Public works were a sixth feature of civilizations. Governments organized workers to build large-scale projects such as roads, water systems, city walls, and granaries where food was stored after harvesting. Building these public works was costly, time-consuming, and often dangerous. Often, workers were injured or killed. Still, public works benefited the society as a whole.

Arts and Architecture Architecture was closely related to public works. Early people built and decorated magnificent temples, tombs, and palaces. Many of these buildings served a public function, but they were also objects of beauty.

[handwritten: Architecture examples]

Early civilizations developed other forms of art as well. In this chapter, you can see a number of examples of statues and paintings that date back thousands of years. Skilled craftworkers also produced fine luxury items for the upper classes, such as gold jewelry and perfume boxes. Music and literature, too, enriched the lives of early people and became a mark of advanced civilization.

[handwritten: Arts resources]

System of Writing The final common feature of many civilizations was a system of writing. Forms of writing varied, from picture writing to symbols representing sounds and letters.

In some early societies, writing was first developed mainly to record numbers, such as the amount of grain harvested. Eventually, however, people used writing to preserve all kinds of information. They recorded laws, wrote down prayers to the gods, and described the mighty deeds of rulers.

Historians have learned much about the early civilizations that left behind written records. With the development of writing, we pass from prehistory to recorded history.

[handwritten: Writing aspects]

READING CHECK **Identify Main Ideas** What are the eight basic features of civilization?

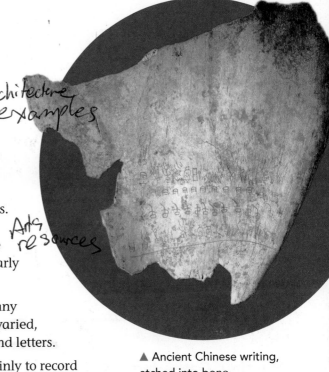

▲ Ancient Chinese writing, etched into bone

☑ Lesson Check

Practice Vocabulary

1. Choose one of the eight features of **civilization** and explain how it still exists in our civilization today.

2. What social classes were common in most early civilizations?

Critical Thinking and Writing

3. **Infer** What would happen to a civilization if it ran out of resources?

4. **Identify Supporting Details** What are public works? Give two examples.

5. **Synthesize** How was job specialization linked to the emergence of social classes?

6. **Writing Workshop: Use Descriptive Details and Sensory Language** Write notes in your 📓 Active Journal about descriptive details and sensory language that you can use in the narrative essay you will write at the end of the Topic.

☑ Review and Assessment

VISUAL REVIEW

Neanderthals and Early Humans

Neanderthals	Homo Sapiens
• Were first to bury their dead	• Had larger brains than predecessors
• May have believed in life after death	• Could form complex language
• Hunted animals	• Cooperated with each other
• Could form language	• Hunted animals
• Used tools and fire	• Used tools and fire

Hunting, Gathering, and Farming

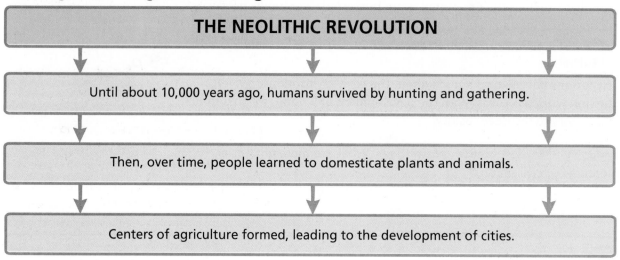

THE NEOLITHIC REVOLUTION

Until about 10,000 years ago, humans survived by hunting and gathering.

Then, over time, people learned to domesticate plants and animals.

Centers of agriculture formed, leading to the development of cities.

READING REVIEW

Use the Take Notes and Practice Vocabulary activities in your Active Journal to review the topic.

INTERACTIVE

Practice vocabulary using the Topic Mini-Games.

Quest FINDINGS

Design Your Village

Get help for designing your Neolithic village in your Active Journal.

ASSESSMENT

Vocabulary and Key Ideas

1. **Explain** How do **archaeologists** and **geologists** help us learn about the past?

2. **Describe** How did **hunter-gatherers** of the Paleolithic Era survive?

3. **Describe** How did people **adapt** to changing climate conditions during the last Ice Age?

4. **Summarize** What was the Neolithic Agricultural **Revolution**?

5. **Explain** How did farming lead to food **surpluses**?

6. **Explain** In early civilizations, how was government connected to religion?

7. **Define** What is a **hieroglyphic**?

Critical Thinking and Writing

8. **Compare and Contrast** How were Stone Age people different and similar to us?

9. **Infer** What do you think happens to species that fail to adapt?

10. **Analyze Cause and Effect** How did farming lead to the development of social classes?

11. **Analyze Cause and Effect** Do you think there could have been civilization without the development of agriculture? Explain.

12. **Revisit the Essential Question** Does geography really shape people's lives? Explain.

13. **Writing Workshop: Write a Narrative Essay** Use the notes you made in your 📖 Active Journal to write a narrative essay in which you travel through time to see how hunter-gatherers, early farmers, and pastoral nomads lived.

Analyze Primary Sources

14. According to the primary source, animals were domesticated in certain ways in order to

   A. be larger.
   B. have keener senses.
   C. be more useful to people.
   D. survive better in the wild.

"Chickens were selected to be larger, wild cattle (aurochs) to be smaller. . . . Most domestic animals . . . have smaller brains and less acute sense organs than do their wild ancestors. Good brains and keen eyes are essential to survival in the wild, but represent a . . . waste of energy in the barnyard, as far as humans are concerned."

—Jared Diamond, *Nature*, August 8, 2002

Analyze Maps

Use the map at right to answer the following questions.

15. Which letter represents Mesopotamia? Which rivers was it settled near?

16. Which letter represents the Indus Valley? Which continent is it on?

17. Which letter represents Egypt? Which body of water does the Nile River flow into?

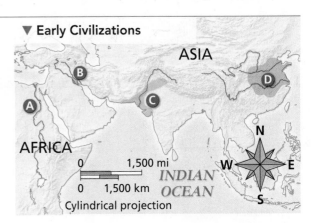

▼ **Early Civilizations**

Civilizations and Peoples of the Fertile Crescent
(3400 BCE–70 CE)

GO ONLINE
to access your
digital course

▶ VIDEO

◀))) AUDIO

📖 ETEXT

👆 INTERACTIVE

✏️ WRITING

🎮 GAMES

📄 WORKSHEET

✅ ASSESSMENT

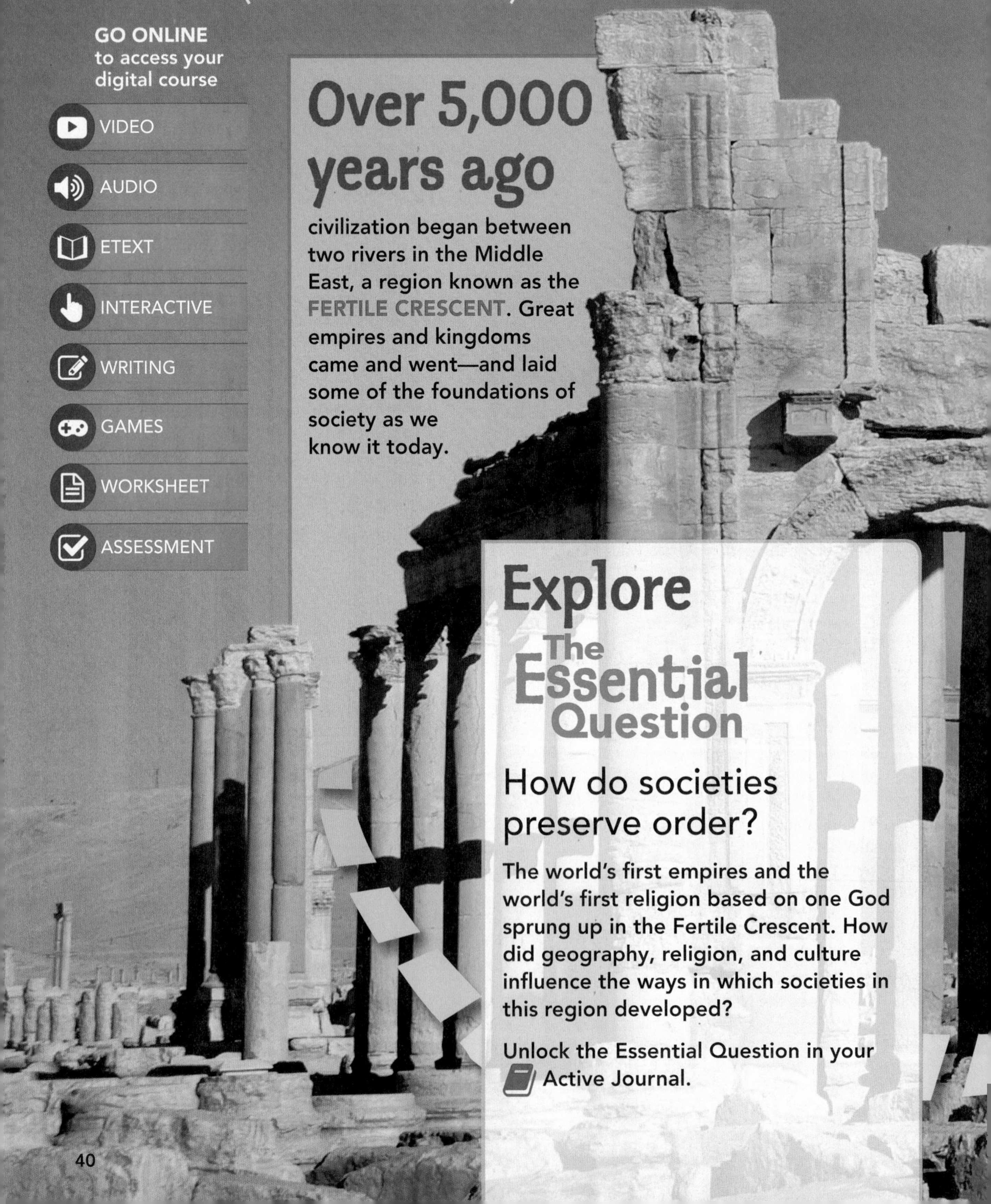

Over 5,000 years ago

civilization began between two rivers in the Middle East, a region known as the **FERTILE CRESCENT**. Great empires and kingdoms came and went—and laid some of the foundations of society as we know it today.

Explore
The Essential Question

How do societies preserve order?

The world's first empires and the world's first religion based on one God sprung up in the Fertile Crescent. How did geography, religion, and culture influence the ways in which societies in this region developed?

Unlock the Essential Question in your 📙 Active Journal.

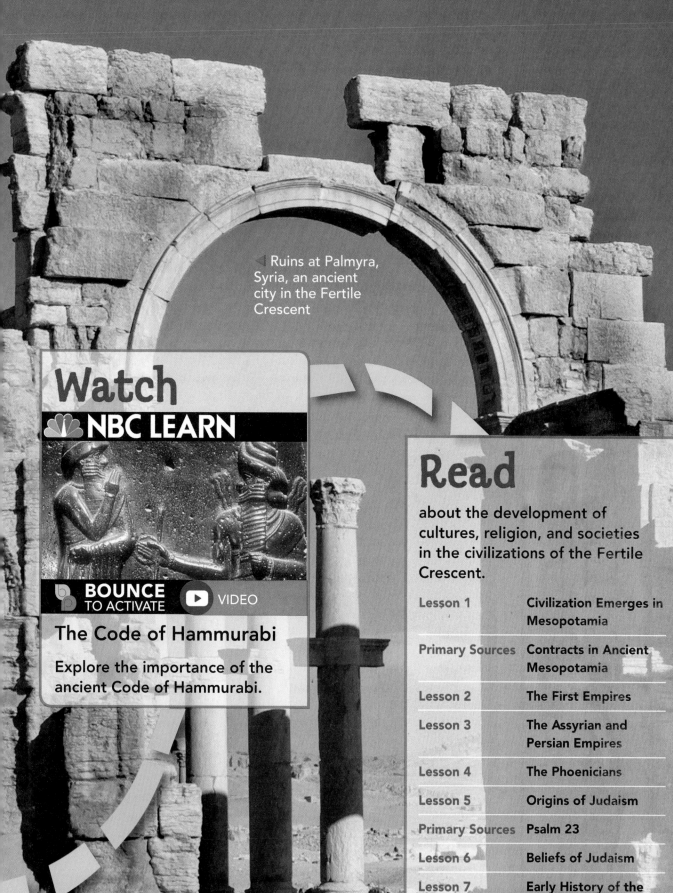

Ruins at Palmyra, Syria, an ancient city in the Fertile Crescent

Watch

NBC LEARN

BOUNCE TO ACTIVATE ▶ VIDEO

The Code of Hammurabi

Explore the importance of the ancient Code of Hammurabi.

Read

about the development of cultures, religion, and societies in the civilizations of the Fertile Crescent.

41

Civilizations and Peoples of the Fertile Crescent

(3400 BCE–70 CE)

Learn more about the Fertile Crescent and early civilizations by making your own map and timeline in your 📓 Active Journal.

🖐 INTERACTIVE

Topic Map

Where is the Fertile Crescent?

The Fertile Crescent extends from the Persian Gulf to the Mediterranean Sea. As its name states, it is both fertile and crescent-shaped. The fertile soil of this part of the world gave rise to the first civilizations.

🖐 INTERACTIVE

Topic Timeline

What happened and when?

Agricultural inventions ... new civilizations ... enormous empires ... and the beginning of Judaism. Explore the timeline to see how civilization began to unfold.

3400 BCE
Sumerian city-states form.

2334 BCE
Sargon unites Mesopotamia under Akkadian empire.

1792-1750 BCE
Hammurabi rules over the Babylonian empire.

TOPIC EVENTS

4000 BCE	3000 BCE	2000 BCE

WORLD EVENTS

3100 BCE
First pharaoh unites Egypt.

1800 BCE
Shang kingdom founded in China.

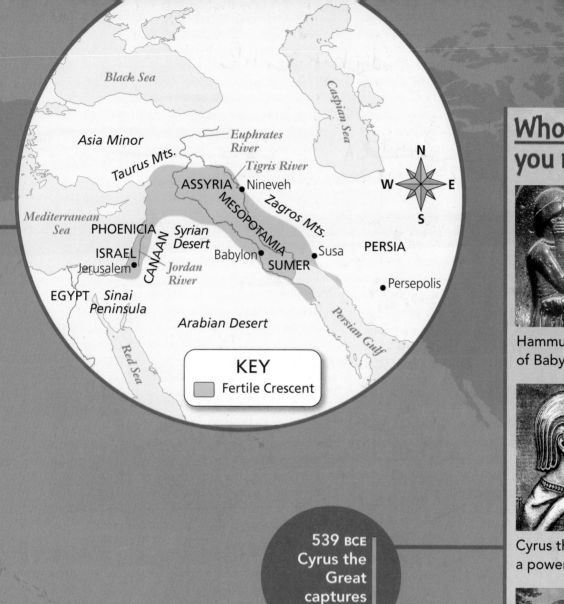

Black Sea

Caspian Sea

Asia Minor

Euphrates River

Tigris River

Taurus Mts.

ASSYRIA · Nineveh

Zagros Mts.

MESOPOTAMIA

Mediterranean Sea

PHOENICIA

Syrian Desert

ISRAEL

CANAAN

Babylon · SUMER

· Susa

PERSIA

Jerusalem ·

Jordan River

EGYPT

Sinai Peninsula

· Persepolis

Arabian Desert

Persian Gulf

Red Sea

N W E S

KEY
Fertile Crescent

Who will you meet?

Hammurabi, a king of Babylon

Cyrus the Great, a powerful leader

Ruth, a central figure in the Bible's book of Ruth

539 BCE
Cyrus the Great captures Babylon.

1200s BCE
Moses leads Exodus (traditional date).

720s BCE
Assyria conquers northern Kingdom of Israel.

586 BCE
Babylonians conquer Judah.

70 CE
Second Temple destroyed.

1000 BCE

1 CE

1200 BCE
Olmec civilization begins in modern Mexico.

400 BCE
Buddhism becomes widespread in northern India.

43

Quest
Discussion Inquiry

Debate Punishments for Crimes

Quest KICK OFF

You are a legal advisor to the president of the United States! The president wants your advice on mandatory minimum sentences. These are sentences a judge must use when someone is convicted of a crime. You need to help answer one of the most important questions of justice in history:

Are harsh punishments necessary for a safe society?

Explore the Essential Question "How do societies preserve order?" in this Quest.

1 Ask Questions
Get started by making a list of questions about how the ancient Babylonians viewed criminal punishments. Write the questions in your 📓 Active Journal.

2 Investigate
As you read the lessons in this topic, look for **Quest** CONNECTIONS that provide information about different ways groups tried to create order. Collect examples in your 📓 Active Journal.

3 Examine Primary Sources
Next, explore a set of sources. They will support differing viewpoints about whether harsh punishments are necessary in today's world. Capture notes in your 📓 Active Journal.

4 Discuss!
After you collect your clues and examine the sources, prepare to discuss this question: **Are harsh punishments necessary for a safe society?** You will use your knowledge of ancient law codes as well as evidence from sources to make convincing arguments to answer the question.

Civilization Emerges In Mesopotamia

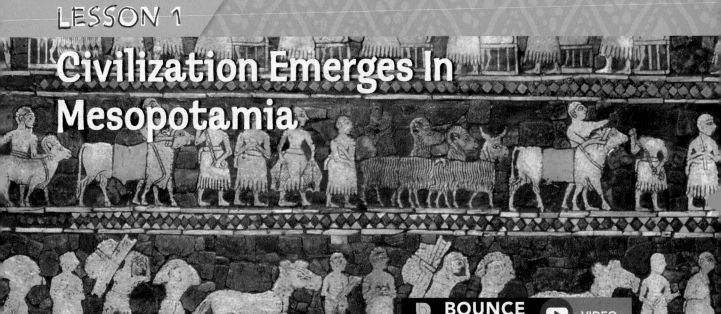

BOUNCE TO ACTIVATE ▶ **VIDEO**

GET READY TO READ

START UP

Study the Standard of Ur, which is a small box covered with mosaics. What can you conclude about daily life in Mesopotamia from this box?

GUIDING QUESTIONS

- How did civilizations develop in Mesopotamia and how did the fertile land support this development?
- What impact did civilization in Mesopotamia have on the surrounding environment?
- Why did priests and kings hold great power in the city-states of Sumer?
- What were the achievements of the Sumerians in technology, writing, and the arts?

TAKE NOTES

Literacy Skills: Identify Main Idea and Details
Use the graphic organizer in your ▨ Active Journal to take notes as you read the lesson.

PRACTICE VOCABULARY

Use the vocabulary activity in your ▨ Active Journal to practice the vocabulary words.

Vocabulary		Academic Vocabulary
Fertile ✓	barter	distinct
Crescent	polytheism	prosper
Mesopotamia ✓	ziggurat	
irrigate ✓	cuneiform	
city-state		

The **Fertile Crescent** is a region of the Middle East that stretches in a large, crescent-shaped curve from the Persian Gulf to the Mediterranean Sea. The Fertile Crescent includes **Mesopotamia** (mes uh puh TAY mee uh), a wide, flat plain in present-day Iraq. This plain lies between two great rivers, the Tigris (TY gris) and the Euphrates (yoo FRAY teez). In fact, *Mesopotamia* means "land between the rivers" in Greek. Here, thousands of years ago, the world's first civilization began to form. This was the civilization of Sumer (SOO mur).

How Was Agriculture Important in Mesopotamia?

As its name suggests, the Fertile Crescent's soil is rich and fertile. Some of the most productive land in the region is in Mesopotamia. This rich soil allowed Sumerian farmers to grow many grains and vegetables. They also raised sheep, goats, and cattle.

Produces silt

natural resources

Geography of Mesopotamia Northern Mesopotamia includes the foothills of the Taurus and Zagros mountain chains. To the south, these foothills flatten into plains that stretch southeast toward the Persian Gulf.

Persian mountain ranges

dry but fertile

Southern Mesopotamia is a hot, dry region with little rainfall. At first glance, the land looks like a desert. But the soils are not desert soils. In fact, they are rich with nutrients.

two rivers

The southern part of Mesopotamia owes its good soil to the Tigris and Euphrates rivers. These rivers begin in the mountains of southeastern Turkey and flow south and east, through present-day Iraq. The rivers carry fine, fertile soil called silt down from the mountains. Each spring, the rivers flood their banks, spreading floodwaters and silt across the plain. When the floods end, they leave behind a fresh layer of moist, fertile earth that is perfect for growing crops.

intro to silt

👆 INTERACTIVE

Sumer and the Fertile Crescent

makes

dry ground

But Mesopotamia's geography also gave Sumerian farmers many challenges. The heavy spring floods could wash away crops and even whole villages. During the summer, the hot sun baked the ground rock hard. With little rain for months, plants died.

Farming the Land Despite these challenges, the Sumerians used technology to turn Mesopotamia into productive farmland. Remember that technology is the practical application of knowledge to accomplish a task.

use of technology

The Sumerians used technology to **irrigate**, or supply water to, their crops. They dug many miles of irrigation canals to bring water from the rivers to their fields. With irrigation, people transformed their environment so that crops could still get water during the hot, dry summer. People began settling in new areas where irrigation made growing crops possible, turning land into fields and building homes.

Irrigation systems are vital

GEOGRAPHY **SKILLS**

A series of early civilizations beginning with Sumer arose in Mesopotamia, the region between the Tigris and Euphrates rivers.

1. **Interaction** What natural features may have limited the expansion of these civilizations?

2. **Contrast** How was the Fertile Crescent different from neighboring areas?

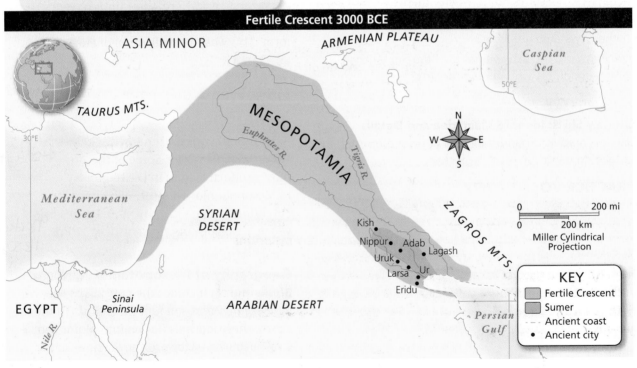

Fertile Crescent 3000 BCE

ASIA MINOR

ARMENIAN PLATEAU

Caspian Sea

50°E

TAURUS MTS.

MESOPOTAMIA

Euphrates R.

Tigris R.

30°E

N
W E
S

Mediterranean Sea

SYRIAN DESERT

ZAGROS MTS.

Kish
Nippur• Adab
Uruk• Lagash
Larsa• Ur
Eridu

0   200 mi
0   200 km
Miller Cylindrical Projection

EGYPT

Sinai Peninsula

ARABIAN DESERT

Nile R.

Persian Gulf

KEY
▢ Fertile Crescent
▢ Sumer
--- Ancient coast
• Ancient city

efficient

Sumerians also developed a new way of planting crops. Earlier farmers used a wooden plow pulled by oxen when planting. The plow cut a long furrow, or trench, in the soil. Then the farmers dropped seeds into the furrow. But Sumerian farmers developed a seed funnel that they attached to their plows. As the plow moved forward, seeds automatically dropped from the funnel into the soil. This made planting faster and easier.

✓ **READING CHECK** **Predict** Predict how irrigation in Mesopotamia led to the development of cities.

City-States of Sumer

Better agricultural techniques helped the Sumerians produce more food. With a dependable food supply, the population began to grow. Around 3400 BCE, cities started to form in southern Mesopotamia. These cities depended on nearby rivers for irrigation to grow crops to support the growing populations. Other major civilizations, such as the Harappa along the Indus River and the Chinese along the Huang River, formed in river valleys for the same reason.

Cities Emerge The first Mesopotamian city was Uruk. Uruk had a population of more than 40,000 people. Other early cities were Ur, Lagash, and Nippur. Some cities grew large and powerful. They became the world's first city-states. A **city-state** is an independent state that includes a city and its surrounding territory. Each Sumerian city-state had its own government and laws, and each had its own main god. Cities had walls and densely packed houses.

Trade Each city-state was a center of trade. Southern Mesopotamia had fertile soil, but it had little wood or stone and no metal ores. Sumerians traveled far to find these important resources. Most trade was done by barter. **Barter** is a trading system in which people exchange goods directly without using money.

Early traders often used the rivers and major canals to transport their goods. They loaded goods onto barges, or large rafts. Workers on land used ropes to pull the barges along the water.

As they had done with agriculture, the Sumerians used new technologies to make trade easier. For example, the Sumerians invented the wheel, which they used on their carts. Many historians include the wheel as one of the most important discoveries of all time. Sumerians also used sails on their boats. With wheeled carts and sailboats, they could more easily transport barley, wheat, dates, and cloth to faraway lands. They could also bring home trade goods like lumber, metals, and precious stones.

Analyze Images Walls and buildings of ancient Mesopotamia were made of mud bricks baked dry. **Synthesize Visual Information** How do these structures show the skill of Mesopotamian builders?

irrigation makes farming efficient, so it gave early people better reasons to settle into houses, then evolving into villages and cities

very important discovery/development

Sumerian Social Hierarchy

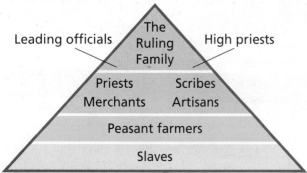

The Ruling Family

Leading officials — High priests

Priests Merchants — Scribes Artisans

Peasant farmers

Slaves

Analyze Diagrams
Sumerian civilization saw the formation of the first social classes. **Use Evidence** What does the chart indicate about how Sumerian society supported itself?

Social classes

vital part of the features of civilization

Social Classes The Sumerians developed a social order with three classes. People of each class had **distinct** roles within Sumerian society. The upper class included the ruler, his top officials, powerful priests, wealthy merchants, and owners of large plots of land. Farmers and skilled workers made up the middle class. The lowest class was mostly enslaved peoples. The city-states' governments and Sumerian religious beliefs, which were firmly connected, helped support this social order.

The rise of social classes was a new development for human societies. Men generally had a higher social position than women, but women in the higher class could gain power. Some could be priestesses, for example, and when kings emerged, their wives had some power.

READING CHECK **Understand Effects** Why did Sumer, Harappa, and the Chinese civilization all form in river valleys?

What Role Did Religion Have in Sumerian Society?

Like most ancient peoples, the Sumerians practiced **polytheism**, the belief in more than one god. Sumerians believed these gods controlled every aspect of life, including rain, wind, and other elements of nature. Some gods represented agriculture or other activities.

Sumerians believed that the gods behaved much like people. They thought that the gods ate, drank, slept, and married. However, Sumerians also believed that the gods lived forever and had great power. If the gods were happy with people's prayers and offerings, they might bring good fortune to the city. If not, they might bring war, floods, or other disasters. As a result, Sumerians felt that they needed to keep the gods happy in order for their cities to grow and **prosper**.

Sumerians believed that only priests knew how to communicate with the gods. They depended on priests to tell them what the gods wanted. As a result, priests had an important role in Sumerian society. Their connection with the gods brought peace and social order.

In larger Sumerian cities, temples were pyramid-shaped brick towers known as **ziggurats** (ZIG OO rats). The largest ziggurats were seven stories tall. They rose upward in steps, with each level smaller than the one below. Some were filled with beautiful paintings and statues.

The area around a temple often included farmland controlled by the temple. Priests kept goods belonging to temples in large storehouses.

READING CHECK **Draw Conclusions** Why did Sumerians believe the success of their society depended on their priests?

What Was the Sumerian Writing System Like?

Sumerian priests needed a system to keep track of their stored goods. At first they drew pictographs on clay. Pictographs are simple pictures that represent objects. To record the number of fish given to a temple, for example, Sumerian priests drew a fish. Then they added marks to represent the number of fish. In time, this way of keeping records developed into the world's first system of writing.

Cuneiform By 3100 BCE, Sumerian priests had created a new writing system called cuneiform. **Cuneiform** is a system of writing that uses triangular-shaped symbols to stand for words, ideas, or sounds.

Cuneiform involved pressing wedge-shaped marks into clay tablets. By combining the marks in different ways, Sumerians could create thousands of symbols.

Epic of Gilgamesh Cuneiform was originally used to record sales, taxes, and agreements. Later, Sumerians began to use writing for more than record keeping. The *Epic of Gilgamesh*, which was written in cuneiform on 12 clay tablets, told the story of a hero.

The stories about Gilgamesh are myths, or made-up tales of gods and heroes. However, some scholars believe that Gilgamesh may have been a real king. These scholars think that he ruled the Sumerian city-state of Uruk sometime after 3000 BCE.

☑ READING CHECK **Identify Main Ideas** How did the use of Sumerian writing change over time?

[handwritten note:] Without cuneiform, I wouldn't be able to write this Note.

Did you know?

The largest surviving ziggurat measures 335 feet (102 meters) on each side and is estimated to have been over 150 feet (45 meters) tall.

[handwritten note:] What !?

Analyze Images The Ziggurat of Ur is an ancient temple built by Sumerians to honor their moon god, Nanna. **Use Visual Information** How might the height of a ziggurat have affected Sumerian people?

CUNEIFORM
STAGES OF DEVELOPMENT

8000 BCE
Sumerians began using different-shaped clay tokens to represent various items of exchange, such as sheep or bread.

3500 BCE
Sumerians began to press the tokens into clay tablets to make signs. They also began to mark the clay with a sharp tool called a stylus.

3100 BCE
Sumerians created a true writing system that included symbols that represented words or syllables. Scribes recorded economic exchanges, myths, prayers, and laws.

SUMERIAN LEGACY
Conquering empires adapted cuneiform into their own cultures. The *Epic of Gilgamesh*, written in cuneiform, is still read today.

Analyze Information
Cuneiform developed over time from a simple system for record keeping into a system of writing. **Understand Effects** How did cuneiform writing allow Sumerians to communicate more effectively?

I thought they were kings!!

I wouldn't want to give up power after only one fight

How Did Sumerian Government Work?

The first leaders of Sumerian city-states were priests, not kings. But when conflicts arose among city-states, the way cities were ruled began to change.

Development of Kingship As city-states grew, people in different cities began to argue with one another over the control of land and water. These conflicts sometimes led to war.

In times of war, priests helped choose the best person to lead the city-state into battle. After the war was over, this leader was expected to give up his power and return to normal life. But some of these military leaders kept control of the city-states even after war ended. These military leaders became the first kings. *← that's cool*

Kings and Priests To stay in power, kings needed the support of the priests. So kings were careful to respect the priests' rights and powers. In turn, priests declared that the gods had sent the king to rule the city. This idea that kings were chosen by the gods became common in Sumer. Together, kings and priests created religious ceremonies that supported royal power.

Sumerian kings eventually took over many jobs the priests once did. They hired workers to build new canals, temples, and roads. Each king also served as the city's chief lawmaker and judge.

Written Laws Some rulers collected city laws into a law code, or a written set of laws. The earliest known law code was issued around 2100 BCE by Ur-Nammu (uhr NAHM OO), the king of Ur. The Ur-Nammu law code included laws about marriage, slavery, and causing harm to other people.

One law read, "If a man knocks out the eye of another man, he shall weigh out half a mina of silver." (A mina is a unit of weight that varied over time but was approximately one pound.)

☑ READING CHECK **Sequence** What steps led to kings replacing priests as rulers of Sumerian city-states?

Sumerian Achievements

Under the rule of priests and kings, Sumerians produced many advances in technology. You have already read about the Sumerians' improvements to farming, such as their use of irrigation and the invention of the seed plow. You have read about their development of cuneiform, which allowed them to keep records. Innovations like the wheel and the sail improved transportation.

The Sumerians also made advances in mathematics and astronomy. Dividing an hour into 60 minutes and a minute into 60 seconds began with the Sumerians. They also divided the year into 12 months of 30 days each, much as we do today. Through trade, many of these Sumerian advances spread to other lands.

Another important advance in technology was the development of bronze. The Sumerians were one of the first cultures to make bronze, which is made by mixing copper and tin. Bronze is a harder metal than copper, so it is better for making tools and weapons. Bronze weapons would later play an important role in the growth of cities into large, powerful states.

☑ READING CHECK **Understand Effects** How did the invention of bronze lead to cities becoming large, powerful states?

Analyze Information
The bull's head decorating a harp shows the skill of Sumerian craft workers. **Infer** Which level of Sumerian society do you think this instrument was meant for? Why?

☑ Lesson Check

Practice Vocabulary

1. How did **city-states** develop?

2. How did **cuneiform** develop?

Critical Thinking and Writing

3. **Use Evidence** How did the priests and kings of Sumer support one another?

4. **Understand Effects** Name two technological advances of the Sumerians and explain why these advances helped Sumer become more prosperous and powerful.

5. **Draw Conclusions** How did irrigation affect Sumer?

6. **Writing Workshop: Introduce Characters** Imagine you are a person living in ancient Mesopotamia. Write a few sentences in your 📓 Active Journal that describe who you are and what your role is in society. You will use this information for a narrative essay you will write at the end of this topic.

Contracts in Ancient Mesopotamia

As civilizations developed in ancient Mesopotamia, so did laws that governed daily life. Contracts, or agreements, from ancient Mesopotamia give us a glimpse into what daily life was like for people living there. The contracts shown here were all signed by the parties involved in the contract.

◀ Cuneiform tablet from 1500 BCE

Reading and Vocabulary Support

① *Shekel, talent,* and *qa* were units of measurement in ancient Mesopotamia.

② Tammuz was a month in ancient Mesopotamia. Other dates are linked to years in the reigns of different kings.

③ Relationships of persons to parents were often given in contracts to identify the people agreeing to the contract. What does this tell you about names in ancient Mesopotamia?

④ What will happen if the emerald falls out of the ring before 20 years have passed?

Quest CONNECTIONS

Read and think about these contracts. How would agreements like these contribute to social order? Record your findings in your 📓 Active Journal.

Akhibte has taken the house of Mashqu from Mashqu, the owner, on a lease for one year. He will pay one shekel ① of silver, the rent of one year. On the fifth of Tammuz ② he takes possession. Date: the fifth of Tammuz, the year of the wall of Kar-Shamash.

One talent one qa of dates from the woman Nukaibu daughter of Tabishna, ③ and the woman Khamaza, daughter of ____, to the woman Aqubatum, daughter of Aradya. In the month Siman they will deliver one talent one qa of dates. Date: adar the sixth, thirty-second year of Darius, King of Babylon and countries.

Bela-akha-iddin and Bel-shunu, sons of Bel-____ and Khatin, son of Bazuzu, spoke unto Bel-shum-iddin, son of Murashu, saying: "As to the ring in which an emerald has been set in gold, we guarantee that for twenty years the emerald will not fall from the gold ring. If the emerald falls from the gold ring before the expiration of twenty years, Bel-akha-iddin, Bel-shunu, (and) Kathin will pay to Bel-shum-iddin ten manas of silver." ④ Date: Nippur. Elul eighth, the thirty-fifth year of Artaxerxes.

Analyzing Primary Sources

Cite specific evidence from the contracts to support your answers.

1. **Infer** What role did women have in society according to the contracts?

2. **Compare and Contrast** How is the third contract different from the first two contracts? How does this difference make that contract stronger than the other two contracts?

3. **Compare Authors' Points of View** What was each person in each of these agreements trying to achieve by having a contract?

Distinguish Cause and Effect

Use the graphic organizer and follow these steps to distinguish cause and effect.

INTERACTIVE

Analyze Cause and Effect

1 Identify the key event. Understanding causes and effects is a matter of finding factors that led to something happening. Those factors are the causes. The event or development they led to is the effect. The Sumerian invention of the wheel was a cause. Greater ease in moving goods was its effect that was also a cause, as it resulted in increased trade.

a. What is the central event or development that is the focus of this graphic organizer?

b. Is it a cause, an effect, or both?

2 Study earlier events or conditions as possible causes. A cause of the key event must happen before the key event. Look for earlier events by asking, Why did the key event happen? or What led to the key event? You may also find such clue words as *because* and *the reason that*, which suggest that one thing caused another. Bear in mind that key events often have more than one cause.

a. What physical feature contributed to there being a surplus of food?

b. What human factor contributed to there being a surplus of food?

3 Study later events or conditions as possible effects. Effects must follow the key event. They may include short-term effects or longer lasting ones. To find later events, ask What did the key event lead to? or What was a result of the key event? You may also find clue words or phrases, such as *brought about, led to, as a result,* or *therefore.* Look at the graphic organizer.

a. What were the effects of having a surplus of food?

b. Which of these was a long-term effect?

c. How did that effect come about?

Causes and Effects of the Rise of Sumerian City-States

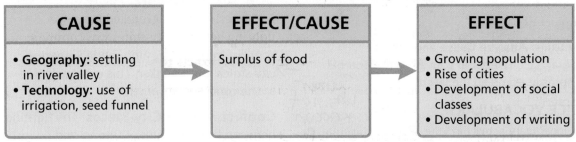

CAUSE	EFFECT/CAUSE	EFFECT
• **Geography:** settling in river valley • **Technology:** use of irrigation, seed funnel	Surplus of food	• Growing population • Rise of cities • Development of social classes • Development of writing

The First Empires

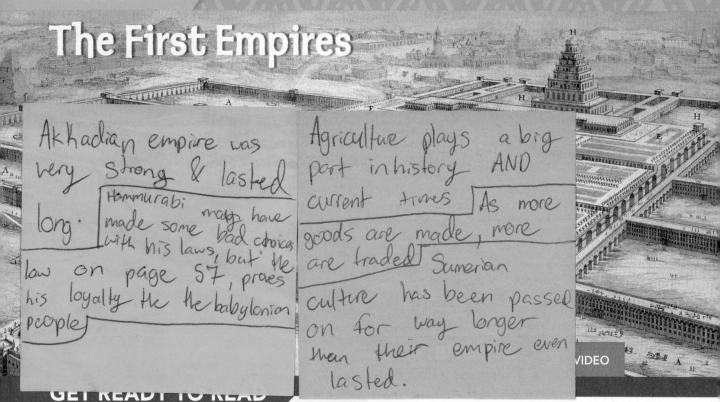

Akhadian empire was very strong & lasted long.

Hammurabi maybe made some bad choices with his laws, but the law on page 57, proves his loyalty the the babylonian people

Agriculture plays a big part in history AND current times

As more goods are made, more are traded

Sumerian culture has been passed on for way longer than their empire even lasted.

VIDEO

GET READY TO READ

START UP

Examine the image of the city of Babylon. Write two questions about what everyday life was like in the city.

GUIDING QUESTIONS

- How did Sargon form the world's first empire in Mesopotamia?
- How did people's lives change when the Babylonian empire conquered Sumer?
- What was the lasting impact of the Babylonian emperor Hammurabi's legal code?

TAKE NOTES

Literacy Skills: Analyze Cause and Effect

Use the graphic organizer in your 📒 Active Journal to take notes as you read the lesson.

PRACTICE VOCABULARY

Use the vocabulary activity in your 📒 Active Journal to practice the vocabulary words.

Vocabulary

empire   Hammurabi's Code
ally   rule of law
cultural trait

Academic Vocabulary

abundant
govern

Sumer was not known for fighting,

Unlike the Babylonians

As the independent city-states of Sumer grew in size, power, and wealth, they became rivals. They each wanted to gain control over more resources. As a result, they often came into conflict. For hundreds of years, the city-states fought among themselves. In time, strong rulers conquered the whole region, creating the world's first empires. An **empire** is a state containing several countries or territories.

The Conquest of Sumer

As Sumerian kings struggled for power, fighting between city-states was common. Years of frequent fighting made Sumerian city-states grow weaker. This eventually led to the conquest of Sumer.

Conflict Among City-States The fighting between the city-states of Umma and Lagash is one example of the widespread conflict in Sumer. For many years, Umma and Lagash and their allies fought to control a fertile region on their shared border. An **ally** is an independent state that works with other states to achieve a shared military or political goal.

Around 2450 BCE, armies from Umma and Lagash met in a major battle. Soldiers used bronze axes and long spears with sharp metal points. Thousands of troops died in the fighting before Lagash won the battle. To celebrate their victory, Lagash soldiers looted and burned Umma. They captured prisoners from Umma to be sold as slaves.

It took years for Umma to recover from the defeat. Around 2375 BCE, a powerful king of Umma finally defeated Lagash and several other Sumerian city-states. His rule soon came to an end, however.

How Did Sargon Build an Empire? While the Sumerian city-states struggled for power, a new society arose in Mesopotamia. The Akkadian people lived to the northwest of Sumer, but they were not related to Sumerians. Akkadians spoke a different language and had different customs.

During the 2300s BCE, an Akkadian man named Sargon became king of the Sumerian city-state of Kish. He changed the language used by the government to Akkadian. Under Sargon's rule, the Akkadian army conquered other Mesopotamian city-states. He placed loyal Akkadians in important government and religious positions. For example, he chose his daughter to be a high priestess in the city-state of Ur. These moves helped him solidify his power. Then Sargon united much of Mesopotamia under his rule, creating the world's first empire, which is called the Akkadian empire.

Akkadian Culture The Akkadians and Sumerians shared some cultural traits. A **cultural trait** is an idea or way of doing things that is common in a certain culture. For example, the Akkadians and Sumerians had similar religious practices, and both societies used the cuneiform system of writing.

As Sargon's troops moved throughout the Fertile Crescent, they brought their cultural traits with them. Furthermore, Akkadians began to trade with people as far away as the Indus Valley in modern day Pakistan. While the Fertile Crescent provided **abundant** crops, it had few trees and did not provide any minerals. Trading to the east and west, Akkadians obtained wood, copper, silver, and precious stones like red carnelian and blue lapis lazuli. Through trade, Akkadian and Sumerian culture spread to other regions and was adopted by other peoples.

How Did the Akkadian Empire End? To control such a large empire, Sargon appointed local rulers. Each local ruler served as king of the land he oversaw. Sargon was able to control the Akkadian empire for more than 50 years.

After Sargon's death in 2279 BCE, the Akkadian empire faced a growing number of rebellions and invasions. Within 100 years, the empire had collapsed. Warriors from the Zagros Mountains, east of the Tigris River, eventually took control of the region.

● **INTERACTIVE**

Akkadian and Babylonian Empires

▲ Sargon, builder of the world's first empire

Academic Vocabulary
abundant • *adj.,* plentiful

Analyze Images
This carving honors the Akkadian king Naram-Sin's victory over enemies. **Identify Supporting Details** What details in the carving glorify the king?

Around 2100 BCE, Sumer was united again, this time by Ur-Nammu, the ruler of Ur. Ur-Nammu issued the world's first known law code. Ur prospered for about 100 years under Ur-Nammu and later rulers. Then, an uprising of rebels from the east managed to destroy Ur and capture its ruler. This ended Ur's rule over Sumer. Once again, the Sumerian city-states fought over power.

☑ **READING CHECK** **Identify Cause and Effect** How did Sargon strengthen his power?

The Babylonian Empire

After the destruction of Ur, many groups invaded Sumer. One of them, the Amorites, came from northern Mesopotamia. The Amorites took control of several Sumerian cities, including Babylon (BAB uh lahn). At the time, Babylon was a small, unimportant city on the Euphrates River near present-day Baghdad, Iraq. But under a king named Hammurabi (hah muh RAH bee), Babylon became the center of a new Mesopotamian empire.

The Empire Forms Around 1792 BCE, Hammurabi became king of Babylon. For 30 years, he solidified his power and built up his army. Then he launched a series of attacks against other Mesopotamian city-states. Within a few years he had united southern Mesopotamia into what we now call the Old Babylonian (bab uh LOH nee uhn) empire, which is also called Babylonia.

Hammurabi was an excellent military leader, and he was also a skilled ruler. Like Sargon, after Hammurabi built his empire he had to create a government strong enough to hold it together. He sent his own governors, tax collectors, and judges to rule distant cities. He spread out his well-trained troops over the empire. Hammurabi also oversaw a number of public building projects and encouraged the growth of trade with other lands.

The Significance of Hammurabi's Code Today, Hammurabi is best remembered for his creation of **Hammurabi's Code**, a set of laws that governed life in the Babylonian empire. Many of these laws had existed since Sumerian times, but Hammurabi wanted to make sure everyone in Babylonia knew the laws they were expected to live by. In the introduction to his code, Hammurabi wrote that he wanted to

Primary Source

bring about the rule of righteousness in the land,
to destroy the wicked and the evil-doers; so that the
strong should not harm the weak—so that I should
. . . further the well-being of mankind.

—Hammurabi's Code

Quick Activity

Explore Hammurabi's Code
and make your own modern
laws in your Active
Journal.

Hammurabi's Code includes nearly 300 laws. Some laws have to do
with crimes such as robbery and murder. The code states specific
punishments for these crimes. For example, one law reads, "If a man
put out the eye of another man, his eye shall be put out." Although
such punishments may sound cruel by modern standards, they did
encourage social order.

Other laws in Hammurabi's Code dealt with private matters such as
business contracts, taxes, marriage, and divorce. Many of these laws
treated various groups of people differently. For example, the penalty
for harming someone of the same rank in society was greater than the
penalty for harming someone of lower rank, such as an enslaved person.

Hammurabi's Code was more detailed than Ur-Nammu's law code. In
fact, it was the first major attempt to organize and write down all the
laws that **governed** a society. It established the **rule of law**, or the
idea that all members of a society must obey the law. This idea is a key
part of modern democratic principles.

Academic Vocabulary

govern • v., to control or
strongly influence

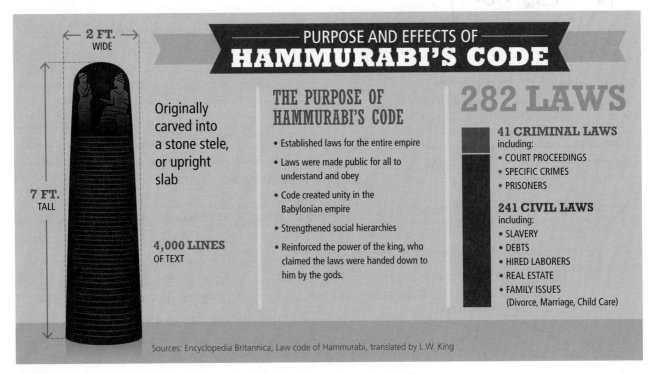

← 2 FT. →
WIDE

7 FT.
TALL

Originally
carved into
a stone stele,
or upright
slab

4,000 LINES
OF TEXT

PURPOSE AND EFFECTS OF
HAMMURABI'S CODE

THE PURPOSE OF
HAMMURABI'S CODE

- Established laws for the entire empire
- Laws were made public for all to
  understand and obey
- Code created unity in the
  Babylonian empire
- Strengthened social hierarchies
- Reinforced the power of the king, who
  claimed the laws were handed down to
  him by the gods.

282 LAWS

41 CRIMINAL LAWS
including:
- COURT PROCEEDINGS
- SPECIFIC CRIMES
- PRISONERS

241 CIVIL LAWS
including:
- SLAVERY
- DEBTS
- HIRED LABORERS
- REAL ESTATE
- FAMILY ISSUES
  (Divorce, Marriage, Child Care)

Sources: Encyclopedia Britannica; Law code of Hammurabi, translated by L.W. King

Analyze Diagrams The purpose of Hammurabi's Code was to create common
rules for the diverse people of the society. **Identify Main Ideas** Why was it
important that Hammurabi's Code was written down?

Analyze Images An artist gave this decorative cup the form of a sheep. **Infer** What can you conclude about the artists of this period from this object?

These technologies helped shape the world to what it is now.

Life in the Babylonian Empire Hammurabi's Code and other Babylonian writings give historians a great deal of information about life in Babylonia. People's lives changed when states and empires took over. There were greater social differences. Now there were kings, priests, and government officials. But still most people were very poor. They were farmers, artisans, or slaves. Many people's lives revolved around agriculture. Food had to be grown and distributed. Irrigation canals had to be kept clear of silt. Wool had to be collected and woven into textiles, or cloth.

In the cities, some people used new technologies to make tools, weapons, pottery, perfumes, and medicines. Babylonian artists were known for their stone and bronze sculptures. They also used gold and precious stones to make jewelry. All the goods were traded within the empire and with other lands.

Legacy of Sumer Sumerian culture stayed alive in Babylonia, just as it had in the Akkadian empire under Sargon. But Hammurabi's empire eventually collapsed after his death in 1750 BCE. In the years that followed, the once-great civilization of Sumer slowly faded away.

Sumer's influence, however, did not disappear. The many peoples who had come into contact with Sumerian civilization adopted ideas and customs from it. In this way, Sumerian advances lived on.

☑ **READING CHECK** **Draw Conclusions** Why was Hammurabi's Code important?

☑ Lesson Check

Practice Vocabulary

1. What Sumerian **cultural traits** did Akkadians share?

2. How did Sargon create Mesopotamia's first **empire**?

3. What is the **rule of law** and why is it important?

Critical Thinking and Writing

4. **Explain** How did Sargon and Hammurabi keep control of large empires?

5. **Identify Main Ideas** Why was trade with other societies important to the Akkadian and Babylonian empires?

6. **Draw Inferences** How did the geography of Mesopotamia help spread Sumerian advances?

7. **Compare and Contrast** the roles of farmers, artisans, and slaves to the roles of rulers and other government officials in the Akkadian and Babylonian empires.

8. **Writing Workshop: Introduce Characters** In your 📓 Active Journal, identify other people from Mesopotamian society that your character would interact with. Explain what these other characters do and how they know your character.

The Assyrian and Persian Empires

BOUNCE TO ACTIVATE ▶ VIDEO

GET READY TO READ

START UP
Examine the carving of Assyrian fighters. What can you conclude about Assyrian warfare from this image?

GUIDING QUESTIONS
- How did Assyrian armies conquer their vast empire?
- How did the Persian empire balance local self-government with central power?
- How did the cultures of Mesopotamia create a rich cultural tradition?

TAKE NOTES
Literacy Skills: Summarize
Use the graphic organizer in your 📓 Active Journal to take notes as you read the lesson.

PRACTICE VOCABULARY
Use the vocabulary activity in your 📓 Active Journal to practice the vocabulary words.

Vocabulary		Academic Vocabulary
cavalry	currency	elite
standing army	stele	reform
tribute		

Invaders swept into Mesopotamia after Hammurabi's death in 1750 BCE. Hundreds of years passed before the Assyrians, a people of northern Mesopotamia, united the region again. In time, the Assyrian empire gave way to the powerful Persian empire.

How Did the Assyrian and Neo-Babylonian Empires Develop?
Assyria (uh SEER ee uh) lay north of Babylon, along the Tigris River. Like much of Mesopotamia, it fell under the influence of Sumer. Later, Assyria was part of the Akkadian and Babylonian empires.

Why Was Assyria Known as a Military State? After Babylonia fell, the Assyrians fought against a steady stream of invaders. Some of them conquered Assyria, but for long periods the Assyrians stayed free.

Assyria's armies included some of the world's earliest **cavalry**, or soldiers who fight while riding horses. Assyrians used iron weapons and tools, which were stronger than the bronze ones.

Provinces are like towns

Analyze Images These archers decorated the palace of a Persian emperor. **Infer** What can you conclude about the Persian armies from this image?

The Assyrians built up a strong military state by the mid-800s BCE. Within 200 years, they turned that state into an empire. By the mid-600s BCE, the Assyrian empire stretched north from the Persian Gulf across the entire Fertile Crescent and southwest into Egypt.

Political Order in the Empire Like Sargon and Hammurabi, Assyrian rulers found that controlling a large empire was difficult. The Assyrians divided the empire into about 70 smaller units of government called provinces. They assigned a governor to each province. Each governor reported directly to the Assyrian ruler. This helped the ruler keep control of distant lands.

An Assyrian ruler named Ashurbanipal (osh ur BANH ee pol) made the city of Nineveh his capital. There, he built a library and filled it with cuneiform tablets. They were mainly texts and letters from Sumer and Babylonia on subjects such as law, literature, mathematics, and science. Some 20,000 of these tablets survive today.

How Was Babylon Restored? After Ashurbanipal's death, civil war and enemy attacks weakened the Assyrian empire. In 604 BCE, Nebuchadnezzar (neb yuh kud NEZ ur) II became king of Babylon. He expanded his power as far west as Egypt. He also captured Jerusalem, destroyed the Jewish Temple, and exiled many Jews to Babylon. Nebuchadnezzar's empire is known as the Neo-Babylonian empire. Nebuchadnezzar spent much money building great walls, gates, and temples. His most famous project was the Hanging Gardens of Babylon. The Hanging Gardens were elaborate gardens built on a series of stone terraces.

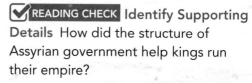

READING CHECK Identify Supporting Details How did the structure of Assyrian government help kings run their empire?

How Did the Persian Empire Rise?

Babylon's thick walls and strong gates were not able to keep out new conquerors. In 539 BCE, Babylon and the rest of Mesopotamia fell under the control of the powerful Persian empire. That empire soon became the largest the world had ever seen. Although the names of the Persian empire changed over time depending on who was ruling, the empire itself stayed in existence for over a thousand years. It dominated much of southwestern Asia and sometimes even Egypt between 500 BCE and 630 CE. It had great political and cultural influence over western Asia during these centuries.

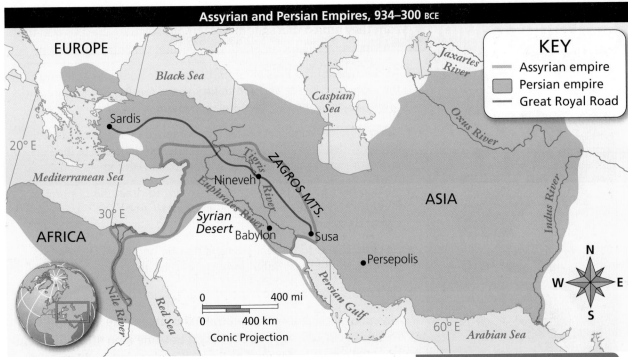

KEY
— Assyrian empire
▨ Persian empire
— Great Royal Road

EUROPE
Black Sea
Jaxartes River
Caspian Sea
Oxus River
Sardis
20° E
Mediterranean Sea
Tigris River
ZAGROS MTS.
Nineveh
ASIA
Indus River
30° E
Euphrates River
Syrian Desert
Babylon
Susa
AFRICA
Persepolis
N
W E
S
Nile River
Red Sea
Persian Gulf
0   400 mi
0   400 km
Conic Projection
60° E
Arabian Sea

Cyrus the Great Persia formed to the east of Mesopotamia, in what is now Iran. For years, the Persians had been ruled by their neighbors to the north, a people called the Medes. But in 550 BCE, Cyrus the Great led the Persians to victory over the Medes. By conquering the Medes, the Persians won an empire.

Cyrus fought to create an even larger empire. He began in Asia Minor, in what is now Turkey, fighting the kingdom of Lydia. He defeated Lydia's rich king, Croesus (KREE sus). Then Cyrus pushed south into Ionia, a region settled by Greeks. One by one, he conquered Ionia's city-states. Later, Cyrus expanded Persia's border in the east, toward India.

Persia's rapid growth was due to its large and highly skilled standing army. A **standing army** is a permanent army of professional soldiers. The core of this army was a force of 10,000 **elite** soldiers known as the "Immortals."

Conquest of Babylon Cyrus and the Persian army captured Babylon in 539 BCE. Under his rule, Babylon grew into the wealthiest province of the Persian empire. In general, Cyrus treated the Babylonians and other conquered peoples well. He allowed them to keep their own customs and religions rather than forcing them to adopt Persian ways. For example, when Cyrus conquered Babylon he allowed the Jewish people to return to Jerusalem and rebuild their Temple.

Further Development Cyrus died in a battle in 530 BCE. His son Cambyses (kam BY seez) II continued his father's dream of increasing the size of the Persian empire. First, Cambyses invaded northeast Africa and conquered Egypt. From there, he traveled south to try to capture Kush, but failed.

GEOGRAPHY **SKILLS**

The Assyrian empire began from a base in northern Mesopotamia. The Persian empire originated further east.

1. **Region** Which empire mainly occupied the Fertile Crescent?

2. **Use Visual Information** What did the Great Royal Road connect?

Are they really important? I doubt it.

Academic Vocabulary
elite • *adj.*, representing the best
would have thought

🖱 **INTERACTIVE**

Assyrian and Persian Empires

BIOGRAPHY
5 Things to Know About

CYRUS THE GREAT
Persian ruler 590/580–c. 529 BCE

- As the ruler of the Persian empire, Cyrus declared himself king of the world in 539 BCE and within fifty years, the Persian empire had grown to cover nearly three million square miles.

- Using his knowledge that horses are frightened by the smell of camels, he swiftly defeated the Lydian army and doubled the size of the Persian empire simply by terrorizing the Lydian horses with camels.

- He had his troops dig trenches overnight to drain the Euphrates River to thigh level, allowing his soldiers to cross and capture the city of Babylon.

- He proclaimed to the Babylonians that he had been chosen by Marduk, the highest Babylonian god, to be their ruler.

- His empire continued to expand after his death, lasting more than a thousand years.

Critical Thinking What did Cyrus do that convinced Persians to call him "the Great"?

Cambyses marched the Persian army through the desert with little food or other supplies. Soon his men were forced to kill and eat their pack animals. Many Persians died of starvation.

After Cambyses died, Darius (duh RY us) took the Persian throne by force. Under his rule, Persia grew even larger, and Darius became known as Darius the Great. He extended Persian rule east to the Indus Valley. In the west, the Persian army defeated Thrace, which was the first Persian victory in Europe. But later campaigns against Greece ended in Persia's defeat at the Battle of Marathon.

Suprising

Quest CONNECTIONS

How did Cyrus and other Persian rulers try to establish social order? Record your thoughts in your 📓 Active Journal.

I guess it was time since they had already grown so much larger.

☑ READING CHECK **Identify Implied Main Ideas** Why was the Persian empire important to the history of southwest Asia?

Persia's Government and Religion

The vast Persian empire included peoples with many different cultures. Persian rulers had to find a way to unify the empire. They might have tried to force people to follow the same customs and same laws. The Persians took a different approach, however.

Local Self-Government Darius created a political structure that gave local people some control over their own government. Darius divided his empire into satrapies, or provinces, and chose a leader for each one. Darius allowed them to keep their local laws and traditions and make many of their own decisions.

Academic Vocabulary
reform • v., to improve

Central Control Darius also **reformed** the empire's central, or overall, government. First, he improved its finances. Conquered peoples had always sent tribute to the Persian ruler. **Tribute** is payment made to show loyalty to a stronger power, but the amount of tribute was often set by the ruler.

Before Darius, Persian rulers often showed no concern for what a region could really afford to pay. Darius created a fairer system in which each province paid according to its wealth.

Next, Darius created a common currency. **Currency** is money that is used as a medium of exchange, usually bills or coins. Darius introduced gold coins—printed with an image of himself—that would be accepted across the Persian empire as payment for goods. The currency helped unify the Persian economy by making it easier for distant provinces to trade with one another.

New Roads Darius used some of Persia's great wealth to build roads across the empire. Trade goods and tribute traveled on these roads. So did armies, government officials, and royal messengers.

The Persians set up postal stations along the 1,500-mile-long Great Royal Road. Messengers on horseback brought messages from one station to the next. It took three months for a message to travel from one end of the road to another. Still, the Persian system was the fastest communication system in the ancient world. The Greek historian Herodotus wrote:

Primary Source

Nothing mortal travels so fast as these Persian messengers. . . . [T]hese men will not be hindered from accomplishing at their best speed the distance which they have to go, either by snow, or rain, or heat, or by the darkness of night.

—from *The Persian Wars* by Herodotus, translated by George Rawlinson

Analyze Images This sculpture from a Persian capital shows conquered peoples carrying tribute. **Draw Conclusions** Why would a Persian ruler want to show a scene like this?

Religion In ancient times, most people worshiped many gods. But beginning around 600 BCE, a Persian man known as Zoroaster (zoh roh AS tur) taught that there is one supreme god, Ahura Mazda, who has an evil opponent. Over time, Zoroaster's beliefs developed into the religion Zoroastrianism. Zoroastrianism eventually became the official religion of the empire, although conquered people could worship their own gods.

The sacred text of Zoroastrianism is the Avesta, which includes prayers, hymns, and other writings. Zoroastrianism's central belief is that the universe is in a state of struggle between the forces of good and evil. Zoroastrians believe that people have an important role to play in this conflict by working for good. They also believe in the existence of an afterlife. Historians think that these teachings later influenced Judaism, Christianity, and Islam.

✓ READING CHECK Identify Supporting Details How did Darius change the Persian empire?

Arts of Mesopotamia

Unlike art produced by earlier world cultures, the arts of ancient Mesopotamia give us a glimpse of daily life, as you saw on the Standard of Ur. They show people engaged in different activities.

Seals The Sumerians often used carved stone seals to identify the owner of an object, especially before the development of cuneiform writing. A seal left the owner's personal mark—such as an animal or a geometric shape—stamped in clay. For example, a sack containing trade goods might be tied closed with a string. Then the owner would cover the knot with wet clay and stamp the clay with the seal.

Some seals were shaped like cylinders, or tubes. When rolled over wet clay, the seals left the image of an entire scene.

Sculptures Sumerians also carved statues of people that, for the first time in history, looked like real humans. Other peoples created a form of sculpture known as relief. In relief sculpture the scene sticks out from the surface of the base material.

Many relief sculptures were carved on steles (STEE lee). A **stele** is a carved stone slab or pillar that stands on end. A famous example is the stele of Hammurabi. At the top of this stele is a relief showing Hammurabi and the Babylonian god Shamash. Below the relief is Hammurabi's Code, carved in cuneiform.

The Assyrians created large, colorful reliefs on the sides of buildings. They decorated structures with colorful tiles and bricks that formed elaborate patterns and images of real and imagined animals. Assyrians also decorated walls with cone-shaped pieces of baked clay painted in white, black, and red.

Analyze Images Creatures like this decorated many Assyrian palaces. **Use Visual Information** What three types of beings make up this imaginary creature?

☑ **READING CHECK** Identify Implied Main Ideas What did the use of stone seals suggest about daily life?

☑ Lesson Check

Practice Vocabulary

1. What was the effect of having a **standing army** on Persia's growth?

2. How did the use of **currency** unify Persia's economy?

Critical Thinking and Writing

3. **Summarize** How did the Assyrians create an empire?

4. **Synthesize Visual Information** What subject do most of the images in this lesson have in common? What does this subject suggest about the societies that created these works of art?

5. **Identify Implied Main Ideas** How did the way the Persian government handled religion throughout the empire help preserve social and political order?

6. **Writing Workshop: Establish Setting** Write a few sentences in your 🗎 Active Journal to describe the setting where your character lives in Mesopotamia. You will use this information in the narrative essay you will write at the end of this topic.

Recognize the Role of Chance, Error, and Oversight

Use the primary source and follow these steps to recognize the role of chance, oversight, and error.

INTERACTIVE

Analyze Primary and Secondary Sources

1 Identify the topic. When studying an event, begin by focusing on what the passage is about. For example, is the passage about a military campaign or the rise of a new leader? Where did the event happen? Who were the key figures? Read the passage from *The History of Herodotus*.

   a. What is the passage about?

   b. Where did the event happen, and who were the key figures?

2 Identify the goal or expected outcome. Ask, What is the leader trying to accomplish? What is likely to happen if everything goes as planned?

   a. In this passage, what is the leader trying to accomplish?

   b. What challenges is he likely to encounter if his plan does not go as he thought it would?

3 Identify any unexpected outcomes. As you consider the event or time period, ask, Did events happen as expected? Did something go wrong? Did key people achieve their stated goals?

   a. Consider what the leader's goals were in the passage. Did he achieve his goals? Explain why or why not.

   b. What problem did his soldiers face?

4 Analyze the cause of the unexpected outcomes. Look for explanations for unexpected outcomes. Did something that nobody could have predicted go wrong—a storm or illness, for example? Did a person make a key mistake? Did someone forget some key steps?

   a. Analyze the passage. What went wrong?

   b. Could the outcome have been prevented? If so, how?

Primary Source

"Cambyses ... set out on his march against the Kush without making any provision for the feeding of his army .... Like a senseless madman ... he began his march. Before he had traveled one-fifth of the distance, all the army's food was gone. The men were forced to eat the pack animals, which were soon gone also. If at this time, Cambyses ... had confessed himself in the wrong, and led his army back, he would have done the wisest thing that he could ... but ... he ... continued to march forward. So long as the earth gave them anything, the soldiers lived by eating the grass and herbs. But when they came to the bare sand, a portion of them were guilty of a horrid deed. By tens they cast lots for a man, who was slain to be the food of the others. When Cambyses heard of these doings ... he gave up his attack on Kush ...."

— from *The History of Herodotus*, Book 3, 440 BCE

The Phoenicians

BOUNCE TO ACTIVATE ▶ VIDEO

GET READY TO READ

START UP

Look at this land that was once part of Phoenicia. How might people have adapted to this land?

GUIDING QUESTIONS

- How did contact, trade, and other links grow among the societies of Mesopotamia and the eastern Mediterranean?
- How did the Phoenicians spread their culture over a wide area?
- What important contribution did the Phoenicians make to the development of writing?

TAKE NOTES

Literacy Skills: Summarize

Use the graphic organizer in your 📘 Active Journal to take notes as you read the lesson.

PRACTICE VOCABULARY

Use the vocabulary activity in your 📘 Active Journal to practice the vocabulary words.

Vocabulary		Academic Vocabulary
import	cultural	assembly
export	diffusion	profit
navigation	alphabet	
colony		

The Mediterranean Sea forms the western boundary of the Fertile Crescent. The Phoenician (fuh NISH un) civilization began here, on a thin strip of land along the Mediterranean coast, in what is now Lebanon. Like Sumer, Phoenicia consisted of city-states. Although Phoenicia was small in size, it had an important influence on the region's history.

Who Were the Phoenicians?

The Phoenicians were fearless sailors who guided ships full of trade goods through ocean waters. For hundreds of years, they dominated sea trade across the Mediterranean, just as the earlier Greek Minoan people had done.

Origins Phoenician society developed from the earlier Canaanites (KAY nun ites). The Canaanites were a people who lived in parts of what are now Israel, Jordan, Lebanon, and Syria. Nearby Egypt had a strong influence on Canaan. In fact, Egypt controlled parts of Canaan off and on from around 1500 BCE to 1150 BCE.

Phoenician society began to emerge after Egyptian rule ended. The independent Phoenician city-states soon prospered. In general, the rulers of Phoenician city-states were priest-kings who shared power with leading merchant families and a citizen **assembly**.

Farming and Manufacturing Geography greatly influenced Phoenicia's development. The Lebanon Mountains formed Phoenicia's eastern border. These heavily forested mountains sloped down close to the Mediterranean coast, leaving little flat land for farming.

Phoenicians manufactured a number of goods. Weavers created cloth that they colored with a rare purple dye made from tiny sea snails. They sold this purple cloth for high prices. Skilled Phoenician craftsworkers made pottery and glass and metal objects. They also used trees to make wood furniture.

Phoenician Traders Phoenicia had few natural resources of its own, so the Phoenicians traded with other cultures for resources and goods. Phoenician traders brought back many imports. An **import** is a good or service sold within a country that is produced in another country. Most Phoenician imports were raw materials, including gold, silver, tin, copper, iron, ivory, and precious stones.

Phoenician craftsworkers used these raw materials to make bronze and silver bowls, iron tools and weapons, and gold jewelry. Traders shipped these goods—as well as pine and cedar logs, wine, olive oil, salt, fish, and other goods—as exports to ports across the Mediterranean. An **export** is a good or service produced within a country and sold outside the country's borders.

☑ READING CHECK **Identify Cause and Effect** Why did the Phoenicians trade?

Academic Vocabulary

assembly • *n.*, group organized for a purpose

GEOGRAPHY SKILLS

The Phoenicians sailed across the Mediterranean Sea and then explored lands to the north and south.

1. **Region** Where were most Phoenician colonies located?

2. **Analyze Maps** What information on the map supports the claim that the Phoenicians were skilled sailors?

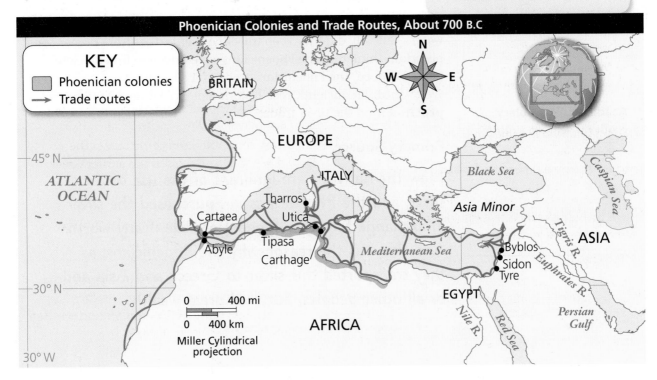

Phoenician Colonies and Trade Routes, About 700 B.C

KEY
- Phoenician colonies
- → Trade routes

BRITAIN

EUROPE

ITALY

Tharros
Cartaea
Utica
Tipasa
Carthage
Abyle

ATLANTIC OCEAN

Black Sea

Asia Minor

Caspian Sea

Mediterranean Sea

Byblos
Sidon
Tyre

ASIA

Tigris R.
Euphrates R.

EGYPT

AFRICA

Nile R.
Red Sea

Persian Gulf

45° N
30° N
30° W

0   400 mi
0   400 km
Miller Cylindrical projection

How Did Phoenicians Use the Sea?

Phoenicia's location was ideal for trade. It lay on the western edge of Asia, within sailing distance of Europe and Africa. Several overland trade routes from the east ended in Phoenicia. As a result, many peoples came to depend on the Phoenicians to ship their trade goods across the Mediterranean Sea.

Navigation Because of Phoenicia's location between the Mediterranean and the Lebanon Mountains, Phoenicians turned to the sea to trade. They became experts at **navigation**, or the art of steering a ship from place to place. Phoenician sailors developed a thorough knowledge of wind patterns and ocean currents. At first, the Phoenicians sailed and traded among nearby lands. Later, they took their ships to new areas.

Exploring Unknown Waters From Phoenicia, the Phoenicians sailed south and west past Egypt and along the North African coast. Others traveled north and west past the Balkan and Italian peninsulas. They explored the Mediterranean islands of Sicily and Sardinia. In time, the Phoenicians reached the Iberian Peninsula, at the western end of the Mediterranean Sea. Today this land includes Spain and Portugal.

▲ Ruins of the Phoenician colony of Carthage in North Africa

After passing the southern tip of Iberia, Phoenician sailors left the Mediterranean for the Atlantic Ocean. Some sailed north along the Iberian coast, and a few traveled all the way to Britain. Others headed south to West Africa.

Phoenician sailors showed great courage by sailing far into unknown waters. But why did they keep traveling ever farther from home? Some historians think that the Phoenicians were driven to find precious metals. Indeed, the Phoenicians traded for silver in Iberia and gold in West Africa. An ancient Greek historian described how Phoenicians **profited** from the silver trade:

Academic Vocabulary
profit • v., to make a gain

Primary Source

Now the natives were ignorant of the use of the silver, and the Phoenicians . . . purchased the silver in exchange for other [goods] of little if any worth. And this was the reason why the Phoenicians, as they transported this silver to Greece and Asia and to all other peoples, acquired great wealth.

—Diodorus Siculus, *Library of History*

Colonies and City-States Phoenician sailors found many sheltered harbors along the Mediterranean coast. At first these places served as trading stations where ships stopped to pick up water, food, and other supplies. Those areas with fertile land or other resources attracted farmers and other settlers. Those settlements grew into colonies. A **colony** is an area ruled by a distant country. When Phoenicia came under attack by Assyrians and others starting in the 800s BCE, many Phoenicians left Phoenicia. They migrated to their colonies for safety.

A few Phoenician colonies developed into wealthy city-states. One was Carthage, on the North African coast. Carthage eventually became rich and powerful, setting up its own colonies and fighting three wars against the powerful Romans. In the last of these wars, the Romans destroyed Carthage. Over time, the Roman empire took over all of the Phoenician city-states and colonies.

✓ **READING CHECK** **Identify Cause and Effect** Why did the Phoenicians form colonies?

What Is the Cultural Legacy of the Phoenicians?

Phoenicia did not survive, but some of its achievements did last. Greece and Rome absorbed parts of Phoenician culture through cultural diffusion. **Cultural diffusion** is the spreading of cultural traits from one region to another. The Phoenicians' legacy included the spread of its culture and a new way of writing.

Links to Other Societies Through trade, the Phoenicians linked the diverse peoples and cultures around the Mediterranean region and beyond. In the process, Phoenicians helped ideas spread. They passed parts of their culture on to the Greeks. For example, the Greeks used the Phoenician standard of weights and measures. Greek culture later spread throughout the entire Mediterranean region, and its influence continues today.

 INTERACTIVE

Development of the Modern Latin Alphabet

Development of the Alphabet

COMPARISON OF WRITING SYSTEMS			
Phoenician	Early Greek	Early Latin	Modern English Capitals
ⴶ	ᐱ	ᐞ	A
୨	8	B	B
⼧	ℸ	⟨	C
٩	Δ	D	D

Analyze Charts As other peoples adopted the Phoenician alphabet, they changed the letter forms. **Analyze Information** How was the alphabet used today in English influenced by the Phoenicians?

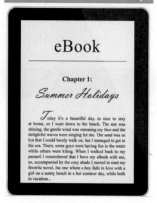
The Alphabet The Greeks also adopted the Phoenician way of writing. Before the Phoenicians, the main writing system in the ancient Near East was cuneiform. In cuneiform, symbols represent syllables or whole words. In order to be able to write, a person had to learn and remember hundreds of symbols.

The Phoenicians developed an alphabet. An **alphabet** is a small set of letters or symbols, each of which stands for a single sound. The Phoenician alphabet had 22 symbols. Each symbol stood for a consonant sound. This new approach to writing was a major improvement over cuneiform. Now, instead of having to memorize hundreds of different symbols, a person only had to know 22 symbols in order to write. This alphabet made writing much easier to learn, making it possible for more people to learn how to write.

People who traded with the Phoenicians learned their alphabet in order to communicate with them. By 750 BCE, the Greeks had begun using the Phoenician alphabet. Around 500 BCE, the Greeks added letters to represent vowels. They also gave the letters names. The word *alphabet* comes from the first two letters in the Greek alphabet—alpha and beta.

Around 100 BCE, the Romans adopted the Greek alphabet. The Romans changed some letters. The result was an alphabet that looks much like ours today. The Romans carried their culture across much of Europe and into other lands. Their language and system of writing was adopted in those lands. Through that process, it passed into widespread use. While it is the Roman form of writing that became the alphabet used to write English, that writing system had its origins in ancient Phoenicia.

☑ READING CHECK **Compare and Contrast** How was Phoenician writing different from cuneiform?

☑ Lesson Check

Practice Vocabulary

1. How did the Phoenicians turn **imports** from other cultures into **exports**?

2. How was the Phoenician **alphabet** similar to the alphabet we use today?

Critical Thinking and Writing

3. **Understand Effects** How is the Greek adoption of the Phoenician way of writing an example of cultural diffusion?

4. **Generate Explanations** Explain how the evolution of language impacted the number of people who could read and write in each of the societies—Phoenician, Greek, and Roman.

5. **Summarize** How did the Phoenicia's location allow Phoenicians to more easily make contact with other cultures?

6. **Writing Workshop: Organize Sequence of Events** Make an ordered list of events in your 📙 Active Journal to show what happens to your character in your narrative essay. You will use this sequence of events when you write your narrative essay at the end of this topic.

LESSON 5
Origins of Judaism

BOUNCE TO ACTIVATE ▶ VIDEO

GET READY TO READ

START UP
Examine the mosaic, which shows the symbols of the 12 tribes of Israel. Choose two of the symbols and write about what you think they might represent.

GUIDING QUESTIONS
- How did the Israelites' belief in one God develop into Judaism?
- How did the environment shape Jewish religion?
- Why are Abraham and Moses important figures in Judaism?

TAKE NOTES
Literacy Skills: Summarize
Use the graphic organizer in your 📓 Active Journal to take notes as you read the lesson.

PRACTICE VOCABULARY
Use the vocabulary activity in your 📓 Active Journal to practice the vocabulary words.

Vocabulary		Academic Vocabulary
monotheism	Exodus	eventually
ethics	commandment	compel
Torah		
covenant		

Judaism first developed as a religion more than 3,000 years ago in the Fertile Crescent. It was the world's first religion based on one God who set down laws about right and wrong. Judaism has helped shape the religions of Christianity and Islam, as well as modern ideas about law and human rights.

The Early Israelites and the Worship of One God

The Israelites were related to other peoples of the Fertile Crescent, but they developed a unique culture. Although their neighbors worshiped many gods, the Israelites practiced **monotheism**, or the belief that there is only one God. They believed that God created each person in God's image.

The Israelites also had important beliefs about the proper way for people to live. They believed that God called on them to act based on **ethics**, or ideas of right and wrong. Their teachings and practices became known as Judaism, the religion of the Jewish people. Judaism is one of the world's oldest religions.

Analyze Images The scroll contains the Torah. **Identify Main Ideas** Why is the Torah important to Judaism?

What Are the Origins of Judaism? Most of what Jews believe about the origins of their religion comes from the Torah (TOH ruh). The **Torah** consists of the first five books of the Hebrew Bible. (These are also the first five books of the Christian Old Testament, which has all of the books of the Hebrew Bible.) The archaeology and history of Egypt and Mesopotamia also help us understand the world of the Torah.

Abraham's Covenant The Torah tells about a man named Abraham, who may have lived about 1700 BCE. He herded animals near Ur in Mesopotamia.

According to the Torah, God told Abraham to leave Ur and travel with his family to Canaan (KAY nun) on the coast of the Mediterranean Sea. The Torah says that God then made a **covenant**, or binding agreement, with Abraham. The land of Canaan would belong to Abraham's descendants, so it became known as the Promised Land.

Primary Source

I will maintain My covenant between Me and you, and your offspring to come, as an everlasting covenant throughout the ages, to be God to you and your offspring to come.

—Genesis 17:7

The Patriarchs The Torah says that Abraham led his people to Canaan. Abraham, his son Isaac, and Isaac's son Jacob are known as the patriarchs, or the forefathers of the Jewish people.

According to the Torah, Abraham's grandson Jacob had twelve sons. Each of Jacob's sons became the ancestor of at least one large group of related families called a tribe. Jacob was later renamed Israel. The twelve tribes descended from Jacob became known as the Israelites.

I knew this! ⟶

Academic Vocabulary
eventually • *adj.,* after a time

Scholars believe that the stories of the patriarchs were passed along by word of mouth for hundreds of years. **Eventually**, they were written down in Genesis (JEH nuh sihs), the first book of the Torah.

☑ READING CHECK **Identify Implied Main Ideas** Why does the Torah contain many references to herding?

What Was the Exodus?

The last chapters of Genesis describe a famine in Canaan. Because Egypt had great supplies of grain, according to the Torah, Jacob's family moved there.

The Book of Exodus (EKS uh duhs) comes after Genesis in the Torah. According to Exodus, as the number of Jacob's descendants grew, a new pharaoh, or king of Egypt, became mistrustful of them. Exodus describes how the pharaoh enslaved and mistreated the Israelites. According to the Torah, the pharaoh **compelled** the Israelites to do harsh work.

Moses Exodus states that Moses was an Israelite who was adopted by the pharaoh's family. According to Exodus, God appeared to Moses and told him to rescue his people. Moses asked the pharaoh to let him lead the Israelites out of Egypt, but the pharaoh refused.

Exodus describes terrible hardships that God brought to Egypt because of the Pharaoh's refusal. The last and worst punishment was the death of every firstborn son of the Egyptians. Moses told the Israelites that God would let their sons live if they marked their doorways with the blood of a lamb.

Finally, the pharaoh allowed the Israelites to leave Egypt. Moses led the Israelites to the Sinai (SY ny) Peninsula, out of the pharaoh's reach. The escape of the Israelites from slavery in Egypt is called the **Exodus**. Each year, Jews celebrate Passover to commemorate the journey from slavery in Egypt to freedom.

The Desert Experience Many biblical scholars believe, the Exodus occurred during the 1200s BCE. According to the Torah, after the Israelites left Egypt, they lived in the Sinai Desert for 40 years. During this time, God prepared them for life in the Promised Land, then called Canaan. They received a series of instructions from God. They also learned ways to worship God and created important religious objects.

Academic Vocabulary

compel • v., force

← Why would he ask?

 INTERACTIVE

The Exodus in Jewish Tradition

GEOGRAPHY **SKILLS**

The ancient history of the Israelites took place in the Fertile Crescent and Mesopotamia.

1. **Movement** Why would Egypt be more appealing to the ancient Israelites in time of drought than Mesopotamia?

2. **Identify Multiple Causes** What made Canaan attractive as a place to live?

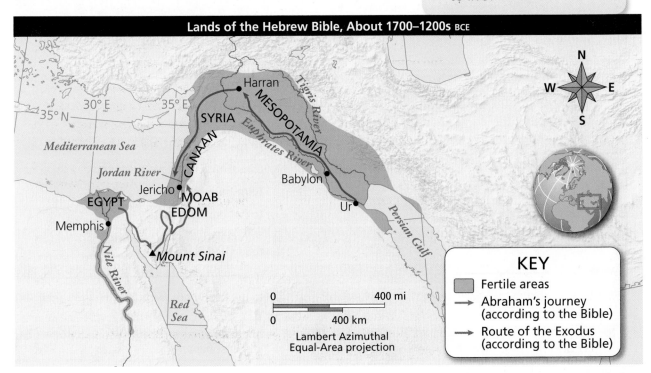

Lands of the Hebrew Bible, About 1700–1200s BCE

KEY

- Fertile areas
- → Abraham's journey (according to the Bible)
- → Route of the Exodus (according to the Bible)

0 — 400 mi
0 — 400 km
Lambert Azimuthal Equal-Area projection

On the journey through the desert to Canaan, according to the Torah, the Israelites faced harsh conditions. Occasionally, the Israelites battled other peoples. Some Israelites questioned the leadership of Moses or of God. However, they came to believe that if they obeyed God's commands, God would provide for them. The Torah states that during their journey, God provided them with water and food.

✔ READING CHECK Identify Main Ideas Why do Jews celebrate Passover?

What Are the Ten Commandments?

The Book of Exodus says that during the Israelites' journey, they stopped at the foot of Mount Sinai. Moses went up the mountain to meet with God. The Torah tells how at Sinai God gave Moses the Torah, which forms the foundation of Judaism. The Torah includes laws, among them those known today as the Ten Commandments. A **commandment** is an order to do something. The Torah contains many other laws, but the Ten Commandments are the most important.

The accounts of the Exodus and the Ten Commandments are important to Jews, Christians, and others. For them, a lesson of the Exodus is that if people believe in God and obey God's laws, God will protect them and support them. Memory of the journey from slavery to freedom teaches Jews to help oppressed people.

✔ READING CHECK Identify Main Ideas What do Jews believe about personal responsibility?

Analyze Charts The Ten Commandments helped shape American laws and people's ideas about right and wrong. **Infer** Based on the explanation of the tenth commandment, what does covet mean?

The Ten Commandments

COMMANDMENT	EXPLANATION
1st I the Lord am your God, who brought you out of the land of Egypt, the house of bondage.	to recognize God as the one and only God and to understand the relationship between people and God
2nd You shall have no other gods besides Me. You shall not make for yourself a sculptured image, or any likeness of what is in the heavens above, or on the earth below, or in the waters under the earth.	to not worship any other God or false idols
3rd You shall not swear falsely by the name of the Lord your God.	to speak the truth, seen today in legal oaths
4th Remember the sabbath day and keep it holy.	to dedicate one day to rest and worship
5th Honor your father and your mother.	to respect and love one's parents
6th You shall not murder.	to not murder others
7th You shall not commit adultery.	to ensure faithfulness to one's spouse; seen today in divorce laws
8th You shall not steal.	to prevent taking another person's belongings
9th You shall not bear false witness against your neighbor.	to prevent lying; seen today by laws against testifying falsely in a court of law
10th You shall not covet your neighbor's house, nor his wife… nor anything that is your neighbor's.	to prevent wanting other people's possessions, life, or spouse.

SOURCE: Book of Exodus 20:2-18, *JPS Hebrew-English Tanakh*, Jewish Publication Society (JPS) 1985.

Return to the Promised Land

After the Israelites received the laws from Moses, according to the Torah, they continued to the Promised Land. Moses saw Canaan from a mountain, but he died without entering the Promised Land. His deputy, Joshua, took his place as the leader of the Israelites. According to the Hebrew Bible, Joshua commanded the Israelites when they were attacked just after leaving Egypt. He also accompanied Moses to the foot of Mount Sinai.

According to the Book of Joshua in the Bible, the Israelites entered Canaan from the east under Joshua's leadership. One of the first cities they conquered was the high-walled city of Jericho (JEHR ih koh). After the defeat of Jericho, the Israelites went on to conquer several other kingdoms in Canaan.

Then each of the tribes descended from Jacob's sons settled in a different area. The tribes of Judah, Simeon, and Benjamin settled in the south. The other tribes settled in lands to the north. They herded their animals and farmed by making terraces on hillsides.

According to the Hebrew Bible, the Israelites maintained their identity. They sometimes strayed from God's commandments, but they always returned to the teachings of the Torah, including the belief in only one God.

▲ A Jewish family celebrates Passover.

☑ **READING CHECK** **Draw Conclusions** How was Moses important to the development of the Jewish religion?

Did you know?

The ancient settlement of Jericho might be the lowest town in the world. It sits 825 feet (251 m) below sea level.

☑ Lesson Check

Practice Vocabulary

1. Explain the relationship between Judaism and **monotheism.**

2. Use the words **commandment** and **ethics** in a sentence about Judaism.

Critical Thinking and Writing

3. **Draw Conclusions** Explain the connection, according to the Hebrew Bible, between Abraham's covenant with God and the Israelites' belief about Canaan.

4. **Identify Main Ideas** What was the lesson of the Exodus, according to the Torah?

5. **Sequence** What did the Israelites do after they reached Canaan?

6. **Understand Effects** Explain how religion helped shape the culture of the ancient Israelites, as presented in the Hebrew Bible.

7. **Writing Workshop: Revise Your Sequence of Events** Revise the sequence of events you prepared in your 🗐 Active Journal to show what happens to your character in your narrative essay. You will use this sequence of events when you write your narrative essay at the end of the topic.

Primary Sources

Psalm 23

While living in Canaan, Abraham and his people herded sheep and other animals. Later, they raised crops. The Torah makes many references to herding flocks or to farming. Psalm 23 is an example. The Psalms are a collection of 150 religious hymns in the Hebrew Bible. These songs reflect the Israelites' belief in God as the powerful savior of Israel. Many of the psalms praise the faithfulness of God to each of his people. In Psalm 23, the speaker describes his faith in God's protection and celebrates the Israelites' sense of a special relationship with a loving God using a herding metaphor.

◀ King David, author of Psalm 23 according to the Hebrew Bible

Reading and Vocabulary Support

① *Renew* means to return to a former condition.

② A *staff* is a walking stick.

③ What does the psalm say the Lord provides to the Israelites? What phrases serve as clues?

④ What do you think it means that the Lord "spread[s] a table" for the Israelites "in the full view of [their] enemies"?

⑤ To *anoint* means to rub oil into a part of the body as part of a religious ceremony.

The LORD is my shepherd, I lack nothing;

He makes me lie down in green pastures;
He leads me to still waters;

He renews ① my life;
He guides me in right paths as befits His name.

Though I walk through the valley of the shadow of death,
I fear no harm,
for You are with me;
Your rod and Your staff ②—they comfort me. ③

You spread a table before me in the full view of my enemies; ④
You anoint ⑤ my head with oil; my drink is abundant.

Only goodness and steadfast love shall
pursue me all the days of my life,
and I shall dwell in the house of the LORD for many long years.

Analyzing Primary Sources

Cite specific evidence from the document to support your answers.

1. **Demonstrate Reasoned Judgment** Given the Israelites' belief in a covenant, does comparing God to a shepherd makes sense?

2. **Analyze Style and Rhetoric** What is the tone of this psalm? How does this tone reflect the relationship the Israelites had with God?

3. **Vocabulary: Analyze Word Choices** What might the poem's speaker hope to convey by using so many metaphors?

Beliefs of Judaism

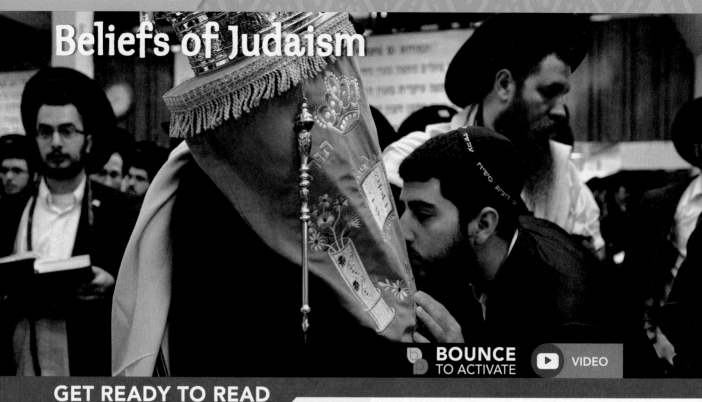

BOUNCE TO ACTIVATE ▶ VIDEO

GET READY TO READ

START UP

Examine the photo of a synagogue service. What aspects of a traditional service may be portrayed here?

GUIDING QUESTIONS

- What is the importance of the Hebrew Bible and the commentaries in Judaism?
- Why do the Jewish people give special importance to study and law?
- What are the ethical teachings and central beliefs of Judaism, including those about righteousness and justice?

TAKE NOTES

Literary Skills: Analyze Cause and Effect
Use the graphic organizer in your ▣ Active Journal to take notes as you read the lesson.

PRACTICE VOCABULARY

Use the vocabulary activity in your ▣ Active Journal to practice the vocabulary words.

Vocabulary		Academic Vocabulary
prophet	righteousness	commentary
rabbi	justice	individual
Talmud	Sabbath	

God's covenant with the Israelites and God's commandments for God's people are described in the Torah. They form the basis for the Jewish religion and its teachings. These teachings mainly have to do with how people should relate to God and to one another.

The Hebrew Bible

The written tradition is very important in Judaism. Jews greatly value scholarship and learning. In fact, Jews are often called "People of the Book." The Torah and the larger Hebrew Bible are Jewish sacred writings and are the source of Jewish teachings. The Hebrew Bible is also known as the Tanakh in Hebrew.

To Jews the Hebrew Bible is not just a history of their ancestors. They believe it reveals God's will as carried out in human events. This shared account unites Jews all over the world with a common set of teachings. The Hebrew Bible also forms the basis for the Christian Old Testament, which includes the books of the Hebrew Bible, but in a different order.

Analyze Images A Jewish boy reads from the Torah during his bar mitzvah, a ritual that marks his coming of age. The ceremony for girls is called a bat mitzvah. **Cite Evidence** What detail in the photograph shows the boy is reading the text with great care?

The Hebrew Bible describes events believed to have happened hundreds of years before the Bible was put into writing. The books of the Hebrew Bible are divided into three sections.

The Torah As you have learned, the first five books of the Hebrew Bible are called the Torah. The Torah begins by telling the story of God's creation of the world and the first people. It tells of a man named Noah who escaped a great flood on an ark, or boat. It tells of the life of Abraham and God's covenant with him.

The Torah then focuses on Abraham's son Isaac, his grandson Jacob, and Jacob's descendants, the Israelites. The Torah follows their journey from Egypt back to the Promised Land. The Torah is also called the Law of Moses because of the many rules and laws it contains.

The Prophets The next section of the Hebrew Bible is called the Prophets. This section contains books by or about Jewish prophets. A **prophet** is a person believed to be chosen by God as a messenger to bring truth to the people. The prophets were preachers, poets, and reformers. They reminded people to obey God's laws. In so doing, they told people how they should relate to God, to other people, to the land in which they lived, and even to themselves.

The Prophets traces the history of Judaism and the Jewish people. Beginning with the Book of Joshua, this section continues the story of the Israelites from the Torah, describing their arrival in the Promised Land. Other books deal with the creation of the kingdom of Israel.

The Writings The last section of the Hebrew Bible is the Writings. This section includes great Hebrew literature such as the Psalms (sahmz). Psalms are poems or songs offering praises or prayers to God.

The Writings also include the Book of Proverbs. It contains wise sayings. Many give advice to young people, such as this example:

Primary Source

Do not envy a lawless man, Or choose any of his ways.

—Proverbs 3:31

Other Writings tell about heroes such as Esther, Ruth, and Job (johb). The Writings also contain books, such as Chronicles, that provide a history of the early Jewish people.

☑ READING CHECK **Summarize** What is contained in the Torah?

What Is the Importance of Law and Learning?

The Hebrew Bible and **commentaries** on the Bible are vitally important to Jews. They are important because they are the source of Jews' most important teachings, including teachings about ethics.

Laws, the Talmud, and Commentaries Respect for God's laws is basic to Judaism. The great leader Moses is known to Jews as "Moses our teacher." The Torah contains many laws in addition to the Ten Commandments. Many of these laws give directions for religious rituals. Others describe how to have a fair society, how to help those in need, and even how to protect the health of the community through cleanliness and sanitation.

Many centuries after the time of Moses, prominent Jewish **rabbis** (RAB yz), or religious teachers, recorded oral laws that they believed had come down from the teachings of Moses. Other rabbis discussed how laws should be interpreted in different situations. Eventually, they wrote down their commentaries, or discussions, about the laws. The **Talmud** (TAHL mood), a text finished around 600 CE, is a collection of oral teachings and commentaries about the Hebrew Bible and Jewish law. Jews still study and discuss it.

The Need to Study The Hebrew Bible and the Talmud are central to Jewish teaching and practice. As a result, Jews value the study of these religious texts. Jewish scholars still write commentaries on the Hebrew Bible and Talmud today.

The Hebrew Bible is mostly written in the Hebrew language. As a result, many Jews people try to learn to read Hebrew. Some also learn Aramaic, the language of most of the Talmud.

☑ READING CHECK **Identify Cause and Effect** Why do Jews value the Hebrew Bible and Talmud?

Academic Vocabulary

commentary • *n.*, a set of comments or a recorded discussion about something

Analyze Images This illustrated manuscript is from a book of Jewish laws written by a scholar of the 1300s. **Cite Evidence** Based on the image, what ceremony is the focus of the laws shown on this page?

KEY TEACHINGS OF JUDAISM

ETHICAL MONOTHEISM	OBSERVANCE OF LAW	LOVE FOR OTHERS
There is only one God.	Laws in the Hebrew Bible and Talmud guide how Jews live and treat other people.	The Hebrew Bible tells Jews to love and help other people.
WEEKLY DAY OF REST	**COMMITMENT TO STUDY & PRAYER**	**CONNECTION TO THE LAND OF ISRAEL**
The idea of a weekly day of rest, or Sabbath, began in Judaism.	Study leads to wisdom and good deeds; people communicate with God through prayer.	Israel has a central role in the Hebrew Bible and is home to Judaism's most sacred sites.

Analyze Charts Several beliefs are central to the teachings of Judaism. **Identify Main Ideas** Why does the belief in ethical monotheism come first?

👆 **INTERACTIVE**

Significance of Major Jewish Holidays

 **CONNECTIONS**

How do the basic teachings of Judaism support social order? Record your thoughts in your 📓 Active Journal.

What Are the Basic Teachings of Judaism?

The idea of God in Judaism was unique in the ancient world. In other early religions, people worshiped many gods. They had images of these gods made of wood, stone, pottery, or metal. People believed that each god lived in a certain place. In contrast, the God of the Israelites did not live in stones, rocks, or the sea. God did not take a human or an animal form. God was invisible, and yet God was everywhere.

Primary Source

Am I only a God near at hand —says the LORD— And not a God far away? If a man enters a hiding place, Do I not see him? —says the LORD— For I fill both heaven and earth — declares the LORD.

—Jeremiah 23:23–24

Ethical Monotheism According to the Hebrew Bible, in the Sinai Desert the Israelites made a covenant with God to follow a code of laws, including the Ten Commandments. Along with the Ten Commandments, Jewish people follow other teachings from the Torah, as interpreted by the Talmud and other commentaries. Many of these teachings have to do with ethics.

Ethical monotheism is probably the most important teaching of Judaism. This is the idea that there is one God who sets down ethical rules, or rules about right and wrong. Being faithful to God means following these rules.

Righteousness and Justice Ethical monotheism calls on Jews to know the difference between right and wrong. For them, actions should be based on righteousness and justice. **Righteousness** is acting or living in a way that is ethically right and obeys God's laws.

As you have learned, Jews maintain that each person has value and worth because he or she is created in the image of God. Along with **individual** worth comes individual responsibility to God. Each individual has the responsibility to act righteously in God's eyes.

Righteousness was a key concern of the prophets. For example, they reminded people that they needed to be honest and kind to each other. They criticized rulers who were cruel to the poor and weak. They urged people to work for **justice**—fairness or fair treatment—for everyone. Jewish teachers also expected everyone to help those in need.

Observance of Law The laws and other rules that Jews follow are seen as part of the Jewish people's covenant with God. According to the Torah, God had a special relationship with the Israelites. In return, the Israelites believed that they had a responsibility to obey God's laws and commandments.

The Jewish idea of individual responsibility means that these laws and commandments apply equally to every Jewish person. This means that God's laws apply equally to leaders such as Moses and to the ordinary people who follow them. This idea of equality in the eyes of God helped shape modern systems of law.

Women in Ancient Judaism In ancient Judaism, as in most ancient religions and cultures, men had the most power. Women rarely owned property, although they did have the right to buy and sell land. Jewish law gave women other important rights and protections, including the right to be consulted about whom they would marry and the right to take cases to court.

Academic Vocabulary
individual • *adj.,* having to do with a single person or thing

◀ These scrolls are the Torah, or the five books of Moses.

Love for Others The Hebrew Bible commands, "Love your fellow [human being] as yourself." Jews are required to help others. As a result, Jews have been involved in many efforts to fight discrimination. Jews also give to charities in response to this teaching. These ideas have influenced modern thinking about basic human rights.

Other Key Teachings Another important Jewish teaching is to observe the **Sabbath**, or a weekly day of rest. This belief is basic to Judaism and is found in the Ten Commandments. For Jews, the Sabbath is the seventh day of the week, or Saturday. According to Jewish teachings, this should be a day free from work. Many nations have adopted the practice of having a weekly day of rest.

Jewish teaching also stresses the importance of study and prayer. You have learned about the importance of studying the Torah and Hebrew Bible and commentaries on them, such as the Talmud. Jews also value prayer as a way of communicating with God.

The Jewish people's ties to the Land of Israel are also central to Judaism. This is the land that was promised to Abraham, according to the Torah. It includes the modern state of Israel. Many Jews feel a deep connection to this land because of its place in the Jewish sacred writings and Jewish history.

Analyze Images Many Jews make donations and volunteer time to assist the needy. **Cite Evidence** How are these people contributing to charity?

☑ **READING CHECK** **Summarize** What is ethical monotheism?

☑ Lesson Check

Practice Vocabulary

1. What is a **prophet**, and what kind of writings are found in the collection of books called the Prophets?

2. What is the relationship between the **Talmud** and the Hebrew Bible? What do they say about Jewish ideas of **righteousness** and **justice?**

3. Why do you think observation of the **Sabbath** is an important Jewish teaching?

Critical Thinking and Writing

4. **Classify and Categorize** What are the three main parts of the Hebrew Bible and how do they differ?

5. **Draw Conclusions** Why is studying the Hebrew Bible and commentaries such as the Talmud so important to Jews?

6. **Cite Evidence** How are God's covenants with the Jewish people related to Jewish teachings about ethics and justice?

7. **Writing Workshop: Use Narrative Techniques** Write a few sentences in your 📓 Active Journal to identify and record some narrative techniques you can use to tell your story. You will use these narrative techniques when you write your narrative at the end of the topic.

Early History of the Jewish People

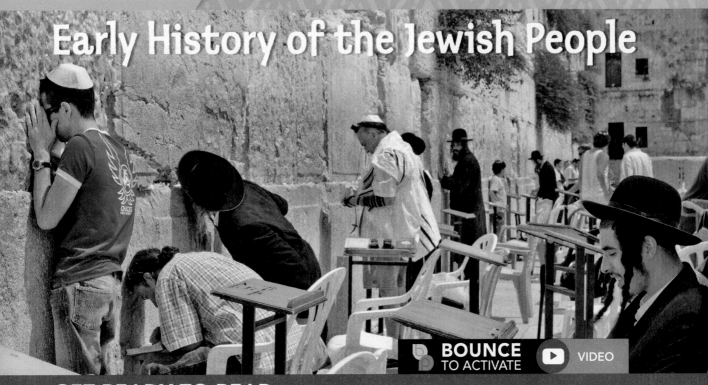

BOUNCE TO ACTIVATE ▶ VIDEO

GET READY TO READ

START UP

Examine the photo of Jews praying at the Western Wall today. What do you think this place means to the Jewish people?

GUIDING QUESTIONS

- How did the environment and history shape Jewish religion and practices over time?
- How did early Judaism support individuals, rulers, and societies?
- Why did Jewish communities spread to many different parts of the ancient world?
- How are the religious and ethical teachings of Judaism reflected in society today?

TAKE NOTES

Literary Skills: Sequence
Use the graphic organizer in your 🗐 Active Journal to take notes as you read the lesson.

PRACTICE VOCABULARY

Use the vocabulary activity in your 🗐 Active Journal to practice the vocabulary words.

Vocabulary		Academic Vocabulary
judge	Diaspora	commission
exile	synagogue	reject

After the Israelites settled in the Land of Israel, they lived as a group of separate tribes before joining to form a kingdom. After about 70 years the kingdom split, and the Israelites were later conquered by foreign empires. The descendants of the Israelites, known as Jews, later spread to many parts of the world.

The Kingdom of Israel

Most of what we know of early Jewish history comes from the Hebrew Bible. Archaeologists also have found evidence for some of the events mentioned in the Hebrew Bible before about 900 BCE. After that date, there is even more evidence from other written sources and from archaeology for events mentioned in the Hebrew Bible.

The Time of the Judges The Hebrew Bible states that Joshua led the Israelites in the conquest of Canaan. After Joshua died, the Israelites remained a group of tribes without a common government. They faced a number of conflicts with other peoples.

In times of distress, the Israelites often rallied around leaders called judges. As used in the Hebrew Bible, a **judge** was a leader who rallied the Israelites to defend their land. Judges were often warriors or prophets. They did not pass leadership to their descendants.

Deborah and Ruth Some women became well known during the time of the judges. The prophet Deborah, who inspired an army to win a great battle, was the only female judge. Other well-known women are Ruth and Naomi. When her husband died, Ruth followed her mother-in-law Naomi back to Israel. She accepted Naomi's religion and joined the tribe of Judah. It was dangerous at the time for Naomi and Ruth to be without male protection, but Naomi was determined to return. Her dedication to the Jewish home and Ruth's loyalty make them significant. The time of the judges ended when the warrior Saul became the first king of Israel.

David and Solomon The Hebrew Bible states that one of Saul's best fighters was David, a young shepherd and musician. David became the next king. Some archaeologists and historians date that to about 1000 BCE. He captured the city of Jerusalem and made it his capital. He extended the kingdom's borders. David is believed to have written beautiful psalms—poems or songs in the Bible—such as this one:

Primary Source

The LORD is my shepherd, I lack nothing; . . .
Though I walk through the valley of the
shadow of death, I fear no harm, for You are with
me; Your rod and Your staff—they comfort me.

—Psalm 23:1, 4

Academic Vocabulary

commission • v., to order the creation of

BIOGRAPHY
5 Things to Know About

Ruth
Biblical figure c. 1100–1000 BCE

- Ruth was from Moab and was not a Jew, but was married to the Jewish son of Naomi for ten years before he died.

- Naomi begged for her to return to Moab, but Ruth would not leave her mother-in-law alone. Leaving her own parents, she followed Naomi to Bethlehem.

- In telling Naomi her plan to return with her to Bethlehem, Ruth said, "Wherever you go, I will go," which is often used during wedding services as an example of love and dedication.

- With Naomi's help, Ruth marries a prosperous relative of Naomi named Boaz, who was impressed by Ruth's loyalty to Naomi.

- Ruth is one of the few women with a book named after them in the Hebrew Bible. Her story became the Book of Ruth.

Critical Thinking Why do you think Ruth's words are used in wedding ceremonies today?

David's son Solomon ruled after him. He **commissioned** the great First Temple in Jerusalem. According to tradition, Solomon wrote many of the wise sayings in the Hebrew Bible's Book of Proverbs.

The Kingdom Divides The Kingdom of Israel split in two after Solomon died, around 900 BCE. Solomon's descendants ruled the Kingdom of Judah in the south. From the name *Judah*, the religion of the Israelites became known as Judaism. The descendants of the Israelites became known as Jews.

A rival, or competing, kingdom in the north kept the name of the Kingdom of Israel. About 722 BCE, the Assyrian Empire conquered Israel. The Assyrians were brutal. Thousands of Israelites were sent to distant parts of the empire. Other Israelites fled south to Judah.

One hundred years later, the city-state of Babylon rebelled against Assyria and began the Neo-Babylonian empire. Babylon's greatest emperor, Nebuchadnezzar (neb yuh kud NEZ ur) conquered Judah. About 587 BCE, the Babylonians destroyed Jerusalem, including Solomon's Temple.

The Babylonian Captivity The Babylonians took thousands of Jews from Judah to faraway Babylon. Many Jewish prophets urged the Jews to obey the Torah while living in exile. **Exile** means separation from one's homeland. According to the Hebrew Bible, some Jews, such as Daniel, became important people in Babylon. Many Jews wished to return to their homeland.

Cyrus the Great, king of the Persians, conquered the Babylonian empire. The Persian empire now controlled most of Southwest Asia. In 538 BCE, Cyrus allowed the Jewish people to go home. Many did return to Judah. Jewish leaders began to build the Second Temple in Jerusalem. They completed the Second Temple in 515 BCE. They later rebuilt the walls of Jerusalem.

✓ READING CHECK **Identify Supporting Details** What are some of the accomplishments that David is known for in Judaism?

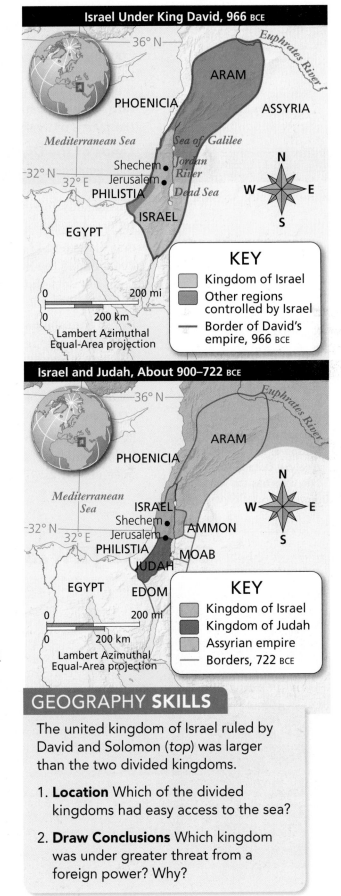

Israel Under King David, 966 BCE

KEY
- Kingdom of Israel
- Other regions controlled by Israel
- Border of David's empire, 966 BCE

0   200 mi
0   200 km
Lambert Azimuthal Equal-Area projection

Israel and Judah, About 900–722 BCE

KEY
- Kingdom of Israel
- Kingdom of Judah
- Assyrian empire
- Borders, 722 BCE

0   200 mi
0   200 km
Lambert Azimuthal Equal-Area projection

GEOGRAPHY **SKILLS**

The united kingdom of Israel ruled by David and Solomon (*top*) was larger than the two divided kingdoms.

1. **Location** Which of the divided kingdoms had easy access to the sea?

2. **Draw Conclusions** Which kingdom was under greater threat from a foreign power? Why?

What Was the Diaspora?

The Babylonian Exile was a turning point in Jewish history. Communities of Jews now lived throughout the Babylonian empire, which stretched across the Fertile Crescent. These communities outside the Land of Israel came to be known as the **Diaspora** (dy AS puh ruh), or communities of Jews living outside of their ancient homeland. *Diaspora* is a Greek word meaning dispersion, or scattering.

Lands of the Diaspora After the Persians conquered Babylon, their empire spread across all of Southwest Asia. The Persian empire included the Land of Israel, but it also included Egypt, Asia Minor (present day Turkey), Mesopotamia, what is now Iran, and parts of central Asia. Jewish people spread across these regions.

One of the best-known Jewish people in the Persian empire was Esther. According to the Hebrew Bible, she married the Persian emperor. One of his advisors planned to kill all the Jews. Esther convinced the Persian king to **reject** this plan.

In 330 BCE, Alexander the Great, from present-day Greece, conquered the Persian empire. After his death, Greek empires ruled the Land of Israel, the rest of Southwest Asia, Egypt, and parts of southern Europe. In the years that followed, Jewish people settled in all of these regions. Some also settled far to the south, in Arabia and Africa. Others settled to the east in many parts of Asia.

By this time, millions of Jews lived inside and outside of the Land of Israel. Nonetheless, Jews everywhere still looked to Jerusalem as their spiritual home.

Academic Vocabulary

reject • *v.*, to decide against, turn away

Analyze Diagrams Israel has the world's largest Jewish population. But a majority of Jews live in the Diaspora, or outside Israel. **Analyze Data** In what two ways has the world's Jewish population changed since 1950?

GLOBAL JEWISH POPULATION

ESTIMATED WORLDWIDE
JEWISH POPULATION 2015
14,310,500

43.4% LIVE IN ISRAEL

39.8% LIVE IN THE U.S.

0.2% OF THE **WORLD POPULATION**

9.7% LIVE IN EUROPE
2.7% LIVE IN CANADA
1.3% LIVE IN ARGENTINA
3.1% LIVE ELSEWHERE

JEWISH POPULATION
IN ISRAEL & IN DIASPORA (MILLIONS)

Year	In Israel	In Diaspora
1950	1.2	10.1
1960	1.9	10.2
1970	2.6	10.0
1980	3.3	9.5
1990	3.9	9.0
2000	5.0	8.1
2010	5.8	7.8
2020 (projected)	6.7	8.0

Sources: DellaPergola, *World Jewish Population, 2015*; Pew Research Center; University of Connecticut, "World Jewish Population, 2012"; Rabinovich and Reinharz, *Israel in the Middle East,* 2008.

New Ways to Worship The Diaspora brought changes in the way Jews worshiped. Many Jews lived too far from Jerusalem to return for worship.

Previously, most Jews could worship at the Temple in Jerusalem. Because of the Diaspora, however, Jews had to practice their faith wherever they were living.

Some Jews had already been used to gathering in a **synagogue**, or meeting place. There they could pray and discuss the Torah and Hebrew Bible. Often, someone who knew the Torah well became the group's rabbi, or teacher. In the Diaspora, synagogues became even more important.

Greek Rule After the Babylonian Exile ended, Jews in Israel tried hard to follow their religion. But that was difficult because they faced harsh and unfair treatment by rulers of the Greek Empires.

Jews rebelled against harsh Greek rule. During the 100s BCE, a family known as the Maccabees rebelled and won independence from Greek rulers who tried to ban important parts of Judaism. The Jewish holiday of Hanukkah celebrates the victory of the Maccabees, freedom of religion, and reclaiming of the Temple.

Roman Rule In 6 CE, the Land of Israel became part of the Roman Empire. By this time, it was called Judaea, or later "land of the Jews." Roman disrespect toward Judaism led Jews to rebel against Rome. In 70 CE, the Romans destroyed Jerusalem, including the Second Temple.

The Romans also killed or enslaved thousands of Jews. Thousands more fled to other lands. During the war, a teacher from the Second Temple named Yohanan ben Zaccai (YOH hah nahn ben ZAH keye) secretly visited the Roman commander. He received permission to set up a center for Jewish scholars in another part of Judaea. The Temple was gone, but learning survived and remained important to Jews.

After another Jewish rebellion, the Romans changed the name of the province in 135 CE to Palaestina, later shortened to Palestine, after the ancient Israelites' enemies the Philistines. The Romans required provinces to pay tributes and taxes to support the rulers and the empire.

Judaism Changes and Develops The religious practices of early Judaism changed as a result of interactions with other societies. The Torah and Jewish law needed interpretation as society changed. For many centuries, details of the interpretation of the laws of the written Torah had been passed down orally from teacher to student. These explanations were called the Oral Torah. Jewish leaders feared that the Oral Torah would be lost in the Diaspora, and that direct passing down of the law might become impossible or unreliable. Because of that, within a few hundred

Analyze Images Jewish families take part in religious services in a modern synagogue. **Identify Main Ideas** What development gave rise to the practice of worshiping in a synagogue?

years after the destruction of the Second Temple, the Oral Torah was set down in writing, which later formed the core of the Talmud.

The preservation of those texts and laws, and of ethical and ritual requirements, was key to the development of Judaism as a religion. Judaism survived outside the homeland by focusing on the Torah and Jewish teachings, and by maintaining its strong religious and historic connection to the Land of Israel. This Judaism, in which traditions could be handed down through the generations in writing, became known as Rabbinic Judaism. Its practices no longer centered on the Temple. But Judaism's main teachings remained unchanged.

☑ READING CHECK Understand Effects How did Yohanan ben Zaccai help the Jewish religion to continue during the war against the Romans?

Judaism's Support for Society

Judaism is given credit for introducing monotheism to society. Beyond monotheism, Judaism's contributions have affected every part of our society. Biblical teachings and laws in both the Written and Oral Torahs have shaped not only early Jewish society, but civilization as a whole. The early Noahide Laws (described in the Oral Torah as given to the Biblical figure of Noah, generations before Abraham) are seven laws that Jews believe apply to society as a whole. They contain some of the elements of the Ten Commandments: to not deny or curse God and to not murder, steal, or engage in improper relationships.

How Does Judaism Help Ensure Social Justice? The Ten Commandments and later teachings contain laws about honoring parents, a day of rest, and justice. The guidelines for social justice, and for rulers and leaders, supported the needs of society and its members. The Hebrew Bible contains guidance and laws that detail how people

Analyze Images The Second Temple is thought to have looked something like this. **Synthesize Visual Information** How would the setting and the Temple itself inspire worshipers?

Religious Holidays in the Jewish Tradition Today

Day	Early Practice	Today
Sabbath	"Remember the Sabbath day, to keep it holy." Exodus 20:7	Jews observe the Sabbath as a day of rest from work, with communal prayer in the synagogue and time spent with family and friends during festive meals in the home.
Rosh Hashanah	"And in the seventh month, on the first of the month, it shall be declared a holiday for you, a day of sounding a teruah [blast of a shofar, or ram's horn] for you." Numbers 29:1	Rosh Hashanah celebrates the world's creation with prayers in the synagogue, reflection on the past year, the blowing of the shofar, and festive meals.
Passover	"You shall not eat any food made with yeast; for seven days you are to eat matzah [unleavened bread], the bread of affliction; for you departed from the land of Egypt hurriedly—so that you may remember the day of your departure from the land of Egypt as long as you live." Deuteronomy 16:3	Passover is a week of remembrance of the Exodus. Its main event is the seder, a ritual meal. Its foods symbolize the simple meal that marked the Israelites' escape from slavery.

should respond to poverty, famine, and injustice. It teaches that one must, above all, respect human life and give generously to the needy. Individuals and society must care for strangers and refugees, respect others' rights and property, and honor parents and respect marriage.

The concept of justice and equality under the law is contained in what may be the earliest legal system, with lower courts for simple disputes, and high courts that examine and rule on the difficult cases. The idea of making amends with money for crimes and debts took the place of a death penalty. Protection from those who would take the law into their own hands was guaranteed by setting up asylum cities in ancient Israel where those who were accused of killing others could safely await trial.

Laws Supporting Animal Rights and the Environment The Written and Oral Torahs also support the needs of animals and the environment. The Torah and Talmud provide instructions on animal rights and humane treatment. The Torah also includes environmental protections. These include introducing the practice of crop rotation to leave fields uncultivated during some seasons. This practice is useful because it helps maintain the nutrients in soil that keep the land fertile. Another protection for the environment found in the Torah is the obligation to not destroy or waste resources.

☑ READING CHECK Identify Main Ideas List three teachings of Judaism and explain why they are important today.

Analyze Charts Jewish religious practice has changed somewhat over time, as shown by the changes with these holidays. **Draw Conclusions** How are the holidays connected to the Hebrew Bible and the history of the Israelites?

What Is the Legacy of Judaism?

Today, nearly 14 million Jews live throughout the world. A large majority of the world's Jews live in either the United States or Israel.

Judaism's legacies, or the concepts and values it has given the world, include teachings about one God who created everything. Christians and Muslims, like Jews, honor Abraham as a founding figure and Moses as a messenger of God. They both share with Jews the belief in a single God. The ethical teachings of Judaism have influenced spiritual leaders in all parts of the world.

The Hebrew Bible is another legacy of Judaism. Its poetic language makes it a classic of world literature, as do its dramatic stories of unforgettable figures such as Moses, David, and Esther.

One of the greatest legacies of Judaism is the set of values that have been incorporated into what many call the Judeo-Christian tradition. These moral and ethical values form a basis for modern democratic societies such as the United States. They relate to such ideas as the worth of the individual and the importance of moral behavior. Examples include the equal importance of every individual, individual freedom and responsibility, community responsibility, and the importance of human rights and justice.

☑ READING CHECK **Summarize** What is the Judeo-Christian tradition?

▲ Rabbi Yitzhak Yosef (left) shakes hands with Pope Francis in Jerusalem. Jews and Christians share many traditions.

☑ Lesson Check

Practice Vocabulary

1. Who were the **judges**, and what role did they play in the lives of the Israelites?

2. What were the Jews who were in **exile** in Babylonia able to do with their sacred texts for the first time?

3. How were **synagogues** important to Jews in the Diaspora?

Critical Thinking and Writing

4. **Support Ideas with Evidence** Why are Naomi and Ruth significant figures?

5. **Draw Conclusions** How did the position of the Land of Israel, in a region conquered by several ancient empires, affect Jewish history?

6. **Understand Effects** Describe some of the ways in which Judaism has influenced modern democratic societies.

7. **Writing Workshop: Use Descriptive Details and Sensory Language** Write notes in your 🗐 Active Journal about descriptive details and sensory language that you can use in the narrative essay you will write at the end of the topic.

Construct a Timeline

Use the secondary source and follow these steps to construct a timeline.

INTERACTIVE

Sequence

1 **Identify the time span.** To organize information in a timeline, identify the earliest date and the latest date at which key events or periods occurred.

a. In the passage, what was the date of the first event?

b. What was the date of the last event?

2 **Identify your timeline's beginning and end points.** Begin the timeline at a date just before the oldest date in your list of events or periods. At the end of the timeline, place a date just after the last date in your list of events or periods.

3 **Divide the timeline into equal time spans.** Calculate the length of your timeline from start to finish. Then, divide that time period into equal segments. Mark each segment on the timeline and label it.

4 **Place items along the timeline.** Write down key events and their dates where they fall along the timeline. For time spans, place them at the point they begin. Make sure to arrange all items in sequence. Be sure to include all of the dates mentioned in the passage.

Secondary Source

"The time of the judges ended when the judges chose Saul to become the first king of Israel in 1021 BCE. He remained king for the next 20 years and is known for defending Israel against its enemies. David, who was considered one of Saul's best fighters, became the next king of Israel around 1000 BCE. David captured Jerusalem and made it the capital city. David's son Solomon followed in his father's footsteps, becoming king in 967 BCE. He extended the kingdom and built the First Temple in Jerusalem. After Solomon died around 900 BCE, the kingdom of Israel split. Solomon's descendants ruled the kingdom of Judah, in the south. The kingdom in the north kept the name of Israel. It stood until about 722 BCE when it was conquered by the Assyrian empire. Many Israelites fled south to Judah to avoid capture by the Assyrians."

☑ Review and Assessment

VISUAL REVIEW

Achievements of Mesopotamian Civilizations and Empires

Sumerian City-States (c. 3500 BCE–2350 BCE)	Akkadian Empire (c. 2334–c. 2154 BCE)	Babylonian Empire (c. 1850 BCE–1595 BCE)
• Irrigation • Cities • Cuneiform • Bronze	• World's first empire • Trade and spread of culture	• Rule of law • Hammurabi's Code • Advances in technology

Assyrian Empire (934 BCE–627 BCE)	Neo-Babylonian Empire (626 BCE–539 BCE)	Persian Empire (539 BCE–330 BCE)
• First cavalry • Iron technology • Library	• Nebuchadnezzar • Hanging gardens • Other structures	• Standing army • Roads • Local control • Common currency

Early History of Judaism and the Israelites

Early Israelites	Jewish Beliefs
• Worship of one God • God's covenant with Abraham • Torah • Exodus and return to Promised Land • Ten Commandments • Prophets, kings	• Ethical monotheism • Observance of law • Love for others • Observance of Sabbath • Study and prayer • Connection to land of Israel

READING REVIEW

Use the Take Notes and Practice Vocabulary activities in your 📘 Active Journal to review this topic.

⊙ INTERACTIVE

Practice vocabulary using the Topic Mini-Games.

Quest FINDINGS

Have Your Discussion About Preserving Order

Use your notes and your sources to make your arguments. Refer to your 📘 Active Journal.

ASSESSMENT

Vocabulary and Key Ideas

1. **Check Understanding** How did Hammurabi's Code establish the **rule of law**?

2. **Draw Conclusions** Why was **cuneiform** important?

3. **Describe** Give three examples of **cultural diffusion** in the Fertile Crescent.

4. **Identify Main Ideas** How were religion and government related in these societies?

5. **Define** What were the **Exodus** and the **Diaspora**?

6. **Identify Main Ideas** What is the connection between the **Torah** and Jewish **ethics**?

Critical Thinking and Writing

7. **Draw Inferences** Why do you think the Phoenicians were better than other civilizations at ocean navigation and trade?

8. **Draw Conclusions** Why did the Phoenician alphabet make writing easier and more efficient than cuneiform?

9. **Analyze Cause and Effect** Why was Sumerians' use of farming technology essential to the development of cities as centers of culture and power?

10. **Draw Inferences** How did the Jews' interactions with other groups affect Judaism?

11. **Revisit the Essential Question** How did the societies of the Fertile Crescent preserve order?

12. **Writing Workshop: Write a Narrative Essay** Using the notes you made in your 🖍 Active Journal to write a narrative essay in which you are a person living in ancient Mesopotamia describing your daily life.

Analyze Primary Sources

13. What was Hammurabi's main reason for publishing his code of laws?
    A. improve trade
    B. end wicked behavior and protect the weak
    C. expand Babylonian territory
    D. show Babylonia's greatness

"[T]hen [the gods] Anu and Bel called by name me, Hammurabi, the exalted prince, who feared God, to bring about the rule of righteousness in the land, to destroy the wicked and the evil-doers; so that the strong should not harm the weak; . . . to further the well-being of mankind."

—*Introduction to Hammurabi's Code, about 1780 BCE*

Analyze Maps

14. Compare and contrast the size and location of the Babylonian empire and Phoenicia.

15. How do you think the location of rivers in the Fertile Crescent influenced the founding and growth of Sumer?

16. Which is the largest empire shown on the map?

17. Where on this map were the Promised Land and the first kingdom of Israel?

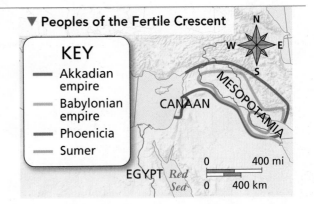

▼ **Peoples of the Fertile Crescent**

KEY
— Akkadian empire
— Babylonian empire
— Phoenicia
— Sumer

MESOPOTAMIA

CANAAN

EGYPT *Red Sea*

0   400 mi
0   400 km

GO ONLINE
to access your
digital course

 VIDEO

 AUDIO

 ETEXT

 INTERACTIVE

 WRITING

 GAMES

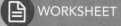 WORKSHEET

 ASSESSMENT

Go back over 5,000 years

to ANCIENT EGYPT AND KUSH. Why? To check out the pyramids and mummies, of course! You will also see how Egypt and its neighbor Kush show us how geography—in this case the Nile River—can be essential to the growth of a civilization.

Explore
The Essential Question

What makes a great leader?

Egypt and Kush were ruled by kings known as pharaohs. How did the pharaohs help build Egypt into one of the world's greatest ancient civilizations?

Unlock the Essential Question in your ✏ Active Journal.

Read

about the complex culture that created the pyramids, the Sphinx, and thousands of mummies.

Watch

 BOUNCE TO ACTIVATE VIDEO

Uncovering Mummies' Secrets in the Artifact Lab

Unravel the mysteries of some of Egypt's most powerful pharaohs.

◀ The Great Sphinx at Giza, Egypt

Ancient Egypt and Kush
(3000 BCE–600 BCE)

Learn more about ancient Egypt and Kush by making your own map and timeline in your Active Journal.

INTERACTIVE

Topic Map

Where were ancient Egypt and Kush?

These ancient kingdoms were located in the northeast corner of Africa, to the west of ancient Mesopotamia. Locate the Nile and its delta on the map in the circle.

INTERACTIVE

Topic Timeline

What happened and when?

Huge stone pyramids built without modern machines . . . riches beyond imagining . . . . Explore the timeline to see some of what was happening in Egypt and Kush and in the rest of the world.

About 3100 BCE
Egypt's first pharaoh unites Upper and Lower Egypt.

About 2450 BCE
The Great Pyramid of Giza is built.

TOPIC EVENTS

4000 BCE	3000 BCE

WORLD EVENTS

About 3000 BCE
The Sumerians invent a written language.

2100 BCE
Xia Dynasty rises in China.

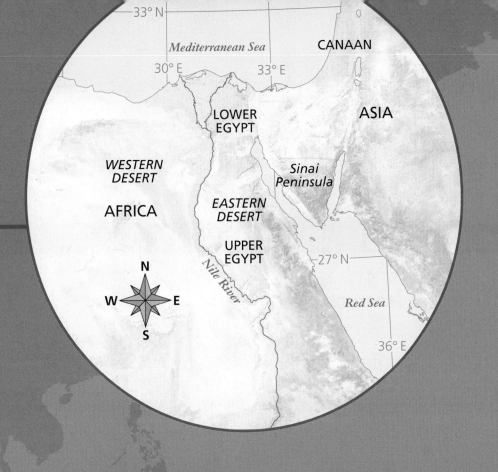

33° N

Mediterranean Sea

CANAAN

30° E   33° E

LOWER
EGYPT

ASIA

WESTERN
DESERT

Sinai
Peninsula

AFRICA

EASTERN
DESERT

UPPER
EGYPT

27° N

N
W   E
S

Nile River

Red Sea

36° E

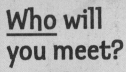

Hatshepsut, the
woman who was
pharaoh

Tutankhamen,
whose magnificent
tomb glittered
with gold

Ramses II, the
conqueror

About 1333 BCE
Tutankhamen
becomes
pharaoh.

1279 BCE
Ramses II
becomes
pharaoh.

343 BCE
Persian invaders
defeat the
last Egyptian
pharaoh.

1473 BCE
Hatshepsut
becomes
pharaoh.

730 BCE
A Nubian
pharaoh
conquers
Egypt.

2000 BCE		**1000** BCE		**1** BCE

About 1700 BCE
Hammurabi writes
early set of laws.

750 BCE
City-states begin
to rise in Greece.

Quest

▼ One of Hatshepsut's obelisks

Become a Pharaoh-in-Training

Quest KICK OFF

The year is **1000** BCE. Your uncle has died suddenly and you have been crowned Pharaoh of Ancient Egypt!

What do you need to learn to become a great pharaoh?

How did the pharaohs rule ancient Egypt? Explore the Essential Question "What makes a great leader?" in this Quest.

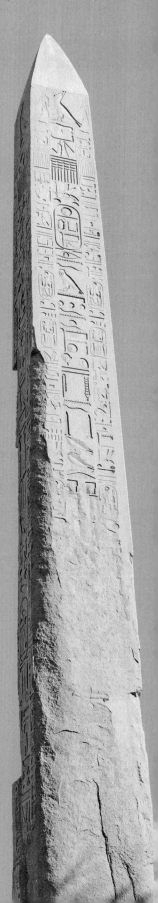

1 Ask Questions
Being a pharaoh is a big job. Get started now by making a list of questions about how best to rule. Write the questions in your 📕 Active Journal.

2 Investigate
As you read the lessons in this topic, look for **Quest** CONNECTIONS that provide information on how Egypt's pharaohs built a highly accomplished civilization. Capture notes in your 📕 Active Journal.

3 Examine Primary Sources
Next explore a set of primary and secondary sources from Ancient Egypt. They'll help you learn even more about how to be a great pharaoh. Capture notes in your 📕 Active Journal.

Quest FINDINGS

4 Write Your Monument Inscription
The pharaohs of ancient Egypt captured records of their great deeds on monuments throughout Egypt. At the end of the topic you'll write a message to appear on a monument built in your honor. The message will celebrate all of your great deeds as pharaoh. Get help for writing your message in your 📕 Active Journal.

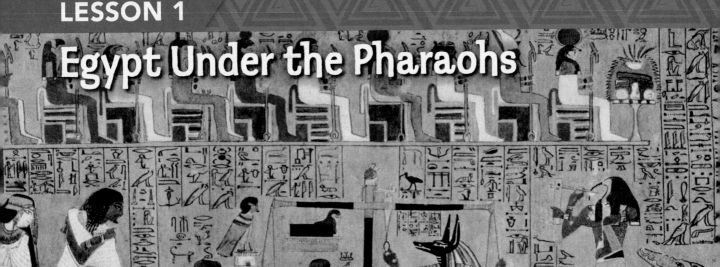

Egypt Under the Pharaohs

BOUNCE TO ACTIVATE ▶ VIDEO

GET READY TO READ

START UP

Examine the Egyptian tomb painting. Notice the symbols, objects, and the clothing and interactions of the people and gods. Write three questions you have about ancient Egypt based on the painting.

GUIDING QUESTIONS

- How did Egypt's unique geography help its civilization grow?
- How did a complex society develop in Egypt?
- How did pharaohs change Egypt?
- How did religion affect the lives of ancient Egyptians?

TAKE NOTES

Literacy Skill: Main Ideas and Details Use the graphic organizer in your 📖 Active Journal to take notes as you read the lesson.

PRACTICE VOCABULARY

Use the vocabulary activity in your 📖 Active Journal to practice the vocabulary words.

Vocabulary		Academic Vocabulary
cataract	dynasty	environmental
delta	bureaucracy	devotion
artisan	mummy	
pharaoh		

Like the Fertile Crescent of Mesopotamia, Egypt was home to one of the world's first great civilizations. As in the Fertile Crescent, Egypt's civilization developed in a river valley with rich soil. However, Egypt's geography and culture differed in many ways from those of the Fertile Crescent.

The Nile River Valley

The ancient Egyptians treasured the Nile River. They knew that without the Nile, their land would be nothing but a sun-baked desert of bright blue skies and dry sand.

The World's Longest River The Nile is the world's longest river. It begins in East Africa and flows about 3,500 miles north to the Mediterranean Sea.

This great river has two main sources—the White Nile and the Blue Nile. The White Nile flows from Lake Victoria. The Blue Nile rushes down from the highlands of present-day Ethiopia. The two rivers meet in present-day Sudan. In ancient times, northern Sudan was known as Nubia, or Kush.

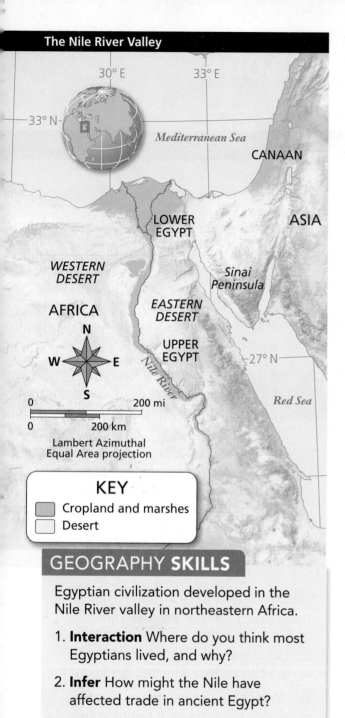

The Nile River Valley

KEY
- Cropland and marshes
- Desert

0 — 200 mi
0 — 200 km
Lambert Azimuthal
Equal Area projection

GEOGRAPHY SKILLS

Egyptian civilization developed in the Nile River valley in northeastern Africa.

1. **Interaction** Where do you think most Egyptians lived, and why?

2. **Infer** How might the Nile have affected trade in ancient Egypt?

In Kush and Egypt, the Nile flows through the Sahara, a vast desert that stretches across most of northern Africa. Before reaching Egypt, the river in ancient times roared through six **cataracts**, or groups of rocky rapids. The rocky cataracts made it impossible for people to travel by ship upstream from Egypt.

Upper and Lower Egypt Below the cataracts, the Nile flows through a narrow valley lined with cliffs. This region is part of an area called Upper Egypt because it is upstream from the Mediterranean Sea.

The river carries silt—fine mineral particles that can form fertile soil—from its sources in East Africa. Near the end of its journey, the Nile slows down and fans out into many streams and marshy areas. As it slows, the river drops its silt. Over thousands of years, this silt has built up to form a large river delta. A **delta** is an area of sediment—soil or minerals carried by water—deposited at the mouth of a river. The Nile delta forms the region known as Lower Egypt.

Floods and the Black Land A narrow strip of fertile soil lines both banks of the Nile and covers its delta. This rich, dark soil was so important to the Egyptians that they called their country *Kemet*, which means "the Black Land."

The yearly flooding of the Nile created the Black Land. Each summer, heavy rainfall in East Africa poured into the Nile's sources. Flood waters surged through Egypt. When the flood waters drained away, they left behind a layer of fresh silt.

However, the Nile floods were unpredictable. If too much water came, the floods could be a natural disaster that swept away soil. If too little water came, Egypt could suffer a drought, or a shortage of water. Droughts could bring hunger by causing crops to fail.

On either side of the Black Land lay vast deserts. Egyptians called these deserts "the Red Land." Unlike the Black Land, the Red Land was a deadly place of hot, burning sands.

READING CHECK **Summarize** Describe the Nile and its importance to ancient Egypt.

How Did Egyptian Civilization Develop?

More than 7,000 years ago, people began growing grains in the fertile soil left behind by the Nile floods. Over time, Egypt's farmers were able to grow more and more food. This food supported a growing population.

Agricultural Techniques Create a Surplus Egyptian farmers learned to build earthen walls around fields to trap the Nile's flood waters. The water soaked into the soil and allowed grains such as wheat to grow. This simple form of crop irrigation allowed farmers to grow more crops and produce a food surplus, or an amount of food greater than their own family's needs. Irrigation of the Nile valley allowed the land to be farmed even though the region received less and less rain over time. Later, you will read how farmers used similar techniques along the Indus River in India and the Huang He in northern China.

Meanwhile, powerful people and families gained control over regions within Egypt. They were able to collect some of the farmers' surplus crop as taxes.

How Did Cities Develop? These local rulers used this surplus to buy rich cloth, jewelry, and luxury goods. These were supplied by merchants and **artisans**, or skilled workers who practice a handicraft.

Farmers' production of a surplus supported these artisans. Some became full-time artisans, such as weavers or potters. Artisans and merchants began to settle around the homes of local rulers. In time, these settlements grew into cities.

Egypt's cities brought together wealthy and skilled people. They became centers of culture and power. Skilled architects built impressive buildings. Artists created great works of art to decorate them. Egyptian cities grew to be large and powerful.

☑ READING CHECK Understand Effects How did growing a surplus of crops affect ancient Egypt?

Not much change

Did you know?

Without the Nile, Egyptian cities would never have developed. Beyond the Nile valley lay a deadly landscape of hot burning sand that the Egyptians called "the Red Land."

Analyze Images The illustration on the left shows croplands during the Nile's yearly flood. The illustration on the right shows the same croplands after the flood. **Identify Effects** How did the yearly floods help Egypt's farmers?

▲ The pharaoh Tutankhamen ruled for nine short years during the New Kingdom era.

Academic Vocabulary
environmental • *adj.,* having to do with natural surroundings

The Kingdoms of Egypt

During the 3000s BCE, two kingdoms developed in Egypt. The kings of Upper Egypt wore white crowns. The kings of Lower Egypt wore red crowns.

Uniting Egypt You might remember that the city-states of Sumer never united under one kingdom. However, Egypt's two kingdoms did unite. Legends say that Narmer brought them together in about 3000 BCE. This made him the first **pharaoh**, or king, of a united Egypt. He wore a double crown of red and white and founded Egypt's earliest dynasty. A **dynasty** is a ruling family.

Normally, control passed between members of a dynasty. Sometimes, however, a new dynasty gained power. Historians divide Egypt's history into periods based on kingdoms and dynasties.

The Old and Middle Kingdoms Historians call the period from about 2686 to 2125 BCE the Old Kingdom. Like later kingdoms, the Old Kingdom was a period of prosperity, political strength, and cultural achievement.

After a period of civil wars, the Middle Kingdom began. It lasted from about 2055 to 1650 BCE. Pharaohs of the Middle Kingdom dealt with one of Egypt's major **environmental** challenges—the Nile floods. As the Sumerians had done in Mesopotamia, the pharaohs built a system of canals that could drain dangerous flood waters and irrigate new farmland.

High Point and Decline The New Kingdom followed more civil wars and invasions. The New Kingdom lasted from about 1550 to 1070 BCE. New Kingdom pharaohs conquered lands in Asia and Africa. This was the high point of ancient Egyptian power and prosperity.

However, the New Kingdom eventually declined and broke apart. Egypt faced foreign invasions. One late dynasty gained power only with the help of the Assyrians. Still later, Egypt was conquered by the Persian empire. In 332 BCE, the Greek army of Alexander the Great conquered Egypt.

The Political Order in Egypt The pharaoh relied on a **bureaucracy**, or a system of offices and officials that handle the business of government. The head of Egypt's bureaucracy was an official called the vizier. The bureaucracy collected taxes from farmers. Farmers paid these taxes mainly in the form of surplus crops.

The bureaucracy took some of this surplus for itself. It distributed the rest to priests, to the pharaoh, and to artisans and merchants who worked for the pharaoh. Egypt's bureaucracy and system of taxation were a model for later governments, including those of today.

✓ **READING CHECK** **Categorize** Name one accomplishment of pharaohs of the Middle and New Kingdoms.

How Was Egyptian Society Organized?

To control Egypt, pharaohs needed the loyalty and labor of the people. Egypt's social order provided both.

Egyptian society was shaped like a pyramid. The pharaoh was at the top of that pyramid. Egyptians believed that gods controlled everything. The pharaoh controlled Egypt, so people saw him as a god-king who deserved loyalty.

Just below the pharaoh were nobles, priests, and officials. They helped the pharaoh govern Egypt. Scribes kept records for Egypt's bureaucracy.

Merchants and artisans made up a middle level. Painters, stonecutters, and builders spent their lives working on temples and tombs.

Farmers were lower on the social pyramid. By far, most of the people of ancient Egypt were farmers. During the growing season, farmers raised Egypt's food. For the rest of the year, many were required to work as laborers on the pharaoh's building projects. Most did so willingly out of religious **devotion**. They believed that if they helped the god-king, they would be rewarded after death.

Slaves were at the bottom of the social pyramid. Many were prisoners of war or debtors who were freed from slavery after serving for a period of time. Slaves were the property of their owners and had to do forced labor.

☑ **READING CHECK** **Identify Main Ideas** Describe how Egyptian society functioned.

Academic Vocabulary
devotion • *n.*, dedication, loyalty

Quest CONNECTIONS

Look at the diagram. How did each of these groups contribute to Egypt's greatness? As a pharaoh, how can you earn their loyalty? Record your findings in your ▱ Active Journal.

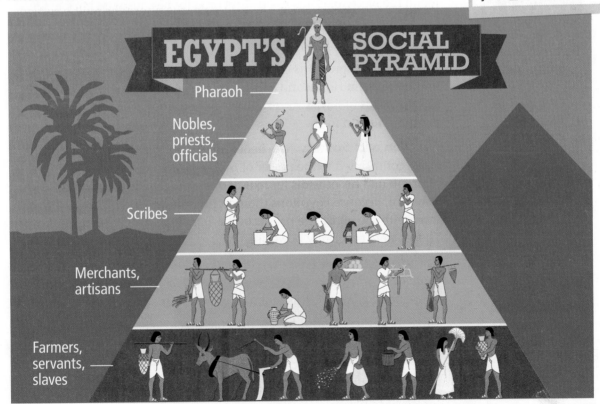

EGYPT'S SOCIAL PYRAMID

Pharaoh

Nobles, priests, officials

Scribes

Merchants, artisans

Farmers, servants, slaves

Analyze Diagrams To control Egypt, pharaohs needed the loyalty and labor of the people. Egypt's social order provided both. **Draw Conclusions** What does the widening nature of the pyramid suggest about the number of people who belonged to each level of society?

Egyptian Religion

Religion played an important role in the life of the people of Egypt. They believed that their gods controlled everything from the flooding of the Nile River to the death of a child. Their gods could be kind or dangerous. To please the gods, Egyptians built them temples and offered prayers and gifts.

Many Gods Like the Sumerians, ancient Egyptians were polytheists. They worshiped hundreds of gods. Many were associated with animals. Statues or other works of art often show a god with the head or body of a lion, a crocodile, or some other creature. Egyptians believed that gods shared the qualities of these animals, such as their strength, speed, or bad temper.

One of the most important gods was Amon-Re, the sun god. Egyptians believed that Amon-Re made a daily journey across the sky. Each night, he died in the west as the land grew dark. Each morning, he was reborn in the east as the sun rose.

Osiris was the god of the underworld, or the world of the dead. According to Egyptian legend, Osiris was killed and chopped into pieces by a rival god named Seth. Isis, the wife of Osiris, was the mother goddess of Egypt. She moved heaven and earth to help her husband. Isis found the pieces of Osiris's body and brought her husband back to life.

Isis represented love, caring, and protection. Egyptians looked to Isis for protection in both life and death.

Horus was the son of Isis and Osiris. Egyptian legends tell of great battles between Horus and Seth. When Horus defeated Seth, he united the two lands of Egypt. As a result, every pharaoh was thought to be Horus in human form.

Religion and Society The belief that the pharaoh was a god on Earth contributed to the power of the pharaoh. People obeyed the pharaoh and his officials for fear of angering a god. Priests were also powerful, because Egyptians thought priests could help a person gain favor with the gods. The priests of the Temple of Amon-Re in the city of Thebes were especially powerful.

Preparing for the Afterlife Egyptians believed that they, like Osiris, could overcome death. Life on Earth could lead to an afterlife, or life after death. However, this required preparation.

The first way to prepare for the afterlife was to live a good life. Egyptians believed that Osiris decided who would have an afterlife. Those who had lived good lives would be allowed to live forever, but the sinful would be destroyed.

▲ After death, a person's body was cleaned, bathed with chemicals, and wrapped in linen bandages to preserve it, making a mummy.

Preserving the Dead The second way that Egyptians prepared for the afterlife was by preserving their bodies after death. Egyptians believed that their spirit would need to recognize their preserved body and use it as a home.

Poor people were buried in the desert, where the hot, dry sand quickly dried out their bodies. Wealthy Egyptians had their bodies made into mummies. A **mummy** is a body preserved by a special process. The knowledge of this process was one of ancient Egypt's great achievements. From mummies, scientists have learned much about life and death in ancient Egypt.

✓ READING CHECK **Identify Cause and Effect**
What role did the afterlife play in the lives of ancient Egyptians?

Great Rulers

Hatshepsut, Ramses II, and Thutmose III were powerful New Kingdom pharaohs who shaped Egypt's history.

Hatshepsut Hatshepsut was one of the few women to rule Egypt. She was the daughter of one pharaoh and the wife of another. When her husband died, he left a son, named Thutmose III, who was too young to rule. So Hatshepsut decided to make herself Egypt's new pharaoh.

Some Egyptians did not want to bow to a woman. To gain their support, Hatshepsut carried out all of the rituals expected of a king. Her statues showed her dressed as a king. She even wore the false beard that was a

⏻ INTERACTIVE

Egyptian religion gallery

Quick Activity

Explore the impact of Egypt's pharaohs in your 📓 Active Journal.

Thutmose III is Hatshepsut's son? That suprises me

BIOGRAPHY
5 Things to Know About ⟩ RAMSES II
Egyptian Pharaoh (c.1303–1213 BCE)

- He became pharaoh when he was very young and ruled for 66 years, the second-longest reign in Egyptian history.

- In addition to ruling as pharaoh, Ramses also led the Egyptian army and conquered a large amount of territory.

- Ramses won his greatest fame in the Battle of Kadesh, where he fought off a surprise attack by a much larger Hittite force.

- He brought tremendous wealth to Egypt and built many temples.

- When Ramses died at over 90 years of age, he was beloved throughout Egypt.

Critical Thinking What qualities of leadership do you think Ramses II had to make him successful?

▲ Hatshepsut ruled as Pharaoh for more than 20 years. **Draw Conclusions** Based on this statue, how do you think the Egyptian people felt about Hatshepsut?

traditional symbol of the pharaoh's strength and power. Most Egyptians came to accept Hapshetsut's rule.

Primary Source

"[T]he god's wife Hatshepsut executed the affairs of the Two Lands according to her counsels. Egypt worked for her, head bowed . . ."

— A government official during Hatshepsut's reign, from "The 18th Dynasty Before the Amarna Period," by Betsy M. Bryan, in *The Oxford History of Ancient Egypt*

Hatshepsut's rule was peaceful. Hatshepsut built Egypt's wealth and power through trade. She sent traders by sea to a land called Punt in East Africa. They returned with precious wood, ivory, gold, and perfumes. Hatshepsut recorded the story of their journey on the stone walls of an enormous temple that she built.

Thutmose III When Hatshepsut died, Thutmose III became ruler of Egpyt. Unlike Hatshepsut, he used war to strengthen and expand the empire. He conquered land in Africa, Syria, and the Fertile Crescent. His conquests gave Egypt more wealth, power, and prestige.

Ramses II Ramses II, who ruled about 150 years after Thutmose III, also used war to build Egypt's wealth and power. He spent the first half of his time as pharaoh fighting in Canaan and Syria, in the Fertile Crescent. In 1275 BCE, Ramses II led his army against the powerful Hittites. The two armies fought in Kadesh in present-day Syria. Ramses II lost many soldiers to the Hittites in the battle of Kadesh. He later made peace with the Hittites by agreeing on a border. Ramses II was a great builder. He built more monuments than any other pharaoh.

✓ READING CHECK **Identify Supporting Details** What actions showed that Hatshepsut, Thutmose III, and Ramses II were great rulers?

☑ Lesson Check

Practice Vocabulary

1. What role did **pharaohs, artisans**, and the **bureaucracy** play in ancient Egypt?

2. How is the creation of **mummies** related to Egypt's dynasties?

Critical Thinking and Writing

3. **Explain** How did the Nile contribute to the growth of ancient Egyptian culture?

4. **Compare and Contrast** Compare and contrast the ways in which farmers and scribes contributed to ancient Egyptian civilization.

5. **Identify Central Ideas** What role did pharaohs play in ancient Egypt's religion?

6. **Writing Workshop: Develop a Clear Thesis** Write a sentence in your 📓 Active Journal that expresses the effects of geography on Egypt. This sentence will become the thesis statement for an essay you will write at the end of the topic.

Primary Sources

The Victory of Ramses II

Around 1273 BCE, Egyptian forces under Pharaoh Ramses II battled the Hittites for control of the city of Kadesh in Syria. In one of the largest chariot battles in history, Ramses fought his way out of a Hittite ambush.

▶ Ramses II is the largest figure in this painting.

Then the king he lashed each horse, . . .
Then he looked behind, and found
That the foe were all around,
Two thousand and five hundred of their chariots of war;
And the flower of the Hittites, and their helpers in a ring. . . .

Then spake Pharaoh, and he cried:
"Father <u>Ammon</u>, ① where are you?
I have built for you tall gates and wondrous works beside the Nile . . . .
It is I who sent for you,
The ships upon the sea,
To pour into your <u>coffers</u> ② the wealth of foreign trade . . . .
To you my cry I send,
Unto earth's extremest end,
Saying 'Help me, father Ammon, against the Hittite horde.' ③

Then my voice it found an echo in <u>Hermonthis'</u> ④ temple-hall,
Ammon heard it, and he came unto my call;
And for joy I gave a shout,
From behind, his voice cried out,

"I have hastened to you, Ramses Miamun,
Behold! I stand with you,
Behold! 'tis I am he,
Own father thine, the great god Ra, the sun.
Lo! mine hand with then shall fight. . . ." ⑤

—From *The Poem of Pen-ta-ur*

Analyzing Primary Sources

Cite specific evidence from the document to support your answers.

1. **Determine Author's Purpose** Why do you think Ramses wanted this poem inscribed on temples?

2. **Use Evidence** Would you consider this poem a reliable source of information? Explain.

Reading and Vocabulary Support

① Recall what you have learned about Egyptian religion. Who is Amon (Ammon in the poem), or Amon-Re? Why do you think Ramses is crying out to Amon?

② A coffer is a box that holds money.

③ What request does Ramses make to Amon? Why does he think he deserves Amon's help?

④ Hermonthis was an important city in Egypt.

⑤ According to this poem, how does Amon respond to the pharoah's request?

Quest CONNECTIONS

Based on the poem, how does Ramses want to be remembered? Record your findings in your 📓 Active Journal.

Identify Physical and Cultural Features

Use the sources below as you follow these steps to identify physical and cultural features.

1 **Identify physical features.** Physical features include bodies of water, coastlines, mountains, valleys, and deserts.

  a. What does the photograph show you about the physical features of the land where the Valley of the Kings is located?

  b. How does the map show this same information?

2 **Identify cultural features.** Cultural features are features created by people, such as cities, borders, buildings, roads, railroads, or canals. What is the main cultural feature of ancient Egypt shown on the map?

3 **Relate physical and cultural features.** Cultural features are often related to physical features. For example, a river (physical feature) can form a border between two countries (cultural feature). The natural landscape may determine where a city is built. Based on the photo and map, why do you think the Valley of the Kings was not located closer to the Nile?

Primary Source

▲ Many of the most powerful pharaohs and nobles of ancient Egypt are buried in the Valley of the Kings.

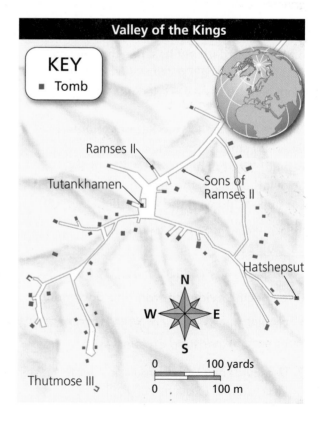

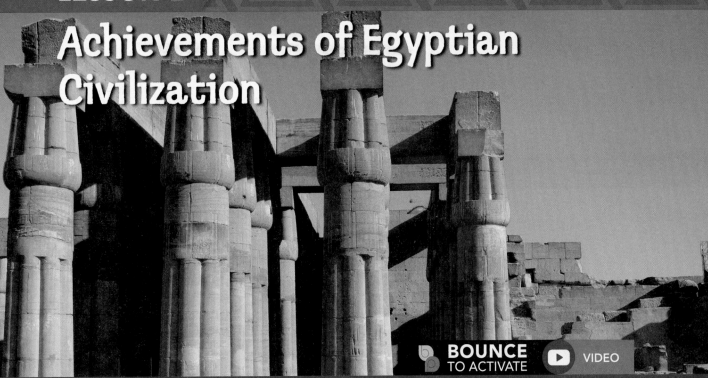

LESSON 2
Achievements of Egyptian Civilization

BOUNCE TO ACTIVATE ▶ VIDEO

GET READY TO READ

START UP

Notice the size and scale of the pillars in the photo. How do you think the ancient Egyptians achieved great feats of architecture without the technology we have today?

GUIDING QUESTIONS

- What was the impact of writing on Egypt?
- What were the main features of Egyptian architecture and art?
- How did advancements in science, mathematics, and technology affect Egyptian society?

TAKE NOTES

Literacy Skills: Summarize

Use the graphic organizer in your 📓 Active Journal to take notes as you read the lesson.

PRACTICE VOCABULARY

Use the vocabulary activity in your 📓 Active Journal to practice the vocabulary words.

Vocabulary	Academic Vocabulary
hieroglyphic anatomy	survive
papyrus	construct
pyramid	
sculpture	

Like the Sumerians, the ancient Egyptians were great inventors. In writing, literature, art, architecture, mathematics, and science, the Egyptians made advances that paved the way for later civilizations.

Writing and Literature

The ancient Egyptians developed one of the world's first writing systems. Egyptian writing preserved some of the world's oldest records and works of literature.

What Was Hieroglyphic Writing?

Ancient Egyptians developed early forms of writing by 3200 BCE. At around the same time, Sumerians in Mesopotamia were developing their own system of writing. Scholars aren't sure who developed writing first. They also don't know if one group borrowed the idea of writing from the other, or if each people came up with the idea separately.

Egyptian writing used hieroglyphics. A **hieroglyphic** is a drawing or symbol that represents a word or a sound.

Sumerians ↓

that's interesting

Mesopotamian cuneiform and Egyptian hieroglyphics shared some similarities. Both systems of writing used signs that represented sounds, or phonemes, and other signs—logograms—that represented the meanings of words or phrases.

Most ancient Egyptians did not know how to write. Scribes, or officials who knew how to write, were valued for their knowledge. With writing, Egyptians could keep records and preserve knowledge. This ability made its complex civilization and advanced technology possible.

The Importance of Papyrus Egyptians invented a material very similar to paper. This material is called **papyrus** (puh PY rus) and was made from the papyrus reed that grew along the Nile. Our word *paper* comes from the word *papyrus*. Scribes wrote in ink on papyrus sheets. This was much easier than pressing letters into wet clay as the Sumerians did. Papyrus sheets were also easier to transport than pieces of clay.

Papyrus sheets had another important quality. They could last a very long time in the dry environment of Egypt. Many documents written on papyrus—including medical books, calendars, stories, poems, and prayers—have **survived** to the present. Wall paintings may show us how Egyptians lived; however, written records give us a fuller sense of what was in their hearts and minds.

Analyze Images Scholars have studied hieroglyphics to learn how the ancient Egyptians lived. **Use Visual Information** List the hieroglyphs you recognize. How is writing with symbols different from using an alphabet?

Papyrus was efficient

Egyptian Literature Ancient Egyptian literature included teachings, stories, poems, religious texts, and histories. Egyptian literature was written on sheets of papyrus, carved on stone monuments, and painted on the coffins of mummies.

One famous text, *The Book of the Dead,* is a guide to the afterlife for dead souls. *The Tale of Sinuhe* tells the tale of an Egyptian official. Hearing that the pharaoh has been killed, he flees Egypt out of fear that he will be blamed for the crime:

Primary Source

"My heart staggered, my arms spread out; trembling fell on every limb. I removed myself, leaping, to look for a hiding place."

—From *The Tale of Sinuhe*, translated by R. B. Parkinson

thats scary + stressful

Academic Vocabulary

survive • *v.,* to last, to continue to live

✓ READING CHECK **Understand Effects** How did writing make Egypt's complex civilization and technology possible?

Architecture and Art

The Egyptians created temples for their gods and tombs for their pharaohs and other important people. The temple complex at Karnak contains the ruins of the world's largest temples, built with massive blocks of stone. These great buildings, and the art they contain, continue to inspire artists to this day.

Why Did the Egyptians Build Pyramids?
Tombs of early rulers were underground chambers, or rooms. The burial chamber contained items that the ruler might want in the afterlife.

An architect named Imhotep designed a new kind of tomb for his pharaoh, with six stone mounds, one on top of the other. The result is known as a step pyramid. Later architects made the sides smoother to create a true **pyramid,** or structure with triangular sides.

During the Old Kingdom, three enormous pyramids were built at Giza for King Khufu, his son Khafre, and his grandson Menkaure. The largest is the Great Pyramid of Khufu. For nearly 4,000 years, this pyramid was the world's tallest building. Nearby stands the Sphinx, a famous statue. The Sphinx guarded the road to Khafre's pyramid.

When they were built, these pyramids were the largest structures on Earth. They were a great achievement. They show Egyptians' command of mathematics and advanced building techniques.

Building the pyramids also required the labor of thousands of workers. Workers cut and placed the huge stones by hand. Scholars once thought that slaves had built the pyramids. They now think that many workers were farmers.

The great age of pyramid building ended about 2200 BCE. Pharaohs who ruled after that time carved massive tombs from the cliffs at the edge of the Nile Valley. Egypt's massive tombs and temples show that Egyptians valued monuments to the gods, including pharaohs.

INTERACTIVE

Egyptian Pyramids

Quick Activity

Explore how the ancient Egyptians moved the stone blocks that created the pyramids in your 📔 Active Journal.

Quest CONNECTIONS

What were Egyptian pharaohs trying to accomplish by building pyramids? Record your findings in your 📔 Active Journal.

Analyze Images The Great Pyramid of Giza is considered one of the seven wonders of the ancient world. **Infer** Why is the Great Pyramid of Giza called a "wonder"?

▲ Statue from the tomb of the Pharaoh Tutankhamun.

Painting and Sculpture Egyptians were skilled artists and builders. Much of what we know about life in Egypt comes from paintings on the walls of tombs that show Egyptians at work and at play; their purpose was not decoration. The paintings were created to provide the person buried in the tomb with all of the objects and pleasures shown on the walls.

Egyptian artists also created wonderful sculptures. A **sculpture** is a statue or other free-standing piece of art made of clay, stone, or other materials. Colossal statues of gods stood in temples. Egyptians placed smaller statues of people in tombs along with their mummies. If a mummy was destroyed, the statue could replace it as a home for the dead person's spirit.

✓ **READING CHECK** Draw Conclusions Why do people still admire the pyramids and art the Egyptians created?

Science and Mathematics

The Egyptians made many great discoveries in science, mathematics, and technology. Later civilizations built on these discoveries.

The Egyptian Calendar Like most early peoples, prehistoric Egyptians probably measured time by the cycles of the moon. The result would have been a lunar, or moon-based, year of about 354 days.

Over the years, the seasons would run ahead of such a calendar, since the seasons follow a solar, or sun-based, year of 365.2422 days. The ancient Egyptians wanted to keep the calendar linked to the seasons to help farmers plan when to plant and harvest crops. They watched for a bright star called Sirius which would appear above the horizon before sunrise about the same time of year as the Nile floods. Sometimes the first appearance of Sirius came too close to the end of the lunar year, so the Egyptians added an extra month to that year to catch up to the seasons.

However, this meant that each year had a different number of days. That made record keeping and planning difficult. So the ancient Egyptians developed a solar calendar with exactly 365 days. They used this calendar for official record keeping.

The seasons still slowly shifted through this solar calendar, too, so the ancient Greeks added leap years when they ruled Egypt in the 200s BCE. Our modern calendar was modeled after this solar calendar.

Mathematics The ancient Egyptians developed a solid understanding of mathematics. Their ability to **construct** the great pyramids proves their command of arithmetic, or addition, subtraction, multiplication, and division. It also shows their skill in geometry, or the measurement of dimensions.

Academic Vocabulary
construct • v., to build or put together

Science, Technology, and Medicine Ancient Egyptians also made advances in science, technology, and medicine. As you have learned, the Egyptians knew that the star Sirius first appeared in the early morning sky at the same time of year as the Nile flood. This was part of their advanced knowledge of astronomy—the study of the stars and other objects in the sky.

The construction of the great pyramids shows the ancient Egyptians' mastery of engineering. No other civilization had been able to plan and build structures so large or so perfectly shaped.

The ancient Egyptians also made many of the earliest discoveries in chemistry. These discoveries led to many new inventions. These included the earliest forms of glass, mortar for setting stones and bricks, and many kinds of cosmetics.

The Great Pyramids were not the only example of Egyptian engineering. To bring the water of the Nile River to their fields, the ancient Egyptians developed complex systems of irrigation, or ways of watering land.

The Egyptians had the most advanced medical knowledge of their time. From their work with mummies, for example, they learned much about human anatomy. **Anatomy** is the study of the structure of the body and its organs. The ancient Egyptians were skilled surgeons. Egyptian doctors also studied diseases and developed effective medicines to treat or cure them.

✓ READING CHECK **Summarize** What were three Egyptian achievements in science and mathematics?

Analyze Images This waterwheel in the Nile delta is similar to the irrigation systems that may have been used by ancient Egyptians. **Infer** How do you think advances in irrigation helped ancient Egyptian society to prosper?

Very Advance for times so long ago.

✓ Lesson Check

Practice Vocabulary

1. How did Egyptians' use of **hieroglyphics** and **papyrus** help advance their society?

2. Why were the Egyptians able to build the **pyramids**?

Critical Thinking and Writing

3. **Infer** If papyrus couldn't last a long time in Egypt's dry environment, how would that have affected our understanding of ancient Egyptian society?

4. **Use Evidence** Why are the pyramids considered one of ancient Egypt's greatest achievements?

5. **Identify Supporting Details** How did the Egyptians' knowledge of astronomy help them farm?

6. **Writing Workshop: Support Thesis with Details** Refer to the thesis statement you wrote in Lesson 1. What details from Lessons 1 and 2 support your point? Write them in an outline in your 📓 Active Journal.

Distinguish Verifiable from Unverifiable Information

INTERACTIVE

Distinguish Between Fact and Opinion

Use the secondary source as you follow these steps to distinguish verifiable information from unverifiable information.

1 Identify statements that could be verified. Historical sources may contain facts, or statements that can be proved to be true. Look at the secondary source from the lesson. How many factual statements—statements that you could prove to be true—does it include?

2 Determine how you might verify these statements. Find ways to verify each statement. For example, you could compare a statement to a reliable online source. Reliable sources often end in .gov, .org, or .edu. Go online and find a reliable source to verify the statement that Egyptians invented papyrus.

3 Identify statements that cannot be verified. It is not possible to verify something like a person's opinion. It is also not possible to prove that tall tales or myths about events from an ancient time are true. Remember, though, that statements can be valuable even though they are not verifiable.

a. Which sentence in the secondary source might be difficult to verify?

b. What makes it difficult to verify?

Secondary Source

Egyptians invented a material very similar to paper. This material, papyrus, was made from the papyrus reed that grew along the Nile. Our word *paper* comes from the word *papyrus*. Scribes wrote in ink on papyrus sheets. Scribes probably found it much easier to write this way than to press letters into wet clay as the Sumerians did. Papyrus sheets were also less heavy to transport than pieces of clay.

Primary Source

▲ Egyptians formed papyrus by pressing together and drying the tissue of papyrus plants.

Egypt and Kush

BOUNCE TO ACTIVATE   ▶ VIDEO

GET READY TO READ

START UP

Examine the photo of Kush pyramids. How do they compare to Egyptian pyramids?

GUIDING QUESTIONS

- How did trade link Egypt and neighboring lands?
- How did its location help civilization in Kush grow?
- What were Kush's achievements?

TAKE NOTES

Literacy Skill: Main Ideas and Details Use the graphic organizer in your 📓 Active Journal to take notes as you read the lesson.

PRACTICE VOCABULARY

Use the vocabulary activity in your 📓 Active Journal to practice the vocabulary words.

Vocabulary	Academic Vocabulary
commerce	rely
ivory	generate
ebony	
interdependence	
Meroitic script	

South of Egypt, farther up the Nile River, was a land that the Egyptians called Kush. Another name for this region is Nubia. Nubia extends from present-day southern Egypt into northern Sudan. Trade and conquest brought Egypt and Kush together.

Why was Trade Important for Egypt and Kush?

Egypt was rich in sunshine and fertile soil, but it lacked the forests, minerals, horses, and other useful natural resources found in Kush and other countries. The people of ancient Egypt had to get these resources through trade, or commerce, with neighboring countries. **Commerce** is the buying and selling of goods and services.

As their country grew in wealth, Egyptians also wanted to buy luxury goods from other lands. Luxury goods are expensive goods that are not needed, but that make life more enjoyable. Egyptian luxury goods included precious stones and perfumes. Trade gave Egypt access to goods it would not otherwise have.

Trade Routes of Egypt and Kush

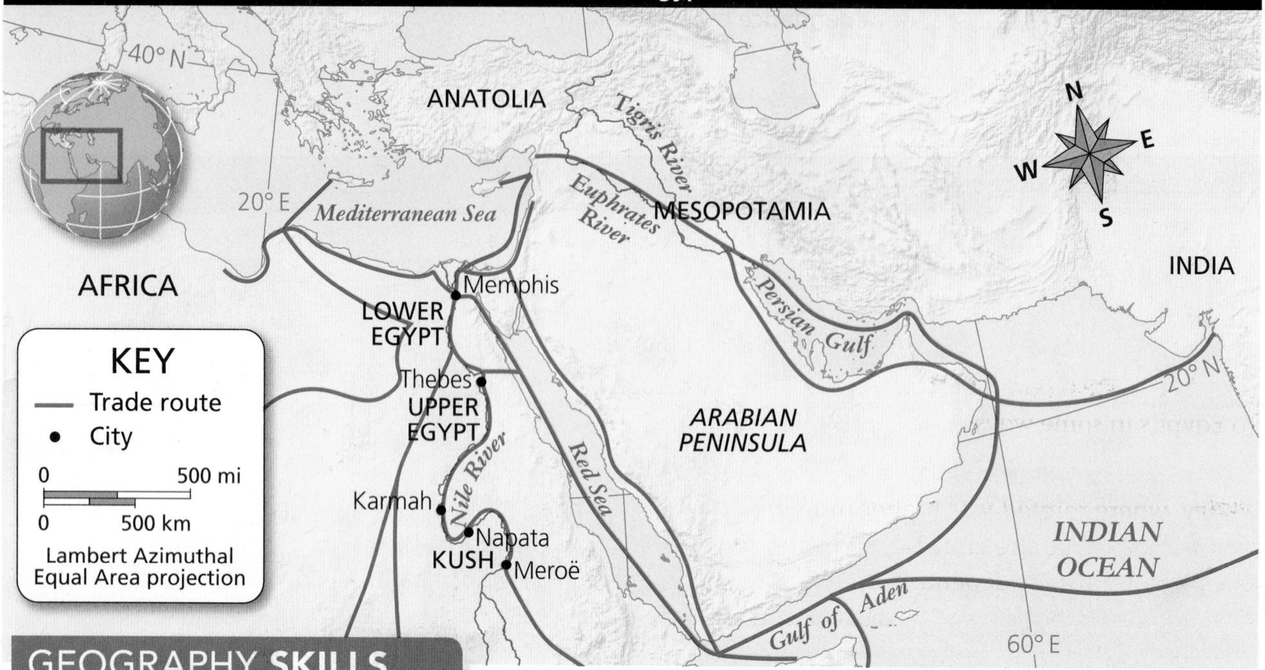
40° N
ANATOLIA
Tigris River
Euphrates River
MESOPOTAMIA
N
E
W
S
INDIA
20° E
Mediterranean Sea
AFRICA
Memphis
LOWER EGYPT
Persian Gulf
KEY
Trade route
City
0 500 mi
0 500 km
Lambert Azimuthal Equal Area projection
Thebes
UPPER EGYPT
Nile River
ARABIAN PENINSULA
20° N
Red Sea
Karmah
Napata
KUSH
Meroë
INDIAN OCEAN
Gulf of Aden
60° E

GEOGRAPHY SKILLS

Egypt traded with its neighbors in Africa and the Middle East.

1. **Movement** Which seas did traders cross to reach Egypt?
2. **Infer** Considering the lands around the Nile Valley, what challenges might land trade routes have posed?

Trade in the Eastern Mediterranean The pharaohs sent merchants and officials to other lands to promote trade. As early as the Old Kingdom, a pharaoh named Snefru promoted trade with lands on the eastern Mediterranean Sea.

The area of modern Lebanon in the eastern Mediterranean had forests that Egypt lacked. The Egyptians crossed the Red Sea because they were eager to buy its cedar wood. In other Mediterranean lands, they bought olive oil and metals such as tin and copper. Rulers in Egypt, Mesopotamia, Syria, and Anatolia sent diplomats from one region to another. The movement of government officials and luxury goods among these royal courts formed one of the world's first trading communities.

NOTES
Trade was extremely important and was well thought out by egyptians

Egypt strengthened its relationships with other lands in other ways. New Kingdom pharaohs made peace by signing treaties with former enemies such as the Hittites. Pharaohs sometimes married princesses from the places they made peace with. As a result, trade with these lands flourished.

Trade in the Nile Valley Snefru also boosted trade between Egypt and Kush. Under later dynasties, trade between Egypt and Kush increased.

INTERACTIVE

Ancient Egypt and Kush trade simulation

The most valuable goods that Egyptians bought in Kush were gold and elephant tusks, which were a source of **ivory**, a hard white material made from these tusks. They also bought incense and a dark, black wood called **ebony**. In return, the Egyptians sold grain, cloth, papyrus, glass, and jewelry.

Present Day, you would never trade gold, for grain.

Egypt **relied** on Kush's gold, and Kush relied on Egypt's grain. Trade created **interdependence**, or dependence by each country or group on the other.

Trade brought the Kushites into closer contact with ancient Egypt. Over time, the Kushites adopted elements of Egyptian culture, including Egyptian religion.

READING CHECK **Use Evidence** Why did Egyptians want to trade with Kush?

How did Kush Develop?

Like Egypt, Kush had an ancient culture. Kush's geography was similar to Egypt's in some ways and different in others.

How Did Geography Affect Kush?
Kush lay in the upper Nile Valley, where rainfall was higher than in Egypt and land for farming and raising cattle stretched beyond the river banks. Like Egypt, however, Kush's farmers depended on the Nile and its annual floods. Their farming methods **generated** a surplus, though a smaller one than Egypt's. This surplus supported cities with artisans and merchants.

However, the Nile's cataracts lay within Kush. While Egyptians used boats, cataracts made it impossible to travel very far by boat in Kush. Instead, people had to travel on foot through the rugged desert.

Another difference from Egypt was that the Kushites had much less land to farm. As a result, the Kushites were sometimes short of food. This made them eager to trade gold, iron, and other products for Egypt's grain.

Kush was also in closer contact than Egypt with the peoples of Africa south of the Sahara. The Kushites traded goods and ideas with these peoples just as they did with the Egyptians.

How Do We Know About Kush?
Scholars have used both historical records and archaeological evidence to learn about Kush. Written records in Egypt document trade with Kush. They also describe a powerful kingdom in Kush modeled on the kingdom of Egypt.

Some of the evidence of trade with Egypt comes from archaeology. Archaeologists have also found that the Kushites and Egyptians both saw kings as gods. This idea was common in Africa and may have come to Egypt through Kush.

READING CHECK **Identify Supporting Details** How did Kush's geography affect its relationship with Egypt?

Notes

How did egypt and kush communicate when they were so far apart?

Analyze Images Kush princes and their servants bring gold to Egypt. **Infer** What do you think princes from Kush hoped to receive in return for the gold they brought to Egypt?

Kush and Egypt

Through trade, the Egyptians discovered that Kush was rich in resources, including gold. The Egyptians realized that the more gold they had, the more wood and other resources they could buy from the eastern Mediterranean.

Egypt Conquers Kush Egypt conquered most of Kush for a time during the Middle Kingdom, and then again during the New Kingdom. The conquered Kushites had to pay tribute to the pharaoh. One year's tribute to the pharaoh Thutmose III included hundreds of pounds of gold, cattle, ivory, and ostrich feathers from Kush. Kush also gave Egypt enslaved people as part of its tribute.

Analyze Images Egyptians used Kush gold to make jewelry. **Infer** Why might Egypt have relied on Kush gold to make jewelry?

Kush & Egypt become one, with the culture peices of culture lasting.

After the rule of Ramses II, Egypt weakened, and the New Kingdom ended. Rival leaders in different cities fought for control of Egypt. Meanwhile, Kush became an independent kingdom ruled by Kushite kings.

Kush Conquers Egypt In the mid-700s BCE, a Kushite king conquered the Egyptian city of Thebes. The next ruler of Kush, a king named Piye (PEE yeh), or Piankhi, expanded the Kushite empire by conquering one Egyptian city after another. Finally, Piye declared himself pharaoh of a united Egypt and Kush.

Primary Source

"O mighty, mighty Ruler, Piankhi, O mighty Ruler, [you come] having gained the dominion of the Northland. . . . [You are] unto eternity, [your] might endure[s], O Ruler, beloved of Thebes."

—Inscription from the victory monument of Piye, translated by James Henry Breasted

Pharaohs from Kush ruled Egypt for almost a hundred years. Kushite rulers promoted the traditional Egyptian ways that they had learned under earlier pharaohs. They built temples to honor Kushite and Egyptian gods. At the same time, the Kushites created painted pottery and other distinctive works of art.

The rulers from Kush might have ruled Egypt longer if they had not tried to expand their power. They went to war with the Assyrians, skillful warriors who had recently conquered the Fertile Crescent. Assyrian troops invaded Egypt around 665 BCE. After losing many battles, the Kushites retreated from Egypt back to Kush.

☑ READING CHECK **Identify Cause and Effect** Why did Egypt conquer Kush?

What Were Kush's Accomplishments?

Kush remained a highly developed civilization for almost a thousand years after it lost Egypt. It developed its own system of writing, economy, and government.

Independent Kush In 591 BCE, the Egyptians destroyed Napata, the capital of Kush. The Kushites moved their capital south to the city of Meroë (MEHR oh ee), which was easier to defend.

Meroë was also located near iron deposits and on a trade route from Central Africa. This region received more rain than did most of Kush. This rain supported the growth of wood that the Kushites could burn to smelt, or melt out, iron from a rock called iron ore.

The Kushites turned Meroë into Africa's first ironworking center. Kush's iron tools and weapons were much stronger than Egypt's soft bronze tools. The Kushites continued to make jewelry and other beautiful objects from their gold.

The Kushites built hundreds of pyramids at Napata and Meroë. These pyramids were built at a steep angle. The pyramids held the tombs of the kings and the queen-mothers of Kush.

The queen-mothers of Kush are also known by their Roman name, candaces. Candaces remained powerful, sometimes more powerful than kings, throughout the history of Kush.

The Kushites created the **Meroitic script**, one of the world's first alphabets. Scholars have learned to read this alphabet but still don't understand the words of the Meroitic language written in it.

Did you know?

The modern country of Sudan includes most of former Kush.

Backwards!!

I thought Sumer had the first

Analyze Images
Civilizations in Africa and the Fertile Crescent developed different writing systems that used either pictures, symbols, or marks to communicate ideas. **Synthesize Visual Information** Describe the differences between the three forms of writing.

Comparing Writing Systems

Hieroglyphs (Egypt)	Meroitic script (Meroë)	Cuneiform (Mesopotamia)
• Pictures of objects (hieroglyphs) to represent both letters and words	• Symbols to represent letters	• Wedge-shaped marks at first to form pictures; later to represent concepts
• Written on papyrus or carved in stone	• Written on papyrus or parchment or carved in stone	• Marks made in clay
• Developed over 5,000 years ago	• Developed over 2,100 years ago	• Developed over 5,000 years ago

Analyze Images The abundant iron in Kush was used to make tools, weapons, and objects like this silver libation bowl found in the tomb of Netaklabah-Amon. **Infer** Why is iron a good material to use for making tools and weapons?

Kush was more advanced than Egypt

Kush's Links to Africa and the World Kush played an important role in ancient Africa. The kingdom may have controlled an area larger than the Egyptian empire. Kush had advanced ironworking technology. The Kushites traded iron goods, cloth, and gold with other African peoples. In return, the Kushites bought ebony and ivory from East and Central Africa. The Kushites also sold slaves from other parts of Africa to the Egyptians.

The Kushites also traded with Greek and Roman Egypt. Kushites sold ebony, ivory, gold, and iron goods and bought grains and cloth in Egypt. The Kushites used irrigation to grow more food for their busy cities, but they still had to trade to meet some of their need for food.

The ancient Greeks and Romans knew the Kushites for their metalworking skills, and they valued Kushite iron tools and weapons. Ports on the Red Sea allowed the Kushites to trade with countries as far away as India.

By the 200s CE, war with the Roman empire, which controlled Egypt, had weakened Kush. Meanwhile, desert peoples raided Kush's cities and disrupted its trade. Finally, in the 300s, Kush was conquered by the kingdom of Axum, centered in the present-day country of Ethiopia to the southeast.

Throughout its history, Kush had linked Africa south of the Sahara with other ancient civilizations. The Kushites created patterns of trade and farming that continued after the conquest by Axum. These traditions have continued in the region to this day.

☑ **READING CHECK** **Understand Effects** What was the impact of Kush moving its capital to Meroë?

☑ Lesson Check

Practice Vocabulary

1. Describe the way **interdependence** had an affect on **commerce** in ancient Egypt.

2. What was different about Kush's **Meroitic script**?

Critical Thinking and Writing

3. **Understand Effects** How did trade cause culture and ideas to spread between Egypt and Kush?

4. **Draw Conclusions** How did trade benefit both Egypt and Kush?

5. **Infer** Why might the Kushites have depended more heavily on trade than the Egyptians?

6. **Writing Workshop: Update Your Thesis** Add details from Lesson 3 to your outline. Examine your outline for details that do not support your thesis. If necessary, update your thesis in your 📓 Active Journal to reflect the details in your outline.

Frame Questions

Use the primary and secondary sources as you follow these steps to frame questions.

INTERACTIVE

Ask Questions

1 Identify your focus. When studying a primary or secondary source about a place or event, begin by focusing on what the passage is about and what you are trying to learn. Use the "5WH" technique—ask "Who? What? Where? When? Why? and How?"—to help you. Based on the sources, what are some questions you might ask about the kingdom of Kush?

2 Identify the information provided. As you review sources, ask, "Which of my questions are answered by these sources?" Which of your questions about Kush are answered by the primary and secondary sources that appear here?

3 Frame remaining questions. Now think about what you still need to learn after you study your sources.

   a. Which questions about Kush remain to be answered?

   b. Which of your 5WH questions are not answered by the excerpt and photo?

4 Plan your research. Use your list of unanswered questions to decide how you will seek answers. Ask yourself, "What kinds of sources would help me answer these questions?"

Secondary Source

Kush had a long history of trade and other contacts with Egypt. But in the mid-700s BCE, a Kushite king conquered the Egyptian city of Thebes. The next king of Kush, Piye, expanded the Kushite empire by conquering one Egyptian city after another. Finally, Piye declared himself pharoah of a united Egypt and Kush.

Kush ruled Egypt for almost one hundred years. Kushite rulers promoted the traditional Egyptian ways that they had learned under earlier Pharoahs. They built temples to honor both Kushite and Egyptian gods. But the rulers of Kush could not maintain their power.

Primary Source

▲ These ruins of Kush pyramids can be found in present-day Sudan.

VISUAL REVIEW

Achievements of Egypt and Kush

Egypt	Kush
• Organized bureaucracy and taxation system • Strong pharaohs • Papyrus and hieroglyphic writing • Massive building projects • Calendar; scientific and medical advances	• Vast trading network • Strong pharaohs • Meroitic script writing system one of world's first alphabets • Massive building projects • Ironworking center and skilled metal workers

Comparing Egypt and Kush

EGYPT
- Engineering and technological advances
- Large surplus of grain
- Lacked forests, minerals, and horses

BOTH
- Complex, ancient culture
- Depended on Nile for crops
- Large trade networks
- Built pyramids
- Influenced one another
- Conquered one another

KUSH
- Linked Africa south of Sahara to other civilizations
- Surplus of gold, ivory, and iron
- Nile's cataracts made travel by boat difficult
- Less land to farm
- Powerful queens

READING REVIEW

Use the Take Notes and Practice Vocabulary activities in your
📕 Active Journal to help you to review the topic.

👆 **INTERACTIVE**

Practice vocabulary using the Topic Mini-Games.

Quest FINDINGS

Write your Monument Inscription

Get help for writing your message in your 📕 Active Journal.

ASSESSMENT

Vocabulary and Key Ideas

1. **Define** What are the **cataracts** of the Nile?

2. **Describe** What did **artisans** in ancient Egypt and Kush do?

3. **Describe** Use the word **bureaucracy** in a sentence describing ancient Egyptian government.

4. **Recall** Why were **papyrus** and **hieroglyphics** important in ancient Egypt?

5. **Identify** Which achievements show Egyptians' mathematical abilities?

6. **Explain** Why is the relationship between Egypt and Nubia described as one of interdependence?

7. **Define** What is Meroitic script?

Critical Thinking and Writing

8. **Understand Central Ideas** Why did the ancient Egyptians want to control the Nile's flood waters?

9. **Cite Evidence** How did Hatshepsut build Egypt's wealth and power?

10. **Classify and Categorize** How were Mesopotamian cuneiform and Egyptian hieroglyphics similar?

11. **Compare and Contrast** How were the civilizations of ancient Egypt and Kush both similar and different?

12. **Revisit the Essential Question** Were Egyptian pharaohs great leaders? Explain.

13. **Writing Workshop: Write an Explanatory Essay** Using the outline you created your 📖 Active Journal, answer the following question in a three-paragraph explanatory essay: How did geography affect the lives of ancient Egyptians and Kushites?

Analyze Primary Sources

14. For whom is the source below likely written?
    A. a king or pharaoh
    B. a young person
    C. a fisherman
    D. a sandalmaker

    "The sandal maker is utterly wretched . . . I mention to you also the fisherman. He is more miserable than one of any other profession. . . .

    See, there is no office free from supervisors, except the scribe's. He is the supervisor! But if you understand writings, then it will be better for you than the professions which I have set before you."

    —from *The Literature of the Ancient Egyptians*, standardized by Adolf Erman

Analyze Maps

Use the map at right to answer the following questions.

15. Which letter represents Lower Egypt? Why is this area known as Lower Egypt?

16. Which letter represents the Red Sea? Which continents does this sea separate?

17. Which letter represents the Mediterranean Sea? Which continent lies north of the Mediterranean Sea?

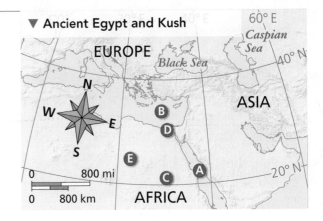

▼ Ancient Egypt and Kush

TOPIC 4

Early Civilizations of India (3100 BCE–540 CE)

GO ONLINE
to access your
digital course

 VIDEO

 AUDIO

 ETEXT

 INTERACTIVE

 WRITING

 GAMES

 WORKSHEET

 ASSESSMENT

India's Early Civilizations

The early civilizations of India built vast empires. Two of the world's major religions developed in the region and spread throughout Asia and the rest of the world.

Explore The Essential Question

What makes a culture endure?

Indian cultural traditions created important thinkers and teachers, who founded schools of thought and religions that still endure today. How did this happen in an era of turmoil and conquest?

Unlock the Essential Question in your Active Journal.

Read

about the empires of ancient India and their complex cultures.

Watch

NBC LEARN

BOUNCE TO ACTIVATE ▶ VIDEO

Indian Classical Dance in the Modern World

Learn about Indian arts that endure today.

▲ Brihadisvara Temple and Chandikesvara shrine, Tanjore, Tamil Nadu, India

Early Civilizations of India (3100 BCE–540 CE)

Learn more about ancient India by making your own map and timeline in your 📖 Active Journal.

INTERACTIVE

Topic Map

Where was ancient India?

These ancient civilizations and empires were located on the Indian subcontinent, which today includes India, Pakistan, Bangladesh, Nepal, Bhutan, Afghanistan, and Sri Lanka.

INTERACTIVE

Topic Timeline

What happened and when?

You may think that most innovation has happened in the last hundred years. You'd be wrong. Thousands of years ago, civilizations were growing, changing, and making new discoveries. Explore the timeline to see what was happening in ancient India and around the world.

1600 BCE
Vedic period emerges.

1900 BCE
Indus Valley civilization begins to break down.

2600 BCE
Indus Valley civilization reaches its peak.

TOPIC EVENTS

3000 BCE	2500 BCE	2000 BCE	1500 BCE

WORLD EVENTS

2630 BCE
The first pyramid is built in Egypt.

2000 BCE
The Middle Bronze Age begins.

1600 BCE
Mycenaean culture develops in Greece.

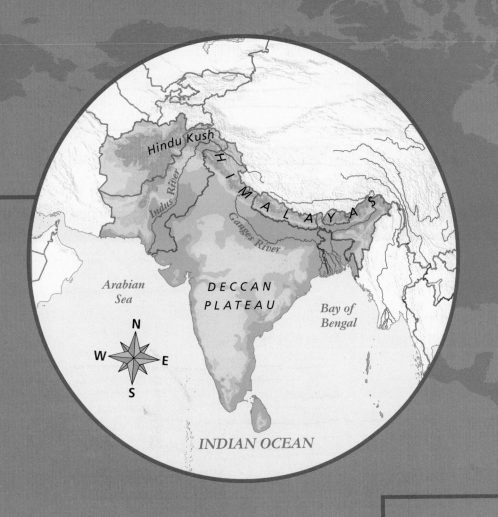

Hindu Kush

H I M A L A Y A S

Indus River

Ganges River

Arabian Sea

DECCAN PLATEAU

Bay of Bengal

N W E S

INDIAN OCEAN

Who will you meet?

Siddhartha Gautama, the Buddha

Chandragupta Maurya, who united India

Asoka, a powerful emperor who gave up war and chose peace.

500s BCE
Buddha gains enlightenment.

500 BCE
Classical Hinduism develops.

321 BCE
Maurya empire founded.

268 BCE
Asoka becomes emperor.

320 CE
Gupta empire is founded.

540 CE
Gupta empire no longer exists.

500
BCE

1
CE

500
CE

551 BCE
Confucius is born in China.

438 BCE
Parthenon is completed.

27 CE
Augustus becomes first Roman emperor.

Quest

A Trip Through India

Quest KICK OFF

You have the amazing opportunity to lead a tour group to India. You get to plan the entire trip!

Where should you visit?

What cultural experiences should not be missed on a visit to India? Explore the essential question "What makes a culture endure?" in this Quest.

1 Ask Questions

India is a large country with a complex history. There are many reasons to visit. Write a list of questions you think someone visiting India for the first time may have about India. Write the questions in your 📓 Active Journal.

2 Investigate

As you read this topic, look for **Quest** CONNECTIONS that provide information on different sites in India. Capture notes in your 📓 Active Journal.

3 Conduct Research

Next, do more research about places to visit and things to do in India. Take notes in your 📓 Active Journal and describe their historic and cultural significance.

Quest FINDINGS

4 Create a Travel Brochure

People look at brochures to plan travel. At the end of the topic, you'll create a brochure of historical and cultural things to do and see in India. Your brochure should include a travel schedule with information about each of the sites you'll visit. Get help for creating your travel brochure in your 📓 Active Journal.

▲ On a trip to India you might see Indians celebrating their culture during one of many festivals.

LESSON 1

The Indus Valley Civilization

BOUNCE TO ACTIVATE — VIDEO

GET READY TO READ

START UP

Examine the photo of the Indus River. What can you predict about the Indus Valley civilization based on what you know about the development of other ancient civilizations in river valleys?

GUIDING QUESTIONS

- How did the environment influence the Indus Valley civilization?
- What were the achievements of the Indus Valley civilization?
- Why do the Indus Valley civilization politics, religion, and history remain a mystery?

TAKE NOTES

Literacy Skills: Identify Main Idea and Details
Use the graphic organizer in your 📓 Active Journal to take notes as you read the lesson.

PRACTICE VOCABULARY

Use the vocabulary activity in your 📓 Active Journal to practice the vocabulary words.

Vocabulary		Academic Vocabulary
subcontinent	granary	achievement
river system	citadel	evidence
monsoon		

[handwritten: India is very Big]

The first civilizations arose near rivers. One such civilization was in South Asia. Its people farmed along the Indus River. Farmers grew plenty of food, and populations grew. In time, some of the people settled in towns and cities and formed governments.

What Is the Indian Subcontinent?

Geographers divide the continent of Asia into regions. One of those regions is South Asia. It looks like a huge triangle jutting out into the Indian Ocean. Today, it includes the countries of India, Pakistan, Bangladesh, Sri Lanka, Maldives, Nepal, and Bhutan. India is by far the biggest country in the region.

For much of its history, all of South Asia was known simply as India. It is still called the Indian subcontinent. A **subcontinent** is a large landmass that is set apart from the rest of the continent. The Indian subcontinent stretches almost 2,000 miles from north to south. In some places, it is nearly as wide from east to west. The subcontinent is separated from the rest of Asia by the towering Himalayas and Hindu Kush, two mountain ranges to the north.

[handwritten: important mountains]

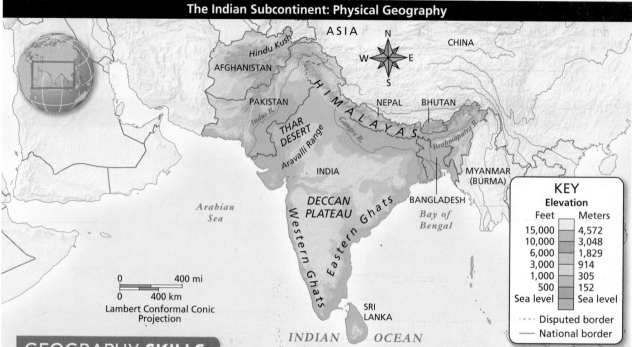

The Indian Subcontinent: Physical Geography

KEY

Elevation

Feet		Meters
15,000		4,572
10,000		3,048
6,000		1,829
3,000		914
1,000		305
500		152
Sea level		Sea level

---- Disputed border
—— National border

0   400 mi
0   400 km
Lambert Conformal Conic Projection

GEOGRAPHY SKILLS

The Indian subcontinent is separated from the rest of Asia by seas and mountains.

1. **Region** What are the names of the physical features of South Asia that make the region a subcontinent?

2. **Infer** In what parts of the subcontinent did the people of ancient India most likely settle?

🖑 INTERACTIVE

Technology of the Indus Valley

Flooding is a huge part of every civilization

River Systems The Indus River flows across the northwestern part of the subcontinent. The Indus forms part of a **river system**, or a main river and all of the other rivers and streams that drain into it. Another river, which is dry, but flowed parallel to the Indus, was the Saraswati. Recently, archaeologists have found almost 600 towns and villages buried in sand along course of this now dry river.

India's first civilization grew around the Indus Valley. This civilization developed in an area that is dry most of the year. When the river flooded, it left behind very rich soil. River water let farmers harvest plentiful crops. These crops fed the cities of the civilization.

To the east, the Ganges River flows more than 1,500 miles across the northern part of the subcontinent. Its floods created a huge, fertile plain. After the Indus civilization died out, the Ganges Plain became the center of Indian civilization.

Climate Much of the Indian subcontinent has a tropical climate. Seasonal winds, known as **monsoons**, help shape life in this region. In the winter, dry monsoon winds blow from the land to the sea. Little rain falls. In the summer, wet winds from the ocean blow onto the land. They bring rain, which provides water for crops and a welcome break from the intense heat.

For much of its history, Indian agriculture depended on the summer monsoon. If the rains came on time, all was well. If the rains came late or not at all, crops died and people could starve.

✅ READING CHECK **Identify Main Ideas** How did rivers and monsoons support the development of India's first civilizations?

Indus Valley Civilization

Farmers began growing crops in hills near the Indus river system around 7000 BCE. With a steady food supply, the population grew. After 3000 BCE, cities began to develop on the broad plains of the Indus Valley. By about 2500 BCE, these cities were the centers of the advanced Indus Valley civilization. However, by around 1700 BCE, the civilization had largely disappeared.

Archaeologists have discovered most of what we know about the Indus Valley civilization. In the 1920s, they discovered the ruins of two great cities: Harappa and Mohenjo-Daro. Since then, archaeologists have found more than a thousand other cities, towns, and villages from this civilization spread across the region.

Technology Indus Valley cities were well planned and organized. The people of the Indus Valley built thick walls around their cities. They also built huge raised mounds of earth and brick in their cities. During times of flooding, these mounds remained above water.

Many houses in these cities had a bathroom and toilet. Wastewater from houses flowed into brick-lined sewage channels. These were the world's first citywide sewer systems. A trash chute in many houses led to a bin in the street.

Many of the **achievements** of the Indus Valley people showed an advanced knowledge of mathematics. Their cities were built with wide, straight streets in a grid pattern. They had an advanced system of weights and measurements using multiples of ten, like the modern metric system.

Farming The dry region of northwest India could not always depend on the monsoon rains. Therefore, farmers built irrigation channels and ditches. These brought river water to the wheat and barley fields. Some

monsoons were so important to life. Very smart advances

Academic Vocabulary

achievement • *n.*, accomplishment that requires effort or skill

Irrigation is part of so many civilizations

▼ Mohenjo-Daro, the largest of the Indus Valley civilization's cities, grew because farmers produced a surplus of food.

relied on water, as well as animals. Advances helped trade, and over all living & well being

scholars think that these farmers stored their surplus crops in a **granary**, or special building used to hold grain. They may have been the first farmers to grow cotton for making cloth.

Farmers also raised cattle, sheep, goats, and chickens for food. They used oxen, or cattle, to pull carts. Animals seem to have been important to the Indus people. They carved wooden animals and painted pictures of animals on pottery.

Trade The Indus Valley environment was rich in resources for trade. Indus Valley jewelers made beautiful jewelry from precious stones. Traders sold this jewelry as far away as Mesopotamia, where they could travel by sea. Traders sold cotton cloth woven in the Indus Valley. They also sold teak, a valuable wood from a tree that grows in India. Indus Valley cities prospered from trade.

Indus Valley traders used stone seals with writing to identify their goods. They stamped their seals on soft clay squares attached to their goods. Accurate weights and measures helped promote trade.

Sumerian writers mentioned trade with people who probably came from the Indus Valley. Trade spread ideas between these two civilizations.

☑ READING CHECK **Identify Main Ideas** How did the environment contribute to the development of the Indus Valley civilization?

GEOGRAPHY **SKILLS**

The Indus Valley civilization was connected to Egypt and Mesopotamia by a network of overland and sea routes.

1. **Movement** How did Mesopotamian traders get to the Indus Valley by water?

2. **Use Visual Evidence** Why were there no trade routes from the Indus Valley that headed to the east?

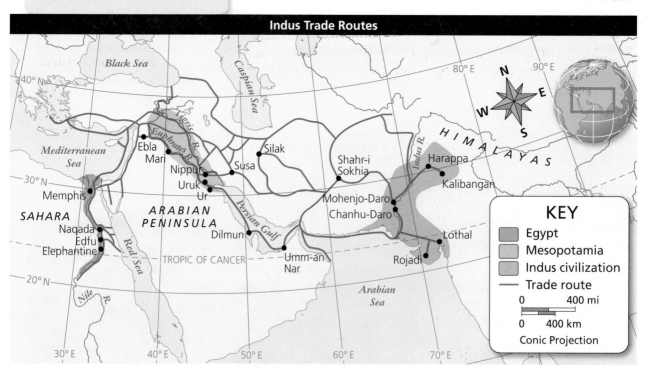

Indus Trade Routes

KEY
- Egypt
- Mesopotamia
- Indus civilization
- Trade route

0 — 400 mi
0 — 400 km
Conic Projection

What Mysteries Surround the Indus Valley Civilization?

Artifacts and ruins of many buildings have been found in the Indus Valley. They provide a lot of information. But scholars still have many questions about this ancient civilization. They want to know more about its rulers, religion, and writing. They wonder about the reasons why it disappeared and where its people went.

Government and Religion

Clearly, the people of the Indus Valley were well organized. Their cities show a surprising level of planning. They all used a common system of weights and measures. These facts suggest that the Indus Valley people had a strong central government. Yet no royal statues or tombs have been found. This makes it seem unlikely that kings ruled the Indus Valley. Based on the available evidence, it just isn't possible to know for sure what kind of government the Indus Valley had.

Most cities had a huge **citadel**, or fortified area. The walled citadel was built on a raised platform of earth and brick that could have protected it from floodwaters or attackers. Scholars are not sure, but the citadel may have been a center of government, a place to lead religious ceremonies, or both.

Religion is another part of the Indus Valley civilization about which little is known. Scholars have found no direct evidence of temples and no clear sign of activity led by religious leaders.

However, some Indus Valley statues and small carvings have features that seem to show practices of what we now know as Hinduism. Some of the artifacts share characteristics of statues of Hindu Gods, though the connection is still debated. Also, some Indus Valley carvings look like people meditating or offering a formal greeting, 'Namaste', important practices in Hinduism today.

Writing Scholars have not yet discovered how to read the symbols found on the stone seals and pottery of the Indus Valley. There are too few examples of each symbol to be sure of its meaning. Most experts think that these marks are a form of writing. However, they do not know if these markings are names, records of sales, or something else.

Analyze Images Traders from the Indus Valley used seals like these. **Use Visual Information** What do you think the animal symbols meant?

A lot about the Indus was unknown and not linked.

So Many Possibilities

Why Did the Indus Civilization Disappear? The greatest mystery is what caused this civilization to disappear. Sometime before 1700 BCE, the Indus Valley people began to abandon their cities. The civilization declined rapidly after that. No one knows why.

There are many possible explanations. Some **evidence** suggests that standing water in drains may have bred mosquitos that spread disease and weakened Indus Valley populations. Indus Valley people may also have stripped forests of trees, leaving them without wood for building or fuel. A lack of forest cover could have caused severe floods that damaged Indus Valley cities. Their cattle may have overgrazed the land, leaving bare soil. Smaller herds could have led to starvation. Salt could also have built up in the soil, making it difficult to grow crops. Another possibility is that a major earthquake wiped out the population.

▲ One explanation for the disappearance of the Indus civilization is a long-term drought. Droughts still challenge the Indian subcontinent.

Academic Vocabulary

evidence • *n.,* information used to prove something

Some historians think that climate change may have brought an end to the civilization. Years of drought could have dried up the rivers and made it impossible to feed city dwellers. The most widespread theory says that many people finally moved away towards the Ganges, where the rains were more regular.

☑ READING CHECK **Identify Cause and Effect** Different possibilities exist for why the Indus civilization disappeared. Which of these were related to environmental changes?

Most of the civilizations are a mystery - Wow!

☑ Lesson Check

Practice Vocabulary

1. Explain why India is called a **subcontinent**.

2. How was a **granary** used?

Critical Thinking and Writing

3. **Identify Main Ideas** How did ancient farmers use the water of the Indus river system to help grow crops?

4. **Classify and Categorize** What were some innovations of the Indus Valley civilization?

5. **Compare and Contrast** What are some similarities and differences between the Indus Valley civilization and other ancient river valley civilizations?

6. **Writing Workshop: Generate Questions to Focus Research** Write three to four questions in your 📖 Active Journal about technological innovations in ancient India. These questions will help you focus your research on the topic of technological innovations in ancient India for a research paper you will write at the end of the topic.

LESSON 2
India's Vedic Age

BOUNCE TO ACTIVATE ▶ VIDEO

GET READY TO READ

START UP
Examine the carving of the God Indra atop a mythical beast. What details do you notice?

GUIDING QUESTIONS
- During the Vedic period, how did connections between the Indian subcontinent and other regions increase?
- What do the sacred hymns known as the Vedas teach us about religion and customs in ancient India?
- How did the varnas and jatis develop into the caste system?

TAKE NOTES
Literacy Skills: Summarize
Use the graphic organizer in your 📖 Active Journal to take notes as you read the lesson.

PRACTICE VOCABULARY
Use the vocabulary activity in your 📖 Active Journal to practice the vocabulary words.

Vocabulary		Academic Vocabulary
Veda	varna	migrate
caste	jati	status

Civilizations linked much more than the firts Indus civilization.

Settlement

After 2000 BCE, another group of people lived in the Indus Saraswati region. They called themselves Aryans Scholars often refer to them as Indo-Aryans. These peoples may have brought with them beliefs and practices that mixed with local groups. This idea is based on the fact they spoke Sanskrit, an Indo-Aryan language. Sanskrit is also the language in which the ancient Indo-Aryans composed religious hymns and poetry. These hymns are known as Vedas and are the reason this period of history is called the Vedic Age.

Who Were the Indo-Aryans and How Did They Live?

Historians have taken different views on the origins of the Indo-Aryans. In the past, many historians accepted the Aryan invasion theory, but many historians today reject this idea. This theory held that the Indo-Aryans were nomadic warriors who crossed the mountains into India. They used horse-drawn chariots and iron weapons to defeat the local people.

Others have argued that the Aryans were India's original inhabitants. They say that if the Indo-Aryans came from a region outside of India, the Vedas would refer to it. The Vedas, however, do not make any mention of such a place.

More recently, scholars suggest a third theory, which suggests Indo-Aryans were originally from what is now Afghanistan and Central Asia. Over many centuries, they **migrated** into India with their livestock, mixed with local people and adopted local beliefs. Local people adopted the Indo-Aryan language. Over time, people across a large part of the Indian subcontinent came to see themselves as Indo-Aryans.

Academic Vocabulary

migrate • v., to move from one region to another in order to live there

What are the Vedas? The Indo-Aryans composed the Vedas. There are four Vedas: the Rig-Veda, Sama-Veda, Yajur-Veda, and Atharva-Veda. Each **Veda** is a collection of hundreds, and even thousands, of sacred hymns.

Ancient Indians, usually priests, memorized and sang or chanted these verses during ceremonies. The Vedas called upon people to make offerings to their gods. Typical offerings might be barley, butter, or milk.

GEOGRAPHY SKILLS

Recent theories suggest that the Indo-Aryans migrated into South Asia through passes in the mountains of the Hindu Kush.

1. **Movement** Why would nomads raising cattle on dry grasslands want to migrate into South Asia?

2. **Draw Conclusions** Where in India do you think the Indo-Aryans settled?

For a thousand years, Indians passed the Vedas down by word of mouth. They sang or chanted them in Sanskrit, which is a distant relative of English. Today, Sanskrit remains a language of sacred literature. Sanskrit is the ancestor of many modern Indian languages, including Hindi and Urdu. Eventually, Indians began to collect the Vedas and put them into writing.

The oldest of the Vedas is the Rig-Veda. It includes about 10,000 hymns. One passage, "The truth is one; the wise call it by many names," is considered a key part of Hindu philosophy. Most of

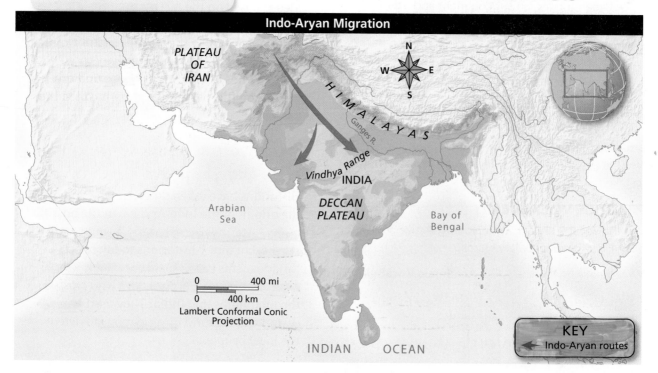

Indo-Aryan Migration

PLATEAU OF IRAN

HIMALAYAS

Ganges R.

Vindhya Range

INDIA

DECCAN PLATEAU

Arabian Sea

Bay of Bengal

0   400 mi
0   400 km
Lambert Conformal Conic Projection

INDIAN   OCEAN

KEY
← Indo-Aryan routes

the hymns also praise various Gods and Goddesses representing natural forces such as the sky, sun, and fire. These deities are viewed as different forms of a single, divine absolute. Another Veda is dedicated to an earth Goddess. She is praised for her bounty. The Vedas are considered to have influenced and and contributed to the development of Hinduism, and are still used in some Hindu rituals today.

How Did the Indo-Aryans Live? The Rig-Veda and the other sacred texts provide a record not only of the Vedic religion, but also of the people themselves. Most of what we know about Indo-Aryan life on the Indian subcontinent during this period comes from the Vedas.

Though scholars do not know the origins of Indo-Aryans, the Vedas show that they lived as herders. They raised cattle, horses, goats, and sheep. Cattle held special importance for them since the herds provided both food and clothing. Early on, ancient Indians measured their wealth by the size of their cattle herds.

The Vedas also mention that the Aryans practiced agriculture, and grew several different crops including barley, wheat, and lentils. The Rig-Veda mentions water channels dug from the banks of the Saraswati and other rivers to irrigate these crops. Milk and its products were a very important part of their diet. As the Indo-Aryans began to focus more on growing crops, however, they gave up dairy farming as their main source of food.

The Vedas show that the Indo-Aryans found joy in their day-to-day lives. They loved music and dancing. They held chariot races and enjoyed gambling. They also questioned the meaning of life and existence through their texts. The following passage from a hymn in the Rig-Veda describes the connection between the human body and a divine power:

Primary Source

The human body is the temple of God. One who kindles the light of awareness within gets true light. The sacred flame of your inner shrine is constantly bright. The experience of unity is the fulfillment of human endeavors. The mysteries of life are revealed.

—Rig-Veda

▲ Page of Sanskrit from the Rig-Veda, or "Knowledge of the Hymns of Praise"

Notes
-Vedas are like oracles bones, telling the future about the past.

-games and events made for joyus pastimes.

INTERACTIVE
Vedic Era Gods

Analyze Images The early Indo-Aryans tended flocks of livestock, much like these modern Indian goat herders. **Draw Conclusions** Why did the Indo-Aryans stop living as nomads and begin settling down in villages?

Notes

The Growth of Vedic Civilization Over many hundreds of years, Vedic civilization slowly spread eastward across the humid and fertile Ganges Plain. The Indo-Aryans carved farms and villages from the forests. Some villages grew into towns and cities.

At first, communities were divided into clans, or groups of people who believe that they share a common ancestor. Each clan had a chief.

Later, clans joined together to form republics. Leaders made decisions in an assembly, but over time powerful leaders gained control and made themselves kings. By 500 BCE, more than a dozen kingdoms and republics covered northern, western, and central India.

As Vedic civilization grew, societies in the southern part of India also developed their own culture. People in this part spoke languages like Tamil, which had no similarity to Sanskrit. Over time, Sanskrit-speaking people eventually mingled with these groups, creating new customs based on a mixture of the different groups.

✓ READING CHECK **Summarize** What is the importance of Sanskrit?

The Caste System

In ancient Indian society, a system of social classes based on birth developed. These evolved over many centuries, and eventually became known as the caste system. They became closely linked to Indian notions of a proper society. While the social groupings might not have begun this way, over time, they became associated with Indian notions of purity. Today, **caste** is a fixed social class into which a person is born.

Over many centuries in India and other parts of the Indian subcontinent, caste became a prominent part of people's lives. One's caste influenced specific rules of behavior, such as where people lived, how they earned a living, whom they could eat with, and whom they could marry.

How Was Caste Determined? Most scholars agree that the caste system did not emerge until much later in Indian history, but its roots are in ancient India, when two social groupings emerged. The Vedas identify four **varnas**, or groupings based on one's skill. The varnas were Brahmins, who were known as priests and teachers; Ksathriyas, or the rulers and warriors; Vaishyas, who were landowners, bankers, and merchants; and Sudras, who did farm work and other manual work.

Another grouping was by occupation. The term for an occupation-based caste is **jati**, meaning "birth group." Some scholars think that these castes began as extended families who may have had a family business or occupation. Today, many people refer to jati when they are referring to caste. All across South Asia, thousands of jatis developed, each with its own rules and restrictions.

By 500 CE or so, another group outside of the jatis emerged. They were known as Untouchables, and later Dalits, who did work considered impure and had a low social **status**. These inequalities did not derive from Hindu teachings, but over time, many Indians of all faiths came to identify with one caste or another.

How Did the Caste System Develop? Scholars are not sure how the caste system developed. They aren't sure whether the status-based varnas or the occupation-based jatis developed first. Most say the fixed nature of caste might be a more recent development in Indian history.

At first, caste may have been mainly based on a person's occupation or family membership. Children might have been able to move into a different caste than their parents. In fact, the evidence suggests that families could sometimes move from one varna to another. Hindu sages like Valmiki and Vyasa were not born Brahmins, while some who were born into Vaisya or Sudra families became warriors.

Over hundreds of years, castes seem to have become more rigid. By the time the Portuguese arrived in India in the 15th century, many people across the Indian subcontinent identified with a caste. Each caste was

Academic Vocabulary

status • *adj.,* position in society

Notes

The Caste System

Caste	Occupation Groups
Brahmins	Priests
Kshatriyas	Rulers and warriors
Vaishyas	Landowners, bankers, and merchants
Sudras	Farmers, laborers, and servants

Analyze Charts Ancient Indian society was grouped by varnas, or groups based on one's skills. These groups are thought to have later developed into the caste system.

given a particular status. People were born into a caste and could not leave it. Though Hindu leaders preached against the fixed nature of the caste system, many Hindus in the Indian subcontinent eventually accepted caste as a part of daily life.

In time, the caste system became the basis for India's social structure. By 1900, almost everyone in the Indian subcontinent identified with a caste, though some groups, such as Muslims, Christians, and Sikhs, did not have as many caste rules as Hindus did. The system brought both costs and benefits. For instance, the system limited people's individual freedom. The patterns of their lives were fixed at birth.

However, some believe that the caste system helped India develop. They feel that it brought stability to Indian society. Indian goods became famous because caste members perfected their skills. The system also allowed different groups to follow their own beliefs.

Analyze Images Meira Kumar, a Dalit, was elected India's first woman parliamentary speaker. **Draw Conclusions** What was the significance of her election?

In India today, the law forbids caste discrimination. Many Hindus in India and the United States do not identify themselves with a caste. People's jobs no longer depend on their caste alone. Brahmins or Kshatriyas may work with their hands. Dalits may work as professionals.

✓ READING CHECK **Summarize** What was the caste system?

✓ Lesson Check

Practice Vocabulary

1. Explain why the **Vedas** are important.

2. Explain the meaning of the term *caste* in Indian history.

Critical Thinking and Writing

3. **Identify Evidence** What evidence would offer proof for the different theories about the origins of the Indo-Aryans?

4. **Compare and Contrast** What are the similarities and differences between jati and varna?

5. **Support Ideas with Evidence** Why can Sanskrit be described as an important Indo-Aryan tradition?

6. **Writing Workshop: Generate Questions to Focus Research** Write two questions in your 📓 Active Journal to focus your research for the research paper you will write about technological innovations in ancient India at the end of the topic.

Notes

Detect Historical Points of View

Compare
Viewpoints

Use the secondary source and follow these steps to detect historical points of view.

1 Identify the topic or issue. What is the author writing about?

   a. What is the overall topic that the author is addressing?

   b. What is his point of view about the subject?

   c. What might be an opposing point of view to this one?

2 Determine the author's position on the topic or issue. What is the author's position? Often, an author will state his or her overall point of view in a topic sentence. What is the author's position on the subject? Are there topic sentences or summary statements that state his point of view? What are they?

3 Identify important background information about the passage. Identifying the author's background and the time and place in which the author lived can help you analyze a historical point of view.

   a. What information is given about the author's area of research? Is he an expert on the topic?

   b. When was the passage written? Does that affect the argument? How?

4 Analyze the possible impact of historical background on the author's beliefs. People's beliefs and opinions may be influenced by the context in which the author is writing. The context is what is happening in the world around the author. Ask, "How might the context have affected this author?"

Secondary Source

Several species of *Equus*, including the true horse, existed in the Indus-Sarasvati civilization, probably in small numbers. Some of them may have entered India over a much longer time span than is usually granted, in the course of the Indus-Sarasvati civilization's interactions with neighbouring areas, but certainly not through any Aryan invasion or migration. There was no epoch exhibiting a sudden, first-time introduction of the animal.

—Michel Danino, quoted in *Archaeology Online* in "The Horse and the Aryan Debate"

LESSON 3

Origins and Beliefs of Hinduism

BOUNCE TO ACTIVATE ▶ VIDEO

GET READY TO READ

START UP

Examine the photo of the Hindu temple. What does it suggest to you about Hinduism?

GUIDING QUESTIONS

- How did Hinduism grow out of the Vedas?
- How did Hinduism support people and society in ancient India?
- How did Hinduism spread and what has been its lasting impact?

TAKE NOTES

Literacy Skills: Sequence

Use the graphic organizer in your 🗐 Active Journal to take notes as you read the lesson.

PRACTICE VOCABULARY

Use the vocabulary activity in your 🗐 Active Journal to practice the vocabulary words.

Vocabulary		Academic Vocabulary
guru	dharma	issue
Brahman	ahimsa	devote
reincarnation	moksha	
karma		

Hinduism is one of the oldest religions in the world and the third largest, with about 1 billion followers. It began in India during the Vedic age, growing slowly and changing into a more popular Hinduism. It is the majority religion of India, Nepal, and Mauritius, and has existed in countries like Indonesia, Vietnam, Cambodia, and Thailand for many centuries.

What Are the Roots of Hinduism?

For thousands of years, Hinduism has been the main religion of India and widely practiced in South and Southeast Asia. Hinduism is based on the word *Hindu*, which is what early Persian traders called the people they encountered in India.

Vedic Age Beliefs and Practices As you have learned, the Vedas are the subcontinent's oldest known religious texts. They were memorized and passed on by word of mouth. They were later written down, though the oral tradition remained important.

The Vedas contain hymns to many Gods and Goddesses. They also describe religious rituals, including offerings of food to specific Gods such as Agni, the God of fire, or Vayu, the God of the wind. These Gods later became part of popular Hinduism, taking lesser roles as other deities such as Vishnu, Shiva, and Devi became more widely worshipped.

What Was Early Hinduism Like?   During the Vedic Age, early Hinduism was based on the principle of Brahman, the all-powerful principle that Hindus believe exists in all beings. It was made up of elaborate rituals to worship the various deities that were seen as manifestations of this divine principle. Much of the ritual authority was given to priests, or Brahmins, though recall that varnas might not have been fixed at that time. Scholars say that non-Brahmin sages also had influence during this period. However, because early Hinduism relied on ritual, it was limited to priests.

✓ READING CHECK **Understand Effects** How is Hinduism related to the Vedas?

How Did Classical Hinduism Develop?

Beginning about or before 500 BCE, Hindu beliefs began to change. Some thinkers emphasized and built on top of the concept of Brahman, a single spiritual power that was manifested in the Gods of the Vedas and resided in all things. Other people began asking questions such as: Why are we born? How should we live? What happens to us when we die? Hinduism evolved from Indians' efforts to answer these difficult questions.

Analyze Images A leader teaches holy law in this painting from the 1800s. **Recognize Multiple Causes** What role did gurus have in developing Hinduism?

Analyze Images An illustration from the *Bhagavad-Gita* shows Krishna and Radha, who often symbolize the love of Brahman for humans. **Identify Main Ideas** Why is the *Bhagavad-Gita* important to Hindus?

New Teachings To find those answers, thinkers and teachers known as **gurus** left their homes to live in the forest, to think, and to talk about religious ideas. In a sense, these gurus and their students were founders of modern Hinduism. The ideas of these teachers were passed down orally at first. Later, they were written down.

Their ideas survive in writings known as the Upanishads (OO PAN uh shadz). The Upanishads made connections between heavenly forces and people's lives. Alongside the Vedas, the Upanishads became Hindu holy scriptures. The oldest Upanishads date to around 800 or 700 BCE. Indian thinkers continued to produce them for several hundred years.

The Upanishads helped connect people to Hinduism. These sacred writings dealt with questions of life and death or right and wrong that concern all people. These teachings are a key piece of Hinduism as it is practiced today.

Epic Poems Two epic poems also emerged during this period, and are revered by Hindus and non-Hindus all over the world. An epic poem is a long story of heroes told in verse. Both of these poems took shape during the period when classical Hinduism emerged. These epic poems are the *Ramayana* (rah MAH yuh nuh) and the *Mahabharata* (muh hah BAH rah tuh). They helped explain religious ideals and how people should live their lives.

The *Ramayana* is the story of a king named Rama and his beautiful wife, Sita. Sita is kidnapped by the demon king Ravana. His niece, the demon Trijata, protects Sita. Aided by his brother Lakshman and the monkey God Hanuman, Rama eventually rescues Sita. This epic emphasizes the importance of dharma, or righteous action.

The *Mahabharata* may be the world's longest poem. It is 200,000 lines long. It tells the story of two families at war for control of a kingdom. Like the *Ramayana*, it deals with moral **issues**. These include the conflict between loyalty to family and duty.

The most widely read section of the *Mahabharata* is the *Bhagavad-Gita* (BUG uh vud GEE tuh). This means "Song of the Lord." Some scholars

Quick Activity

Explore Hindu poetry in your 📔 Active Journal.

Academic Vocabulary

issue • *n.,* problem or subject to be discussed or decided

consider the *Bhagavad-Gita* to be Hinduism's most important religious, text, and its impact goes beyond Hinduism. It has influenced world leaders like Mahatma Gandhi and Nelson Mandela, and has been translated into hundreds of languages across the world.

This text deals with key Hindu beliefs. These beliefs have to do with the nature of the soul and its relationship to God, and different ways to live a good life. These ways are called yoga.

✔ READING CHECK **Summarize** Explain the significance of the *Mahabharata* and *Ramayana*.

INTERACTIVE

Hindu Temple 3D model

What Are Hindus' Beliefs About God?

Hinduism is like a great river. Over thousands of years, many beliefs and traditions have flowed into it. As a result, Hindus may have different practices, but they share certain basic beliefs.

The Upanishads contain two beliefs that lie at the heart of Hinduism. The first is that there is one supreme cosmic consciousness, spiritual force, or God known as **Brahman**. The Upanishads teach that all of the Gods that Indians worship are forms of Brahman. Brahman, they say, is the source of all things.

Many Hindus worship individual Gods or Goddesses as forms of Brahman. Some Hindus worship Brahman as Vishnu. Others worship Brahman as Shiva. Still others worship Brahman as the Goddesses Shakti or Sarasvati, the Goddess of learning. These Gods and Goddesses may have other named forms. For example, the God Krishna is a form of Vishnu.

The second core Hindu belief is that every person is born with a soul, which is also a form of Brahman. According to the Upanishads:

Analyze Images This statue of Shiva overlooks the Arabian Sea in western India. **Use Visual Evidence** How does this statue show the importance of Shiva to Hindus?

Primary Source

This soul of mine within the heart is smaller than a grain of rice.... This soul of mine within the heart is greater than the earth,... greater than the sky.... This soul of mine within the heart, this is Brahman.

—*The Thirteen Principal Upanishads*

✔ READING CHECK **Summarize** What do Hindus believe about Brahman and the soul?

What Do Hindus Believe About Life?

Hindu scriptures such as the Upanishads and the *Bhagavad-Gita* also teach important Hindu beliefs about life.

Reincarnation and Karma Hinduism teaches that when people die, most will undergo reincarnation. **Reincarnation** is the rebirth of a soul in a new body.

In the *Bhagavad-Gita,* the god Krishna explains the process of reincarnation to Arjuna, the hero of the *Mahabharata:*

Primary Source

As a man discards worn-out clothes to put on new and different ones, so the embodied self (soul) discards its worn-out bodies to take on other new ones.

—*Bhagavad-Gita*

Analyze Images A dharma wheel symbolizes the Hindu belief in a cycle of birth, life, and death and the concept of doing right. **Identify Cause and Effect** How would dharma have a positive influence on Indian society?

The law of karma determines how a person is reborn. **Karma** is the effect of a person's actions in this and in previous lives. Hindus believe that bad karma—evil deeds—will bring more suffering in a next life, while good karma can lead to a clearer path to liberation.

What Are Hinduism's Four Goals? Hindus believe that people have four basic goals in life. People should pursue all four, but not everyone achieves all of these goals in one lifetime.

The first goal is doing what is right. For Hindus, **dharma** is a person's duty or what is right. Dharma includes the duties that come with one's age or position in life. Dharma also includes the rule of **ahimsa**, or avoiding doing harm to any living thing, truthfulness, and moderation and self-control. Following dharma brings good karma. Violating dharma brings bad karma.

The second goal is striving for well-being, or earning a livelihood with dignity. This goal can involve making a good living and raising a family. It can involve starting or running an honest business. However, Hindus say, material well-being by itself does not bring true happiness.

The third goal is pleasure. This includes eating good food or taking a hot bath. However, seeking nothing but pleasure, can leave a person feeling empty.

The final goal is **moksha**, or liberation from reincarnation. When this happens, many Hindus believe a person's soul becomes one with Brahman, while others believe the soul lives close to Brahman forever. For Hindus, the purpose of life is to achieve moksha. A soul that achieves moksha lives forever in a state of joy.

What Are the Paths to Moksha? Hinduism lays out four main paths to moksha. These paths are all forms of yoga, defined as a way of seeking moksha. These paths are the way of knowledge, the way of works, the way of devotion, and the way of meditation.

For a person following the way of knowledge, moksha comes with a true understanding of one's soul and its oneness with Brahman—or God. The Upanishads say that such understanding does not come easily.

▲ A Hindu woman worships at a temple shrine.

The way of works means carrying out the religious rituals and duties that will improve one's karma. To follow the way of works, Hindus must carry out duties within their family. They also offer prayers and food to the Gods. Those who do good deeds without expecting any reward are especially praised.

The way of devotion is also known as the path of love. People on this path **devote** themselves to loving God. For most Hindus, following the path of love means worshiping one of the Hindu Gods or Goddesses. These Gods and Goddesses have human forms and personalities, as well as those of animals and nature.

Academic Vocabulary
devote • *v.*, to set aside for a purpose

The way of devotion takes many forms. People on this path may present offerings to their God at a temple. They may travel to sites sacred to their God. In all of these ways, Hindus try to move closer to God in their hearts.

The path of meditation teaches that the mind can be disciplined with the help of spiritual practices like yoga meditation. Such a mind turns away from desires and towards Brahman.

☑ READING CHECK **Draw Inferences** Explain Hinduism's four goals in your own words.

What Is the Impact of Hinduism?

More than a billion people live in India today. About 80 percent of them follow Hinduism. The rest follow other religions. Hindus also live and worship in many places outside of India. The spread of Hinduism has had a lasting impact on India and on the world.

The Spread of Hinduism Long ago, the people of India lived under many separate rulers, spoke different languages, and worshipped different Gods. Yet most Indians practiced Hinduism, supported by Hinduism's shared values of devotion and following dharma.

Several things helped the growth of Hinduism in India. One was Hinduism's flexibility. Because Hinduism views all Gods as forms of a single, supreme God, it can accept the worship of new Gods. People did not have to give up their old religion when they became Hindus. Instead, Hinduism adopted their traditions and Gods or viewed their Gods as forms of existing Hindu Gods.

Hinduism also did not require regular attendance at religious services. Instead, Hindus could pray or make offerings to the gods at a local temple during special celebrations or whenever it was convenient. They could also pray or make offerings at shrines in their homes. A shrine is a place of worship that is often dedicated to a sacred object or being. So no matter where Indians went, they could easily practice their religion.

While Hinduism is the only major world religion in which God is thought of as having a female as well as a male form, women were sometimes not treated as equals in the Indian subcontinent. This often went against core Hindu teachings about equality of genders. Women had rights to their own personal wealth, but in most cases, had fewer property rights than men. This was similar to other ancient societies. Women could also participate in religious ceremonies, and there were some women who became Hindu sages.

GEOGRAPHY **SKILLS**

Hinduism began in India and spread into other parts of Asia.

1. **Movement** In which direction did Hinduism expand between 1 CE and 1100 CE?

2. **Synthesize Visual Information** Based on the map, do you think Hinduism expanded during that time mainly by land or mainly by sea? Explain.

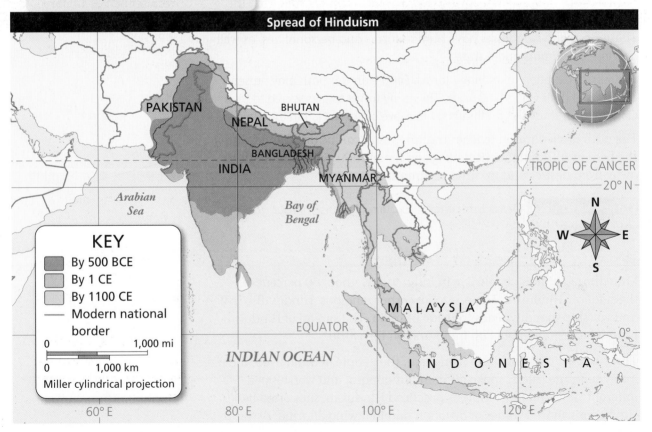

Spread of Hinduism

KEY
- By 500 BCE
- By 1 CE
- By 1100 CE
- Modern national border

0 — 1,000 mi
0 — 1,000 km
Miller cylindrical projection

Over time, Hinduism spread to other lands. For more than a thousand years after 1 CE, Indian traders and priests carried Hinduism to Southeast Asia. Hinduism left a lasting influence on Thailand and Indonesia, where the *Ramayana* remains popular. Today, most people on the Indonesian island of Bali are Hindus.

Indians also took Hinduism with them when they moved across the seas. Many migrated to Great Britain, the United States, and Canada. More than two million Hindus now live in the United States.

Hindu Traditions Today Hindus live in some 150 countries, but most Hindus still live in India. Hindu traditions remain an important part of Indian life. Hindu festivals draw huge crowds. One festival takes place on the Ganges River. It is one of India's holiest sites. Every year, millions of Indians line the banks of the Ganges and bathe in its waters. They believe that those waters can wash away bad karma and cure disease.

Hinduism's openness to all religions has shaped India's political system. It guarantees religious freedom.

Hinduism has also influenced India's art and literature. Beautiful carvings of Gods and Goddesses decorate Hindu temples. The temples are places of worship, but they also serve as centers of art, music, and dance.

The *Mahabharata* and the *Ramayana* were India's first great literature. They have inspired other literature for hundreds of years. In India, comic books and movies still retell the stories of these epic poems today.

▲ Parade in Venice, California, celebrating the Hindu Festival of Chariots

READING CHECK Draw Conclusions Why do you think Hinduism is still practiced throughout the world?

☑ Lesson Check

Practice Vocabulary

1. Describe how **gurus** helped Hinduism to grow.

2. Use the terms *Brahman*, *karma*, and *moksha* to describe Hindu beliefs.

Critical Thinking and Writing

3. **Identify Implied Main Ideas** How did the Upanishads and the Hindu epic poems contribute to the growth of Hinduism?

4. **Analyze Cause and Effect** Why might a Hindu offer food or flowers to a God such as Shiva?

5. **Draw Conclusions** Why is the *Bhagavad-Gita* considered by some scholars to be the most important text of Hinduism?

6. **Writing Workshop: Find and Use Credible Sources** Find credible sources for your research paper on technological innovations in ancient India. Begin reading these sources and taking notes in your 📓 Active Journal.

The Ramayana

The *Ramayana*, an epic poem, tells the story of Rama's quest. The *Ramayana* is often used to instruct people on how to live a morally perfect life. Kaikeyi is Rama's stepmother and Bharata is Kaikeyi's son. Kaikeyi has just told Rama that Bharata will become king instead of him.

◀ Kaikeyi tells Rama he will not be king.

Reading and Vocabulary Support

① *Inviolable* means sacred or holy.

② What is Rama sad about in this part of the poem?

③ Kings and queens are crowned during a *coronation* ceremony.

④ Why do you think the king is crying and unable to speak to Rama?

⑤ *Maternal* means related through a mother.

Rama the annihilator of enemies heard those harsh and deadly words but was unruffled. He spoke these words to Kaikeyi: "Let it be, as you said it. I shall fulfill the king's promise, go to the forest from here to reside there, wearing braided hair and covered with a hide. But I want to know why the king, the inviolable ① and the subduer of enemies, is not greeting me today as before. Oh, queen! you need not be indignant. I am telling before you that I shall go to the forest, wearing rags and braided hair. Become delighted as well. How can I not do faithfully an action dear to my father, as commanded by him as well-wisher, venerable man, as person with right conduct and as king. My heart is burning indeed with one sorrowful ② feeling that king himself has not directly informed me about Bharata's coronation ③. Without being asked, I myself would have gladly offered even Sita with kingdom, even my life, loved ones and wealth. Being directed by [the] king, who is my father himself, how much more should I tell that I can give everything to Bharata, duly obeying father's promise to fulfill your beloved desire. That is why, you console him. Why indeed the king is thus slowly shedding tears, with eyes gazed upon the floor? ④ Let messengers go now itself on fleet horses to bring Bharata from maternal ⑤ uncle's house as per orders of the king. I am glad that he would certainly go and urged him to make haste at once. Immediately, I shall go to live in forest of Dandaka for fourteen years, without reflecting on whether my father's words are right or wrong."

Analyzing Primary Sources

Cite evidence from the poem to support your answers.

1. **Analyze Information** What is Rama's dharma in the passage according to Rama?

2. **Cite Evidence** What can you conclude about Kaikeyi's role in Bharata being made king instead of Rama? Cite evidence from the passage.

3. **Analyze Style and Rhetoric** What are Rama's first words in the passage? How do they set the tone for his response to the news about Bharata?

LESSON 4

Origins and Beliefs of Buddhism

BOUNCE TO ACTIVATE ▶ VIDEO

GET READY TO READ

START UP

Look at the statue of Buddha. What do you think the Buddha meant to his followers in ancient India?

GUIDING QUESTIONS

- Why did the Buddha give up a life of luxury, and how did he find enlightenment?
- Why do Buddhists follow the eight-step path?
- How did Buddhism support those who followed the teaching of the Buddha?
- How did Buddhism spread?

TAKE NOTES

Literacy Skills: Compare and Contrast

Use the graphic organizer in your 📓 Active Journal to take notes as you read the lesson.

PRACTICE VOCABULARY

Use the vocabulary activity in your 📓 Active Journal to practice the vocabulary words.

Vocabulary

meditate
enlightenment
nirvana
monastery

Theravada Buddhism
Mahayana Buddhism

Academic Vocabulary

consequences
widespread

At the end of the Vedic period, around 600 BCE, many Indians left their homes and families to become wandering teachers of new philosophies of life. Two well-known teachers were Siddhartha Gautama (sid DAHR tuh GOW tuh muh), and Mahavira (muh hahVEE ruh). Siddhartha became known as the Buddha (BOO duh). Buddhism is a religion based on the teachings of the Buddha. We call his followers Buddhists. Mahavira was the founder of Jainism. Both faiths arose in ancient India and, like Hinduism, spread elsewhere.

The Life of the Buddha

Scholars know few hard facts about the Buddha. The story of his life comes mainly from Buddhist texts. Those texts include the teachings of the Buddha, which his followers memorized and passed down by word of mouth. But they also include many legends.

A Pampered Youth Siddhartha Gautama was probably born during the 500s BCE in what is now Nepal. A Hindu prince, he was raised in wealth and luxury. According to legend, Siddhartha's mother had a dream.

▲ Young Prince Siddhartha shows off his archery skills, thus pleasing his father.

She dreamed that an elephant came to her from heaven. Based on the dream, a prophet predicted that the child would grow up to be a holy man. This disturbed Siddhartha's father. He wanted his son to be a ruler.

To keep Siddhartha from becoming a holy man, his father shielded him from everything unpleasant or disturbing. The prince never saw anyone who was poor, sad, or sick. When he rode out of the palace in his chariot, guards traveled ahead of him to clear beggars and sick people from the streets.

Buddhist tradition says that one day when Siddhartha was about 29, he rode out of the palace without any guards. During that ride, Siddhartha saw an old, bent, toothless man leaning on a stick. On a second ride, Siddhartha saw a man shrunken by disease. On a third, the prince saw a dead man. Siddhartha was shocked. He realized that he, too, faced old age, sickness, and death.

A few days later, Siddhartha rode out of the palace again. He came upon a fourth sight, a wandering holy man. The holy man was homeless and owned nothing. Still, he seemed content. Siddhartha decided to search for the same sense of peace that the holy man showed.

A Search for Truth That night, Siddhartha cut his hair and traded his rich clothing for the simple robe of a religious seeker. He set out to find the truth about life, suffering, and death.

Siddhartha began his search by studying with Hindu gurus. They taught him meditation techniques and the different teachings of the Upanishads which he was to later build upon with his own insights. Then he joined a band of religious ascetics. Ascetics deny themselves physical comforts to seek a spiritual goal.

For five years, Siddhartha wore scratchy clothes and fasted, or went without food, for long periods. He lost weight and became very weak. After six years of self-denial, he realized that going to such extremes was not the path to truth.

Finding Enlightenment Siddhartha renewed his search. One day Siddhartha sat down under a fig tree to meditate. To **meditate** means to calm or clear the mind, often by focusing on a single object. The fig tree would come to be known as the Bodhi Tree, or Tree of Knowledge.

According to legend, Siddhartha meditated under the tree for 49 days and nights. During this time, he came to understand the cycle of birth, death, and rebirth. Finally, Siddhartha reached an awareness that freed him from his ties to the world. He entered a new life free of suffering. He had, at last, achieved **enlightenment**—a state of perfect wisdom. Siddhartha had become the Buddha, which means "the Enlightened One."

According to Buddhist texts, the Buddha had freed himself from the "wheel of existence." He could have enjoyed freedom from the world's suffering. Instead, he went back into the world to teach others what he had learned.

For the next 45 years, the Buddha traveled across India sharing his message. He attracted many followers and students. He trained some of them to be teachers and religious leaders.

The Buddha died at about the age of 80. According to legend, his dying words to his followers were these:

Primary Source

This is my last advice to you. All . . . things in the world are changeable. They are not lasting. Work hard to gain your own salvation.

—Rev. Siridhamma, *Life of the Buddha*

✔ READING CHECK **Identify Cause and Effect** How did Siddhartha achieve enlightenment?

Analyze Images The Buddha meditates beneath the Bodhi Tree. **Use Evidence** What details in the painting point to the Buddha having reached a state of peace and enlightenment?

Analyze Images A Buddhist nun walks out of a temple in Kathmandu, Nepal. **Infer** What does this image suggest about Buddhism today?

What Are Buddhist Beliefs?

Buddhists believe that when the Buddha gained enlightenment, he had a flash of insight. He understood why people suffer. He also saw how people could escape the cycle of death and rebirth.

The Buddha accepted the Hindu idea of karma—the idea that a person's actions have **consequences** in this or in future lives. However, the Buddha did not accept the Hindu idea of a permanent soul. He believed that a "self" might be reborn in a new body, but he thought that the "self" was an illusion. He believed that it would disappear and cease to exist when a person achieved enlightenment.

The Buddha moved even further away from other Hindu beliefs. For example, the Buddha did not believe in the existence of any god. He also did not accept specific varna roles. The Buddha believed that good and bad actions were more important than social roles. Like Hinduism, however, his teachings supported a moral and ethical society.

The Middle Way The Buddha had lived in luxury, as a wealthy prince. He had also lived in poverty, as an ascetic. One was "a life given to pleasures." The other was a life of suffering. Neither way of life had led him to enlightenment. To gain enlightenment, the Buddha advised people to follow a Middle Way. Buddhism supports individuals in their quest to find enlightenment through the Middle Way and other teachings. Following the Middle Way meant accepting four truths.

The Four Noble Truths These Four Noble Truths were among the insights the Buddha had when he achieved enlightenment under the Bodhi Tree.

The First Noble Truth is that all of life involves suffering. Birth, sickness, old age, and death bring suffering.

The Second Noble Truth is that wanting or desiring things for oneself causes suffering. Not all desires are bad. It is not wrong to desire the happiness of others. However, selfish desires lead to suffering.

The Third Noble Truth is that people can end their suffering. The way to do this is to give up all selfish desires.

The Fourth Noble Truth is that there is a way to overcome selfish desires. The way to overcome those desires is to follow the Eightfold Path.

The Eightfold Path was another of the Buddha's insights. By following this path, he believed, people could end their desires and suffering. The Buddha taught that this path was open to anyone. People of any caste could follow it.

The Eightfold Path The Eightfold Path takes its name from its eight steps. These steps lead to Three Qualities.

The first two steps are Right Belief and Right Purpose. They involve preparing one's mind for spiritual growth. These steps produce the first of the Three Qualities, wisdom.

The next three steps are Right Speech, Right Conduct, and Right Livelihood (or profession). These steps call for taking charge of one's behavior. These steps produce the quality of morality, or right action.

The last three steps train the mind to gain enlightenment. The third quality produced is the same as the eighth step—meditation.

Reaching Nirvana The goal of a person who follows the Eightfold Path is to reach nirvana. **Nirvana** is a state of blissful peace without desire or suffering. Those who reach nirvana are at peace with themselves. They are also freed from having to go through reincarnation. A person can reach nirvana without dying but will not be reborn after dying.

Some Buddhists believe that enlightenment always brings nirvana. Others believe that nirvana only sometimes follows enlightenment.

☑ READING CHECK **Compare and Contrast** How were the Buddha's beliefs different from Hindu beliefs?

Analyze Charts The Eightfold Path is the way to end suffering, according to Buddha. **Identify Supporting Details** How might the steps on this path help Buddhists overcome selfish desires?

THE EIGHTFOLD PATH		
The First Two Steps involve preparing one's mind for a new way of life.	**1. Right Belief**	The first step is belief and understanding of the Four Noble Truths.
	2. Right Purpose	The second step is to make spiritual growth the purpose of one's life.
The Next Three Steps involve taking charge of one's behavior.	**3. Right Speech**	The third task is to become aware of what one says. This means avoiding lies in statements that hurt others.
	4. Right Conduct	The next task is to understand one's behavior and to work to improve it. Right conduct means not killing, stealing, lying, or hurting others.
	5. Right Livelihood	This involves choosing a livelihood, or profession, that supports one's spiritual growth. A person should earn a living in a way that does not harm other living things.
The Last Three Steps help train the mind to gain enlightenment.	**6. Right Effort**	The sixth step involves making an effort to avoid bad thoughts and to hold only good thoughts in one's mind.
	7. Right Mindfulness	Mindful means becoming aware of what one thinks and feels. A person with right mindfulness controls his or her thoughts and emotions.
	8. Right Meditation	The last step is to practice meditation that can lead to enlightenment. Buddhists say that those who complete this step will experience a new reality.

How Did Buddhism Spread?

For hundreds of years, the Buddha's followers memorized his teachings. After many years, they wrote those teachings down. Those written teachings make up the sacred scriptures of Buddhism today. Different branches of Buddhism accept different collections of these scriptures. However, all Buddhists accept the Four Noble Truths and the Eightfold Path.

Monasteries and Missionaries As the Buddha preached, he gained many followers. At first they followed him from place to place. After a while, the Buddha found places for them to stay during the rainy season. These became Buddhist **monasteries**, or religious communities. The most devoted Buddhists lived in monasteries. There they had time to study and meditate.

The Buddha urged his followers to carry his teachings to all corners of Earth. A person who spreads religious ideas is a missionary. Buddhist missionaries carried Buddhism across India and to Sri Lanka, then throughout Asia. Some traveled north to Central Asia. Then missionaries followed trade routes east into China. From China, Buddhism spread to Korea and Japan. Buddhism arrived later in Tibet.

What Are the Two Branches of Buddhism? As Buddhism spread, its followers split into two major branches, or sects. The two branches share basic beliefs, but they see the Buddha's life and teachings differently.

One branch is **Theravada Buddhism** (thehr uh VAH duh). This sect focuses on the wisdom of the Buddha. Members think that the Buddha's greatest achievement was his enlightenment and entry into nirvana.

Mahayana Buddhism (mah huh YAH nuh) is the other branch. It focuses on the Buddha's compassion. For its members, the Buddha's greatest achievement was returning from nirvana to share his wisdom out of compassion for others.

INTERACTIVE

Origins and Beliefs of Buddhism

Analyze Images The Paro Taktsang Buddhist monastery in Bhutan is also called "Tiger's Nest." It was built alongside a rocky cliff 3,000 feet above the Paro valley. **Identify Main Ideas** What is the purpose of a monastery?

The Legacy of Buddhism Today, there are about 400 million Buddhists throughout the world. Most live in Asia. Theravada Buddhism is the main religion of Sri Lanka, Myanmar (or Burma), Thailand, and Cambodia. Mahayana Buddhism is **widespread** in Bhutan, Vietnam, China and Taiwan, Mongolia, the Koreas, and Japan.

More than two million Buddhists live in the United States. Few Buddhists remain in India, but the Buddha's teachings made a lasting impact on Hinduism.

Buddhism has inspired beautiful art and architecture. It has been a source of wisdom even for some non-Buddhists.

READING CHECK Identify Main Ideas How did Buddhism spread in India and Sri Lanka, and later across Asia?

▲ Women from the Jain community attend a prayer meeting for world peace.

What Is Jainism?

Mahavira, another successful wandering teacher around the same time as Siddhartha, was a teacher of Jainism. Jainism and Buddhism developed at the same time. A main characteristic of Jainism was the idea of ahimsa, which is nonviolence to all life. As such, Jainism encourages vegetarianism. The path to enlightenment in Jainism comes through nonviolence. Jainism continues to play a role in India today. Mohandas Gandhi, a well-known peace activist in India in the first half of the twentieth century, practiced nonviolent protest. He protested against British rule in India.

Academic Vocabulary

widespread • *adj.*, common, spread across a large area

READING CHECK Identify Supporting Details Why did people who followed Jainism practice *ahimsa*?

☑ Lesson Check

Practice Vocabulary

1. Explain the meaning of the term **nirvana** for Buddhism.

2. Describe the difference between **Theravada Buddhism** and **Mahayana Buddhism.**

Critical Thinking and Writing

3. **Infer** How does Buddhism support individuals who want to achieve enlightenment?

4. **Synthesize** What are Buddhism's moral teachings, or teachings about right and wrong?

5. **Analyze Information** What role did missionaries play in Buddhism in India, Sri Lanka, and Central Asia?

6. **Writing Workshop: Support Ideas with Evidence** Use your sources to complete gathering credible evidence to support your ideas about technological innovation in ancient India by taking notes in your 📓 Active Journal.

🔍 Primary Sources

The Life or Legend of Gaudama

The Life or Legend of Gaudama is a Burmese text that tells the story of the Buddha's life and relates his teachings. The early section discusses his birth and his growing desire to gain spiritual wisdom. In the passage prior to this excerpt, the young Siddartha sits under a tree to meditate.

◀ A sculpture of the enlightened Buddha

Reading and Vocabulary Support

① *Contemplation* means to think deeply about.

② A *vortex* is a whirlpool, a swirling body of water.

③ What does this phrase suggest?

④ *Benevolent* means kind or caring.

⑤ Why does this thought delight the Buddha?

"Buddha continued to remain . . . in a cross-legged position, with a mind absorbed into contemplation ① during seven days. Mental exertion and labor were at an end. Truth, in its [bright] beauty, encompassed his mind and shed over it the purest rays. Placed in that [shining] center, [Buddha] saw all beings entangled in the web of passions, . . . whirling in the vortex ② of endless miseries, . . . sunk into the dark abyss of ignorance, the wretched victims of an illusory, unsubstantial, and unreal world. He said then to himself,: 'In all the worlds, there is no one but me who know how to break through the web of passions, . . . to save them from the whirlpool of miseries, . . . to [drive away] the mist of ignorance by the light of truth, to teach all intelligent beings, the unreality and non-existence of this world, and thereby to lead them to the true state of [enlightenment].' ③ Having thus [expressed] the feelings of compassion that pressed on his benevolent ④ heart, [Buddha] . . . delighted in contemplating the great number of beings who would avail themselves of his preachings, and labor to free themselves from the slavery of passions." ⑤

Analyzing Primary Sources

Cite evidence from the text to support your answers.

1. **Analyze Information** How does the Buddha come to view the world as a result of his meditation?

2. **Cite Evidence** What constitutes enlightenment, according to the Buddha?

3. **Determine Author's Point of View** What attitude does the author of this text show toward the Buddha?

Quest CONNECTIONS

Based on the text, what does the Buddha decide to do? How do you think that affected ancient India and the culture of present-day India? Record your findings in your 📖 Active Journal.

LESSON 5

The Maurya Empire Begins

BOUNCE TO ACTIVATE   **VIDEO**

GET READY TO READ

START UP
Examine the statue of Chandragupta Maurya. Write two things you think may have been true about Chandragupta and his rule based on how he is portrayed.

GUIDING QUESTIONS
- How did Chandragupta use military strategy to unite much of India for the first time?
- How did Chandragupta develop a bureaucracy, a tax system, and a system of spies to help rule his empire?

TAKE NOTES
Literacy Skills: Analyze Cause and Effect
Use the graphic organizer in your 📙 Active Journal to take notes as you read the lesson.

PRACTICE VOCABULARY
Use the vocabulary activity in your 📙 Active Journal to practice the vocabulary words.

Vocabulary	Academic Vocabulary
strategy	mission
province	welfare
bureaucracy	
subject	

By the end of the Vedic age, many kingdoms and chiefdoms covered India. The strongest of the kingdoms was Magadha (MUH guh duh). Around 321 BCE, a rebel army overthrew the king of Magadha. The leader of the rebels was a young man named Chandragupta Maurya (chun druh GOOP tuh MOWR yuh).

How Did Chandragupta Unite India?

Most of what we know about Chandragupta's life comes from ancient writings and legends. Some legends say that he was born into Magadha's royal family but was left with poor farmers when he was young. Historians may never know the real story.

Seizing Power As a young man, Chandragupta depended on the advice of an older, educated Brahmin named Kautilya (kow TIL yuh). Legends say that Kautilya searched for a leader to drive Greek invaders out of northwestern India. In one story, Kautilya saw Chandragupta playing as a boy and knew that he could be trained as a leader.

Wow Scary!

Kautilya helped Chandragupta raise an army and develop a strategy to gain power. A **strategy** is a long-term plan for achieving a goal. Their strategy was to take control of the northwest from the Greeks and then attack Magadha from the northwest.

Success on the Battlefield Kautilya trained his pupil to become a brilliant military leader. Chandragupta armed his men with powerful weapons, including the Indian bow. This bow was as tall as a man. Its arrows could pierce a strong shield.

A story says that Chandragupta saw a mother scold her child for starting to eat from the center of the plate. She said the center is too hot. So Chandragupta weakened Magadha by attacking its borders, then moved in to take its capital city.

After Chandragupta conquered Magadha, he attacked other kingdoms. By 305 BCE, he ruled much of the Indian subcontinent. After Chandragupta forced the Greeks out of northwestern India, his Maurya empire stretched from the Bay of Bengal to present-day Afghanistan. For the first time, one state controlled all of northern India.

✓ READING CHECK Draw Conclusions How did Chandragupta start the Maurya empire and make it grow?

GEOGRAPHY SKILLS

At its height, the Maurya empire controlled almost the entire Indian subcontinent.

1. **Place** On which river was Pataliputra located?

2. **Infer** In which kingdom —Magadha, Kalinga, or Bactria—did Chandragupta fight the Greeks?

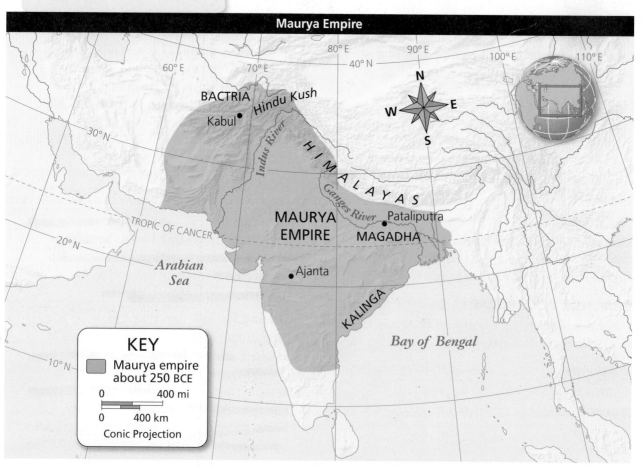

Maurya Empire

KEY

Maurya empire about 250 BCE

0   400 mi
0   400 km
Conic Projection

How Did Chandragupta Rule an Empire?

[handwritten: Similar lifes & challenges, different empires & civilizations]

As emperor, Chandragupta faced the same problem as other empire builders: How could he rule over a large area with many different needs and traditions?

Building a Government Chandragupta solved this problem by dividing his empire into four regions. He divided each region into smaller provinces A **province** is a region with its own government.

The emperor also set up a **bureaucracy**, or a system of offices that carries out government rules and regulations. Appointed officials in each region, province, and village carried out the emperor's orders. In this way, he was able to control every village in his empire.

Chandragupta also set up a tax system. Tax workers collected 25 percent of the crops raised by farmers. They also collected a sales tax on goods. Chandragupta used the taxes to pay government workers. He used them to support a large army.

This system gave the Maurya empire an efficient government. However, its strength depended on the power and authority of the ruler. The government was only as strong as the emperor.

Connections to Other Regions The Maurya empire also maintained strong connections to other regions. Chandragupta was friendly with a Greek kingdom to the west, though relations were not good at first. After conquering northwestern India, Chandragupta sent troops west of the Indus River. They clashed with the forces of Seleucus, a Greek general who ruled Persia. Rather than engaging in an all-out war, the two leaders agreed to a peace treaty in which Seleucus gave up territory west of the Indus in exchange for 500 elephants.

This was the beginning of relationships with many neighbors to the empire. These governments often sent envoys to each other. An envoy is a messenger or representative. An envoy is usually sent on **missions** concerning relations between governments.

Subjects and Spies Chandragupta ruled a vast empire, but he lived in constant fear of his enemies. He had servants taste his food for poison. He slept in a different bed every night.

To ease his fears, Chandragupta had specially trained female warriors guard his palace. He set up a huge spy network to watch his **subjects**, or people under his rule. He even hired spies to watch other spies. The emperor set aside time every day to receive reports from his spies.

Analyze Images
Chandragupta issued gold coins with his image on them. **Infer** How could placing his image on coins help Chandragupta rule his empire?

 INTERACTIVE

Village Life in India

Academic Vocabulary
mission • *n.*, journey with a purpose

[handwritten: wealthy/powerful/fearful]

[handwritten: rare for this time]

So rude + unfair

Chandragupta's subjects had no right to privacy or freedom of speech.

Some members of the empire had absolutely no freedom of any kind. Slavery existed in Maurya India. Most slaves were prisoners of war or people who could not pay what they owed. Laws protected slaves from harsh treatment in India, unlike in other countries.

Kautilya's Advice Many of Chandragupta's ideas about ruling came from his advisor Kautilya. Kautilya was the author of a book called the *Arthashastra*. The book gives advice on how to be a good ruler. "The primary duty of a king," the *Arthashastra* says, "is the protection of his subjects." He went on to give more detail about what he saw as a ruler's responsibility:

Primary Source

In the happiness of his subjects lies the king's happiness. In the welfare of his subjects, his welfare. A king's good is not that which pleases him, but that which pleases his subjects.

—Kautilya, *Arthashastra*

▲ Portrait of Chandragupta

A good king also has self-control, consults with elders, stays up-to-date about threats to his kingdom, and enhances his knowledge in all areas of learning.

Academic Vocabulary

welfare • *n.,* well-being, comfort, prosperity

READING CHECK **Identify Cause and Effect** What did Mauryan rulers do to maintain connections with other nearby governments?

☑ Lesson Check

Practice Vocabulary

1. Use the terms **bureaucracy** and **subject** to describe Maurya government.

2. How did **strategy** help Chandragupta Maurya's rise to power?

Critical Thinking and Writing

3. **Identify Main Ideas** How did Chandragupta Maurya conquer Magadha?

4. **Use Evidence** How did a bureaucracy help the Maurya emperors rule?

5. **Draw Conclusions** What was the relationship between the Maurya government and the people it governed?

6. **Writing Workshop: Cite Sources** Cite sources for your research paper in your 📓 Active Journal. You will write your research paper at the end of the topic.

Assess Credibility of a Source

Use the primary source and follow these steps to assess credibility of a source.

INTERACTIVE

Analyze Primary and Secondary Sources

1 **Identify who created the source and when it was created.** Read the passage. Determine who wrote it. The information may or may not state when it was created. Use information about the source to determine when it was created. What can you conclude from this source about when it was created?

2 **Identify the topic.** What is the creator of the source writing about? Sometimes the subject will be named directly and other times it will be implied. Does this source tell who or what it is about specifically? Who or what is the topic of this source?

3 **Identify the facts, opinions, and possible inaccuracies or biases.** What facts are present? Are any important ones left out? What opinions are stated? You can look for words that show a strongly favorable or unfavorable view of the topic. Does the author take a balanced approach to the subject? Is more than one point of view given about the subject? Read the passage again.

a. State the facts included in this source.

b. Is there any reason to doubt Megasthenes' description of these facts?

c. Does Megasthenes seem to have an opinion about the subject of the passage? If so, what is his opinion?

d. What evidence does Megasthenes give in the passage that supports this opinion?

4 **Assess the credibility of the source.** Compare the source to other sources on the same subject. Evaluate the facts included, the fairness of their presentation, and the opinions or points of view. A source that seems heavily biased or incomplete may not be a reliable source. A primary source is generally more reliable than a secondary source because the person actually witnessed the event.

a. Is Megasthenes a primary or a secondary source?

b. Does Megasthenes have a strong opinion? If so, what is it?

c. Do you think this is a credible source? Why or why not?

Primary Source

"Outside the gates of the palace stand the bodyguards and the rest of the soldiers. . . . Nor does the king sleep during the day, and at night he is forced at various hours to change his bed because of those plotting against him. . . . When he leaves to hunt, he is thickly surrounded by a circle of women, and on the outside by spear-carrying bodyguards. The road is fenced off with ropes, and to anyone who passes within the ropes as far as the women death is the penalty."

—Megasthenes, a Greek ambassador to Chandragupta's court at Pataliputra

Asoka's Rule

BOUNCE TO ACTIVATE ▶ VIDEO

GET READY TO READ

START UP
Examine the painting of Asoka as a Buddhist. What does it tell you about the kind of ruler Asoka was?

GUIDING QUESTIONS
- Why did the emperor Asoka turn from war to peace?
- How did Asoka promote the growth of Buddhism and encourage morality among his subjects?
- How did Buddhism support Asoka's hopes for his empire?

TAKE NOTES

Literacy Skills: Sequence
Use the graphic organizer in your ▤ Active Journal to take notes as you read the lesson.

PRACTICE VOCABULARY
Use the vocabulary activity in your ▤ Active Journal to practice the vocabulary words.

Vocabulary
tolerance
stupa

Academic Vocabulary
eventually

Power in the Maurya empire passed from grandfather, to father, to son. Chandragupta's son, Bindusara, expanded the empire farther across India. When his son, Asoka, gained power, at first he waged war. Then he turned to peace.

Why Did Asoka Turn to Peace?

As Chandragupta grew older, he became a Jain—a follower of Jainism (JY niz um). Like Buddhists, Jains aim for enlightenment. However, they accept the reality of the soul like Hindus. According to legend, Chandragupta gave up being emperor to enter a Jain monastery.

Asoka Rises to Power Asoka was one of Bindusara's seven sons. Legends say that Bindusara did not like him. As soon as Asoka was old enough to hold a job, Bindusara sent him away to be the ruler of a faraway province.

When Bindusara died, there was a struggle for the Maurya throne. One legend says that Asoka killed his own brothers in order to become emperor. After four years of fighting, Asoka became the third Maurya emperor.

[handwritten: Asoka = Ruthless. He did bad things for power]

Asoka spent the next eight years strengthening his hold on power. Then, he went to war again. His target was the kingdom of Kalinga, which had resisted conquest. The war between Maurya and Kalinga was long and terrible. **Eventually**, Asoka conquered Kalinga, but at a terrible cost. Thousands of soldiers died. Another 150,000 people were captured and sent to other parts of the empire.

Asoka was shocked by the suffering caused by the war. "The slaughter, death, and carrying away of captive people," he later wrote, "is a matter of profound sorrow and regret to His Sacred Majesty."

Academic Vocabulary
eventually • *adv.*, after a long time

[handwritten: is that remorse I see?]

New Rules for the Empire The suffering that Asoka saw during the war made him think hard about how he wanted to rule. Asoka began trying to follow Buddhist values. He turned away from violence.

Supported with Buddhist ideals, Asoka replaced rule by force with rule based on dharma, or moral law. His rule of moral law included three principles. The first was the principle of ahimsa, or the belief that one should not hurt any living thing. Asoka gave up hunting and banned the cruel treatment of animals.

The second principle was tolerance. **Tolerance** is a willingness to respect different beliefs and customs. Asoka was a Buddhist, but he respected Hinduism, Jainism, and other religions.

The third principle was the people's well-being. Asoka believed that a ruler must be careful to rule his people well. As a result, Asoka made many decisions to make his empire a better place to live.

INTERACTIVE
Asoka's Life

BIOGRAPHY
5 Things to Know About

ASOKA MAURYA
Emperor

- Asoka reportedly studied Buddhism at a Buddhist monastery while recovering from his wounds from the conquering of Kalinga.

- Asoka built hospitals for animals as well as hospitals for people.

- Mahinda, who was either a son or brother of Asoka, was the first Buddhist monk on the island of Sri Lanka.

- Asoka created a special group of high officers who went out into communities to encourage dharma work.

- Asoka built many stupas, which were Buddhist commemorative burial mounds.

Critical Thinking Explain how one of Asoka's actions directly reflected one or more of his three principles of moral law.

▲ Ceremonies celebrating the introduction of Buddhism to Sri Lanka

Quest CONNECTIONS

Look at the ceremony at the Buddhist monastery in Sri Lanka. What could visitors learn about Buddhism today from visiting such a monastery? Explore more about these monasteries and record your findings in your 📓 Active Journal.

Asoka's Stone Pillars To share his ideas, Asoka had stone pillars, or columns, set up across his empire. Each pillar rose 40 feet into the air and weighed 50 tons. Some of Asoka's stone pillars are still standing today.

These pillars were not just decorative. Asoka had messages carved into the polished pillars. In some of these messages, he assured his subjects that he was focused on their well-being. He apologized for making war on Kalinga, and he explained his new goals. He urged people to respect their parents and to be generous to other people. He urged respect for all religions. Most of all, Asoka encouraged people to live moral lives.

Buddhism Expands While Asoka respected all religions, he became a follower of Buddhism. His support for Buddhism helped the religion spread. With Asoka's backing, Buddhists were able to build monasteries and shrines throughout India. They also built **stupas**, Buddhist commemorative burial mounds, that still exist.

Buddhists also sent missionaries to neighboring countries, such as Sri Lanka. The support of the powerful Maurya emperor gave the religion prestige. This encouraged other rulers to adopt it.

✅ READING CHECK **Understand Effects** How did each of the three principles of Asoka's rule of law improve life for his people?

What Was Asoka's Legacy?

Asoka ruled India for nearly 40 years. During that time, he did much to improve life for his people. He set up hospitals and dug wells. He built an excellent road system.

The roads promoted trade within the empire. They also increased trade with neighboring lands, such as the Greek-controlled kingdoms of southwest Asia.

The longest of these roads—the Royal Road—stretched more than a thousand miles across northern India. Trees along the road provided shade for travelers. Rest houses offered food and shelter.

As a result of Asoka's efforts, India prospered. The country was at peace. There was little crime. People could leave their homes unguarded and travel the country without fear.

Asoka died in 232 BCE. After his death, the Maurya empire struggled. The emperors that followed Asoka were weak. As you have read, the Maurya government depended completely on the emperor's ability to make good decisions and command loyalty. As emperors lost control of parts of the empire, they lost support. In 185 BCE, the last Maurya ruler was murdered. After 136 years, the Maurya empire had come to an end.

☑ **READING CHECK** **Use Evidence** Which of Asoka's achievements do you think was his greatest? Why?

▼ Stupa in Sanchi, India

☑ Lesson Check

Practice Vocabulary

1. Use the term **tolerance** to describe the rule of Asoka.

Critical Thinking and Writing

2. **Analyze Information** What role did the stone pillars Asoka created play in his rule?

3. **Draw Conclusions** How did Asoka incorporate the well-being of his people into activities such as trade along the Royal Road?

4. **Understand Effects** How did Asoka's rule promote Buddhism?

5. **Writing Workshop: Develop a Clear Thesis** Think about the information you have collected on technological innovations in ancient India for your research paper. What conclusions can you draw about how technology was used, the process by which it was developed, or the areas of life affected by new technology? Write a clear thesis on the subject in your 📓 Active Journal.

The Gupta Empire

BOUNCE TO ACTIVATE ▶ VIDEO

GET READY TO READ

START UP

Look at the photo of modern Indian dancers performing a traditional dance. Why might ancient arts still be practiced in India today?

GUIDING QUESTIONS

- How did the Gupta dynasty create the second major Indian empire?
- During Gupta rule, how did India make advances in the arts, science, and mathematics, including our modern system of numerals?

TAKE NOTES

Literacy Skills: Summarize

Use the graphic organizer in your 📓 Active Journal to take notes as you read the lesson.

PRACTICE VOCABULARY

Use the vocabulary activity in your 📓 Active Journal to practice the vocabulary words.

Vocabulary	Academic Vocabulary
citizenship	drama
numeral	extract
decimal system	
metallurgy	

After the collapse of the Maurya empire, India broke into many small kingdoms. Armies from the north and west invaded India repeatedly but many invasions were repelled. Meanwhile, trade brought Indians into contact with China, Southeast Asia, and the Roman empire. Invaders and traders brought new ideas from the ancient Greeks and other peoples. Indians built on these ideas to make their own advances in art, literature, math, and science.

A New Empire in India

About 500 years after the Mauryas, the Gupta dynasty reunited northern India. Chandra Gupta I, the first Gupta ruler, may have been named after the founder of the Maurya empire, Chandragupta. Like the first Maurya emperor, Chandra Gupta I dreamed of building an empire. He gained power over a kingdom in the Ganges Basin and ruled from about 320 CE to 335 CE. He expanded his territory across the Ganges Basin through alliances and wars of conquest.

Chandra Gupta's son, Samudra Gupta, conquered most of the remaining small kingdoms of northern India. Samudra Gupta also conquered lands to the south and west.

Under Samudra's son, Chandra Gupta II, the Gupta empire reached its greatest size. He conquered areas along the west coast. Then, like Asoka, he tried to bring peace and prosperity to India. Unlike the Mauryas, the Guptas did not try to rule their entire empire directly. Instead, they left most decisions in the hands of local leaders. Governors controlled provinces. Village and city councils made decisions at the local level.

In each village, the leading families sent representatives to the council. In the cities, guilds, or groups of merchants or craftsmen working in the same line of business, sent representatives to the city council. People living in the Maurya empire were subjects, with a duty to obey. The people of the Gupta empire were also subjects, but some also had a kind of **citizenship**, or a status with political rights and obligations.

A Buddhist monk from China named Fa Xian (fah shen) visited India under the Guptas. He wrote:

Notes
grew and grew.
could lead to
a rebellion

Did you know?

The name Gupta is a common last name in India today. It means *ruler* or *protector*.

Notes

The gupta family
was very, very powerful
and conquered lots of
land

Primary Source

The people are numerous and happy. . . . If they want to go, they go. If they want to stay, they stay. The king governs without . . . corporal [physical] punishments[.]

—Fa Xian, *A Record of the Buddhistic Kingdoms*

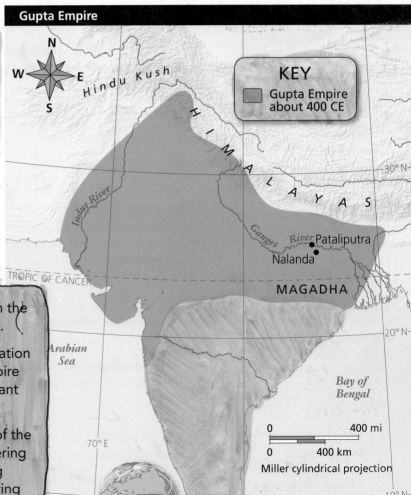

Gupta Empire

KEY

Gupta Empire about 400 CE

Hindu Kush

HIMALAYAS

Indus River

Ganges River — Pataliputra

Nalanda

MAGADHA

TROPIC OF CANCER

Arabian Sea

Bay of Bengal

| 0 | 400 mi |
| 0 | 400 km |

Miller cylindrical projection

30° N
20° N
10° N
70° E
80° E
90° E

GEOGRAPHY SKILLS

The Gupta empire stretched from the Arabian Sea to the Bay of Bengal.

1. **Movement** How might the location and expanse of the Gupta empire have promoted trade with distant lands?

2. **Sequence** Place these events of the Gupta empire in order: conquering of northern kingdoms; allowing local decision making; conquering areas along the west coast.

▲ Murals in the Ajanta caves are examples of Buddhist art produced during the Gupta empire.

Under later Gupta rulers, the empire faced new invaders from the west. Parts of the empire broke away. The last Gupta ruler died around the year 540.

☑ READING CHECK **Sequence** How did the Gupta empire develop from a warring empire to a peaceful land?

What Was Gupta Culture Like?

Around the time of the Guptas, artists produced great literature, painting, and architecture. The art and literature of the Gupta period still influence Indian culture today. Much of this art was religious. While Buddhism remained important under the Guptas, the Guptas favored Hinduism.

A Flowering of Literature Under Gupta rule, literature flourished. The greatest writer of the time was the poet Kalidasa, who wrote plays and poetry in the ancient language of Sanskrit.

A popular form of literature was the fable. A fable is a short story with a moral, or lesson, at the end. One Indian fable describes two frogs that fell into a pail of milk and could not jump out. They swam for a long time. Then, one of the frogs gave up hope and drowned. The other frog kept swimming. Eventually, the swimming frog churned the milk into butter and was able to jump out easily. The lesson of this fable is to keep trying even when things look hopeless.

Music, Dance, and Entertainment Music and dance thrived during the Gupta period. Dancers created works based on Hindu literature. Musicians played stringed instruments and drums.

Quest CONNECTIONS

Travelers to India want to see the art created during the Gupta Era. Think about why travelers would want to see a painting such as these murals in the Ajanta caves. Capture notes about them in your 📓 Active Journal.

NOTES
art, architecture, literature, very important, made large advances in the Gupta period.

Some forms of Indian **drama** combined stories, dance, and music. Performers with elaborate makeup and costumes told stories through song and dance.

The game of chess was invented under the Guptas. From India, the game moved along trade routes both east, into other parts of Asia, and west, into the Middle East and Europe.

Architecture and Painting Hindus and Buddhists built many temples and monasteries during this time. Stonecutters carved some temple buildings from rock. Architects also built impressive free-standing temples and monasteries. Both rock-carved and free-standing temples show good engineering skills.

Just after the Gupta period, Indians carved temples and monasteries into the rocks of cliffs. In central India, the rock-cut shrines of Ellora contain brilliant sculptures and paintings.

✔ READING CHECK **Compare and Contrast** How did a fable differ from poems or plays in the Gupta empire?

Mathematics and Science

During the Gupta period, trade and invasion brought the learning of Greece and Persia to India. Indian scholars drew on this learning to make advances of their own in mathematics and science.

The Decimal System Indian mathematicians developed the concept of zero as a number and as a **numeral**, or a symbol used to represent a number. Probably the greatest advance was the **decimal system**, a counting system based on units of ten. Together these advances were the basis for what we know as the Hindu-Arabic, or Arabic, numerals, in use worldwide today.

A New World of Mathematics Combining a decimal system with a numeral for zero transformed mathematics. With the new Indian system of numerals, multiplication and division became much easier. This new system opened the way for other advances in mathematics, such as algebra.

Aryabhata (ahr yuh BUH tuh) was an important Indian astronomer

Academic Vocabulary
drama • *n.*, plays or performances that tell stories

INTERACTIVE

A Golden Age in the Arts

Origins of Arabic Numerals

Late Gupta (India, 500s)	Gwalior (India, 800s)	Western Arabic (North Africa and Spain, 900s)	Western Arabic (Worldwide, Today)
O	o	o	0
—	1	1	1
=	2	2	2
≡	3	3	3
४	४	✗	4
ん	५	५	5
६	६	6	6
?	?	?	7
?	?	8	8
?	?	?	9

Analyze Charts Gupta mathematicians developed numerals 1,500 years ago that evolved into the shapes we use today. **Identify Main Ideas** Which numeral especially transformed mathematics? Why?

Analyze Images
Eighteenth-century sundial in Jaipur, India, built in the style used by Indian astronomers

Academic Vocabulary
extract • *v.*, remove, draw out

and mathematician. In 499 CE, Aryabhata wrote a mathematics book on arithmetic, algebra, and trigonometry.

Hundreds of years later, mathematicians in Europe relied on Aryabhata's work to calculate the area of triangles and the volume of spheres.

Astronomy Aryabhata was the first astronomer to state that the Earth rotates, or spins, on its axis to create day and night. He discovered that eclipses were caused by the motion of Earth and the moon. Aryabhata also discovered that the moon shines because it reflects sunlight.

Medicine Indian doctors made progress in medical science as well. They developed a system of medicine known as Ayurveda. Ancient Ayurvedic medical textbooks describe many different diseases and how to treat medical problems. They also explain how to make hundreds of medicines from plants, animal parts, and minerals.

Metallurgy Gupta artisans also made progress in **metallurgy**, the science that deals with **extracting** metal from ore and using it to create useful objects. The Iron Pillar of Delhi is a famous example of their skill in producing metal compounds of great quality. This 23-foot-high column was made from a single piece of iron. It has stood outside for more than 1,500 years without turning to rust.

✓**READING CHECK** **Understand Effects** Why are the decimal system and the development of the concept of zero considered the greatest advancements of Indian mathematicians?

☑ Lesson Check

Practice Vocabulary

1. How is a **numeral** different from a number?

2. Which Gupta advances were related to the **decimal system** and **metallurgy**?

Critical Thinking and Writing

3. **Compare and Contrast** How was the Gupta system of government different from the Maurya system of government?

4. **Summarize** Which Gupta traditions continue to influence the art of India today?

5. **Cite Evidence** How do historians know that metal workers in the Gupta empire made great progress in metallurgy?

6. **Cite Evidence** What proof do historians have of how medicine was practiced in the Gupta empire?

7. **Writing Workshop: Write an Introduction** Write an introductory paragraph for your research paper on technological innovation in ancient India in your 📓 Active Journal. Explain what you concluded from your research and how you are going to show it in the body of the paper.

Interpret Thematic Maps

Follow these steps to review the ways to analyze a thematic map.

INTERACTIVE

Read Special Purpose Maps

1 **Identify the topic of the thematic map.** A thematic map shows information about an area. The map title indicates the type of map and its topic. The key also gives information.

   a. What is the title of this map? What does it tell you about the map?

   b. What does the key to this map tell you about the information the map shows?

   c. How can you use the key to help you find specific information on the map?

2 **Determine the place on the map.** Map titles indicate the map's region. When it does not, use the map or nearby text to understand what area is being shown.

   a. Does the title indicate the region?

   b. What information tells you the place or places shown on the map?

3 **Determine the time shown on the map.** Look for dates in the map title or key. If no dates are shown, look for clues in the title and key. Look also at information around the map to find clues about the time. Read the text that accompanies the map. What information lets you know the period?

4 **Explain what the map shows.** Use the key to understand colors and symbols.

   a. What does the shaded area show?

   b. Where did Buddhism start?

Secondary Source

The Buddha urged his followers to carry his teachings to all corners of Earth. A person who spreads religious ideas is a missionary. Buddhist missionaries carried Buddhism across India and to Sri Lanka, then throughout Asia. Some traveled north to Central Asia. Then missionaries followed trade routes east into China. Buddhism spread to Korea and Japan. Buddhism arrived later in Tibet.

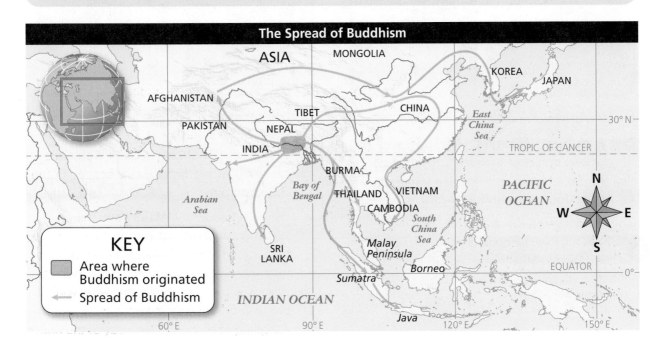

The Spread of Buddhism

KEY
- Area where Buddhism originated
- ← Spread of Buddhism

☑ Review and Assessment

VISUAL REVIEW

Comparing Hinduism and Buddhism

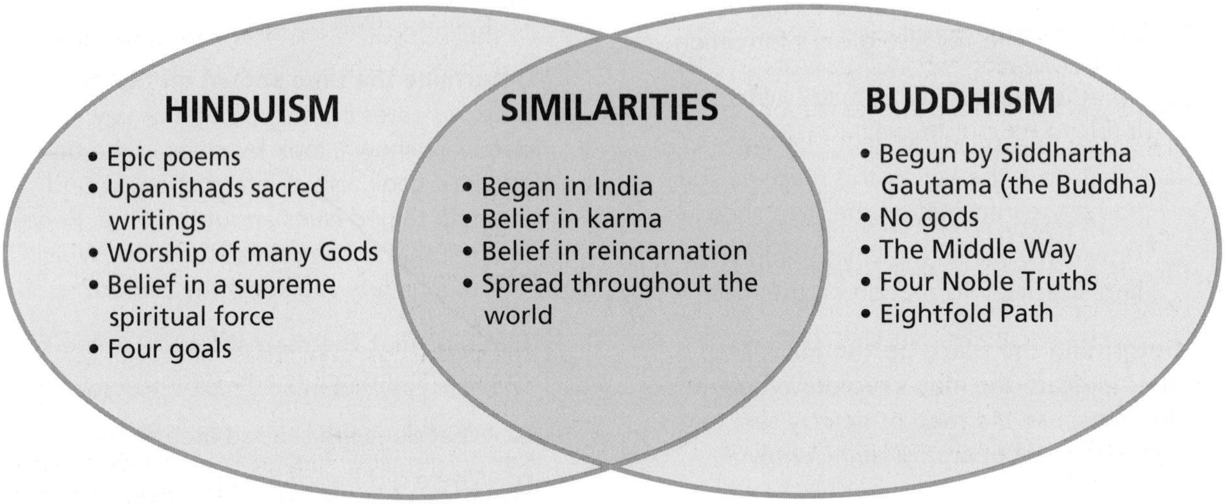

HINDUISM
- Epic poems
- Upanishads sacred writings
- Worship of many Gods
- Belief in a supreme spiritual force
- Four goals

SIMILARITIES
- Began in India
- Belief in karma
- Belief in reincarnation
- Spread throughout the world

BUDDHISM
- Begun by Siddhartha Gautama (the Buddha)
- No gods
- The Middle Way
- Four Noble Truths
- Eightfold Path

Early Indian Civilizations and Empires

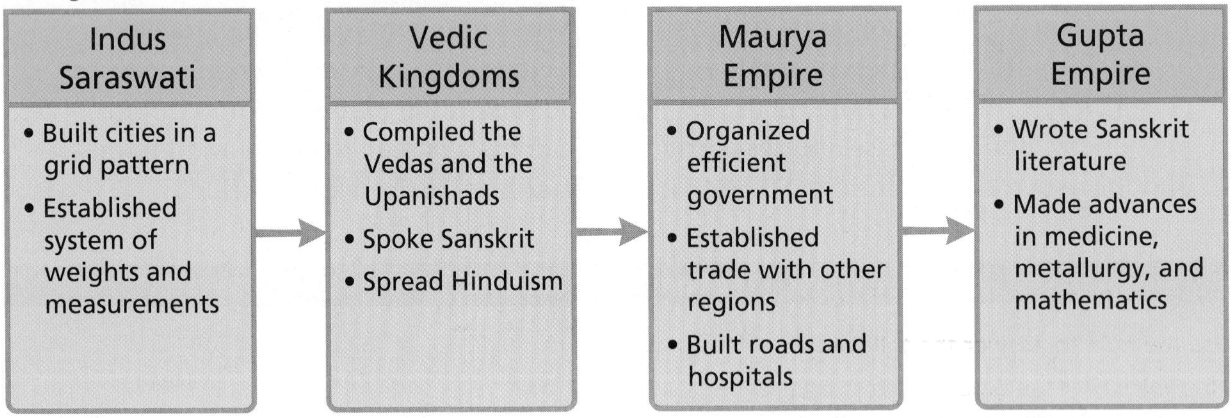

Indus Saraswati	Vedic Kingdoms	Maurya Empire	Gupta Empire
• Built cities in a grid pattern • Established system of weights and measurements	• Compiled the Vedas and the Upanishads • Spoke Sanskrit • Spread Hinduism	• Organized efficient government • Established trade with other regions • Built roads and hospitals	• Wrote Sanskrit literature • Made advances in medicine, metallurgy, and mathematics

READING REVIEW

Use the Take Notes and Practice Vocabulary activities in your 📓 Active Journal to review the topic.

INTERACTIVE

Practice vocabulary using the Topic Mini-Games.

Quest FINDINGS

Make Your Travel Brochure

Get help for making your travel brochure in your 📓 Active Journal.

ASSESSMENT

Vocabulary and Key Ideas

1. **Describe** How did Chandragupta's **bureaucracy** work?

2. **Check Understanding** What **citizenship** rights did people have in the Gupta empire?

3. **Describe** Describe the **citadels** of the Indus Saraswati civilization and their possible function.

4. **Identify Main Ideas** How was life for **Kshatriyas** different from life for **Vaishyas**?

5. **Identify Supporting Details** How are **dharma** and **ahimsa** related in Hinduism?

6. **Recall** How did early Indian civilizations depend on **monsoons**?

7. **Describe** Kautilya's **strategy** for governing and how it differed from Asoka's strategy.

Critical Thinking and Writing

8. **Identify Main Ideas** Why are important aspects of the rise and decline of the Indus Saraswati civilization so mysterious?

9. **Infer** What are the main paths to moksha in Hinduism, and how might the acceptance of these paths have contributed to the spread of Hinduism?

10. **Compare and Contrast** How is Buddhism similar to and different from Hinduism?

11. **Infer** Why would discoveries in metallurgy be important to a civilization?

12. **Revisit the Essential Question** How have cultures of ancient India endured to today?

13. **Writing Workshop: Write a Research Paper** Using the notes you have made and the sources you have found, write a research paper on technological innovations in ancient India.

Analyze Primary Sources

14. For whom is the source below likely written?

"In the happiness of his subjects lies the king's happiness. In the welfare of his subjects, his welfare. A king's good is not that which pleases him, but that which pleases his subjects."

—Kautilya, Arthashastra

Analyze Maps

Use the map to answer the following questions.

15. Which of these empires was most likely significantly stronger than its neighbors? Why?

16. Why might both empires have wanted access to both the Arabian Sea and the Bay of Bengal?

17. How is the location of these two empires related to the geography of the Indian subcontinent?

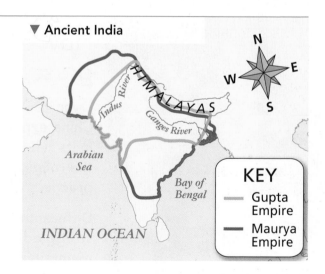

▼ Ancient India

KEY

— Gupta Empire

— Maurya Empire

Early Civilizations of China

(1700 BCE–220 CE)

GO ONLINE
to access your
digital course

▶ VIDEO

◀)) AUDIO

📖 ETEXT

👆 INTERACTIVE

✍ WRITING

🎮 GAMES

📄 WORKSHEET

☑ ASSESSMENT

It began at the edge

of a great river over 7,000 years ago. Sounds familiar, right? Like other early civilizations, the **EARLY CIVILIZATIONS OF CHINA** depended on rivers to grow and thrive. In time, China emerged as a great empire with a rich and complex history and culture.

Explore

The Essential Question

How do societies preserve order?

Over its rich history, ancient China experienced many changes in its ruling dynasties and in the religious and cultural practices of its people.

Different rulers and religions struggled with the challenge of maintaining order in what became a great empire.

Unlock the Essential Question in your 📓 Active Journal.

Watch

NBC LEARN

BOUNCE TO ACTIVATE ▶ VIDEO

Shi Huangdi, First Emperor of Unified China

Learn about the controversial figure who unified China under his firm command.

◀ Emperor Shi Huangdi's tomb, containing thousands of life-sized terra cotta soldiers

Read

about the beginnings and rise of an empire of great cultural, scientific, and cultural achievement.

Early Civilizations of China (1700 BCE – 220 BCE)

Learn more about the early civilizations of China by making your own map and timeline in your 📙 Active Journal.

INTERACTIVE

Topic Map

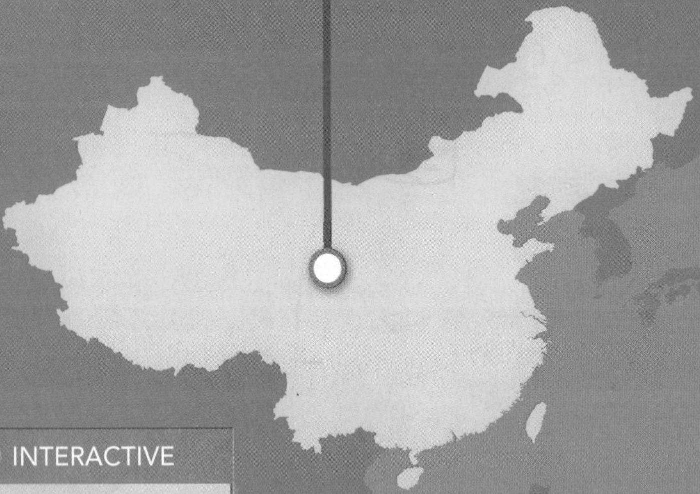

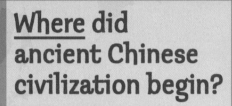

Where did ancient Chinese civilization begin?

Ancient China was born in the valleys of great rivers, the Huang and Chang. The early civilization grew up in these valleys and in the broad area between the vast deserts and towering mountains that helped cut off China from the rest of the world.

INTERACTIVE

Topic Timeline

What happened and when?

Great dynasties are founded ... brilliant philosophers are born. Explore the timeline to see some of what was happening in China and in the rest of the world.

About 1400 BCE
The Shang begin writing oracle bones.

1800 BCE
Shang kingdom founded; Shang artisans make bronze tools.

5000 BCE
Farmers settle villages along the Huang River.

TOPIC EVENTS

5000 BCE — 2000 BCE

WORLD EVENTS

1600 BCE
Aryans begin to compose Vedas.

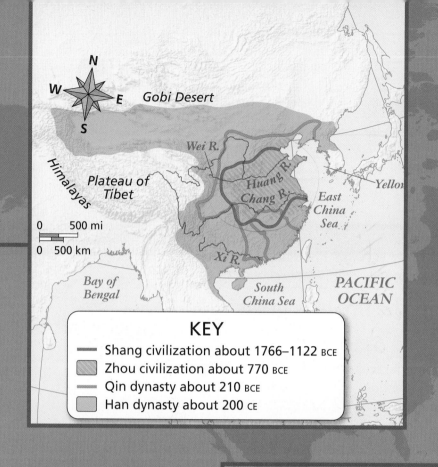

KEY

 ═══ Shang civilization about 1766–1122 BCE
 ▦ Zhou civilization about 770 BCE
 ─── Qin dynasty about 210 BCE
 ▨ Han dynasty about 200 CE

Who will you meet?

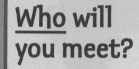

King Wu, first Zhou king

Confucius, a philosopher whose teachings changed the course of Chinese history

Shi Huangdi, first emperor to unify China

551 BCE
Confucius is born.

475 BCE
The Warring States period begins.

206 BCE
Han Dynasty begins.

221 BCE
Qin Dynasty begins.

103 BCE
Trade begins on Silk Road.

1050 BCE
The Zhou Dynasty begins.

1000 BCE

1 CE

934 BCE
Assyrian empire begins.

700 BCE
Greek colonies spread.

44 BCE
Julius Caesar becomes dictator of Rome.

Quest

Document-Based Writing Inquiry

Evaluating a Leader's Legacy

Quest KICK OFF

The year is 210 BCE. The great Shi Huangdi has died, and you have been given the job of writing his obituary.

How do you sum up the life of a great but harsh leader?

What challenges did Shi Huangdi face, and how did he meet them? Explore the Essential Question "How do societies preserve order?" in this Quest.

1 Ask Questions
The life and rule of Shi Huangdi was successful—but controversial. What questions do you have about the challenges he faced and the decisions he made? Write your questions in your 📓 Active Journal.

2 Investigate
As you read the lessons in this topic, look for **Quest CONNECTIONS** that provide information about the rule of Shi Huangdi and how he united China. Capture your notes in your 📓 Active Journal.

3 Examine Primary Sources
Next explore a set of primary sources from Qin China. They'll help you learn more about the rule of Shi Huangdi. Capture your notes in your 📓 Active Journal.

Quest FINDINGS

4 Write Your Obituary
An obituary sums up the achievements and highlights of a person's life. At the end of this topic, you'll write an obituary for the leader who first unified all of China—sometimes through controversial means. Your obituary will help summarize this ruler's life—the good, the bad, and the ugly. Get help for writing your obituary in your 📓 Active Journal.

▲ Statue of Emperor Shi Huangdi

The Huang Valley

BOUNCE TO ACTIVATE ▶ VIDEO

GET READY TO READ

START UP

Write two predictions about how the geographic features you see in this picture of the Huang Valley might have influenced the development of Chinese civilization.

GUIDING QUESTIONS

- How did location and the environment influence the development of civilization in China?
- Why did Chinese society emerge along the Huang River?
- What were the major achievements of the Shang dynasty?

TAKE NOTES

Literacy Skills: Summarize

Use the graphic organizer in your 📓 Active Journal to take notes as you read the lesson.

PRACTICE VOCABULARY

Use the vocabulary activity in your 📓 Active Journal to practice the vocabulary words.

Vocabulary		Academic Vocabulary
loess	pictograph	interpret
dike	logograph	challenge
oracle bone		

Chinese civilization arose along the Huang (hwong) River, also called the Yellow River. By around 5000 BCE, farmers had settled in a number of villages in this river valley. Over time, powerful rulers united these villages to create large kingdoms. Among these, the Shang kingdom rose to become the most influential.

Geography of China

Today, the country of China is a huge land, similar in size to the United States. Much of China is covered by rugged mountains and vast deserts. Despite the challenges of the geography, early people found the resources they needed along China's river valleys.

River Systems Rivers helped China's development, just as they aided the development of civilizations in Mesopotamia, Egypt, and India. China has two main rivers: the Huang and the Chang (chahng). They provide water for farming. People move goods along these waterways. Both rivers begin in the mountains of western China.

The Chang, also called the Yangtze River, is China's longest river. But the Huang River

[handwritten annotations: "certain civilizations would have ended if not for rivers" and "great for trade"]

The Chang River is China's longest river. It is almost twice as long as the Missouri River, the longest river in the United States.

Woah!

GEOGRAPHY SKILLS

Ancient Chinese civilization developed in the North China Plain and was affected by other geographical features.

1. **Region** What two rivers flow through the North China Plain?

2. **Recognize Multiple Causes** What multiple geographic land features might have caused ancient China to be isolated from other civilizations?

was especially important to China's early history. It flows east to the Yellow Sea and crosses the flat North China Plain. Winds from the Gobi Desert blow loess (LOH es) onto the Huang River valley. **Loess** is a fine, dustlike material that can form soil. The Huang River cuts through deep deposits of loess and picks it up. The loess makes the river muddy and turns it yellow. The name of the Huang River comes from this mud. In Chinese, *huang* means yellow.

When the river overflows its banks, it deposits the loess on the surrounding plain. The floods can be unpredictable. However, this fertile soil makes the North China Plain well suited for agriculture. Even with simple tools, ancient farmers could easily plant their crops in the soft soil. Here, people created the first large settlements in China.

fertile soil makes settling easier

How Did Isolation Affect China's Development?

China is nearly surrounded by physical barriers. Two great deserts, the Taklimakan (tah kluh muh KAHN) and the Gobi, lie to the north and west of China. The towering Himalayas form a wall between China and India. To the south lie more mountains, and to the east the Pacific Ocean.

China's geography slowed the spread of information and ideas, which made governing the vast land difficult. It was difficult for ideas and goods to travel between China and other civilizations. Some early innovations, such as the domesticated horse, may have come to China from western Asia. However, ancient China was largely cut off from other civilizations.

✓ **READING CHECK** **Cause and Effect** What geographic features affected settlement patterns and government in early China?

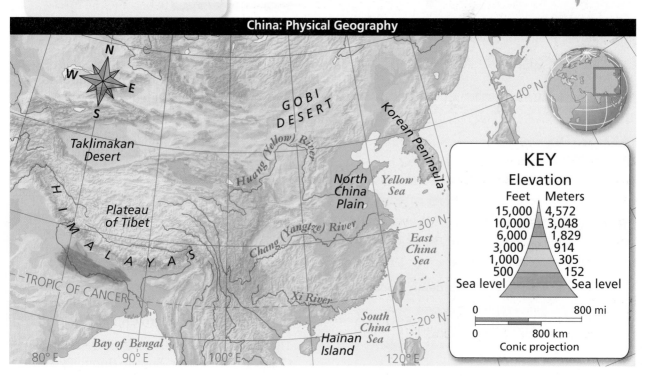

China: Physical Geography

GOBI DESERT

Korean Peninsula

40° N

Taklimakan Desert

Huang (Yellow) River

North China Plain

Yellow Sea

Plateau of Tibet

HIMALAYAS

Chang (Yangtze) River

30° N

East China Sea

TROPIC OF CANCER

Xi River

South China Sea

20° N

Bay of Bengal

Hainan Island

80° E   90° E   100° E   120° E

KEY
Elevation

Feet	Meters
15,000	4,572
10,000	3,048
6,000	1,829
3,000	914
1,000	305
500	152
Sea level	Sea level

0   800 mi
0   800 km
Conic projection

The Shang Dynasty

From the early settlements along the Huang River, the Shang kingdom rose to dominate a large part of the region. The language and culture of the Shang would have a lasting influence on China.

The Shang Rise Farming villages grew along the Huang River. The people used stone tools and made pottery and silk cloth. Some of these villages had chiefs, or rulers, who organized workers and commanded warriors. Strong chiefs led their warriors to take control of nearby villages, creating small kingdoms.

Around 1700 BCE, one of those kingdoms began to expand. A ruler from this kingdom founded the Shang dynasty. A dynasty is a ruling family that holds power for many years. This dynasty lasted some 600 years. It is the earliest dynasty for which we have a written record.

How Did the Shang Government Rule? Strong rulers ran the government. The Shang kept power within the family. Rule passed from brother to brother and from the youngest brother to his oldest son.

The Shang leaders organized groups of farmers to clear and prepare new land. The result was larger harvests. With extra food, Shang rulers could support many soldiers. They attacked neighboring lands and expanded their territory. Soldiers fought with bows, lances, and bronze axes. Some rode into battle in chariots.

Shang rulers used their wealth to build a number of large walled cities. They also tried to control the floods along the Huang River. They built **dikes**, or walls to hold back water.

Writing The earliest written records from China are **oracle bones** from the Shang dynasty. Oracle bones are animal bones or turtle shells carved with written characters that the Shang kings used to try to tell the future.

Questions were written on the bone, which was then heated until it cracked. The king or a priest would **interpret** the cracks to get an answer. No one knows exactly how the cracks were read.

At times, the Chinese also used oracle bones to record important events related to their questions. From these written records, scholars have learned much about ancient China and its rulers.

The Shang did not use an alphabet for their written words, which are called characters. Instead, some characters were **pictographs**; that is, pictures that represent words or ideas. Other characters were a combination of symbols. Some symbols stood for the meaning of the word while others represented the sound.

Shang was well military trained

▲ Religious leaders would carve outcomes on bones or shells like this one, then crack it and interpret the cracks for the king.

I rember learning about the turtle shells. :)

Academic Vocabulary
interpret • v., to explain, give the meaning of

were used in many other ancient times

🔘 INTERACTIVE

Chinese Writing

Analyze Images Shang dynasty artisans were skilled in creating detailed objects in bronze and jade. This was a ceremonial bronze axe head. **Infer** Why do you think ancient Chinese ceremonial objects were made of bronze, but everyday objects were not?

Academic Vocabulary
challenge • *n.*, something that is difficult or demanding to do

By 1300 BCE, the Shang had a fully developed writing system. Many ancient characters became the writing Chinese people use today. The sound changed, but their meaning can still be understood.

Chinese characters use a logographic script. A **logograph** is a written character that represents a complete word or phrase. By contrast, in an alphabet such as the one used in the United States, written characters represent sounds. Chinese writing requires more memorization because it has thousands of characters , making it a **challenge** to learn.

Still, this system is useful in a country where people speak many languages. Spoken Chinese is different across the country, but all Chinese speakers use the same characters. In a sense, Chinese characters are like numbers. A number has the same meaning in many languages even if the spoken word used for that number is different in each of those languages.

Bronze Metalworking Shang artisans created pottery and jade carvings, but they are best known for their bronze metalworking. These objects included finely decorated pots, cups, and weapons.

Most tools used on a daily basis were not made out of bronze. The Shang used the expensive, beautiful bronzes in religious ceremonies. Human and animal sacrifices were prepared with bronze blades. They also offered food and wine to their gods and ancestors in the hope that these spirits would help them.

☑ **READING CHECK** **Summarize** How and from where did the Shang dynasty develop?

☑ Lesson Check

Practice Vocabulary

1. What is **loess**?

2. Use the terms **oracle bones**, **pictograph**, and **logograph** to describe the Chinese language.

Critical Thinking and Writing

3. **Identify Cause and Effect** How did the geography of the Huang River valley affect the lives of the Chinese who settled there?

4. **Draw Conclusions** How did organization allow the leaders of the Shang dynasty to increase their power?

5. **Writing Workshop: Introduce Claims** Examine what values you think made the Shang dynasty successful. Write a sentence in your 📓 Active Journal that states what values you think a government needs in order to successfully lead. This will become the basis for an argumentative essay that you will write at the end of this topic.

The Zhou Dynasty

BOUNCE TO ACTIVATE ▶ VIDEO

GET READY TO READ

START UP
Examine the illustration of Zhou emperor Mu Wang riding in his chariot. Write three questions you have about Zhou rulers based on the picture.

GUIDING QUESTIONS
- How did the Zhou dynasty gain power?
- How did the idea of the Mandate of Heaven explain the rise and fall of dynasties?
- What were the successes and failures of the Zhou?

TAKE NOTES
Literacy Skills: Identify Main Ideas
Use the graphic organizer in your 📓 Active Journal to take notes as you read the lesson.

PRACTICE VOCABULARY
Use the vocabulary activity in your 📓 Active Journal to practice the vocabulary words.

Vocabulary	Academic Vocabulary
Mandate of Heaven	survived
warlord	minor
chaos	

Around 1050 BCE, a group called the Zhou (joh) attacked the Shang kingdom from the west. They overthrew the Shang ruler and established a new dynasty. The Zhou dynasty ruled for about 800 years. For much of the second half of its rule, however, the Zhou struggled to keep its large kingdom united. The widespread use of iron had much to do with the Zhou dynasty falling. Iron became readily available, and even the peasants had access to iron tools and weapons. With iron weapons readily available to the masses, the result was wars and upheavals.

Rise and Fall of the Zhou

Most of what is known about the fall of the Shang comes from sources written during the Zhou. According to these sources, the Zhou gained power because the Shang kings had grown corrupt. The last Shang king governed badly. He cared only about his own enjoyment, and many people came to resent him. When the Zhou attacked the Shang, many Shang warriors refused to fight. They surrendered and accepted the Zhou king as their new ruler.

[handwritten annotations: "Took advantage of the Shang's mistakes"; "Sides were into play with power"]

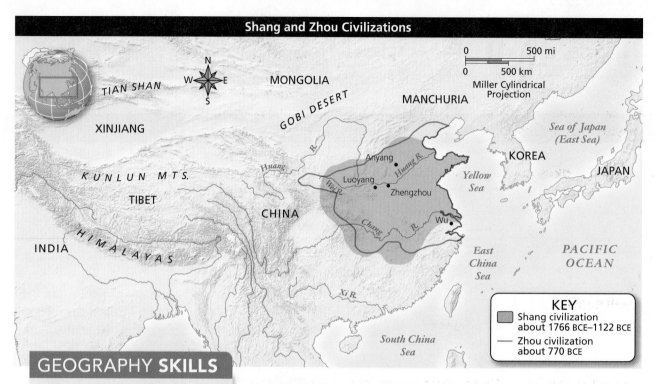

Shang and Zhou Civilizations

KEY
▪ Shang civilization
about 1766 BCE–1122 BCE
— Zhou civilization
about 770 BCE

GEOGRAPHY **SKILLS**

This map shows the locations of Shang and Zhou civilizations.

1. **Locate** Where was the Shang dynasty located? Why was it located there?

2. **Infer** What do you think prevented Shang and Zhou civilizations from expanding further west?

The Right to Rule After taking power, the Zhou leaders declared that their success proved that they had heaven's support. In their view, heaven was the highest force of nature that gave dynasties the right to rule. They called this right to rule the **Mandate of Heaven**. If a dynasty failed to act properly, it lost this right. This mandate would then pass to a new dynasty. The Mandate of Heaven permitted a leader to seize control by force, if necessary. Victory served as proof that heaven supported the change in leadership.

The concept of the Mandate of Heaven became a tradition of Chinese government. Under this tradition, the ruler was called the Son of Heaven. If he acted virtuously, there would be harmony between heaven and earth. Emperors were supposed to care for their people and stop corruption. Uprisings and natural disasters were seen as possible omens that the current dynasty had lost the Mandate of Heaven and its right to stay in power.

One ancient Chinese source, the *Book of History*, explains why the Zhou kings received and kept the Mandate of Heaven:

Primary Source

. . . our kings of Zhou treated the people well . . . and presided over services to spirits and to Heaven. Heaven therefore instructed the Zhou kings, chose them . . . and gave them the decree to rule.

—*Book of History*

Zhou kings were said to be chosen by heaven, which gained respect.

Quick Activity

As a new Zhou ruler, use your 📓 Active Journal to convince your subjects you have the Mandate of Heaven.

Governing the Zhou Through conquest, the Zhou expanded its lands. At its height, the Zhou ruled a territory that reached to the Chang River. This large kingdom included many different cultures. To keep control, the king placed family members in charge of individual regions or states. As with the Shang, some of China's geographical features slowed travel and communication, making governing from a central location difficult. Over time, the ties between the Zhou king and local nobles weakened.

In 771 BCE, a group of nobles joined with nomadic invaders to try to overthrow the king. With the help of other nobles, the Zhou **survived** this attack. But the power of the Zhou king decreased. From that point on, the Zhou kings were weak and dependent on the nobles who had helped them to stay in power.

States that had once been tied to the Zhou grew more independent. Fighting broke out between **warlords**. Warlords are military rulers of small states. Although these warlords claimed loyalty to the king, they often really sought power for themselves. Many increased their military might by learning to make iron weapons.

The Warring States Period Eventually, **minor** battles escalated into full-scale warfare. China entered an era of **chaos**—total disorder and confusion. This era, from about 475 to 221 BCE, became known as the Warring States period. Brutal and destructive conflict marked the period. Battles ravaged the countryside. Millions of people died.

Stronger states conquered weaker ones. Over time, a few large states emerged. Loyalty to the Zhou dynasty disappeared. In 256 BCE, the last Zhou ruler was overthrown. Fighting continued for years, however, before a new dynasty managed to unite China.

✓ READING CHECK **Identify Central Ideas** What made governing the Zhou kingdom difficult?

Zhou Society

The Zhou adopted much of Shang culture. They followed the same basic laws, wore similar clothing, and spoke the same language. They produced bronze art that rivaled that of the Shang. However, great changes also occurred in the Zhou dynasty. For example, the Zhou kings gave up the practice of human sacrifice and stopped using oracle bones.

Structure of Society The Zhou kings, just as the Shang rulers before them, occupied the center of government. The Zhou, however, gave more power to individual states and the nobles who led them. Those states set up their own walled capital cities, from which they controlled the lands of lesser nobles. The nobles were expected to serve the king and raise armies to support him.

INTERACTIVE

The Dynastic Cycle

Academic Vocabulary

survive • *v.*, to last, to continue to live

minor • *adj.*, not serious, not important

needed a stronger government

Analyze Images This image shows Zhou king You using gunpowder to frighten his enemy. **Use Visual Information** What do other details from this image you tell about how battles were fought at the the time of the Zhou?

why change now?

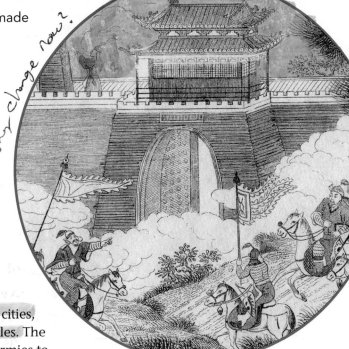

Analyze Images Zhou coins were made in many shapes including knives and spades, and some had holes so they could be carried on a string. **Compare and Contrast** How are Zhou coins like and unlike the coins we use today?

Same as so many early civilizations

Their version of Jail or community service

The majority of Zhou people, as in most ancient societies, were peasants. They farmed the land and served as soldiers. There were also a small number of merchants, artisans, and slaves. People were sold into slavery as punishment for crimes and to pay debts.

Family Relationships The ancient Chinese put a high value on family. Society demanded that individuals show loyalty to their family. Older family members had more power and privileges than younger ones. As in most ancient societies, men had higher status than women.

Economy and Technology During the Zhou, there were many technological advances. For weapons, one important invention was the crossbow. Artisans learned to make iron, which is stronger than bronze. The Zhou used iron to make weapons.

Innovations also helped strengthen the Zhou economy. Iron was used to make stronger, more effective farm tools. Crop yield also increased as the Zhou used irrigation and fertilizer for more of their farmland. The Zhou built a network of roads, which helped travel and trade. A number of new cities sprang up. *Lots of great ways to spread + grow civilization*

Coins were also used for the first time in the Zhou dynasty. Coins made trade across the large Zhou empire easier.

Cultural Life The Zhou dynasty was a time of great creative energy. As the leaders of the Warring States vied for influence, they supported poets and artists. They looked for wise men to help them to rule. The writings of thinkers from this time became the foundation of much of Chinese thought for centuries.

☑ **READING CHECK** **Understand Effects** How did technological advances strengthen Zhou society?

☑ Lesson Check

Practice Vocabulary

1. What is a **warlord**?

2. Use the term *chaos* to write a sentence about the Warring States period.

Critical Thinking and Writing

3. **Compare and Contrast** How was the Zhou dynasty similar to and different from the Shang dynasty?

4. **Draw Conclusions** How did China's geography make it difficult for the Zhou kings to keep their large kingdom united?

5. **Infer** How did the invention of coins help make trade easier?

6. **Writing Workshop: Support Claims** What values did Shang and Zhou societies have that you think helped their governments to lead effectively? Write down examples in your 📓 Active Journal that support your claim.

📖 Primary Sources

Sun Tzu, The Art of War

The Art of War is a classic text on military strategy, written by Sun Tzu during the Warring States period. According to legend, a Chinese king named Helu (514–496 BCE) had a small army of 30,000, but was facing an invasion by an army of more than 300,000. To survive and prevail, he turned to Sun Tzu to train his army in the art of war and deception.

▶ Sun Tzu

All warfare is based on deception.

Hence, when able to attack, we must seem unable; when using our forces, we must seem inactive; when we are near, we must make the enemy believe we are far away; when far away, we must make him believe we are near.

Hold out baits ① to entice the enemy. Feign ② disorder, and crush him.

If he is secure at all points, be prepared for him. If he is in superior strength, evade ③ him.

If your opponent is of choleric temper, ④ seek to irritate him. Pretend to be weak, that he may grow arrogant.

If he is taking his ease, give him no rest. If his forces are united, separate them.

Attack him where he is unprepared, appear where you are not expected.

These military devices, leading to victory, must not be divulged ⑤ beforehand.

—Sun Tzu, *The Art of War*

Analyzing Primary Sources

Cite specific evidence from the document to support your answers.

1. **Explain an Argument** Soldiers are taught to stand tall and strong and to always be ready for action. Why then does Sun Tzu advise them to pretend to be inactive, disorganized, or weak?

2. **Generate Explanations** *The Art of War* has been studied for more than 1,000 years and by armies around the world. What makes these deceptive strategies so effective?

Reading and Vocabulary Support

① People often use worms as bait to lure fish. What type of bait might an army use to entice an enemy?

② To feign is to pretend. What would an army look like if it feigned disorder?

③ When you evade people, you avoid or escape them.

④ A person with a choleric temper is proud, impatient, and short-tempered.

⑤ Why would it be important not to divulge, or reveal, these military tactics?

Distinguish Fact from Opinion

Follow these steps to distinguish fact from opinion.

INTERACTIVE

Distinguish Between Fact and Opinion

1 Identify the facts. A fact is something that can be proved to be true. A fact often provides information such as *who, what, where, when,* or *how.* The source is from *The Book of History,* and it describes the actions of the first Zhou ruler, King Wu, who ruled from approximately 1046 to 1043 BCE.

   a. What are some facts you find in this passage?

   b. How do you know they are facts?

2 Confirm that the facts can be verified. Use reliable sources to confirm the accuracy of any facts. These include strong online sources, such as sites ending in *.gov, .edu,* or *.org.* Print sources from the library can also confirm facts. In the case of this excerpt, historical records about King Wu could be used. Where are some places you would look to verify the facts you found in the primary source?

3 Identify the opinions. An opinion is a personal belief or judgment. Opinions cannot be proved to be either true or false. Writers may introduce opinions using the words *I think, I feel,* or *I believe.* Other clues that indicate something may be an opinion are words that describe qualities such as *honorable, attractive,* or *generous.*

   a. What are some examples of opinions in this passage?

   b. How do you know they are opinions?

4 Evaluate opinions. While opinions are not true or false, some are stronger than others. A strong opinion is supported by facts. For example, the opinion that people submitted joyfully to the king's rule could be supported with facts about the absence of conflict or opposition during his reign. What facts would be needed to support the opinion that the king showed that he was truthful?

Primary Source

He overthrew the existing government of Shang, and made it resume its old course. He delivered the count of Qi from prison, and raised a tumulus [earthen mound] over the grave of Bi Gan. He bowed in his carriage at the gate of Shang Yong's village. He dispersed the treasures of the Lu Dai, and distributed the grain of Zhu Jiao, thus conferring great gifts throughout the empire, and all the people joyfully submitted. He arranged the orders of nobility into five. . . . He gave offices only to the worthy, and jobs only to the able. He attached great importance to the people being taught the duties of the five relations of society. . . . He showed that he was truthful, and proved that he was righteous. He honored virtue, and rewarded merit. Then he had only to let his robes fall down, fold his hands, and the kingdom was orderly ruled.

— Shu Jhing, *Book of History,* Chapter 21

Chinese Belief Systems

BOUNCE TO ACTIVATE ▶ VIDEO

GET READY TO READ

START UP

Study the photograph of the Daoist monastery. Why do you think it was built in this location? Write one prediction about how the monastery's location might influence people who lived or visited there.

GUIDING QUESTIONS

- What role did belief in spirits and reverence for ancestors play in early Chinese religion?
- How did the philosophical system of Confucianism support individuals, rulers, and societies?
- What values did Daoism affirm?

TAKE NOTES

Literacy Skills: Compare and Contrast

Use the graphic organizer in your 🗐 Active Journal to take notes as you read the lesson.

PRACTICE VOCABULARY

Use the vocabulary activity in your 🗐 Active Journal to practice the vocabulary words.

Vocabulary	Academic Vocabulary
philosophy	income
filial piety	stable

Isolated by its geography, ancient China had a unique culture. Two important belief systems, Confucianism and Daoism, developed during the Zhou. Each is a **philosophy**, that is, a set of beliefs about the world and how to live. These philosophies influenced all aspects of society. Religious practices, such as the worship of certain gods, became connected to these philosophies. Today, Daoist and Confucian temples are found across China. Before these philosophies appeared, the Chinese followed ancient spiritual traditions.

Spiritual Traditions

Some ancient Chinese viewed Earth as a flat square. Heaven stretched above. Both heaven and Earth were populated by a variety of spirits.

Many Spirits The ancient Chinese viewed heaven as the home of the spirits of the sun, moon, stars, and storms. On Earth, spirits lived in hills, rivers, rocks, and seas. These spirits ruled the daily lives of people.

Good spirits made crops grow, kept sailors safe, and brought happiness. Harmful spirits might harm travelers at night or hide in a house, bringing bad luck. During festivals, people used loud sounds to frighten evil spirits away.

Honoring Ancestors The most important spirits to many ancient Chinese were those of their ancestors. They believed that family members lived on after death in the spirit world and remained part of the family. If family members took care of their ancestors, then the ancestors would protect and guide the living. Ancestor spirits who were not honored could cause people trouble.

Over the centuries, the Chinese developed many rituals to honor their ancestors. Families had shrines with tablets inscribed with ancestors' names. They set out food for their ancestors on special occasions to welcome them home. After paper money came into use, they burned fake "spirit" money to give the ancestors **income** in the afterlife. Practices of honoring the dead are often called ancestor veneration. Many rituals related to ancestor veneration are performed at holidays and funerals in China today.

Analyze Images According to Chinese tradition, the Kitchen God is a friendly spirit who lives in a family's kitchen. **Formulate Questions** What else do you want to know about the Kitchen God and the role of spirits in the lives of ancient Chinese? What questions could you ask to help you find out more?

✓ **READING CHECK Identify Central Ideas** Why was it important to the ancient Chinese to honor their ancestors?

Life and Teachings of Confucius

Confucianism, the teachings of the thinker Confucius, is one of the most important philosophies that developed in China. Confucius lived just before the Warring States period. He and later thinkers at the end of the Zhou dynasty looked for solutions to China's problems. Among these thinkers, Confucius had the greatest effect on Chinese culture. He is known as the "First Teacher" and is honored for his great wisdom.

Life of a Philosopher Confucius was born into a poor family in 551 BCE. He held several low-level government jobs that allowed him to see greed and cruelty. Officials often did not enforce the law. Some took bribes, or illegal payments, to do favors for the rich. Peasants starved while rulers taxed them to pay for wars.

Confucius believed that the cause of disorder was that the Chinese had turned away from the traditional roles and values of the early Zhou. Only a return to those ideals could bring order to China. Confucius made his life's work teaching the wise ways of the ancestors.

Academic Vocabulary
income *n.,* payments of money

Confucius started his own school. Students of Confucius collected his teachings and wisdom in a book called the *Analects.*

Though Confucius never achieved great wealth or influence in his lifetime, his students spread his teachings. In later centuries, the *Analects* became central to political and ethical thought across China and East Asia. Chinese students still memorize passages from it today.

What Were the Five Confucian Relationships? The heart of Confucianism lay in a vision of a **stable**, orderly society based on five relationships: (1) ruler and subject, (2) father and son, (3) husband and wife, (4) older and younger brothers, and (5) two friends.

Especially important was the relationship between father and son, or parents and their children. Elders care for and teach younger family members. In return, children respect and obey their elders. The devotion of children to their parents is called **filial piety**. Confucians referred to this as "the source of all virtues."

The relationship between parents and children was the model for the other four relationships. The person of higher status in each of the five relationships should respect the senior person. Confucius believed order and harmony would come to society once all people acted according to their roles.

Teaching by Example Confucius believed that the best way for a ruler to lead people was by setting a good example. He taught:

Primary Source

If they people are led by laws . . . they will try to avoid the punishment but have no sense of shame. If they are led by virtue . . . they will have the sense of shame and will become good.

—Confucius, *Analects*

Did you know?

Under Confucianism, women were instructed to play subordinate roles to fathers, husbands, and brothers. Despite this, some Chinese women produced Confucian literary works.

Analyze Charts Confucius stressed the importance of five basic relationships that shape behavior. Most relationships are between family members who are different ages or status. **Use Visual Information** According to Confucius, which is the only relationship that is between equals?

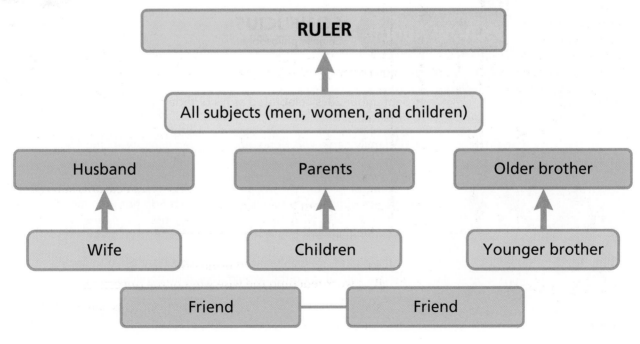

RULER

All subjects (men, women, and children)

| Husband | Parents | Older brother |

| Wife | Children | Younger brother |

Friend — Friend

Confucius believed that the chün-tzu, or "gentleman," must set the moral example for others by being kind and benevolent. He also stressed that traditional rituals and education supported social order.

✓ READING CHECK **Explain** What is the most important virtue in Confucianism?

Beliefs of Daoism

Another group of thinkers saw the disorder during the Zhou dynasty and responded differently. Their reaction led to the development of Daoism. Daoism is an ancient Chinese way of life that emphasizes a simple and natural existence. It is a philosophy of following the Dao (dow); that is, the natural way of the universe.

The Legend of Laozi According to legend, a man named Laozi (LOW dzuh) founded Daoism. Laozi is known as a sage, or wise person. He is said to have written down his beliefs in a book called the *Dao De Jing* (DOW deh jing).

Historians do not know whether Laozi actually lived. They believe that the *Dao De Jing* was probably written by many people. It is a small book, made up mostly of poems. People throughout the world still read the *Dao De Jing* for its wisdom.

Yin and Yang Daoism reflects ancient Chinese beliefs about the world such as the quiet order in the changing seasons and the violence of nature in floods and storms.

Daoists believed that two great forces called yin and yang were at work in nature. They are opposites. Yin is female, dark, cool, and quiet. Yang is male, bright, warm, and active. Chinese thinkers believed balance between yin and yang was key to harmony in the universe.

BIOGRAPHY
5 Things to Know About CONFUCIUS
Chinese philosopher

- Confucius was only three when his father died.

- September 28 is celebrated as his birthday. It is an official holiday in Taiwan.

- His family name was Kong, and his given name was Qui. The name Confucius is not a meaningful term in Chinese. It was coined in Europe around the eighteenth century.

- One of his most famous sayings is, "What I do not wish men to do to me, I also wish not to do to [other] men." Versions of this "Golden Rule" are found in many cultures.

- At the age of 56, Confucius left his home state of Lu to find another feudal state that would accept his services.

Critical Thinking Why do you think Confucius left Lu?

The Dao Daoists saw the Dao, which means "the way" or "the path," as the source of yin and yang. The Dao is mysterious and impossible to define clearly. However, Daoists felt people should try to understand the Dao. Often, they saw evidence of the Dao in natural things, like water:

Primary Source

There is nothing in the world more soft and weak than water, and yet for attacking things that are firm and strong, nothing is better than it . . .

—Laozi, *Dao De Jing*

Water, through patient effort over time, is even stronger than rock. By acting like water, people are following the Dao.

People can upset order with their actions. Order comes when people keep to a simple life, instead of competing for wealth and power. Daoists believed a good leader took little action, leaving people to live a simple life. Daoists were not concerned with the morals, rituals, and learning that the Confucians valued. Also unlike Confucians, Daoists believed in the possibility of life after death or even immortality.

Most Chinese thinkers studied and used ideas from both philosophies. Throughout Chinese history, Confucianism and Daoism influenced Chinese culture even as new ideas came from abroad.

☑ **READING CHECK** **Compare and Contrast** What is one difference between Confucianism and Daoism?

▲ This symbol represents yin and yang.

Quick Activity

Examine how the ideas of Confucius and Laozi from ancient China shape lives in your 📓 Active Journal.

☑ Lesson Check

Practice Vocabulary

1. What is a **philosophy**?

2. Use the term *filial piety* to describe the ideas of Confucius.

Critical Thinking

3. **Draw Conclusions** What role did ancestors play in ancient Chinese religion?

4. **Summarize** How would you summarize the main teachings of Confucius?

5. **Solve Problem** How did Confucianism and Daoism develop different solutions to the chaos of the Warring States period?

6. **Writing Workshop: Support Claims** Write a list in your 📓 Active Journal of beliefs that Confucius and Daoists had about what values help governments to lead effectively. Identify which values support your claim and which oppose it.

Confucius, *The Analects*

Confucius lived at a time of conflict and change. He developed a doctrine that he hoped leaders would adopt to restore harmony. Although leaders of his time refused to practice his ideas, Confucius became a revered teacher whose ideas have inspired followers for thousands of years.

◀ Statue of Confucius

Reading and Vocabulary Support

① *Virtue* means goodness, or the quality of being good to others.

② The word *propriety* means the proper way to behave.

③ How would you summarize the steps of the process of a "return to propriety" described by the Master?

④ To be deficient means to be in short supply of something.

⑤ Sacrifices are very important rituals. When Confucius says to treat others as if assisting at a great sacrifice, what do you think he means?

Yen Yuan asked about perfect <u>virtue</u> **①**.

The Master said, "To subdue one's self and return to <u>propriety</u> **②**, is perfect virtue. If a man can for one day subdue himself and return to propriety, all under heaven will ascribe perfect virtue to him. . . .

Yen Yuan said, "I beg to ask the steps of that process." The Master replied, "Look not at what is contrary to propriety; listen not to what is contrary to propriety; speak not what is contrary to propriety; make no movement which is contrary to propriety. **③** Yen Yuan then said, "Though I am <u>deficient</u> **④** in intelligence and vigor, I will make it my business to practice this lesson."

Chung-kung asked about perfect virtue. The Master said, "It is, when you go abroad, to behave to every one as if you were receiving a great guest; to employ the people as if you were <u>assisting at a great sacrifice</u> **⑤**; not to do to others as you would not wish done to yourself; to have no murmuring against you in the country, and none in the family. Chung-kung said, "Though I am deficient in intelligence and vigor, I will make it my business to practice this lesson."

—*The Analects of Confucius*

Analyzing Primary Sources

Cite specific evidence from the document to support your answers.

1. **Determine Author's Point of View** Confucius suggests that all under heaven would consider a person to have perfect virtue if he or she could master correct behavior for a full day. What does Confucius suggest about the difficulty of mastering this behavior?

2. **Infer** Do you think the students really consider themselves unintelligent and lacking in vigor, as they state in the passage? What do these words suggest about the Confucian attitude toward modesty?

3. If both the leaders and the citizens of a state were to adopt these behaviors, how could these principles lead to harmony among people?

Quest CONNECTIONS

Based on Confucius teaching of perfect virtue and propriety, does Shi Huangdi meet the standard of the right way to govern a state? Record your findings in your 📓 Active Journal.

The Unification of China

BOUNCE TO ACTIVATE   ▶ VIDEO

GET READY TO READ

START UP

Look closely at the photograph of the Great Wall, then preview the lesson. Write down several facts you already know about the Great Wall.

GUIDING QUESTIONS

- What steps did Shi Huangdi take to unite China?
- Why was Shi's centralized government so powerful?
- How did Legalist principles shape the Qin dynasty?

TAKE NOTES

Literacy Skills: Use Evidence

Use the graphic organizer in your 📖 Active Journal to take notes as you read the lesson.

PRACTICE VOCABULARY

Use the vocabulary activity in your 📖 Active Journal to practice the vocabulary words.

Vocabulary	Academic Vocabulary
Great Wall	uniform
standardize	collapse
Legalism	
censor	

The Warring States period came to an end when the kingdom of Qin (chin) unified China. King Zheng (jung) of Qin, who became the First Emperor, is remembered as a leader determined to build a great empire. Although his dynasty lost power soon after his death, later dynasties built upon his methods for ruling a large empire.

Unity Under the Qin

Qin was a mountainous kingdom located in northwestern China. Beyond Qin lay the foreign lands of Central Asia. The Qin rulers built a strong kingdom with an efficient government. By the late Zhou dynasty, Qin was the strongest kingdom in western China. Still, King Zheng, who came to power in 247 BCE, thirsted for more power.

How Were the Warring States United? Under King Zheng's leadership, Qin brought down rival kingdoms. In 221 BCE, Qin forces defeated their last enemy and united China, yet many challenges remained. Languages and customs varied.

[Handwritten annotations: "King Zheng was very influential and important", "most important part"]

(handwritten margin note: King Sheng wanted a lot of power & recognition.)

Rebellion was always a danger, as was invasion by nomads from north and west of China. The king needed to make the Chinese into one people ruled by one government.

Who Was the First Emperor? The Qin ruler decided that "king" was too small a title for the leader of such a vast empire. He thus declared himself to be Shi Huangdi, or "First Emperor." The word "Huangdi" was tied to the gods and rulers of China's past. Shi Huangdi unified China from the Yellow River to the Yangtzee River.

How Was the Empire Defended? Before the Qin unification, the many Chinese kingdoms built walls to protect themselves from other kingdoms. Shi Huangdi had these walls torn down to make rebellion more difficult. Without these walls, local leaders could not defend their territory and break away from Qin rule.

The First Emperor also began work on one of the largest public works projects in history—the **Great Wall**, a long wall running east and west along his empire's northern border to defend the empire from nomads living to the north.

> **INTERACTIVE**
>
> Terra Cotta Army of Shi Huangdi

(handwritten margin note: How did people die Buiding the Wall?)

(handwritten margin note: Shi Huandi did not stop building his empire. Very Wealthy Dynasty.)

The wall went up quickly. Already, there were shorter walls along the border. Workers connected these old walls together, making a huge stone barrier. Building the wall was hard and dangerous. Many died while working on the wall. These workers included the many prisoners and citizens Hangdi uprooted from their homes to work on various projects.

The Great Wall did not always keep nomads out. Determined invaders were able to get around it. Still, the emperors of dynasties that followed the Qin also relied on the wall as a way to protect their northern border. Later emperors made the wall stronger, adding towers in key locations along its length.

Uniform Standards Shi Huangdi knew he needed to standardize many aspects of daily life in order to unify China's economy and culture. To **standardize** is to set rules that make things more similar. Anyone who did not follow the standards was punished as a traitor.

Perhaps most importantly, the Qin government established a single written language with standard characters. These characters are the basis of the written language in China today.

(handwritten margin note, vertical: So many things were standardized)

Transportation was also standardized. The government established a standard length for the axles of all vehicles. As a result, all ruts made in Chinese roads by the wheels of carts would be the same width. This made travel between different areas easier. The Qin government also created a uniform set of weights and measures for use in trade. It made uniform coins to be used as currency across China.

▲ Shi Huangdi had workers build an enormous tomb filled with thousands of statues of soldiers, like the one above. He may have believed this terra cotta army would protect him in the afterlife.

SHI HUANGDI UNITES CHINA

CHINA'S 1ST EMPEROR wanted to bring all of China under his control. He sought to create order by **STANDARDIZING** many aspects of daily life.

The **banliang** became the single form of currency.

Rules specified how to write **characters** so that everyone could read them.

Weights and measures that merchants used were made standard.

The **space between wheels** was specified so all roads would have the same ruts.

The Great Wall around Qin lands helped define the empire.

How Was the Empire Organized? Shi Huangdi introduced the concept of centralization, or a central governing system. He organized China into 36 provinces. Each province was divided into counties. County leaders were responsible to the heads of provinces. Province heads reported to the central government which, in turn, reported to the emperor. The emperor dismissed any official who failed to carry out his policies.

To prevent rebellion, Shi Huangdi forced thousands of noble families to move to the capital. There, government spies could watch over them.

Analyze Charts The chart shows ways Shi Huangdi standardized certain aspects of Chinese life. **Generate Explanations** How do you think having the same currency and weights and measures helped to unify the empire?

long chain
Protection only over nobles

✔ **READING CHECK** Explain Why did Shi Huangdi call himself the First Emperor?

from what was said before, I didn't realize how cruel he was!

Rule of the First Emperor

Shi Huangdi is remembered as a cruel leader. He believed strict rules were necessary to end the chaos in China. The laws he created helped unite the empire, but his harsh rule was also one cause of the fall of the Qin dynasty. Although he built roads, dikes, and palaces, he forced tens of thousands of people to leave their homes to work on these projects.

A Legalist Government In the late Zhou, the Qin rulers brought in advisors from other kingdoms to help make Qin stronger. Shang Yang (shahng yahng) was one important advisor. He belonged to a school of thought called Legalism. According to **Legalism**, a strong leader and a strong legal system are needed to create social order. *Laws?*

Following Shang Yang's advice, the Qin kings took more direct control over the common people. Heavy taxes and required labor service increased the wealth of the Qin kings.

Quest CONNECTIONS

Why did Shi Huangdi make great efforts to standardize and centralize so many aspects of Chinese life? Record your findings in your 📖 Active Journal.

The kingdom became stronger and more orderly. Shi Huangdi set out to extend this Legalist government over the rest of China.

Harsh Laws Shi Huangdi was especially interested in the teachings of the Legalist Han Feizi (hahn FEY zuh). Han Feizi did not agree with Confucianism. Confucius and his followers believed people could be led by setting a good example. Han Feizi believed people must be forced to be good. This could be done by making and enforcing strict laws.

Shi Huangdi made a **uniform** legal code across his empire. Penalties for breaking a law were severe. A thief could face punishment as harsh as having the feet or nose cut off. A less serious theft might be punished by hard labor, such as helping to build roads and walls. Other punishments included execution by beheading or cutting the criminal in half. According to one account, the emperor had 460 scholars executed for disobeying an order. Han Feizi explained the reason for these harsh punishments:

Academic Vocabulary

uniform • *adj.*, unchanging; fixed

Just for stealing!?

Primary Source

Punish severely light crimes. People do not easily commit serious crimes. But light offenses [crimes] are easily abandoned by people. . . . Now, if small offenses do not arise, big crimes will not come. And thus people will commit no crimes and disorder will not arise.

—Han Feizi

He has a good point, but it's extremely harsh

Did you know?

Shi Huangdi appointed inspectors, who were actually more like spies, to check on local officials and tax collectors to make sure they were carrying out his laws.

Why would he do that?????

BIOGRAPHY
5 Things to Know About SHI HUANGDI
Chinese Emperor (259 BCE–210 BCE)

1. • Shi Huangdi was only 13 years old when he took the throne.

2. • He standardized Chinese writing and built much of the Great Wall of China.

3. • Later Confucian scholars condemned Shi Huangdi for his harsh rule and for burning Confucian texts.

4. • He was guarded in death by 6,000 life-sized terra cotta guards in a secret tomb.

5. • His empire fell less than four years after his death.

Draw Conclusions Why did Shi Huangdi's empire fall less than four years after his death? What does that tell you about the state of China at the time?

Thought Control The First Emperor also tried to control Chinese thought. He decided to **censor**, or ban, ideas he found dangerous or offensive. Censorship took many forms. Debate about the government was banned. People were not allowed to praise past rulers or criticize the present one. The emperor ordered the burning of all books that did not support his policies.

The Fall of the Qin Dynasty These policies were not popular, but they did help create a single nation from China's diverse regions. The First Emperor believed that his dynasty would last forever, but it **collapsed** about three years after his death.

The Qin Dynasty was undone by its unbending enforcement of its harsh laws. A rebellion was sparked by a soldier named Chen Sheng, who led a band of men north to guard China's border. Along the way, heavy rains delayed the band. Chen knew that the penalty for arriving late would be severe. So he and his men decided that they had nothing to lose by rebelling.

As news of Chen's uprising spread, thousands rose up to support him. Qin generals tried to put down the uprisings, but the rebellions spread rapidly. Knowing the punishments for failure, some generals joined the rebellions. The rebels joined together long enough to overthrow the Qin, but then began fighting amongst themselves. China again slid into chaos.

✓ READING CHECK Describe How did Shi Huangdi try to stop people from criticizing him?

Analyze Images Scholars who disobeyed Shi Huangdi were buried alive. He also had many books burned, but preserved those about agriculture and medicine. **Draw Conclusions** Why do you think these books were not burned?

Books are history, why do such a thing?

Academic Vocabulary
collapse • *v.*, to break down or fall down

✓ Lesson Check

Practice Vocabulary

1. Use the terms *standardize* and *censor* to describe how Shi Huangdi united his empire.

2. Why did Shi Huangdi build the **Great Wall**?

Critica Thinking and Writing

3. **Compare and Contrast** How is Legalism different from Confucianism?

4. **Analyze Cause and Effect** Why did Shi Huangdi create harsh laws?

5. **Identify Cause and Effect** What was one cause of the fall of the Qin dynasty?

6. **Writing Workshop: Use Credible Sources** Where can you find credible sources of information to support your argument? Research at a library and on reputable websites or use the primary and secondary sources in this book. Make sure to consider the point of view of each source and remain alert for bias. Take notes from your sources in your 📕 Active Journal.

Draw Sound Conclusions from Sources

Follow these steps to learn how to draw sound conclusions from sources.

INTERACTIVE

Draw Conclusions

1 **Study the facts and main ideas in a source.** This primary source came from the prime minister, Li Si to the Qin emperor, Shi Huangdi.

a. What seems to be the main idea of this passage?

b. What facts or evidence does the author include to support the main idea?

2 **Formulate questions about the source.** Asking questions about the source can help you uncover its purpose and meaning. For example, with this source you might ask, "What is Li Si proposing about books of poetry, history, and philosophy?" What is another question you could ask about the purpose or meaning of the source?

3 **Draw conclusions from the source.** This source provides some insight in the rule of Shi Huangdi and the methods he used. What can you conclude about Shi Huangdi based on this passage?

4 **Test any conclusions for soundness.** Ask, "Do the facts in the source support my conclusions?"

a. What have you learned about Shi Huangdi?

b. Does what you learned match the conclusions you have drawn from the source?

c. Do you need to adjust your conclusion based on what you learned?

Primary Source

I humbly propose that all historical records but those of Qin be burned. If anyone who is not a court scholar dares to keep the ancient poems, historical records, or writings of the hundred schools of philosophy, these books shall be confiscated and burned by the provincial governor and army commander. Those who in conversation dare to quote the old poems and records should be publicly executed; those who use old precedents to oppose the new order should have their families wiped out; and officers who know of such cases but fail to report them shall be punished in the same way. If thirty days after the issuing of this order, the owners of these books still have not destroyed them, they shall have their faces tattooed and be condemned to hard labor at the Great Wall. The only books which need not be destroyed are those dealing with medicine, divination, and agriculture.

— Sima Qian, *Records of the Grand Historian*

Quest CONNECTIONS

What does this excerpt from Sima Qian tell you about how Shi Huangdi faced challenges during his rule? Record your findings in your 📓 Active Journal.

LESSON 5
The Han Dynasty Expands

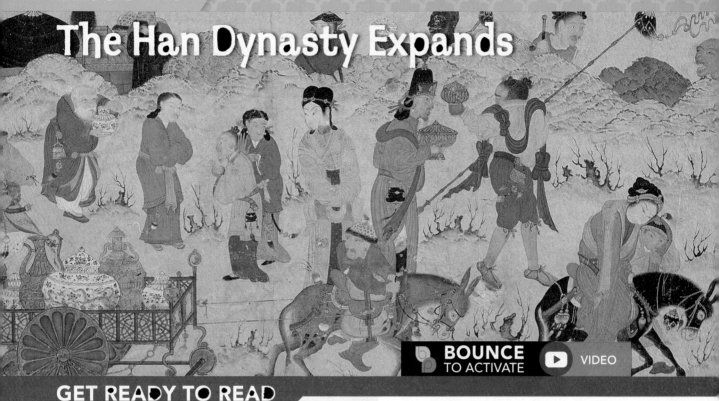

BOUNCE TO ACTIVATE ▶ VIDEO

GET READY TO READ

START UP
Look at the photograph of this scene along the Silk Road. Write down several facts you know or questions that you have about the Silk Road.

GUIDING QUESTIONS
- What social customs and government policies helped China unify under the Han?
- What role did Confucianism play in the development of the civil service?
- How did the Silk Road increase trade, the spread of Buddhism, and connections between China and other regions of Afroeurasia?

TAKE NOTES
Literacy Skills: Analyze Cause and Effect
Use the graphic organizer in your 📓 Active Journal to take notes as you read the lesson.

PRACTICE VOCABULARY
Use the vocabulary activity in your 📓 Active Journal to practice the vocabulary words.

Vocabulary		Academic Vocabulary
official	envoy	assigned
civil service	cuisine	obtained
Silk Road		

Besides founding China's first empire, Shi Huangdi also laid the foundation for a system of government to rule a large empire. The next dynasty was the Han. The Han emperors built on the successes of the Qin to create one of the most influential dynasties in Chinese history.

How Did the Han Govern China?
The fighting that toppled the Qin dynasty lasted for several years. Finally, a rebel general named Liu Bang (LYOH bahng) gained control of China. In 206 BCE, he founded the Han dynasty. The Han ruled China for about 400 years. Today, the largest ethnic group in China still call themselves the "Han." Later dynasties were established that were governed by Confucian principles using scholar-officials. Maintaining the philosophy laid out in the Mandate of Heaven was crucial to following Confucian principles.

Reuniting and Expanding China The first Han emperor came from a poor family. His success was, in part, due to his ability to surround himself with capable advisors.

As emperor, he consulted with a Confucian scholar who pointed out that the Qin lost power because of cruel policies. The emperor encouraged learning, lowered taxes, and ended many of the Qin's harsh rules.

Confucian scholars throughout the Han gave practical advice and encouraged rulers to set an example of mercy and proper behavior. Han emperors kept many of the Qin laws and policies to standardize Chinese life, but avoided the harsh rule that had caused unrest.

The Han not only stayed in power, they expanded China's territory. Much of this expansion took place under the fifth Han emperor, Wudi (woo dee). Remembered as one of the country's greatest emperors, Wudi ruled for more than 50 years. Wudi sent his armies west to conquer lands far into Central Asia. He extended his empire north to the Korean peninsula and south into what is now Vietnam.

Analyze Images Han Emperor Wudi rides in a chariot as he prepares to exit his walled palace. **Draw Conclusions** What can you infer about life in a Han palace, based on the picture? Cite evidence to support your conclusion.

Han was time to redeem & rebuild

Academic Vocabulary

assign • v., to give as a job or task

Han Government Han emperors followed the example of the Qin by creating a strong central government. In this way, they avoided the problem of disunity that the Zhou dynasty had faced. As the Zhou dynasty had expanded, local noblemen became more powerful than the Zhou king. The Han emperors tried to make sure that local leaders remained too weak to challenge their authority. When the Han emperors conquered new lands, they administered this land directly rather than giving it to a nobleman.

The Han government was organized like a pyramid. The broad base of the pyramid was made up of China's many towns and villages. At the top of the pyramid were the emperor and his chief advisors. Many layers of government lay between. At each level, **officials**, that is, people **assigned** to a position in the government, took orders from those above them and gave orders to those below them.

How Did Civil Service Strengthen the Han Government? The strength of the Han government lay in its civil service. A **civil service** is a system of government employees mainly selected for their skills and knowledge. In the first 200 years of Han rule, the civil service grew to more than 130,000 officials.

Positions in the civil service were not hereditary; that is, they were not passed down from father to son. Officials were appointed to their positions. Han emperors asked their officials to recommend people for the civil service. From those recommendations, the emperors selected officials from across the empire.

Emperor Wudi also created exams to find talented people for the civil service. These exams were based on the ideas of Confucius. In later dynasties, the exam system would become even more important for selecting officials.

Han officials enjoyed high salaries and a life of comfort and influence. They wore special clothes that indicated their rank. They collected taxes, organized labor, and enforced laws. They could even force people to move. If there were too many people in one area, officials could relocate them to lands with fewer people.

The Han emperors placed limits on the powers of officials. For example, officials were not allowed to serve in their home districts. This prevented them from organizing against the emperor with family and friends. The emperors knew that to rule successfully, they needed their officials' loyalty.

Decline of the Han At its height, the Han dynasty ruled some 60 million people. It ruled China for over 400 years. Then, like other powerful empires, it went into a decline. Once again, the central government weakened and warlords competed for power. China was plunged into disunity for several centuries. Still, the idea of a unified China never died. Future dynasties eventually emerged, modeling themselves on the Han.

✓ READING CHECK **Identify** Name one achievement of Wudi.

The Silk Road

One of the most lasting contributions of the Han dynasty was establishment of the Silk Road. The **Silk Road** is a network of trade routes that crossed Asia, connecting China to Central

🖑 INTERACTIVE

Ancient Chinese Dynasties

GEOGRAPHY **SKILLS**

The Silk Road stretched from China to the Mediterranean with trade routes by both land and sea.

1. **Movement** Name the locations of two different routes Chinese travelers could take to get to Rome.

2. **Use Visual Information** Based on the map, how do you think the growth of the Han dynasty was impacted by trade on the Silk Road?

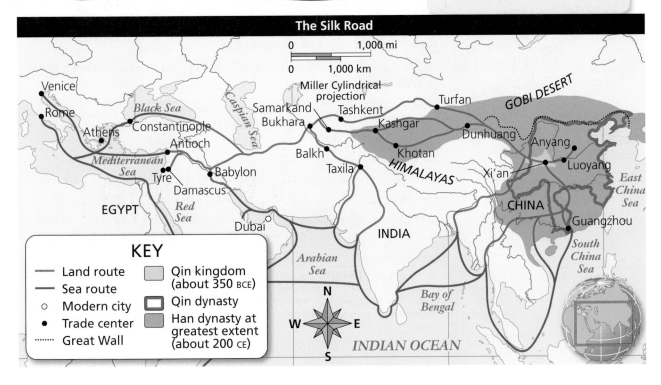

The Silk Road

KEY
— Land route
— Sea route
○ Modern city
● Trade center
⋯⋯ Great Wall

Qin kingdom (about 350 BCE)
Qin dynasty
Han dynasty at greatest extent (about 200 CE)

Lesson 5.5 • The Han Dynasty Expands **205**

Did you know?

The Silk Road was not a road. It was a network of many routes over land and water that connected Asia with Europe and Africa.

[handwritten note] Conquring lead to allys, made kingdoms stronger.

Analyze Diagrams More than just goods were exchanged along the Silk Road. **Recognize Multiple Causes** What are two reasons why you think ideas like religion and philosophy traveled in both directions along the Silk Road?

and Southwest Asia. Trade routes across Central Asia had existed before the Han, but during the reign of Wudi, contact between China and regions to the west increased. Merchants made their fortunes along the Silk Road, but it was also a path for the spread of ideas.

The Journey of Zhang Qian At first, the Chinese traveled to Central Asia not to trade, but to seek an ally in their fight against a fierce group of nomads, the Xiongnu (shong noo). Emperor Wudi heard of a people from Central Asia called the Yuezhi (yooeh jur) who were also enemies of the Xiongnu. Wudi hoped the Yuezhi would help fight the Xiongnu. He asked for a volunteer to find the Yuezhi. Zhang Qian (jahng chyen) stepped up to take on this challenge.

Zhang set out to the west. He was captured by the Xiongnu and held prisoner for ten years. He escaped and found the Yuezhi, but could not persuade them to ally with the Han against the Xiongnu.

Still, Wudi was interested in Zhang's account of his travels. Zhang described exotic lands where horses sweat blood and "the inhabitants ride elephants when they go into battle." Wudi and later Han emperors sent **envoys**, that is, representatives of the emperor, to create relations with kingdoms to the west. The Han also sent troops to the west. With the Han army protecting the region, trade flourished. Merchants could trade with less fear of being attacked by bandits.

A Major Trade Route The name "Silk Road" comes from China's most important export: silk. It is made from the cocoon of a caterpillar called the silk worm. It is strong, soft, and can be dyed many colors. Only the Chinese knew how to make silk. They guarded this secret closely. It was illegal to export silk worms. However, toward the end of the second century BCE, the Han Dynasty began to exchange

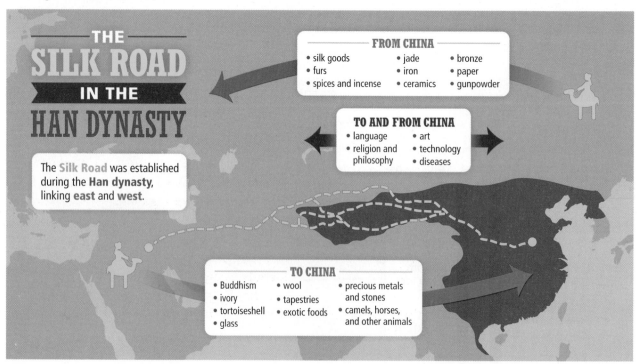

THE SILK ROAD IN THE HAN DYNASTY

The **Silk Road** was established during the **Han dynasty**, linking **east** and **west**.

FROM CHINA
- silk goods
- furs
- spices and incense
- jade
- iron
- ceramics
- bronze
- paper
- gunpowder

TO AND FROM CHINA
- language
- religion and philosophy
- art
- technology
- diseases

TO CHINA
- Buddhism
- ivory
- tortoiseshell
- glass
- wool
- tapestries
- exotic foods
- precious metals and stones
- camels, horses, and other animals

ambassadors with other Asian and African states. Chinese ambassadors and merchants gave gifts of silk cloth to Persia, Kush, and the Maurya empire of India. As a result, other central Asian states began to trade regularly with Chinese merchants.

The Chinese exchanged silk and other luxury goods for a wide range of products. The Chinese particularly valued the strong horses of central Asia. The Silk Road also enriched Chinese **cuisine**; that is, the style of cooking. Grapes, sesame, and onion were all brought into China along the Silk Road. The emperor also **obtained** rare animals, such as elephants, lions, and ostriches, from abroad. In addition to the Silk Road, Chinese merchants also traded along seas that ran along the coast of Asia from China to the Red Sea.

Exchanges of Ideas The Silk Road was a path for the exchange of ideas. Chinese inventions, such as paper, spread west along the Silk Road.

Foreign ideas, such as Buddhism, entered China during the Han along these trade routes. The religion of Buddhism started in India and spread into Central Asia. The Chinese, then, learned about this religion from Buddhists in Central Asia. Over time, Buddhism became very popular in China. After the Han, Chinese Buddhists traveled to India to study the religion. Chinese Buddhists also brought new ideas and practices to the religion.

Along with Confucianism and Daoism, Buddhism is one of the most influential belief systems in China. Chinese scholars mixed ideas from the three belief systems in their writings and art.

✔ READING CHECK **Identify Cause and Effect** How did the Silk Road benefit China?

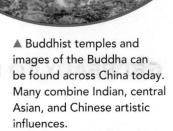

▲ Buddhist temples and images of the Buddha can be found across China today. Many combine Indian, central Asian, and Chinese artistic influences.

Academic Vocabulary
obtain • *v.*, to get or to receive something

✔ Lesson Check

Practice Vocabulary

1. Use the terms **official** and **civil service** to describe the government of the Han.

2. What was the **Silk Road**?

Critical Thinking and Writing

3. **Compare and Contrast** How was the Han dynasty similar to and different from the Qin dynasty?

4. **Classify and Categorize** How did Emperor Wudi organize the Han government to make it stronger?

5. **Understand Effects** How did the Silk Road lead to the spread of Buddhism into China?

6. **Writing Workshop: Shape Tone** Draft your argument in your 📕 Active Journal. Then evaluate your argument. Is your claim effectively presented in a clear and logical manner? Does the tone of your argument help you to make a strong argument? Identify places in your argument where you can use strong verbs and supporting evidence to more strongly make your point.

LESSON 6

Han Society and Achievements

BOUNCE TO ACTIVATE ▶ VIDEO

GET READY TO READ

START UP

Many modern Chinese ideas, such as garden design, were influenced by Han ideas. What does this picture of a Chinese garden tell you about how the Chinese came to value the natural world?

GUIDING QUESTIONS

- How did Confucian teachings about relationships shape Han society?
- Why was China's economy strong under the Han?
- What were the major achievements of Han China in the arts, science, and technology?

TAKE NOTES

Literacy Skills: Summarize

Use the graphic organizer in your 📗 Active Journal to take notes as you read the lesson.

PRACTICE VOCABULARY

Use the vocabulary activity in your 📗 Active Journal to practice the vocabulary words.

Vocabulary		Academic Vocabulary
monopoly	acupuncture	exempt
calligraphy	seismometer	benefit
lacquer		

The Han dynasty was a time of innovation and economic development. The production of many goods increased and trade flourished. More people worked as craftsmen and merchants. Many important inventions also date to this dynasty.

Han Society

Han China was a mixture of peoples and cultures, but the country became more unified during this dynasty. Han emperors continued many of the Qin policies that standardized life in China, such as using a common currency. Shared values also bound the people together.

The Social Order China's social order was based on Confucian values. Confucius and his followers valued mental work more than physical labor. Scholars, therefore, were highly respected. Farmers were also highly respected because they produced the most important and basic goods: food and cloth. Artisans were valued for their skill and hard work.

Confucius and many other early Chinese thinkers had little respect for merchants because merchants do not produce anything. As a result, merchants fell lower in the social order. The government placed restrictions on merchants. They were not allowed to wear fine clothing or own land. Their children could not become officials. Still, many merchants became wealthy and powerful. They lived comfortable lives despite the lack of respect for trade.

At the bottom of the social order were a small number of slaves. When someone committed a serious crime, family members might be punished with slavery. Other people were sold into slavery when their families fell deep into debt.

Family Life Confucian teachings about family loyalty and respect for elders were key values. During the Han, ancestor worship continued. People made offerings to show respect and gain support from their ancestors.

Also, the Han legal code enforced Confucian values. Parents could report children who did not behave with filial piety. Adult children would be punished harshly. Younger children, though, were usually **exempt** from punishment.

The Role of Women The status of women was generally lower than that of men. Most worked in the home, weaving and caring for their children and elderly family members.

One exceptional woman was Ban Zhao (bahn jow). Unlike most Han women, she received a good education. Ban became a historian in the royal court. She wrote that young women deserved an education, yet she also accepted the higher status of men in society.

Primary Source

If a wife does not serve her husband, then the proper relationship between men and women . . . [is] neglected and destroyed.

—Ban Zhao, *Lessons for Women*

✓ READING CHECK **Cite Evidence** What evidence supports the generalization that merchants held a low place in Chinese society?

Academic Vocabulary
exempt • *adj.*, to be free from a punishment or duty

Analyze Images This image recreates what a pottery workshop may have looked like at the time of the Han. **Synthesize Visual Information** What can you tell about the work and lives of Han artisans from this picture?

Economic Life

China under the Han was peaceful compared to the chaotic Warring States period. The Han emperors lowered the high taxes that Shi Huangdi had collected. China prospered in this more stable time.

Agriculture Farmers were the backbone of China's economy. They made up about 90 percent of the population. As one Han emperor said,

Primary Source ~~Crops were~~

Agriculture is the foundation of the world. No duty is greater. *important*

—Emperor Wen, *Hanshu*

Most farms in Han China were small. Farmers grew wheat, millet, barley, beans, and rice. Farmers with more land might also grow fruit or bamboo. Farming families often made their own cloth.

Analyze Images
This image shows a method of ancient Chinese silk production. **Synthesize Visual Information** What does this image tell you about how ancient Chinese silk was produced and who produced it?

Silk production was especially important as trade along the Silk Road increased. On small farms, the women of the family tended silkworms and wove silk. In wealthy households, the women hired workers to help make silk. Workshops in cities also employed many weavers. Workshops bought silk thread from farms. They specialized in making the most expensive, high-quality cloth.

Industry Industries, such as iron production, also became important. Iron was useful for making tools and weapons. Salt mining was another key industry.

These industries became so important that one Han emperor, Wudi, turned them into state monopolies. A **monopoly** is when a single group controls the production of a good or service.

The monopolies brought in money. Profits from selling iron and salt helped support Wudi's military adventures.

Controlling Production and Prices Wudi's monopoly was also a way to try to keep important producers and merchants from becoming too powerful. Some producers of salt and iron had become very wealthy. They bought huge areas of land and employed large numbers of people. The Han emperors worried that these producers could become so influential that they could challenge the emperor's power. The emperors also worried that too many farmers were leaving their fields to work for these producers. Without enough farmers, China might face food shortages.

Had to control others power

🖐 **INTERACTIVE**

Silkmaking in Ancient China

The Han emperors also made policies to try to control prices. For example, in years when crops were good, the government bought up the extra grain. In years when the harvest was bad, the grain harvest decreased and grain became expensive. The government then sold back the stored grain to keep prices lower and avoid a shortage.

Despite the **benefits** of these policies, there were many problems. Some officials tried to make money by selling stored goods at high prices. Also, there were complaints that iron tools produced by the government monopoly were poor quality. Many emperors after Wudi either changed or gave up these policies.

☑️ **READING CHECK** **Explain** Why did Wudi take control of the iron and salt industries?

Han Achievements

The prosperity of Han China helped support many cultural achievements. Artists, writers, and musicians created works of beauty. Scientists and inventors also made important advances.

China's Traditional Arts The traditional arts of China include painting, sculpture, and poetry. Han artists painted colorful murals. Sculptors created beautiful works in stone, clay, and bronze. Poets wrote about the Chinese countryside.

Because Confucius believed that music was good for the spirit, Han rulers created an official Bureau of Music. Musicians played drums, bells, flutes, and harps. Music and dancing were common at public festivals and ceremonies.

Two other traditional arts were garden design and **calligraphy**, the art of beautiful writing. Calligraphers expressed emotions in the way they wrote Chinese characters. Garden designers carefully arranged plants, rocks, and water to resemble scenes in nature.

Perhaps the greatest craft of the Han period was lacquerware. **Lacquer** is a protective coating made from the sap of a special tree. Han artists brushed it on wood or metal objects to create a hard finish. The process required many layers of lacquer and many hours of work. When color was added, the lacquerware seemed to glow.

Advances in Science Han China is also known for scientific advances. Astronomers studied the sky and made precise calculations of the length of the solar year.

Academic Vocabulary
benefit • *n.*, something good or helpful

life depend on the harvest

Analyze Images This example of Han dynasty lacquerware is a vessel painted with a cloud design. **Infer** Based on the detail and design, what can you infer about the skill Chinese artisans must have needed in order to create such a piece?

Analyze Images In this seismometer, earthquake tremors cause a pendulum to open the jaw of the dragon, which drops a ball into the mouth of the toad below. **Generate Explanations** Why must it have been important to the early Chinese people to detect and measure earthquakes?

Paper was good, 2 Suprised it wasn't popular

Han doctors made progress in medicine. They studied ancient texts on medicine and developed new theories to explain and treat illness. Herbal medicines were one important treatment. Another was **acupuncture**, a therapy that uses needles to cure sickness and stop pain.

Chinese Inventions Han inventors produced important new tools. One was the **seismometer**, a tool to detect earthquakes. The seismometer was a metal jar that dropped small balls when a tremor from an earthquake was felt.

Another invention was the wheelbarrow. This human-powered cart appeared in China about 100 BCE. It was so useful for moving heavy loads that it was called the "wooden ox."

Perhaps the most important innovation of the Han was paper. Early paper was made from rags and bark. Paper was probably not widely used at first. Documents continued to be written on more durable wood and silk. In later dynasties, printing on paper became a way to make cheap books. More people could afford books, and new ideas spread quickly.

☑ **READING CHECK** **Make Connections** What kinds of workers might have found the wheelbarrow useful?

☑ Lesson Check

Practice Vocabulary

1. What is a **monopoly**?

2. Use the terms *acupuncture* and *seismometer* to describe the achievements of the Han dynasty.

Critical Thinking and Writing

3. **Understand Effects** How did Confucian beliefs affect the structure of Han society?

4. **Identify Cause and Effect** How do you think the relative peacefulness of the Han era is related to its successful economy?

5. **Identify Implied Main Ideas** What do the achievements of Han society say about its success as a dynasty?

6. **Writing Workshop: Write a Conclusion** Write a concluding sentence in your 📓 Active Journal. Your conclusion should restate your claim about what values a government needs to successfully lead.

Identify Sources of Continuity

Follow these steps to learn to identify the sources of continuity in a society.

INTERACTIVE

Develop Cultural Awareness

1 **Gather information about the society.** Look at a variety of resources to learn about life in the society that you are studying. Examine the primary and secondary sources below. What is the subject of these sources?

2 **Identify possible sources of continuity in the society.** Look for information about the society's government, values, family life, economy, religion, philosophy, language, and culture.

a. What do the sources below have to say about Chinese family life?

b. What else do the sources say about Chinese values?

3 **Determine which sources of continuity are important in the society.** Think about what these sources are saying about the treatment of parents, elders, and people of authority. What sources of continuity do you observe? You may want to take notes about each one.

4 **Summarize what you discover.** Use the information you have learned to make a general statement. What are the sources of continuity in Chinese society?

Primary Source

"They are few who, being filial and fraternal [devoted to their parents], are fond of offending against their superiors. There have been none, who, not liking to offend against their superiors, have been fond of stirring up confusion."

— *The Analects of Confucius*

Secondary Source

This passage from the Analects of Confucius reflects a key aspect of the great philosopher's system. It helps explain why even today Chinese children grow up with a deep respect for authority starting with their relationship with parents, then teachers, and later with employers and government officials. While in many countries students are encouraged to debate ideas with their teachers, in China it is dishonorable to disagree with a teacher. In fact, the Chinese word for teacher, *laoshi,* meaning "old master," conveys the deep respect people have for their teachers. Elderly people in China are esteemed, too. A person's 60th birthday is one of the most festive celebrations of a person's life.

☑ Review and Assessment

VISUAL REVIEW

Early Chinese Dynasties

Zhou Dynasty	Qin Dynasty	Han Dynasty
• Ruled by "Mandate of Heaven" • Expanded lands under Zhou control • Developed iron tools and weapons, irrigation and fertilizer, and system of roads	• First emperor Shi Huangdi– unified China • Established uniform standards for all China • Ruled with brutal control of thought, behavior • Rejected Confucianism in favor of Legalism	• Expanded Chinese territory • Organized government based on Confucian ideals, strengthened civil service • Started the Silk Road

Development of Government in China

The Shang	The Zhou
Established family control over government, with power passed from brother to brother, then to oldest son	Claimed "Mandate of Heaven" to rule, which required rulers to act in a virtuous way

Warring States period	Shi Huangdi and the Qin	The Han
Warlords fought for power in a declining Zhou dynasty	Used Legalism to control a vast empire	Established a vast civil service based on Confucian ideas to aid in government

READING REVIEW

Use the Take Notes and Practice Vocabulary activities in your 📔 Active Journal to help you to review the topic.

INTERACTIVE

Practice vocabulary using the Topic Mini-Games.

Quest FINDINGS

Get help for writing Shi Huangdi's obituary in your 📔 Active Journal.

ASSESSMENT

Vocabulary and Key Ideas

1. **Discuss** According to Chinese beliefs, how did rulers have to act in order to keep the **Mandate of Heaven?**

2. **Explain** When was the Warring States period and what happened during this time?

3. **Recall** What problems did Confucius address in Chinese society?

4. **Summarize** What are the basic ideas of Daoism?

5. **Explain** Why did Shi Huangdi's harsh rules lead to the fall of the Qin dynasty?

6. **Describe** Describe the civil service created during the Han dynasty.

7. **Recall** Why is Wudi considered a great ruler?

8. **Summarize** How did the Chinese begin trading along the **Silk Road?**

Critical Thinking and Writing

9. **Identify Cause and Effect** What is one political effect of the geography of China?

10. **Core Concepts: Citizenship** Confucius compares the role of the king to the role of a father. Do you agree that the role of a leader is similar to a parent? Explain why or why not?

11. **Analyze Cause and Effects** What effect did Shi Huangdi's policies have on the culture and government of China?

12. **Compare Viewpoints** Why might a Confucian scholar and a Legalist scholar have different viewpoints about censorship?

13. **Revisit the Essential Question** What were some of the different ways Chinese rulers maintained order in ancient China?

14. **Writing Workshop: Write an Argument** Using the notes and draft in your 📕 Active Journal, write an argumentative essay on the following topic: Which ancient Chinese values or belief system helped produce the most effective government in ancient China?

Analyze Primary Sources

15. According to the source below, what does wisdom result in?
    A. unhappiness
    B. harmonious relationships
    C. remedies
    D. simple happiness

    "Forget about knowledge and wisdom, and people will be a hundred times better off.

    Throw away charity and righteousness, and people will return to brotherly love. Throw away profit and greed, and there won't be any more thieves. Renounce knowledge and your problems will end."

    —Dao De Jing

Analyze Maps

Use the map at right to answer the following questions.

16. What does the red line represent?

17. What rivers did the Zhou civilization form around?

18. What geographic feature lay to the north of the Zhou civilization?

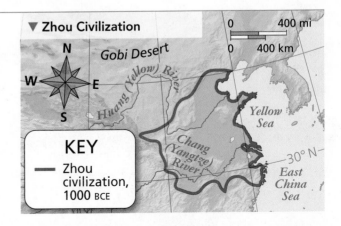

▼ Zhou Civilization

KEY
— Zhou civilization, 1000 BCE

Ancient Greece
(2000 BCE–300 BCE)

GO ONLINE
to access your
digital course

▶ VIDEO

◀)) AUDIO

📖 ETEXT

👆 INTERACTIVE

✍ WRITING

🎮 GAMES

📄 WORKSHEET

☑ ASSESSMENT

Go back over 2,600 years

to a high point of **ANCIENT GREECE'S CIVILIZATION.** Why go there? To see the birth of democracy! Greece's great thinkers influenced generations, from the Roman republic up to today.

Explore
The Essential Question

What is the best form of government?

Ancient Greece was not one nation, but a collection of city-states, ruled by different forms of government. How did the leaders of these governments mold Greece into one of the world's greatest civilizations?

Unlock the Essential Question in your 📙 Active Journal.

Read

about the culture, science, and various forms of government that made ancient Greece the birthplace of Western civilization.

Watch

NBC LEARN

BOUNCE TO ACTIVATE   ▶ VIDEO

Pericles, the Golden Age of Athens

Learn how Pericles ruled over the Golden Age of Athens.

▲ The Acropolis of Athens, Greece

Ancient Greece
(2000 BCE–300 BCE)

Learn more about the development of ancient Greece by making your own map and timeline in your  Active Journal.

INTERACTIVE

Topic Map

Where was ancient Greece?

Ancient Greece was centered on the Balkan Peninsula in the Mediterranean Sea in Europe.

INTERACTIVE

Topic Timeline

What happened and when?

Epic battles...thinkers with immortal ideas... Explore the timeline to see some of what was happening in ancient Greece and in the rest of the world.

508 BCE Democracy develops in Athens.

750 BCE New city-states appear in Greece.

TOPIC EVENTS

800 BCE	700 BCE	600 BCE

WORLD EVENTS

650 BCE Ironworking begins in China.

525 BCE Persia conquers Egypt.

Pericles, the great Athenian statesman

Socrates, the ancient philosopher

Hypatia, a Hellenistic mathematician, philosopher, and astronomer

Who will you meet?

490 BCE
Battle of Marathon is fought.

431 BCE
Peloponnesian War begins.

399 BCE
Socrates is sentenced to death.

334 BCE
Alexander the Great invades Asia.

| **500 BCE** | **400 BCE** | **300 BCE** | **200 BCE** |

500 BCE
Hinduism develops.

400 BCE
Buddhism begins to spread.

Quest
Project-Based Learning Inquiry

The Influence of Ancient Greece

Quest KICK OFF

It's the year 30 BCE, and the golden age of ancient Greece is drawing to a close, leaving behind a rich, living legacy of ideas. Your quest, as part of a team, is to create a television news magazine about ancient Greece based on the question:

Why has ancient Greece's culture endured?

How did one of the forms of government developed in ancient Greece leave a lasting legacy? Explore the Essential Question "What is the best form of government?" in this Quest.

▶ Athena, the Greek goddess of wisdom and war

1 Ask Questions

First, you'll need to research the five story segments that will combine to form your news magazine. Begin by making a list of the questions you need to answer in your news magazine. Write these questions in your ▤ Active Journal.

2 Investigate

As you read the lessons in the Topic, look for **Quest CONNECTIONS** that show how ancient Greece still influences life today in government and politics. Record notes in your ▤ Active Journal.

3 Conduct Research

Next, begin researching aspects of ancient Greece, using print and online sources. Capture notes in your ▤ Active Journal.

Quest FINDINGS

4 Create Your News Magazine

Next, work with your team to fully research, write, and produce the news magazine, either recorded or performed live for your class. Each team member will research and write one segment. Get help for this task in your ▤ Active Journal.

The Early Years of Greek Civilization

▶ VIDEO

GET READY TO READ

START UP

The photograph shows part of the coastline of Greece. What challenges might people living here face?

GUIDING QUESTIONS

- How did physical geography help shape the development of Greek societies?
- How did the Minoans and Mycenaeans influence Greek culture?
- How did city-states develop, and how did they interact with one another?

TAKE NOTES

Literacy Skills: Analyze Cause and Effect
Use the graphic organizer in your 📓 Active Journal to take notes as you read the lesson.

PRACTICE VOCABULARY

Use the vocabulary activity in your 📓 Active Journal to practice the vocabulary words.

Vocabulary		Academic Vocabulary
polis	politics	eventual
citizen	aristocracy	exclude
acropolis		

[handwritten annotation: Surrounded by a LOT of water.]

The ancient Greek world was spread across the coasts and islands of the Mediterranean Sea. Greeks interacted with older societies in Mesopotamia and Egypt and built on the accomplishments of those civilizations. At the same time, the Greeks developed their own unique ways of living. The Greeks made contributions to art, drama, philosophy, and political science. Greek culture helped form Western civilization—the civilization of Europe and the Americas. The Greeks gave us words and concepts such as *democracy, geometry,* and *politics.* How did the Greeks come to have so much influence on our world?

[handwritten annotation: many helpful contributions]

[handwritten annotation: main idea/ topic]

How Did Geography Shape the Greek World?

In ancient times, there was no country called Greece. Instead, there were communities of Greek speakers scattered across the islands and coasts of the Mediterranean Sea. This early Greek world lay on the fringe of two continents—Europe and Asia. Travelers and traders passed through the region exchanging goods, ideas, and customs.

[handwritten annotation: trade = expansion = super important]

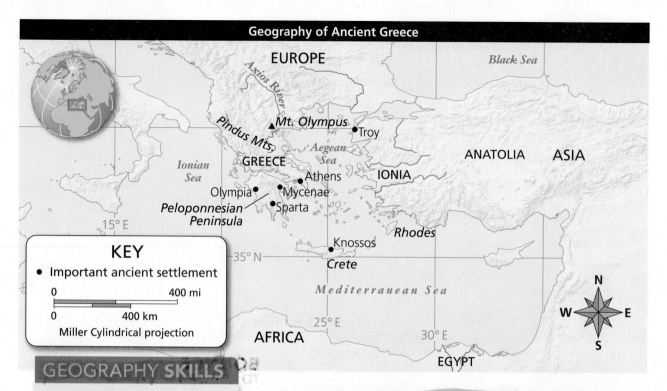

Geography of Ancient Greece

EUROPE

Black Sea

Axios River

Pindus Mts.

▲ Mt. Olympus

Troy

Aegean Sea

ANATOLIA   ASIA

Ionian Sea

GREECE

Athens

IONIA

Olympia

Mycenae

Sparta

Peloponnesian Peninsula

Rhodes

15° E

Knossos

35° N

Crete

Mediterranean Sea

25° E

30° E

N
W   E
S

AFRICA

EGYPT

KEY

• Important ancient settlement

0 ———————— 400 mi
0 ———————— 400 km
Miller Cylindrical projection

GEOGRAPHY SKILLS

Ancient Greek civilization developed among the islands clustered around the Aegean, Mediterranean, and Ionian Seas.

1. **Location** What continents lie to the east and south of Greece?

2. **Analyze Cause and Effect** What effect did Greece's location near so many seas have on the Greek way of life? What information in the text does the appearance of Greece's islands support?

Small amount of crops, means scarce food source.

Where is Greece? Modern Greece occupies a large peninsula that juts into the Mediterranean Sea. A peninsula is a land area surrounded by water on three sides. A number of other peninsulas also extend from the peninsula of mainland Greece. The largest of them, in southern Greece, is called the Peloponnesian (pel uh puh NEE shun) Peninsula.

About 2000 BCE, Greek-speaking peoples entered these lands from the north. They settled on mainland Greece. A mainland is an area of land that is part of a continent. Greek speakers also settled on the islands of the Aegean (ee JEE un) Sea.

Mainland Greece is divided by mountain ranges. Between these ranges lie narrow valleys and small plains. The mountains were good for grazing sheep and goats, but they were too steep and rocky for farming. Less than one quarter of the land could be used to grow crops. The only fertile land was in the lowland valleys and plains. Here people settled in farming communities.

The mountains isolated these lowland communities, so a fiercely independent spirit developed among the Greeks. They never attempted to unite under a single government. In fact, Greek cities were often at war with one another.

Surrounded by the Sea Although mountain ranges isolated communities, the sea brought contact with the wider world. The Greeks became skillful sailors and merchants. Greek fishing and trading ships crisscrossed the waters of the Mediterranean Sea to the south, the Aegean Sea to the east, and the Ionian (eye OH nee un) Sea to the west. This led to contact with the older, more complex cultures of North Africa and Asia.

A Mediterranean Climate Greece has a Mediterranean climate, with mild, wet winters and hot, dry summers. The lack of rain made it difficult to grow shallow-rooted crops such as grains, which need frequent watering. So the mainland Greeks were always searching for foreign sources of grain. On the other hand, the Mediterranean climate was ideal for growing deep-rooted plants such as olive trees and grape vines. Olive oil and wine became important trade goods and brought in wealth.

growing crops was very hard given the many obstacles.

☑ **READING CHECK** **Identify Cause and Effect** How did physical geography shape Greek culture?

Who Influenced the Early Greeks?

The early Greeks were influenced by an early civilization—the Minoans. Minoan culture developed on Crete, an island south of mainland Greece. It spread across the Aegean islands and influenced mainland Greece around 2000 BCE.

Trade flourished over seas.

The Minoans Minoan civilization was highly advanced. The Minoans had a writing system and built huge stone palaces with running water, like the one at Knossos (NAH sus). They traded goods throughout the Mediterranean. Around 1450 BCE, Minoan palaces and towns were mysteriously destroyed. Most historians believe that mainland Greeks were responsible.

The Mycenaeans The Minoans influenced a civilization that developed among Greek speakers on mainland Greece. This civilization, known as Mycena (my suh NEE uh), developed around 1600 BCE. Each Mycenaean town was governed by a monarchy, a government headed by a king. Mycenaean rulers lived in stone fortresses on hilltops overlooking their towns.

The Mycenaeans made fine bronze weapons and pottery. They traded these goods for copper, ivory, and luxury goods from other lands. Mycenaeans sometimes raided other peoples and one another for gold and other goods.

Eventually, the Mycenaean kingdoms grew weak. Then, around 1100 BCE, this civilization was destroyed by newcomers from the north known as Dorians.

The Dark Age With the fall of the Mycenaeans, Greek culture declined. People lost the ability to read and write. The following period, which lasted roughly from 1100 to 750, has been called a dark age. During these centuries, mainland Greeks migrated across the Aegean, settling the islands and the west coast of Anatolia, an area that became known as Ionia (eye OH nee a).

Analyze Images Ruins from a Minoan palace at Knossos still stand. **Identify Supporting Details** What is impressive about this palace?

Analyze Images Trojans celebrate the gift of the wooden horse in this scene from a recent movie. **Draw Conclusions** What about the story of the Trojan horse do you think interests audiences so many years later?

Academic Vocabulary
eventual • *adj.,* final

Greeks were smart (horse)

The Greeks in Ionia brought their culture with them through several waves of migration. They never forgot the "heroic age" of the Mycenaeans. They told stories and sang songs of the world that existed before the dark age. One of these stories was about the Trojan War.

☑ **READING CHECK** Identify Supporting Details How were the Minoans and Mycenaeans advanced cultures?

The Trojan War

In the legend of the Trojan War, warriors from Mycenaean kingdoms sailed across the Aegean to attack Troy, a city in Anatolia, also called Asia Minor (now the country of Turkey). The ten-year-long conflict ended when the Greeks tricked the Trojans into accepting a "gift" of a large wooden horse. Greeks hiding in the horse crept out and opened the city gates. The Greek army entered and burned Troy to the ground.

For centuries, the stories of the Trojan War were recited or sung, as the Greeks could no longer read or write. Then, in the 700s, the Greeks developed an alphabet based on the Phoenician alphabet. According to tradition, a poet named Homer shaped the stories of the Trojan War into a long epic poem, the *Iliad.* The poem was eventually written down.

The *Iliad* tells of events during the war, but stops before the Greeks' **eventual** victory. Homer's *Odyssey* is another epic poem, which describes the adventures of the hero Odysseus on his journey home after the war. Both the *Iliad* and the *Odyssey* imagined a Mycenaean world of fearless warriors.

The *Iliad* and the *Odyssey* shaped Greek culture. Students learned the verses by heart. The values expressed in these poems became part of Greek identity, including bravery, strength, and honor. In the *Iliad,* the warrior Achilles speaks to his troops before battle:

Primary Source

"Every man make up his mind to fight And move on his enemy! Strong as I am, It's hard for me to face so many men And fight with all at once. . . . And yet I will!"

—Homer, the *Iliad*

The ancient Greeks tried to live up to the ideals of the poems' warriors, who sought glory through courageous feats.

☑ **READING CHECK** Identify Supporting Details How did Homer preserve the memory of Mycenaean civilization?

👆 **INTERACTIVE**

The Journey of Odysseus

Emergence of City-States

By the time Homer's epics were composed, each Greek community had begun to organize itself into a **polis**, or city-state. The city-state became one of the most important features of Greek culture. The Greeks created such city-states everywhere they settled, mostly along the coast.

Geography played an important role in the emergence of the city-state. Greek cities were cut off from one another by mountains and water. The remoteness of these cities did not allow for a huge empire to be grow as in Egypt or Persia. Instead, the cities flourished on their own, each establishing its own system of commerce, government, and culture. The seas allowed city-states to trade their unique products with one another and the outside world.

What was the Polis? A polis was more than just a city. It was a community with its own government. The government of a polis ruled a wide area that included not only the city but its surrounding villages and countryside as well.

Each Greek city-state usually had a marketplace and government center. Here members of the city-state who had legal rights—the **citizens**—would meet to make laws and discuss issues affecting the entire community.

The area and population of a polis were generally small. All the citizens of the polis could gather to make decisions as a single group.

The Acropolis: "The High City" A typical polis was usually built on two levels. On a high hill stood the **acropolis** (uh KRAH puh lis), a word meaning "high city." Public buildings and marble temples were located in this area. The acropolis also served as a fortress in times of danger. On lower ground, below the hill, lay people's homes, shops, and farms. In Athens, the lower city included the agora, or marketplace. There people gathered to discuss public affairs.

Analyze Images The ruins of the Parthenon, an ancient temple, sit on the acropolis of Athens, high above the modern city. **Use Visual Information** How does this view of Athens help you understand the idea of an acropolis?

▲ Bronze discs used in Athens for voting

Polis was very important (handwritten note)

Academic Vocabulary

exclude • *v.*, to shut out, keep from participating

Politics in the Polis The word *polis* gave rise to the term **politics**, the art and practice of government. Each city-state had a different kind of government. Some city-states were monarchies, ruled by a king. In early times the polis was governed by an **aristocracy**, a hereditary class of rulers. Aristocracy meant "rule by the best people."

But in some city-states an extraordinary thing happened—the citizens began governing themselves. Rule by citizens made such Greek city-states unique. By contrast, in most of the world, priests and kings held all the political power.

Even though self-government was a feature of most city-states, not everyone was allowed to participate in making decisions. Women, slaves, and foreigners were all **excluded** from the process. The polis had three kinds of inhabitants: citizens (who could vote), women and free foreigners (who could not vote), and slaves, who had few rights at all.

"The Framework of Greek Life" Citizens felt strong pride and loyalty toward their polis. Greeks believed that a good citizen should always be willing to sacrifice for his city. He should be prepared to die for his polis, if necessary.

As one historian wrote, "The polis was the framework of Greek life." Greeks identified with their city. If their polis was a success, so were they. Throughout the history of ancient Greece, the polis played a key role in Greek life.

✓ **READING CHECK** **Identify Supporting Details** Why was a Greek person's polis important to his or her identity?

✓ Lesson Check

Practice Vocabulary

1. How did **citizens** take part in the running of their **polis**?

2. What role did the **aristocracy** play in **politics**?

Critical Thinking and Writing

3. **Synthesize** What changes took place in the Greek world during the dark age?

4. **Compare and Contrast** Compare the advantages and disadvantages of Greece's physical geography for settlers.

5. **Writing Workshop: Consider Your Purpose** You will write an explanatory essay exploring why independent Greek city-states rose, peaked, and ultimately, fell. Who is your audience for this essay? How will that affect how you write it? Consult your 📓 Active Journal for help.

Democracy in Athens

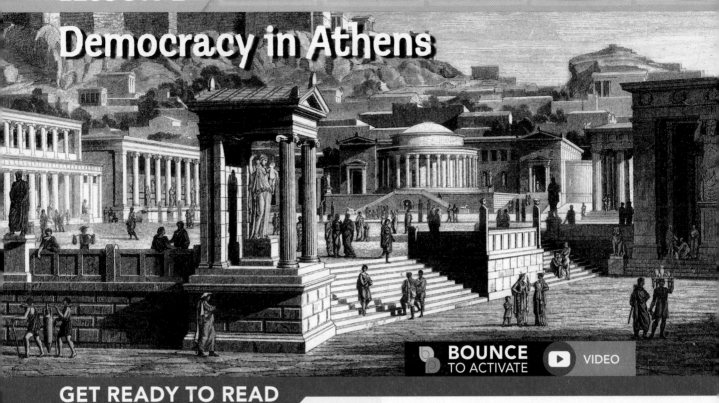

BOUNCE TO ACTIVATE ▶ VIDEO

GET READY TO READ

START UP

Look at the picture of the agora in Athens, the open marketplace where people could gather. How do meeting places like this help new ideas develop and grow?

GUIDING QUESTIONS

- What political forms did Greek city-states experiment with?
- How did Athenian democracy work?
- What were the benefits and limitations of the democracy practiced in Athens?

TAKE NOTES

Literacy Skills: Summarize

Use the graphic organizer in your 📖 Active Journal to take notes as you read the lesson.

PRACTICE VOCABULARY

Use the vocabulary activity in your 📖 Active Journal to practice the vocabulary words.

Vocabulary

oligarchy citizenship

phalanx direct democracy

tyranny representative

democracy democracy

Academic Vocabulary

maintain

lecturer

One night in 508 BCE, the sounds of a power struggle echoed through the streets of Athens. Isagoras, the city's leading judge, was trying to crush a movement for democracy. He had invited warriors from the city-state of Sparta to help him defeat this dangerous new trend. He forced the popular leader Cleisthenes (KLYS thuh neez) to flee the city. Isagoras also exiled 700 families who supported democratic reform.

But now some Athenians were fighting back. The Spartans were excellent soldiers, but they were overwhelmed by the Athenian people. After the Spartans surrendered, Cleisthenes returned, and Athens continued building its democracy.

Experimenting with Forms of Government

Isagoras and the Spartans were trying to keep government in the hands of the aristocrats, a type of government the Greeks called an **oligarchy** (AHL ih gahr kee). In an oligarchy, political power is held by a small group of people.

Analyze Images The phalanx was a formation of soldiers that might be as deep as eight lines. **Draw Conclusions** How might such a battle formation create a spirit of equality?

Academic Vocabulary
maintain • *v.*, to keep and support

Handwritten notes:
- draco was a cruel person.
- armies were very organized & strategic
- city-states play a large role in all ancient civilizations, especially Greece.

Oligarchies Oligarchies were usually headed by a council of leaders who belonged to the aristocracy. One of these aristocratic leaders was a lawgiver named Draco. He created a legal code that specified harsh punishments for all offenses, from serious to minor crimes. Today, people still use the word *draconian* to describe laws that seem unnecessarily harsh or severe.

A Military Tactic Changes Government In many city-states, power began to shift into the hands of more people. This process may have been sparked by a change in the way Greek armies were organized. In earlier times, the outcome of battles depended on fights between individual aristocratic warriors.

Around 700 BCE, a new military formation called the phalanx was introduced. The **phalanx** was a formation of heavily armed foot soldiers who moved together as a unit. Before battle, these citizen-soldiers lined up to form a row of overlapping shields. Each man's shield helped protect his neighbor. He held the shield with his left arm. In his right hand he held a spear or sword.

As foot soldiers, fighters in a phalanx did not need to be rich enough to buy and **maintain** a horse. More men could afford the necessary weapons and armor. As city-states came to depend on the phalanx formation for defense, citizen-soldiers may have gained more political power. Some historians believe this gave more men a voice in government. Aristocratic leaders risked losing the support of their army if they did not consider the interests of these men.

Each city-state set up a different form of government. With so many city-states, great political variety characterized the Greek world.

Tyrannies At first tyrants, or strong leaders, emerged to champion the interests of ordinary citizens. Tyrants were usually members of the aristocracy. But by promising land and other benefits to the poor, they won popular support. Then they were able to set up a **tyranny**, or government run by a strong ruler.

Tyrants did not allow others to play a significant role in government. Nevertheless, Greek tyrants were not always bad rulers. In some city-states, they governed fairly and worked to improve life for ordinary people.

Many tyrants, however, found that they could not fulfill their promises. Other tyrants ruled harshly. Eventually, other forms of government replaced tyrannies.

✓ READING CHECK **Compare and Contrast** How are oligarchies and tyrannies different?

The World's First Democracy

Most city-states adopted tyranny, but some moved toward rule by the many. The Greeks called this form of government **democracy**, which means "rule by the people." In these new democracies, large numbers of men participated in civic affairs.

When Did Democracy in Athens Begin? In the year 594 BCE, the aristocrats of Athens chose Solon to lead the polis. Solon ended the practice of selling into slavery poor people who could not pay their debts. He also gave some non-aristocratic men the right to vote for officials. These measures set Athens on the path to democracy.

Later Reforms In 508 BCE, a leader named Cleisthenes made several reforms that reduced the power of the rich. By increasing the number of citizens who could vote, he brought in many new voters from the lower classes. Cleisthenes also increased the power of the assembly, which included all male citizens. The assembly met to discuss political issues and make decisions for the city-state.

Another major reform took place in 461 BCE. In that year, Athens created citizen juries. A jury is a group of people who hear evidence and decide a court case. The new system put legal decisions in the hands of the people.

The Age of Pericles More reforms followed in the 450s BCE under Pericles. His first major change was to pay citizens for participating in jury service and in other civic duties. These payments helped poor people to take part in government. These reforms created the world's first democracy. Athenians were proud of what they had achieved.

One factor that encouraged democracy in Athens was the idea of citizenship. **Citizenship** is membership in a community. Elsewhere in the ancient world, people lived as subjects of a ruler whom they were expected to obey without question. In contrast, the Greeks gave ordinary people the right to help make government decisions.

Education's Role in Democracy Education helped promote the growth of democracy in Athens. The education students received was designed to produce well-rounded citizens.

Although some girls could read and write, most education was reserved for boys. They attended school from the age of seven and studied literature, physical education, and music.

By the 420s BCE, there was also higher education. Commonly, a **lecturer** taught students subjects such as mathematics and public speaking.

✓ READING CHECK **Identify Main Ideas** What important political development occurred in Athens?

Academic Vocabulary

lecturer • *n.,* person who gives an informative talk to students

▼ Athenian leader Solon ended the practice of enslaving people who could not pay debts.

[handwritten note: majoraty of tyrangs were harsh and unfair.]

INTERACTIVE

Athenian Democracy

Courts made decisions based on different democracy

Quest CONNECTIONS

Look at the diagram of Athenian democracy. In what ways did Athenian democracy influence the U.S. government? Record your findings in your Active Journal.

How Did Athenian Democracy Work?

Political reforms produced a golden age of democracy in Athens. Citizens ran all parts of the government. The most important were the assembly, the council, and the courts.

The Business of Government The main political body of Athens was the assembly, which all free adult male citizens had the right to attend. Meetings took place 40 times a year. Everyone who attended the assembly had the right to speak, from the poorest farmer to the richest aristocrat.

A 500-person council, known as the boule, was the second key component of the Athenian government. The council helped decide which issues should come before the assembly. Members of the council were chosen by lot, or at random, from among the citizens. As a result, every male citizen had a chance of serving on the council.

The Courts The government's third key component was the court system. Athens had many different courts, each of which decided different types of cases. Juries made up of citizens served in the courts, deciding cases by majority vote.

Juries in Athens were much larger than modern juries. Many people, from several hundred to several thousand, might serve on a single jury! Additional laws were passed to discourage bribery.

As democracy grew stronger in Athens, older governmental bodies lost power. For example, the Areopagus (ar ee OP uh gus), a council of advisers who decided some court cases, lost all its functions except the right to judge murder cases.

ATHENIAN DEMOCRACY

DEMOCRACY FIRST DEVELOPED IN ATHENS BEFORE SPREADING —TO OTHER— GREEK CITY-STATES.

CITIZENS
In the mid-400s BCE, there were about 45,000 Athenian citizens. From this group, people were chosen for various government positions.

ASSEMBLY
Voted on laws and determined foreign policy

JURIES
Decided rulings in trials

ARCHONS
Served as judges

COUNCIL OF 500 (BOULE)
Prepared bills to be voted on by the assembly and enforced the assembly's decision

COUNCIL SUBCOMMITTEES
Handled finances and religious rituals

Analyze Diagrams The Athenian assembly was open to all male citizens. **Draw Inferences** Why do you think the boule and its subcommittees were created?

Did Athenian Democracy Have Limitations? Athens was not completely democratic. Women could not vote or hold office. Foreigners, even if they came from another Greek city-state, could not be citizens and had no voice in the government. Slaves had no rights.

Athens, then, did not have rule by all the people. Compared to most places in the ancient world, however, Athens included far more people in government.

Direct and Representative Democracy: The Differences

Athenian democracy depended on active citizen involvement. A political system in which citizens participate directly in decision making is called a **direct democracy**. Direct democracy worked in Athens because the population of the city-state was small and because of the commitment and hard work of its citizens.

Direct democracy is less practical in large countries like the United States. In countries spread over a wide area of land, citizens live too far apart to meet. In addition, nations like the United States have so many citizens that Athenian-style assemblies would be too big.

For this reason, most democracies today are representative democracies. In a **representative democracy**, citizens elect others to represent them in government. These representatives then make the decisions and pass laws on behalf of all the people. Despite the differences, modern democracies share the Athenian ideal of rule by the people.

Analyze Images Greek men used stones to vote. Here, two men vote under the watchful eye of the Greek goddess Athena. **Draw Conclusions** What does artwork showing a goddess watching over voting tell you about Athenians' views on the practice?

Athenians had different say in govermnet

☑ READING CHECK Identify Supporting Details How did the assembly provide Athenians with a direct role in government decisions?

☑ Lesson Check

Practice Vocabulary

1. How did the **phalanx** help encourage **democracy** in Athens?

2. How do an **oligarchy** and **tyranny** differ?

3. What are the differences between **representative democracy** and **direct democracy**?

Critical Thinking and Writing

4. Draw Conclusions Why did the use of the phalanx affect politics?

5. Compare and Contrast How is the modern democracy of the United States different from Athenian democracy?

6. Writing Workshop: Pick an Organizing Strategy How did Athens' government contribute to its rise? Start thinking about how you might organize your essay. Take notes in your 📕 Active Journal.

◀ A statue of Pericles

Pericles, Funeral Oration

In the years after the Persian Wars, Pericles guided Athens to a golden age, when the economy thrived and the government became more democratic. At the end of the first year of the Peloponnesian War (431–404 BCE), Pericles gave a famous speech that Thucydides recounted. It was a funeral oration Pericles gave at a public funeral for the war dead where he compares Athens to Sparta.

Reading and Vocabulary Support

① According to Pericles, what determines a man's ability to advance in Athenian society?

② What do you think Pericles meant by "jealous surveillance"?

③ A magistrate is a judge or high government official.

④ Elegance means richness.

Our constitution does not copy the laws of neighboring states; we are rather a pattern to others than imitators ourselves. Its administration favours the many instead of the few; this is why it is called a democracy. If we look to the laws, they afford equal justice to all in their private differences; if no social standing, advancement in public life falls to reputation for capacity, class considerations not being allowed to interfere with merit; nor again does poverty bar the way, if a man is able to serve the state, he is not hindered by the obscurity of his condition. ① The freedom which we enjoy in our government extends also to our ordinary life. There, far from exercising a jealous surveillance ② over each other, we do not feel called upon to be angry with our neighbor for doing what he likes, or even to indulge in those injurious looks which cannot fail to be offensive, although they inflict no positive penalty. But all this ease in our private relations does not make us lawless as citizens. Against this fear is our chief safeguard, teaching us to obey the magistrates ③ and the laws, particularly such as regard the protection of the injured, whether they are actually on the statute book, or belong to that code which, although unwritten, yet cannot be broken without acknowledged disgrace.

Further, we provide plenty of means for the mind to refresh itself from business. We celebrate games and sacrifices all the year round, and the elegance ④ of our private establishments forms a daily source of pleasure. . . .

—From *The History of the Peloponnesian War, Book 2,* by Thucydides

Analyzing Primary Sources

Cite specific evidence from the document to support your answers.

1. **Determine Author's Purpose** After reading this document, what do you think is Pericles' point of view regarding Athenian society?

2. **Determine Central Ideas** What are some of the main ideas expressed by Pericles in this document?

Distinguish Relevant from Irrelevant Information

Follow these steps to distinguish relevant from irrelevant information.

1 Identify your focus or topic. By clearly defining your topic, you can better determine which pieces of information will be relevant or irrelevant. If you were preparing a report on Pericles' character, what types of information would you look for to support your points?

2 Locate sources and read about the topic. Based on the topic you identified, select a number of sources that will likely offer information on this topic. You may find sources online or in your school's media center.

a. What is the source of the passage below?

b. What other types of sources might offer relevant information about Pericles' character?

3 Identify the information that is relevant to your topic. Scan your sources to find passages that may relate to your topic. Then, read these passages closely to determine whether or not they provide relevant information.

a. What is one piece of relevant information found in this passage?

b. What does this information tell you about Pericles' character?

4 Identify the information that is irrelevant to your topic. Irrelevant information, such as anecdotes, may be interesting, but it is not central to the topic. Give one detail from the passage that is irrelevant to the topic.

Primary Source

The Character of Pericles

"Pericles was born into the best families of Athens, both on his father's and mother's side. He received a good education from his teachers, including the philosopher Zeno....One day, Pericles was in the marketplace of Athens doing business. All day long some noisy pest followed him around, yelling at him and calling him names. He even followed Pericles home. Throughout the ordeal, Pericles stayed calm. It was dark by the time Pericles arrived home. So he gave orders for one of his servants to take a torch and guide this pest safely back to wherever he lived. Some people said that Pericles was only trying to fool the public with a false front of virtue. But Zeno replied that if Pericles were faking virtue, they should do the same."

—from Plutarch's *Lives*

Oligarchy in Sparta

BOUNCE TO ACTIVATE ▶ **VIDEO**

GET READY TO READ

START UP

What does the image of Spartan king Leonidas tell you about the role of warfare in Spartan society?

GUIDING QUESTIONS

- What type of government developed in Sparta?
- What was life like in Sparta?
- How did Sparta differ from Athens?

TAKE NOTES

Literacy Skills: Compare and Contrast
Use the graphic organizer in your ▰ Active Journal to take notes as you read the lesson.

PRACTICE VOCABULARY

Use the vocabulary activity in your ▰ Active Journal to practice the vocabulary words.

Vocabulary	Academic Vocabulary
ephor	authority
helot	innovation
military state	
barracks	

very military based

Life was simple in Sparta. Most decisions were made for you. If you were a Spartan boy, the state would take you from your family at the age of seven. You would spend more than 20 years training for and serving in the professional army. If you were a girl, you would be raised for the sole purpose of bearing strong children for the state.

The Spartan State: A Contrast to Athens

Other Greeks regarded Sparta with a mix of fear and admiration. In contrast to democratic Athens, Sparta felt like an army camp, its male citizens obligated to full-time military training. Its government was an odd mixture of monarchy, oligarchy, and democracy. People in city-states such as Athens were amused by Sparta's strange customs. They were also frightened by its growing power.

Government in Sparta Sparta was a city-state on the Peloponnesian Peninsula. The center of Sparta was inland, so Sparta was not a sea power. Neither was it a democracy.

No democray

Sparta was ruled by two kings who served as military leaders. The kings headed Sparta's governing body, the council of elders. The council included 28 men over the age of 60. This oligarchy was the true government of Sparta.

Sparta did have a democratic assembly made up of some free adult males, but it had only about 9,000 citizens, compared to about 45,000 in Athens. The Spartan assembly also had far less power than the Athenian assembly. It could pass laws, but the council had to approve them.

However, the Spartan assembly did have one important power. It elected five ephors. An **ephor** (EH for) was responsible for the day-to-day operation of the government. The five ephors made sure that the kings and the council acted within the limits of Spartan law. Ephors could remove a king who broke the law.

Military Conquests Without the resources and trading opportunities of the sea, Sparta turned to conquest to meet its growing needs.

The Spartans conquered the neighboring city-state of Messenia. Some conquered Messenians became a kind of slave called a **helot** (HEL ut). The helots belonged not to individual Spartans but to the polis as a whole. They were forced to farm the land and turn over half the food they raised to Sparta. Helots were treated harshly.

The helots produced enough food to support the Spartans. As a result, the Spartans did not have to farm for a living. Spartan men were free to become professional warriors.

The Helot Revolts In the early 400s BCE, the helots launched a violent revolt. Although the Spartans put down the revolt, they lived in fear of further unrest. The helots outnumbered them.

The Spartans faced a choice. They could give up control of the helots and the food they produced, or they could strengthen their control by turning Sparta into even more of a military state. A **military state** is a society organized for the purpose of waging war.

The Spartans chose the second option. Not only did they emphasize the military even more than before, they also tried to control the helots through terror. Every year, the ephors declared war on the helots. This gave any Spartan the right to kill any helot without fear of punishment. At the same time, secret police watched over the helots.

READING CHECK Draw Conclusions What did the existence of helots say about life in Sparta?

GEOGRAPHY **SKILLS**

Helots revolted in Messenia, next to Sparta.

1. **Place** What is Sparta's location relative to the sea?

2. **Draw Conclusions** Why might Messenia's location have made it a valuable region for Sparta to control?

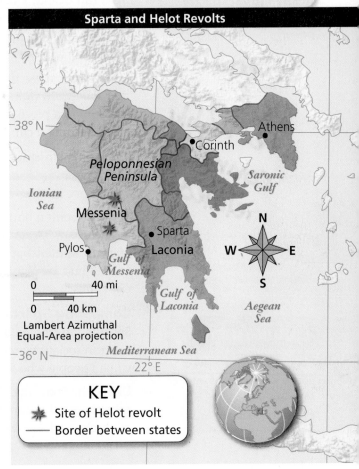

Sparta and Helot Revolts

38° N

Athens

Corinth

Peloponnesian Peninsula

Saronic Gulf

Ionian Sea

Messenia

Sparta

N

Pylos

Laconia

W   E

Gulf of Messenia

S

0   40 mi

0   40 km

Gulf of Laconia

Aegean Sea

Lambert Azimuthal Equal-Area projection

Mediterranean Sea

36° N

22° E

KEY

✳ Site of Helot revolt

— Border between states

Military Training in Sparta

Because of their history of conquest and their need to control the helots, Spartans valued military discipline. Even today, the adjective *spartan* means "highly disciplined or lacking in comfort." Unlike Athenians, Spartans did not value luxury goods or beautiful buildings.

Education in Sparta With the helots working the fields, Spartan males had plenty of time to train for military service. At seven, they were taken away from their homes to live together in **barracks**, or military housing.

Spartan boys did not receive a well-rounded education. They spent most of their time exercising, hunting, and training. They were taught to obey orders rather than to think for themselves. As Greek writer Plutarch wrote, "All their education was directed toward prompt obedience to **authority**, stout endurance of hardship, and victory or death in battle."

▲ A Spartan helmet, armor, and shield

Academic Vocabulary

authority • *n.*, people in power

Government & military were highly connected/related.

At the age of 18, young men began a two-year program of military training. During this time the trainees could marry, but they were allowed little time for a life at home. Even after the age of 30, when they left the army, they spent most of their time with other men.

Spartan Social Classes When they left the school system, Spartan men faced another test. In order to become full citizens, they had to gain entry to a men's club of soldiers. If they failed, they became "inferiors" who would never gain citizenship and would live as outcasts.

Men who won election to a men's club became known as "equals." They had full citizen rights. This included membership in the assembly and the right to a piece of state-owned land worked by helots. At age 60, an equal became a candidate for election to the council of elders.

Women's Unique Role in Sparta Spartan women were raised to be strong and vigorous. They participated in sports. By staying fit, they could have healthy babies who would grow into good soldiers.

Spartan women had a good deal of freedom and responsibility because their husbands spent almost their entire lives away at military camp. Spartan women were responsible for raising future soldiers for the state, so they had greater independence than women had in other Greek city-states.

Comparing Sparta and Athens The discipline and training of Spartan life created a powerful army and a stable government. But Spartan society feared individual differences and change. The Spartans valued people who fit in, not those who stood out.

Unlike the Spartans, the Athenians valued individual expression and new ideas. Athenian democracy evolved over time. Sparta's rigid oligarchy and society changed very little. These differences led the

Quick Activity

Compare Pericles' view of Sparta with those of another Athenian, Xenophon, in your 📕 Active Journal.

Governments of Athens and Sparta

Athens	Sparta
• Main political body is a large assembly • Members of smaller council chosen at random to serve one-year terms • Assemblies made up of free males • Large citizen-juries run court system	• Government led by two kings • Smaller and less powerful assembly than in Athens • Councils made up of free adult males • Council members elected for life • *Ephors* monitor both kings and council

Greek historian Thucydides to describe the Athenians as "addicted to **innovation**." In contrast, he viewed the Spartans as having "a genius for keeping what you have got." The opposing values of Athens and Sparta helped create tensions between the two city-states.

Economically, Sparta and Athens were very different. Because of their lack of natural resources, neither city-state was able to produce enough food to feed its growing population. Athens, however, had vast amounts of silver and relied on trade to obtain food for its citizens. Sparta relied on conquest and slave labor in the conquered territories to obtain its food. When food was scarce, the Athenians traded with others to get what they needed, while the Spartans conquered more territory.

Athenian leader Pericles believed that Athenian democracy was far superior than life in Sparta. Pericles was the leader of Athens during the Peloponnesian War against Sparta (431-404 BCE). He tried to raise morale by contrasting the two cities in his famous funeral oration.

☑ **READING CHECK** **Identify Cause and Effect** How did Sparta's rigid society affect the lives of women?

Analyze Charts The Athenian and Spartan governments differed significantly. **Summarize** What is the main difference between the two?

Academic Vocabulary
innovation • *n.*, new ways of doing things

INTERACTIVE

Comparing Sparta and Athens

☑ Lesson Check

Practice Vocabulary

1. What role did an **ephor** play in Spartan government?

2. What is the purpose of **barracks**?

3. What is a **military state** like?

Critical Thinking and Writing

4. **Make Inferences** Why did Sparta become a military society?

5. **Compare Viewpoints** What might have bothered Spartans and Athenians about each other's society?

6. **Writing Workshop: Develop a Clear Thesis** How did Spartans develop their society? Begin to draft a thesis statement about the rise and peak of Greek city-states in your 📓 Active Journal.

Ancient Greek Society and Economic Expansion

BOUNCE TO ACTIVATE ▶ VIDEO

GET READY TO READ

START UP
Study the image and briefly describe what it shows about trade and the economy in ancient Greece.

GUIDING QUESTIONS
- What roles and rights did women have in the Greek city-states?
- How was Greek society organized?
- Why did the Greeks expand through trade, conquest, and colonization?
- How did the Greeks' expansion affect connections within the ancient world?

TAKE NOTES
Literacy Skills: Use Evidence
Use the graphic organizer in your 📓 Active Journal to take notes as you read the lesson.

PRACTICE VOCABULARY
Use the vocabulary activity in your 📓 Active Journal to practice the vocabulary words.

Vocabulary	Academic Vocabulary
tenant farmer	obtain
metic	symbolize
slavery	

A Greek traveler in ancient times would have felt at home in any Greek port city. Greeks spoke the same language and worshiped many of the same gods.

However, our ancient traveler might also have been startled at the differences between city-states. He or she would have observed a variety of governments, economies, and ways of organizing society.

What Was the Role of Women in Ancient Greece?

In the Greek world, women had different rights and roles, depending on the city-state. In Sparta, they had a good deal of freedom. However, in city-states such as Athens, they had few rights.

Family Life The typical Greek family consisted of husband, wife, and children. As head of the house, the man had control over his family. Poorer women worked outdoors on farms or sold goods in markets. But in city-states like Athens, women from richer families were expected to stay at home while the men took part in public life. Although women did play public roles in religious ceremonies, for the most part their lives were restricted. The Greek philosopher Xenophon described Greek gender roles:

Primary Source

"The gods have ordered and the law approves that men and women should each follow their own capacity. It is not so good for a woman to be out of doors as in. And it is more dishonorable for a man to stay indoors than to attend to his affairs outside."

—Xenophon, *Economics*

In most Greek homes, women supervised the household, raised the children, kept track of money and spending, and managed the slaves. Many Greek women made most or all of the clothing family members needed. They had to spin wool or flax into yarn, weave fabric, and sew or knit the clothes. Greek women also supervised the preparation of meals.

Spartan Women In Sparta, women enjoyed more rights and freedoms than did women in other city-states. Spartan women could sell their property. Like their brothers, Spartan girls were educated and trained in sports. Such Spartan customs shocked the Greeks of other city-states.

✓ READING CHECK Compare and Contrast How did the lives of women in Athens and Sparta differ?

What Were the Social Divisions in Greek Society?

Ancient Greek society had a complex class system, with rich landowners at the top and slaves at the bottom. Between these two extremes were ranked the small landowners, merchants and artisans, and the landless poor of Greek society.

The Aristocracy Early city-states were controlled by aristocrats or kings. Some aristocrats claimed descent from kings or gods. They believed this gave them the right to hold political power. Their wealth came from owning large plots of land, where they raised crops and livestock. Slaves did most of the work on these estates. This left aristocrats with free time for politics and leisure activities.

Analyze Images Pottery shows a scene of women collecting water at a tap. **Identify Main Ideas** How does this piece of art reflect one of the roles women had in ancient Greece?

Citizens and Noncitizens Society was divided between citizens (who were all adult males) and noncitizens, whose rights were limited. All citizens had the right to vote.

Farmers who owned large areas of land enjoyed a relatively high status, or rank in society. Although such landowners were rich, they made up only a minority of citizens. Many more citizens were small farmers—farmers who owned smaller plots of land. Small farmers rarely had enough land to raise livestock or produce a food surplus. On a lower social scale were tenant farmers. A **tenant farmer** was someone who paid rent, either in money or crops, to grow crops on another person's land. These tenant farmers were called *thetes*.

Merchants and artisans were often resident aliens. One of these resident aliens, called a **metic**, might be a Greek from another city-state or someone who was not Greek. Metics were noncitizens. Although they were free, they enjoyed fewer rights than the native-born men of the polis.

Slavery in Ancient Greece The lowest class in Greek society was made up of enslaved people. **Slavery** is the ownership and control of other people as property.

Enslaved people became slaves in various ways. Most were prisoners of war. Others were bought from slave traders or sold into slavery by their families. Sometimes parents who could not care for their children abandoned them. These children often become slaves. Many enslaved people in Greek city-states came from other lands. Some slaves were Greeks themselves.

Analyze Diagrams Identify the different social divisions in Greek society, using the images in the diagram. **Classify and Categorize** Which three groups shown could take part in government?

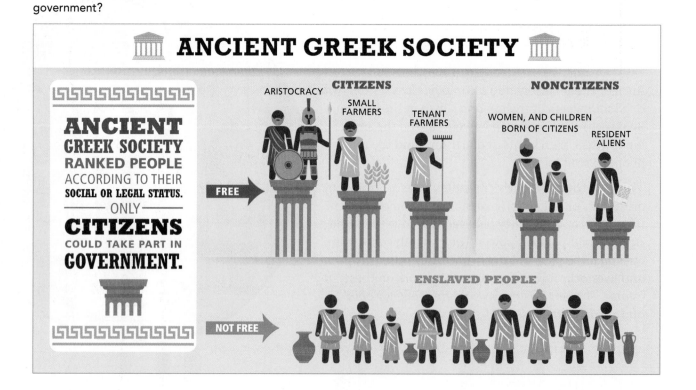

ANCIENT GREEK SOCIETY

ANCIENT GREEK SOCIETY RANKED PEOPLE ACCORDING TO THEIR SOCIAL OR LEGAL STATUS. ONLY CITIZENS COULD TAKE PART IN GOVERNMENT.

FREE

NOT FREE

CITIZENS
ARISTOCRACY
SMALL FARMERS
TENANT FARMERS

NONCITIZENS
WOMEN, AND CHILDREN BORN OF CITIZENS
RESIDENT ALIENS

ENSLAVED PEOPLE

By the 500s BCE, slavery was widespread in Greece. In some city-states, enslaved people made up one third of the population. Slaves did many jobs in Greek society. Household slaves cooked, cleaned, and took care of children. Some enslaved people were teachers. Others worked on farms, ships, or in mines. Their labor helped the Greek economy grow.

Some slaves were treated kindly. A few were even freed. But slaves had no legal rights and could be punished harshly by their owners. Enslaved people were sometimes worked to death under cruel conditions.

✓ READING CHECK Identify Supporting Details What were some social divisions in ancient Greece?

The Greek Economy

As you have read, the Greeks lacked good farmland and some basic resources. When the population of Greek city-states increased, the Greeks had to find ways of feeding their people.

Conquest Some city-states **obtained** more land and resources by conquering their neighbors. Sparta, located inland on the Peloponnesian Peninsula, decided not to depend on trade for growth. Spartan troops conquered the neighboring city-state of Messenia and turned its conquered people into non-free laborers. The Messenians were forced to raise crops for the Spartans.

This captive workforce freed Spartan men from their farming chores. So the Spartans were able to form a professional army that was the most feared in Greece. By the mid-500s BCE, Sparta controlled most of the Peloponnesian Peninsula.

Colonization Migration—moving to a new area—was another solution to the population problem. Beginning in the 700s BCE, new waves of Greek colonists sailed off to find new places to settle. Leaving home was not an easy decision. Colonists faced danger and uncertainty on the voyage and the challenge of building new homes. As historian Donald Kagan notes, "Only powerful pressures like overpopulation and land hunger" drove people to take such risks.

The ideal site for a colony was on the coast. There, the settlers could anchor their ships. They could also set up a port for trading with other ports. The best spot would have good land for farming. It needed to be near important resources such as timber or minerals that could be exported. Homer described the founding of a fictional colony:

Use Visual Information
In a scene from the *Odyssey*, enslaved women do work for Odysseus's wife, Penelope. **Use Visual Information** What kind of jobs did these women have?

Academic Vocabulary
obtained • *v.*, gained

Primary Source

"So [the founder] led them away, settling them in [a place called] Scheria, far from the bustle of men. He had a wall constructed around the town center, built houses, erected temples for the gods, and divided the land."

—Homer, the *Odyssey*

Academic Vocabulary

symbolized • *v.*, represented

Greek colonists brought a flame from home to light fires in the new colony. This flame **symbolized** their ties to their old city-state. They often traded with the home city. But most colonists never returned home. They made new lives in their new city-state.

By the 500s BCE, there were hundreds of Greek colonies around the Mediterranean Sea and the Black Sea. They stretched from the shores of what is now Russia all the way west to Spain.

Currency Trade led to an important new development. Around 650 BCE, the kings of Lydia began making the world's first gold and silver coins. Lydia was in Anatolia (also called Asia Minor, in present-day Turkey), near the city-states of Ionia. Using coins led to a kind of economic revolution. Coins of standard size and value gradually replaced the old bartering system, in which some goods would

GEOGRAPHY **SKILLS**

Greeks took advantage of their location on the water to trade with other lands.

1. **Interaction** How did Greek traders interact with the people who lived along the Black Sea?

2. **Draw Conclusions** How might the city-states of Athens and Sparta have focused on different regions when trading?

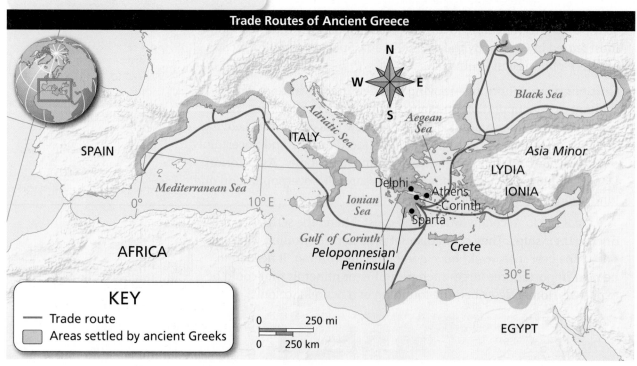

Trade Routes of Ancient Greece

KEY
— Trade route
▢ Areas settled by ancient Greeks

be traded for other goods. These coins were used as currency, a way of exchanging value. Thanks to the use of coins, trade became easier.

Greeks learned about coins from trading with Lydia. Several city-states set up their own mints, or places where coins are made. Each city-state stamped its coins with symbols of the city or an image of the god or goddess who protected the city. The coins of Athens, for instance, were marked with an owl. This bird was associated with Athena, the goddess for whom Athens was named.

Trade in Athens Trade made the city-state of Athens rich. Athens had very little farmland, so it relied on commerce to meet the need for food and other resources. Athenians founded colonies around the Black Sea, on the coast of North Africa, and in other regions. They came to rely on grain that was shipped from ports on the Black Sea. They traded silver for much-needed food.

To pay for the grain, Athenian workshops also produced pottery, jewelry, and other trade goods. These products, along with olive oil and wine, were also shipped to other lands. Ships returned to Athens with timber, minerals, and luxury goods such as ivory, glass, and perfume. Streets and markets bustled with activity.

The Effects of Expansion Greek colonization affected both trade and culture. Just as colonization spread Greek culture and goods across the Mediterranean world, it also drew new customs and ideas back to Greece. As a result, cultural borrowing increased throughout the Mediterranean region. The Greek alphabet was likely influenced by the Phoenician alphabet. Stories of Egyptian gods and goddesses mingled with the stories of Greek mythology, with some Greeks choosing to worship Egypt's deities as well.

▲ Athenian coins

The establishment of colonies had economic effects on Greece. Many colonies became successful through active trade with Greece. They also introduced Greeks to new goods from foreign lands.

 READING CHECK Identify Supporting Details How did Greek city-states gain needed resources when their populations grew?

INTERACTIVE

Expansion and Trade in the Greek World

☑ Lesson Check

Practice Vocabulary

1. How would a **tenant farmer** earn his living?

2. What was the difference between a citizen, a **metic**, and a slave?

Critical Thinking and Writing

3. **Make Inferences** Why did the physical geography of Greece encourage colonization?

4. **Draw Conclusions** How did the adoption of coins help increase Greek wealth?

5. **Writing Workshop: Support Thesis with Details** How did ancient Greece's society and economy affect the rise and peak of the independent city-states? Collect details to support your thesis in your 📘 Active Journal.

Warfare in Ancient Greece

BOUNCE TO ACTIVATE ▶ VIDEO

GET READY TO READ

START UP

The boat pictured is a model of an ancient Greek warship. Why would the ancient Greeks have needed to develop a strong navy in order to fight with other nations?

GUIDING QUESTIONS

- How did the Greek city-states defeat the mighty Persian empire?
- What role did Athens take after the Persian Wars?
- What were the causes and effects of the Peloponnesian War?

TAKE NOTES

Literacy Skills: Compare and Contrast
Use the graphic organizer in your 📓 Active Journal to take notes as you read the lesson.

PRACTICE VOCABULARY

Use the vocabulary activity in your 📓 Active Journal to practice the vocabulary words.

Vocabulary	Academic Vocabulary
Battle of Marathon	pursue
Battle of Salamis	ally
Delian League	
Peloponnesian League	

Warfare was frequent in ancient Greece. The quarrelsome city-states battled one another over land and resources. In addition to all their minor conflicts, the Greeks fought three major wars in the 400s BCE. Twice they united long enough to defeat the Persian empire.

The Persian Wars

After 546 BCE., Persia conquered the Greek city-states of Ionia in western Asia. The Ionian city-states were used to governing themselves, so they rebelled in 500 BCE. To help them, Athenian soldiers burned the Persian city of Sardis. This enraged Darius, the Persian king. After his troops recaptured the Ionian cities, Darius set out to conquer the rest of Greece.

War and conquest were second nature to the Persians. They established a vast empire after defeating Babylon in 539 BCE. The Persians eventually controlled a vast territory from Anatolia to India. Although it was the greatest empire of its time, Persia's rulers had a difficult time defeating the Greeks on their home soil.

The Battle of Marathon In 490 BCE, about 20,000 Persian soldiers sailed for Greece. They landed by the plain of Marathon, near Athens. Athenian soldiers rushed to Marathon, but they were outnumbered by about two to one. Also, unlike the Persians, they had no archers or soldiers on horseback.

Despite these disadvantages, the Athenians attacked the day after the Persian landing. At dawn, Greek phalanxes raced across the plain, taking the Persians by surprise. In panic, the Persians fled to their ships. The unexpected Greek victory at the **Battle of Marathon** ended the First Persian War. In ancient times, a legend told of a messenger who died after running 26 miles to carry the news of the victory back to Athens. Ever since then, the word "marathon" has been used to describe a challenging footrace.

The Second Persian War Darius died before he could launch another attack. But his son, Xerxes (ZURK seez), was determined to defeat the Greeks and began the Second Persian War.

In 480 BCE, Xerxes assembled an invasion force of about 100,000 men. The Persian empire was the superpower of its day. Because it controlled Egypt, Persia was able to add the Egyptian army to its ranks. Although the Persians did not have a navy, they used the ships of the Phoenicians, who were part of their empire.

The Spartans moved north to block the huge army. Led by King Leonidas, a small Spartan force stopped the Persians at a narrow mountain pass called Thermopylae (thur MAHP uh lee). The Spartans held off the invaders for days. Then, a Greek traitor showed the Persians another path through the mountains. Attacked from both sides, the Spartans died heroically, in defense of Greece.

Analyze Images Athenians and Persians do battle at the Battle of Marathon. **Use Visual Information** What mood was the artist trying to convey about this battle?

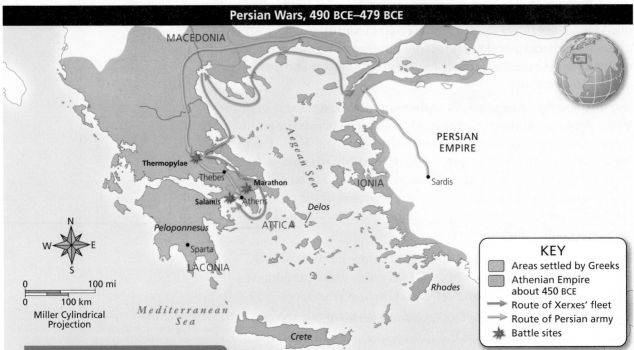

Persian Wars, 490 BCE–479 BCE

MACEDONIA

Thermopylae
Thebes
Salamis • Athens
Marathon
ATTICA
Delos
IONIA
Sardis

PERSIAN
EMPIRE

Peloponnesus
• Sparta
LACONIA

Aegean Sea

Rhodes

Mediterranean
Sea

Crete

N
W E
S

0   100 mi
0   100 km
Miller Cylindrical
Projection

KEY
▢ Areas settled by Greeks
▢ Athenian Empire
about 450 BCE
→ Route of Xerxes' fleet
→ Route of Persian army
✸ Battle sites

GEOGRAPHY SKILLS

Xerxes sent his army and navy to attack Greece after Athenians burned down the city of Sardis.

1. **Movement** Where was the last battle for the Persians?

2. **Draw Conclusions** Why did it make sense for Xerxes to send his army and navy in two different directions?

Academic Vocabulary
pursue • *v.*, to chase

INTERACTIVE

Persian Wars

The Greek historian Herodotus recorded the events:

Primary Source

"King Xerxes pitched his camp in the region of Malis called Trachinia, while on their side the Greeks occupied the straits . . . . [T]he Greeks in general call Thermopylae (the Hot Gates) . . . . Here then the two armies took their stand. . . ."

—Herodotus, *The Histories*

Victory for Athens The Persians advanced on Athens. The Athenian leader Themistocles (thuh MIS tuh kleez) convinced Athenians to flee to nearby islands. When the Persians reached Athens, they found the city almost empty.

Xerxes burned Athens and sent his ships to **pursue** the Greek navy. Confident of victory, Xerxes had his throne placed on a hill to watch the naval battle in the Strait of Salamis.

But Themistocles had set a trap. He kept his Greek ships hidden until Persian ships filled the narrow strait. Suddenly, the Greeks attacked. They rammed the crowded Persian ships, splintering their hulls. By nightfall, the strait was clogged with more than 200 broken Persian ships. The Greeks lost only about 40 ships. The **Battle of Salamis** broke Persian naval power. After another defeat for Xerxes on land, the Persians returned home.

✓ READING CHECK **Identify Cause and Effect** How did Xerxes' over-confidence lead to a Persian defeat?

Why Were Athens and Sparta Rivals?

After defeating the Persians at Salamis, Athens enjoyed a "golden age." The Athenian leader Pericles began rebuilding the city, which became famous for its art and learning. The wealth and power of the city grew.

However, trouble was brewing. Greece now had two rival powers—Athens, with the strongest navy, and Sparta, with the strongest army. Each wanted to be the supreme power in Greece. Their rivalry would lead to deadly conflict.

Athens's Alliance Soon after the Persian wars, Athens formed an alliance with other city-states. An alliance is an association of nations formed to achieve a goal. Because Athens and its **allies** met together on the island of Delos, their alliance was called the **Delian League**. Members promised to protect one another from Persia and provide ships or money for defense. This money was kept in the League's treasury on Delos.

Academic Vocabulary

ally • *n.*, member of an alliance

The Delian League had about 150 members. All of the allies were supposed to be equal. However, Athens was by far the most powerful member. Athenian ships protected Greek traders and travelers. By building an alliance of city-states that bordered the Aegean Sea, Athens was able to protect its grain supply.

Athens ran the Delian League as if it were its own empire rather than an alliance of equals. The Athenians brought some cities into the League by force and blocked others from leaving. When Naxos tried to leave, Athens attacked the city-state and forced it to stay.

▼ A Greek military helmet

The arrogant behavior of the Athenians angered other League members. Rather than asking city-states to contribute ships, Athens requested money. Athens used the money to build its navy. It continued to collect these funds even when there was no fighting with Persia. Athens also forced League members to use Athenian currency instead of their own.

In 454 BCE, Athenian leaders moved the League's treasury from Delos to Athens. Soon after, money from League members was used to rebuild Athens. Some of this money went to constructing the Parthenon, the great temple to Athena that stood on the Acropolis. Other members of the Delian League came to resent this use of the League's funds.

Sparta's Alliance The Spartans had already formed their own alliance on the Peloponnesian Peninsula. It is known today as the **Peloponnesian League**. Like Sparta, other members of the Peloponnesian League feared the power of Athens and its style of government. In contrast to democratic Athens, Sparta and most of its allies were oligarchies.

In 433 BCE, Sparta's Peloponnesian League and Athens's Delian League came into conflict. That year, Athens placed a ban on trade with Megara, a member of the

Peloponnesian League. This angered Sparta and its allies, who prepared for war. Athens and its allies did the same. Both sides were confident of a quick and easy victory.

✓ **READING CHECK** **Identify Cause and Effect** Why did Athens form the Delian League?

The Peloponnesian War

War between the two Greek alliances broke out in 431 BCE. Known as the Peloponnesian War, the conflict lasted on and off for 27 years.

Sparta's Siege of Athens The Peloponnesian War began when an army led by Sparta marched into Athenian territory. Pericles, the leader of Athens, instructed farmers living in the Athenian countryside to move inside the walled city for safety.

The Spartans settled down around Athens for a long siege. The goal of a siege is to force the enemy to surrender by cutting off its food and other supplies. Athenians had prepared for just such an event, however. They had built two long walls to line the four-mile road that connected Athens to its port city. While these long walls stood, Athenians could receive supplies by sea.

Supplied with food by ship, the Athenians held out for more than a year. Then, a plague, or contagious disease, broke out in the overcrowded city. Thousands of people died in Athens.

However, the war dragged on. Sparta, with its powerful army, and Athens, with its strong navy, found it difficult

GEOGRAPHY SKILLS

The Peloponnesian War was fought between Athens and Sparta.

1. **Place** Where were Sparta and its allies located? Where was the Athenian empire located?

2. **Draw Conclusions** Why would a defeat in a location like Aegospotami be so damaging to the Athenian economy?

Peloponnesian War

Black Sea
MACEDONIA
Hellespont (Dardanelles)
Aegospotami
40° N
THESSALY
Aegean Sea
0   200 mi
0   200 km
Miller Cylindrical projection
N
W   E
S
PERSIAN EMPIRE
Megara   Athens
20° E
Peloponnesian Peninsula
Delos   Naxos
Sparta
IONIA
35° N
Crete
25° E   *Mediterranean Sea*   30° E

KEY
- Sparta and allied states
- Athenian Empire around 431 BCE
- Athenian ally
- ✴ Battle

to defeat each other. In 421 BCE, both sides agreed to a truce, or an agreement to stop fighting, while they discussed peace terms.

Athens Surrenders Within a few years, however, the truce was broken. Athens launched an invasion of Sicily. With help from Sparta, the Greeks of Sicily destroyed the Athenian forces. Athens lost a large part of its navy at Syracuse.

Athens was now desperately weakened. The Persians saw a chance to deal Athens a fatal blow. They gave money to Sparta so it could build its own powerful navy. With this new fleet, Sparta defeated the Athenian navy at the Battle of Aegospotami in 404 BCE. After that, the Spartans attacked Athens itself.

Once again, the Athenians resisted. But with its new navy, Sparta was able to keep food from reaching Athens by sea. The following year, Athens was forced to surrender.

The peace terms were harsh. Sparta even made the Athenians give up their democratic government. Although democracy was soon restored, Athens had lost its power.

The Peloponnesian War hurt all the city-states, bringing Athens to its knees and ending the golden age of Greece. Throughout the 300s, the Greeks persisted in fighting amongst themselves. The constant fighting among city-states opened the door to the military conquest of Greece by Macedonia, a powerful kingdom to the north. As you will read, Macedonian rulers united the Greek city-states by force. After a rich period of democracy, Athenians were back to living under one powerful ruler.

▲ In this illustration created in the early 1900s, the Spartan navy defeats Athens at the Battle of Aegospotami.

☑ READING CHECK Identify Cause and Effect Why did Athens lose the Peloponnesian War?

☑ Lesson Check

Practice Vocabulary

1. Who fought at the **Battle of Marathon** and the **Battle of Salamis**?

2. What groups made up the **Delian League** and the **Peloponnesian League**?

Critical Thinking and Writing

3. **Compare Viewpoints** Why did other Greek city-states resent Athens's power?

4. **Draw Conclusions** Why was it so difficult for Athens and Sparta to defeat each other?

5. **Writing Workshop: Update Your Thesis** What does the information about conflict in ancient Greece tell you about the downfall of the independent Greek city-states? Update your thesis with new information in your 🗎 Active Journal.

Compare Different Points of View

Follow these steps to detect historical points of view.

INTERACTIVE

Compare Viewpoints

1 Identify the topic or issue. The first source is an inscription on a monument in Persepolis, one of Persia's ancient capitals. The monument shows tribute bearers bringing tribute to Persian king Darius I. The second source was written by Greek historian Herodotus. He wrote about how he viewed Darius I. What is the main idea of each passage?

2 Determine the author's position on the topic or issue. What is each author's position on the subject? Sometimes an author will state his or her overall point of view in a topic sentence. Other times the point of view is expressed over a whole passage or work. How do the two sources describe Darius I differently?

3 Identify important background information about the passage. Identifying facts such as the author's background and the time and place in which the author lived can prove valuable when analyzing a historical point of view. Where did the authors of the following pieces of text come from?

4 Analyze possible impact of historical background on the author's beliefs. People's beliefs and opinions may be influenced by what is happening in the world around them—the context.

a. How does the inscription show the Persian point of view?

b. How did Herodotus' background as a affect his point of view of Darius I?

Primary Source

"I am Darius the great king, king of kings, king of countries containing all kinds of men, king on this great earth far and wide. . . . If now you shall think that 'How many are the countries which King Darius held?' look at the sculptures (of those) who bear the throne. . . ."

—Inscription on the stairs of Apandana at Persepolis

Primary Source

"[Darius I] divided his dominions into twenty provinces, which they call satrapies; and having divided his dominions and appointed governors, he instructed each people to pay him tribute....It is because of this fixing of tribute, and other similar ordinances, that the Persians called Darius the merchant, Cambyses the master, and Cyrus the father; for Darius made petty profit out of everything, Cambyses was harsh and arrogant, Cyrus was merciful and always worked for their well-being."

—Herodotus, Greek historian

Ancient Greek Beliefs and Arts

GET READY TO READ

START UP

The image shows a scene from a Greek myth in which dangerous creatures called sirens tempted sailors into shipwrecks with their loud singing. What myths have you learned in school?

GUIDING QUESTIONS

- What effect did religion and mythology have on Greek people and their society?
- In what ways have Greek art and architecture remained influential today?
- How does Greek literature continue to influence our literature and language today?

TAKE NOTES

Literacy Skills: Synthesize Visual Information
Use the graphic organizer in your 📙 Active Journal to take notes as you read the lesson.

PRACTICE VOCABULARY

Use the vocabulary activity in your 📙 Active Journal to practice the vocabulary words.

Vocabulary		Academic Vocabulary
polytheism	lyric poetry	cease
mythology	chorus	submission
Olympic games		

Greek children grew up hearing many stories about their gods. In one tale, a proud girl named Arachne boasts that her weaving skills are better than those of the goddess Athena. Athena challenges Arachne to a weaving competition. When Arachne creates a tapestry, or cloth with pictures, that mocks the gods, Athena is furious. The goddess changes the girl into a spider, condemned to weave webs forever. The Greeks told the story of Arachne as a warning against the sin of excessive pride.

Greek Religion and Mythology

The ancient Greeks practiced **polytheism**, the worship of many gods, or deities. A deity is a being with supernatural powers. Unlike the gods of Egypt, however, Greek gods were believed to look and behave like human beings. They were portrayed as human-like in art and literature.

What Was Greek Mythology? Greeks expressed their religious beliefs in their mythology. **Mythology** is the collection of myths or stories that people tell about their gods and heroes. These rich and powerful tales influenced all forms of literature and art.

Some myths explained the changing of the seasons. Others revealed why so much suffering exists in the world. Many myths explained human behavior or taught moral lessons. Some told the stories of heroes, such as Hercules, who was described as having amazing strength. Homer's *Odyssey* tells the story of Odysseus' decade-long struggle to return to Ithaca from the Trojan War. Written in the late 700s BCE, the *Odyssey* was an epic poem that was recited to a listening audience.

Greek myths and stories are still read and retold today. Some of the ancient stories describe entertaining adventures. They also reveal important truths about human nature and why people act in certain ways.

Primary Source

"Look you now, how ready mortals are to blame the gods. It is from us, they say, that evils come, but they even of themselves, through their own blind folly, have sorrows beyond that which is ordained."

—Homer, the *Odyssey*, Book 1

Analyze Charts This chart shows eight of the most important gods and goddesses in Greek mythology. **Determine Relevance** What do their roles tell you about what was important to the ancient Greeks?

Greek Gods and Goddesses In Greek mythology, Zeus was the supreme ruler of the gods, as well as the lord of the sky and the god of rain. He lived on Mount Olympus and threw thunderbolts at those who displeased him. His wife, Hera, protected married women and their households.

Zeus had two brothers. The first, Poseidon, was god of the sea. Zeus' other brother, Hades, ruled and lived in the underworld, which was inhabited by the souls of the dead.

Olympian Gods

Name	Characteristics
Zeus	Father of many of the other gods; conjurer of storms and god of justice
Hera	Wife of Zeus and queen of the gods; goddess of marriage
Athena	Daughter of Zeus; goddess of wisdom and protector of cities
Apollo	God of prophecy, music, poetry, and god of light
Artemis	Twin sister of Apollo; goddess of hunting and childbirth
Poseidon	Brother of Zeus; god of the sea
Ares	God of war
Aphrodite	Goddess of love and beauty

Other major gods included Apollo, god of the arts, prophecy, and healing, and Ares, god of war. Aphrodite was goddess of love and beauty, and the goddess Artemis oversaw hunting and childbirth.

Athena was a popular goddess because, according to one myth, she had given the Greeks the gift of the olive tree. Athena was also the guardian of the city of Athens. When the Greeks fought against other peoples, they believed Athena would appear to help them.

Greeks believed that their gods and goddesses behaved like human beings. The deities fell in love, got married, and had children. They liked to celebrate and play tricks. They also felt jealousy and rage.

What was Greek Religion's Role in Everyday Life? The Greeks honored their gods with public and private religious rituals. Public meetings began with prayers and animal sacrifices. Women played important roles in some of these public ceremonies. In private homes, families maintained household shrines.

Each city-state built temples to its patron deity. On holy days, citizens made sacrifices in front of the gods' temples. They asked the gods for favors, such as good crops or good health.

The Olympic Games Some religious festivals included athletic contests. Athletes competed in sports such as boxing, wrestling, and running. They displayed their skill to honor the gods.

The leading competitions brought together athletes from many city-states. The most famous sports event was the **Olympic games**, which honored Zeus. These games took place every four years. During the games, all conflicts between city-states **ceased**. Travelers came from all over the Mediterranean to attend the games. The festival site at Olympia was crowded with merchants, food sellers, and artisans. Successful athletes were rewarded not with money, but with privileges and fame.

Sacred Sites The Greeks considered groves of trees, springs, and other places to be sacred because they were home to a god or spirit. Mount Olympus, in northern Greece, was an important sacred spot. The Greeks believed it was home to the major gods.

Another sacred site was Delphi, on the slopes of Mount Parnassus. Delphi contained many shrines, but the most important building was the holy temple of the god Apollo. The temple of Apollo housed Apollo's priestess, who was known as the Delphic oracle. An oracle is someone who predicts what will happen in the future. People traveled to Delphi from all over Greece and other lands to ask the priestess questions about the future.

☑ **READING CHECK** **Draw Conclusions** Why are the stories of ancient Greece still influential today?

Academic Vocabulary
ceased • *v.*, stopped

▼ A statue of a Greek discus thrower

Arts in Ancient Greece

The Greeks had a strong appreciation of beauty. They expressed this in their painting, sculpture, and architecture. Even ordinary objects such as vases and jugs were carefully designed. Although most of their paintings have not survived, Greek statues and buildings have been admired for generations.

Painting and Sculpture

From the descriptions of ancient writers, we know that ancient painting was realistic. Painters created an impression of depth and perspective in their work.

Early Greek sculpture shows strong Egyptian influence. However, Greek sculptors gradually developed a style that was much more realistic than any other sculpture in the ancient world. At the same time, Greek sculptors created images of humans and deities that seemed to inhabit an ideal world of calm and peace. They often used this ideal style to decorate their temples and gravestones.

The Greeks honored their deities by creating huge statues of gods and goddesses for shrines and temples. They also carved scenes to decorate temple walls.

Architecture

Like Greek sculpture, Greek architecture was inspired by the proportions of the human body. Architects also tried to achieve perfection in their work. They created buildings that gave a sense of balance and harmony of parts. The finest example of classical Greek architecture is the temple known as the Parthenon, built to honor Athena. The architects Ictinus and Callicrates designed graceful marble columns to support the roof. Above the columns, bands of sculptures showed images of gods and humans. Inside the temple stood a giant statue of the goddess Athena, designed by the sculptor Phidias.

People today think of Greek buildings and statues as dazzling white marble. In ancient times, however, these works would have been painted. Statues would have had colored eyes, skin, and hair, making them appear startlingly real. Over time, however, the ancient colors have faded.

INTERACTIVE

Art and Architecture in Ancient Greece

Analyze Images These ruins once belonged to the Temple of Apollo at Delphi. **Cite Evidence** What considerations would the architects of this temple have taken into account? Find evidence in the text to support your answer.

READING CHECK Identify Main Ideas What makes Greek sculpture unique?

Greek Literature

Like the other arts, Greek literature was linked with religion. Religious festivals often included contests between poets. Others included plays based on myths. The *Iliad* and the *Odyssey,* Homer's great epic poems, reflected the Greeks' belief that the gods controlled human lives.

Analyze Images The ruins of the Parthenon in Athens are on the left. On the right is pictured the Lincoln Memorial in Washington, D.C. **Compare** What similarities do you see between the structures?

Lyric Poetry Some Greek poets who came after Homer wrote shorter poems. Performers often sang these poems while playing a stringed instrument known as a lyre. As a result, these poetic songs became known as **lyric poetry**.

Greeks wrote lyric poetry on many different subjects. Pindar praised victorious athletes while Alcaeus wrote about politics and war. In contrast, Sappho wrote about human emotions. Although most of her poetry has been lost, she was greatly admired in ancient times.

Greek Drama The roots of modern Western theater reach back to ancient Greece. The word *drama*, which means a play or performance on stage, is a Greek word. The words *theater, tragedy, comedy,* and *scene* also come from Greek.

Greek drama developed from performances honoring the god Dionysus. In the earliest plays, a few individual actors performed the character roles. The **chorus** commented on the action and advised the characters. In time, plays became a central feature at festivals. Prizes were awarded for the best play, the best chorus, and the best actor.

Greek dramatists wrote two types of plays: tragedy and comedy. The plot of a tragedy often came from mythology or Homer's epics. Tragedies often traced the downfall of heroic figures caught in violent conflict with their family, their city, or the gods. In the tragedy *Antigone* by Sophocles, the chorus offers the audience this advice:

Primary Source

"There is no happiness where there is no wisdom; No wisdom but in **submission** to the gods. Big words are always punished, And proud men in old age learn to be wise."

—Sophocles, *Antigone*

Quest CONNECTIONS

Study the photographs of the two buildings. How has ancient Greek architecture endured in the modern age? Record your observations in your ▱ Active Journal.

Academic Vocabulary
submission • *n.*, obedience

▲ In this scene from one of Aesop's fables, a fox tries to trick a rooster into leaving a tree.

Quick Activity

Explore the moral lesson of Aesop's fable "The Fox and the Crow" in your ▤ Active Journal.

Two other famous authors of Greek tragedies are Aeschylus and Euripides. Theater groups still stage some of the tragedies of these dramatists. In addition, modern playwrights continue to draw inspiration from the plots and themes of ancient Greek tragedies.

Greek comedies ended happily. They dealt with current events and made amusing observations about Greek culture, society, and politicians. Aristophanes was perhaps the most famous comic playwright. Two of his comedies are still performed today.

What did Aesop's Fables Teach? Another lasting form of Greek literature is the fable, a story that teaches a moral lesson. The most famous of these fables are by Aesop. According to some legends, Aesop was a slave who lived on the Greek island of Samos during the 500s BCE. Freed as a reward for his learning, Aesop traveled widely, collecting and retelling his fables.

Many of Aesop's fables are still familiar. A tale about a tortoise and a hare shows the Greeks' love of athletic competition. In this fable, a hare mocked the slow speed of a tortoise, so the tortoise challenged the hare to a race. The hare was so confident of winning that he took a nap. When he awoke, the tortoise had won. The moral: "Slow and steady wins the race!"

☑ READING CHECK **Compare and Contrast** Compare the two main types of Greek drama.

☑ Lesson Check

Practice Vocabulary

1. How was Greek **mythology** a form of **polytheism**?

2. What role did a **chorus** have in Greek drama?

Critical Thinking and Writing

3. **Synthesize** What were some qualities that the Greeks admired?

4. **Draw Conclusions** Why are Greek myths and dramas still important to us today?

5. **Writing Workshop: Support Thesis with Details** How do ancient Greece's achievements in literature and the arts show a society at its peak? Collect details to support your claims in your ▤ Active Journal.

Homer, the *Odyssey*

The *Odyssey* is one of the first great works of Western literature, alongside the *Iliad*. According to tradition, both were written by the Greek poet Homer. The *Odyssey* is a tale of the Greek hero Odysseus, also called Ulysses, and his epic journey home after the fall of Troy. Homer's works provided the foundations of Greek education and culture. They still impact Western ideas today.

▶ This mosaic shows Odysseus with his men.

Tell me, O muse ①, of that ingenious hero who travelled far and wide after he had sacked the famous town of Troy. Many cities did he visit, and many were the nations with whose manners and customs he was acquainted; moreover he suffered much by sea while trying to save his own life and bring his men safely home; but do what he might he could not save his men, for they perished through their own sheer folly in eating the cattle of the Sun-god Hyperion; so the god prevented them from ever reaching home. Tell me, too, about all these things, O daughter of Jove ②, from whatsoever source you may know them.

So now all who escaped death in battle or by shipwreck had got safely home except Ulysses, and he, though he was longing to return to his wife and country, was detained by the goddess Calypso, who had got him into a large cave and wanted to marry him ③. But as years went by, there came a time when the gods settled that he should go back to Ithaca; even then, however, when he was among his own people, his troubles were not yet over; nevertheless all the gods had now begun to pity him except Neptune ④, who still persecuted him without ceasing and would not let him get home.

—Homer, the *Odyssey*, Book 1

Reading and Vocabulary Help

① The narrator of the story asks the muse for inspiration as he prepares to tell the story.

② In this context, Jove is the Greek god Zeus and his daughter is Athena.

③ Why does Calypso detain Odysseus?

④ Neptune is the Roman god of the sea; however, in Greek mythology his name is Poseidon.

Analyzing Primary Sources

Cite specific evidence from the document to support your answers.

1. **Determine Author's Point of View** How does Homer use the second paragraph to foreshadow the rest of the poem?

2. **Use Evidence** From the reading, which god do you suppose will give Odysseus the most trouble on his journey?

3. **Analyze Style** This text is the very beginning of the *Odyssey*. How does the author introduce the hero of the story?

Ancient Greek Learning

BOUNCE TO ACTIVATE ▶ VIDEO

GET READY TO READ

START UP

In the image, Greek philosophers exchange ideas and share their teachings. List several reasons why education is important to a society.

GUIDING QUESTIONS

- What enduring contributions did Greek scholars make to philosophy and history?
- What scientific and medical discoveries did the ancient Greeks make?
- How did Greek thought affect individuals, states, and societies?

TAKE NOTES

Literacy Skill: Summarize

Use the graphic organizer in your 📙 Active Journal to take notes as you read the lesson.

PRACTICE VOCABULARY

Use the vocabulary activity in your 📙 Active Journal to practice the vocabulary words.

Vocabulary		Academic Vocabulary
Socratic method	Hippocratic oath	reason
Academy		concept
hypothesis		

Just as the Greeks appreciated beauty and the arts, they saw the value of learning about the world. Scholars, scientists, and great thinkers were honored members of society. Some of their scientific findings lay the foundation for future discoveries. Greek philosophers, thinkers who explored the nature of knowledge, came up with ideas that we still use to understand our world.

Greek Philosophy

As you read earlier, Chinese thinkers were among the world's first philosophers. Their goal was to pursue wisdom. Greek philosophers had the same goal. In fact, the word *philosophy* comes from Greek words meaning "love of wisdom."

The Importance of Reason The Greeks began their search for wisdom by asking questions similar to those the Chinese asked, such as: "What is the nature of the universe? What is a good life?" The Greeks, however, took their search a step further. They also asked: "How do we know what is real? How can we determine what is true?"

The Greeks believed that they could answer these questions by using the human power of **reason**. Reason is the power to think clearly. To increase their thinking power, the Greeks developed a system of reasoning known as logic. Logic involves a step-by-step method of thinking through a problem or question.

Academic Vocabulary

reason • *n.*, the power to think clearly

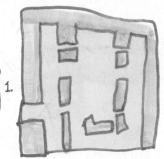

knowledge

Socrates and Plato Several important philosophers lived in Athens. One of them, Socrates, wandered around the city, drawing other Athenians into discussion. In these discussions, Socrates asked question after question to force his listeners to think more clearly. Today, this question-and-answer method of teaching is called the **Socratic method** and is used to instruct students in a variety of subjects.

1.

Socrates' discussions challenged accepted beliefs. Eventually, this got him into trouble with the leaders of Athens. They charged him with corrupting the young. Socrates was also accused of not believing in the gods that the city recognized. In the trial that followed, Socrates defended himself:

Primary Source

"I have never set up as any man's teacher. But if anyone, young or old, is eager to hear me . . . I never grudge [deny] him the opportunity. . . . If any given one of these people becomes a good citizen or a bad one, I cannot fairly be held responsible."

Modist

—Socrates, quoted in Plato's *Apology*

Plato, a student of Socrates, recorded his teacher's ideas in a series of conversations called dialogues. Plato went on to found a school of

Analyze Images In 399 BCE, Socrates was sentenced to death for teaching his beliefs to his students. In this painting, he takes the poison that will kill him, as his students look on. **Analyze Images** How would you describe Socrates' attitude as he faces his death? How did the artist portray the reaction of his followers?

- He was the son of a stonemason and a midwife, not an aristocrat.
- Many people considered him annoying.
- Plato said he was the "wisest, justest, and best of all I have ever known."
- He said "an unexamined life is not worth living."
- Fairly or not, Socrates was found guilty and sentenced to death in 399 BCE.

Critical Thinking What do you think Socrates meant by saying that "an unexamined life is not worth living"?

philosophy called the **Academy**. Today, the word *academy* often means a school of higher learning. Plato was interested in the nature of reality. He remains one of the most influential thinkers in history.

INTERACTIVE

Greek Philosophers

What did the Stoics Believe? During the Hellenistic period, new philosophies arose. One group, founded by Zeno, was called the Stoics.

To the Stoics, divine reason governed the universe so people needed to live in harmony with nature. Stoics tried to master their emotions through self-control.

✓ READING CHECK **Identify Main Ideas** How did Socrates change how teachers and students interacted?

How did History and Politics Shape Greece?

The Greeks' search for wisdom also led them to study the past. Greek historians did more than record events, however. Most importantly, they examined why these events took place.

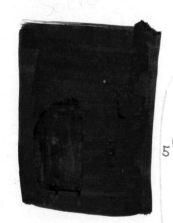

Three Great Historians The Greek writer Herodotus is often called "the father of history" because he asked why certain events happened. Born about 484 BCE, Herodotus lived during the Second Persian War. The Persian Wars, and the cultures of both peoples, are carefully described in his masterwork, *The Histories*. In this work, he investigates the causes of the conflict between the Greeks and the Persians.

Thucydides, of Athens, was another important Greek historian, whose contributions still endure. Born in 460 BCE, Thucydides lived during the Peloponnesian War. He began writing his history of the war while the events were fresh in people's memories. Before writing about a battle, he would visit the battle site. He would also interview people who had participated in the event. He hoped that his history would be accurate—and that it would help people avoid repeating the mistakes of the past.

Xenophon lived from about 427 to around 355 BCE. He traveled widely in the Persian empire and Greece. He wrote the first known autobiography in world history. An autobiography is a book about a person's life written by the subject of the book. Xenophon believed that the study of history could teach people how to live moral lives.

Political Thinkers Greek writers also discussed politics and government. For example, Plato wrote a book called *The Republic*, which presented his views about the ideal government. Plato did not approve of the way democracy functioned in Athens. He thought that the ideal city-state would be led by philosopher-kings, who had the wisdom to make the right decisions. Such leaders would not be elected by the people.

The philosopher Aristotle also wrote a book about government, called *Politics*. In this book, Aristotle compared existing governments. He argued that the best government would be a balanced one that avoided extremes. Aristotle also believed that citizens must participate in politics in order to be happy.

Great Orators Greece was also brimming with great orators, or gifted public speakers. These orators included Demosthenes, and Pericles, who was discussed in earlier lessons. Demosthenes was an Athenian statesmen who overcame a stammer to become one of the greatest orator of his day. Many of his speeches, especially those against Philip II of Macedonia, still survive.

☑ READING CHECK **Identify Main Ideas** Why did the Greeks study the past?

Science and Technology

Most ancient peoples associated everyday occurences, like the rising of the sun or common illnesses, with the activities of various gods or spirits. While most Greeks shared these beliefs, some began to look for natural causes of such events.

The Power of Observation Like modern scientists, the Greeks first made observations of nature. They then formed a **hypothesis**, or logical guess, to explain their observations. This way of thinking represented something new in the ancient world. It laid the foundations of modern science, mathematics, and medicine.

The Study of Nature Greek philosophers began the scientific study of nature. These early scientists believed that natural laws governed the universe. They set out to identify and explain those laws.

One of the first scientific thinkers was a philosopher named Thales of Miletus. Thales was born around 624 BCE. Thales asked questions such as: How big is the Earth? What is its shape? What holds it up in space? In each case, he based his answer on his observations of nature.

▲ Demosthenes practices a speech by speaking to the sea.

These early Greek scientists were not always correct. For example, Thales believed that all things are made of water. Thales also believed that Earth was a disk that floated on water. Even though Thales's ideas were incorrect, he inspired other thinkers to use logic to develop answers. For example, the philosopher Democritus said that the universe was made up of tiny particles that could not be split. He called them "atoms."

Aristotle The most famous natural philosopher was the scholar Aristotle. He was born in 384 BCE and studied at Plato's Academy. Later, he set up his own school, called the Lyceum.

Unlike Plato, who distrusted the senses, Aristotle sought knowledge through observation. He analyzed data about plants, animals, and rocks. He studied mathematics and logic. He analyzed government and the arts. A modern historian summarized Aristotle's work:

Analyze Images This artwork, *The School of Athens* by Raphael, shows Plato and Aristotle surrounded by other philosophers. Raphael painted this between 1509 and 1511 CE. **Draw Conclusions** What does the large gap in time between these philosophers' time and Raphael's painting say about Plato and Aristotle's importance?

Primary Source

"He was a great collector and classifier of data. . . . What he wrote provided the framework for the discussion of biology, physics, mathematics, logic, literary criticism, aesthetics, psychology, ethics, and politics for two thousand years."

—J. M. Roberts, *History of the World*

How Did the Greeks Improve Technology? The Greeks put their powers of observation to practical use as they developed sophisticated technology. From the 400s on, the Greeks invented all kinds of mechanisms, including water clocks, watermills, and locks. They understood the principle of steam power, which they used to operate mechanical statues, gadgets, and toys. The inventor Archimedes is said to have created a weapon that used mirrors to redirect the sun's light to set fire to enemy ships—an early laser! *extremely inventive*

☑ READING CHECK **Identify Main Ideas** How did Greek science develop?

Quest CONNECTIONS

Read the information about Thales and the quote about Aristotle. How did these scientists influence how we study science today? Record your findings in your 📓 Active Journal.

Aristotle was very influential 2,000 years!?

A Golden Age for Mathematics and Medicine

Greek thinkers often excelled in many different fields. For example, Thales, the philosopher, was also a leading mathematician. The Greeks also believed that Thales had studied geometry in Egypt. Later, in the Hellenistic period, this kind of cultural exchange helped produce a golden age of Greek mathematics and medicine.

Mathematics The Greeks first discovered many basic **concepts** in mathematics. Pythagoras of Samos was an early Greek mathematician. Pythagoras thought that numbers were the key to understanding the universe. He developed the idea of "square numbers." Today students of geometry still learn the Pythagorean theorem, which bears his name. A theorem is a statement in mathematics that can be proved to be true.

Hypatia was one of the world's leading mathematicians and astronomers. She was the daughter of Theon of Alexandria, himself a leading mathematician. She carried on his work and even became a popular philosopher. Another mathematician, Euclid, has endured as the "father of geometry." He taught in Alexandria and compiled a number of works including *The Elements*, a textbook that became the basis for modern geometry.

Medicine The Greeks also made contributions in the field of medicine. Greek doctors looked for natural causes of illnesses instead of blaming them on the gods. Their success at treating patients brought them fame throughout the Mediterranean world. Greek doctors practiced surgery and dentistry.

Hippocrates became the best-known Greek doctor. He also wrote many medical books and ran a school that trained new doctors. Hippocrates taught his students to diagnose patients by asking them questions and making observations so they could learn about their symptoms.

Hippocrates also had his students swear an oath. In this oath, medical students promised to use their knowledge only in ethical ways. The **Hippocratic oath** still guides doctors today.

Academic Vocabulary
concept • *n.*, idea

Greek Mathematicians' work is still studied today.

3. The oath is practiced at many doctors, & is entirely logical

▶ Hypatia, a leading mathematician and astronomer

Primary Source

"I will prescribe treatment for the good of my patients according to my ability . . . and never do harm to anyone. To please no one will I prescribe a deadly drug nor give advice which may cause his death. . . . In every house where I come I will enter only for the good of my patients. . . . All that I learn from my patients . . . I will keep secret. If I keep this oath faithfully, may I enjoy my life and practice my art, respected by all men and in all times."

—Hippocrates, from *The Hippocratic Oath*

▲ This carved sculpture shows a Greek doctor and his patients.

Hippocrates had a similar mindset as Socrates.

Medicine in Alexandria The city of Alexandria, Egypt, became an important center for the study of medicine. The Greeks benefited from the medical knowledge of the Egyptians. Egyptian doctors carefully examined patients and recorded their symptoms. But the Greeks went further and sought to understand the reasons for a patient's illness.

Although Greek societies frowned on dissection of the human body, two scientists working in Alexandria, Herophilus and Erasistratus, studied human anatomy. It was in Alexandria that doctors realized that the optic nerve linked the eye to the brain. Ancient Greek doctors also discovered that the brain was the center of thought, and that the pulse sent blood through the arteries.

☑ **READING CHECK** Identify Supporting Details Why were medical students required to take an oath?

They discovered all about the most important things we know now.

☑ Lesson Check

Practice Vocabulary

1. What does a teacher do when using the **Socratic method**?

2. What do scientists need to do to form a **hypothesis**?

3. What do doctors promise by taking the **Hippocratic oath**?

Critical Thinking and Writing

4. **Evaluate Explanations** Why is learning about a scholar like Thales still valuable, even though some of his ideas were later proved to be incorrect?

5. **Synthesize** What methods of the early Greek historians might be useful to historians today?

6. **Writing Workshop: Draft your Essay** Review your thesis and supporting details, then begin drafting your essay. Consult your 📓 Active Journal.

Update an Interpretation

Using the secondary source, follow these steps to learn ways to update interpretations of history as new information is uncovered.

INTERACTIVE

Synthesize

1 Identify the interpretation that may need to change. For a long time, scholars believed the ancient city of Troy as described by Homer in the *Iliad* was a Greek settlement.

2 Study new information about the subject. Read about the evidence found by archaeologists in the article below.

  a. What question of history is the source discussing?

  b. Does the source suggest new information that may require a new interpretation of events?

3 Revise the interpretation, if needed, to reflect the new information. Remember that the original interpretation was that Troy was a Greek settlement. What does the new evidence suggest about Troy?

Secondary Source

"We know today, from our own excavations and even from earlier ones, that in all main respects, Bronze Age Troy had stronger ties with Anatolia than with the Aegean. We've learned this from the tons of local pottery and small finds, such as a seal with a local hieroglyphic inscription, as well as the overall settlement picture, mud-brick architecture, and cremation burials. . . .

. . . [I]t is now more likely than not that there were several armed conflicts in and around Troy at the end of the Late Bronze Age. At present we do not know whether all or some of these conflicts were distilled in later memory into the "Trojan War" or whether among them there was an especially memorable, single "Trojan War." However, everything currently suggests that Homer should be taken seriously, that his story of a military conflict between Greeks and the inhabitants of Troy is based on a memory of historical events—whatever these may have been. If someone came up to me at the excavation one day and expressed his or her belief that the Trojan War did indeed happen here, my response as an archaeologist working at Troy would be: Why not?"

—Manfred Korfmann, *Archaeology*, May/June 2004

Alexander and the Hellenistic World

BOUNCE TO ACTIVATE   ▶ VIDEO

GET READY TO READ

START UP

Look at the image of the leader Alexander the Great, who conquered many lands. In what way can military conquest spread the culture of one civilization?

GUIDING QUESTIONS

- How did Macedonian rulers defeat the Greek city-states?
- In what ways did Alexander's conquests affect connections between cultures in the ancient world?
- How did Hellenistic learning expand the impact of Greek culture?

TAKE NOTES

Literacy Skills: Sequence
Use the vocabulary activity in your 📕 Active Journal to take notes as you read the lesson.

PRACTICE VOCABULARY

Use the graphic organizer in your 📕 Active Journal to practice the vocabulary words.

Vocabulary	Academic Vocabulary
sarissa	period
Hellenistic	acquire
classical civilization	

The Greeks told a story about Alexander the Great, the young man who set out to conquer the world. The story begins one afternoon as 12-year-old Alexander, the prince of Macedonia, watched his father, King Philip II, barter over a horse. It was a fine black stallion, but it was also angry and unruly. The king decided that the horse could not be tamed. As the king turned away, Alexander grabbed the reins. Alexander sensed that the horse's wildness was caused by fear. He turned the horse to face the sun so that it would no longer be frightened by its own shadow. Alexander quickly calmed and mounted the horse, to everyone's astonishment. The king bought the horse for Alexander, who named him Bucephalus. Bucephalus never allowed anyone else to ride him. He carried Alexander into many battles as the young Macedonian fought for world conquest.

What Fueled Macedonia's Rise?

Macedonia was a land in the north of the Greek peninsula. The Macedonians had their own traditions, which the Greeks considered old-fashioned. Unlike most Greek city-states, the Macedonians were still governed by kings. Despite their different customs, the Macedonians were influenced by Greek culture.

Philip of Macedonia Macedonia was briefly part of the Persian empire. But after Persia's defeat during Xerxes' invasion of Greece, the Macedonians regained their independence. Their kingdom expanded over the lands north of Greece.

One of the rulers of Macedonia was a brilliant and ambitious leader named Philip. Philip gained power after his brother, the Macedonian king, was killed in battle in 359 BCE. The king's son, who was heir to the throne, was only an infant, so the nobles of Macedonia elected Philip as king.

To strengthen his power, Philip built up a powerful army and developed new tactics. Like the Greeks, Philip organized his infantry into phalanxes. Then he armed each man with an 18-foot-long pike. The Macedonian pike, or **sarissa**, was much longer than the spears used by the Greeks. It gave the Macedonians an advantage in battle, as the Macedonian pikes could be used to keep enemies at a greater distance. Philip also trained his men to change directions in battle without losing formation. Armed with long pikes and fighting with greater discipline, Philip's soldiers were a powerful force.

Philip proved the value of his ideas soon after becoming king. His powerful army defeated the Illyrians, who had won a victory over the Macedonians just a few months before.

Philip Conquers Greece Philip then turned to conquer Greece. First, he tried to win the loyalty of each city-state with diplomacy. When these tactics failed, he went to war.

Analyze Images
Macedonians use sarissas in battle. **Use Visual Information** How would these long pikes be an advantage in a battle like this?

start of alexanders reign.

Started to gain power + Motivation.

In 338, Philip, along with his son Alexander, who led the cavalry, won a decisive battle in central Greece over the combined armies of Thebes and Athens. Philip gained control of almost all of mainland Greece. The city-states were allowed to keep their governments. However, they were expected to support Philip in his next goal—a war against Persia. But as preparations were being made for the invasion of Asia, Philip was assassinated, or murdered, during his daughter's wedding.

✓ READING CHECK **Identify Supporting Details** How did Philip strengthen his power?

Alexander on the March

Alexander, Philip's 20-year-old son, now gained the throne. Alexander was already a military leader. His brilliant mind had been shaped by the famous scientist and philosopher, Aristotle. Alexander was filled with dreams of glory. As a boy, Alexander's favorite book was a copy of the *Iliad* that Aristotle had given to him. Alexander wanted to be like the book's hero, Achilles. This ambition would inspire his spectacular conquests.

Alexander would lead his armies through Persia, central Asia, and Europe. His conquests would spread Greek culture well beyond Greece, but his first task was to secure its control.

Conquering Greece After Philip's death, some city-states in Greece tried to regain their independence. Alexander quickly crushed these revolts. To discourage future rebellions, he burned Thebes to the ground.

With Greece secure, Alexander turned eastward. In 334, he took his army of 30,000 foot soldiers and 5,500 cavalry troops into Asia. Alexander inspired fierce loyalty among his soldiers by personally leading them in battle.

Did you know?

Alexander was the first Greek ruler to shave his beard—a fashion that lasted 500 years!

BIOGRAPHY
5 Things to Know About

ALEXANDER THE GREAT
King and Conquerer (356 BCE–323 BCE)

- His mother, Olympias, was the daughter of King Neoptolemus of Epirus, a region in northwest Greece and southern Albania.

- He left with his mother on the day his father married a new wife.

- He won his first victory against the Persians at the Granicus River in 334 BCE.

- After conquering Egypt, Alexander let Egyptians practice their own religion.

- Although he named many cities for himself, he also named one for his horse.

Critical Thinking Looking at Alexander's lifespan, what was so remarkable about his many victories?

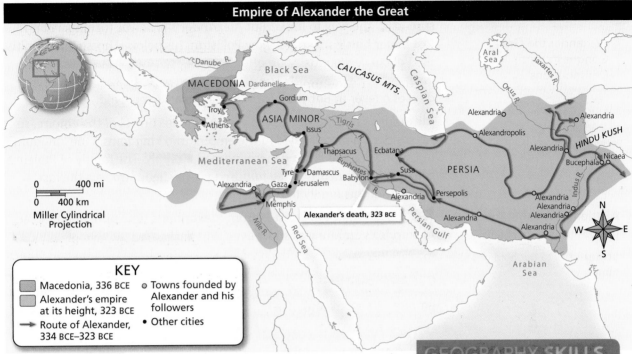

Empire of Alexander the Great

KEY
- Macedonia, 336 BCE
- Alexander's empire at its height, 323 BCE
- → Route of Alexander, 334 BCE–323 BCE
- ○ Towns founded by Alexander and his followers
- • Other cities

Alexander's death, 323 BCE

0   400 mi
0   400 km
Miller Cylindrical Projection

Hoping for World Conquest In Asia, Alexander freed the Ionian city-states from Persian rule. He marched south to capture the cities along the Mediterranean coast. Then the army marched to Egypt. The Egyptians welcomed Alexander for liberating them from the Persians. Before leaving Egypt, he founded the city of Alexandria on the edge of the Nile delta.

From Egypt, Alexander headed back toward Persia. By the end of 330, he had defeated the Persian king.

Alexander was not satisfied with the defeat of the Persian empire. His eyes were fixed on a greater goal—world conquest. He led his army farther east, into Afghanistan and India. These were lands no Greek had ever seen. Because he built a vast empire in only 11 years, people called him "Alexander the Great."

The Hellenistic Period Alexander founded Greek-style cities everywhere he went. In these cities, Greek customs mingled with the ideas and art of other lands. Greek soldiers, traders, and artisans settled in these new areas. From Egypt to India, the Greeks built temples and filled them with Greek statues. Those already living in these lands absorbed Greek ideas and customs. Out of this exchange emerged a new form of Greek culture called **Hellenistic**, or Greek-like. The word *Hellenistic* comes from the Greeks' word for themselves: Hellenes.

Greek culture mixed with local cultures in Egypt, Persia, and India. For example, the Egyptian goddess Isis was given a place in Greek mythology and was honored across the Hellenistic region.

GEOGRAPHY SKILLS

Alexander built a vast empire in only 11 years.

1. **Location** How far south did Alexander's empire extend?

2. **Identify Cause and Effect** Across which three continents did Alexander's empire stretch? What effect did this conquest have on these lands?

Alexander longed for more power, even after many defeats

INTERACTIVE

Alexander the Great's Conquests and Contributions

The Fall of the Greek Empire Because of Alexander, Greek culture spread all the way to India. But Alexander's luck was turning. After his last major battle in what is now Pakistan, his beloved horse Bucephalus died of battle wounds. Soon after, his army mutinied and refused to conquer any more lands. The army headed west. In 323, Alexander died of a fever in Babylon. He was not quite 33 years old.

Alexander's infant son was too young to take control of the empire, so Alexander's generals divided the empire into kingdoms. One kingdom, in Egypt, was ruled by a general named Ptolemy. The family of Ptolemy ruled Egypt for nearly three hundred years. Cleopatra was the last member of this family to rule Egypt.

The Hellenistic **period** lasted from Alexander's time until about 30 BCE. Alexander's empire was short-lived, but the world was forever changed by his conquests.

Academic Vocabulary

period • *n.*, a span of time

acquire • *v.*, to get hold of, obtain

✔ READING CHECK **Identify Cause and Effect** Why was Alexander's empire so short-lived?

What was the Impact of Hellenistic Learning?

Alexander the Great had been deeply impressed by his teacher Aristotle's interest in the world. When Alexander led his army into Asia, he brought scientists to study local plants and animals. Alexander's support for research flourished in one of the cities that he founded—Alexandria, the Greek capital of Egypt.

Hellenistic Egypt Alexandria became an important site of encounter as the city grew rich from handling the trade between peoples of Europe, Africa, and Asia. The wealth of the city helped fund projects like the Great Library. The Library was founded by the Ptolemies, the Hellenistic rulers of Egypt. Their goal was to **acquire** a copy of every book in the world. Over the years, the collection grew to about 500,000 book rolls, or scrolls.

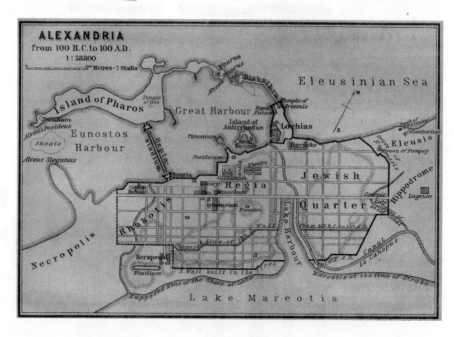

Analyze Images This map of Alexandria shows the grids created by the layout of its main streets. **Draw Conclusions** What does the street grid tell you about how the city was planned and built?

City of Scholars Alexandria's library and museum attracted some of the most important scholars in history. It was here that Jewish scholars created the Septuagint, a translation of the Hebrew Bible into Greek. Euclid, Theon, and Hypatia, who you read about in the last lesson, all lived and worked in Alexandria.

Although the inventor and mathematician Archimedes spent most of his life in Syracuse, he may have studied in Alexandria. Archimedes created many useful inventions. One of them, the Archimedean screw, is still used to lift water for irrigation or to drain swamps. Archimedes also made important contributions to mathematics.

93

▲ A diagram of an Archimedean screw shows a method of draining water.

Greek Culture Spreads Greek culture spread during Alexander's conquests. In Italy, Greek culture influenced the Romans, long before they conquered Greek lands. The union of Greek and Roman culture created what we call Greco-Roman or **classical civilization**. As you will read later, the Romans spread this civilization across even larger parts of the world.

Exchange Between Continents During the Hellenistic period, many cities along the Silk Road became sites of encounter for people of different religions, cultures, and regions across Europe, Africa, and Asia. The Silk Road connected people from the Mediterranean Sea to China. As a result, cities from Athens to Alexandria to Luoyang in China became great gathering places for traders, artisans, and merchants of different cultures. Each brought new ideas and new ways of life.

✓ READING CHECK **Identify Cause and Effect** How did Alexandria become so rich?

☑ Lesson Check

Practice Vocabulary

1. How did Alexander's men use the **sarissa**?

2. What cultures influenced **Hellenistic** culture?

Critical Thinking and Writing

3. **Draw Inferences** Why did Alexander burn Thebes to the ground?

4. **Draw Conclusions** How was Alexandria a site of encounter?

5. **Writing Workshop: Revise** Now that you have read about the fall of the independent Greek city-states, make revisions to your essay to include these new details. If possible, exchange drafts with a partner and comment respectfully on one another's work.

☑ Review and Assessment

VISUAL REVIEW

Comparing Athens and Sparta

ATHENS
- Democracy
- Open to change
- Focus on individual expression
- Value placed on luxury
- Acquired resources through trade

BOTH
- Spoke Greek
- Worshiped some of the same gods
- Had class system
- Government included assemblies made up of free men

SPARTA
- Oligarchy
- Focus on discipline
- Value placed on military life
- Acquired resources through conquest
- More independence for women

Notable Greek Achievements

Field	Achievement
art	realistic depictions
architecture	details such as columns and sculptures
sports	founding of the Olympic games
literature	lyric poetry, comedy and drama, Aesop's fables
philosophy	Socratic method, focus on reason, Stoicism
science and technology	the use of observation and hypothesis
mathematics	Pythagorean theorem
medicine	Hippocratic oath

READING REVIEW

Use the Take Notes and Practice Vocabulary activities in your 📓 Active Journal to review the topic.

INTERACTIVE

Practice vocabulary using the Topic Mini-Games.

Quest FINDINGS

Present Your News Magazine

Get help for writing your news magazine in your 📓 Active Journal.

ASSESSMENT

Vocabulary and Key Ideas

1. **Trace** How did the geography of Greece give rise to city-states?

2. **Define** What is a **polis**?

3. **Describe** Why did Greek colonists settle along coastal areas?

4. **Define** What is an **oligarchy**?

5. **Describe** What is the difference between a lyric poem and epic poem?

6. **Recall** What regions became part of Hellenistic Greece?

Critical Thinking and Writing

7. **Determine Relevance** How did trade contribute to the development of the Minoan and Mycenaean cultures?

8. **Compare and Contrast** What were the key differences between Athens and Sparta?

9. **Draw Conclusions** What caused the Greek city-states to become part of the Macedonian empire?

10. **Revisit the Essential Question** Of the forms of government you learned about in this topic, which do you think was the best form? Explain your reasoning.

11. **Writing Workshop: Write an Explanatory Essay** Using the thesis statement and details you recorded in your 📓 Active Journal, complete an essay on this question: Why did the power of the independent Greek city-states rise, peak, and fall?

Analyze Primary Sources

12. In the view of Aristotle in the selection below, what is the role of government?
    A. to conquer other governments
    B. to do the least for their citizens
    C. to do the greatest amount of good
    D. to rule only for the aristocracy

    "Every state is a community of some kind, and every community is established with a view to some good; for mankind always act in order to obtain that which they think good. But, if all communities aim at some good, the state or political community, which is the highest of all, and which embraces all the rest, aims at good in a greater degree than any other, and at the highest good."
    —Aristotle, *Politics*

Analyze Maps

Use the map at the right to answer the following questions.

13. Locate Athens and Sparta on the map.
14. Which body of water is west of the Peloponnesian Peninsula?
15. What body of water does the letter D mark?

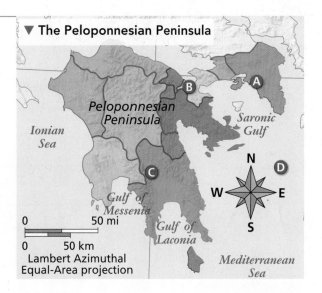

▼ **The Peloponnesian Peninsula**

Peloponnesian Peninsula

Ionian Sea

Saronic Gulf

Gulf of Messenia

Gulf of Laconia

Mediterranean Sea

0   50 mi
0   50 km
Lambert Azimuthal Equal-Area projection

TOPIC 7

The Roman Republic
800 BCE – 30 BCE

GO ONLINE
to access your
digital course

 VIDEO

 AUDIO

 ETEXT

 INTERACTIVE

 WRITING

 GAMES

 WORKSHEET

 ASSESSMENT

Go back 2,500 years

to **THE ROMAN REPUBLIC** to discover the beginnings of one of the ancient world's greatest civilizations. You won't be surprised to find that its government, with a senate, judges, and a strong executive, had a major influence in shaping our own.

Explore
The Essential Question

What is the best form of government?

Rome developed a new way of governing. How was the Roman republic different from the monarchies that came before it?

Unlock the Essential Question in your Active Journal.

◀ The Temple of Saturn in Rome

Watch

NBC LEARN

BOUNCE TO ACTIVATE ▶ VIDEO

Cicero and the Roman Republic

Discover one of the republic's greatest statesmen and orators.

Read

about the world's first great republic and the people who created it, along with the challenges they faced.

The Roman Republic

800–30 BCE

Learn more about the Roman republic by making your own map and timeline in your Active Journal.

 INTERACTIVE

Topic Map

Where was the Roman republic?

The ancient city of Rome was located on the Tiber River on the west coast of the Italian peninsula. Over several centuries, the republic expanded into much of western and southeastern Europe and the eastern and southern shores of the Mediterranean Sea. Locate the city of Rome on the larger map.

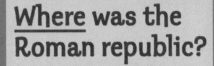 INTERACTIVE

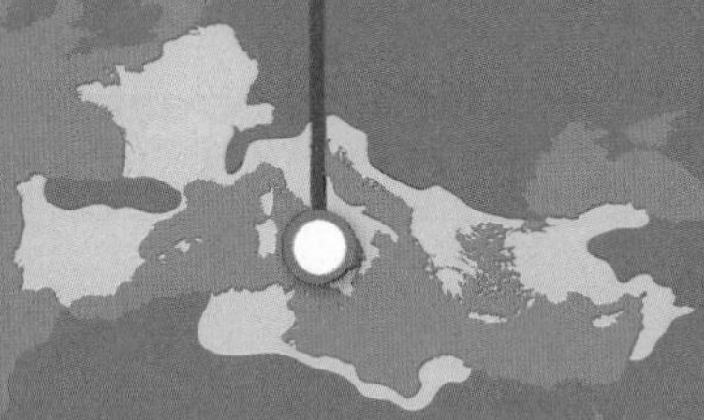

Topic Timeline

What happened and when?

A town founded on seven hills grows into the biggest city in the world...epic power struggles...Explore the timeline to learn what was happening in Rome and the rest of the world during this period.

509 BCE
The Roman republic is founded.

800 BCE
People first settle in Rome.

TOPIC EVENTS

900 BCE	700 BCE	500 BCE

WORLD EVENTS

586 BCE
Nebuchadnezzar II destroys the Temple in Jerusalem.

400 BCE
Olmec civilization disappears in Central America.

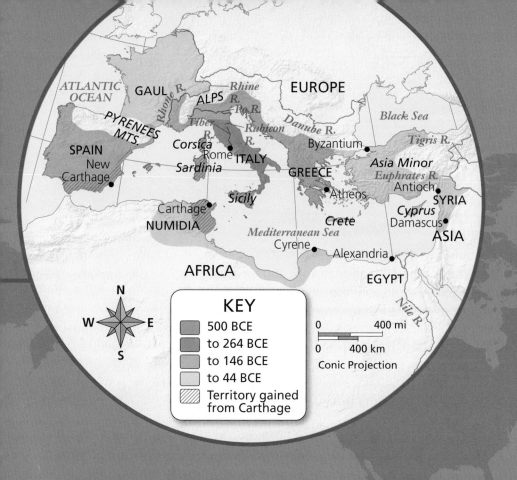

ATLANTIC OCEAN

GAUL
Rhone R.
ALPS
Rhine R.
Po R.
Danube R.
EUROPE
Black Sea
Tigris R.
PYRENEES MTS.
SPAIN
New Carthage
Corsica
Tiber R.
Rubicon
Rome ITALY
Sardinia
GREECE
Byzantium
Asia Minor
Euphrates R.
Antioch
SYRIA
Sicily
Athens
Cyprus
Damascus
ASIA
Carthage
NUMIDIA
Crete
Mediterranean Sea
Cyrene
Alexandria
EGYPT
AFRICA
Nile R.

KEY
- 500 BCE
- to 264 BCE
- to 146 BCE
- to 44 BCE
- Territory gained from Carthage

0 — 400 mi
0 — 400 km
Conic Projection

N W E S

Who will you meet?

Aeneas, Trojan prince and legendary founder of Rome

Cicero, scholar, writer, and defender of the Roman republic's ideals

Julius Caesar, soldier-politician who dealt a final blow to the republic

146 BCE
Rome destroys Carthage.

30 BCE
Augustus becomes Rome's first emperor.

44 BCE
Julius Caesar becomes dictator for life.

218 BCE
Hannibal's army invades Italy and threatens Rome.

| 300 BCE | 100 BCE | 100 CE |

221 BCE
Shi Huangdi founds Qin Dynasty in China

185 BCE
Last Maurya emperor dies in India

Quest
Document-Based Writing Inquiry

The Roman Influence

Quest KICK OFF

In 509 BCE, ancient Romans overthrew their king and established a republic, a form of government in which citizens vote and elect officials. In fact, the word *republic* come from Latin, the language the Romans spoke. What other influences did the Roman republic have?

How did Rome's government influence later governments?

Explore the Essential Question "What is the best form of government?" in this Quest.

▼ Statue of a Roman Senator

1 Ask Questions

First, you'll need to review the elements of Rome's government discussed in the topic. Then think about past and current governments in Europe, the Americas, Africa, and Asia to focus on in your explanatory essay. How do their governments compare to Rome's? Make a list of the questions you need to answer in your essay in your 📔 Active Journal.

2 Investigate

As you study the topic, look for **Quest CONNECTIONS** that indicate elements of Rome's government that have influenced the United States government or governments of other countries. Record your notes in your 📔 Active Journal.

3 Examine Primary Sources

Next explore a set of sources of information that reveal the influence of Rome's government on later governments. Capture your thoughts in your 📔 Active Journal.

Quest FINDINGS

4 Write Your Explanatory Essay

Next, develop an answer to the Guiding Question, and shape it into an essay explaining how Rome's government influenced later governments. Get help for this task in your 📔 Active Journal.

The Roman Republic Rises

BOUNCE TO ACTIVATE ▶ VIDEO

GET READY TO READ

START UP

Study the photograph of the Tiber River valley and quickly preview the headings and images in the lesson. What do these images add to what you already know about Rome? Write down two facts you already know.

GUIDING QUESTIONS

- In what ways did geography affect Rome's growth?
- How did the Etruscans and Greeks influence Roman culture?
- What form of government did the Romans found?
- How did the Romans gain control of the Italian peninsula?

TAKE NOTES

Literacy Skills: Analyze Cause and Effect
Use the graphic organizer in your 📓 Active Journal to take notes as you read the lesson.

PRACTICE VOCABULARY

Use the vocabulary activity in your 📓 Active Journal to practice the vocabulary words.

Vocabulary		Academic Vocabulary
forum	legion	identify
republic	maniple	diplomacy

You have learned how civilizations developed in the eastern Mediterranean in Mesopotamia, Egypt, and Greece. Around 800 BCE, along the Tiber River in present-day Italy, a village called Rome was built. This settlement became the world's largest city and center of a mighty empire.

Italy's Varied Geography

Rome lies near the center of the Italian Peninsula. A high mountain range called the Alps separates Italy from the rest of Europe. The Apennines run down the center.

Despite its many mountains, Italy has a less rugged landscape than Greece. Soldiers could march from one place to another relatively easily. This made it easier for Rome to unite the peninsula. In addition, Italy has several rivers that ships can use. Since ancient times these rivers have provided water and transportation routes.

Italy has large, fertile, flat plains. These gave it plenty of land suited for farming. Roman farmers produced such products as olive oil, wheat, grapes, and wine. They raised sheep and goats for milk and wool.

INTERACTIVE

Growth of the Roman Republic

Ancient Rome was part of a region called Latium. This region gave its name to the Latin people and their language, also called Latin.

READING CHECK Identify Main Ideas What advantages did Italy's plains give Rome?

The Earliest Days of Rome

Archaeologists have discovered that people first settled in Rome around 800 BCE. They built villages on the tops of seven hills overlooking the Tiber River, near where the river flows into the sea. Over time these villages formed a single town that grew into a small city.

Historians do not know exactly *how* Rome was founded, or established. The Romans themselves told a legend about the beginning of their city.

According to the legend, Rome was founded by twins named Romulus and Remus. Their mother was a Latin princess. The twins' father was Mars, the god of war. The king, their uncle, was jealous of the twins. He had the babies placed in a basket and thrown into the Tiber. They were saved from death by a she-wolf and raised by a shepherd.

As adults, the twins gathered a group of men to found a new city. However, they quarreled and Romulus killed Remus. Romulus lived and gave his name to the city he built—Rome.

Historians do not believe this legend. However, we can learn from the story that the Romans believed their city had a special origin and a connection to the gods.

GEOGRAPHY SKILLS

Roman civilization began by the Tiber River, close to the center of the Italian Peninsula and the Mediterranean Sea.

1. **Location** How was Rome's location relative to bodies of water an advantage?

2. **Infer** How might the Tiber have interfered with the development of Rome?

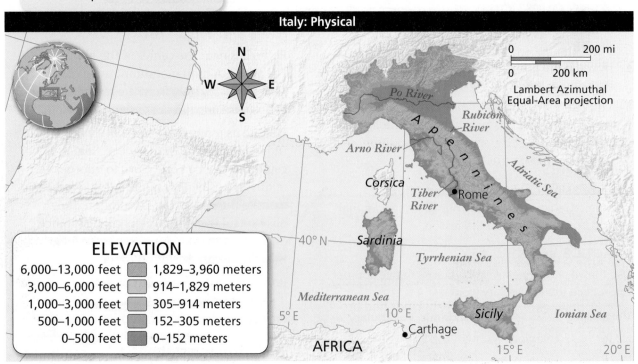

Italy: Physical

ELEVATION

6,000–13,000 feet	1,829–3,960 meters
3,000–6,000 feet	914–1,829 meters
1,000–3,000 feet	305–914 meters
500–1,000 feet	152–305 meters
0–500 feet	0–152 meters

0 200 mi
0 200 km
Lambert Azimuthal Equal-Area projection

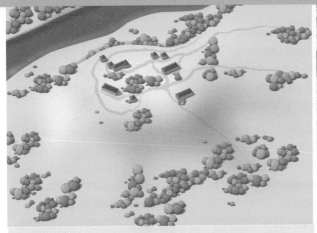

Rome began in the 800s BCE as a group of villages on top of hills overlooking the Tiber River, like the one shown here.

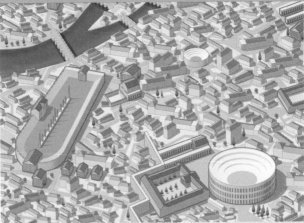

By the 300s CE, Rome was the largest city in the world.

A Roman writer made this point.

Primary Source

Now, if any nation ought to be allowed to claim a sacred origin. . . that nation is Rome.

—Livy, *History of Rome*

What Was the Forum? The early Romans drained a swampy area between two of the town's hills. This became the Roman Forum. A **forum** is an open area in a city filled with public buildings, temples, and markets. The Roman Forum was the center of Rome's government, religion, and economy. When the Romans founded new cities in later years, they usually built a forum at the center.

What Were Rome's Natural Advantages? Several factors in Rome's geography helped the city grow and prosper. The city's hills gave the Romans a natural defense. Because Rome was located on the Tiber River, it had access to a nearby port. Although the river was shallow, small boats could reach the city. However, the river was too fast and dangerous for large boats. Seagoing ships could not attack Rome.

Rome was also located on key trade routes. The Tiber Valley was a natural east–west route for trade. In addition, several north–south trade routes crossed the Tiber just south of Rome.

READING CHECK **Summarize** What were Rome's natural advantages?

Rome Becomes a Republic

Like Athens and Sparta, Rome began as an independent city-state. Its first form of government was a monarchy.

The Roman Kings Rome's early kings had broad powers. They served as head of the army, chief priest, and supreme judge. The Roman kings helped the city grow. They built the first buildings in the Forum and led wars against nearby villages.

Analyze Diagrams
The two diagrams show Rome's growth over hundreds of years. **Make Predictions** What factors caused Rome to grow?

▼ Romans built aqueducts, like this one in Spain, in Rome and in many other places under their control.

Quest CONNECTIONS

How did the government of the Roman republic resemble ours? How was it different? Record your findings in your 📓 Active Journal.

The kings ruled with the consent of Rome's wealthy aristocrats. Older male aristocrats formed a body called the senate. The senate advised the king on important matters. The word *senate* comes from the Latin word *senex*, which means "old man."

Founding the Republic Over time, Roman aristocrats grew tired of royal rule. The seventh king of Rome, Tarquin the Proud, mistreated his people. In 509 BCE, leading Romans overthrew the king and formed a **republic**. A republic is a government in which citizens have the right to vote and elect officials. As in other spheres, Romans were strongly influenced by Greek forms of government, particularly Athens' democracy.

The word *republic* comes from the Latin term *res publica*, which means "public thing" or "public business." In the Roman republic, all free adult male citizens could play a role in the city's government.

☑️ READING CHECK **Identify Supporting Details** What does *res publica* mean?

The People of Italy

As Roman power grew, the Romans came into contact with different Italian peoples and borrowed from their cultures.

Greek Colonies Greeks settled in Italy starting around the 700s BCE. They founded cities in southern Italy. Rome came into contact with these cities and learned about Greek culture. The Romans admired the Greek city-states, especially Athens. Many Hellenistic traditions also were adopted by the Romans.

Academic Vocabulary

identify • *v.*, consider or treat as the same

The Greeks of Italy had a strong influence on Roman culture. Romans made Greek mythology their own by **identifying** their gods with those of the Greeks. For example, the Greek Zeus was identified with Roman Jupiter, Hera with Juno, and Athena with Minerva.

The Romans also adopted Greek legends. According to legend, Romulus and Remus were Aeneas's descendants. Aeneas was a Trojan hero in the *Iliad,* a Greek poem. His story was written down during the first century CE by the Roman writer Virgil in a poem called the *Aeneid.*

Analyze Images Early writing systems had both similarities and differences. **Compare and Contrast** Which are more similar, Etruscan and Latin letters or Latin and Roman letters?

Who Were the Etruscans? The Etruscans were the most powerful people in central Italy when Rome was founded. They lived in Etruria, just north of Latium. The Etruscans were skilled artists and builders. They sailed around the Mediterranean as traders. They learned from the Greeks and the Phoenicians. The Etruscans developed their own alphabet based on Greek. From this, the Romans developed an alphabet. Today we use Roman letters in English and many other languages. The Etruscans also influenced Roman religion and architecture.

Early Alphabets

Etruscan	Early Latin	Modern Roman
∩	A	A
⊟	H	H

SOURCE: *Blackwell Encyclopedia of Writing Systems*

☑️ READING CHECK **Identify Cause and Effect** How did the Greeks influence the Romans?

How Did Rome Expand?

The Roman people were feared conquerors. They also made skillful use of **diplomacy**. By using both force and diplomacy, the Romans ruled all of Italy by the late 200s BCE.

Rome's Army The basic unit of the Roman army was the **legion** (LEE jun). Each legion had from 4,500 to 5,000 heavily armed soldiers. Most served as infantry, or foot soldiers.

Each legion was broken up into maniples. A **maniple** was a unit of between 60 and 160 soldiers. On flat plains, all the maniples in a legion formed a solid battle line. But in rough country, each maniple could move and fight on its own. This flexibility gave the Roman legions a great advantage over enemies who fought in a single square block, including Greek phalanxes. Phalanxes were less flexible.

The Roman military did not just use Roman innovations. It was open to good ideas wherever they came from. For example, maniples were first used by the Samnites, a mountain people who lived in the Apennines in central Italy.

Roman soldiers were builders as well as fighters. When a Roman army was on the move, its soldiers would build a temporary fort every night. Soldiers also built roads and bridges. These helped armies move faster.

Rome's Friends and Allies Rome gained power with the help of its allies. The Romans signed treaties with other peoples, often defeated enemies. The treaties required allies to send troops to fight alongside the Romans in their campaigns. Eventually, many loyal allies were given Roman citizenship and the right to vote.

☑ **READING CHECK** What methods did Roman leaders use to expand their territory?

Academic Vocabulary

diplomacy • *n.,* managing relationships with other countries through negotiation

▲ Roman legions, clad in armor and helmets, were feared all over the Mediterranean.

☑ Lesson Check

Practice Vocabulary

1. What is a **republic**?

2. What was the role of the Roman **Forum**?

3. What was the basic unit of the Roman army?

Critical Thinking and Writing

4. **Compare and Contrast** How was a Roman legion different from a Greek phalanx?

5. **Draw Conclusions** Find evidence to support the idea that the Romans were open to the influences of foreign cultures.

6. **Identify Cause and Effect** In what ways did Rome's geography help it grow?

7. **Writing Workshop: Develop a Clear Thesis** Recall what you know or have learned about Rome and other earlier or contemporary societies, such as Egypt, Persia, Greece, and China. Write a thesis statement that compares Rome to one of these societies in terms of the environment, political system, citizenship, or cultural connections in your 📓 Active Journal.

Livy, *History of Rome*

Titus Livius, known as Livy, wrote a history of the Roman republic in the early days of the Roman empire. His work was huge—142 volumes long! However, only about a quarter of the work survives. Livy started his history at the beginning, with the legendary founders Romulus and Remus.

◄ Romulus and Remus were the legendary founders of Rome.

Reading and Vocabulary Support

① Recall what you have learned about early Roman history. Who is Romulus? Why do you think he is calling people together?

② What is Romulus's attitude toward the people he is leading?

③ Lictors were Roman officials who cleared the way for chief magistrates in public and caught and punished criminals.

④ Sovereignty is supreme power and authority, especially political authority.

⑤ Where does Livy think Romulus got the idea to have twelve lictors?

⑥ How did the Etruscans influence the early Romans?

After the claims of religion had been duly acknowledged, Romulus ① called his people to a council. As nothing could unite them into one political body but the observance of common laws and customs, he gave them . . . a body of laws which he thought would only be respected by a <u>rude and uncivilised race</u> ② of men if he inspired them with awe by assuming the outward symbols of power. He surrounded himself with greater state, and in particular he called into his service twelve ③ <u>lictors</u>. Some think that he fixed upon this number from the number of the birds who foretold his <u>sovereignty</u>; ④ but I am <u>inclined</u> ⑤ to agree with those who think that as this class of public officers was borrowed from . . . their neighbours, the <u>Etruscans</u> ⑥ . . . . Its use amongst the Etruscans is traced to the custom of the twelve sovereign cities of Etruria when jointly electing a king furnishing him each with one lictor.

—Livy's *History of Rome*, Book I, Chapter 8

Analyzing Primary Sources

Reread the excerpt to find evidence to support your answers.

1. **Determine Author's Purpose** Why does Livy discuss the origin of lictors?

2. **Identify Main Ideas** Why does Romulus give a body of laws to his people?

3. **Write a Summary** In your own words, summarize the main ideas of this passage. Avoid letting your own opinions influence the summary.

Government of the Republic

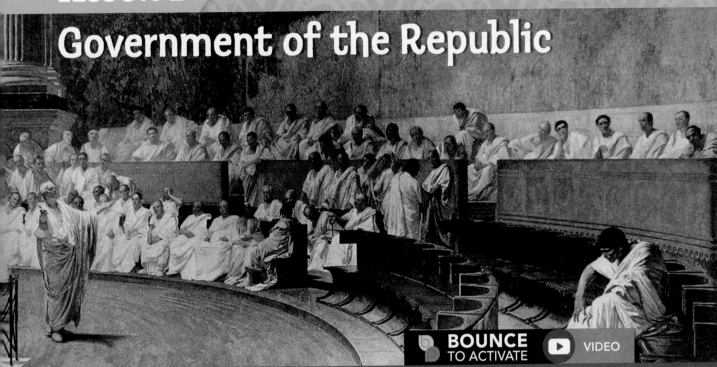

BOUNCE TO ACTIVATE ▶ **VIDEO**

GET READY TO READ

START UP

Examine the painting of Cicero addressing Roman senators. Write one prediction about how the Roman Senate may be similar to the United States Senate and one prediction of how it was different.

GUIDING QUESTIONS

- Why and how was power divided among different groups in the Roman republic?
- How did the Romans view of the concept of citizenship?
- How did the Roman republic function?
- What influence did the Roman republic have on later governments?

TAKE NOTES

Literacy Skills: Identify Main Ideas
Use the graphic organizer in your ⬛ Active Journal to take notes as you read the lesson.

PRACTICE VOCABULARY

Use the vocabulary activity in your ⬛ Active Journal to practice the vocabulary words.

Vocabulary		Academic Vocabulary
constitution	toga	violate
veto	consul	policy
magistrate		

The Roman republic was a unique system of government that lasted for 500 years. It led the Roman people from humble origins to conquest of the Mediterranean world.

What Were the Principles of Roman Government?

The ancient historian Polybius said about the Roman republic that "it was impossible even for a native to pronounce with certainty whether the whole system was aristocratic, democratic, or monarchical." Rome's system combined all three forms of government. Strong leaders, wealthy aristocrats, and average citizens all had a role to play.

Rome's Constitution Roman government was structured by a **constitution**. This is a system of rules by which a government is organized. Unlike the United States' constitution, the Roman constitution was unwritten. It was based on tradition, custom, and a collection of laws.

unique, yet effective

THREE BRANCHES OF ROMAN GOVERNMENT

Each branch of the Roman government had its own powers and could "check and balance" the others.

MAGISTRATES
- Elected **officials** who enforced the law and judged cases
- The two most powerful magistrates were the **consuls**

ASSEMBLIES
Groups of adult male Roman **citizens** who **passed laws** and elected **magistrates**

THE SENATE
- Wealthy, **important citizens**
- Helped pass laws, controlled **foreign policy** and government **money**

Analyze Charts The Roman government was made up of three different parts. **Apply Concepts** How could the assemblies check the magistrates?

Similar to government in US

Quest CONNECTIONS

Look at the diagram. What influence on modern government do you see? Capture your notes in your 📓 Active Journal.

Academic Vocabulary

violate • *v.*, break a rule or agreement

What Was the Separation of Powers? The main idea in Rome's system of government was the separation of powers. Power was shared among different people with set roles. After overthrowing the last king, Romans did not want to be ruled by a single man. They built their new system of government to make sure no one person could become too powerful. For centuries, it worked.

One way in which the Romans limited officials' power was by splitting offices between two or more men. The Romans did not elect one top leader. Instead, they elected two leaders called consuls. They held equal powers. Each could veto the action of the other. To **veto** means to stop or cancel the action of a government official or body. In Latin, *veto* means "I forbid."

The Romans also limited an official's time in office to one year. Even a powerful official could not do much harm in that short time.

How Do Checks and Balances Work? Power was also divided among the three branches of government. They were the assemblies, the senate, and the **magistrates**, or elected officials who enforce the law. A government with three parts is called a tripartite government.

Each branch had its own set of powers. One branch could check, or stop, another branch from misusing its power. No branch could hold total power, though the senate was often the most powerful branch.

The Roman Rule of Law Another key principle was the rule of law. This means the law applied to everyone. Even elected officials could be tried for **violating** the law after their term of office was over.

✅ **READING CHECK** Identify Main Ideas What are checks and balances?

Who Were the Citizens of Rome?

Free Roman men were citizens of the Roman republic. If both his parents were Roman citizens, males could be Roman citizens at birth. Women and slaves were not citizens and had no direct role in government. The symbol of Roman citizenship was the **toga**, a garment that adult men wore wrapped around their bodies. Only citizens could wear togas. Citizenship could also be granted by the Roman people and later on by generals and emperors.

Rights and Responsibilities Roman citizens had the right to a trial. Any adult male citizen had the right to vote. He had to pay taxes. Citizen also were obligated to serve in the military and in Roman courts as legal guardians, witnesses, jurors, or judges, both at their own expense. Roman culture stressed civic duty, meaning the responsibility of a citizen.

Patricians and Plebeians Roman citizens were divided into two orders. One was the patricians, members of the oldest families in Rome. They were usually wealthy. In the early days of the republic, they may have controlled all government offices.

The other order was made up of the plebeians, who were a majority of Romans. They did not come from famous old families like the patricians. Most were common farmers or artisans. However, some plebeians were wealthy.

The plebeians forced patricians to open up political offices to them. According to Roman tradition, they did so by going on strike. During a war, the plebeians walked out of the city and sat down on a nearby hill. Rome could not fight on without them, so the patricians had to give in.

☑ READING CHECK **Summarize** Who had the right to vote during the Roman republic?

What did the Assemblies and the Senate Do?

Patricians and plebeians alike had a role to play in Roman government.

The Assemblies Assemblies of Roman citizens were the democratic part of Roman government. All adult male citizens could participate in assemblies, though the votes of the wealthy usually counted for more than those of the poor.

At assemblies, Roman citizens elected officials and passed laws. This was a form of direct democracy, like the assembly in Athens. However, the power of the assemblies was checked by the powers of the senate and of elected officials.

The Senate The senate was the part of Roman government that worked like an oligarchy. It was made up of the wealthiest and best-known older Roman men, often former magistrates. Senators were chosen by an official called the censor. They did not represent the people. They were supposed to guide the state. Rich, older senators were thought to be wiser than other citizens.

citizens had priveledge + power

Quick Activity

Discover how the Romans used numerals in your 📓 Active Journal.

▼ This silver coin from around 100 BCE shows Romans voting.

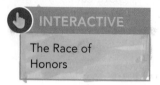

INTERACTIVE

The Race of Honors

The senate advised the assemblies and magistrates. Its advice was almost always followed. It also ran foreign **policy** and decided how to spend the state's money. It was the most powerful part of the Roman government.

☑ READING CHECK **Cite Evidence** What did the senate control directly?

Who Were the Magistrates?

The Romans elected a number of powerful magistrates. The power of these high officials made them almost like monarchs. Magistrates were wealthy men. Their ancestors had usually held high offices. For men from elite families, politics was a key part of life.

Politicians usually moved from lower offices to higher offices. This path was called the Race of Honors. It changed over time, but by the later years of the republic, it followed a standard form.

What Were the Lower Offices? The Race of Honors started with the lowest office, the quaestor (KWY stor). Quaestors were accountants who kept track of the state's money. They also served as assistants to higher officials. If a citizen did well as a quaestor, he might seek election as an aedile (ee dile). Aediles were in charge of holding festivals and maintaining public buildings. These lower offices were stepping-stones to greater power.

Tribunes of the Plebs Plebeians could run for the powerful office of tribune of the plebs before moving on to higher offices. Tribunes acted as the protectors of the plebeians. Sometimes they took radical or even revolutionary positions.

Analyze Charts During the Roman republic, citizens could rise through a variety of roles to become consul. **Draw Conclusions** Do you think this competitive set-up was an effective way of training government officials? Use evidence to support your answer.

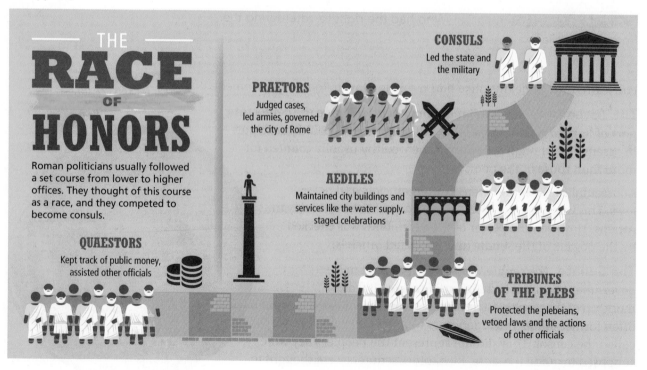

THE RACE OF HONORS

Roman politicians usually followed a set course from lower to higher offices. They thought of this course as a race, and they competed to become consuls.

CONSULS
Led the state and the military

PRAETORS
Judged cases, led armies, governed the city of Rome

AEDILES
Maintained city buildings and services like the water supply, staged celebrations

TRIBUNES OF THE PLEBS
Protected the plebeians, vetoed laws and the actions of other officials

QUAESTORS
Kept track of public money, assisted other officials

LUCIUS QUINCTIUS CINCINNATUS
Roman Statesman (Born c. 519? BCE)

- Cincinnatus was a historical figure who became a Roman legend for his devotion to his country.

- According to tradition, in 468 BCE, the Roman senate called on Cincinnatus to save a surrounded Roman army. He left his plow standing in the field, said good-bye to his wife, and went to war.

- He defeated the enemy in one day, legend says, and held power only as long as the emergency lasted, then returned to his farm.

- George Washington's contemporaries thought of him as an American Cincinnatus. He left retirement to lead the Continental Army. In 1783, with the war won, he returned to his farm.

- To Romans and Americans, the story of Cincinnatus demonstrated an ideal of republican patriotism.

Critical Thinking Why was George Washington thought of as an American Cincinnatus?

Tribunes had the right to veto any law, or the action of any magistrate. The veto gave the tribunes great power over all other parts of the government. It was also strictly forbidden to harm a tribune or stop him from doing his job.

Praetors and Consuls After serving as an aedile or tribune, men could try to be elected as a praetor (PRY tor). Praetors judged cases, managed the city of Rome, and led armies in times of war.

After serving as a praetor, a politician could be elected consul. The **consuls** were the top officials in the Roman republic. Their most important job was to lead the army. They also presided over the senate and assemblies and were the highest judges.

Consuls and praetors had visible symbols that showed their authority. They wore special togas and sat on ivory chairs. They were followed around by bodyguards called lictors. The lictors carried the consul's or praetor's fasces, a symbol of power.

Dictators In the modern world, when we call someone a dictator we usually mean that he is a cruel tyrant. But in ancient Rome, a dictator was an important public official. The senate could vote to name a dictator in times of great emergency. Dictators held complete power, but only for a limited time. They served for a maximum of six months.

A man named Cincinnatus was one famous dictator. Cincinnatus was working his farm when he heard that he had been chosen dictator. He quickly defeated Rome's enemies, resigned his office, and went back to his fields. He was thought of as a model citizen.

☑ **READING CHECK** **Infer** Why did Cincinnatus become famous?

▼ Elected in 2016, Tammy Duckworth of Illinois is one of the U.S. Senate's 21 female Senators.

How Did the Romans Set an Example?

The Roman republic was the most successful and long-lasting republic until modern times. The writers of the American constitution knew a great deal about Roman history and government. They followed the Roman example in many areas.

For instance, like Roman citizens, American citizens have the right to vote and stand for office. The United States government has three branches with separate powers, like the Roman republic had. Checks and balances limit the power of each branch. The rule of law applies equally to every American, as it did to every Roman citizen. Like tribunes of the plebs, presidents have the power to veto laws. The United States has a senate, as ancient Rome did.

Still, many parts of American government are different. As you read, the Roman republic did not have a written constitution, while the United States does. Ancient Rome also practiced forms of direct democracy. In contrast, the United States practices representative democracy. Roman citizens voted directly on laws. In the United States, laws are usually passed by representatives elected by the citizens.

In the United States today, women participate equally in the government. In ancient Rome, women did not have a role in politics. While slavery has been illegal in the United States since the 1860s, many people in ancient Rome were slaves who had no political rights.

☑ **READING CHECK** Compare and Contrast How was a tribune of the plebs like an American president?

☑ Lesson Check

Practice Vocabulary

1. What is a **constitution**? Did the Romans write theirs down?

2. What was a **toga** a symbol of?

3. What do **magistrates** do?

Critical Thinking and Writing

4. Identify Main Ideas In what ways were the tribunes of the plebs especially powerful?

5. Compare and Contrast How is direct democracy in the Roman republic different from representative democracy in the United States?

6. Draw Conclusions What do you think America's founders thought of the Roman republic? Explain.

7. Writing Workshop: Support Thesis with Details Compare Rome's government with those of other societies, such as Egypt, Persia, Greece, or China. Gather details to support the thesis for your essay. Write these supporting details in your 📕 Active Journal.

Society in the Republic

BOUNCE TO ACTIVATE ▶ VIDEO

GET READY TO READ

START UP

Look at the photo. Think about the different groups in your school, such as students, teachers, and staff members. How do they work together? Predict how groups of people in ancient Rome worked together.

GUIDING QUESTIONS

- What roles did men and women hold in Roman society?
- How did life differ for different classes of Romans?
- In what ways were religion and citizenship connected in Romans' lives?

TAKE NOTES

Literacy Skills: Classify and Categorize

Use the graphic organizer in your 📖 Active Journal to take notes as you read the lesson.

PRACTICE VOCABULARY

Use the vocabulary activity in your 📖 Active Journal to practice the vocabulary words.

Vocabulary		Academic Vocabulary
patriarchal society	villa	minority
paterfamilias	established religion	tenant

Like other ancient societies, Rome was divided by gender and class. Men and women had their own social roles. The lives of wealthy Romans were very different from the lives of poor Romans and slaves.

women did not have privileges

Roman Men and Women

Rome was a **patriarchal society**. This means that men ruled their families and that people traced their origins through male ancestors.

What Power Did Fathers Have? The oldest man in a Roman family was called the **paterfamilias**, or head of the household. He owned all the family's property. In theory, a father had absolute, or unlimited, power over his wife, children, slaves, and underage siblings. He could sell his children into slavery. He could even kill them if he chose. In practice, however, a father's power was limited by custom. In fact, many fathers felt that doing one's duty to their families was one of the highest Roman virtues. This duty also included honoring ancestors and continuing the family name through sons.

male figure held all power

→Main Idea →example
→explanation

▲ A Roman husband and wife

What Was the Role of Women? Roman women enjoyed more freedom than Greek women. Unlike most Greek women, they could own personal property. Also unlike many Greek women, Roman women took an active role in social life. Women went to parties, enjoyed the theater, and participated in religious rituals. They could make wills, divorce their husbands, and go out in public. In addition, rich wives and mothers could sometimes influence public decisions through their husbands and sons. But, as you have read, women could not vote, attend assemblies, or hold public office.

According to the Romans, the most important role of a Roman woman was to bear children and raise them to follow traditions. The ideal woman was a faithful wife and mother, devoted to her family.

☑ **READING CHECK** Identify Supporting Details Could Roman women own property?

How Did the Rich and Poor Live?

Most Romans were poor free people or people who were enslaved. A tiny **minority** were wealthy.

Living the Good Life Most wealthy Romans earned their money from agriculture. They owned huge farms worked by poor Romans or slaves. The landowners grew rich from what these people produced. Other wealthy Romans earned their fortunes through business.

Upper-class Romans lived in one- or two-story houses as large as a city block. These homes had courtyards, gardens, private baths, beautiful decorations, and even running water. Many elite families also owned **villas**, or large country homes.

What Was Life Like for the Common People? Life was different for poor Romans. In the city, most poor people lived in cramped apartments without running water. Crime, disease, and fire were serious dangers. Apartment buildings were often badly built, and sometimes collapsed.

Common men and women worked at a variety of jobs. Many were **tenant** farmers who rented land from wealthy landlords. Others worked as day laborers in construction or at the city docks. Some ran stores, taverns, or restaurants.

☑ **READING CHECK** Identify Main Ideas Were the majority of Romans rich or poor?

INTERACTIVE

Roman Villa

Academic Vocabulary

minority • *n.,* a group that is less than half the population

tenant • *n.,* person who rents land or a home

Roman Slavery

Slavery was very common in ancient Rome. As Rome became richer and more powerful, Romans bought or captured more and more slaves. As many as 40 percent of people in Rome in the year 1 BCE may have been enslaved.

How did Enslaved People Live? For most of Roman history, enslaved people had no rights. They were bought and sold as property. They could be beaten or killed by their masters for any reason. Children born to slaves were also slaves. Many slaves worked in mines or on large farms. These enslaved people often died quickly due to brutal treatment.

Other slaves led easier lives. Some enslaved people worked in the homes of their wealthy masters. They performed housework for their masters. They probably had a more reliable source of food and shelter than the poor free Romans.

Some educated slaves worked as secretaries or teachers. These slaves were usually Greeks. Although they lived in much better conditions than other enslaved people, they could still be treated very cruelly.

Enslaved people who served loyally could be freed as a reward. They could also save up to buy their freedom. Freed slaves became citizens and had the right to vote.

Did Enslaved People Fight Back? Some slaves fought back against their masters. One famous fighter was Spartacus, who led an army of rebel slaves in the 70s BCE. They fought the Roman army and threatened to capture Rome before the Romans defeated them.

☑ READING CHECK Summarize Could slaves become free? If so, how?

Quick Activity

This painting shows a Roman slave who worked in a kitchen. Compare the social hierarchy of Roman society with other civilizations in your 📖 Active Journal.

Analyze Diagrams Like other early societies, Rome had a strict social order. **Compare** What roles did both poor citizens and enslaved people fulfill?

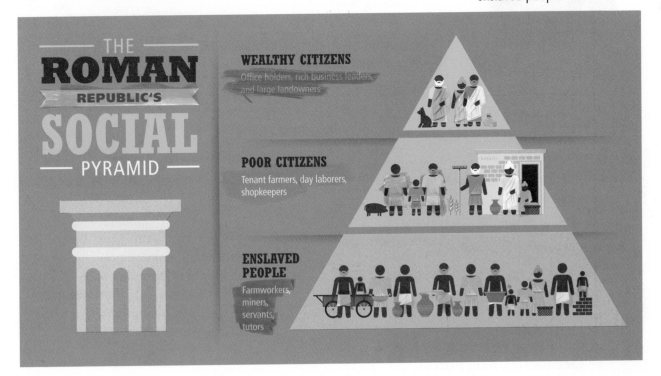

THE ROMAN REPUBLIC'S SOCIAL PYRAMID

WEALTHY CITIZENS
Office holders, rich business leaders, and large landowners

POOR CITIZENS
Tenant farmers, day laborers, shopkeepers

ENSLAVED PEOPLE
Farmworkers, miners, servants, tutors

Roman Religion

Religion was an important part of everyday life in ancient Rome. Religious practices were at the center of the lives of Roman citizens, both with their families at home altars, where they offered sacrifices, and at many public events.

Origins of the Gods The Romans worshipped hundreds of gods. Many were adapted from the Greeks or Etruscans. Others came from Latin traditions. Some came from people the Romans conquered.

What Was Government's Role in Religion? Rome had an **established religion**, an official religion supported by a government. Government officials also served as priests. They often consulted religious experts before making decisions. Romans believed that maintaining good relations with the gods was part of the government's job. Rome was also home to thousands of Jews, and Judaism was recognized by Julius Caesar as an officially permitted religion.

The Romans tried to placate their gods, or keep them happy. They believed that if they did certain things, the gods would give them what they asked for. They prayed, worshiped at home, built temples, offered animal sacrifices, and held games in the gods' honor. Romans like Cicero believed that their success was due to their attention to the gods.

▼ Minerva, the goddess of wisdom.

Primary Source

I am quite certain that . . . [Rome] would never have been able to be so great had not the immortal gods been placated.

—Cicero, from *The Nature of the Gods*

☑ **READING CHECK** **Identify Cause and Effect** Why did the Romans sacrifice to their gods?

☑ Lesson Check

Practice Vocabulary

1. In what way was Rome a **patriarchal society**?

2. What class of people owned **villas**?

3. Who was the **paterfamilias** of a Roman family?

Critical Thinking and Writing

4. **Compare Viewpoints** How might a wealthy Roman view the growth of Roman power differently from a slave?

5. **Identify Main Ideas** What were three important influences on Roman religion? Which do you feel was the most powerful? Why?

6. **Writing Workshop: Draft Your Essay** Draft your explanatory essay comparing Rome to other societies. Start your essay with an introduction and develop your strongest points in the body paragraphs. Get help in your 📔 Active Journal.

Interpret Economic Performance

Follow these steps to learn how to interpret economic performance using the information in a source.

INTERACTIVE

Analyze Data and Models

1 **Identify the type of economic information being presented.** Economists often refer to different kinds of statistics or theories to explain economic performance. For example, they may use a graph showing the rate of unemployment, tables about the standard of living, or statements about levels of income inequality.

a. In the passage below, what kinds of economic information are presented?

b. Could any of the information be presented in a chart, graph, or diagram?

2 **Summarize the main points of your source.** Try to identify the key economic points that the source is presenting. If there are graphs or tables, you can often find key information there. In discussions like the one below, pay close attention to the first and last sentences of the paragraphs. What do you consider the key points of this passage to be?

3 **Interpret the information presented in your source.** Using your source, formulate a conclusion about the economic information presented.

a. Is the author noting positive or negative economic performance?

b. Based on this passage, what conclusions about the state of Rome's farmers can you draw?

c. What effect might the economic situation described have on the stability of the Roman republic?

Secondary Source

The growth of Rome's territory through the conquest of lands outside of Italy affected the republic's poorer classes in surprising ways. As the republic grew, food was brought into the city from distant provinces. For example, grain was imported from Egypt. As the food supply increased, prices fell. Low prices were disastrous for Italian farmers, many of whom were not able to make a living off their small plots and land. They had little choice but to sell their property to rich landowners.

At the same time, large numbers of prisoners-of-war, now slaves, came to Italy. Rather than hire landless farmers to work their growing estates, wealthy landowners bought slaves. Therefore, farmers ended up with no land and no jobs. As a result, these farmers joined a growing class of poor, jobless Romans.

LESSON 4
The Republic Struggles

BOUNCE TO ACTIVATE   ▶ VIDEO

GET READY TO READ

START UP
Look closely at the illustration of one of Rome's enemies attacking Roman soldiers at the Battle of Zama. How do you think the Roman legions felt to be confronted with these strange African animals?

GUIDING QUESTIONS
- What changes resulted in Rome after the Punic Wars?
- What were the strengths and weaknesses of the Roman republic?
- Why did the Roman republic fall?

TAKE NOTES
Literacy Skills: Summarize
Use the graphic organizer in your 📓 Active Journal to take notes as you read the lesson.

PRACTICE VOCABULARY
Use the vocabulary activity in your 📓 Active Journal to practice the vocabulary words.

Vocabulary	Academic Vocabulary
empire	equipment
province	professional
civil war	
Augustus	

Rome began as a small city-state. It conquered a large area around the Mediterranean Sea, but its system of government did not survive this change.

Conflict with Carthage
Rome fought Carthage for control of the western Mediterranean in a series of three wars. These are known as the Punic Wars.

How Did Hannibal Invade Italy?
Carthage was a city in North Africa that also controlled parts of Spain and Sicily. The second of Rome's wars with Carthage nearly destroyed the Roman republic. Hannibal, Carthage's greatest general, led his city's troops. In 218 BCE he marched from Spain into Italy over the Alps mountains with 40,000 soldiers and about 40 war elephants. Despite the long, difficult, and dangerous trip, his army reached Italy.

Through clever tactics, Hannibal defeated three Roman armies. He probably expected Rome to give up after these crushing defeats, but the Romans kept up the fight. They wore down Hannibal's men.

In 204 BCE, the Roman general Scipio crossed the sea into Africa. His army attacked Carthage. Hannibal had to sail home from Italy to protect his city. In Africa, Scipio defeated Hannibal and won the war.

The End of Carthage Although Rome had defeated Hannibal, many Romans still feared Carthage. One senator ended every speech with the words, "Carthage must be destroyed." Rome attacked Carthage in 146 BCE, and Roman troops burned and looted the city. They sold its people into slavery. From Carthage, Rome gained fertile land for growing wheat in Sicily and North Africa, as well as silver deposits in Spain.

Rome now controlled most of the lands along the western half of the Mediterranean Sea. Rome also sent armies to the east. They conquered Greece and parts of southwest Asia. Rome did not yet have an emperor, but it ruled an **empire**, or a state containing several countries or territories. It was divided into **provinces**, or areas within a country or empire. Roman magistrates were sent out to govern these provinces. Many governors were corrupt and cruel.

✓ READING CHECK **Identify Main Ideas** Who was Hannibal?

What Were Rome's Growing Pains?

Conquest brought Rome power and wealth, but the vast riches from trade and the conquest of new territories also caused problems. As the Romans conquered more land, huge numbers of slaves were brought to Italy. The gap between the rich and powerful senators, patricians, and some plebeians and poor plebeians, conquered foreigners, and enslaved people grew. This tension began to affect the Roman political system.

GEOGRAPHY **SKILLS**

During the republic, Rome grew from a city to a power controlling nearly the whole Mediterranean.

1. **Location** Use the compass rose to describe Carthage's location relative to Rome.

2. **Sequence** When did Rome unite Italy?

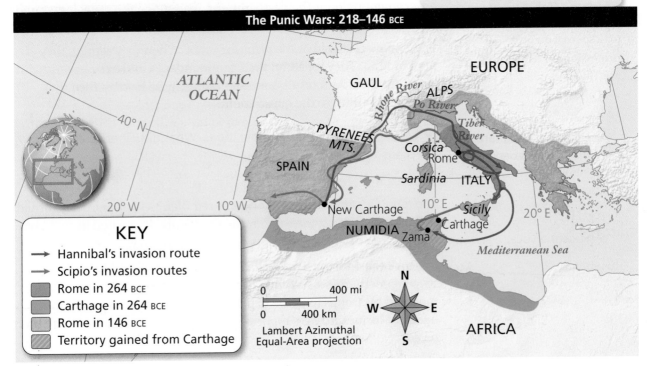

The Punic Wars: 218–146 BCE

ATLANTIC OCEAN

EUROPE

GAUL Rhone River ALPS Po River Tiber River

40° N

PYRENEES MTS.

Corsica

Rome

SPAIN

Sardinia ITALY

20° W   10° W   10° E   Sicily   20° E

New Carthage   Carthage

NUMIDIA Zama

Mediterranean Sea

AFRICA

KEY
- → Hannibal's invasion route
- → Scipio's invasion routes
- ▢ Rome in 264 BCE
- ▢ Carthage in 264 BCE
- ▢ Rome in 146 BCE
- ▢ Territory gained from Carthage

0 ——— 400 mi
0 ——— 400 km
Lambert Azimuthal Equal-Area projection

N W E S

Breaking the Rules In the later years of the republic, magistrates often became very wealthy by stealing from people in the provinces and looting from rich foreign enemies they fought overseas. Wealth made them more powerful at home. Because politicians could become so powerful in this way, they became willing to break the rules of politics or use violence to win elections. Government slowly stopped working.

The Urban Poor Although Rome was growing richer, many Romans were getting poorer. Landowners and employers bought slaves to do work that used to be done by poor Romans. Tenant farmers lost their livelihood. Poor people came to the city in search of work.

Analyze Images Mobs rioted in Rome as the gap between rich and poor widened. **Infer** What kinds of pressures would lead poor people to respond by rioting?

The government feared that Rome's poor could riot or start a revolution. It gave out free grain to keep the peace. Some politicians supported reforms. They appealed to the poor to win office. More traditional elite politicians opposed them. Politicians supported gangs that fought one another. In the 120s BCE, Tiberius and Gaius Gracchus tried to give land to the poor. Their opponents killed them.

The Power of the Army Gaius Marius was a powerful consul. He reformed, or changed and improved, the Roman army. Until around 100 BCE, only citizens who could afford their own armor served in the military. But Marius allowed even the poorest citizens to join. The government paid for their **equipment**. This made the army larger and more **professional**. It also helped the poor.

These soldiers stayed in the army for years. When they retired, they needed land. They relied on their commander to make the government give it to them. As a result, soldiers became more loyal to their commander than to the government.

Academic Vocabulary

equipment • *n.*, things used for a specific purpose

professional • *adj.*, trained, expert

☑ **READING CHECK** **Identify Main Ideas** What did Tiberius and Gaius Gracchus try to do?

How Did Rome Change From Republic to Empire?

The republic's military commanders used their new power. They turned their armies against their rivals and the senate. Rome had its first **civil war**, or war between groups from the same country.

Who Were Marius and Sulla? In 87 BCE, an assembly voted to strip a general named Sulla of his power and give it to Marius. Sulla marched his troops to Rome to get his job back. He won a civil war against Marius and his supporters. Sulla ruled as dictator for more than a year.

Why Did Pompey and Caesar Fight? New commanders rose up to take Sulla's place. Gnaeus Pompey conquered parts of southwest Asia. Gaius Julius Caesar conquered Gaul. The two men teamed up and used their influence to run the government together, ignoring laws and customs. Caesar invited the brilliant lawyer, scholar, and famous speaker, Marcus Tullius Cicero, to join his political alliance with Pompey. Cicero thought the alliance was unconstitutional, so he turned Caesar down. He chose instead to support the senate and to hold fast to the principles of the republic. In Cicero's *The Republic*, he describes the traditional authority and role of the senate:

Primary Source

... the senate governed the commonwealth [community] in those days.... Public affairs were principally managed under the authority, and by the rules and customs of the senate. And although the consuls possessed their power only for a year, it was royal in its nature and effect. And this was strenuously preserved, as necessary to the preservation of the influence of the nobles and principal chiefs....

—Cicero, *The Republic*, Chapter XXXII

Quest CONNECTIONS

Cicero made many great speeches in the Senate. Do leaders today still use speeches as a way of communicating? Record your answer in your 📓 Active Journal.

BIOGRAPHY
5 Things to Know About

CICERO
Roman Statesman, Scholar, Writer (106 BCE–43 BCE)

- Marcus Tullius Cicero was a famous Roman lawyer, speaker, and writer. Much of what we know of the decline and fall of the Roman republic comes from his writings about events he observed or participated in.

- Cicero won fame for his warnings against armed uprisings planned by his rival Catiline.

- He made his way along the *cursus honorum*, becoming a consul in 63 BCE and later governor of the province of Cilicia.

- During the civil war, when Pompey and Caesar seized the Roman government, Cicero tried to avoid taking sides. He remained loyal to the senate and the idea of the republic.

- When Cicero was exiled, he studied philosophy. Eventually, he was allowed to return. He was assassinated in 43 BCE.

Critical Thinking Why might Romans hungry for power consider Cicero an enemy?

▲ Julius Caesar was a brilliant military commander. His numerous victories allowed Caesar to force the senate to make him dictator. This painting shows Caesar receiving the surrender of a Gallic tribal leader.

But later the two commanders fought. The senate sided with Pompey. It ordered Caesar to give up his legions. Caesar marched his army across the Rubicon River into Italy. This began a civil war. Caesar defeated Pompey and the senate.

Caesar took control of Rome. He used his power to help the poor, but he was also made dictator for life. This angered many senators who wanted to keep the republic as it was. A group of senators murdered Caesar in 44 BCE.

The End of the Republic Caesar's death did not save the republic. In his will, Caesar made his teenage relative Octavian his heir. Octavian became a leader of Caesar's many followers. He swore to avenge Caesar's death. He defeated Caesar's murderers in a civil war.

Octavian defeated Mark Antony and Antony's ally Cleopatra, the queen of Egypt. By 30 BCE, he ruled Rome. The republic became a monarchy, the Roman empire. Octavian became the first emperor. He took the title **Augustus**, meaning honored one.

Augustus made new rules for senate membership. He increased the property requirement and prohibited senators from being directly involved in business. The emperor could call for and lead senate discussions, introduce laws, and appoint new senators. Augustus pretended to respect republican traditions, but as emperor he held all the real power. The senate became merely a group of advisors.

Why did the Roman republic fall? And why were Julius Caesar and Augustus allowed to take control of Rome? The empire's swift expansion, with its increasing wealth and the growing gap between rich and poor, put pressure on the republic's government and society. As the military's power grew, commanders were tempted to seize power for themselves. These conflicts led to a long civil war. Augustus ended the civil wars, but at the cost of the republic's freedom.

 INTERACTIVE

Who Was Julius Caesar?

☑ READING CHECK **Identify Cause and Effect** What was decided when Caesar crossed the Rubicon?

☑ Lesson Check

Practice Vocabulary

1. Who is involved in a **civil war**?

2. Who first led the Roman **empire**?

Critical Thinking and Writing

3. **Summarize** How did Rome defeat Hannibal?

4. **Compare and Contrast** Compare and contrast the Roman army before and after Marius's reforms.

5. **Identify Main Ideas** What was the main reason why the Roman republic fell?

6. **Writing Workshop: Write a Conclusion** Review what you've written already for your explanatory essay that compares Rome to earlier and contemporary societies. Write a strong conclusion that sums up your ideas. Consult your 📓 Active Journal for help.

Analyze Sequence, Causation, and Correlation

INTERACTIVE

Analyze Cause and Effect

Read the passage and then follow these steps to help you identify sequence and to distinguish between causation and correlation.

1 Choose an event or a condition as a starting point. You might want to choose an event at the beginning of the passage.

2 Identify sequence. Look for clue words or phrases like *first*, *next*, and *then*. These terms signal sequence. Make a rough timeline of events that led up to that event and events that occurred after that event. Note that all the events in the passage took place in BCE. This means that more recent years have *smaller* numbers than earlier years.

3 Identify cause-and-effect relationships. Look for clue words or phrases that signal cause-and-effect like *because*, *for this reason*, *brought about*, *led to*, *as a result*, and *therefore*. Which cause-and-effect clues do you see in the passage?

4 Look at other events or conditions for possible correlations. Look for clue words or phrases like *meanwhile*, *at the same time*, and *also*. Terms like these suggest that although events and conditions may have something in common, one thing has not *caused* the other. Which correlation clue words or phrases do you see in the passage?

5 Summarize the cause-and-effect relationships and correlations. Make a table or chart of the events. Indicate which events were causes of another event and which were correlations, or events happening at the same time.

Secondary Source

The Roman republic faced many conflicts as it gained territory and power. Beginning in 264 BCE, Rome fought three Punic wars against Carthage, a rival city-state in North Africa. The Romans won the First Punic War in 241 BCE and as a result gained control of Sicily, Corsica, and Sardinia.

For revenge, the Carthaginian general Hannibal started the Second Punic War in 218 BCE and won battles in Italy for the next 15 years, but the Romans wore his army down and eventually captured Carthage. Then, in 149 BCE, the Third Punic War erupted, and the Romans burned and looted Carthage in 146 BCE. Survivors were killed or sold into slavery.

Meanwhile, Roman armies also conquered Greece and parts of southwest Asia. The magistrates who governed these new Roman territories were often corrupt and brutal. At home, the growing gap between rich and poor led to gang wars in Rome's streets. In 123 BCE, when the tribune Tiberius Gracchus tried to give land to the poor, his enemies killed him and his brother.

☑ Review and Assessment

VISUAL REVIEW

Rome: Comparing Monarchy and Republic

MONARCHY

King served as head of the army, chief priest, and supreme judge

Older male aristocrats formed a body called the Senate that advised the rulers

REPUBLIC

- All free adult male citizens took part in government
- Separation of powers
- Citizens = patricians and plebeians

Roman Citizenship

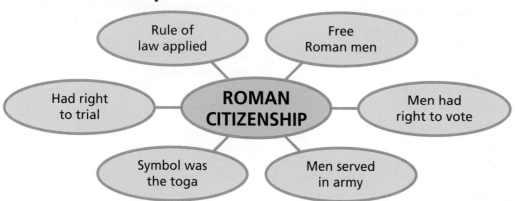

Rule of law applied

Free Roman men

Had right to trial

ROMAN CITIZENSHIP

Men had right to vote

Symbol was the toga

Men served in army

READING REVIEW

Use the Take Notes and Practice Vocabulary in your 📕 Active Journal to review the topic.

- Reading Skill Graphic Organizers

- Practice Vocabulary Activities

Complete an interactivity to help you practice vocabulary.

 **INTERACTIVE**

Practice vocabulary using the Topic Mini-Games

Quest FINDINGS

Write Your Explanatory Essay

Get help for writing your essay explaining the Roman republic's influence on later governments in your 📕 Active Journal.

ASSESSMENT

Vocabulary and Key Ideas

1. **Describe** How did Italy's geography help Rome unite the peninsula?

2. **Identify Main Ideas** How did the Greeks influence Roman religion?

3. **Recall** Who could wear a **toga**?

4. **Check Understanding** How did Rome's allies help it expand?

5. **Check Understanding** How did Rome's expansion lead to a rise in the number of enslaved people in Rome?

6. **Define** What does it mean to say that ancient Rome had an **established religion**?

Critical Thinking and Writing

7. **Identify Implied Main Ideas** Why are Roman beliefs about the founding of their city, such as those about Romulus and Remus and Aeneas, important?

8. **Compare and Contrast** List one similarity and one difference between the governments of the Roman republic and the United States.

9. **Identify Central Issues** Suppose that you could travel back in time to ancient Rome. List one question you would ask each of the following: a man, a woman, a rich person, a poor person, and an enslaved person.

10. **Revisit the Essential Question** Defend the statement that the Roman republic was structured to keep a single person from holding too much power. Support your answer with evidence from this lesson.

11. **Writing Workshop: Write a Research Paper** Using the preparatory work you've done in your ▯ Active Journal, conduct research in order to answer the following question in a research essay: How did other societies influence and affect the Romans? Consider the Greek, Hellenistic, Chinese, and Persian civilizations you've already studied in this course in your essay.

Analyze Primary Sources

12. Why does Polybius believe the Roman constitution worked so well?
    A. because it gave all power to a single ruler
    B. because different parts of the government balanced one another
    C. because it was a pure democracy
    D. because one part of the government had total power over all other parts

"The three kinds of government, monarchy, aristocracy and democracy, were all found united in the common wealth [government] of Rome. . . . Such being the power that each part has of hampering the others or co-operating with them... it is impossible to find a better political system than this."
—Polybius *Histories*, 200s BCE

Analyze Maps

Use the map to answer the following questions.

13. Which letter represents the eastern Mediterranean? How did Rome's location near this area help it develop?

14. Which letter represents Carthage?

15. Which letter represents Rome? Which part of Europe did the Romans conquer after Italy?

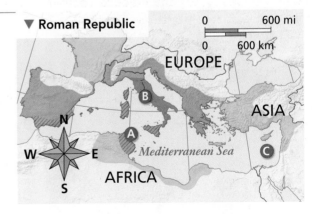

▼ Roman Republic

TOPIC 8

The Roman and Byzantine Empires

(30 BCE – 1453 CE)

GO ONLINE to access your digital course

- VIDEO
- AUDIO
- ETEXT
- INTERACTIVE
- WRITING
- GAMES
- WORKSHEET
- ASSESSMENT

Journey to

the mighty Roman empire and its successor, the Byzantine empire. Historians have tried for 15 centuries to unlock the mystery of the fall of Rome. Read and look for the answer yourself.

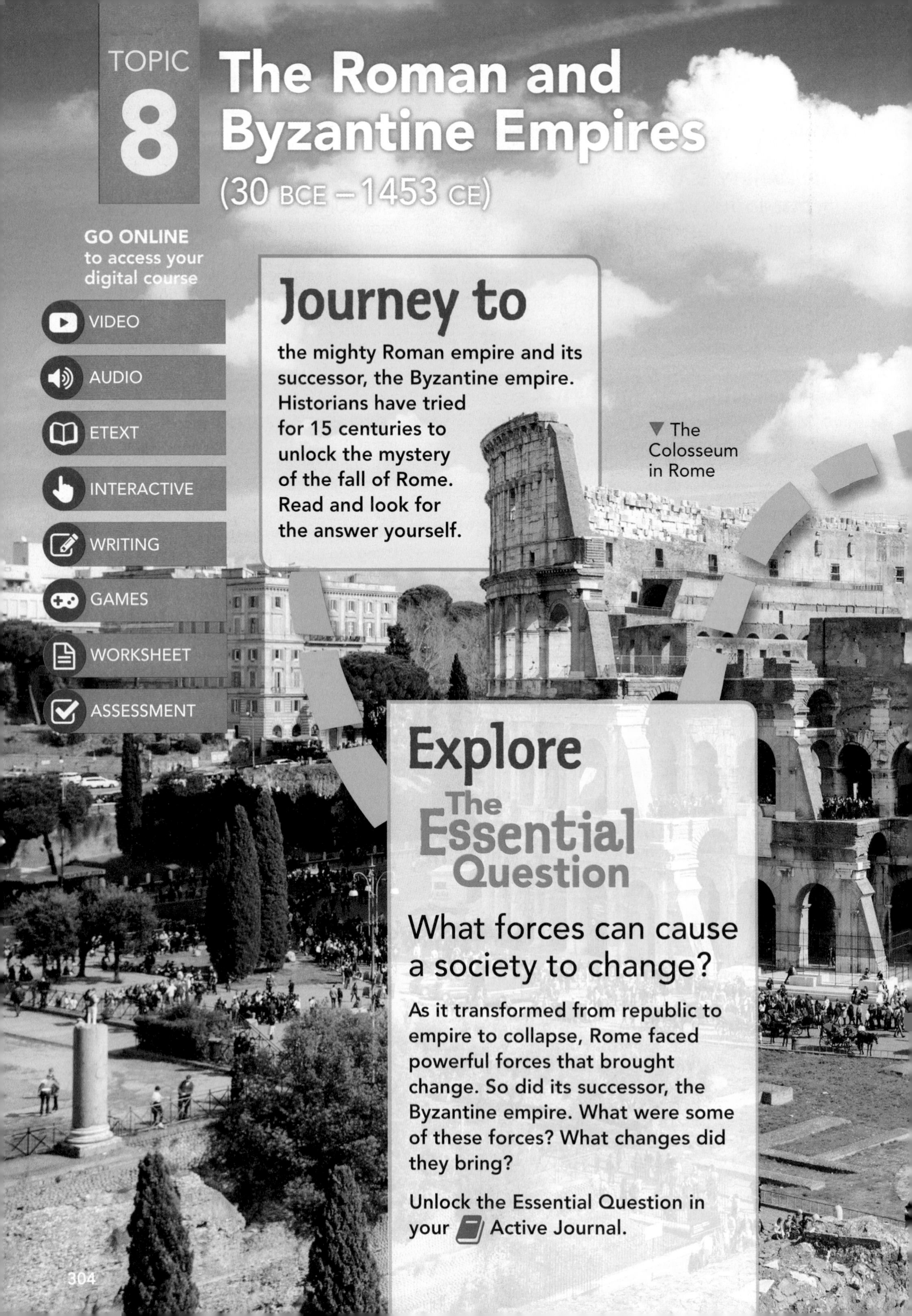

▼ The Colosseum in Rome

Explore The Essential Question

What forces can cause a society to change?

As it transformed from republic to empire to collapse, Rome faced powerful forces that brought change. So did its successor, the Byzantine empire. What were some of these forces? What changes did they bring?

Unlock the Essential Question in your Active Journal.

Watch

NBC LEARN

BOUNCE TO ACTIVATE ▶ **VIDEO**

Augustus and the Pax Romana

Learn about the glorious period of peace and prosperity that began with Rome's first emperor.

Read

about the rise of the Roman empire, its glory years, and its decline and transformation into the Byzantine empire.

TOPIC 8

The Roman and Byzantine Empires (30 BCE – 1453 CE)

Learn more about the Roman and Byzantine empires by making your own map and timeline in your 📓 Active Journal.

👆 INTERACTIVE

Topic Map

Where were the Roman and Byzantine empires?

These empires covered much of western and southeastern Europe and the eastern and southern shores of the Mediterranean Sea. In the detailed map, yellow shading shows Rome at the end of the republic; other colors show the empire's later growth. Locate Rome and Constantinople on the larger map.

👆 INTERACTIVE

Topic Timeline

What happened and when?

The Roman republic gave way to an even mightier empire. But even a great empire declines. Explore the timeline to see what was happening in the Roman empire and its successor, the Byzantine empire, along with the rest of the world.

27 BCE
Augustus becomes the first Roman emperor.

c. 1 BCE
According to Christian tradition, Jesus is born.

117 CE
The Roman empire reaches its largest extent.

313
Emperor Constantine ends the persecution of Christians in the empire.

476
The western Roman empire collapses.

TOPIC EVENTS

| 250 BCE | 1 CE | 250 |

WORLD EVENTS

87 BCE
Long reign of Chinese emperor Wu Di ends.

320 CE
Gupta emperors create a Golden Age in India.

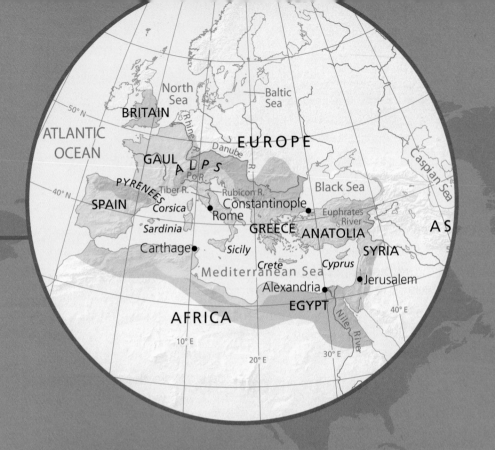

Paul helped spread Christianity throughout the Roman empire.

Constantine transformed the Roman empire.

Theodora ruled with her husband Justinian at the height of the Byzantine empire.

527
Justinian becomes Byzantine emperor.

1054
Great Schism divides Eastern Orthodox and Roman Catholic churches.

1453
Constantinople falls to the Ottoman Turks. Byzantine empire ends.

| 500 | | 1000 | 1250 | 1500 |

1325 CE
Aztecs found their capital at Tenochtitlan in Mexico.

Quest

Discussion Inquiry

The Fall of Rome

Quest KICK OFF

As the Roman empire continued, political, social, and economic conflicts built up over time within and along its borders. These conflicts eventually led to important changes in the empire.

Your quest is to study these conflicts to understand their consequences, and prepare to take a position in one-on-one discussions based on the question:

Could the fall of Rome have been prevented?

How did different events and forces affect the empire? Consider the Essential Question, What forces can cause a society to change? in this Quest.

▼ Julian, emperor of Rome for less than two years in the late 300s

1 Ask Questions
Recall what you know about the Roman empire. List questions you need to answer to understand why the empire fell. Write down these questions in your 📙 Active Journal.

2 Investigate
As you read the topic, look for **Quest CONNECTIONS** that reveal major conflicts that over time had an effect on the Roman empire.

3 Examine Primary Sources
Next, closely study the positions of historians on this question in sources provided to you online.

Quest FINDINGS

4 Prepare Your Position
After reading the sources, discuss the strongest arguments with your partner or small group. Discuss first taking one side of the question, then taking the other side. Get help for this task in your 📙 Active Journal.

The Roman Empire Begins

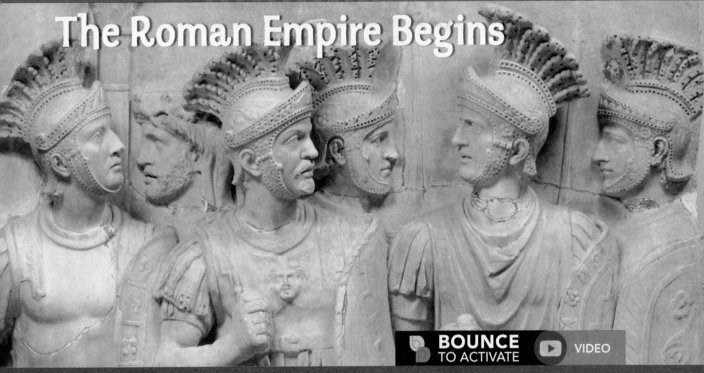

GET READY TO READ

START UP
Look at the carving of elite Roman troops known as Praetorian Guards. Why might an emperor need elite guards?

GUIDING QUESTIONS
- What was the Pax Romana and how did it affect Rome?
- How did the Roman empire gain and maintain power over people and territories?
- How did Rome's achievements in architecture and technology encourage its growth?
- How did Rome's environment affect its growing economy and trade networks?

TAKE NOTES
Literacy Skills: Analyze Cause and Effect
Use the graphic organizer in your 🗐 Active Journal to take notes as you read the lesson.

PRACTICE VOCABULARY
Use the vocabulary activity in your 🗐 Active Journal to practice the vocabulary words.

Vocabulary		Academic Vocabulary
deify	concrete	succession
Pax Romana	aqueduct	structure

Rome began as small settlements along the Tiber River. Mediterranean Europe has mild, rainy winters and hot, dry summers. Early farmers transformed southern Europe's forests into wheat fields, olive orchards, and vineyards. Italy's geography included mountains, rivers that supplied water and offered transportation routes, and plains that provided farmland. The early settlements joined together and became a city. The city's soldiers conquered its neighbors, and in time Rome ruled all of Italy.

The Rise of the Roman Empire

Free adult male citizens of the Roman republic had the right to vote to elect their officials. Through war and diplomacy, Rome's power and wealth grew rapidly. The republic, however, did not survive the new challenges brought by its armies' successes. After the fall of the Roman republic, Rome was ruled by all-powerful individuals—emperors. They helped bring about two centuries of peace.

In 30 BCE Octavian took control of the Roman world. He became Augustus, the first and one of the greatest Roman emperors.

Power of the people

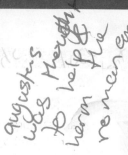

Who Was Augustus? After Augustus won the civil wars that had torn apart the Roman republic, he brought peace to the Roman world. He held nearly total power over the empire, although Rome still had a senate. Augustus made the empire more stable. He shrank the size of the army and raised soldiers' pay. By bringing peace, Augustus gave the economy a boost, improving life for ordinary people. He also fought corruption. He was considered an ideal emperor. After his death he was **deified**, or officially declared to be a god, and worshiped. Most later emperors were also deified, some while they were still alive.

INTERACTIVE

Roman Rulers Who Made History

Who Were the Other Emperors? When Augustus died, his stepson Tiberius became emperor. Rome was now clearly a monarchy. The republic was not coming back. Later, a law was passed stating that the emperor had nearly total power, though in fact this had already been the case.

Primary Source

"Whatever he considers to be in accordance with the public advantage and . . . public and private interests he shall have the right and the power to do and to execute, just as had the deified Augustus."

—Law concerning the power of Vespasian, from *Ancient Roman Statutes*

Academic Vocabulary

succession • *n.*, one person or thing following another

Rome had no formal or set way to choose a new emperor. **Succession** was a serious problem. Members of the imperial family and other powerful Romans schemed and even killed to become emperor. Sometimes the Roman army made the final decision.

BIOGRAPHY
5 Things to Know About

AUGUSTUS

Roman Emperor (c. 62 BCE–14 CE)

- He founded the Roman empire and became its first, and one of its greatest, emperors.
- His great-uncle, Julius Caesar, won a civil war and was named Rome's dictator in 46 BCE. Without a son and needing an heir, Caesar adopted Octavian.
- Augustus was named Octavius at birth. When Julius Caesar adopted him, his name changed to Octavian. In 26 BCE, the Roman Senate renamed him Augustus.
- After Caesar was murdered in 44 BCE, Augustus formed alliances and fought bloody battles to win control of the empire.
- He pretended to the senate that he ruled according to the traditions of the republic. In fact, he held all power. His long reign as emperor was prosperous and peaceful.

Critical Thinking What methods did Augustus use to gain total power over Rome?

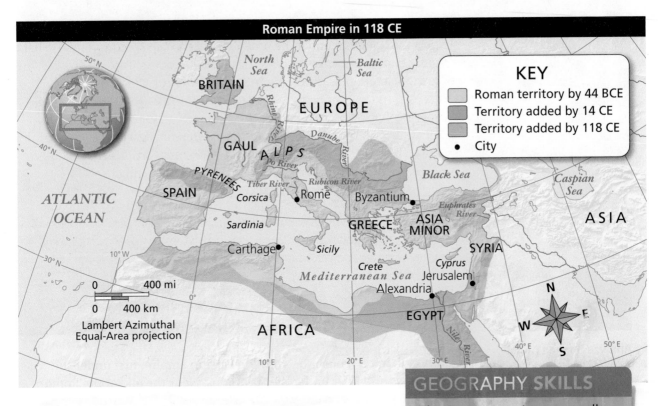

Roman Empire in 118 CE

KEY
- Roman territory by 44 BCE
- Territory added by 14 CE
- Territory added by 118 CE
- • City

Lambert Azimuthal Equal-Area projection

0 — 400 mi
0 — 400 km

Some of the emperors after Augustus were successful. Trajan conquered new territory for Rome. Hadrian travelled around the empire. He also built walls that separated Roman provinces from non-Roman lands. Marcus Aurelius wrote a famous book of philosophy. Many emperors built aqueducts, public baths, temples, stadiums, and other large buildings in Rome and across the empire.

Other emperors were considered failures. Some are still known for their cruelty. For example, Nero was accused of killing Roman citizens without cause, even his close relatives. He was also the first emperor to persecute Christians.

What Was the Pax Romana? Still, Augustus's rule began a long period of peace and prosperity known as the **Pax Romana**, or the "Roman Peace." It lasted from 30 BCE to around 180 CE. During that time as many as 65 million people were able to go about their lives in relative peace. No major wars threatened most of the people of the empire.

The Empire at Its Height During the Pax Romana, at its farthest expansion, the Roman empire reached from Britain in the north to Egypt in the south and from the Atlantic in the west to present-day Iraq in the east. The Romans were the first (and only) empire to unite all the territories that border the Mediterranean. However, dense forests to the north, deserts to the south and southwest, and the Atlantic Ocean to the west blocked further Roman conquests.

That left only Rome's eastern border available for the empire's further growth. In the east, however, the Romans faced continuing conflict,

Analyze Images About 73 miles long, Hadrian's Wall was designed to protect Roman Britain from attacks. **Use Visual Information** How effective do you think this wall would have been in the 100s CE?

although not a major war, with the Persian empire, first under the Parthians and later under the Sasanians. Near the end of the Roman republic period, the Parthians defeated the Roman army at Carrhae. The emperors Trajan and Severus had minor battles with them during and after the Pax Romana. The Romans could not secure their empire's eastern border against the Persian threat.

READING CHECK Identify Main Ideas What was the Pax Romana and why was it important?

What Were Rome's Practical Achievements?

The Romans were a practical people. They excelled at using technology to improve daily life.

Roman Roads Link the Empire "All roads lead to Rome" is an old saying. In ancient Italy, it was true. Major roads extended out from the city like the spokes of a wheel. More than 50,000 miles (80,467 km) of paved roads crisscrossed the Roman empire, linking cities and forts. Roman roads were built to last. Some are still used today.

Roman roads were built mainly so that soldiers could march quickly from place to place. Military engineers traveled with the army. So did architects, stonemasons, and surveyors. Roman soldiers often worked on the roads when not fighting.

Roman roads were superbly engineered. Main roads were hard-paved and well drained. Smooth, all-weather roads were a considerable improvement over dirt paths. They sped up communication throughout the empire. This made government and trade more efficient. Good roads from ports to large inland cities also helped supply food.

Roman Architecture Roman architects devised new building methods and materials, such as concrete. **Concrete** is a building material made by mixing cement (a gray powder made from different materials) with small stones, sand, and water. The thick, soupy mixture is then poured into molds, where it hardens. Many Roman concrete harbors have survived for more than 2,000 years.

Concrete was lighter and easier to work with than stone. Workers needed less skill to pour concrete than to carve stone. Using this new material, workers built large **structures** covered with domes. The largest dome covered the Pantheon.

In addition to domes, Roman engineers and soldiers also built large, sturdy bridges, supported by rounded, semi-circular arches. Such arches allowed for longer bridge spans. In fact, a rounded arch is the most typical feature of Roman architecture.

Aqueducts Transport Water A good water supply is as important to city life as are bridges and roads. Roman engineers designed water systems to supply towns with clean water. They built hundreds of miles of aqueducts. An **aqueduct** is a channel that moves water over land.

Roman aqueducts were usually made of stone or concrete channels. They flowed mostly underground. When aqueducts needed to cross valleys, the Romans built long arched bridges to pipe the water along. Some of these bridges still stand today.

In the city, water flowed into public fountains. Some wealthy people had water piped directly into their homes. Aqueducts also supplied public baths. The baths were an important part of the Roman lifestyle. Many Romans went to the baths every day to bathe, exercise, see friends, and even conduct business.

Analyze Charts Human activity increased methane levels, which raised temperatures slightly during the Roman empire. **Draw Conclusions** What connections might this chart have to today's environment?

IMPACT OF THE ROMANS ON THE ENVIRONMENT

	BEFORE 100 BCE	AFTER 100 BCE
EXPANSION OF **AGRICULTURE**	**COOLER CLIMATE** Roman farming and grazing generated small amounts of methane.	**WARMER CLIMATE**  Massive expansion of farming and grazing created far more methane.
GROWTH OF **METALWORKING**	Making small numbers of tools and weapons required burning wood that produced some methane.	Making many more tools and weapons required burning much more wood and released far more methane.

Sources: *Smithsonian* magazine

trade was complicated and important to roman to daily life

Aqueducts were only part of the water system. Sewers carried waste away from the cities. Roman water and sewer systems were not equaled until modern times.

✓ **READING CHECK** Draw Conclusions What were some of Rome's greatest engineering achievements?

Trade and the Roman Economy

Roman roads were usually built for military purposes, but goods also moved across the empire by road. Merchants also traveled by sea. Trade increased across the empire. Cities became centers of industry and commerce. The Roman empire was based on a network of such cities that depended on trade with the empire's other regions. This network of cities was unusual in the ancient world.

Trade Grows Before the Romans built a navy, piracy was a problem. It made shipping dangerous and expensive. But the Romans cleared the sea of most pirates. This made trade by sea safer, faster, and cheaper than travel by land. Ships carried grain, wine, olive oil, and pottery across the empire.

At the empire's height, imported grain and olive oil fed Rome's population of between one and two million people. A web of land and sea trade routes served the city. Romans had access to the varied resources and products of Europe, Greece, Anatolia, Syria, Egypt, and North Africa. Roman roads linked the empire's regions.

Merchants brought goods from other civilizations along trade routes across Afroeurasia on land, like the Silk Road between Central Asia and China, and over the

GEOGRAPHY **SKILLS**

By 117 CE, the Roman trade network extended throughout most of Europe and into parts of Asia and North Africa.

1. **Location** How far to the east did the Roman trade routes extend by sea? How far to the west?

2. **Draw Conclusions** What advantages did such wide-ranging trade routes bring to Rome?

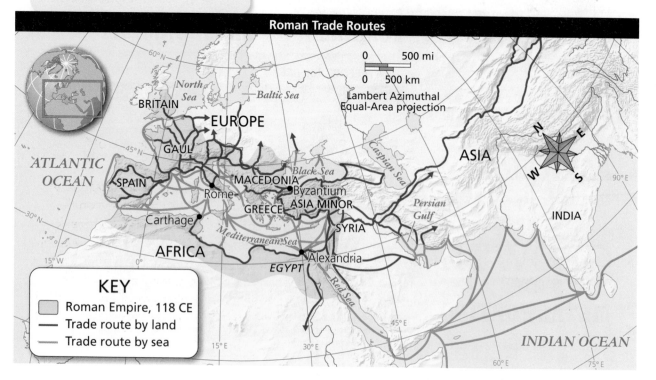

Roman Trade Routes

0 — 500 mi
0 — 500 km
Lambert Azimuthal Equal-Area projection

BRITAIN
North Sea
Baltic Sea
EUROPE
GAUL
ATLANTIC OCEAN
SPAIN
MACEDONIA
Black Sea
Byzantium
Rome
GREECE ASIA MINOR
Carthage
Mediterranean Sea
SYRIA
AFRICA
Alexandria
EGYPT
Red Sea
Caspian Sea
ASIA
Persian Gulf
INDIA
INDIAN OCEAN

KEY
Roman Empire, 118 CE
Trade route by land
Trade route by sea

Mediterranean Sea and the Indian Ocean. These goods included medicine and jewels from India, silk from China, and frankincense and animals from Africa. Small groups of wealthy people purchased these imported luxury items. As travelers journeyed between cultures, they also brought along various ideas and technologies.

Agriculture and Crafts Farming was the base of the Roman economy. Grains like wheat were key. Grain was shipped to Rome to feed its massive population. Imported grain also fed Rome's armies. By the time of the Pax Romana, food for Roman cities depended on the work of enslaved or poor laborers on vast agricultural estates.

In return, money flowed from Rome to the provinces. The owners of provincial farms grew rich. Many used their new wealth to develop their provinces. They built temples, theaters, and baths. Some wealthy provincial people joined the Roman elite. They became senators and even emperors.

Craft industries were also part of the economy. Skilled workers produced cloth, glass, pottery, metalwork, and ships. The construction industry supplied building projects with marble, terracotta tiles, and lead plumbing pipes.

Currency Aids Trade Economic growth in the empire was helped by a stable currency. A stable currency is a system of money that does not change much in value over time. It is more quickly and widely accepted in trade and commerce. Rome's stable currency made it easier to conduct long-distance trade than in the past.

Analyze Images Roman glassware in the 200s and 300s CE included bottles and amphoras, two-handled storage jars. **Infer** What do you think the Romans stored in vessels like these?

☑ READING CHECK **Identify Cause and Effect** Why was it important for Rome's government to import grain to feed its population and armies?

☑ Lesson Check

Practice Vocabulary

1. How were **aqueducts** used?

2. What is **concrete** made from?

Critical Thinking and Writing

3. **Infer** How did the Pax Romana spur economic growth?

4. **Summarize** How did roads, aqueducts, and concrete affect city life?

5. **Summarize** What was the role of farming in the Roman economy?

6. **Writing Workshop: Gather Details** In this topic, you will write an argument on the question: Which was greater, the Greek city-states or the Roman empire? Consider the following factors: size, longevity, economic power, cultural achievements, and influence. Begin to record details about Greece and Rome in your 📓 Active Journal.

📖 Primary Sources

Augustus, *The Deeds of the Divine Augustus*

Augustus, also known as Octavian, ruled the Roman empire for 40 years. Under Augustus's leadership, the size of the Roman empire doubled. *The Deeds of the Divine Augustus* is a document that Augustus wrote about his accomplishments.

◄ Roman coin showing the head of Augustus

Reading and Vocabulary Support

① Do you think it is possible to swear allegiance to someone involuntarily?

② A standard in this sense is a flag carried by a military unit.

③ Augustus says he waged no unjust war. Who determined whether his wars were just or unjust?

④ The Cimbri, Charydes, and the Semnones were Germanic groups living in Europe at the time of Augustus.

⑤ An envoy is a person who represents one government in dealings with another.

1. In my nineteenth year, on my own initiative and at my own expense, I raised an army with which I set free the state...

25. I restored peace to the sea from pirates.... All Italy swore allegiance to me <u>voluntarily</u> **①**, and demanded me as leader of the war which I won at Actium; the provinces of Gaul, Spain, Africa, Sicily, and Sardinia swore the same allegiance. And those who then fought under my <u>standard</u> **②** were more than 700 senators, among whom 83 were made consuls either before or after, up to the day this was written, and about 170 were made priests.

26. I extended the borders of all the provinces of the Roman people which neighbored nations not subject to our rule. I restored peace to the provinces of Gaul and Spain, likewise Germany, which includes the ocean from Cadiz to the mouth of the river Elbe. I brought peace to the Alps from the region which is near the Adriatic Sea to the Tuscan, with no <u>unjust war</u> **③** waged against any nation. I sailed my ships on the ocean from the mouth of the Rhine to the east region up to the borders of the Cimbri, where no Roman had gone before that time by land or sea, and the Cimbri and the Charydes and the <u>Semnones</u> **④** and the other Germans of the same territory sought by <u>envoys</u> **⑤** the friendship of me and of the Roman people. [3]

—Caesar Augustus, *The Deeds of the Divine Augustus*

Analyzing Primary Sources

Cite specific evidence from the document to support your answers.

1. **Draw Conclusions** What does Augustus mean when he says "All Italy swore allegiance to me voluntarily, and demanded me as leader"?

2. **Support Ideas with Examples** Review the passage and identify an example of propaganda.

3. **Analyze Information** What does Augustus suggest are key accomplishments necessary for an emperor to be successful?

🔍 *Quest* CONNECTIONS

What evidence can you find in the reading that Augustus was concerned about maintaining the strength of the empire? Record your findings in your 📓 Active Journal.

Identify Central Issues and Problems

Follow these steps to learn ways to identify central issues and problems.

INTERACTIVE

Solve Problems

1 **Identify the subject of the passage.** Read the passage to find out what it is about.

   a. What is the subject of the passage?

   b. Which sentence or sentences identify the subject?

2 **Identify the people, time, and place discussed in the passage.** Look for clues telling you what people and time period are being discussed.

   a. Who is being discussed in the passage? What is the time period?

   b. Where are the events in the passage taking place?

3 **Determine the central issue or problem.** Read the details of the passage.

   a. What problem or issue is the main focus of the passage?

   b. What facts or details support your answer?

4 **Explain why this issue was important.** Look for information that suggests why this issue was important at that time.

   a. Why was this issue important at that time and place?

   b. Have people at other times and places faced similar issues? Explain.

Secondary Source

After the end of the Pax Romana, the Roman empire began to struggle with many problems. One of the biggest problems was the transition from one emperor to another, which was rarely smooth. Civil war broke out multiple times. War and instability hurt the economy and allowed foreigners to threaten Rome's borders.

How could emperors make the empire more stable? In 284 CE, a solider named Diocletian became emperor of Rome. Diocletian faced serious challenges. After years of civil war, the army was divided. The machinery of government barely worked. Prices were rising. Taxes were no longer being paid. The frontiers were not well guarded. The emperor believed harsh measures were necessary to meet these challenges. He knew that reforms he had in mind would not be popular. But he believed only strong action on his part would be the empire back under control.

Origins of Christianity

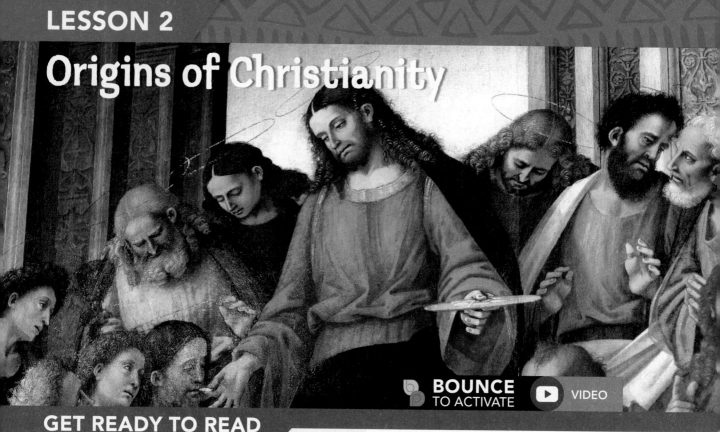

BOUNCE TO ACTIVATE   ▶ VIDEO

GET READY TO READ

START UP

Look at the painting of Jesus and his disciples at their last meal together. Write a prediction on how the Roman authorities will respond to the new religion of Christianity.

GUIDING QUESTIONS

- What was the relationship between Rome and Judea like?
- Who was Jesus and what did he teach?
- How did the religion of Christianity develop and change?
- How did Christianity spread?

TAKE NOTES

Literacy Skills: Sequence

Use the graphic organizer in your 📓 Active Journal to take notes as you read the lesson.

PRACTICE VOCABULARY

Use the vocabulary activity in your 📓 Active Journal to practice the vocabulary words.

Vocabulary		Academic Vocabulary
resurrection	conversion	isolated
baptism	martyr	authorities
crucifixion		

Despite Rome's power and influence, many people in the empire opposed Roman rule. A Jewish spiritual leader named Jesus arose during the Pax Romana. He was executed by the Romans. A new religion soon emerged based on his teachings and the writings of his early followers.

What Was Judea Like Under Roman Rule?

Although centered in the Jewish kingdom of Judea, Jewish people had migrated throughout the Greek and Roman world since the third century BCE. By the late first century BCE, large Jewish communities existed in Egypt, Syria, Anatolia, Greece, Italy (including Rome), and southern France.

In 63 BCE, the Romans took control of Judea, including the city of Jerusalem. A large number of Jews opposed Roman rule.

Zealots Many Jews saw the Romans as foreigners who occupied their land and treated them cruelly. They hoped that God would send a Messiah, or specially chosen king, who would save the Jews from oppression. The Messiah would drive the Romans from their homeland. One group of Jews called the Zealots resisted the Romans by force. They refused to pay taxes and killed Roman officials.

Jewish Groups in Judea Different religious groups existed among Jews during this time. The Pharisees (FARuh seez) were educated people who observed Jewish law. They believed that good people could be resurrected after the Messiah came. **Resurrection** means coming back to life. The Sadducees, another large group, came from the elite and supported the traditions of the Temple in Jerusalem. They generally cooperated with Roman rule.

Other, smaller, groups of Jews withdrew from society and lived in **isolated** communities in the desert. Many of these groups practiced ritual cleansing by plunging into water. Christianity later adopted this ritual as **baptism**.

Academic Vocabulary
isolated • *adj.*, set away from other people or places

✓ **READING CHECK** Identify Supporting Details Who were the Sadducees? Did they support the Zealots?

Jesus' Life and Teachings

During this time, a Jewish man named Jesus of Nazareth lived and taught. He gained a large following.

Early Life of Jesus Most of what we know about Jesus comes from early Christian writings known as the Gospels. According to the Gospels, Jesus was a descendant of the great Jewish king, David, and his birth was miraculous. According to tradition, Jesus was a carpenter, like his father.

Jesus the Teacher The Gospels tell us that as an adult, Jesus was baptized by a prophet named John in the Jordan River. Afterward, he began teaching from the Hebrew Bible. For three years, Jesus traveled throughout Judea, telling people that God would soon come to establish his kingdom.

Jesus became known as a champion of the poor and the outcasts of society. Word spread that he could heal sick people. His closest followers began to wonder whether Jesus was the Messiah.

Jesus preached about how to live a good life. In one famous passage in the Gospels, Jesus lists what he considered the two most important commandments from the Hebrew Bible.

▲ This painting shows Jesus as an infant.

Jesus told his followers:

Primary Source

"'You shall love the Lord your God with all your heart, and with all your soul, and with all your mind.' This is the greatest and first commandment. And a second is like it: 'You shall love your neighbor as yourself.'"

—Matthew 22:37–39

Opposition, Arrest, and Death The Gospels say that Jesus went to Jerusalem around 33 CE to celebrate the Jewish holiday of Passover. Roman **authorities** in Jerusalem worried about the large holiday crowds. Local leaders also feared trouble. A riot might provoke the Romans into destroying the city.

In response to these concerns, the Roman governor Pontius Pilate acted. He had Jesus arrested, beaten, and executed by being crucified. **Crucifixion** was a slow and painful Roman method of execution. The victim was nailed or tied to a large wooden cross and left to hang until dead.

The Resurrection After Jesus died, his body was taken down from the cross and laid in a tomb. The Romans sealed the tomb and posted guards around it. According to the Gospels, some of Jesus' followers visited the tomb three days later. They found the guards gone and the tomb empty. They ran to tell the other disciples. Many claimed to have seen him after his death. They believed that God had resurrected Jesus and that he was indeed the Messiah. The Greek word for *Messiah* is "Christ."

✓ **READING CHECK** **Identify Main Ideas** Which groups did Jesus champion in his teachings?

How Did Christianity Spread?

Jesus and his early followers were Jews. But those who believed Jesus was the Messiah eventually formed a new religion known as Christianity. During his life, Jesus chose twelve trusted followers, called disciples or apostles. After his death, they spread his teachings.

The Early Church When Jesus died, Peter, a key apostle, became a leader of the new church. The word *church* can refer to the community of all Christians, a specific group of Christians, or a building Christians worship in. Peter and other apostles such as James and, a few years later, Paul, spread belief in Jesus as the Messiah. They carried their faith to many parts of the world. They visited Europe, Asia, and North Africa.

Christians and Jews The first followers of the new faith considered themselves Jews. They respected Jewish laws and traditions, read the Hebrew Bible, and prayed in Jewish synagogues.

But differences grew between Jewish followers of Christianity and other Jews. Christians began sharing their beliefs with non-Jews outside of Judea. The apostle Peter even traveled to Rome itself. People from different backgrounds heard the apostles' message. More and more gentiles, or non-Jews, became Christians.

In 66 CE, the Zealots you have already read about led a huge rebellion against Rome. With difficulty, the Romans defeated them and destroyed the Temple in Jerusalem. After a later rebellion, Jews were forbidden to live in Jerusalem. Many left Judea as migrants or were taken away as slaves. They settled around the empire.

Travels of the Apostle Paul A man named Paul helped spread Christianity around the Roman empire. Early in

GEOGRAPHY **SKILLS**

Christianity spread throughout most of the Roman empire.

1. **Interaction** Did Christianity spread first in Asia Minor or Britain? Why do you think this might be so?

2. **Region** What Christian areas were outside of the Roman empire in 476?

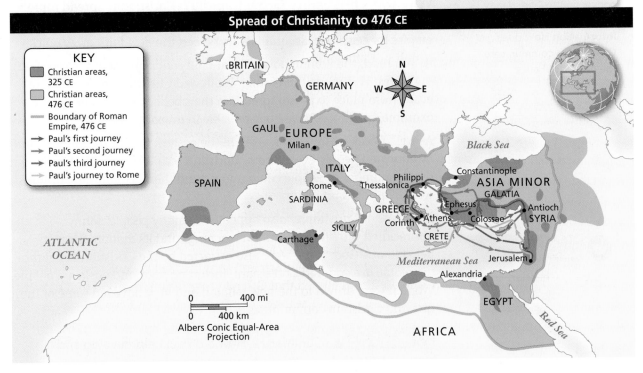

Spread of Christianity to 476 CE

KEY
- Christian areas, 325 CE
- Christian areas, 476 CE
- Boundary of Roman Empire, 476 CE
- Paul's first journey
- Paul's second journey
- Paul's third journey
- Paul's journey to Rome

BRITAIN
GERMANY
GAUL
EUROPE
Milan
SPAIN
ITALY
Rome
SARDINIA
GREECE
Athens
Corinth
SICILY
Carthage
ATLANTIC OCEAN
Black Sea
Constantinople
ASIA MINOR
GALATIA
Philippi
Thessalonica
Ephesus
Colossae
Antioch
SYRIA
CRETE
Mediterranean Sea
Jerusalem
Alexandria
EGYPT
Red Sea
AFRICA

0   400 mi
0   400 km
Albers Conic Equal-Area Projection

his life he was opposed to Christians. He had an experience that led to his conversion to Christianity. A **conversion** is a heartfelt change in one's opinions or beliefs. Paul believed that Jesus had appeared to him and told him to spread the new faith. Paul is called an apostle, even though he was not one of the original twelve.

Paul helped both to spread and define Christianity. Paul traveled to Greece and other areas. He founded churches and preached. Paul also wrote letters called epistles to various Christians. He helped spread the belief that non-Jews did not need to follow all Jewish laws to become Christians. They still needed to live moral lives and could not worship other gods. He taught many basic Christian beliefs, including the resurrection of Jesus. He also preached that Jesus' death saved believers from sin and guilt. Almost half of the text of the New Testament comes from Paul's epistles or writings of those he influenced.

Analyze Images This dramatic painting by Italian Renaissance artist Caravaggio shows Paul's conversion to Christianity. **Synthesize Visual Information** How does Caravaggio communicate the power of Paul's experience?

As more non-Jews came into the church, Christianity became a separate religion and no longer a part of Judaism. Christian communities soon arose around the Mediterranean as well as in Persia and Central Asia.

Why Did Christianity Grow Rapidly? Christianity spread rapidly during the Pax Romana, although it remained a minority faith in the empire for centuries. Several factors helped the new faith grow quickly.

As you read, the Roman government built roads and kept the seas free of pirates. This made travel safer. It allowed Christians to move more easily from place to place, spreading their beliefs. Paul's journeys, for example, might not have been possible in an earlier period.

As well, Greek was widely spoken in the eastern half of the empire, and by educated people everywhere. Christian scriptures were in Greek, so a large number of people could understand them. Later, the scriptures were translated into Latin.

The ideas of Christianity also appealed to many people. Many appreciated Christianity's moral teachings and its monotheism, or belief in one God. Some were also attracted by the Christian belief that all people are equal in God's sight, including poor and enslaved people. Women were drawn to the new religion and may have led some of the growing Christian communities.

INTERACTIVE

Early Christian Symbols

☑ READING CHECK **Summarize** How did Paul help develop and contribute to the growth of Christianity?

Christianity and the Empire

The growth of Christianity worried Roman officials. They sometimes persecuted, or mistreated, Christians.

A New Faith Faces Opposition The Romans generally allowed people to worship their own gods, so long as they also worshiped Roman gods and emperors as a sign of loyalty. Jews did not worship Roman gods, but this did not greatly bother the Romans. They respected the Jewish traditions that forbade worshiping more than one God.

Christianity, however, was a new religion. The government opposed it because when non-Jews became Christians they stopped worshiping the old gods. Officials feared that Christians were disloyal and that the gods would be angry if people who became Christians stopped worshiping them. It was considered the government's job to keep the gods happy.

Christians Are Persecuted A fire destroyed much of Rome in 64 CE. Emperor Nero falsely blamed Christians. Many Christians were killed. After 250 CE, emperors persecuted Christians. Persecution scared some away from Christianity. However, it caused others to bond to their faith. Persecution produced **martyrs**, or people who die for their beliefs. Their courage strengthened many Christians' faith.

Persecution continued, on and off, until the reign of Emperor Constantine. According to tradition, he had a dream just before a battle that told him to fight under the sign of the cross. He won the battle. In 313, he ended persecution of Christians and eventually became a Christian himself.

Constantine thought the Christian Church could help hold together the divided Roman empire. A later emperor made Christianity Rome's official religion around 380. Church leaders chose a Roman structure to organize the Church. They also chose the gospels and letters to be included in the Christian Bible. As the western Roman empire declined, Roman cities were often led by Christian bishops.

READING CHECK **Draw Conclusions** Which emperor ended the persecution of Christians? Why?

☑ Lesson Check

Practice Vocabulary

1. What is **baptism?**

2. What does it mean to be **resurrected?**

3. How did Christian **martyrs** help strengthen the faith of other Christians?

Critical Thinking and Writing

4. Identify Main Ideas Why did the Romans persecute Christians?

5. Summarize Summarize the events of Jesus' life according to the Gospels.

6. Analyze Cause and Effect According to tradition, how did Constantine's dream change the course of Roman history?

7. Writing Workshop: Gather Details In your 📓 Active Journal, add details about Rome's size, longevity, economic power, cultural achievements, influence, expansion, and trade.

Detect Changing Patterns

Follow these steps and use the source to identify
a changing pattern in Roman society.

INTERACTIVE

Identify Trends

1 **Gather information about the society.** Carefully read the source provided here. What are some details that describe Roman society during the time of the Roman empire?

2 **Identify possible sources of change in the society.** Consider the sources of change described in the passage.

   a. Which individuals contributed to the rise and spread of Christianity during the Roman empire?

   b. What specific factors helped make this change happen?

3 **Determine how the sources of change led to new patterns of living.** Using the people and factors you identified in step 2, analyze how a new pattern of living emerged during the Roman empire.

   a. How did Paul and Constantine change Romans' lives?

   b. How did trade, language, and Rome's social system encourage this new pattern?

4 **Summarize what you discover.** Use the information you have learned to identify trends. What general statement can you make about the rise and spread of Christianity during the Roman empire?

Secondary Source

During the time of the Roman empire, several factors contributed to the rise and spread of Christianity throughout the region. In the early years of Christianity, one of Jesus' apostles, Paul of Tarsus, spread the Christian faith through his preaching and leadership.

As the Roman empire grew larger and more powerful, established trade routes made it easier for people to travel. Because the members of the Roman empire often shared a common language, communication among strangers was possible, furthering the spread of ideas and beliefs. Additionally, despite the wealth of the Roman empire, many people remained poor or enslaved. The message of Christianity brought hope to those whose lives were burdened by a lack of freedom or poverty.

Finally, important leaders of the Roman empire embraced Christianity. In 312 CE, Emperor Constantine converted to Christianity. Within 70 years, Christianity had become the official religion of the Roman empire.

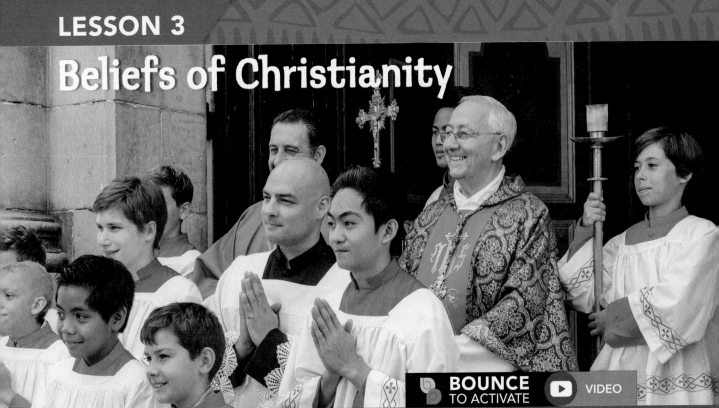

LESSON 3
Beliefs of Christianity

GET READY TO READ

START UP
The photograph shows a Catholic church in France. What can you infer about Christianity today from this photograph?

GUIDING QUESTIONS
- What writings form Christianity's scripture?
- What core set of beliefs do most Christians share?
- How do Christians practice their religion?

TAKE NOTES

Literacy Skills: Analyze Text Structure

Use the graphic organizer in your 📓 Active Journal to take notes as you read the lesson.

PRACTICE VOCABULARY

Use the vocabulary activity in your 📓 Active Journal to practice the vocabulary words.

Vocabulary

New Testament
Gospel
parable
epistle

Trinity
ethics
denomination

Academic Vocabulary

controversial
element

In the centuries after the death of Jesus, Christians gathered their sacred writings and developed their faith. Their writings centered on the life of Jesus and the Christian belief in Jesus as the son of God.

The Christian Bible

You have already read about the Hebrew Bible, which contains Jewish history, religious laws, and many other writings. Like Jews, early Christians read the Hebrew Bible as their scripture, or holy writings.

The Old and New Testaments At first, the Hebrew Bible was the Christians' only sacred text. Then they began to add their own body of writings. Jews did not and still do not accept these as scripture. Christians called the Hebrew Bible the Old Testament, and this new body of work the **New Testament**. They read both together as their holy text.

The works that became the New Testament were written down between 50 CE and 150. By the 300s they were collected and began circulating in the form that Christians recognize today. Jesus and his early followers probably spoke Aramaic. But the New Testament was written in Greek. Greek was the most widely spoken language in the eastern part of the Roman empire. The New Testament contains 27 separate documents, called books.

What Are the Gospels? The first four books of the New Testament are the **Gospels**. They describe the life and teachings of Jesus from four different points of view. The Gospels do not all describe the same events in exactly the same way. Together, however, they create a powerful portrayal of Jesus and his teachings.

Many of Jesus' teachings are presented in the form of **parables**, or stories with a moral. Jesus often used parables to explain important lessons.

Teachings in Other Books After the Gospels come a number of other books. Most of them are **epistles**, or formal letters. These are letters that apostles and other early leaders wrote to the newly established churches.

Most epistles were written to explain Christian teachings or to solve problems in the church. Paul wrote many of these epistles to churches he had started himself. His letters explained many Christian beliefs—such as the Trinity, resurrection, and salvation—in great detail. Paul's life and the lives of other early Christians are described in another book in the New Testament, the Acts of the Apostles.

The last book of the New Testament is the Book of Revelation. It is written like an epistle, but makes predictions about future events. It uses complicated images to predict Jesus' return to Earth and a final battle between good and evil.

READING CHECK **Compare and Contrast** What are the first four books of the New Testament called? How do they differ in describing their subject?

BIOGRAPHY
5 Things to Know About   PAUL THE APOSTLE
Missionary, Saint (4 BCE?–c. 62–64 CE)

- He spoke Greek.

- His Hebrew name was Saul. He changed it to Paul when he converted to Christianity about 33 CE.

- He learned, as he says, to "work with [his] own hands" as a tent maker.

- He traveled widely by ship and by foot as a missionary in the 40s and 50s CE, aiming to convert non-Jews.

- He emphasized belief in the resurrection of Jesus.

Critical Thinking Why might Paul have been a particularly effective spokesperson for the new religion of Christianity?

What Do Christians Believe About God?

Christians use the New Testament as a source for their teachings. Throughout the centuries, Christians have disagreed about some parts of their faith. But most Christians today share many basic beliefs in common.

The Son of God The Gospels refer to Jesus not only as the Messiah, but also as the Son of God. Christian belief holds that Jesus was God in human form. To the early Christians, Jesus' death proved he was human. His resurrection proved that he was divine, or godlike. For some, the idea of Jesus as both human and divine was puzzling or **controversial**. But Christians could have faith that they, too, would be resurrected after death. Christians believe that by believing in Jesus, they will be rewarded with eternal, or endless, life in the presence of God.

Analyze Images This is a page from the Book of Kells, an illuminated manuscript created in the British Isles around 800. It contains the gospels and other material. **Use Visual Information** How did creations like this help keep Christianity alive during the Middle Ages?

The Soul and Salvation Christians believe that everyone has a soul, or spirit. To a Christian, what happens to the soul after death depends on how that person has lived and whether that person believes in Jesus. Christians believe that people need God to forgive their sins, or wrongdoings, so that their souls can live on in the presence of God after death. They have faith that God may forgive people who are truly sorry for their sins and choose to follow Jesus. They believe Jesus promised eternal salvation to those who believe in him as their savior.

Many Christians view Jesus' death and resurrection as key to forgiveness. In the ancient world, some peoples atoned, or made up for sins, by offering animal sacrifices to their gods. Many Christians believe that Jesus, by being crucified, became the sacrifice for everyone's sins.

The Trinity Like Jews, Christians are monotheists. As you have read, this means that they worship one God. Most Christians, however, believe that God exists as three forms, called persons. Together, these three forms are known as the **Trinity**. The Trinity includes God the Father, Jesus the Son, and the Holy Spirit.

Christians believe that God the Father created the universe. They believe that Jesus is God's son. He is God in human form. The Holy Spirit, also called the Holy Ghost, is described as the power of God as experienced on Earth. To early Christians, the Holy Spirit allowed them to sense the presence of God after Jesus was no longer with them.

Academic Vocabulary
controversial • *adj.,* subject to disagreement or argument

☑ **READING CHECK** What do Christians believe about Jesus' death and resurrection?

INTERACTIVE

Christianity Today

Practicing Christianity

In daily life, Christians try to follow Jesus' teachings. Most Christians also observe similar rituals and holidays.

Following Jesus' Teachings Much of Jesus' teaching has to do with **ethics**, or issues of right and wrong, and how to treat people. Jesus taught that God loved all his creations no matter who they were or what they did. Jesus urged his followers to reflect that love in their relationships with others and to treat others as they would like to be treated. This is called the "Golden Rule."

Primary Source

"In everything, do to others as you would have them do to you."

—Matthew 7:12

Jesus also showed great concern for poor and humble people. He accepted even those with the lowest social standing among his followers.

As well as following Jesus' teachings, most Christians believe religious faith is also important. To most Christians, Christianity means believing in Jesus, in his sacrifice for other people's sins, and in his resurrection.

Christianity Today Today, Christianity is the world's largest religion. There are about 2 billion Christians in the world. They are divided into thousands of **denominations**, or religious groups. Different groups share some beliefs and rituals but disagree about others. The largest single groups are Roman Catholicism and Eastern Orthodoxy. Protestantism is a large family of groups. Some Protestant

Christianity in the World Today

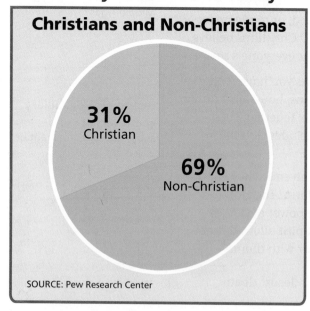

Christians and Non-Christians

31% Christian

69% Non-Christian

SOURCE: Pew Research Center

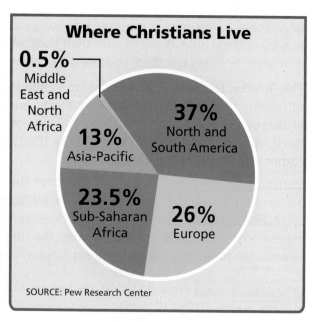

Where Christians Live

0.5% Middle East and North Africa

13% Asia-Pacific

37% North and South America

23.5% Sub-Saharan Africa

26% Europe

SOURCE: Pew Research Center

Analyze Diagrams These graphs illustrate facts about Christians in the world today.
Analyze Graphs Which region of the world has the most Christians? The fewest?

denominations are the Baptist, Methodist, Lutheran, Presbyterian, Pentecostal, and Episcopalian churches.

Christian Rituals and Holidays

Many practices are shared by nearly all groups of Christians. Most Christians observe Sunday as the special day of rest and prayer. At worship services, many Christians participate in a ritual meal called a Holy Communion or Eucharist. This usually includes bread and wine or grape juice. Many Christians are baptized.

Christmas and Easter are two important holidays for most Christians. Christmas celebrates the birth of Jesus, a miracle according to Christian tradition. Easter celebrates Jesus' resurrection.

☑ **READING CHECK** Draw Conclusions Why is ethics important to a religion?

What Is the Judeo-Christian Tradition?

Judaism and Christianity are separate religions. They have many important differences, but the two faiths also have much in common. Both Jews and Christians worship one God. Both read the Hebrew Bible (Old Testament) as scripture. They share a similar ethical tradition. Members of both groups respect the Ten Commandments.

The common **elements** of Judaism and Christianity are called the Judeo-Christian tradition. It has helped shaped much about life in Europe, the Americas, and other areas. It has contributed to art and literature. For example, stories from parts of the Bible read by members of both faiths are common themes in art. The tradition also helps shape law. For example, it teaches the equality of all people before the law.

☑ **READING CHECK** Compare and Contrast What is one element that Judaism and Christianity have in common?

▲ These Christians in Honduras celebrate Palm Sunday, the Sunday before Easter.

Academic Vocabulary
element • *n.*, part

☑ Lesson Check

Practice Vocabulary

1. When was the **New Testament** written down?

2. Who do Christians believe are the members of the **Trinity**?

Critical Thinking and Writing

3. **Summarize** What is the relationship between the Hebrew Bible and the Christian scriptures?

4. **Identify Main Ideas** What do Christians believe about atonement, or making up for sins?

5. **Infer** What is the "Golden Rule"? Why do you think it is called "golden"?

6. **Writing Workshop: Use Credible Sources** You might need more information to make a decision for your essay. List three credible sources of information you could use to compare the Greek city-states and the Roman empire in your 📓 Active Journal.

Primary Sources

The Gospel of Matthew, The Sermon on the Mount

The Sermon on the Mount is a collection of teachings that Jesus gave in a speech on a mountain. The teachings, recorded in the New Testament, emphasized that Jesus' followers should love one another and welcome even the most humble of believers.

◀ Jesus speaks to his disciples.

Reading and Vocabulary Support

① Jesus' disciples were twelve of his closest followers.

② To be meek is to be humble and not boastful or loud.

③ Righteousness is being good and moral.

④ Why might Jesus specifically mention people who are persecuted?

⑤ Why do you think Jesus mentions the fate of the prophets who came before him?

When he saw the crowds, he went up the mountain, and after he had sat down, his disciples ① came to him. He began to teach them, saying:

"Blessed are the poor in spirit, for theirs is the kingdom of heaven.

Blessed are they who mourn, for they will be comforted.

Blessed are the meek ②, for they will inherit the land.

Blessed are they who hunger and thirst for righteousness ③, for they will be satisfied.

Blessed are the merciful, for they will be shown mercy.

Blessed are the clean of heart, for they will see God.

Blessed are the peacemakers, for they will be called children of God.

Blessed are they who are persecuted ④, for the sake of righteousness, for theirs is the kingdom of heaven.

Blessed are you when they insult you and persecute you and utter every kind of evil against you [falsely] because of me.

Rejoice and be glad, for your reward will be great in heaven. Thus they persecuted the prophets who were before you ⑤.

—Matthew 5:1-12, *New American Bible*

Analyzing Primary Sources

Cite specific evidence from the document to support your answers.

1. **Analyze Information** What encouragement does Jesus give his followers when he says, "Blessed are you when they insult you and persecute you and utter every kind of evil against you [falsely] because of me./ Rejoice and be glad, for your reward will be great in heaven"?

2. **Draw Conclusions** Which of these statements do you think would have been most threatening to the Roman authorities of Jesus' time? Why?

LESSON 4
Roman Culture and Its Legacy

BOUNCE TO ACTIVATE ▶ VIDEO

GET READY TO READ

START UP
Tourists visit a Roman ruin in present-day Turkey. Why do you think Roman civilization continues to fascinate people?

GUIDING QUESTIONS
- What cultural exchanges took place between Rome and other ancient civilizations?
- What were Roman achievements in art, literature, and science?
- How did ancient Rome influence language, government, and ideas of citizenship?

TAKE NOTES
Literacy Skills: Identify Main Ideas
Use the graphic organizer in your 📔 Active Journal to take notes as you read the lesson.

PRACTICE VOCABULARY
Use the vocabulary activity in your 📔 Active Journal to practice the vocabulary words.

Vocabulary		Academic Vocabulary
site of encounter	Romance language	achievement
Greco-Roman	oratory	tradition
mosaic	satire	
	gladiator	

The Roman empire may be ancient history, but Roman culture is still with us in many ways. Rome's art, language, entertainment, and law continue to influence the modern world. Also, in the city of Rome, people from different cultures mixed and interacted creatively, adding to Rome's cultural legacy.

Rome as a Site of Encounter
Ancient Rome was a **site of encounter**. Sites of encounter are places where people from different cultures meet and exchange products, ideas, and technologies.

good lyrics [handwritten annotation]

A Multicultural Empire The Roman empire contained many different cultures. The Latin-speaking Romans had conquered Egyptians, Greeks, Syrians, Jews, Celts, and Gauls. These peoples had dozens of religions and spoke hundreds of languages, including Greek, Aramaic, and Hebrew. Roman emperors brought to Rome the best of everything they could find from their empire and the world. The emperors used what they found to enrich Rome and their empire.

▲ This painting from the 1800s shows Rome at its height.

International Influences International trade both spread Rome's influence and brought influences to Rome from other cultures. By the end of the first century BCE, a major expansion of international trade brought Rome into contact with the Parthian Persian, Kushan, Xiongnu (Central Asia), and Han empires. Ideas, customs, and beliefs spread as valuable goods moved long distances between empires.

Arab merchants brought frankincense, myrrh, spices, gold, ivory, pearls, precious stones, and textiles from Africa, India, and East Asia by camel caravan. Chinese silk, much desired by wealthy Romans, traveled to Rome along sea routes and the Silk Road. In return, the Chinese traded for Roman metalwork and glassware. Mithraism, a religion from Persia and the east, attracted many Romans. Roman emperors encouraged this religion's idea of loyalty to the king. In turn, Christianity spread into Persia and parts of Africa.

☑ **READING CHECK** **Identify Main Ideas** What is a site of encounter?

What Was Greco-Roman Culture?

You have read that the Romans borrowed from Greek civilization. They adopted Greek cultural practices and spread their own as well. A combined **Greco-Roman** culture emerged that included Greek and Roman elements. Many people in the empire combined Greco-Roman culture with other local traditions.

Some Roman practices in this joint culture were visiting public baths and worshiping the emperors. Greek traditions included seeing plays by Greek authors and studying Greek philosophy.

Government Spreads Culture Some actions of the Roman government helped spread Greco-Roman culture. For military purposes, it built roads and founded cities called colonies in the provinces. Roads made it easier to travel and spread ideas. Colonies looked like Rome in many ways. Each had a forum, amphitheater, and baths. Roman culture spread from colonies to nearby lands.

The government also spread Roman culture when it allowed more people to become Roman citizens. By 212 CE, almost every free person in the empire was a citizen. As citizens, they lived under Roman law. They used Roman courts to settle disputes. Male citizens could serve in the Roman army.

The Army Shares Culture Roman soldiers helped spread Greco-Roman culture as well. Many soldiers were sent to the far reaches of the empire. They often married local women and settled where they had served. Military outposts on the frontiers grew into towns and cities, which introduced the local people to Greco-Roman culture.

✔️ **READING CHECK** Identify Implied Main Ideas How did colonies help spread Greco-Roman culture?

Roman Art and Language

The arts flourished in the Roman empire. Roman art is still widely admired. The Latin language also remains important.

The Arts of the Empire In Roman towns, art filled public buildings and the homes of the wealthy. Colorful mosaics brightened up floors. A **mosaic** is a design formed with small tiles of glass, stone, or pottery. Public buildings and the homes of the wealthy boasted colorful painted murals on the walls and ceilings. These showed beautiful landscapes, events from mythology and history, and scenes from daily life.

The Romans built statues of their gods, great heroes, and important people. They stood in markets, temples, and other public places. Many were copies of Greek originals. But the Romans also developed their own style. Greek sculptors usually idealized their subjects, or made them look like ideal people. In contrast, earlier Roman sculptors usually showed their subjects as they were in real life.

Analyze Images Roman art, as in this painting from near Pompeii, often showed scenes of daily life. **Synthesize Visual Information** What are some words you would use to describe the lives of upper-class Romans?

Skillful Roman artisans used various materials to make beautiful objects. They crafted vases and jars of blue glass and mirrors of polished silver. Romans wore jewelry made of silver, gold, and gems.

The Influence of Latin Roman soldiers, colonists, and merchants took their language to many parts of Europe. Latin, the Roman language, became the spoken language across much of the western part of the empire. Over centuries, local ways of speaking of Latin changed into new languages, including Spanish, Italian, French, and Portuguese. These are called **Romance languages**, or languages that developed from Latin. Millions of people speak Romance languages today.

English is not a Romance language, but as many as half of all English words may come from Latin. For example, the word *educate* comes directly from Latin, while *labor* comes indirectly from Latin by way of French.

Latin was the language of education in Europe for many centuries. Scientists still use it to name plants and animals. Latin also served as the language of the Roman Catholic Church. All Catholic services were held in Latin into the 1900s.

☑ READING CHECK **Understand Effects** In what ways does the Latin language continue to influence English speakers today?

Literature and Science in Ancient Rome

The Romans prized literature and science. They built on Greek **achievements**.

Oratory and Poetry Flourish The Romans developed **oratory**, the art of giving speeches. Rome's most famous orator was Cicero, a politician during the last days of the Roman republic. Cicero spoke about the great political issues of his time. He used his powers of persuasion to win election to high office. Many of his speeches were written down and used as models by later orators.

The poet Virgil lived around the same time as Cicero. He wrote the *Aeneid*, an epic poem. It was modeled on Homer's Greek epics, the *Iliad* and the *Odyssey*.

Horace was another famous Roman poet. He is best known for a collection of poems called *Odes*. Some are about friendship and love. Others give advice, which is still relevant today.

The poet Ovid wrote witty verses. Many of his poems explored the theme of love. Some retold stories from Greek and Roman myths.

▲ The Roman poet Virgil whose epic poem the *Aeneid* influenced many later writers

Academic Vocabulary

achievement • *n.*, accomplishment that requires effort or skill

Satire and Biography The author Juvenal wrote **satires**, works of literature that make fun of their subject. Juvenal mocked Roman life. For example, he complained that the Roman people accepted the rule of the emperors instead of having a republic. He wrote that in his day Roman citizens only wanted free food and entertainment.

Primary Source

"The people that once bestowed [gave out] commands, consulships, legions, and all else, now . . . longs eagerly for just two things—bread and circuses!"

—Juvenal, *Satire 10*

Quest CONNECTIONS

Read the quote from Juvenal's *Satire 10* again. How do you think the Roman citizenry's attitude towards the government affected the empire's stability? Record your thoughts in your 📓 Active Journal.

The biographer and essayist Plutarch wrote about 227 works. *Parallel Lives* is his most famous book. He compares the characters and lives of pairs of Greek and Roman soldiers, orators, and politicians. These popular biographies provided models for good behavior. Plutarch also wrote many essays on political, religious, ethical, philosophical, and literary subjects. His works were a major influence on the development of essays and biographies.

Philosophy Develops The Romans also continued developing philosophy, inspired by the Greeks. One famous Roman philosopher was Seneca. He wrote about Stoic philosophy. Stoicism urges people to accept suffering and practice self-control.

Roman Advances in Science and Medicine Like philosophy, the Romans also contributed to science and medicine. One important scientist during this period was an astronomer and mathematician named Claudius Ptolemy (KLAWdee uhs TAHLuh mee). He lived in Egypt, which was part of the Roman empire.

Ptolemy wrote a famous book called the *Almagest*. It shaped the way astronomers viewed the universe until the 1400s, although its main idea was wrong. Ptolemy also wrote important works on geography and optics, or the study of light.

The scholar and writer Pliny the Elder wrote the famous *Natural History*, an encyclopedia of scientific matters. Although not always accurate, it was accepted as an authority until the Middle Ages. Pliny carefully names his more than 100 sources, an unusual feature. *Natural History* also provides much valuable information about Roman life for modern scholars.

Analyze Images This drawing illustrates Ptolemy's idea that the earth is at the center of the solar system. **Compare and Contrast** How has Ptolemy's theory been disproved today?

The best-known physician in the Roman empire was a Greek named Claudius Galen. Galen carefully dissected, or cut open, animals such as monkeys. He did this to study how bodies work. Galen was the first to discover that arteries and veins carry blood. Earlier, people believed that they carried air. Doctors used Galen's writings for more than a thousand years.

READING CHECK **Classify and Categorize** What is each of these writers known for: Horace, Ovid, Juvenal?

Popular Entertainment on a Massive Scale

The Greeks staged public entertainments, including plays and athletic events. But the Romans developed a taste for public entertainment on a massive scale. They invented the round amphitheater and built stadiums across the empire.

Gladiatorial Games The Romans enjoyed fights between **gladiators**, or men and sometimes women who fought one another and wild animals as part of a public entertainment. Fights were held in the arenas such as the Colosseum in Rome.

Gladiatorial matches were first held in southern Italy before Rome existed. Originally, these games were staged at funerals. The death of a gladiator was meant as a sacrifice to the spirit of the person whose death was being mourned. Later, the games lost this connection with funerals and were held just to entertain.

The word *gladiator* means swordsman in Latin, though gladiators used a variety of weapons. Gladiators were usually slaves or criminals. They

Analyze Images This drawing shows the Colosseum in cutaway. **Synthesize Visual Information** In what ways does this building resemble modern ones?

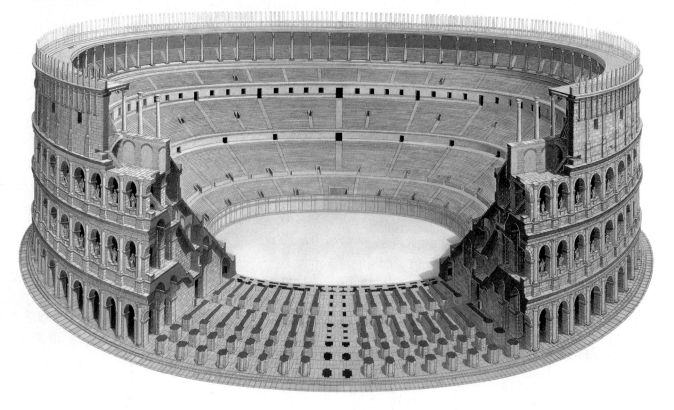

were trained both to fight and to entertain a crowd. Skilled or lucky gladiators who survived many matches could win their freedom. They could even become celebrities.

Sometimes, huge battles between teams of gladiators were staged. Special arenas were flooded so that gladiators could fight one another on boats, recreating famous naval battles from history. Exotic animals like lions and elephants were brought to Rome. Special fighters, condemned criminals, and prisoners of war were made to fight these wild animals.

▲ Events like this chariot race thrilled Roman spectators.

Emperors or wealthy aristocrats paid for these extravagant games. Expensive events showed off the wealth and power of the person who sponsored them.

Chariot Races One of the most popular events in ancient times was chariot racing. In Rome, chariot races took place at the Circus Maximus. The Circus Maximus was a huge racecourse that could seat as many as 270,000 people.

Races were held far more often than gladiatorial games. Horses pulled charioteers seven times around the course. Cheering fans encouraged their favorite team of charioteers.

✓ **READING CHECK** **Compare and Contrast** How did Roman entertainments differ from Greek ones?

Roman Government and Law

You have read that the government of the Roman republic influences governments today. Similarly, Roman law shapes the laws of many modern countries.

Government by Citizens The Roman republic's innovative system of government provided its citizens with roles to play. Power was shared by different people with set roles. Officials' time in office was limited to one year to prevent anyone from gaining too much power. The government had three parts—the assemblies, the senate, and the magistrates. Each part had powers that limited the powers of other parts. These ideas were adapted by many later governments.

Roman culture emphasized civic duty. During the republic, free adult Roman men were citizens. Free Roman women were considered citizens, but could not vote or take part in the government. Slaves were not citizens. Male citizens had the right to vote and to a trial. Male citizens had a responsibility to take part in the life of the Roman community.

▲ Roman laws, like those inscribed on these tablets, influenced later societies.

Academic Vocabulary

tradition • *n.*, a custom or practice that is handed down over generations

 **INTERACTIVE**

3-D Model: The Pantheon

This included serving in the military (paying their own way) and in Roman courts. Much changed after Rome became an empire. The Roman idea of citizenship, however, remained strong. Many wealthy Romans acted to improve city life. They often paid for the construction of buildings or funded public events out of their own money to improve their city.

What Were the Twelve Tables? In the early years of the Roman republic, there were no written laws. Judges decided what the law was in each case. They based decisions on custom and **tradition**. In the 400s BCE, the Romans wrote down a law code called the Twelve Tables. It set down laws relating to family relations, property, inheritance, and other important issues.

What Was the Influence of Roman Law? Roman law lasted longer than the empire itself. It changed a great deal over the centuries. Over time it developed into a system called civil law. Today, civil law is used in many parts of the world. For example, it is used in some countries that were once Roman provinces, such as France, Spain, and Portugal. It is also used in nations that were once colonies of these countries, including Algeria, Mexico, and Brazil. Even today, one American state uses a legal system partly based on civil law. This is Louisiana, which was founded as a French colony.

☑ READING CHECK **Identify Cause and Effect** How did the Twelve Tables change the Roman legal system?

☑ Lesson Check

Practice Vocabulary

1. What are **mosaics** made from?

2. Were Roman **gladiators** usually slaves or usually free men?

3. What is a **Romance language**? Is English one of these?

Critical Thinking and Writing

4. Compare and Contrast How are Cicero's writings different from Juvenal's?

5. Identify Main Ideas In what ways is the legacy of the Latin language important to scientists today?

6. Classify and Categorize In what ways were gladiatorial games entertainment and in what ways were they combat?

7. Writing Workshop: Introduce a Claim As you continue to add information to your chart, start to think about which civilization you feel was greater, Greece or Rome. Form your thoughts into a claim, or thesis statement for your argument. Make a list in your 📓 Active Journal.

The Decline of the Roman Empire

BOUNCE TO ACTIVATE   ▶ VIDEO

GET READY TO READ

START UP

Look at the photograph of the ruins of the Roman Forum. Do you think all civilizations must eventually decline? Why or why not?

GUIDING QUESTIONS

- What factors led to the Roman empire's decline?
- How did Rome's leaders attempt to hold the empire together?
- What happened to the two halves of the empire?

TAKE NOTES

Literacy Skills: Analyze Cause and Effect
Use the graphic organizer in your 📓 Active Journal to take notes as you read the lesson.

PRACTICE VOCABULARY

Use the vocabulary activity in your 📓 Active Journal to practice the vocabulary words.

Vocabulary

inflation   mercenary
barbarian   orthodoxy

Academic Vocabulary

communication
collapse

For centuries, the Roman empire ruled the Mediterranean region. In the 200s CE, however, Rome began to decline.

Why Did the Pax Romana End?

In 180 CE, the emperor Marcus Aurelius died. He was the last of five powerful emperors who had kept the empire strong and united for many years. His death marks the end of the Pax Romana. Over the next 300 years, the empire slowly declined and finally collapsed.

After 200 CE, the empire began to struggle with continuing problems from outside and within its long borders. The Romans came face to face with the limits of their empire. Without conquering new territories, Rome did not receive the large streams of income it had come to depend upon. Other internal weaknesses included widespread corruption, depending too heavily on slave labor, a general lack of education, and the restless poor in the cities. The divide between rich and poor undermined the Roman traditions of citizenship. Depopulation from epidemics also contributed to the empire's decline.

The peace of the Roman empire depended on one emperor following another without violence. Starting in the late 100s CE, military commanders, supported by their armies, began to challenge emperors, hoping to become emperor themselves. Civil wars broke out more frequently.

A general named Septimius Severus briefly restored peace. Severus became emperor after winning a civil war. He understood he was emperor because the army supported him, not because the people liked him. His strategy for holding on to power was simple. He said, "Enrich the soldiers, scorn all other men." While many earlier emperors had tried to win over the people and the senate, later emperors cared less for their opinions and focused on the military.

✓ READING CHECK Identify Main Ideas By what part of society were many emperors after Marcus Aurelius challenged? Explain.

What Was the Imperial Crisis?

Severus's successors lost power. The empire soon fell again into civil wars. The years 235 to 284 are called the Imperial Crisis. During the crisis, Rome was torn apart by civil wars and even split into pieces. Generals quickly became emperor one after another. Each killed or defeated the previous emperor.

Economic Problems Worsen Civil wars created massive economic problems. Wars were expensive. Men who wanted to be emperor needed to convince soldiers to support them. They increased soldiers' pay or gave them bribes. Emperors raised taxes to support these expenses. That hurt common people and the economy.

Emperors also tried to get the money they needed by making coins with less gold or silver and more copper or other less valuable metals. When merchants realized that coins had less precious metal than before, they raised their prices. This caused **inflation**, or a general rise in the cost of goods.

Wars also hurt the economy by making trade dangerous. The trade networks that had made Rome wealthy were disrupted.

Foreign Invaders Threaten the Empire During this period, Rome's foreign enemies became more dangerous. Roman armies were often tied up fighting civil wars. Troops were pulled away from the borders.

As Romans fought other Romans, people from outside the empire took advantage of the bad situation. They raided Roman lands more often.

The empire's size made it hard to defend the borders. Despite good roads, **communication** and travel were much slower than they are

▲ This eagle clasp was made by Visigoths, or West Goths, around 500 CE. The Visigoths were one group who began to invade the Roman empire during the Imperial Crisis.

Quest CONNECTIONS

How do you think the economic problems described here contributed to the empire's decline? Record your findings in your 📕 Active Journal.

Academic Vocabulary

communication • *n.*, way of passing on information

today. Troops could not be moved quickly to fight invaders. It took a long time to bring word of an invasion to the emperor.

In the 200s, the Sassanian empire rose up in Persia. The Sassanian Persians took advantage of Roman civil wars to raid Roman lands. In 260, they captured and executed the Roman emperor Valerian. The Romans could not defeat the Sassanian Persians in the east.

The Germanic Tribes The Romans called the people who lived across the empire's northern borders Germans. They were made up of many different groups. Some were the Franks, Vandals, and Goths.

Like the Persians, the Germans also raided Roman territory more often during the Imperial Crisis. They saw Rome as a rich, easy target. Many Germans also wanted to settle in the empire. Living conditions were often better there.

Romans called the Germans **barbarians**. This is the word Greeks and Romans used for all people who did not share their cultures. They believed that barbarians were savage or uncivilized.

In fact, many Germans adopted parts of Greco-Roman culture. They lived in or near the empire for generations. After Rome became Christian, many Germans converted as well. During and after the Imperial Crisis, tens of thousands of Germans joined the Roman army. By the end of the empire, Germans had become leading Roman generals.

☑ READING CHECK **Identify Cause and Effect** What were some of the factors that made it difficult to defend the Roman empire against foreign invasion?

The Late Empire

The Roman empire did not recover from the Imperial crisis until the late 200s. Diocletian (dy uh KLEE shun), a military leader, became emperor in 284. For the first time in decades, a single man ruled the whole empire. He held on to power for many years.

Diocletian Divides the Empire During his rule, Diocletian tried to make Rome more stable. He reorganized the imperial government. He sent troops to restore peace to frontier regions. Diocletian also persecuted Christians, since many Romans believed that Christians had made the gods angry and that this had caused Rome's problems.

Diocletian's most important contribution was to divide the empire into two halves. He chose a co-emperor to help him manage the empire. Diocletian ruled over the eastern part of the empire, while Maximian ruled in the west.

Constantine Builds a "New Rome" But Diocletian's reforms failed. After his death, military leaders again fought for power. In time, Constantine

▼ Diocletian and his co-emperor Maximian ruled over the two halves of the Roman empire.

became emperor. As you read, Constantine converted to Christianity and made it a legal religion in the empire.

In 324, Constantine began work on an impressive new capital for the eastern half of the empire. He built his "New Rome" in what is now Turkey. It was on the site of an old Greek city called Byzantium. After his death, the city was called Constantinople, city of Constantine.

✓ READING CHECK **Sequence** What key emperor ruled soon after Diocletian, and what changes did he make to the empire?

The West Collapses

Rome declined after Constantine's death. Its enemies took advantage of its weakness and caused it to **collapse**.

The Huns Arrive Nomads from the plains of Central Eurasia, known to the Romans as the Huns, triggered a crisis along the empire's northern borders. These fierce mounted warriors attacked Rome and other large empires of the time, such as those in China, Persia, and India.

The Huns' attacks helped cause a decline in trade on the silk roads and other land routes across Eurasia between 300 and 600. The Huns moved into Europe in the 300s. Later, in the 400s, they attacked Rome under their leader Attila. The Romans defeated that invasion at the battle of Châlons. But the arrival of the Huns was still dangerous. Germans fled ahead of them into Roman lands.

The Germans Invade By 376, some Germans had reached the Danube River, the border of the empire. The German Goths crossed the river. They entered the empire, looking for refuge.

Academic Vocabulary

collapse • v., fall apart, break into pieces

GEOGRAPHY SKILLS

The empire's weakened borders made it vulnerable to invasions by tribal groups from across Europe.

1. **Movement** In what direction did most tribes flee from the Huns?

2. **Draw Conclusions** What appears to be the common goal of all the tribes' invasions?

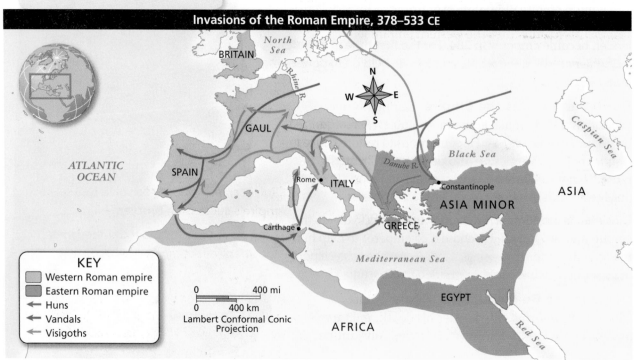

Invasions of the Roman Empire, 378–533 CE

KEY
- Western Roman empire
- Eastern Roman empire
- ← Huns
- ← Vandals
- ← Visigoths

0 ____ 400 mi
0 ____ 400 km
Lambert Conformal Conic Projection

The Romans attacked the Goths and tried to control them, but the Goths defeated them at the battle of Adrianople. Gothic invasions followed. Goths and other Germans crossed into the empire.

Romans tried to pay some tribes of Germans to fight others. They hired **mercenaries**, or soldiers who fight for pay rather than for their country. But these mercenaries were not always loyal. They sometimes turned against the empire. Rome failed to stop the invasions.

The emperor Theodosius took over after the disaster at Adrianople. He was the last person to rule both the eastern and western halves of the Roman empire. Theodosius became a strong supporter of Christian **orthodoxy**, meaning traditional or established religious beliefs. He made Christianity the official Roman religion.

After Theodosius's death, German tribes began to seize whole provinces. In 410, Roman troops pulled out of Britain. They abandoned the province to German invaders. As the western empire fell apart, German generals dominated western Roman emperors from behind the scenes. The emperors lost power.

The Fall of Rome In time, the city of Rome itself was attacked. Goths captured Rome in 410 and looted the city. In 455, the Vandals plundered Rome. Rome never recovered from these attacks. The western Roman empire ended in 476. In that year, a German general named Odoacer deposed, or removed from power, Romulus Augustus, the last western Roman emperor. Odoacer became king of Italy.

As the government of the western Roman empire collapsed, cities came under attack. People moved from the cities to the country for safety. Trade and learning declined. For 500 years in Europe few except the clergy, or church workers, could understand Latin.

The Roman empire survived in a smaller form in the east, however. The eastern Roman empire, called the Byzantine empire, survived for almost 1,000 years after the western empire fell.

✅ READING CHECK **Compare and Contrast** How did the result of foreign invasions differ between the two halves of the empire?

Quick Activity

Odoacer became king of Italy in 476. Did Rome "fall"? Gather evidence in your 📓 Active Journal and decide for yourself.

☑ Lesson Check

Practice Vocabulary

1. When **inflation** occurs, do prices rise or fall?

2. Why do **mercenaries** fight?

Critical Thinking and Writing

3. **Identify Cause and Effect** How did civil wars lead to economic problems?

4. **Identify Main Ideas** What changes did Diocletian make to try to solve the Roman empire's succession problem?

5. **Understand Effects** How did the Huns' movement affect the Roman empire?

6. **Writing Workshop: Support a Claim** To be persuasive, you must support your claim with evidence. Record the three best examples of your chosen society's greatness in your 📓 Active Journal.

The Byzantine Empire Rises

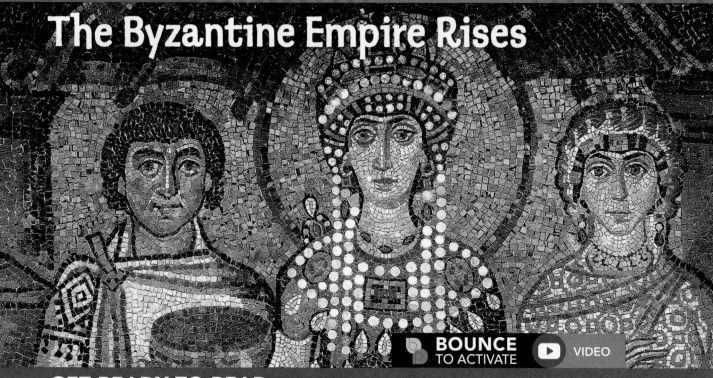

BOUNCE TO ACTIVATE ▶ VIDEO

GET READY TO READ

START UP
Examine the image. Who might the woman in the center be? What details give you clues about her identity?

GUIDING QUESTIONS
- In what ways did the Byzantine empire differ from the Roman empire?
- What were Justinian's achievements?
- What caused the Byzantine empire to decline?
- How did the Byzantine empire influence the cultures around it, including early Russia?

TAKE NOTES
Literacy Skills: Use Evidence
Use the graphic organizer in your 📖 Active Journal to take notes as you read the lesson.

PRACTICE VOCABULARY
Use the vocabulary activity in your 📖 Active Journal to practice the vocabulary words.

Vocabulary		Academic Vocabulary
Byzantine	missionary	successor
strait	Cyrillic	core
moat	alphabet	
Greek fire		

By the year 500 CE, the western Roman empire had collapsed, but the eastern Roman empire lasted nearly 1,000 years more.

What Was the New Rome?
During the later years of the Roman empire, power shifted from the western part of the empire to its east and the empire changed. Emperor Constantine built Constantinople as a new capital for the empire.

Who Were the Byzantines? The people of this empire did not call themselves "Byzantines" (BIZ un teens). They thought of themselves as Romans. But their empire was different from the ancient Roman empire. Most of the time, it did not control the city of Rome. Most of the empire's people were Christians, unlike people in the early Roman empire. They also spoke Greek, not Latin.

Because of these and other differences, historians needed a separate name for this empire. They called it the **Byzantine** empire because its capital, Constantinople, was built at a place called Byzantium.

The City's Location Constantine built his new capital on the Bosporus Strait. A **strait** is a narrow body of water that cuts through land, connecting two larger bodies of water. The Bosporus and other waterways link the Black and Mediterranean seas. On one side of the Bosporus is Asia. On the other side is Europe.

Defense and Trade Because of its location, Constantinople was easier to defend than Rome. It was built on a peninsula. The city was surrounded on three sides by water. Two rings of thick walls and a **moat**, or trench filled with water, protected the city on land.

Constantinople's strategic location and good harbors made it an ideal trading center. Merchants brought spices from India, furs from Russia, silk from China, and grain from Egypt. Traders from Western Europe came to Constantinople to buy products from Asia. Trade made Constantinople rich.

☑ READING CHECK **Compare and Contrast** How did the Byzantine empire differ from the western Roman empire?

Who Were Justinian and Theodora?

One great Byzantine emperor was Justinian, who ruled for nearly 40 years, from 527 to 565. He and his wife, Theodora, who is portrayed on the previous page, were a colorful and unusual royal couple.

Justinian was born to a family of peasants. His uncle Justin began his career as an impoverished soldier. He worked his way up through the army to the throne. Justinian was his **successor**. Theodora also came from a lower-class family. Her father worked

Academic Vocabulary

successor • *n.*, person who follows another in an office or role

GEOGRAPHY **SKILLS**

Constantinople's location made it the political and economic center of the Byzantine empire.

1. **Location** On what continent was Constantinople located?

2. **Synthesize Visual Information** Summarize how Constantinople's location helped protect it.

The Byzantine Empire

EUROPE
Kiev • *Dnieper River*
Danube River
SLAVS
LOMBARDS
FRANKS • Milan
BULGARS
45° N
Rhône River
Po River • Ravenna
Black Sea
Corsica • ITALY BALKANS *Bosporus*
SPAIN Rome • Naples • Constantinople ASIA
VISIGOTHS Sardinia ANATOLIA
• Córdoba Sicily Athens *Tigris River*
Carthage • GREECE
Crete Cyprus
Mediterranean Sea Damascus •
Cyrene • Babylon • PERSIANS
Alexandria • Jerusalem
Cairo • 30° N
AFRICA EGYPT ARABS *Euphrates River* *Persian Gulf*
S A H A R A
Nile River *Red Sea* • Medina — TROPIC OF CANCER —
• Mecca

0   500 mi
0   500 km
Miller Cylindrical Projection

N W E S

KEY
☐ Byzantine empire, about 550
☐ Byzantine empire, about 1020
☐ Byzantine empire, 1360
• City

0°   15° E   30° E   45° E   60° E

Analyze Images
Stout walls like these protected the Byzantine capital. **Identify Main Ideas** What other natural and constructed features helped defend Constantinople?

as a bear trainer at the circus. When she grew up, she became an actress. Both Justinian and Theodora were intelligent, bold, and ruthless.

Justinian's Conquests Justinian dreamed of restoring Rome's lost empire. He wrote:

Primary Source

"We have good hopes that [God will help us to establish] our empire over the rest of those whom the Romans of old ruled from the boundaries of one ocean to another and then lost by their negligence."

—Justinian

He worked for more than 30 years trying to do just that. Justinian's generals won back lands around the Mediterranean, such as Spain, Italy, and North Africa. He even recaptured the city of Rome. During Justinian's reign, the Byzantine empire reached its greatest size.

Justinian's many wars, however, left the empire with money problems. Disease broke out across the empire as he was trying to complete his conquests. After his death, invaders chipped away at the territory he had gained. The Byzantine empire lost the areas he conquered.

Justinian's Legacy Although Justinian could not restore the Roman empire, he did leave an important legacy. He rebuilt Hagia Sophia, the empire's central church. He also collected a law code. You will read more about Justinian's accomplishments later in this topic.

✓ READING CHECK Identify Main Ideas What was Justinian's goal for the Byzantine empire? How did he try to achieve it?

The Shrinking Empire

After the death of Justinian, the Byzantine empire slowly shrank. Over the next 800 years, it declined and fell.

Foreign Invaders Many outside groups took parts of the empire. Germans took back lands in the west that Justinian had conquered. Slavic peoples invaded from the north. The Roman empire's conflicts with the Persians on its eastern frontier continued under the Byzantines. Weakened from the long conflict, the Byzantine and Persian empires were open to attack by Muslim armies in the mid-600s.

Arab Muslim invaders conquered the Sassanian Persian empire, and the Byzantines lost huge territories in Syria, Egypt, and North Africa. The Turks, a Muslim Central Asian people, seized much of modern-day Turkey and other areas from the Byzantines.

However, the Byzantine emperors kept control of the **core** of their empire, modern-day Greece and western Turkey. They also continued to rule Constantinople. Toward the end, they controlled little else. The empire was more like a city-state. The once powerful emperors had to hire Italian ships and soldiers to help defend their capital.

Constantinople's Defenses Invaders often tried to capture the city of Constantinople. Nearly all failed. Those who attacked by land could not get past the city's strong walls. Those who came by sea were stopped by a heavy chain across the city's harbor. The Byzantines also used a secret weapon against ships. This was **Greek fire**, a chemical mixture that burned furiously, even in water. The Byzantines shot Greek fire at enemy ships or against troops attacking the city walls. The result was terrible to see.

The Defenses Fail Still, Constantinople could not hold out forever. In 1204, soldiers from Western Europe called *crusaders* took the city. They looted it and did great damage. You will read more about the crusaders later. The Byzantine empire eventually retook its capital.

The final attack came from the Turkish Ottoman empire. Constantinople's walls were built in an age before gunpowder. The Ottomans used cannons that helped them break down the walls. In 1453, Constantinople fell to the Ottomans. The Byzantine empire was no more.

✔ **READING CHECK** **Compare and Contrast** How was the fall of the Byzantine empire similar to the end of Rome?

INTERACTIVE

Interactive Map
The Byzantine Empire

▼ The Ottomans used cannons like this one in the siege of Constantinople.

The Empire's Influence

The politics of the Byzantine empire were often violent. The imperial court was known for its plots and power struggles. Some rulers were blinded or poisoned by rivals. Even so, the Byzantine empire was so wealthy and its culture was so attractive that its influence spread far beyond the empire's borders.

The Lure of Constantinople Byzantine culture spread in two ways. One was by attracting visitors to Constantinople. Merchants came to trade. Scholars came to study. Artists came to work. Visitors were amazed. Byzantine leaders impressed their visitors with elaborate ceremonies, glittering jewels, and rich clothing. One visitor was impressed by Byzantine religious practices.

Primary Source

"We knew not whether we were in heaven or on earth. For on earth there is no such splendour or such beauty . . . We know only that God dwells there among men."

—The Russian Primary Chronicle

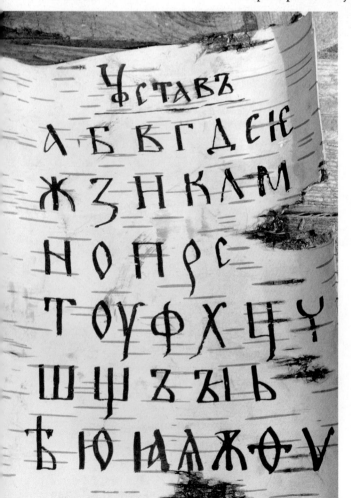

▼ This sample of the Cyrillic alphabet, developed by Byzantine missionaries, is written on birch bark, a tree common in the cold climate of Russia.

The visitors took ideas home with them. Many Eastern Europeans adopted parts of Byzantine culture.

Spreading the Faith Byzantine culture was also spread by Eastern Orthodox missionaries. A **missionary** is someone who tries to convert others to a particular religion. Beginning in the late 800s, Eastern Orthodox missionaries began to travel among non-Christians in southeastern Europe, the home of people called Slavs.

Byzantine missionaries converted many Slavs to Christianity. Many Eastern Europeans practice Eastern Orthodox Christianity today.

The best-known Eastern Orthodox missionaries were two brothers named Cyril and Methodius. They came from a noble family, but gave up their wealth to become priests. They made a major contribution to Slavic culture. Cyril and Methodius invented the **Cyrillic alphabet** (suh RIL ik), which allowed the Slavs to write down their language. It was based on the letters of the Greek alphabet. Today it is used mostly for Slavic languages such as Russian and Bulgarian.

✓ READING CHECK **Classify and Categorize** What are two ways that Byzantine culture spread?

Early Russia

The early history of Russia was strongly influenced by the Byzantine empire. The first large state in what would become Russia and Ukraine was the Kievan Rus (KEEehvun ROOS). It was based in the city of Kiev and founded by a people called the Rus. The Rus were Vikings, a people from northern Europe. The Rus joined with local Slavs to form a powerful state. They controlled trade routes along Russia's rivers south to Constantinople.

Trade made the Kievan Rus rich. It also brought Russians into contact with the Byzantines. Eventually the rulers of the Rus converted to Eastern Orthodox Christianity.

As in the Byzantine empire, icons were very important to Russian Christians. In addition, Russian architecture was influenced by Byzantine building styles.

Over time, the power of Kiev declined just as the Byzantine empire was also declining. Although the Byzantine empire fell in 1453, in time a new Russian empire developed. The Russian empire considered itself the "third Rome," taking up the legacy of ancient Rome and the Byzantine empire. Russian emperors even took the title *tsar*, the Russian version of *caesar*, a title used by both Roman and Byzantine emperors.

▼ The Golden Gate of Kiev greeted visitors to the city.

☑ **READING CHECK** **Identify Main Ideas**
Who were the Kievan Rus and where did they live?

☑ Lesson Check

Practice Vocabulary

1. What is a **strait**?

2. What was the **Cyrillic alphabet** based on?

Critical Thinking and Writing

3. **Identify Evidence** Why might Justinian be considered a successful emperor? Why might he be considered a failure?

4. **Identify Main Ideas** Which two influences helped shape Byzantine culture?

5. **Infer** What are some ways that a written language helps cultures develop?

6. **Writing Workshop: Distinguish Claims from Opposing Claims** Part of a good argument is countering an opposing claim. Plan out how you will do so in your essay in your 📓 Active Journal.

Conduct a Cost-Benefit Analysis

Follow these steps to conduct a cost-benefit analysis on the question: Should Emperor Constantine move the capital of the Roman empire?

INTERACTIVE

Make Decisions

1 **Identify the decision that has to be made.** A decision often starts with a problem. For example: How can I make my government stronger? How can I improve the economy? In the early 300s, Constantine needed to strengthen the eastern empire. What decision did Constantine have to make?

2 **Identify a possible solution.** Next, consider what steps you could take that might solve your problem. What did Constantine do to solve his problem?

3 **Identify the costs and benefits of your solution.** Ask, "What might this solution cost to put into place?" Then ask, "What

are the benefits that might occur?" Be thorough in listing costs and benefits. Review the passage.

a. What are the costs of moving the capital of the Roman empire from Rome to Byzantium?

b. What are the benefits of the move?

4 **Compare the benefits to the costs.** A good solution offers benefits that are far greater than the costs. Compare the list of costs to the list of benefits you identified from Step 3. Do the costs of building the new capital outweigh the benefits?

Secondary Source

Constantine was emperor of both the eastern and western Roman empires. At the time, Rome was the capital. Constantine had an important decision to make: should he build a new capital in Byzantium? There were many benefits to doing this. For one thing, Constantine was a Christian. If he built a new city, he could fill it with Christian churches. He could establish a new senate, and make other changes in government. Byzantium was in a good location for military defense and was also an established trade center.

There would be costs in moving to Byzantium, though. Constantine would have to impose high taxes to pay for all the new buildings. Moving the center of power to the East would impact the West because it could hurt its economy and weaken its government and defenses.

Constantine decided to build a new capital in Byzantium. This important decision would affect the history of the world.

Byzantine Religion and Culture

BOUNCE TO ACTIVATE ▶ VIDEO

GET READY TO READ

START UP

Look at the photograph of Hagia Sophia in Istanbul (formerly Constantinople), Turkey. What conclusions can you draw about the Byzantine empire based on this building?

GUIDING QUESTIONS

- What differences arose between Christians during this period?
- In what ways did the Eastern Orthodox Church and the Roman Catholic Church differ?
- How was Byzantine culture unique?

TAKE NOTES

Literacy Skills: Compare and Contrast
Use the graphic organizer in your 📔 Active Journal to take notes as you read the lesson.

PRACTICE VOCABULARY

Use the vocabulary activity in your 📔 Active Journal to practice the vocabulary words.

Vocabulary		Academic Vocabulary
creed	Great	unified
icon	Schism	discriminated
iconoclast	Justinian's	
pope	Code	

By the late 300s, Christianity was the official religion of the Roman empire. However, various groups of Christians held different religious beliefs and views about important issues. Christianity split into two churches, Roman Catholic and Eastern Orthodox.

Religious Differences

As Christianity grew, Christians began to argue about the beliefs of their faith. These arguments divided Christians into different groups.

The Nicene Creed Early Christians disagreed over exactly who Jesus was. Some argued that he was fully human. Others believed that he was fully divine, or that he was both human and divine. The emperor Constantine called a council of bishops in 325. They met in the city of Nicea (nySEEuh) and adopted a statement of beliefs, or a **creed**, called the Nicene Creed. It said that Jesus was both human and divine. Most Christian groups accepted it. But over time, Eastern and Western Christians came to disagree over the creed's exact wording.

Analyze Images This Byzantine icon shows St. Michael holding a sword. **Identify Implied Main Ideas** What role did icons play in creating tension between Eastern and Western Christians?

The Controversy Over Icons

Christians also argued over the use of icons. An **icon** is a holy image, usually a portrait of Jesus or a saint. Many Christians displayed icons in their homes and churches. For them, honoring an icon was a pathway to God. But to others, praying to icons seemed like worshiping objects, which is forbidden in the Bible.

In the 700s, several Byzantine emperors tried to stop icon use. People who opposed icons were called **iconoclasts**, meaning "image-breakers." They went into churches and smashed icons. Violence broke out between iconoclasts and their opponents.

Attacks on icons angered Christians in Western Europe. There, Church leaders saw holy images as a way to teach people about God, not as objects of worship. Eventually, Byzantine emperors who opposed the iconoclasts took power. Today, icons are an important part of worship in Eastern Orthodox churches. But the issue left bitterness between Eastern and Western Christians.

READING CHECK Compare and Contrast Describe two important views about the use of icons.

Church Organization

Christianity spread and grew in part because of its strong organization. But Christians came to disagree about who should lead the Church.

Bishops and Patriarchs The most important Christian leaders were called bishops. In early days each church was led by its own bishop. Later, a single bishop took charge of all the churches in a city, aided by members of the community. Eventually, bishops gained authority, or power, over all the churches in a region. The bishops of the five most important cities were known as patriarchs. These cities were Constantinople, Rome, Alexandria, Antioch, and Jerusalem.

The bishops' authority was based on a tradition known as apostolic succession. According to this tradition, Jesus gave authority over his Church to the original apostles. They then passed this authority down to each generation of bishops.

The Power of the Pope At first, the five patriarchs were equal in authority. Over time, however, the bishop of Rome claimed authority over Christians everywhere. He began to be called **pope**, which means father, or head, of the Church.

The popes based their claim on the idea that they were the successors to the apostle Peter. They argued that Jesus had made Peter head of the Church. According to tradition, Peter had traveled to Rome to become its first bishop. After his death, his authority as head of the Church passed on to the bishops who followed him. The popes pointed to a passage in the Bible to back up their case. Here, Jesus spoke to Peter, whose name means "rock" in Greek.

Primary Source

"You are Peter, and on this rock I will build my church. . . . I will give you the keys of the kingdom of heaven, and whatever you bind on earth shall be bound in heaven."

—Matthew 16:18–19

Did you know?

There are at least 233 million Eastern Orthodox Christians in the world.

Eastern patriarchs and the Byzantine emperors rejected this view of the pope. Eastern emperors wanted to be in charge of the church in their empire. If the pope was the head of the Church, this would take away from their authority.

READING CHECK **Identify Main Ideas** How did Eastern and Western Christians feel about who should lead the Church?

What Was the Great Schism?

Over time, differences between the Eastern and Western churches grew. Two religious traditions developed. In 1054, these two traditions formally split. The split is known as the **Great Schism** (SIZ um). The word *schism* comes from a Greek word meaning split, or division.

Two Christian Churches The Eastern branch of the church came to be called the Eastern Orthodox Church. *Orthodox* means following established beliefs.

In the Eastern Orthodox tradition, the Byzantine emperor was head of the Church. Patriarchs handled the churches' day-to-day affairs. They were all equals, though the Patriarch of Constantinople was considered first among equals. The Byzantine emperor had the power to remove a patriarch if he chose to.

Analyze Charts The chart shows key differences between two branches of Christianity. **Understand Effects** Which church has divided authority? What effects might this fact have on church policies?

The Christian Church Splits

Roman Catholic Church	Eastern Orthodox Church
• The pope headed the Church.	• The Byzantine emperor headed the Church.
• The pope was the highest Church official.	• All patriarchs had equal authority in their regions.
• Rituals and teaching were in Latin.	• Rituals and teaching were in Greek.
• Priests could not marry.	• Priests could marry.

The Western tradition became known as the Roman Catholic Church. *Roman* refers to the fact that it was based in Rome. *Catholic* means universal, or concerned with all people. This church shaped the culture of Western Europe.

The pope was the head of the Roman Catholic Church. As the spiritual leader of the Church, the pope claimed authority over all secular, or nonreligious, rulers. He did not take orders from any secular ruler, including the Byzantine emperor. This was the most important issue dividing the Eastern Orthodox and Roman Catholic churches.

Different Traditions There were other differences between the two churches. The language of the Eastern Orthodox Church was Greek. The language of the Roman Catholic Church was Latin. Orthodox priests were allowed to be married. Catholic priests were not. The churches also differed in some rituals.

Today there is no Byzantine emperor. Eastern Orthodox churches in different countries are led by their own patriarchs. Eastern Orthodox Christians still do not recognize the pope's power. Since 1054, the two churches have been separate. Recently, relations between the churches have improved, but the division remains.

✔️ **READING CHECK** **Identify Main Ideas** What was the most important issue contributing to the Great Schism?

A Unique Culture

The people of the Byzantine empire maintained some of the Greco-Roman traditions you read about previously. But their society was also strongly shaped by Eastern Orthodox Christianity. The result was a cultural blend that was unique, or distinct from other cultures.

Architecture and Literature Byzantine civilization produced its own styles of architecture. The most famous example is Justinian's church, Hagia Sophia. Similar domes can be seen on churches and other houses of worship in southern Europe and the Middle East.

INTERACTIVE

Hagia Sophia

Analyze Images In its almost 1,500-year history, Hagia Sophia has been a Christian church, a mosque, and, today, a museum. **Cite Evidence** What details can you find in the photograph of Hagia Sophia's changing roles in the past?

Byzantine librarians and monks copied and preserved the manuscripts, or handwritten documents, of ancient Greece and Rome. Many of these works would have been lost if Byzantine librarians and monks had not preserved them.

Organizing Roman Law You have read about Roman law and its later influence. It was preserved and updated in the Byzantine empire. This effort was largely the work of the emperor Justinian.

Jnapit lib secūd9 de edēdo

peaūia quā te deposuisse diais deberi tibi pbes · nā qd desideras / vt rōes suas ad usaria tua exhibeat / id ex cā ad offm mdiaf ptiné solz m · Seue · 7 · Antom9 · aa · Ifausto · I s apud quē res agit acta publica taz auilia qm crimialia exhibei m spidenda / ad muestigan, dam veritatis fidē mbebit; dem Augusti Valentima no · O dita actio / speciem future litis monstrat · quā emendari vel mutari licet

mpa · pi9 Antonin9 emilio I pse dispice quéadmodū

▲ A page of Justinian's Code from the 1400s

Justinian found the vast legal legacy he inherited from Rome to be a confusing jumble of local laws, imperial decrees, and judges' decisions. He ordered a group of lawyers to organize this material. He had them produce a **unified** code, or systematic body of law. His code brought order to the system of Roman law. **Justinian's Code** was published in 529. It gave great power to the emperor. The code said "that which seems good to the emperor has the force of law."

The code reveals ways people were treated in the empire. For example, the code **discriminated** against Jews and other non-Christians. On the other hand, it allowed women to inherit property and protected some individual rights.

☑ READING CHECK **Analyze Cause and Effect** Why did Byzantine lawyers try to organize a new system of laws?

Academic Vocabulary

unified • *adj.*, joined together as a single whole

discriminate • *v.*, treat some people differently or worse

☑ Lesson Check

Practice Vocabulary

1. Why did **iconoclasts** oppose the use of icons?

2. Which city has the **pope** for its bishop?

Critical Thinking and Writing

3. **Compare and Contrast** List three differences between the Roman Catholic and Eastern Orthodox churches.

4. **Summarize** the difference in leadership between the Eastern and Western churches.

5. **Identify Main Ideas** Which two influences helped shape Byzantine culture?

6. **Writing Workshop: Shape Tone** In your essay, take a firm but tactful tone. Answer opposing arguments effectively and respectfully.

VISUAL REVIEW

Pressures on the Roman Empire

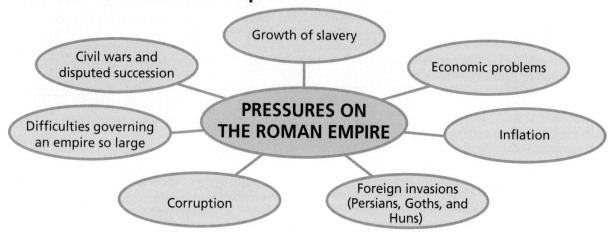

Growth of slavery

Civil wars and disputed succession

Economic problems

Difficulties governing an empire so large

PRESSURES ON THE ROMAN EMPIRE

Inflation

Corruption

Foreign invasions (Persians, Goths, and Huns)

Comparing the Roman and Byzantine Empires

ROMAN EMPIRE

- Based in western Mediterranean
- Spread through Western Europe
- Collapsed in 400s
- Embraced Catholicism
- Latin was key language

- Emperors were Christians after 300s
- Developed strong trade networks
- Gained empires through military victories
- Empires slowly disintegrated

BYZANTINE EMPIRE

- Based in eastern Mediterranean
- Spread through eastern Europe and Western Asia
- Collapsed in 1400s
- Embraced Eastern Orthodox Christianity
- Greek was key language

READING REVIEW

Use the Take Notes and Practice Vocabulary activities in your 📓 Active Journal to review the topic.

 INTERACTIVE

Practice vocabulary using the Topic Mini-Games.

Quest FINDINGS

Hold your discussion on Rome's fall and whether it could have been prevented. Get help for your discussion by using the evidence you collected in your 📓 Active Journal.

ASSESSMENT

Vocabulary and Key Ideas

1. **Recall** What do the words **"Pax Romana"** mean in Latin?

2. **Check Understanding** What is the purpose of **satire**?

3. **Identify** List two everyday situations in which a person would have to think about **ethics**.

4. **Describe** What caused **inflation** in the Roman empire?

5. **Recall** What are two important ways in which Constantine changed the Roman empire?

6. **Identify Main Ideas** What made Constantinople a good location for a new city?

7. **Check Understanding** What were the most important accomplishments of Emperor Justinian?

8. **Identify Supporting Details** In Byzantine times, what aspects of the pope's powers did Roman Catholic and Eastern Orthodox Christians disagree about?

Critical Thinking and Writing

9. **Compare and Contrast** How did the government of the Roman empire differ from that of the republic?

10. **Infer** In what ways did the Roman government help the spread of Christianity, despite its persecution of Christians?

11. **Identify Cause and Effect** In what way did civil wars lead to economic problems?

12. **Infer** How did the appeal of Constantinople help spread Byzantine culture?

13. **Revisit the Essential Question** What forces brought about changes in the Roman empire?

14. **Writer's Workshop: Write Arguments** Using the notes you made in your 📓 Active Journal, write an essay that presents and supports your argument on this question: Which was greater, the Greek city-states or the Roman empire? Keep in mind the following factors: size, longevity, economic power, cultural achievements, and influence.

Analyze Primary Sources

15. Use your knowledge of the Byzantine empire to answer the question.
Why did Justinian create his law code?
A. to gain more power
B. to make Roman law less confusing
C. to help him recapture the western Roman empire
D. to support Eastern Orthodox Christianity

"We have found the entire arrangement of the law which has come down to us ... to be so confused that it ... is not within the grasp of human capacity; and hence We [worked to] make them more easily understood."

—Justinian's Code

Analyze Maps

Use the map at right to answer the following questions.

16. Which letter represents Constantinople? Who made this the capital of an empire? Why?

17. Which letter represents Jerusalem? This city was the capital of which Roman province?

18. Which letter represents Rome? What was the Pax Romana?

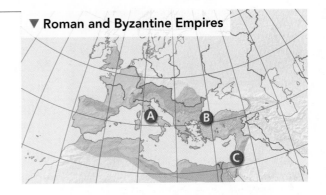

▼ **Roman and Byzantine Empires**

TOPIC 9

Life in Medieval Christendom (486–1300)

GO ONLINE
to access your
digital course

- ▶ VIDEO
- 🔊 AUDIO
- 📖 ETEXT
- 👆 INTERACTIVE
- ✍️ WRITING
- 🎮 GAMES
- 📄 WORKSHEET
- ☑️ ASSESSMENT

Go back 1,500 years

to **MEDIEVAL EUROPE**. You know about the castles, kings, and knights. But there's a lot more to learn about. Medieval Europeans wrestled with issues we still struggle with today, such as how to establish order in a society and the role of faith in everyday life.

Explore The Essential Question

How did societies preserve order?

Medieval Europeans faced a crucial problem after the fall of the Roman empire. What ideas did they adopt to create and preserve order in their unruly society?

Unlock the Essential Question in your 📔 Active Journal.

Watch

Women In Medieval Times

What was it like to be a woman in medieval Europe?

Castle Katz on the Rhine River in Germany

Read

about the ordered society that replaced the mighty Roman empire in Europe.

Life in Medieval Christendom (486–1300)

 INTERACTIVE

Topic Map

Learn more about medieval Europe by making your own map and timeline in your 📖 Active Journal.

Where was medieval Europe?

This region was located north of the Mediterranean Sea. Locate Europe on the larger map.

 INTERACTIVE

Topic Timeline

What happened and when?

One powerful empire fades away, while a new society takes shape. Explore the timeline to see some of what was happening in medieval Europe and in the rest of the world.

792
Vikings make their earliest known raid on Ireland.

732
Charles Martel defeats Muslim invaders in the battle of Tours.

800
Pope Leo III crowns Charlemagne emperor.

486
Clovis defeats the last Roman army in Western Europe.

529
Benedict of Nursia founds the first Benedictine monastery.

TOPIC EVENTS

500   750

WORLD EVENTS

618
Tang dynasty returns China to glory.

630
Muhammad returns to Mecca from Medina.

1088
The University of Bologna is founded.

1209
The Franciscan order forms.

1100
Cahokia civilization thrives in North America.

1235
Sundiata Keita founds the empire of Mali in Africa.

Who will you meet?

Charlemagne helped unite medieval Europe after Rome's fall.

Clare of Assisi created a religious order in the early 1200s.

Thomas Aquinas was a leading scholar of the Middle Ages.

Quest
Discussion Inquiry

Freedom vs. Security?

Quest KICK OFF

The land is in chaos! The social and economic order is in danger of collapse. Invaders are attacking on all sides. You are an adviser to the rulers and must answer this question:

Is it worth trading freedom for security?

Europe faced this very situation in the Middle Ages. As part of your research, you will look at how lords protected vassals under feudalism, and how vassals had obligations to the lords in return. You will also look at how peasants were forced to give up all freedom in return for protection.

1 Ask Questions

You are determined to know how best to advise the government. Get started by making a list of questions about how lords and vassals exchanged duties and about the role of peasants, or serfs. Write the questions in your 📔 Active Journal.

2 Investigate

As you read the lessons in this Topic, look for **Quest** CONNECTIONS that provide information about the ways in which people brought order to the land, and what they had to give up to do so. Collect examples in your 📔 Active Journal.

▼ A vassal pledges his allegiance to his king.

3 Examine Sources

Next, explore a set of sources. They will support differing viewpoints about whether freedom should ever be traded for security. Capture notes in your 📔 Active Journal.

Quest FINDINGS

4 Discuss!

Discuss this question: **Is it worth trading freedom for security?** You will use your knowledge of European feudalism as well as evidence from sources to make convincing arguments to answer YES or NO to the question. You may also come up with your own answers.

LESSON 1

The Early Middle Ages in Europe

BOUNCE TO ACTIVATE   ▶ VIDEO

GET READY TO READ

START UP
Look at this painting of the Christian baptism of Clovis, pagan king of the Franks, in 496. What does this painting tell you about the relationship of kings and the Church in the Middle Ages?

GUIDING QUESTIONS
- How did Europe's varied geography attract many different people?
- What role did Germanic tribes play after the fall of Rome?
- How did Charlemagne unite a large part of Western Europe?

TAKE NOTES
Literary Skills: Sequence
Use the graphic organizer in your 📓 Active Journal to take notes as you read the lesson.

PRACTICE VOCABULARY
Use the vocabulary activity in your 📓 Active Journal to practice the vocabulary words.

Vocabulary		Academic Vocabulary
Middle Ages	clergy	migrate
medieval		unite
topography		

After the western Roman empire collapsed, Western Europe began an era of social, political, and economic decline. But from the ruins of the Roman empire, a new European civilization emerged. Historians call this period of European history between ancient times and modern times—roughly from 500 CE to 1500 CE—the **Middle Ages**. Its culture is called **medieval** civilization, from the Latin words meaning "middle age."

The Geography of Europe
Geographers sometimes describe Europe as a "peninsula of peninsulas." A quick glance at a map of Europe explains why: Europe is a large peninsula that sticks out from the larger Eurasian landmass. Smaller peninsulas extend from the main European peninsula into the surrounding seas. In the north, the Scandinavian Peninsula divides the Atlantic Ocean and the Baltic Sea. In southern Europe, the Iberian, Italian, and Balkan peninsulas push into the Mediterranean Sea. Europe's location, surrounded by so many bodies of water, has a powerful effect on the continent's climate.

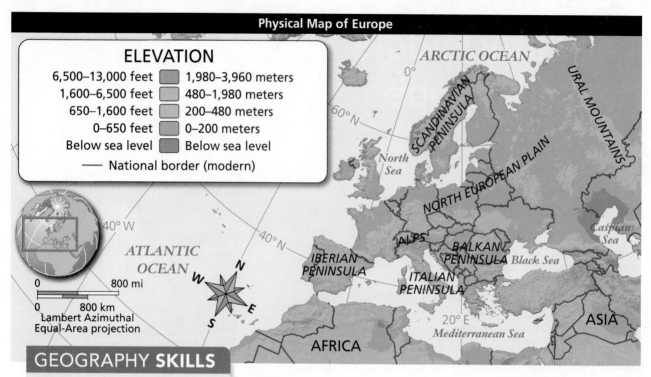

ELEVATION

6,500–13,000 feet	▨	1,980–3,960 meters
1,600–6,500 feet	▨	480–1,980 meters
650–1,600 feet	▨	200–480 meters
0–650 feet	▨	0–200 meters
Below sea level	▨	Below sea level

— National border (modern)

40° W

ATLANTIC OCEAN

0   800 mi

0   800 km
Lambert Azimuthal
Equal-Area projection

N W E S

ARCTIC OCEAN

0°

60° N

SCANDINAVIAN PENINSULA

URAL MOUNTAINS

North Sea

NORTH EUROPEAN PLAIN

40° N

Caspian Sea

ALPS

IBERIAN PENINSULA

BALKAN PENINSULA   Black Sea

ITALIAN PENINSULA

20° E

Mediterranean Sea

AFRICA

ASIA

GEOGRAPHY **SKILLS**

Medieval civilization developed on Europe's plains and near rivers, mountains, and seacoasts.

1. **Place** What peninsulas are labeled on this map?

2. **Synthesize Visual Information** How does elevation vary across Europe?

Mountains and a Vast Plain Europe's **topography**, or the physical features of its surface, is varied. To the north, mountains run along the Scandinavian Peninsula. The Alps form an arc across southern Europe. The Pyrenees divide Spain and France. To the east, the Ural Mountains separate Europe and Asia.

The North European Plain stretches from France through Germany and into Eastern Europe. Some migrating peoples from Eastern Europe used this broad plain to travel west.

Europe's topography affects its climate. Except in the far north, moist westerly winds blow inland from the oceans, bringing rain. Those winds give most of Western Europe a relatively warm, moist climate year-round. However, mountains block the winds from reaching the Mediterranean countries. As a result, they have a Mediterranean climate, with hot, dry summers.

Vital Waterways Europe's rivers flow from the central mountains and highlands. These rivers bring water to farmland and form natural boundaries. They make trade easier. Most early European cities formed near major rivers.

The longest rivers in Western Europe are the Rhine and the Danube. The Danube flows eastward across the broad central plains into Eastern Europe. The Rhine runs northward through Germany and the Netherlands. Its waters carry fine soil that is deposited along the way, building up rich farmland.

☑ READING CHECK **Synthesize Visual Information** Why is Europe referred to as a "peninsula of peninsulas"?

What New Kingdoms Formed in Europe?

Over time, the favorable geography of Western Europe attracted different peoples into the region. The Huns and Germanic tribes began to **migrate** into the Roman empire by around 300. Some, such as the Lombards, settled in Europe's river valleys. Others, such as the Angles, Saxons, and Jutes, moved across the North Sea to the British Isles. These tribes divided Europe into a collection of small, warring kingdoms.

Unlike Rome, these small kingdoms lacked a strong central authority. Most power was in the hands, not of monarchs, but of local leaders and landholders. One major exception was in Iberia (most of today's Spain, Portugal, and Southern France), where a Muslim dynasty established a strong state in the 700s.

During this period, the cities and vast trade networks of the Roman empire largely vanished. Trade slowed to a trickle.

The Rise of the Franks In 486, the Frankish leader Clovis I defeated the last Roman army in Western Europe. Next, he took over several of the Germanic kingdoms. By the early 530s, the Franks controlled much of the land in Gaul (present-day France) and Germany. Although the Franks grew rich from their conquests, their central government did not last long. Eventually, the Frankish lands broke into smaller local kingdoms.

Charles Martel Takes Power In 717, a leader named Charles Martel—or Charles the Hammer—**united** the Frankish lands under his rule. His most important victory was the battle of Tours in 732, when he led Frankish warriors to defeat a Muslim army from Spain. The battle of Tours ended one of the last Muslim military invasions of Western Europe. Muslim troops did not advance any farther into Western Europe, although they did rule most of what is now Spain.

☑ READING CHECK **Identify Main Ideas** How did the Franks take power in Europe?

Academic Vocabulary

migrate • v., to move from one region to another in order to live there

united • v., brought together

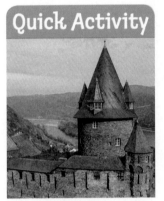

Quick Activity

Explore the importance of the Rhine in medieval Europe in your 📕 Active Journal.

Analyze Images Frankish king Charles Martel led his army against Muslim invaders at the battle of Tours in 732. **Use Evidence** What evidence can you see in the image that the illustrator was aware of Charles Martel's nickname?

INTERACTIVE

Europe Before and After the Fall of Rome

What Was the Age of Charlemagne?

In 768, Charles Martel's grandson—also named Charles—became king of the Franks. Today we call him Charlemagne (SHAHR luh mayn), or Charles the Great. By 800, Charlemagne had built an empire that stretched across what is now France, Germany, and Italy.

A Strong Ruler Charlemagne spent much of his 46-year reign fighting to increase his power and territory. He fought Saxons in the north, Avars and Slavs in the east, and Lombards in Italy. He fought Umayyad Muslims in Spain, but he also made alliances with other Muslim rulers. His military victories reunited much of the original western Roman empire.

Like other Germanic kings, Charlemagne appointed powerful nobles to rule local regions. He sent out officials to make sure that these nobles were ruling fairly and well.

Charlemagne thought that education could help unite his kingdom. Educated officials would be able to keep accurate records and write clear reports. Charlemagne encouraged the creation of schools. He himself studied widely, learning to read Latin and understand Greek.

Charlemagne Spreads Christianity Charlemagne held strong Christian beliefs. Many of his advisers were members of the **clergy**, or the group of people who are trained and ordained for religious services. Charlemagne wanted to create a unified Christian Europe. He worked closely with the Catholic Church to spread Christianity throughout Europe.

One person at Charlemagne's court described his religious habits in this way:

Primary Source

"He cherished . . . the principles of the Christian religion. . . . Hence it was that he built the beautiful chapel at [Aachen, Germany], which he adorned with gold and silver. . . . He was a constant worshipper at this church as long as his health permitted, going morning and evening."

—Einhard, *The Life of Charlemagne*, translated by Samuel Epes Turner

Analyze Images
Charlemagne united most of Western Europe for the first time since the fall of the Roman empire. **Use Visual Information** How does the illustration show you that Charlemagne was both a military and religious leader?

A New Empire in Europe In the summer of 799, Pope Leo III appeared unexpectedly at Charlemagne's castle in what today is Germany. He sought the king's protection against threats by his enemies. Charlemagne provided an armed escort to safeguard the pope as he returned to Rome. Then, a few months later, Charlemagne himself visited the pope there. This demonstrated the powerful king's strong support for Leo. In 800, the pope showed his thanks by crowning Charlemagne emperor of the Romans.

The crowning of Charlemagne was very important. In the Christian Roman tradition begun by Constantine, the emperor had much authority over the Church. But by crowning Charlemagne, Pope Leo III established the idea that only the pope had the power to name an emperor. This strengthened the Church's power.

Leo's action angered the Byzantine empire and the Eastern Orthodox Church. The disagreement over who could crown an emperor worsened the split between the eastern and western Christian worlds.

Europe After Charlemagne After Charlemagne died in 814, his son Louis I took the throne. Louis' sons struggled among themselves for power. Finally, in 843, they agreed to the Treaty of Verdun, which split Charlemagne's empire into three parts.

Charlemagne left a lasting legacy in Europe. He extended Christianity into northern Europe and contributed to the blending of Germanic, Roman, and Christian traditions. He also set up strong, efficient governments. Later rulers looked to his example when they tried to strengthen their own kingdoms.

✓ READING CHECK **Identify Cause and Effect** How did Charlemagne extend his rule?

✓ Lesson Check

Practice Vocabulary

1. What does **topography** describe?

2. What were the **Middle Ages**?

Critical Thinking and Writing

3. **Identify Cause and Effect** How did Europe's geography attract people to different regions?

4. **Identify Main Ideas** How did the arrival of Germanic tribes affect Europe?

5. **Support Ideas with Examples** How did Charlemagne work to unite much of Western Europe?

6. **Writing Workshop: Use Credible Sources** Write a Narrative: Brainstorm in your 📓 Active Journal several sources you could look at to learn about the daily life of a person in medieval Europe.

Primary Sources

Einhard, *The Life of Charlemagne*

Charlemagne (747?–814) is famous for spreading Christianity, preserving ancient knowledge, and supporting education. Throughout his reign, however, he fought many difficult wars to expand his power and territory, including against the Saxons. This excerpt is from a biography written by Einhard, a scholar who became an adviser and friend of the king.

◀ Charlemagne leading troops in battle

Reading and Vocabulary Support

① Why do you think Charlemagne fought in only two battles during this long war?

② Something protracted lasts a long time.

③ How did Charlemagne's leadership in battle affect the Saxons?

④ A grievous war causes great pain and suffering.

⑤ If something is arduous, it is difficult.

⑥ How did Charlemagne learn to face difficulty?

Quest CONNECTIONS

How did wars threaten security in the Middle Ages? Record your findings in your 📔 Active Journal.

Charles himself fought but two pitched battles ① in this war, although it was long protracted ② one on Mount Osning, at the place called Detmold, and again on the bank of the river Hase, both in the space of little more than a month. The enemy were so routed and overthrown in these two battles that they never afterwards ventured to take the offensive or to resist the attacks of the King, unless they were protected by a strong position ③. A great many of the Frank as well as of the Saxon nobility, men occupying the highest posts of honor, perished in this war, which only came to an end after the lapse of thirty-two years. So many and grievous ④ were the wars that were declared against the Franks in the meantime, and skillfully conducted by the King, that one may reasonably question whether his fortitude or his good fortune is to be more admired. The Saxon war began two years before the Italian war; but although it went on without interruption, business elsewhere was not neglected, nor was there any shrinking from other equally arduous ⑤ contests. The King, who excelled all the princes of his time in wisdom and greatness of soul, did not suffer difficulty to deter him or danger to daunt him from anything that had to be taken up or carried through, for he had trained himself to bear and endure whatever came, without yielding in adversity, or trusting to the deceitful favors of fortune in prosperity ⑥.

—Einhard, *The Life of Charlemagne*, translated by Samuel Epes Turner

Analyzing Primary Sources

Choose details from the excerpt to support your answers.

1. **Determine Author's Purpose** Why do you think Einhard wrote this description of Charlemagne at war?

2. **Vocabulary: Use Context Clues** How can context clues help you find the meaning of *adversity*?

Detect Changing Patterns

Follow these steps to learn to analyze bar graphs that show change over time.

INTERACTIVE

Read Charts, Graphs, and Tables

1 **Read the title to see what type of information the graph provides.** What is the graph's title?

2 **Read the labels.**

  a. What does the vertical side (called the vertical axis) of the graph show? How are the measurements marked out? If the measurements are given in thousands, what number is actually shown at the top of the axis? How did you determine this actual number?

  b. What does the horizontal axis show? What is the earliest year shown? The latest?

3 **Bar graphs are good for showing changes over time and comparing one thing at different times.** Look for patterns, trends, and changes in the size of the bars on the graph.

  a. In what year was Rome's population the highest? The lowest?

  b. Between what years did the city's population drop the most?

4 **Draw a conclusion from the information in the graph.** What conclusion can you draw about the general trend of Rome's population from the information on the bar graph?

Primary Source

When historians study a society, they look at these possible sources of change:

- War
- Collapse of government or social order
- Inventions
- Religion and philosophy
- Natural disasters
- Human disasters

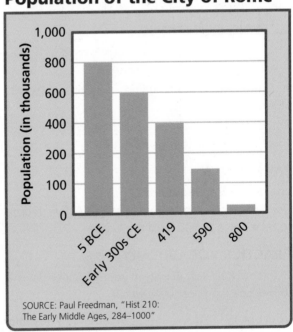

Population of the City of Rome

SOURCE: Paul Freedman, "Hist 210: The Early Middle Ages, 284–1000"

LESSON 2
Christianity Spreads

BOUNCE TO ACTIVATE • ▶ VIDEO

GET READY TO READ

START UP
Examine the photograph of the medieval Greek monastery. Write three questions about how Christianity spread through Europe.

GUIDING QUESTIONS
- How were Christian teachings spread throughout northern Europe?
- What kinds of communities did Christian monks and nuns form?
- How did the Catholic Church become a center of authority in medieval Europe?

TAKE NOTES
Literary Skills: Sequence
Use the graphic organizer in your 📕 Active Journal to take notes as you read the lesson.

PRACTICE VOCABULARY
Use the vocabulary activity in your 📕 Active Journal to practice the vocabulary words.

Vocabulary		Academic Vocabulary
pagan	convent	convert
missionary	sacrament	generally
saint	Christendom	
monastery		

The Roman emperor Constantine ended the persecution of Christians in the 300s. At this time, most Christians lived in the Mediterranean region. During the Middle Ages, Christianity spread throughout much of Europe.

How Did Europe Become Christian?

When the Roman empire collapsed, Christianity had not spread far beyond the empire's borders. Many Europeans were pagans. A **pagan** is a follower of a polytheistic religion, or a religion with more than one god. During the early Middle Ages, Catholic missionaries traveled across Europe to **convert** pagans to Christianity. A **missionary** is a person who tries to convert others to a particular religion.

Converts **generally** chose Christianity freely. Sometimes, however, people did not have a choice. For example, Charlemagne forced the Saxons to become Christians in the early 800s.

Patrick Converts Ireland One important early missionary was a man named Patrick. Some of the stories about Patrick are probably legendary, but we do know that Patrick was born in Britain in the late 300s. As a teenager, he was sold into slavery in Ireland. Patrick eventually escaped, but he later returned to Ireland to convert its people to Christianity.

Patrick began his missionary work in northern and western Ireland. At first, Irish people resisted his teachings. But over time, he gained the trust and friendship of the local tribes. Many Irish people became Christians. In fact, Patrick and other early missionaries founded hundreds of Christian churches in Ireland. After Patrick's death, the Catholic Church recognized him as a **saint**, or an especially holy person.

Missionaries Arrive in Britain During the early Middle Ages, many missionaries were sent by popes, or the leaders of the Catholic Church. In 597, for example, Pope Gregory I sent a group of monks as missionaries to Britain. They were welcomed by the king of Kent, whose wife was already a Catholic. After the king converted to the new faith, his subjects followed his example. Over the next hundred years, most of Britain became Catholic as well.

Christianity Spreads Through Europe By the 700s and 800s, Catholic missionaries were traveling to other parts of Europe. In Central and Eastern Europe, monks worked to convert Slavic peoples. In the 900s, for example, they brought Christianity to the West Slavs. In northern Europe, the British monk Boniface worked to establish the Catholic Church in Germany and the Netherlands. The new shared faith helped bring people together and led to the formation of new states. For example, Poland began to take shape after its first king converted to Christianity in 966.

Academic Vocabulary

convert • v., to switch from one belief system to another

generally • adv., on the whole, as a rule

BIOGRAPHY
5 Things to Know About ST. PATRICK
Catholic Missionary and Irish Bishop (circa 401–circa 500)

- The Britain-born Patrick was sold into slavery in Ireland as a youth.

- He worked for six years as a shepherd before finally escaping back to his home.

- Shortly after returning home, Patrick is believed to have had a dream in which he received a letter from Ireland begging him to return to serve the Irish people's spiritual needs.

- He later did return to Ireland, traveling widely and converting many people to Christianity.

- Patrick wrote an account of his life and work called the *Confessio*.

Critical Thinking How might Patrick's youth as a slave have made him receptive to the message of Christianity?

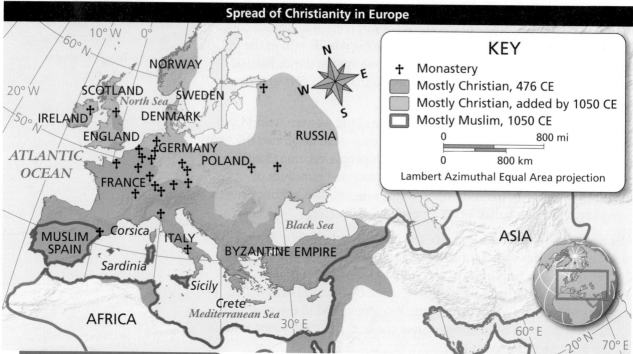

KEY

✝ Monastery

▨ Mostly Christian, 476 CE

▨ Mostly Christian, added by 1050 CE

☐ Mostly Muslim, 1050 CE

0   800 mi

0   800 km

Lambert Azimuthal Equal Area projection

GEOGRAPHY SKILLS

Missionaries spread the Christian faith far and wide during the Middle Ages.

1. **Location** Summarize the spread of Christianity throughout Europe and beyond.

2. **Synthesize Visual Information** Which areas of Europe were mostly Muslim in 1050?

Over time, the Catholic faith became part of everyday life in most parts of Europe. Daily life revolved around the Catholic calendar, which included many holidays, such as Easter, as well as local holy days dedicated to saints. The church became the center of European society as well as a place of worship.

☑ READING CHECK Identify Main Ideas What did missionaries do?

The Role of Monasteries and Convents

During the early Middle Ages, some Christian men and women chose lives of religious study and prayer. In time, those people formed monasteries and convents. A **monastery** is a secluded community where men called monks focus on prayer and scripture. A **convent** is a religious community for women known as nuns. Monks and nuns devote their lives to spiritual goals.

The Benedictine Rule The first Christian monasteries developed in Egypt in the 300s CE. Later, an Italian monk named Benedict established a new European version of monastic life. About 529, Benedict organized a monastery in central Italy. There, he created a series of rules for monastic life. In time, these rules—known as the Benedictine Rule—were adopted by monasteries and convents throughout Europe.

Under the Benedictine Rule, monastic life was a shared experience that balanced prayer and work. Monks and nuns made vows, or solemn promises, to live and worship within their communities for the rest of their lives. They also promised to obey their leaders, work for the good of their community, remain unmarried, and own nothing individually.

Everyday Life in Monasteries The monastic day was busy—and long. It began early, with prayers before dawn, and ended late in the evening. Each day was divided into periods for worship, work, and study. Monks used chants to mark the canonical hours, or religious divisions, of the day.

Monasteries and convents were not only places where monks and nuns lived and prayed, but were also places of work and study. Many were self-contained communities that grew their own food. They made many of the things people needed in daily life. Monks worked in the monastery's gardens and workshops. They worked in libraries where they copied and illustrated religious manuscripts.

Early medieval Europe had no hospitals or public schools. As a result, monasteries and convents often provided basic health and educational services. Monks and nuns helped care for poor or sick people. They set up schools for children.

Monasteries and convents helped keep ancient learning alive. Their libraries contained Greek, Roman, and Christian works, which monks and nuns copied. Some monks created illuminated manuscripts. They decorated texts with elaborate illustrations of biblical scenes or Christian concepts. Monks and nuns also wrote and taught Latin, which was the language of the Church and of educated people.

INTERACTIVE

Medieval Monastery

Analyze Images Benedict (center, with beard) and other monks lived and worked in monasteries. **Infer** What is a reason why the Benedictines and other orders of monks wore special clothing?

One visitor to a medieval French monastery wrote the following:

Primary Source

"For my part, the more attentively I watch them day by day, the more do I believe that they are perfect followers of Christ in all things. When they pray and speak to God in spirit and in truth, by their friendly and quiet speech to Him, as well as by their humbleness of demeanor, they are plainly seen to be God's companions and friends. . . . As I watch them, therefore, singing without fatigue from before midnight to the dawn of day, with only a brief interval, they appear a little less than angels, but much more than men."

—William of St. Thierry, Description of Clairvaux Abbey, about 1143

 **READING CHECK** **Summarize** What services did monks and nuns provide?

The Medieval Church

As Christianity spread, the Catholic Church gradually became a powerful force in Europe. Church leaders influenced not only the spiritual life of medieval Catholics, but also many aspects of secular, or nonreligious, life.

Catholic Teachings As you read in an earlier chapter, the Church taught that people should live lives based on the teachings of Jesus. Sins, such as stealing or doing harm to others, were violations of God's law. Catholics believed that the way people lived would affect what happened to their souls after death.

The concepts of heaven and hell were central to medieval Catholic beliefs. Heaven was described as a perfect place of peace and beauty, where the souls of those who followed God's laws would go after death. Hell was described as a fiery place of punishment for sinners.

Catholics believed that the only way to avoid hell was to do good deeds, believe in Jesus, and participate in the sacraments. The **sacraments** are the sacred rites of the Christian Church, such as baptism and communion. Baptism is a rite that uses water as a sign of spiritual purification and admits a person to the Christian community. Communion is a rite in which people consume consecrated bread and wine, or bread and wine that has been made sacred and which Catholics believe thus becomes the body and blood of Jesus.

Analyze Images
Medieval worshipers attend a church service in southern Germany. **Draw Conclusions** How did services like this one help create a sense of unity among medieval Christians?

The Power of the Medieval Church The pope and other Catholic leaders had significant influence in medieval Europe. Medieval Europeans believed that the Church was the highest authority and the guardian of God's truth. Because the Church controlled the administration of the sacraments, it could punish people by denying them the sacraments. Medieval Catholics believed that people who did not receive the sacraments would be condemned to hell.

The Church also controlled some land and wealth directly. The pope controlled vast lands in central Italy, and many high-ranking clergy were nobles who had their own territories and armies. Some wealthy monasteries held large areas of land.

Secular rulers sometimes struggled against the influence of the Church. For example, they argued over whether the pope or secular leaders had the right to choose local bishops.

What Was Christendom? Eventually, most peoples of Europe were united under the Catholic faith. Although Christians might speak different languages and follow different customs, they saw themselves as part of Christendom. **Christendom** is the large community of Christians spread across the world. The idea of Christendom gave the peoples of Europe a common identity and a sense of purpose. Over time, this sense of common purpose would bring some Christians into conflict with their pagan, Jewish, and Muslim neighbors.

☑ **READING CHECK** **Identify Main Ideas** Why did the Catholic Church have great power over medieval life?

Analyze Images The Church administered sacraments, such as this couple's marriage ceremony, during medieval times. **Infer** What can you infer about the role of the village priest in the everyday lives of villagers?

☑ Lesson Check

Practice Vocabulary

1. What characterizes **pagans**?

2. In what ways do **monasteries** and **convents** differ?

Critical Thinking and Writing

3. **Draw Conclusions** How did monasteries help keep classical Greek and Roman civilization alive?

4. **Summarize** How did Christian teachings affect the lives of medieval Europeans?

5. **Identify Main Ideas** Why was the Catholic Church a center of authority?

6. **Writing Workshop: Develop a Clear Thesis** Write a Narrative: Write in your 📓 Active Journal a main idea about each of the three people whose diary entries you will write.

Relate Events in Time

Follow these steps to relate events in time.

INTERACTIVE

Sequence

1 **Identify the topic and the years covered.** Look at the timeline that appears below.

a. What is the topic of this timeline? What years does it cover?

b. What are the first and last events?

2 **Identify important terms used in the timeline.** The terms used to present a date or event on a timeline can provide information that is essential to understanding the timeline and the way events relate in time. For instance, what does *CE* mean when it is placed after a date?

3 **Use the timeline to analyze how different events are related to one another. Use words such as *before, after, during,* or *while* to answer the questions.**

a. Which events show Roman resistance to the spread of Christianity?

b. About how many years after the date Jesus was believed to have died did the Roman empire officially end its persecution of Christians?

c. Which events show that Christianity was spreading beyond the Mediterranean area?

Early History of Christianity

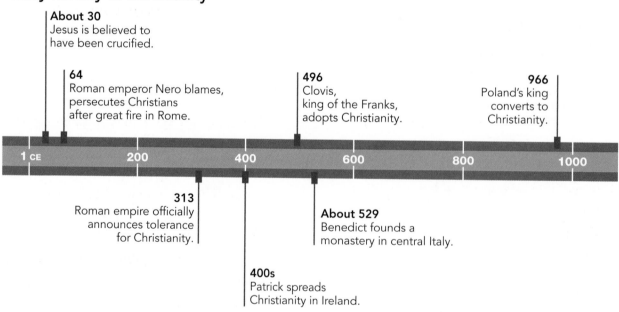

About 30
Jesus is believed to have been crucified.

64
Roman emperor Nero blames, persecutes Christians after great fire in Rome.

496
Clovis, king of the Franks, adopts Christianity.

966
Poland's king converts to Christianity.

1 CE   200   400   600   800   1000

313
Roman empire officially announces tolerance for Christianity.

400s
Patrick spreads Christianity in Ireland.

About 529
Benedict founds a monastery in central Italy.

Feudalism and the Manor Economy

BOUNCE TO ACTIVATE ▶ VIDEO

GET READY TO READ

START UP

Study the image of a king knighting a young man. How does this illustration add to or change what you already know about knights?

GUIDING QUESTIONS

- What impact did invasions by Vikings and other groups have on Europe?
- How did feudalism provide order, control people, and weaken state power?
- How did manoralism create many small, self-sufficient economic units?

TAKE NOTES

Literacy Skills: Identify Main Ideas and Details
Use the vocabulary activity in your 📓 Active Journal to take notes as you read the lesson.

PRACTICE VOCABULARY

Use the vocabulary activity in your 📓 Active Journal to practice the vocabulary words.

Vocabulary		Academic Vocabulary
vassal	chivalry	impact
fief	manor	loyalty
knight	serf	

Charlemagne was able to unite much of Western Europe. After his death, however, his empire split apart. The collapse of Charlemagne's empire left Western Europe open to invasion. It also led to the development of a new system of life called feudalism.

A Violent Time

The period following the death of Charlemagne and the collapse of his empire was a difficult one for people living in Western Europe. During the years between 800 and 1000, invaders threatened Western Europe from all directions. From the east came a people called the Magyars, who conquered what is now Hungary. They made fearsome raids into Germany, Italy, and other parts of Western Europe. From the south and east came Muslim soldiers from Spain, North Africa, and southwest Asia. In the late 800s, they conquered the island of Sicily, which became a thriving center of Muslim culture. The order created by Charlemagne's empire was gone. The even more distant stability of the Roman empire seemed only a dream.

GEOGRAPHY SKILLS

The Vikings and other invaders attacked Western Europe for centuries.

1. **Movement** Describe the Vikings' invasion routes.

2. **Use Visual Information** Label the following places in your ▣ Active Journal: Atlantic Ocean, Scandinavia, Black Sea.

👆 **INTERACTIVE**

Invasions of Europe

Map labels: ICELAND, ARCTIC CIRCLE, 60° 20° W N, ATLANTIC OCEAN, SCANDINAVIA, SCOTLAND, North Sea, IRELAND, 50° N, ENGLAND, RUSSIA, GERMANY, HUNGARY, Caspian Sea, FRANCE, MUSLIM SPAIN, Corsica, ITALY, Black Sea, ASIA, Sardinia, Sicily, BYZANTINE EMPIRE, AFRICA, Mediterranean Sea

0 — 600 mi
0 — 600 km
Lambert Azimuthal Equal-Area projection

KEY
- Viking
- Magyar
- Muslim

The Vikings Invade The boldest and most successful invaders were the Vikings. They were from Scandinavia, a region of northern Europe that now includes Norway, Sweden, and Denmark. In the late 700s, Viking sailors began raiding monasteries in Scotland, England, and Ireland. Monasteries were ideal targets because they were often wealthy and poorly defended. Viking raiders also looted and burned farms and villages. They sailed up rivers into the heart of Europe, where they attacked villages and burned churches in Paris.

The Vikings Explore and Trade The Vikings were not just destructive raiders. They were also farmers, traders, and explorers who sailed throughout the North Atlantic Ocean. Some ventured into the Mediterranean Sea. Around the year 1000, Vikings established a short-lived colony in North America. They also settled in England, Ireland, northern France, and parts of Russia, where they mixed with the local populations. Viking travel in Russia helped open up trade routes between southwest Asia and Western Europe.

✔ READING CHECK **Summarize** What areas of Europe did the Vikings invade?

▼ This is a modern replica, or copy, of a Viking ship built around 820.

How Did Feudal Society Provide Protection?

In the early Middle Ages, kings and emperors were too weak to protect their people from the **impact** of Magyar, Muslim, and Viking invasions. Instead, powerful local lords took over the responsibility of protecting people's homes and lands. The result was a system of feudalism.

Lords and Vassals Make Promises European feudalism was a system of rule in which powerful lords divided their lands among lesser lords, or **vassals**. In exchange for the land, a vassal pledged his service and **loyalty** to the more powerful lord.

In the feudal system, a powerful lord granted a **fief** (feef), or estate, to a vassal. Fiefs ranged in size from a few acres to hundreds of square miles. A fief included any towns or buildings on the land, as well as peasants to farm it. The lord also promised to protect the vassal. In return, the vassal provided military support and money or food for the lord. In many cases, a vassal had his own vassals below him.

European lords built castles from which they ruled nearby lands. Over time, these castles became larger and grander, with high walls, towers, and drawbridges over wide moats. These castles were fortresses in times of war. When fighting broke out, local peasants took shelter behind castle walls.

Academic Vocabulary

impact • *n.*, to have a strong and often bad effect on (something or someone)

loyalty • *n.*, the state of being faithful

Quest CONNECTIONS

Look at the diagram of feudal relationships. How might these relationships have helped protect members of this society? How might they have restricted freedom? Record your findings in your 📓 Active Journal.

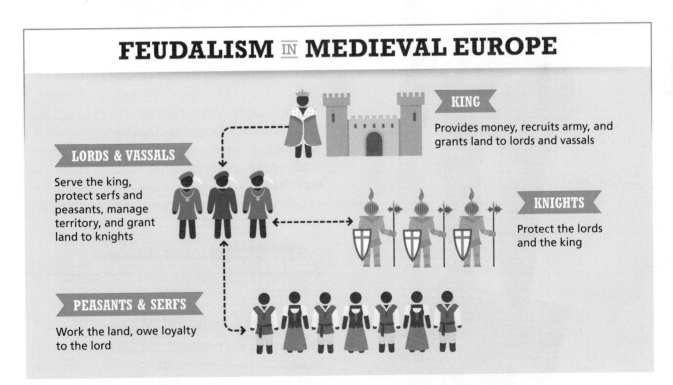

FEUDALISM IN MEDIEVAL EUROPE

KING
Provides money, recruits army, and grants land to lords and vassals

LORDS & VASSALS
Serve the king, protect serfs and peasants, manage territory, and grant land to knights

KNIGHTS
Protect the lords and the king

PEASANTS & SERFS
Work the land, owe loyalty to the lord

Analyze Charts Describe the relationships among different levels of society under feudalism. **Draw Conclusions** Who do you think produced food in the feudal system of medieval Europe?

Warfare as a Way of Life

For medieval lords and vassals, warfare was a way of life. Lords battled constantly for power. As a result, many boys and young men from noble families trained to become **knights,** or warriors mounted on horseback.

Around the age of seven, a boy who was to become a knight was sent to the castle of his father's lord. There, he learned how to fight and ride a horse. After years of training, he pledged his loyalty to the lord and became a knight.

Knights were expected to live by a code of conduct called **chivalry**, which required them to be brave, loyal, and generous. They had to fight fairly in battle. A medieval poet described the ideal knight:

Primary Source

"A knight there was, and that a worthy man, Who . . . vowed himself to chivalry, Honour and truth, freedom and courtesy . . . He was a very perfect gentle knight."

—Geoffrey Chaucer, *The Canterbury Tales*

During war, knights served their lords in battle. Knights usually fought on horseback. They used swords, axes, and lances, or long spears. Early medieval knights wore armor made of chain mail with thousands of small metal rings. Later in the Middle Ages, knights wore heavy plate armor made of solid metal.

✓ READING CHECK **Identify Supporting Details** In what ways did lords have power over medieval life?

How Did Medieval Manors Work?

The heart of the medieval economy was the **manor**, or the agricultural estate of a medieval lord. Manors were centered around the lord's house or castle. In addition to the lord's house, a manor usually included one or more villages and the surrounding fields and forests.

▲ A suit of armor

Quest CONNECTIONS

Look at the diagram of the medieval manor. How might this kind of living arrangement have provided protection to peasants? How might it have restricted their freedom? Record your findings in your 📕 Active Journal.

Analyze Images Medieval manors, such as this one, were almost completely self-sufficient. **Draw Conclusions** How did manors shape medieval life? ❶ Manor house ❷ Peasant fieldworkers ❸ Mill ❹ Sheep ❺ Peasant house ❻ Village church ❼ Vegetable garden ❽ Well

What Peasants and Serfs Did Peasants made up the majority of the medieval population. Most people who lived and worked on a manor were peasants. Many of these peasants were **serfs**, or peasants who were legally bound to the lord's land. Serfs were not slaves who could be bought and sold, but they were not free. They could not leave the manor without the lord's permission. If the manor was given to a new lord, the serfs went along with it.

Daily Life on the Manor Manors produced a wide range of goods and services, but they could not produce everything people needed. For that, people traveled to nearby market towns. Still, in the early Middle Ages, most peasants spent much of their lives in the places where they were born.

The peasants on a manor worked together to plant, care for, and harvest crops on the lord's lands. They generally worked about two or three days a week on the lord's land. At planting and harvest time they worked longer.

Peasants spent much of the remainder of their time growing crops for themselves and their families. They did so on land that the lord allowed them to use for this purpose. Peasants were also allowed to cut wood from the lord's forests to use for fuel and for building. They ground grain into flour at the lord's mill.

Peasants raised sheep, pigs, and cattle for meat. Women spun sheep's wool or linen fibers into thread. They wove woolen and linen cloth into clothing. Specialists such as carpenters and blacksmiths also lived and worked on the manor.

How Manors Were Managed In the early Middle Ages, the lord's wife ran the household. Because the lady was from a noble family, she probably was educated. She had learned Latin and her own language, as well as music, astronomy, and herbal remedies.

As the manor system developed during the Middle Ages, male officials gradually took over the running of the manor. The lord of the manor judged minor crimes and settled arguments among people on his manor. His officials looked after day-to-day affairs. The bailiff kept the estate's accounts and served as judge when the lord was away. The bailiff also collected taxes from the peasants, often in the form of farm products. Another official was the reeve, who was usually elected by the villagers. He had jobs such as repairing buildings and overseeing peasants at work.

✔ READING CHECK **Identify Cause and Effect** Why did ordinary people rarely leave the manor on which they lived?

✔ Lesson Check

Practice Vocabulary

1. Did **serfs** or **vassals** have more power in medieval Europe?

2. What was a **fief**?

Critical Thinking and Writing

3. **Use Evidence** In what ways were manors self-sufficient?

4. **Understand Effects** How did the concept of chivalry affect knights?

5. **Synthesize** In what way did feudalism shape medieval Europe?

6. **Writing Workshop: Use Narrative Techniques** Write in your ▤ Active Journal a paragraph describing how a person in medieval Europe might write about his or her daily activities.

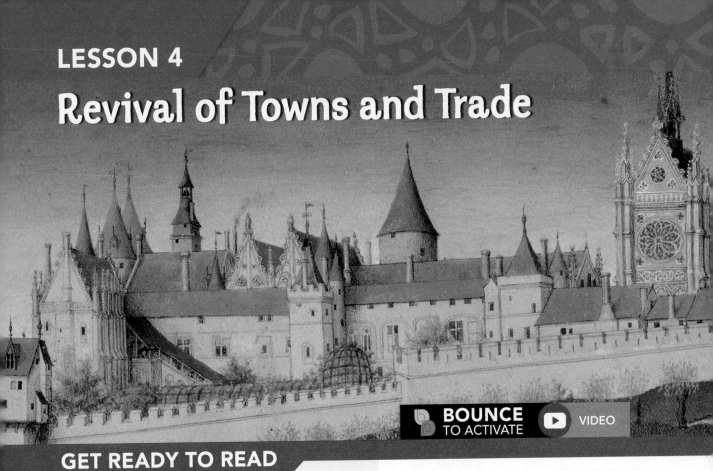

LESSON 4
Revival of Towns and Trade

GET READY TO READ

START UP
Look at the illustration of Paris, France, in the Middle Ages. How do you think a medieval peasant would feel seeing this city for the first time?

GUIDING QUESTIONS
- How did environment and technological innovations support the growth of medieval Christendom?
- What were the results of expanding trade?
- Why were guilds important to the medieval economy?

TAKE NOTES

Literacy Skills: Compare and Contrast
Use the graphic organizer in your 📓 Active Journal to take notes as you read the lesson.

PRACTICE VOCABULARY
Use the vocabulary activity in your 📓 Active Journal to practice the vocabulary words.

Vocabulary		Academic Vocabulary
crop rotation	three-field system	draft
fallow	guild	cease

Picture yourself in this scene of life in the Middle Ages. You would have labored with your parents in fields that belonged to the local lord. Like most people of your age, you would not have attended school. You and your family would have lived without much hope of freedom or change.

But in the distance you might have glimpsed something that promised a better life–the walls of a town. In towns, peasants found more opportunity. Towns offered markets where peasants could sell crops. Crops could also be traded for other goods. By the 1000s, the towns were growing richer as trade increased. The increase in trade was brought about, in part, by better ways of farming.

What Were the New Ways of Farming?
From 1000 to 1300, the period known as the High Middle Ages, the number of people in Europe grew steadily. This population boom was fueled by an increase in food supplies that resulted from improvements in agriculture.

Analyze Images A new kind of harness spread the pressure across the shoulders of the horse. This allowed farmers to plow heavier soils. **Infer** Why would being able to plow heavier soils be a benefit to farmers and others?

Academic Vocabulary

draft • *adj.,* drawing or pulling, as of a load

The Plow and the Horse Ever since Roman times, peasants had used wooden plows that only scratched the surface of the ground. These plows worked well on the thin soils of southern Europe. But new plows had iron blades that could turn over the thicker soils of northern Europe. With the iron plow, people could farm more land.

To pull this iron plow, farmers began using horses instead of oxen. Horses were faster and did more work for the amount of food they ate.

In order to use horses as **draft** animals, peasants developed a harness that helped horses pull heavier loads without injury. The increasing use of horseshoes protected horses' soft hooves.

Horse power and the new plow allowed peasants to cultivate more land. They cleared forests, planted new fields, and produced more food.

What Was the Three-Field System? Farmers also developed a system of **crop rotation**, the practice of changing the use of fields over time. In the early Middle Ages, peasants usually divided their farmland into two large fields. Each year, only one field was planted. The other was left **fallow**, or unplanted. The following year, the fallow one was planted. This process allowed the soil to recover some of its natural fertility.

Later, farmers developed a **three-field system** of crop rotation. In this system, a third of the land was planted with spring crops, such as oats and barley. A third was planted with winter crops, such as winter wheat and rye, and the final field was left fallow. This system had great advantages. It increased the amount of land that could be planted each year. It protected farmers from starvation if one of the crops failed.

Cistercians Advance Farming During the 1200s, an order of monks called the Cistercians (sis TUR shuns) helped expand farming in Europe. The Cistercians embraced poverty and simplicity. They sold surplus agricultural products, such as wool.

Many Cistercian monasteries were built in the countryside. With the help of peasants, Cistercians cut down forests, drained marshes, and brought land under cultivation for the first time. By introducing sheep farming to many regions, the Cistercians increased wool production. This strengthened the textile, or cloth, industry and trade.

More Food Fuels Growth Thanks to the new farming methods, the supply of grains increased. This helped feed the growing population in Europe. Scholars estimate that the population of Europe nearly doubled between 1000 and 1300 CE, rising from 39 million to 74 million people. This surge in population transformed the medieval world.

☑ READING CHECK **Classify and Categorize** On what kind of food did the growing population of medieval Europe depend?

How Did Trade and Industry Increase?

Population growth and advances in farming brought about important changes, especially in trade and industry. The medieval economy boomed.

Trade Revives As food became plentiful, surplus crops from one area were traded for surplus crops from another. Regions specialized in crops that grew best in particular climates and soils. In Spain, olive orchards supplied olive oil. In France, grapes were processed into wines. Surplus crops could also be traded for manufactured goods from distant lands.

Industry Flourishes Some places became famous for a specific manufactured product. For example, the region of Flanders in northern Europe produced fine woolen cloth. This textile industry made northern towns rich. In southern Europe, Italian merchants set up a booming trade with the East.

As population and wealth increased, so did the demand for trade goods. The families of rich merchants and the nobility wanted expensive clothes, weaponry, and jewelry. The market for such goods encouraged specialization and long-distance trade.

Trade Goes Global In the early Middle Ages, trade networks had shrunk. Few people ventured far from their village. But after 1000, commerce revived.

Trade began tying Europe to the wider world, bringing the cultures of Europe, Asia, and Africa into contact once again.

GEOGRAPHY SKILLS

As the demand for trade goods increased, trade networks revived.

1. **Location** Which towns profited from their location on crossroads? On waterways?

2. **Use Visual Information** Label the following places on the outline map in your 📓 Active Journal: Flanders, Bruges, Venice, Genoa, Florence, Toledo.

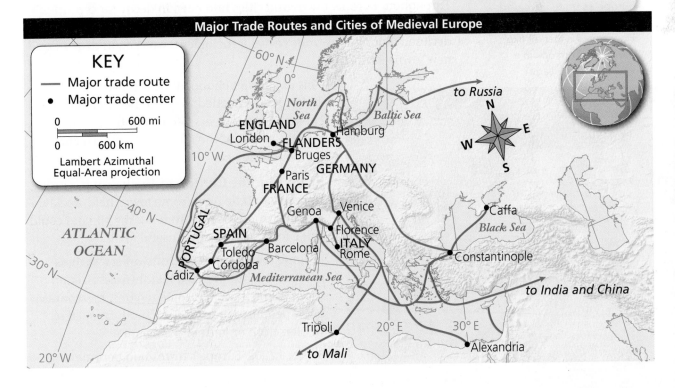

Major Trade Routes and Cities of Medieval Europe

KEY
— Major trade route
• Major trade center

0   600 mi
0   600 km
Lambert Azimuthal Equal-Area projection

The Crusades contributed to this revival of trade. The Crusades were a series of wars fought against Muslims in the Holy Land, today's Middle East. (You will learn more about the Crusades in the next topic.) Crusaders returned to Europe with a taste for Asian spices, perfumes, silks, and other goods. Italian merchants worked to satisfy these tastes by importing trade goods from Asia in their ships.

Merchant Banking Expands As trade increased, merchants needed to transfer large sums of money. Merchants often traveled long distances to buy and sell their goods. Such journeys were difficult and risky. A merchant carrying coins could lose a fortune through a shipwreck or a robbery.

Italian merchants solved this problem by creating a system that included bills of exchange. This was a system similar to the one used by Muslim traders. Bills of exchange allowed a merchant to deposit money in a bank in one city and withdraw money from a bank in a different city. Merchants no longer needed to carry money on dangerous journeys.

The banking system made many Italian families rich, especially in cities such as Florence. In Italy, banking also contributed to one of the most important developments of the High Middle Ages—the revival of towns and urban life.

☑ **READING CHECK** **Identify Cause and Effect** Why was there a need for a banking system?

Towns Grow and Spread

Throughout Europe, towns and cities had been in decay for centuries. Although trade between towns had never completely **ceased**, it had declined. But now, as trade revived, the older towns began to grow and new towns were built.

Analyze Images Markets like this one in Bologna, Italy, spread throughout Europe as trade increased. **Compare and Contrast** How would a market like this differ from one in a small farming village?

This expansion changed the landscape. Townspeople needed wood for heating and cooking, and farmers needed land for farming. As a result, many of the forests of Northern Europe fell under the axe.

From Market Center to Busy Town During the early Middle Ages, some towns held weekly markets where people from nearby villages could trade for food and other useful items.

In time, merchants and craftworkers–such as shoemakers, tailors, and metalworkers–set up shops in the towns. In some regions, merchants hired people to manufacture products such as woolen cloth or leather goods.

By the 1200s, Europe's towns had become bustling centers of trade where people came to buy and sell goods. Some became famous

CRAFT GUILDS OF PARIS

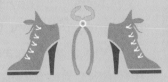

BY **1292**, PARIS HAD **130 REGULATED CRAFTS** (GUILDS). AMONG THE THOUSANDS OF GUILD MEMBERS WERE:

366 shoemakers

54 hat makers

34 blacksmiths

24 innkeepers

62 bakers

for their great fairs. Merchants from all over Europe brought goods to sell at these fairs. Jugglers, musicians, and animal trainers came to entertain. In France during the 1100s and 1200s, fairs were held in the province of Champagne. At the Champagne fairs, cloth from northern Europe was exchanged for spices and other desirable objects from the Mediterranean.

Guilds Protect Crafts As the demand for goods increased, the number of skilled craftworkers in towns grew. Artisans with the same skills often banded together to form guilds. A **guild** is a group of workers practicing the same craft, who have joined together to protect their economic interests. Merchants, grocers, and shoemakers–along with many other kinds of workers–all formed guilds.

Craft guilds were financed by their members, who paid fees. In return, the guild protected workers and their families. If a guild worker died, the guild would pay for the worker's funeral and often care for the worker's family. Some guilds provided free schooling. Guilds also financed building programs.

Guilds regulated businesses. For example, only those who had been properly trained and tested by the guild could set up their own businesses. The guild carefully controlled quality. If a member produced shoddy goods or cheated customers, the guild had the power to punish him. To prevent unfair competition, the guild set the price for all the goods its members sold.

The guild also had other ways of regulating its members' trade practices. For example, the guild controlled where and to whom a member could sell goods.

Analyze Diagrams Guilds in medieval cities formed to protect the economic interests of their members. **Infer** What other guilds might have existed in a medieval town?

INTERACTIVE

Comparing Characteristics of Manor Life and Town Life

Analyze Images Dancers celebrate in a medieval town. **Classify and Categorize** Do you think these townspeople are poor or prosperous? How can you tell?

The rules of the Weavers Guild in Beverley, England, from the year 1209 sternly issued the following warning:

Primary Source

"Weavers . . . may sell their cloth to no foreigner, but only to merchants of the city. . . . And if any weaver . . . sell his cloth to a foreigner, the foreigner shall lose his cloth."

—Beverley Town Documents

Freedom in the Air In the very local world of manors ruled by lords, towns offered new freedoms. Towns were often beyond the control of manorial lords. In some places, wealthy townsmen, not lords, controlled local governments.

The commerce of the towns brought increasing wealth and prosperity to society. Many townspeople grew rich through their labor. Rural peasants, many of whom lived in poverty, could not help but notice that towns offered a better life.

The promise of freedom and prosperity was hard to resist. Peasants began deserting the manors, weakening the feudal system.

Peasants arriving in the towns must have been awed by their first view of urban life. Around the busy marketplaces, huge buildings were rising–houses, guildhalls, and mansions. But soaring even higher were the churches and cathedrals, whose spires drew the eye up toward heaven. The High Middle Ages was a time not only of economic growth, but of deep religious faith. In the next section, you will learn how this faith shaped the medieval world.

☑ READING CHECK **Identify Cause and Effect** Why was there more freedom in the towns than in rural areas?

☑ Lesson Check

Practice Vocabulary

1. For each key term, write a sentence explaining its importance to the revival of trade and towns: **crop rotation, fallow, three-field system, guild.**

Critical Thinking and Writing

2. **Identify Cause and Effect** How did technology help increase food supply?

3. **Understand Effects** How did increasing wealth in towns affect church building?

4. **Identify Main Ideas** How did increasing trade affect society?

5. **Understand Effects** Why would the increase in trade have improved communication?

6. **Writing Workshop: Identify Supporting Details** Writing in your 📙 Active Journal, make a list of three details you could add to your diary entries that would make them more vivid and interesting.

Identify Physical and Cultural Features

Follow these steps to identify physical and cultural features.

1 **Identify physical features** Physical features include bodies of water, coastlines, mountains, valleys, and deserts.

   a. What physical feature is shown in the photograph?

   b. What areas of the map show this type of physical feature?

2 **Identify cultural features** Cultural features are features created by people, such as cities, borders, buildings, roads, railroads, or canals.

   a. What cultural features of medieval Europe are shown on the map?

   b. What kind of cultural feature is represented by the solid black dot? What are some examples of this cultural feature shown on the map?

3 **Relate physical and cultural features** Cultural features are often related to physical features. For example, a river (physical feature) can form a border between two countries (cultural feature). The natural landscape may determine where a city is built.

   a. What physical feature might explain the location of the city of Constantinople?

   b. Which physical feature might have influenced where the city of London was founded and grew up?

Primary Source

▲ Europe's varied geography includes the jagged peaks of the Alps.

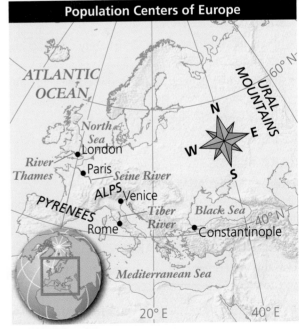

▲ Physical and cultural features of medieval Europe

The Church and Medieval Culture

BOUNCE TO ACTIVATE   ▶ VIDEO

GET READY TO READ

START UP

Look closely at the illustration of everyday life in the Middle Ages in Western Europe. Work with a partner to identify people from different social and economic levels. What clues help you make these distinctions?

GUIDING QUESTIONS

- How did the religion of Christianity develop and change over time?
- How did Christianity influence medieval society and culture?
- What were the characteristics of medieval universities?

TAKE NOTES

Literacy Skills: Analyze Text Structure
Use the graphic organizer in your 📓 Active Journal to take notes as you read the lesson.

PRACTICE VOCABULARY

Use the vocabulary activity in your 📓 Active Journal to practice the vocabulary words.

Vocabulary		Academic Vocabulary
mendicant	university	establish
order	natural law	dramatically

Religion shaped life in the Middle Ages. In the countryside, the pealing of church bells was one of the few sounds that echoed over the quiet fields. Country roads carried the traffic of pilgrims and crusaders on their way to worship sacred relics or fight in a holy war. In this age of devotion, even the natural world looked very different. A rose, for example, was much more than just a beautiful flower. To the medieval mind, it might symbolize some spiritual truth.

In the growing towns, too, the sights and sounds of faith were part of daily life. The streets were crowded with frequent processions—solemn lines of people walking to or from the churches. On holy days, in particular, the air smelled of incense and carried the sounds of religious chanting.

Forms of Devotion

Religion was so important in the Middle Ages that this period is sometimes called the Age of Faith. In most of the countries of Western Europe, Roman Catholicism was the dominant form of Christianity.

Christian Europe expressed its devotion to God through personal prayer and public worship. As the Middle Ages went on, the forms of Christianity changed. Christians came to play different roles in society, and new kinds of Christian community developed.

Religious Orders In early Christianity, monks and nuns pursued personal salvation through prayer and meditation. They lived in monasteries that were often set in remote spots, cut off from contact with the world.

However, by the 1200s, monasteries played a more active role in the world. Monasteries were centers of agricultural production and owned large areas of land. Some monasteries were located in towns, where they provided education or charity to ordinary people.

Also in the 1200s, new forms of Christian community emerged. For example, the **mendicant orders** were founded to fight heresy and to preach to ordinary people. The mendicants, or beggars, owned no property. Mendicants survived by begging for food and drink.

Francis and Clare One of the best-known mendicant orders was founded by Francis of Assisi. As a young man, Francis was rich and spoiled. Then, he had a powerful religious experience. He felt called to live as simply as Jesus had lived. Francis believed that all nature was a reflection of God. Because of this, he felt compassion for all living things and referred to animals as his "brothers" and "sisters." An account of his life written after 1228 tells this story:

Primary Source

"One day he came to a town called Alviano to preach the word of God. . . . The people became quiet and waited reverently, but a flock of swallows . . . continued to chatter away, making it impossible for the people to hear. Francis spoke to them, 'My sisters the swallows, it's my turn to speak now. . . . Listen to the word of God. Stay still and be quiet until it's over.' To the people's amazement, the little birds immediately stopped chattering and did not move until Francis had finished preaching."

—Thomas of Celano, *First Life of Saint Francis*

▼ Medieval painting of St. Francis and St. Clare in the church of Saint Francis, Assisi

Explore how monks created illuminated manuscripts in medieval Europe in your Active Journal.

Academic Vocabulary
established • *adj.*, set up officially

Francis's pure and simple life of devotion attracted many followers. In 1209, he **established** the Franciscan order.

Women were also attracted to the kind of life preached by Francis. In 1212, a noblewoman later known as Clare of Assisi founded an order based on the teachings of Francis. Clare and her followers took a vow of poverty and aimed to live a life of devotion to God. Their order became known as the Poor Clares and spread first through Italy and then across Europe.

☑ READING CHECK **Identify Main Ideas** What were the mendicant orders?

How Did Religion Affect Medieval Culture?

Religion also had a great influence on the arts during the Middle Ages. The Church shaped cultural values and helped form codes of conduct.

Revival of Drama Since the fall of Rome, the Church had disapproved of drama because of its association with the pre-Christian world. Eventually, however, the Church allowed plays based on stories from the Bible. These "mystery plays" marked the revival of European drama.

New Architecture Religion also inspired some of the greatest architecture since ancient times. A new building style that came to be known as Gothic emerged. Gothic combined religious symbolism with engineering advances. Cathedrals built in the Gothic style were higher than any seen before in Western Europe.

Gothic was a revolutionary new architecture. Earlier churches were dark and gloomy. They had massive walls, thick columns, and narrow

---

BIOGRAPHY
5 Things to Know About

CLARE OF ASSISI
Roman Catholic Abbess (1194-1253)

- Born in Assisi, Italy, Clare was strongly influenced by the example of St. Francis.

- Rather than marry, Clare ran away from home in 1212 to become a nun.

- She was the founder of the Second Order of St. Francis, known as the Poor Clares because of their vows of poverty.

- Clare's mother and sister Agnes joined Clare's order. (Both Clare and Agnes were later recognized as saints by the Church.)

- Many miracles were credited to Clare, including saving the city of Assisi from attackers, who were driven off by a strong storm.

Critical Thinking Why might medieval women have found life as a nun appealing?

Analyze Images Gothic cathedrals, like this one in Milan, Italy, featured breathtaking design. Many also had grotesque carved stone creatures known as gargoyles (lower left). **Infer** What might a medieval peasant have felt seeing a Gothic cathedral for the first time?

windows. By the mid-1100s, building technology had advanced. European architects found a way of concentrating the weight of the roof on certain points in the wall. This meant that huge areas of wall could now be opened up. Windows could be larger, filling buildings with light. This architectural breakthrough allowed masons to build stone structures that were spacious and airy.

Gothic churches first appeared in France, but they soon rose all over Europe. Rich townspeople funded their construction. The Gothic cathedral was a breathtaking sight. Rising high above the rooftops, it could be seen for miles.

The Church Shapes Chivalry The Church also influenced cultural values and social behavior. Medieval Europe was a place of almost constant conflict. In this violent world, a code of conduct known as chivalry helped control the behavior of knights. Some values of chivalry, such as bravery and loyalty to the king, were military and feudal in origin. However, the Church tried to shape chivalry to reflect Christian values of generosity, humility, and mercy. Knights were expected to defend the Church and to protect weaker members of society. While the conduct of knights was often far from chivalrous, the values of chivalry left a permanent mark on European manners.

☑ READING CHECK **Summarize** What was the purpose of chivalry?

The High Middle Ages saw expansion not only in trade and culture but also in education. Once again, the Church influenced this growth of learning.

Medieval Universities Students were trained for the priesthood at schools attached to the cathedrals. Gradually, schools were set up to provide further education. These grew into **universities**—schools, or groups of schools, that train scholars at the highest levels.

The medieval university was itself a kind of guild. Professors and students organized to form the university. Classes were held in rented rooms or in churches. Books were expensive and were often rented or shared by students.

Despite these discomforts, there was a new excitement about learning. Many works of ancient Greece had been preserved in the Byzantine empire and in lands under Islamic rule, where they had been studied by Muslim, Jewish, and Christian scholars. Copies of these books traveled to Europe, along with Arabic books of science and philosophy. Such books were added to the monastery libraries, which had preserved other works of classical learning.

Analyze Images Students listen to a professor at the University of Bologna. **Compare and Contrast** What are some ways this school is different from a modern school? In what ways is it similar?

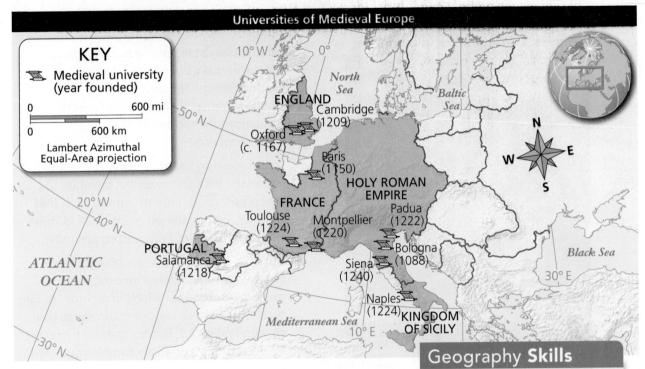

Universities of Medieval Europe

KEY

📜 Medieval university (year founded)

0 — 600 mi
0 — 600 km
Lambert Azimuthal Equal-Area projection

North Sea
Baltic Sea
Black Sea
ATLANTIC OCEAN
Mediterranean Sea

ENGLAND
Cambridge (1209)
Oxford (c. 1167)
Paris (1150)
FRANCE
HOLY ROMAN EMPIRE
Toulouse (1224)
Montpellier (1220)
Padua (1222)
Bologna (1088)
Siena (1240)
PORTUGAL
Salamanca (1218)
Naples (1224)
KINGDOM OF SICILY

10° W, 0°, 50° N, 20° W, 40° N, 30° N, 10° E, 30° E

N E W S

Young men from all over Europe came to study at the universities of Bologna in Italy, Paris in France, and Oxford in England. They studied the "liberal arts," subjects such as grammar and logic, meant to develop their powers of reasoning. Although these students spoke different languages, communication was not a problem. The Church had preserved Latin as the language of learning. Students who spoke Latin could understand courses taught at any university.

Thomas Aquinas The universities attracted the best minds in Europe. One of the greatest medieval scholars was a professor at the University of Paris named Thomas Aquinas (uh KWEYE nus). He was deeply impressed by the writings of the ancient Greek philosopher Aristotle.

Aristotle had emphasized the use of human reason to discover knowledge. In contrast, many Church scholars emphasized faith as the path to truth. Aquinas wanted to show that there is no conflict between the two. He argued that both faith and reason come from God.

Aquinas believed in **natural law**. Unlike human-made law, natural law does not change over time or from one society to another. Aquinas believed that natural laws could be discovered through the power of human reason.

An Age of Confidence A growing confidence in human reason is one of the main features of the High Middle Ages. During this time, conditions in Europe improved **dramatically**. Towns grew, trade increased, and populations boomed. The universities created an educated class that helped run the Church and state.

Geography Skills

1. **Location** Locate: (a) France, (b) the Holy Roman Empire, (c) England.

2. **Synthesize Visual Information/Draw Conclusions** Which areas had the greatest number of universities? What factors do you think contributed to this?

Academic Vocabulary
dramatically • *adv.*, greatly

Analyze Images Lady Fortune spins her wheel, while a wealthy man and a woman await their fates. **Infer** What characteristics of medieval life led people to believe their fortunes could change in a moment?

Europe's growing prosperity influenced religious practices and attitudes. In art, painters began to show a more human Jesus—a Jesus who suffered, like ordinary human beings. The desire to help humanity, and to improve conditions in the world, influenced the formation of the new mendicant orders.

In the growing towns, soaring cathedrals expressed both the medieval devotion to God and a new confidence in human skills and abilities. Europeans felt great pride in these mighty symbols of faith and community.

But even in these centuries of confidence, Europeans remembered an even more ancient symbol—the wheel of fortune. At one turn of the wheel, fortune could make you rich and powerful. But another turn and the wheel could just as easily tumble you down into poverty and ruin. As the 1200s came to an end, there were signs that fortune's wheel was turning again. This time, it was spinning all Europe toward disaster.

✔ **READING CHECK** **Identify Cause and Effect** How did universities develop?

✔ Lesson Check

Practice Vocabulary

1. For each key term, write a sentence explaining its importance to the age of faith: **mendicant order**, **university**, **natural law**.

2. How did monks of the **mendicant orders** survive?

Critical Thinking and Writing

3. **Identify Main Ideas** What were the mystery plays about?

4. **Synthesize** How did Thomas Aquinas blend ancient and medieval thought?

5. **Infer** Why was the concept of the wheel of fortune meaningful to people in medieval Europe?

6. **Writing Workshop: Draw Conclusions** Think about what you have learned about everyday life in medieval Europe. List in your 📓 Active Journal three conclusions about the people you have chosen, based on your learning.

Thomas Aquinas, *Summa Theologica*

Thomas Aquinas (1224–1274) described natural law as the particular way humans, by the way they are made, take part in the laws of God. Aquinas believed thinkers could accept the Church's authority and Christian faith and then draw conclusions using reason. As a medieval scholar, he organized his ideas as questions that he discussed in arguments.

▶ Aquinas taught at the University of Paris.

ARTICLE 4. WHETHER THE NATURAL LAW IS THE SAME IN ALL MEN?

I answer that . . . to the <u>natural law</u> ① belongs those things to which a man is inclined naturally: and among these it is <u>proper</u> ② to man to be inclined to act according to reason. Now the process of reason is from the common to the proper, as stated in [Aristotle's] *Physics*, 1.7. The <u>speculative</u> ③ reason, however, is differently situated in this matter from the practical reason. For, since the speculative reason is busied chiefly with the necessary things, which cannot be otherwise than they are, its proper conclusions, like the universal principles, <u>contain the truth</u> ④ without fail. The practical reason, on the other hand, is busied with <u>contingent</u> ⑤ matters, about which human action are concerned: and consequently, although there is necessity in the general principles, the more we descend to matters of detail, the more frequently we encounter defects. Accordingly then in speculative matters truth is the same in all men, both as to principles and as to conclusions: although the truth is not known to all as regards the conclusions, but only as regards the principles which are called <u>common notions</u> ⑥. But in matters of action, truth or practical rectitude [correctness of judgment] is not the same for all, as to matters of detail, but only as to the general principles. . . .

—Thomas Aquinas, *The Summa Theologica*, translated by the Fathers of the English Dominican Province

Analyzing Primary Sources

Cite specific evidence from the document to support your answers.

1. **Analyze Structure** How does Aquinas organize his answer to the question of whether natural law is the same in all men?

2. **Analyze Style and Rhetoric** How does Aquinas connect Article 4 with ideas in his own and in other texts?

Reading and Vocabulary Support

① Recall what you have learned about natural law. How is natural law different from human-made law? How can it be discovered?

② Something is proper, in this context, when it belongs or applies only to one individual or thing.

③ Speculative means "based on guesses rather than on facts you know to be true."

④ Why do the conclusions of speculative reasoning always contain the truth?

⑤ Contingent things, which include human actions depend on, are associated with, or conditioned by something else.

⑥ According to Aquinas, is truth the same in all people?

VISUAL REVIEW

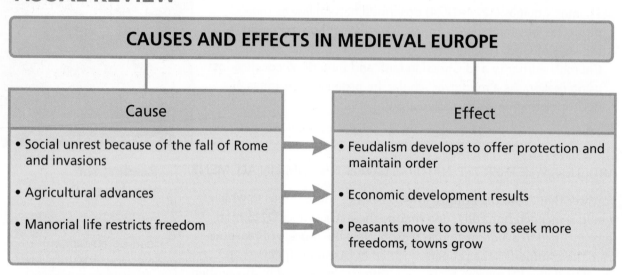

CAUSES AND EFFECTS IN MEDIEVAL EUROPE

Cause	Effect
• Social unrest because of the fall of Rome and invasions	• Feudalism develops to offer protection and maintain order
• Agricultural advances	• Economic development results
• Manorial life restricts freedom	• Peasants move to towns to seek more freedoms, towns grow

Church Influence in Everyday Life

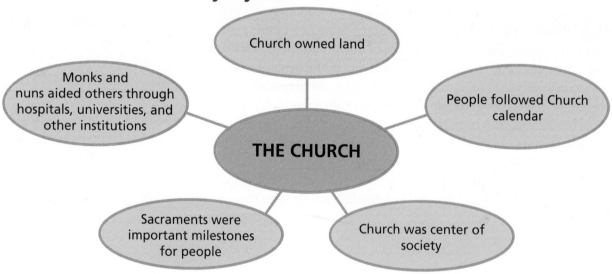

Church owned land

Monks and nuns aided others through hospitals, universities, and other institutions

People followed Church calendar

THE CHURCH

Sacraments were important milestones for people

Church was center of society

READING REVIEW

Use the Take Notes and Practice Vocabulary activities in your 📕 Active Journal to review the topic.

INTERACTIVE

Topic Mini Games

Quest FINDINGS

Write your response to the question "Is it worth trading freedom for security?" Use the notes you made in your 📕 Active Journal.

ASSESSMENT

Vocabulary and Key Ideas

1. **Define** What is a **missionary**?

2. **Describe** How did Charlemagne expand his power and territory?

3. **Check Understanding** What was **manor** life like for serfs and peasants?

4. **Recall** How did **missionaries** work to expand **Christendom**?

5. **Identify Main Ideas** What did the code of **chivalry** require of medieval **knights**?

6. **Check Understanding** How did new technology and **crop rotation** lead to an increase in population?

7. **Explain** How did **universities** develop?

8. **Describe** Why did the growth of towns encourage the rise of the **mendicant orders**?

Critical Thinking and Writing

9. **Draw Conclusions** How did Europe's geography affect the Viking, Magyar, and Muslim invasions between the years 800 and 1000?

10. **Summarize** How and why did Christianity spread through Europe during the early Middle Ages?

11. **Infer** Why did towns offer greater freedom to peasants?

12. **Identify Cause and Effect** How do the great cathedrals reflect the prosperity and optimism of the 1200s?

13. **Revisit the Essential Question** How did the distribution of power under feudalism help preserve order?

14. **Writer's Workshop: Write Narratives** Using the outline you created in your 📓 Active Journal, write three diary entries from the viewpoint of a medieval knight, serf, monk or nun, describing events from his or her day and their reaction to important events.

Analyze Primary Sources

15. What is Bishop Fulbert describing in the following quotation?
    A. the Benedictine rule
    B. the sacraments of the Catholic Church
    C. the manor system economy
    D. the feudal obligations of lord and vassal

    "He who swears [loyalty] to his lord ought always to have these six things in memory: what is harmless, safe, honorable, useful, easy, practicable. . . . The lord also ought to act toward his faithful vassal [in the same way] in all these things."

    —*Bishop Fulbert of Chartres, letter to William V, Duke of Aquitaine, 1020*

Analyze Maps

16. Which letter represents southern Spain? Which religion dominated this area in 1050?

17. Which letter shows the location of Charlemagne's capital? What two large European countries of today made up most of his empire?

18. Which letter shows Scandinavia? Which group of invaders called this region their home?

▼ **Medieval Europe**

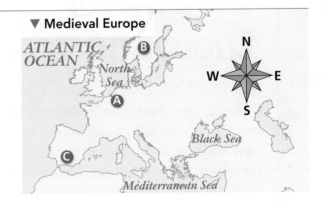

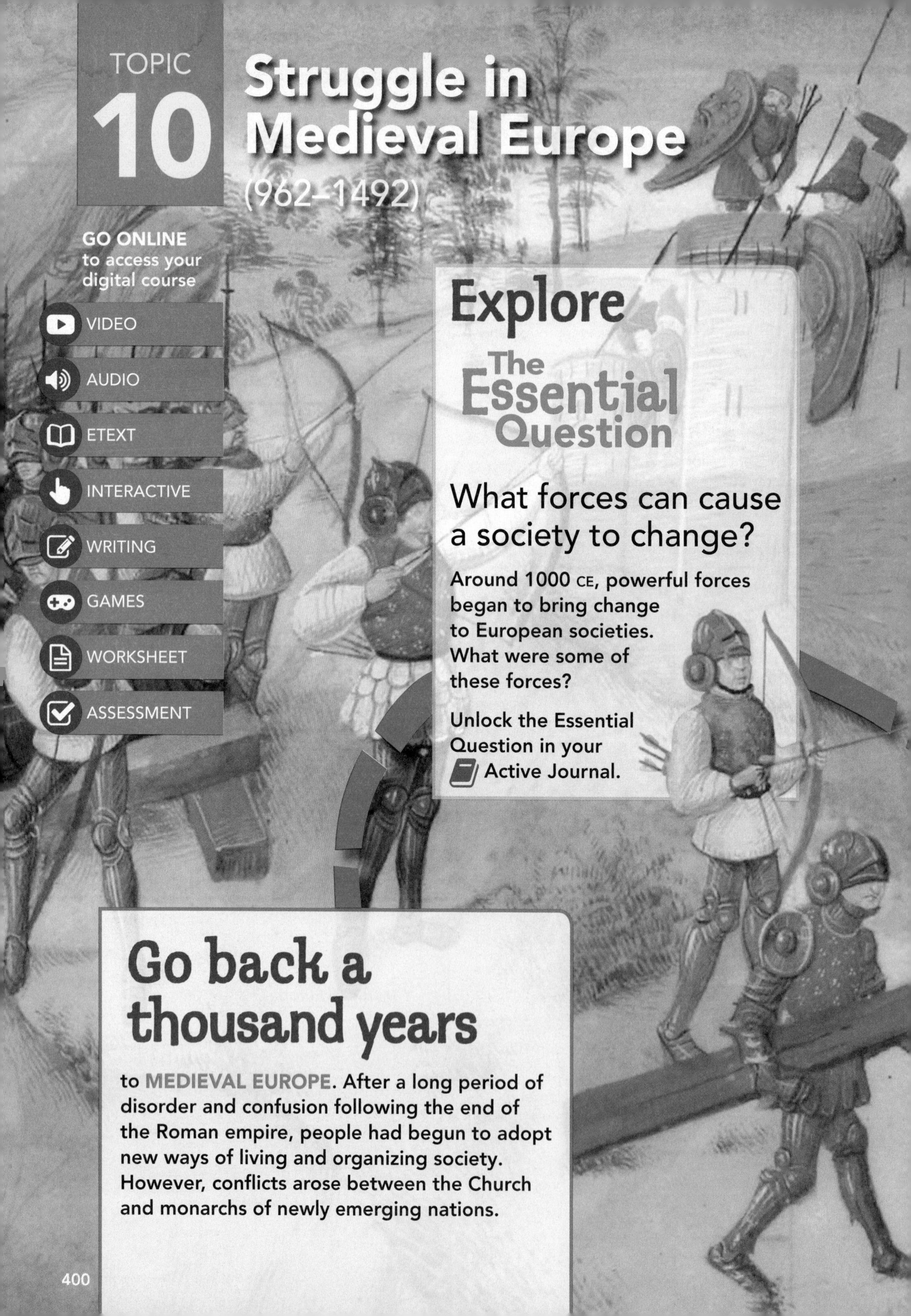

Struggle in Medieval Europe

(962–1492)

GO ONLINE
to access your
digital course

▶ VIDEO

🔊 AUDIO

📖 ETEXT

👆 INTERACTIVE

✏️ WRITING

🎮 GAMES

📄 WORKSHEET

☑️ ASSESSMENT

Explore

The Essential Question

What forces can cause a society to change?

Around 1000 CE, powerful forces began to bring change to European societies. What were some of these forces?

Unlock the Essential Question in your 📓 Active Journal.

Go back a thousand years

to **MEDIEVAL EUROPE**. After a long period of disorder and confusion following the end of the Roman empire, people had begun to adopt new ways of living and organizing society. However, conflicts arose between the Church and monarchs of newly emerging nations.

Read

about the forces that brought major changes to medieval Europe.

Watch

NBC LEARN

BOUNCE TO ACTIVATE ▶ VIDEO

The Black Death

Experience the horrors of the disease epidemic that convinced many in Europe that the end of the world had arrived!

Crusaders attack Jerusalem in 1099

Struggle in Medieval Europe (962–1492)

Learn more about late medieval Europe by making your own map and timeline in your Active Journal.

INTERACTIVE

Topic Map

Where was medieval Europe?

This region was located north of the Mediterranean Sea, reaching from the British Isles and Scandinavia in the north to Poland and, Russia in the east. Locate Europe on the larger map.

INTERACTIVE

Topic Timeline

What happened and when?

From the rise of powerful nation-states to the horrors of the Black Death, explore the timeline to see some of what was happening in medieval Europe and in the rest of the world.

1066 Normans conquer England.

1170 English archbishop Thomas Becket is murdered.

962 Pope crowns Otto I emperor.

1096 First Crusade begins.

TOPIC EVENTS

| 900 | 1000 | 1100 |

WORLD EVENTS

1192 Minamoto Yoritomo is appointed shogun of Japan.

Pope Gregory VII defended the rights of the Church.

Isabella married Ferdinand and united Spain.

Joan of Arc led the French to a glorious victory.

1492
Isabella and Ferdinand conquer Granada.

1347
Plague arrives in Europe.

1215
Magna Carta is signed.

1291
Crusades end.

| 1200 | 1300 | 1400 | 1500 |

1206
Delhi sultanate establishes Muslim rule in northern India.

1325
Aztecs found their capital city, Tenochtitlan.

1453
Ottoman sultan Mehmet II captures Constantinople.

Medieval Monarchs Face Conflicts

Quest KICK OFF

In the late Middle Ages, kings and emperors encountered conflicts that led to important changes in European society.

Your quest, as part of a team, is to create a comic book about a conflict involving a monarch in the late Middle Ages based on the question:

What events marked significant changes in late medieval society?

How did the conflicts involving monarchs in the Middle Ages impact late medieval society? Explore the Essential Question "What forces can cause a society to change?" in this Quest.

▼ A young King Richard II of England in about 1390

1 Ask Questions

First, you'll need to research the lives of monarchs of the late Middle Ages to select one to focus on. Begin by making a list of the questions you need to answer in your comic book. Write down these questions in your 📘 Active Journal.

2 Investigate

As you read in the Topic, Look for **Quest** CONNECTIONS that indicate important issues and events European monarchs confronted. Record your notes in your 📘 Active Journal.

3 Conduct Research

Now begin your research by finding and absorbing additional valid primary and secondary sources of information on your own, such as online or in libraries.

4 Create Your Comic Book

Next, work together as a team to fully research, write, and illustrate the cover, an illustrated page, and a summary of a comic book about a specific event covered in this Topic. Get help for this task in your 📘 Active Journal.

Conflicts Between Popes and Monarchs

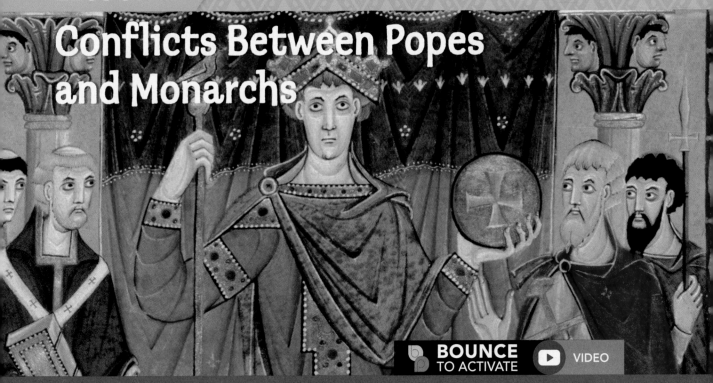

GET READY TO READ

START UP

Examine the illustration from medieval Europe. Who do you think the man in the middle is? Who are the people around him? How do you know?

GUIDING QUESTIONS

- Why did popes and German emperors clash in the 1000s and 1100s?
- What were the causes and effects of the conflict between Henry IV and Pope Gregory?
- How did a strong monarchy emerge in France?

TAKE NOTES

Literacy Skills: Compare and Contrast
Use the graphic organizer in your 📔 Active Journal to take notes as you read the lesson.

PRACTICE VOCABULARY

Use the vocabulary activity in your 📔 Active Journal to practice the vocabulary words.

Vocabulary
secular
excommunicate

Academic Vocabulary
clearly
authority

For centuries after the decline of Rome, people in Europe were still awed by the memory of the Roman empire. Churchmen and kings all claimed the authority of Rome. The Church continued to use Latin, the language of Rome. The popes governed the Church from Rome itself. At a time when Europe was split into hundreds of states, many longed for the political unity of the Roman empire.

As you have read, the Frankish king Charlemagne took the title of "emperor" in the year 800. He hoped to revive not only the Roman empire, but classical learning as well. Even though Charlemagne's empire did not last, later rulers pursued the same goals.

Reviving an Empire

After Charlemagne's empire collapsed, the eastern, German part of the kingdom was divided among a number of dukes. Following Germanic tradition, they chose one of their own to be king.

Academic Vocabulary

clearly • *adv.*, in a clear manner, without doubt or question

Otto the Great A German king known as Otto the Great increased his power by making alliances with other German nobles. In 962, he persuaded the pope to crown him emperor. By adopting this title, Otto was claiming to be the successor of Charlemagne.

Otto's empire included the land that came to be known as Germany, and also extended into Italian lands. In time, German emperors claimed authority over much of central and Eastern Europe. But their empire was not like an ancient empire, controlled by a single government. Instead, it was a collection of states ruled by princes who were loyal to the emperor.

Despite his limited power, Otto created a stable kingdom. His empire was prosperous and saw a great revival in the arts.

Like Charlemagne, Otto worked closely with the Church and strengthened the Church within his empire. In fact, the Church became so strong that eventually it rivaled the authority of the state.

The Holy Roman Empire After the death of Otto the Great, his empire continued to be ruled by his descendants, who became known as the Ottonian kings. The empire itself came to be called the Holy Roman Empire. The name of the empire **clearly** showed that the German kings wanted to create a Christian, or holy, version of the Roman empire. In addition, by claiming to be Roman, the German kings were challenging the Byzantine rulers, who also called themselves Roman emperors.

READING CHECK **Infer** How did the creation of the Holy Roman Empire set the stage for future power struggles?

GEOGRAPHY SKILLS

The Holy Roman Empire occupied the middle of Europe.

1. **Region** What role might the empire have played in linking west and east?

2. **Use Visual Information** Which bodies of water bordered the Holy Roman Empire?

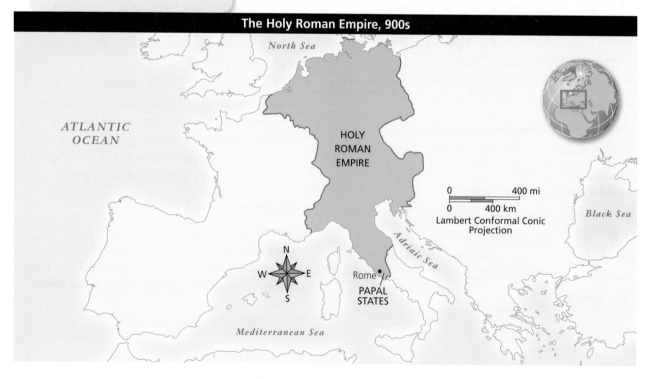

The Holy Roman Empire, 900s

North Sea

ATLANTIC OCEAN

HOLY ROMAN EMPIRE

0 — 400 mi
0 — 400 km
Lambert Conformal Conic Projection

Black Sea

Adriatic Sea

Rome
PAPAL STATES

Mediterranean Sea

GREGORY VII
Pope (c. 1025–1085)

- Pope Gregory VII became pope after a significant career in the papal court.

- As an archdeacon, he managed the Church's affairs as reformers sought to detach the papacy from the control of local aristocratic families.

- Gregory was one of the most controversial popes of the Middle Ages. For a long time, historians called his lifetime the period of "Gregorian Reform." Now it is usually termed the "Reform Papacy."

- He fought against the buying and selling of sacred offices and objects, the unlawful marriage of the clergy, and the right of monarchs and nobles to appoint church officials.

- He first excommunicated Henry IV in 1076, officially forgave him in 1077, and then excommunicated him again in 1080.

Critical Thinking How might Gregory's early career in the Church have been a warning of conflict to come with secular officials?

Why Did Pope Gregory and Henry IV Come Into Conflict?

The early rulers of the Holy Roman Empire controlled and protected the Church. In time, however, the popes gained more power. Thus began a long conflict between rulers and popes.

Pope vs. Emperor In 1073, an Italian monk named Hildebrand became Pope Gregory VII. Gregory believed that the emperor should not have power over the Church. This led to conflict with Henry IV, the Holy Roman emperor at the time.

Gregory insisted that only the Roman pontiff, or pope, had the right to choose bishops. This became an important political issue in the Middle Ages. Bishops controlled much land and wealth. Both kings and popes wanted to appoint bishops who would support their policies.

Pope Gregory issued a list of rules declaring his supreme **authority** over both Church and **secular**, or non-Church, leaders. He asserted that the Church was founded by God alone and claimed the power to depose, or remove from office, any public official, including bishops and even emperors.

Henry IV must have been stunned. Gregory was claiming the right to remove emperors from the throne! The stage was set for a clash of wills between the two men.

Academic Vocabulary
authority • *n.*, the power to make decisions and rules

INTERACTIVE

The Papacy in the Middle Ages

A Ruler Defies the Pope The struggle began when Henry ignored the pope's rules. The emperor named his own bishop for the city of Milan, Italy. In response, Pope Gregory appointed a rival bishop. When Henry tried to remove Gregory from his position as pope, Gregory excommunicated Henry. To **excommunicate** means to exclude a person from a church or a religious community. The pope freed Henry's subjects from their feudal oaths of loyalty to the emperor.

Without the support of his subjects, Henry had no power. Desperate to end his excommunication, Henry visited the pope in an Italian castle. The pope kept Henry waiting in the snow, outside the castle, for three days. Though the pope forgave Henry, their conflict continued. Henry later marched his army to Rome and forced the pope from the city.

Analyze Images Holy Roman Emperor Henry IV is forced to wait in the snow. **Draw Conclusions** What does the picture tell you about Henry's situation at that time?

PA PRIORE OANERTE. De vovet etpvisvs. cler
inricus. iiii.   Gvz   —bertvs.   Gregor. vii
c crvi iec3. PARet ovrabz1z5 evz.
Gregor. vii.   Gregor. vii. oorivr.

Analyze Images A medieval drawing shows Henry driving Gregory from Rome (top). Other scenes include Gregory excommunicating Henry (bottom left) and Gregory on his deathbed (bottom right). **Use Visual Information** How does the artist use visual clues to identify each person in the drawing?

Continuing Conflicts The struggle between popes and rulers continued long after Gregory and Henry died. Eventually, in 1122, the Church and the Holy Roman Empire reached an agreement called the Concordat of Worms (kon KOR dat of vurmz). This agreement gave the Church the sole authority to appoint bishops, but it also allowed emperors to give fiefs, or grants of land, to bishops in order to win their loyalty. Despite this agreement, conflicts between popes and rulers continued.

✓READING CHECK **Identify Main Ideas** How did Pope Gregory try to destroy Henry IV's authority?

How Did the French Monarchy Grow?

Between the 900s and 1200, there were few strong rulers in Europe. Political power lay with aristocrats, whose castles helped them control their lands. Then, in England and France, power began to shift into the hands of monarchs.

Trade Increases By the 1100s, trade was increasing throughout Europe. As trade boomed, kings benefited from taxes on the profits. The kings' new riches strengthened them politically.

Analyze Images The coronation of Philip II at the cathedral of Reims in 1179. **Infer** How does this painting show the close relationship of the Church and royal authorities?

King of France The ancestors of the French kings were merely aristocrats with little power. One family, the Capetians (kuh PAY shunz), established their capital in Paris. Over time, their kingdom grew stronger. One Capetian ruler, King Philip II Augustus, came to the throne in 1180. He acquired large holdings of land. Royal documents refer to him with the new title of "King of France" rather than the old title of "King of the Franks."

Philip II created new officials to oversee justice. He also gained more control over the French Church. By the end of his reign, France had the strongest monarchy in medieval Europe.

✓ READING CHECK **Identify Cause and Effect** What factor helped increase the power of French kings?

✓ Lesson Check

Practice Vocabulary

1. Use the following terms to describe the struggle between popes and rulers: **secular, excommunicate**.

2. What **authority** did popes have that kings did not have?

Critical Thinking and Writing

3. **Infer** Why did so many rulers try to claim the authority of ancient Rome?

4. **Draw Conclusions** Why did kings want the right to appoint bishops?

5. **Identify Main Ideas** How did popes try to control monarchs?

6. **Writing Workshop: Generate Questions to Focus Research** What do you know about Jewish life in medieval Europe—such as impact of the Crusades or the Plague on Jewish populations, Jewish life in Spain before or after the Reconquista, or Jewish migration? Write in your 📔 Active Journal three questions about an aspect of Jewish life in medieval Europe that you would like research more about.

Compare Different Points of View

A point of view is the way an individual looks at an event or issue. Participants in a historic event will have different point of view, depending on many factors, such as background and religion.

Follow these steps to compare different points of view. Then, answer the questions based on the two text excerpts.

INTERACTIVE

Compare
Viewpoints

1 Identify the event or issue being discussed. The title of the account may tell you directly what the subject is, or you may have to use your existing knowledge.

a. What is the main idea of the Dictatus Papae? Of the emperor's letter to the pope?

b. The two documents are both related to what major issue of medieval times?

2 Identify the factors that may have influenced each writer's point of view. You may have to infer some of this information from what they say.

a. Why do you think Gregory would have favored the principles he listed?

b. How was Henry's point of view shaped by his background and position?

3 Identify facts and opinions in each account. Facts can be checked and proven. Opinions vary depending on point of view.

a. How does Henry use Gregory's real name to express an opinion?

b. Would both men agree that authority to rule comes from God?

4 Develop your own opinion about the event. Your opinion should be based on the facts and what you know about the event.

a. How easy do you think it will be for the men to settle their differences?

b. What additional information might help you draw conclusions about the conflict?

Primary Source

Pope Gregory VII listed principles relating to the authority of the pope:

That the Roman church was established by God alone.

That the Roman [pope] alone is rightly called universal.

That he alone can depose and reinstate bishops. . . .

That he may be permitted to depose emperors. . . .

—Gregory VII, *Dictatus Papae*, March 1075

Primary Source

This excerpt is from Henry's reply that Henry sent in January 1076:

Henry . . . to Hildebrand, not pope, but false monk. . . .

You have attacked me, who, unworthy as I am, have yet been anointed [or chosen] to rule among the anointed of God, and who, according to the teaching of the fathers, can be judged by no one save God alone, and can be deposed for no crime except infidelity[lack of faith].

—Letter of Henry IV to Gregory VII, January 1076

England Takes Shape

BOUNCE TO ACTIVATE ▶ VIDEO

GET READY TO READ

START UP

Look closely at the tapestry showing the invasion of England by Norman soldiers from France. Why do you think France and England have such a long history of conflict?

GUIDING QUESTIONS

- What impact did the Norman Conquest have on the history and culture of England?
- Why did Henry II and Becket clash?
- How did the Magna Carta support the development of a limited monarchy?

TAKE NOTES

Literacy Skills: Use Evidence
Use the graphic organizer in your 📖 Active Journal to take notes as you read the lesson.

PRACTICE VOCABULARY

Use the vocabulary activity in your 📖 Active Journal to practice the vocabulary words.

Vocabulary		Academic Vocabulary
pilgrimage	writ	standardized
Magna Carta	parliament	transform
common law	judiciary	
habeas corpus		

On Christmas Day in 1066, William, Duke of Normandy, was about to be crowned king of England at Westminster Abbey, near London. But William and his Norman knights were nervous. They had just seized power and were afraid of an uprising. When the English crowds outside began to cheer, the Normans misunderstood and panicked. They attacked the people and set fire to nearby houses.

Inside the great coronation church, the ceremony continued. As the crown was placed on William's head, the firelight from the burning houses flickered over the church walls. It was a fitting coronation for a warlord who had gained power by sword and flame.

England Before the Conquest

The roots of the kingdom of England reach back to a time before England existed. In the 400s, Germanic tribes began settling in the east of Britain. These tribes became known as Anglo-Saxons. Anglo-Saxon kingdoms formed, and the land occupied by these kingdoms became known as "England," or the land of the Angles.

During the 900s and 1000s, England became much more organized under a centralized government. A **standardized** system of coinage came into use throughout the kingdom.

By 1066, England was a stronger state. But despite the growing power of the English monarchy, the king was unable to resist the invasion led by William, Duke of Normandy. This invasion changed the history of Europe forever.

Academic Vocabulary
standardized • *adj.*, the same everywhere

☑ READING CHECK Identify Main Ideas Who were the Anglo-Saxons?

What Was the Norman Conquest?

William was descended from Viking raiders called Northmen, or Normans, who settled in northern France. This area of France came to be called Normandy, after the Normans. The dukes of Normandy became great feudal lords. They grew rich collecting taxes from traders who crossed their lands. In time, they wanted new lands to rule.

Norman Claims on England For some time, the Normans had been interested in the wealth of nearby England. Duke William of Normandy was related to the Anglo-Saxon king, Edward the Confessor. But Edward was a weak ruler. The real power in England was held by a noble family called the Godwins. Harold Godwin, Earl of Wessex, expected to inherit the throne.

GEOGRAPHY **SKILLS**

Invaders in the north influenced events in southern England.

1. **Movement** Which armies fought at York? Which armies fought at Hastings?

2. **Draw Conclusions** Why might Harold's army have been exhausted by the time they reached Hastings?

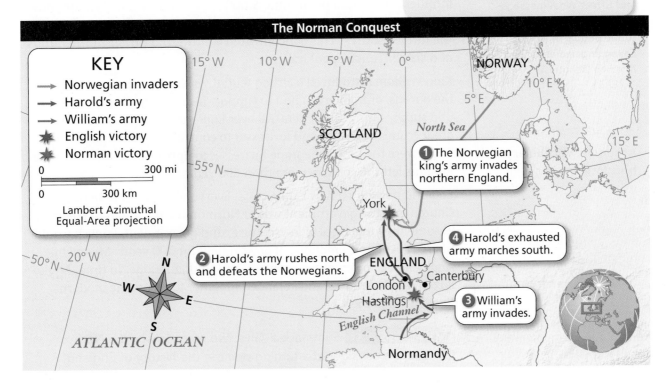

The Norman Conquest

KEY
→ Norwegian invaders
→ Harold's army
→ William's army
✹ English victory
✹ Norman victory

0   300 mi
0   300 km
Lambert Azimuthal Equal-Area projection

❶ The Norwegian king's army invades northern England.

❷ Harold's army rushes north and defeats the Norwegians.

❸ William's army invades.

❹ Harold's exhausted army marches south.

NORWAY
North Sea
SCOTLAND
York
ENGLAND
London • Canterbury
Hastings
English Channel
Normandy
ATLANTIC OCEAN

Analyze Images The Tower of London was one of the castles built to control England. **Identify Cause and Effect** What message might this castle have sent to the people of Anglo-Saxon England after the Norman Conquest?

Academic Vocabulary

transform • v., to change

As Edward lay dying, he supposedly promised the English Crown to Harold. But William claimed that Edward had already promised the Crown to him. The Norwegian king also claimed the English throne. So when Harold became king, he faced two strong and threatening rivals.

William the Conqueror In late September 1066, the Norwegian king landed his army in northern England. The English king, Harold, and his army rushed north and defeated the Norwegian invasion. But a few days after Harold's victory, William of Normandy invaded southern England. Harold was forced to march his exhausted army 250 miles south to confront William's forces.

On October 14, the two armies met near the village of Hastings, on the south coast of England. The English were on foot, fighting with swords and spears. The Normans' excellent cavalry and skilled archers easily defeated them. Harold and his brothers were killed in the battle, ending Anglo-Saxon rule in England.

The Norman duke William was now "the conqueror" of England. He and his army fought their way across the land, burning and looting. On Christmas Day 1066, William the Conqueror was crowned king of England in Westminster Abbey.

Norman England The Norman Conquest **transformed** England. English language and culture would never be the same.

The Battle of Hastings wiped out many great Anglo-Saxon noble families. There had been some 5,000 local landowners. William now gave their lands to about 180 Norman barons. The king's family got the largest shares. This concentrated wealth and power in the hands of a small French-speaking elite.

King William introduced a strong feudal system. As vassals of the king, the barons, or noblemen, had to support him with military service and supply him with soldiers. All over England, Norman barons built great castles as homes and fortresses to control the native population. These were the first large stone fortresses to appear in Britain since the Romans left the country more than 600 years earlier.

England now had a new ruling class. Everyone in power in both the Church and the government was of Norman birth. Latin and French became the languages of law, culture, and government. English would not reappear as a language of government for 300 years. Meanwhile, Anglo-Saxons maintained their customs and language. In time, Anglo-Saxon and Norman French blended together to create the modern English language.

✓ READING CHECK **Summarize** Give two reasons why the Norman Conquest is considered a turning point in the history of England.

How Did Church and State Clash in England?

In England, as in the Holy Roman empire, conflict emerged between Church and state. A long struggle set King Henry II against his old friend, Thomas Becket, the archbishop of Canterbury.

Henry and Thomas Becket had once been allies. In 1162, King Henry appointed Becket to be the archbishop of Canterbury. Becket was now the most important bishop in the land.

Henry wanted to expand royal power. He thought that Becket would support his policies. But to the king's dismay, Becket grew more loyal to the Church than to the monarchy. Becket resisted Henry's attempt to limit the power and independence of the Church. The struggle became so fierce that Becket excommunicated Henry.

At last, Henry became so angry that he uttered words that he later regretted. At a royal banquet he cried out, "How can you all allow me, your king, to be treated with such contempt?" Some of his knights believed that the king was calling for Becket's death. They traveled to Canterbury and murdered the archbishop in the church itself.

The murder of an archbishop shocked Christendom. People felt Becket was a martyr, a person who died for his beliefs. A shrine was set up where Becket had been killed. The cathedral of Canterbury became a destination of **pilgrimage**—a journey undertaken to worship at a holy place.

☑ READING CHECK **Identify Cause and Effect** What wider conflict led to the murder of Becket?

🔘 INTERACTIVE

Key Events in Medieval English History

Analyze Images Knights strike down Thomas Becket at the altar in Canterbury cathedral despite the attempt at defense by another priest. **Identify Main Ideas** How did the murder increase friction between Henry and the Church?

Analyze Images King John signs the Magna Carta. **Use Visual Information** What is John's attitude about signing the document? How can you tell?

How Was Royal Power Limited in England?

The Norman kings were always trying to strengthen the central government, but powerful feudal lords often opposed them. Kings had to ask their barons for money and soldiers to wage wars and crusades. In return, the barons could make demands on their king.

King John John, the son of Henry II, became king of England in 1199. As a descendant of William the Conqueror, King John also claimed Normandy in France. However, claiming and ruling were very different things. By 1204, John had lost control over most of his French lands. To get them back, he needed to raise an army. To raise that army, he needed money from taxes. His efforts to fund his army led to conflict with his barons over taxes and royal power.

Signing the Magna Carta By 1215, England's leaders had had enough of King John's high taxes and failures. Rebellious barons forced the king to sign a document that promised them certain rights. This document came to be known as the **Magna Carta**, which is Latin for "Great Charter."

In the Magna Carta, King John agreed to recognize the rights of barons. He promised he would not collect more taxes without the approval of a council of barons and churchmen. He also promised to recognize the right of trial by jury. The charter stated that the king:

Primary Source

"[will not] proceed against [the accused], or send others to do so, except according to the lawful sentence of his peers and according to the Common Law."

—Magna Carta, translated by Xavier Hildegarde

The Magna Carta set a historic example. It made it clear that even a king must abide by the law of the land. Over time, the rights in the Magna Carta were extended to ordinary people. With only a few changes, they became part of English law. Later, other governments—including that of the United States—adopted its basic principles: rule of law, trial by jury, and the right of the people to have a voice in their laws and taxation.

English Law When the Magna Carta referred to "the law of the land," it meant English, rather than Roman, law. In many countries, medieval law was based on Roman law. In England, the law of the land was a mix of Norman French feudal law, Church law, and old Anglo-Saxon common law. **Common law** is law that has developed from custom and judges' decisions, rather than acts of a lawmaking assembly.

An important legal practice to come out of English common law is known as **habeas corpus**, a Latin phrase that means "you shall have the body." Habeas corpus refers to a court order to bring an arrested person before a judge or court. A jailer who receives this **writ**, or court order, must either release the prisoner or present a good reason for keeping that person in jail. The writ helps prevent secret arrests and imprisonment without trial. However, throughout British and American history, the writ of habeas corpus has often been suspended during times of war.

Parliament and an Independent Judiciary During the 1200s, English kings began seeking advice from county representatives. This was the beginning of Parliament, one of the oldest representative assemblies in Europe. A **parliament** is an assembly of representatives

THE RULE OF LAW IN MEDIEVAL ENGLAND

ARREST
The state arrests, or holds, a person.

WRIT OF HABEAS CORPUS
This ensures the person is held only for lawful reasons.

COURT TRIAL BY JURY
The person's case is heard at a court by a group of fellow citizens.

ACQUITTAL— OR CONVICTION!
- The jury decides whether the accused person is guilty or not.
- Punishment could be harsh—for example, thieves might have their hands cut off.

Analyze Diagrams A system of justice gradually developed in medieval England. **Understand Effects** Which step ensures that people are not held in jail for long periods of time without being convicted of a crime?

Analyze Images Queen Elizabeth II of the United Kingdom opens a meeting of Parliament. **Use Visual Information** What evidence can you see in the photograph that the United Kingdom values its heritage and traditions?

who make laws. At first, the king called meetings of Parliament when he needed to raise taxes. Eventually, Parliament became a true lawmaking body, divided into two houses. The House of Lords represented nobles. The House of Commons represented more ordinary people such as knights and town leaders.

Even before Magna Carta, England took another important step toward a more democratic government. In 1178, King Henry II chose five members of his personal household, including two clergy, "to hear all the complaints of the realm and to do right." These judges were supervised by the "King and the wiser men of the realm." So began the Court of Common Pleas, England's most active common law court in the Middle Ages. Later, the Magna Carta directed that this court should sit permanently "in some certain place." As a result, the monarch's direct control over the courts was greatly reduced. This was the beginning of England's independent **judiciary**, or system of courts outside the control of other branches of government.

England never did develop a written constitution. However, the collected decisions, judgments, and actions of its governments make up an unwritten constitution that continues to guide the country today.

READING CHECK **Draw Conclusions** How did the signing of the Magna Carta and the development of Parliament have a similar impact?

☑ Lesson Check

Practice Vocabulary

1. Use the following terms to describe the struggle for power that developed between kings and nobles: **Magna Carta, common law, habeas corpus, writ, parliament.**

2. What is the **Magna Carta**?

Critical Thinking and Writing

3. **Understand Effects** How did the Norman Conquest affect land ownership?

4. **Synthesize** Why would habeas corpus strengthen a free society?

5. **Make Inferences** How did the Magna Carta help lay the foundation of democracy?

6. **Writing Workshop: Find and Use Credible Sources** Where can you find credible and accurate information about Jewish life in medieval Europe? Write a list of possible sources in your ▰ Active Journal.

The Magna Carta

The Magna Carta was the first document to place limits on the power of the English monarch. It also helped set up a basic framework for England's judiciary, or system of courts.

▶ The Magna Carta

(18) . . . We ourselves, or in our absence abroad our chief justice, will send two justices to each county four times a year ① , and these justices, with four knights of the county elected by the county itself, shall hold the assizes ② in the county court, on the day and in the place where the court meets. . . .

(20) For a trivial offence [or crime], a free man shall be fined only in proportion to the degree of his offence ③ , and for a serious offence correspondingly, but not so heavily as to deprive him of his livelihood. . . .

(55) All fines that have been given to us unjustly and against the law of the land, . . . shall be entirely remitted ④ or the matter decided by a majority judgment of the twenty-five barons . . . together with [the] archbishop of Canterbury ⑤ . . . .

(60) All . . . that we have granted shall be observed in our kingdom in so far as concerns our own relations with our subjects. Let all men of our kingdom, whether clergy or laymen, observe them similarly ⑥ . . . .

—Magna Carta, 1215

Analyzing Primary Sources

Review the excerpt to find details for your answers.

1. **Infer** Why do you think locally elected knights attended county courts?

2. **Draw Conclusions** If overly heavy fines for trivial offenses ruined people's livelihoods, what effects do you think might result?

3. **Identify Cause and Effect** How might steps such as those described in this document weaken the power of a king?

Reading and Vocabulary Support

① How does the king establish county courts?

② Assizes are county court sessions.

③ Why do you think it is important for fines to be in proportion to crimes?

④ To remit is to give something back.

⑤ What will be the procedure for challenging unjust fines given by the king?

⑥ According to the Magna Carta, to whom do these rights and procedures apply?

Quest CONNECTIONS

Based on the excerpt, what role does King John offer his barons for dealing with potential conflicts with him? Record your findings in your 📖 Active Journal.

LESSON 3

The Crusades

BOUNCE TO ACTIVATE | VIDEO

GET READY TO READ

START UP

Study the illustration of a the capture of the city of Antioch in 1098 during the First Crusade. Tell a partner how you think the participants might have felt.

GUIDING QUESTIONS

- Why did Europeans launch the Crusades?
- How did the Crusades lead to increased persecution of Jews, Muslims, and Christian heretics?
- What were the lasting social and economic effects of the Crusades?

TAKE NOTES

Literacy Skills: Sequence

Use the graphic organizer in your 📓 Active Journal to take notes as you read the lesson.

PRACTICE VOCABULARY

Use the vocabulary activity in your 📓 Active Journal to practice the vocabulary words.

Vocabulary	Academic Vocabulary
Crusades	establish
heresy	region
Inquisition	

In March 1096, farmers in northern France paused in their plowing to listen to a distant roar. It was the sound of a vast crowd of people singing hymns and calling others to join them. The farmers watched the approaching mob of peasants, some 20,000 strong, led by a man dressed as a hermit. The farmers immediately knew who he was. For months, Peter the Hermit had been calling on all Christians to join his fight to free Jerusalem. His preaching had inspired thousands to follow him. Like so many others before them, the farmers left their fields and became part of Peter the Hermit's army.

The **Crusades**, a series of military campaigns to establish Christian control over the Holy Land, had begun. Over the next few centuries, wave after wave of peasants, soldiers, and kings would travel from Europe to the Middle East in pursuit of this goal. Their campaigns would reshape both Europe and the Middle East.

The First Crusade

The Crusades began with high hopes. One goal was to protect Christian pilgrims as they visited the Holy Land, the lands in Palestine where Jesus had lived and taught. Muslim caliphs, or leaders, had generally allowed Christian pilgrims to visit holy places. But in the early 1000s, the Fatimid Arabs started destroying churches and killing pilgrims. Then, in 1071, Seljuk (SEL jook) Turks took over Jerusalem from the Fatimids. The Turks harassed pilgrims and marched on the Christian city of Constantinople, so the Byzantine emperor in Constantinople asked Pope Urban II for help.

Why Did the Pope Call for a Crusade? In 1095, Pope Urban II called for a crusade to free the Holy Land. He called on the "soldiers of Christ" to defend Constantinople and liberate Jerusalem from the Turks. People answered the pope's call with enthusiasm. Their slogan was *"Deus le veult!,"* which means "God wills it!"

The Crusader's Creed Some religious leaders used feudal concepts to explain the idea of a holy war: Since Jesus was every Christian's Lord, Jesus' vassals were obliged to defend his lands and shrines. So they saw a crusade was a just, or righteous, war.

The word *crusade* comes from the Latin word *crux*, or "cross." Crusaders sewed a cross on their clothing. They took a vow to make a pilgrimage to Jesus's tomb. Like other pilgrims, crusaders were promised forgiveness for sins.

People who "took the cross" made many sacrifices. Crusaders faced robbers, hunger, and disease before even encountering the enemy. Knights sold estates and borrowed money to pay for the long and dangerous trip. Although many crusaders were members of the nobility, others hoped to gain land and wealth by joining the Crusades.

INTERACTIVE

Conflicts and Crusades

Analyze Images This painting from the 1400s shows Pope Urban II calling for support from noblemen and monarchs to launch the First Crusade. **Infer** How does this image suggest the authority of the Pope?

On his way to the Holy Land, one crusader, the French noble Jean de Joinville, wrote:

Primary Source

I never once let my eyes turn back . . . for fear my heart might be filled with longing [for] my lovely castle and the two children I had left behind.

—Jean de Joinville, *Life of Saint Louis*

Academic Vocabulary
establish • *v.*, to set up

The First Crusade Begins Up to 150,000 people hurried to join. The first group of crusaders to leave for the Holy Land was a ragged mob of peasants led by Peter the Hermit. Peter's "army" of untrained men, women, and children was not prepared for the long journey to the Middle East. Most were killed by the Turks before ever reaching the Holy Land. Professional armies followed, traveling by land and sea.

Despite setbacks, the First Crusade was a military success. The crusaders had one important advantage—they took the Muslim kingdoms by surprise. The Muslims were too divided to resist. By 1099, the crusaders had captured Jerusalem and **established** four crusader states in the Holy Land. The crusaders also turned back the Turks' advance on Constantinople.

☑ READING CHECK **Recognize Multiple Causes** Why did people join the Crusades?

Second and Third Crusades

In 1144, the Muslims counter-attacked and conquered the crusader state of Edessa. The fall of Edessa alarmed Europeans so much that the pope called for a second crusade.

GEOGRAPHY **SKILLS**

The Crusades brought people from many areas of Europe into contact with the cultures of the Middle East.

1. **Place** Which Byzantine city was on the crusaders' route?

2. **Synthesize Visual Information** Which European ports were used by crusaders heading for the Holy Land?

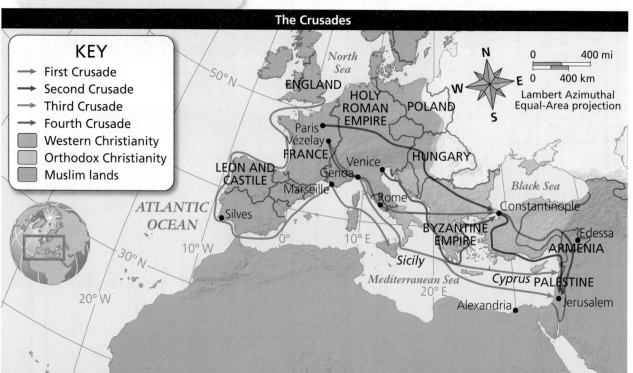

The Crusades

KEY
→ First Crusade
→ Second Crusade
→ Third Crusade
→ Fourth Crusade
■ Western Christianity
■ Orthodox Christianity
■ Muslim lands

The Crusades

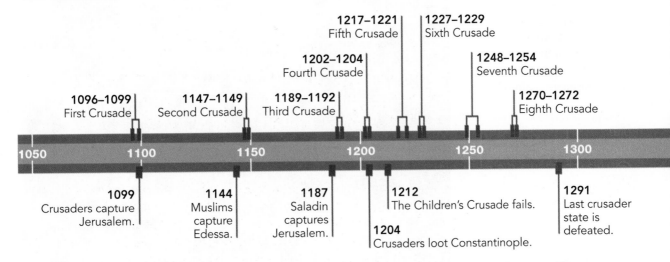

1096–1099	First Crusade
1147–1149	Second Crusade
1189–1192	Third Crusade
1202–1204	Fourth Crusade
1217–1221	Fifth Crusade
1227–1229	Sixth Crusade
1248–1254	Seventh Crusade
1270–1272	Eighth Crusade

1099 Crusaders capture Jerusalem.

1144 Muslims capture Edessa.

1187 Saladin captures Jerusalem.

1204 Crusaders loot Constantinople.

1212 The Children's Crusade fails.

1291 Last crusader state is defeated.

Analyze Timelines The Crusades spanned almost two centuries. **Infer** What event sparked the Third Crusade?

Second Crusade King Louis VII of France and the German emperor organized the Second Crusade. Other monarchs, such as Louis' wife, Eleanor of Aquitaine, joined this crusade, but the Second Crusade failed. The Crusade's leaders argued. The crusaders, who often treated the Muslim majority in the Palestine region with disrespect and cruelty, were unable to gain local support. After the Second Crusade failed, the Muslim leader Saladin grew stronger. In 1187, he recaptured Jerusalem.

Third Crusade The fall of Jerusalem provoked the Third Crusade in 1189. Because it was organized by the rulers of England, France, and Germany, it was called the "Crusade of the Kings." Richard I of England, called the "Lionheart," won important victories.

Saladin's noble character inspired respect. One of Saladin's officials told how a terrified prisoner was brought before Saladin:

Primary Source

The interpreter asked him [the prisoner]: 'What are you afraid of?' [He replied,] 'At first I was afraid of seeing that face, but after seeing it . . ., I am sure that I shall see only good in it.' The Sultan was moved . . . and let him go free.

—Baha' ad-Din Ibn Shaddad

Saladin and Richard signed a truce that ended the Third Crusade. Christian pilgrims were free to travel, and Saladin agreed to respect crusader lands, but Jerusalem remained in Muslim hands.

✓ **READING CHECK** **Identify Main Ideas** Why might the Third Crusade be considered a failure?

▲ This illustration from the 1800s depicts Eleanor of Aquitaine, who participated in the Second Crusade.

Analyze Images This painting from the 1800s shows crusaders attacking Constantinople **Infer** Why would the Byzantine emperor have felt betrayed by the crusaders' actions?

The Fourth and Later Crusades

The Fourth Crusade embarrassed the pope who had launched it. The crusaders never reached the Holy Land. Instead, they tried to fund their campaign by looting Christian cities along the route.

Crusaders Loot Constantinople In 1204, crusaders stormed Constantinople, the rich Byzantine capital. For three days, they smashed Christian icons, stole relics, and attacked women. The pope was furious. He wrote that crusaders who "should have used their swords against the infidel [unbeliever], have bathed those swords in the blood of Christians." The Byzantines never forgave the Catholic Christians.

The Final Crusades In 1212, a popular crusading movement swept through France and Germany. The so-called Children's Crusade attracted poor people of all ages. Most never got farther than Italy.

Although several more crusades were launched, the crusaders were slowly forced out of the Holy Land. Finally, in 1291, Egyptian Muslims defeated the last crusader state.

The Muslim View Muslims in the Middle East were caught off guard by the first waves of crusaders. The Muslim world was too divided politically to organize a strong defense. Most Muslims regarded the crusaders as soldiers hired to win back Byzantine lands.

However, Muslim counterattacks became more successful. Like the crusaders, Muslims described their own campaigns in religious terms, as holy war.

☑ READING CHECK Understand Effects What was the lasting impact of the Fourth Crusade?

Quick Activity

Explore the experience of the crusaders in your 📓 Active Journal.

How Did Religious Persecutions Arise?

In Europe, the Crusades fueled dangerous passions. Religious fervor against Muslims led to brutal attacks against all whose beliefs differed from Church teachings. Campaigns were soon launched against Muslims and other religious minorities in Europe itself.

Attacks on Jewish Communities Jewish groups were a main target of attacks in Europe. Some Europeans had falsely labeled Jews as enemies of Christianity, and used the Crusades as an excuse for violence. Mobs of Christian peasants turned on those Jews who would not instantly convert to Christianity. During the First Crusade, these mobs terrorized and slaughtered the Jewish communities along crusader routes to the Middle East.

The worst violence occurred in German cities along the Rhine River, such as Mainz and Cologne. More than 5,000 Jews were murdered in Germany in several different attacks. Thousands of Jews killed themselves and their families to escape torture and murder. When the knights of the First Crusade took Jerusalem in 1099, they slaughtered Jews and Muslims alike.

A few Christian clergymen tried to protect the Jews, but the public mood led to more persecution in crusader countries. Jews were expelled from England in 1290, and from France in 1306.

Crusades Against Heretics Jews and Muslims were not the only victims of religious persecution in Europe. Other targets included Christians who followed various heresies. A **heresy** is a belief that is rejected by official Church teaching. Medieval Christians would not tolerate even minor differences in beliefs. Heretics were considered dangerous, because their ideas might influence others.

At first, heretics were excommunicated. This was a serious punishment, because the Church was the center of medieval life. However, some heretics clung to their beliefs. The pope called on nobles to organize local crusades against them. In the Languedoc (lang DOK) **region** of southern France, entire communities of Christians were massacred or exiled for disagreeing with Church teachings.

Accusations of heresy were used to destroy the Knights Templars, who had once been the military heroes of the Crusades. The Templars were an order of military monks approved by the Church in 1127. As warriors, they were greatly admired during the Crusades. However, they also set up an

Did you know?

Crusader knights wore heavy armor and rode large warhorses. Their cavalry charges were greatly feared. Muslim warriors, however, were lightly clothed and rode speedy Arabian horses. Their speed and mobility gave them an advantage.

Academic Vocabulary

region • *n.*, area with at least one unifying physical or human feature such as climate, landforms, population, or history

Analyze Images Jewish communities were frequent victims of persecution in medieval Europe during the Crusades. **Use Visual Information** Based on the painting, what forms did the persecutions take?

Analyze Images The Spanish Inquisition judges an accused heretic. **Summarize** Why was the Inquisition created?

Quest CONNECTIONS

How do you think the Crusades and their effects will change the medieval society of Europe? Record your findings in your ▱ Active Journal.

international banking system, which made them rich—and envied. The king of France, who owed them money, had their leaders arrested in 1307. The Templar leaders were accused of heresy, tortured, and burned alive.

The Inquisition Begins In the 1200s, Pope Gregory IX created the **Inquisition**, a series of investigations designed to find and judge heretics. Accused heretics who did not cooperate were punished. This Inquisition later targeted Jews, first burning copies of the Talmud and then burning Jews at the stake starting in France in 1288.

Minor heresies might be forgiven with a fast or a whipping. More serious accusations could lead to fines or imprisonment. If a heretic would not confess, often under torture, he or she was executed.

☑ **READING CHECK Identify Cause and Effect** Why were Jewish communities targeted during the Crusades?

What Were the Effects of the Crusades?

The Crusades failed to achieve their goal of forcing the Muslims out of the Holy Land. In addition, centuries of fighting weakened the Byzantine empire, which had protected Europe from Turkish invasion. However, the Crusades did have some lasting effects in Europe.

Seeing a Wider World The Crusades opened Europeans' eyes to the rest of the world. People who had never been farther from home than the next village suddenly saw new lands, peoples, and ways of life.

The Crusades may have encouraged Europeans to explore distant parts of the world. Some historians believe that the adventurous spirit of the Crusades helped lead to the great European voyages of discovery that began in the late 1400s.

Trade With the East Increases The Crusades brought wealth and trade to European port cities. Italian cities such as Venice and Genoa had always traded by sea. They were eager to supply the needs of the crusader states in the Holy Land. The crusader states were surrounded by hostile populations and had to depend on goods shipped from Europe. In the process, old trade routes between Europe and the Middle East were reopened. The merchants of Venice and Genoa also opened trading colonies in Egypt.

Even while the Crusades continued, peaceful exchanges of goods and ideas took place between Muslims, Jews, Latin Roman Christians, and Greek Byzantine Christians. In the twelfth century, for example, the Norman island kingdom of Sicily became a major site of encounter.

Norman Sicily had a multicultural population and tolerant rulers. Located in the central Mediterranean, Sicily was connected to Islamic trade routes to the south and east. In addition, Latin Christian merchants traveled to Sicily. Over time, they bought increasing amounts of Asian products from Muslim and Jewish merchants.

As trade routes reopened, trade increased. Crusaders returned home with silks, spices, and other exotic goods. Demand for these products at home encouraged European merchants to expand trade with Asia and to search for faster routes to China and India.

Cultural Exchange Grows The Crusades led to cultural exchange between Europe and Muslim states, in places such as Sicily and elsewhere. Europeans benefited greatly from this contact with the Middle East. The Crusades may have introduced Europeans to the Muslim hygienic practice of washing with soap. Scientific knowledge also expanded. Muslim medicine was more advanced than that of Europe. In addition, Muslims had preserved much ancient Greek and Roman knowledge that had been lost in Western Europe. This ancient wisdom, along with Muslim advances in science and medicine, now spread across Europe. This knowledge would one day help Europeans themselves make great advances in the sciences and the arts.

☑ **READING CHECK** **Understand Effects** Why did Italian cities benefit from the Crusades?

Analyze Images An Italian merchant watches goods being loaded onto a ship. **Identify Cause and Effect** How did the Crusades influence Europe's demand for exotic and luxury goods?

☑ Lesson Check

Practice Vocabulary

1. Use the following terms to describe medieval conflicts and crusades: **Crusades, heresy, Inquisition**.

2. In what **region** was the Holy Land of the Crusades located?

Critical Thinking and Writing

3. **Understand Effects** How did the Crusades affect Europe economically?

4. **Hypothesize** How might the development of medieval Europe have been different if the Crusades had never happened?

5. **Make Inferences** Why were religious minorities in Europe persecuted during the Crusades?

6. **Writing Workshop: Support Ideas With Evidence** Examine your credible sources for evidence that supports what you have learned about Jewish life in this Topic. Do research and write a brief account of some aspect of Jewish life in medieval Europe. Write a brief outline of your ideas with their supporting details in your 📕 Active Journal.

The Reconquista

BOUNCE TO ACTIVATE ▶ VIDEO

GET READY TO READ

START UP

Examine the illustration from the 1200s. It shows Arab and Christian musicians playing instruments called ouds together in Muslim Spain. What does this illustration tell you about cultural mingling in Muslim Spain?

GUIDING QUESTIONS

- How did Spain's Muslim conquerors build a sophisticated culture?
- How did Christians, Muslims, and Jews interact in Iberia?
- Why did powerful new rulers drive Muslims and Jews from Spain in the late Middle Ages?

TAKE NOTES

Literacy Skills: Summarize
Use the graphic organizer in your 📙 Active Journal to take notes as you read the lesson.

PRACTICE VOCABULARY

Use the vocabulary activity in your 📙 Active Journal to practice the vocabulary words.

Vocabulary	Academic Vocabulary
Iberian Peninsula	legal
Moors	determined
Reconquista	

By the early 700s, Muslims ruled most of the **Iberian Peninsula**, the peninsula where present-day Spain and Portugal are located. Under Muslim rule, a culture of great diversity developed there. Muslim, Jewish, and Christian communities exchanged knowledge and customs. But the political situation on the peninsula was unstable. Christian kingdoms waged a long campaign against the Muslims. In 1492, Spain's multicultural society was finally swept away.

Spain Under Muslim Rule

The Umayyad rulers of the Muslim empire in the Middle East and northern Africa were overthrown and murdered in 750, but one survivor fled to Spain. In 756, Abd al-Rahman established a new dynasty at Córdoba. The dynasty ruled most of Spain for nearly 300 years. A few small Christian kingdoms controlled the northern part of Spain.

Moorish Culture in Spain To European Christians, the Muslims in Spain were known as **Moors**. The Moors governed an extremely advanced, dynamic, and diverse society centered in what is now southern Spain. In Arabic, this region was called "al-Andalus," which became the modern name Andalusia.

In the tenth century, the Muslim capital of Córdoba was Europe's largest city. It had many mosques, bookshops, and public baths. Houses had mosaic floors, gardens, and fountains. Its great library may have contained about 400,000 volumes.

Traders carried leather goods, silk cloth, and jewelry from Córdoba to markets in Europe. Moorish Spain was home to the Great Mosque of Córdoba and the Alhambra palace in Granada, two masterpieces of Muslim architecture.

A Multicultural Society Advances The golden age of Moorish culture reached its peak in the 800s and 900s. Science and medicine were far more advanced in Muslim Spain than in the rest of Europe. Foreign students flocked to Córdoba. They studied philosophy, music, and medicine with Muslim and Jewish scholars.

Academic Vocabulary
legal • *adj.*, having to do with the law

Córdoba was home to two of the most famous philosophers of the Middle Ages. One was the Muslim **legal** scholar and judge Ibn Rushd, or Averroës. The other was the Jewish legal scholar Moses Maimonides (my MAHN nah deez).

By medieval standards, most of Spain's Muslim rulers were tolerant of Jews and Christians, as all three religions worshiped one God. Muslim leaders wanted to create a prosperous, stable society. They accepted the religious diversity of their subjects. In fact, some Jews and Christians held high official positions.

Still, there were restrictions. Non-Muslims had to follow certain rules and pay a special tax. Later Muslim rulers were even less tolerant. They imposed strict new rules. Christians could not carry Bibles in public. Jews also were persecuted.

☑ READING CHECK Identify Main Ideas How did religious toleration strengthen Moorish Spain?

▲ Profits from the silk trade allowed Muslim rulers to build palaces like the Alhambra in Granada.

What Was the Reconquista?

The decline of Muslim rule in Spain began in 1002 with a civil war. The Córdoba caliphate was split into small, weak kingdoms. In contrast, by 1050, the Christian kingdoms in northern Spain were more united. Long before the Crusades, popes urged Christians in Spain to wage war against the Muslims. The movement to drive the Muslims from Spain was called the **Reconquista** (re kon KEES tah), or "Reconquest."

The Reconquista helped create a new kingdom, Portugal. In the mid-ninth century, Portugal began as a border county of Asturias recaptured from the Umayyad Muslims by Vimara Peres, a vassal of the King Alfonso III of Asturias. Then, In 1097, it was incorporated into the Kingdom of Léon. After the battle of São Mamede in 1128, Portugal became an independent kingdom ruled by the Counts of Portugal.

Military Campaigns in Iberia The first major victory in the Reconquista was the capture of the city of Toledo in 1085. In 1139, a victory over the Muslims led to Portugal becoming a separate, Christian kingdom. Over time, the Christian kingdoms in Spain formed a powerful alliance against the Muslims. They attacked the Muslim city of Córdoba, which fell in 1236. Córdoba's Great Mosque became a Catholic cathedral.

In 1229, James I of Aragon also captured Majorca, a small island off the east coast of Iberia, from its Muslim rulers. Like Sicily, Majorca had an excellent location on Mediterranean trade routes. Moreover, its varied population made Majorca an important trading and shipping center. Merchants from

GEOGRAPHY SKILLS

Christian armies gradually drove Muslim rulers from Spain.

1. **Region** Which part of Muslim Spain resisted the Christians the longest?

2. **Use Visual Information** From which direction did Christian forces advance over the centuries?

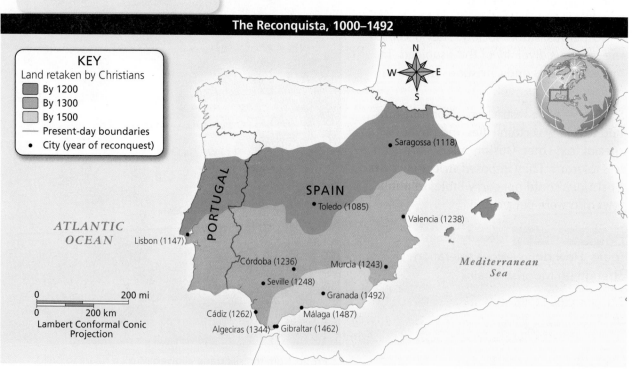

The Reconquista, 1000–1492

KEY
Land retaken by Christians
By 1200
By 1300
By 1500
— Present-day boundaries
• City (year of reconquest)

ATLANTIC OCEAN

PORTUGAL

SPAIN

Saragossa (1118)
Toledo (1085)
Valencia (1238)
Lisbon (1147)
Córdoba (1236)
Murcia (1243)
Seville (1248)
Granada (1492)
Cádiz (1262)
Málaga (1487)
Algeciras (1344)
Gibraltar (1462)

Mediterranean Sea

0   200 mi
0   200 km
Lambert Conformal Conic Projection

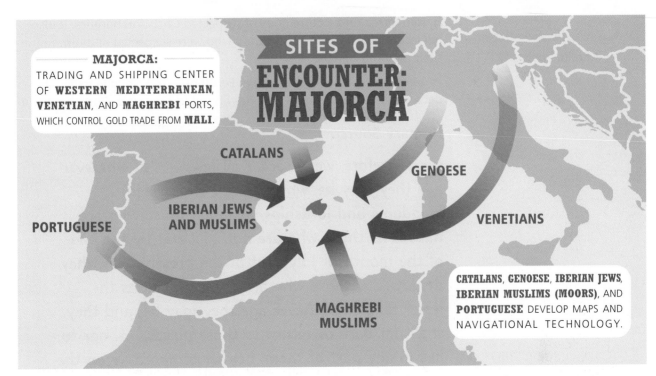

ENCOUNTER: MAJORCA

MAJORCA: TRADING AND SHIPPING CENTER OF **WESTERN MEDITERRANEAN**, **VENETIAN**, AND **MAGHREBI** PORTS, WHICH CONTROL GOLD TRADE FROM **MALI**.

CATALANS

GENOESE

IBERIAN JEWS AND MUSLIMS

PORTUGUESE

VENETIANS

MAGHREBI MUSLIMS

CATALANS, GENOESE, IBERIAN JEWS, IBERIAN MUSLIMS (MOORS), AND **PORTUGUESE** DEVELOP MAPS AND NAVIGATIONAL TECHNOLOGY.

Catalonia (in Aragon), Italian city-states (such as Genoa and Venice), and North Africa journeyed to Majorca to trade. Muslims, Latin Christians, and Jews exchanged their valuable goods and ideas there.

By the middle of the 1200s, all that was left of Moorish Spain was the kingdom of Granada. By paying tribute, it managed to survive for a few hundred years more. However, most of Spain was now under Christian rule.

Uniting the Kingdoms In 1469, an important royal marriage took place. Ferdinand of Aragon married Isabella of Castile-León. Their marriage united Spain's largest Christian kingdoms. It laid the basis for a Spanish state.

Ferdinand and Isabella now concentrated on conquering Granada, the last Muslim territory. When the city fell in 1492, the pope was delighted. But the Catholic monarchs' crusade against the Muslims in Spain led to terrible persecutions of non-Christians.

Religious Persecutions Jewish people had lived quite peacefully in the Christian kingdoms until the late 1300s, when anti-Jewish attacks began. Thousands died in massacres. Terrified, many Jews converted to Christianity. Isabella's reign, however, made life even more dangerous for Jews.

Isabella and Ferdinand were **determined** to unite Spain as a Catholic country. To do so, they brought in a Dominican friar named Torquemada (tor kay MAH duh) to head the Spanish Inquisition. The Inquisition had begun as a series of Church investigations to find and punish heretics. In Spain, it became a permanent institution.

Analyze Diagrams
Majorca was a center of trade in the Mediterranean.
Use Visual Information
What important trade good came from Africa to the Mediterranean?

Academic Vocabulary
determined • *adj.,* to have a strong feeling about doing something

INTERACTIVE

Muslim Spain

It used terror and torture against suspected Christian heretics. It also persecuted converts to Christianity who were suspected of maintaining their previous beliefs.

In 1492, Spain took a radical step. Ferdinand and Isabella issued a decree that banished all Jews who refused to convert to Christianity.

Primary Source

. . . Therefore, we . . . order all Jews . . . of whatever age they may be, who live, . . . in our said kingdoms and lordships, as much those who are natives as those who are not, . . . that by the end of the month of July next of the present year, they depart . . . , those who are great as well as the lesser folk, of whatever age they may be, and they shall not dare to return to those places, . . . nor to live in any part of them, neither temporarily on the way to somewhere else nor in any other manner, under pain that if they do not perform and comply with this command and should be found in our said kingdom and lordships and should in any manner live in them, they incur the penalty of death and the confiscation of all their possessions.

—King Ferdinand and Queen Isabella, *Edict of the Expulsion of the Jews*, March 31, 1492.

Analyze Images In this 1882 painting, the last Muslim ruler in Spain hands to King Ferdinand the keys to the city of Granada in 1492. **Identify Main Ideas** Why was this event a turning point in European history?

Many Spanish Jews fled to other parts of Europe and the Mediterranean area, especially Italy and the Ottoman empire. Later, the Muslims were also ordered to leave the country. A few years later, Portugal followed its Iberian neighbor and also banished Jews.

The loss of these two groups of people did great harm to the Spanish economy and culture. Spain lost more than 160,000 of its people. However, even those Jews and Muslims who had converted to Christianity and remained in Spain were not safe. Generations later, their families were still being persecuted for having a practicing Jewish or Muslim ancestor.

✓ **READING CHECK** **Identify Cause and Effect** What were some of the the intended and unintended effects of the Reconquista?

Analyze Images Maimonides (1135–1204) was a leading Jewish philosopher, theologian, legal scholar, physician, and astronomer in Muslim Spain. **Identify Main Ideas** How did the expulsion of Jews like Maimonides, along with Muslims, affect Spain's culture?

✓ Lesson Check

Practice Vocabulary

1. Use the following terms to describe Christians and Muslims in Spain: **Moors**, **Reconquista**.

2. Where was the **Iberian Peninsula** located? What lands did it include?

Critical Thinking and Writing

3. **Identify Cause and Effect** Why was culture in the Iberian Peninsula so diverse?

4. **Synthesize** What connection do you see between the Crusades and the Reconquista?

5. **Draw Conclusions** Why do you think minorities were persecuted as Christian kingdoms united?

6. **Writing Workshop: Cite Sources** Make sure to record full and accurate information about all sources you use. This information should be cited at the end of your research paper. Write down information about your sources in your 📓 Active Journal.

Decline of Medieval Society

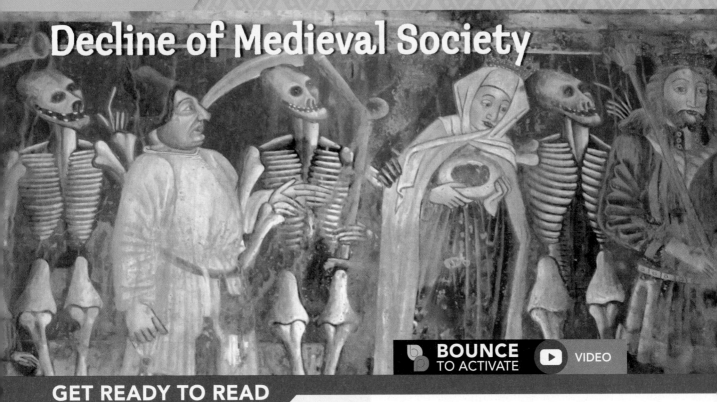

BOUNCE TO ACTIVATE ▶ VIDEO

GET READY TO READ

START UP

Look at this painting of a medieval concept called the Dance of Death. What does the painting suggest about life and death in the Middle Ages?

GUIDING QUESTIONS

- How did the Hundred Years' War threaten the stability of medieval society?
- Why did the Black Death spread rapidly across Europe and Asia in the 1300s?
- What impact did the Black Death have on the medieval social order?

TAKE NOTES

Literacy Skills: Identify Cause and Effect

Use the graphic organizer in your 📓 Active Journal to take notes as you read the lesson.

PRACTICE VOCABULARY

Use the vocabulary activity in your 📓 Active Journal to practice the vocabulary words.

Vocabulary	Academic Vocabulary
famine	invisible
Hundred Years' War	network
bubonic plague	
Black Death	
Peasants' Revolt	

In the 1340s, rumors reached Europe about a terrifying illness in the Far East. These stories described a plague that was killing millions as it swept through China and India. Then, in 1347, ships began drifting into Italian ports filled with dead or dying crews. Very quickly, thousands in the port cities fell ill, often dying within days. From the ports, the plague spread inland. Soon, every corner of Europe was infected. With few people remaining healthy enough to grow food, medieval society was shaken. Villages were abandoned as people tried to escape the disease. All lived in fear of human contact. For those who witnessed these terrifying events, it seemed that the end of the world had come.

Famine and Warfare Strike

The plague was only one of a series of disasters to strike Europe in the 1300s. By 1300, Europe had enjoyed two centuries of economic growth, but now Europeans faced troubled times. A change in the weather may have played a part. From 1315 to 1317, it rained so much that crops were ruined.

Cattle died of diseases brought on by the wet weather. In northern Europe, many people died of starvation, and the years became known as the Great Famine. A **famine** is a serious shortage of food. Europe had barely recovered from the famine when war broke out.

The Hundred Years' War The conflict began when Edward III of England claimed the throne of France. He was supported in this claim by the Flemish, whose textile industry depended on the wool exported from England to Flanders. The conflict between the kingdoms of England and France lasted from 1337 to 1453 and became known as the **Hundred Years' War**. Although few battles were fought during this war, rural areas in particular suffered as roaming armies destroyed crops and brought starvation to peasant communities.

In the early 1300s, England and France were becoming unified states, or nations. The Hundred Years' War increased the sense of patriotism that was developing in each kingdom. So the war was a new kind of conflict—a war between nations.

Deadly New Weapons The English won key battles early in the war, partly because of a powerful weapon: the longbow. Arrows from the English longbow struck with great force, piercing the armor of French knights. In the battle of Crécy in 1346, the French army disintegrated under a thick rain of arrows. In the battle of Agincourt (AH jin cor), fought in 1415, the longbow brought the English another major victory. Thousands of French soldiers were massacred, and France lost important members of its nobility.

Soon, both sides were using even deadlier new weapons: guns and cannons. Guns shot through armor, and cannon blasts pierced even the strongest castle walls. Clearly, the age of mounted knights and castles was ending.

Analyze Images Arrows shot from an English longbow (at right in the illustration) could travel a distance of about 500 yards. **Infer** What advantage would such a weapon provide the English, at the Battle of Crécy, against the French, with their less-powerful crossbows?

JOAN OF ARC
French heroine c. 1412–1431

- Joan of Arc was a farmer's daughter from northeastern France. She could not read or write but had a very strong faith in Christianity.

- Joan claimed that, from the age of thirteen, voices from God gave her a mission: to save France.

- At sixteen, Joan cut her hair short, dressed in men's clothes, and made an 11-day journey across enemy territory to meet Charles, the French crown prince.

- She persuaded Charles that she would get him crowned king. He let her lead an army against the English at Orléans, where she won a miraculous victory.

- In the spring of 1430, Joan was captured. After a trial for heresy, she was burned at the stake at age 19.

Critical Thinking How do you think Joan was able to accomplish so much, in spite of her lack of military training?

Joan of Arc Inspires the French By the early 1400s, France was losing the war. The tide was turned by a young peasant woman known as Joan of Arc. Joan claimed that voices from heaven had told her to dress in knight's clothing and lead the French army to victory. Joan led French soldiers against the English and won important victories. Joan was eventually captured by the English, tried for heresy, and burned at the stake. The French honor her today as a national heroine. The Catholic church declared her a saint.

Joan of Arc turned the fortunes of France during the Hundred Years' War. In 1453, England was finally defeated. However, the war had caused much suffering in France. During the early years of the war, the French suffered from the attacks of an even greater and **invisible** enemy—the plague.

Academic Vocabulary
invisible • *adj.*, not visible

☑ READING CHECK **Identify Main Ideas** Why did the Hundred Years' War decrease the value of armed knights?

What Was the Black Death?

In 1347, ten years after the start of the Hundred Years' War, Europe was struck by a terrible epidemic, a disease that spreads quickly through a population. The epidemic was the **bubonic plague**, a deadly infection. Victims usually died within a few days, often in terrible agony, with their bodies covered in buboes, or swellings. At the time, people called the epidemic the Great Dying. Much later it came to be known as the **Black Death.**

No one knew what caused the plague. It may have been carried by infected fleas that lived on rats. However, one form of the plague was transferred through the air and inhaled.

Quick Activity

Investigate the awful effects of disasters of the late Middle Ages in your 📓 Active Journal.

The Spread of the Disease The epidemic began in Central Asia. From there, it slowly spread along the trade **networks** that linked China, India, and the Middle East. Before reaching Europe, the Black Death had killed millions in Asia. In 1331, the plague struck in China and perhaps contributed to the end of Mongol rule there. Hubei province, near present-day Beijing, lost five million people, about 90 percent of its population. Western Central Asian cities, including Talas, Sarai, and Samarkand, suffered Black Death outbreaks. It is estimated that these cities lost at least 40 percent and up to 70 percent of their populations. The bubonic plague eventually killed an estimated 75 million people globally.

People infected with the plague rode merchant ships from the East to ports throughout Europe. The disease swept toward southern Europe from ports on the Black Sea, such as Caffa. First Italy, and then France, Spain, and England were struck. Travelers carried the plague up rivers and on overland trade routes, deep into the heart of Europe. In the decades that followed, the plague would often seem to ease, before returning with terrifying force.

The plague slowly tore apart European society. All societies are based on human contact; but as the plague spread, fear of contact drove many into isolation. The rich fled the towns, often taking the town doctors with them. In the towns, entire families were wiped out. As many as one third of all Europeans—tens of millions of people—died between 1347 and 1352, when the first wave of the plague finally ran its course. Thousands of villages throughout Europe became ghost towns. During the 1300s, the population of the Muslim world also dropped temporarily by about a third.

Academic Vocabulary

network • *n.*, a closely interconnected group of people or things

GEOGRAPHY **SKILLS**

The Black Death spread quickly throughout Europe from Asia.

1. **Region** Which areas of Europe were first affected by the plague?

2. **Use Visual Information** From which direction did the plague travel across Europe?

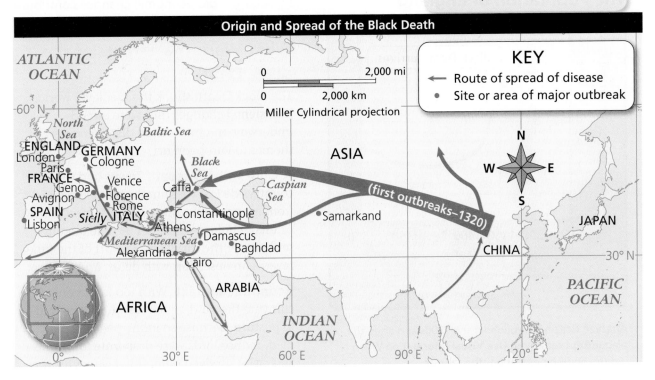

Origin and Spread of the Black Death

KEY
← Route of spread of disease
• Site or area of major outbreak

0   2,000 mi
0   2,000 km
Miller Cylindrical projection

INTERACTIVE

The Black Death

The Search for Scapegoats In the midst of this horror, terrified people looked for scapegoats. Scapegoats are people who are blamed for a problem that they did not cause. A friar in Paris reported how many Christians falsely blamed Jews for spreading the plague:

Primary Source

"Some said that this pestilence was caused by infection of the air and waters, since there was at this time no famine nor lack of food supplies, but on the contrary great abundance. As a result of this theory of infected water and air as the source of the plague, the Jews were suddenly and violently charged with infecting wells and water and corrupting the air. The whole world rose up against them cruelly on this account."

—Jean de Venette, *Chronicle*

In many European towns, Jews were exiled or massacred in anti-Jewish riots. In Strasbourg, the town council ordered that the city's 2,000 Jews convert to Christianity or be burned to death. Nine hundred Jews were burnt alive. The pope issued an order that Jews should not be killed or forced to convert. However, his order was widely ignored, and hundreds of Jewish communities were destroyed.

☑ READING CHECK Identify Cause and Effect How did economic changes contribute to the Black Death?

What Were the Effects of the Black Death?

The Black Death shook the medieval world. It hastened changes that were already underway and introduced disturbing new themes to European art.

A Culture of Despair Towns and the countryside lost vast numbers of people from every social rank: peasants, merchants, priests, scholars, nobles. A terrible gloom settled over the survivors. The art of the time reveals an obsession with death and disease.

Economic Impact With too few people to cultivate the land, much farmland reverted to pasture. Because so many peasants had died, manor lords were desperate for workers. Serfs who survived demanded wages for their

The Population of England

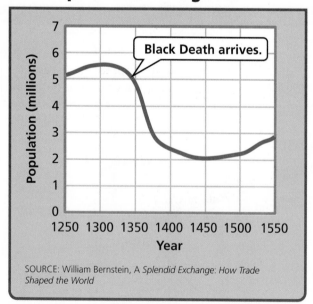

SOURCE: William Bernstein, *A Splendid Exchange: How Trade Shaped the World*

Analyze Graphs Throughout the 1200s and after, the plague kept returning. **Use Visual Information** When did the English population stop falling?

work and left manors to work where wages were highest. In response to such changes, manor lords tried to limit the serfs' movements and freeze wages at pre-plague levels.

As social tensions rose, peasants and townspeople across Europe revolted. In 1381, English peasants mounted the **Peasants' Revolt**, killing lords and burning manors. Although such revolts were crushed, feudalism never recovered.

Effects on the Church The Black Death also affected the Church. England, for example, lost an estimated 40 percent of its clergy. The Church was forced to hire men who were often uneducated. This in turn encouraged a movement to reform Church practices.

Toward a New World In the pre-plague medieval world, everyone's place in society was fixed at birth. After the Black Death, Western Europeans were less tied to a stable social and spiritual community. As social tensions increased, serfs defied manorial lords, and many began criticizing medieval traditions. Throughout Western Europe, the shock of the Black Death hastened the end of the Middle Ages and the arrival of the modern world.

Analyze Images A monk falls ill during a procession to pray for the end of the plague. **Infer** Why did the Black Death leave Europeans feeling helpless?

☑ READING CHECK **Understand Effects** What were the social effects of the Black Death?

☑ Lesson Check

Practice Vocabulary

1. For each key term, write a sentence explaining its role in the breakdown of medieval society: **Hundred Years' War, bubonic plague, Black Death, Peasants' Revolt**.

2. At first, the plague spread from Central Asia along trade **networks** that linked what areas?

Critical Thinking and Writing

3. **Analyze Cause and Effect** How did the Black Death help to end manorialism?

4. **Draw Inferences** Why did famine and wars weaken medieval society?

5. **Draw Conclusions** How did the Black Death shake people's confidence in the Church?

6. **Writing Workshop: Use Technology to Produce and Publish** Make use of appropriate technology to create and distribute your research paper. Consider your desired audience as you   decide in what form(s) to publish your work. Write notes about production and publishing your research in your 📓 Active Journal.

Giovanni Boccaccio, *The Decameron*

In *The Decameron,* Italian author Giovanni Boccaccio (1313–1375) described two different ways people of Florence reacted to the danger posed by the plague in 1348. Among the victims were his own father and stepmother.

◀ The plague ravages Florence, Italy, in 1348.

Reading and Vocabulary Support

① To live temperately is to avoid extremes.

② *Viands* are food. What challenges might people have faced in finding food during the plague?

③ Why did this group of people decide to talk only with themselves?

④ *Revel* means having fun.

⑤ A sovereign remedy is the best or only remedy.

⑥ *Aught* means anything.

Among whom there were those who thought that to live temperately ① and avoid all excess would count for much as a preservative against seizures of this kind. Wherefore they banded together, and, dissociating themselves from all others, formed communities in houses where there were no sick, and lived a separate and secluded life, which they regulated with the utmost care, avoiding every kind of luxury, but eating and drinking very moderately of the most delicate viands ② and the finest wines, holding converse with none but one another, lest tidings of sickness or death should reach them, ③ and diverting their minds with music and such other delights as they could devise. Others, the bias of whose minds was in the opposite direction, maintained, that to drink freely, frequent places of public resort, and take their pleasure with song and revel, ④ sparing to satisfy no appetite, and to laugh and mock at no event, was the sovereign remedy ⑤ for so great an evil: and that which they affirmed they also put in practice, so far as they were able, resorting day and night, now to this tavern, now to that, drinking with an entire disregard of rule or measure, and by preference making the houses of others, as it were, their inns, if they but saw in them aught ⑥ that was particularly to their taste or liking; which they were readily able to do, because the owners, seeing death imminent, had become as reckless of their property as of their lives; so that most of the houses were open to all comers, and no distinction was observed between the stranger who presented himself and the rightful lord.

—Boccaccio, *The Decameron*

Analyzing Primary Sources

Choose details from the excerpt to support your answers.

1. **Compare and Contrast** Describe the two responses that Boccaccio noted among his fellow Florentines to the threat of the plague.

2. **Draw Conclusions** What does this passage suggest about people's understanding of how to stop the plague?

3. **Synthesize** Using what you have learned about how the plague spread, which group of Florentines do you think gave themselves a better chance of avoiding sickness? Why?

Quest CONNECTIONS

Why was the plague likely to cause major changes to medieval society? Record your findings in your 📕 Active Journal.

Assess Credibility of a Source

Follow these steps to assess the credibility of a source.

1 **Identify who created the source and when it was created.** The first step in assessing the credibility of any source is identifying who wrote it and under what circumstances.

a. Who wrote this account?

b. When was it written?

2 **Identify the topic.** Define the specific subject matter the author is writing about. What contrast does Villani describe?

3 **Identify the facts, opinions, and possible inaccuracies or biases.** What facts are present, and are any important ones left out? What opinions are stated?

a. Does the author have an apparent point of view on the subject?

b. How would you describe Villani's attitude towards those who believe that God no longer has the power to punish them ("unstrung" refers to a bow string that can no longer fire an arrow)?

4 **Assess the credibility of the source.** Compare the source to other sources in terms of the facts included, the evenhandedness of their presentation, and the nature of the opinions and points of view. A source that seems heavily biased or incomplete may not be a reliable primary source.

a. What similiarities can you see between this account of the plague and the one by Boccaccio in the Primary Source feature?

b. What differences?

Primary Source

"Those few discreet folk who remained alive... believed that those whom God's grace had saved from death, having beheld the destruction of their neighbors,... would guard themselves from iniquity and sins, and would be full of love and charity one towards another. But no sooner had the plague ceased than we saw the contrary;... they forgot the past as though it had never been, and gave themselves up to a more shameful and disordered life than they had led before... Thus, almost the whole city, without any restraint whatsoever, rushed into disorderliness of life; and in other cities or provinces of the world things were the same or worse.... [T]here was no part of the world wherein men restrained themselves to live in temperance, when once they had escaped from the fury of the Lord; for now they thought that God's hand was unstrung."

—Matteo Villani, *Chronicle, 1348–1363*

TOPIC 10

Review and Assessment

VISUAL REVIEW

CONFLICTS IN MEDIEVAL EUROPEAN STATES

England	Holy Roman Empire	Spain
King John versus nobles leads to Magna Carta, Henry II versus Becket shows church-state conflict	Henry IV versus Gregory VII shows church-state conflict	Muslim-Christian tensions lead to war, Spain expels Muslims, Jews after Reconquista

THE CRUSADES

Causes	Effects
Christian pilgrims harassed in Holy Land, Byzantine emperor asks Pope for help, Pope calls for a Crusade to defend Constantinople and liberate Jerusalem, crusaders long for adventure, riches, and absolution	Many deaths of soldiers and civilians of people of all faiths, increased tension between Rome and Constantinople over sack of Byzantine capital, religious persecution rises in Europe, Byzantine empire is weakened, trade increases, ports grow rich, Europeans develop interest in other cultures, cultural exchange grows

READING REVIEW

Use the Take Notes and Practice Vocabulary activities in your Active Journal to review the Topic.

INTERACTIVE

Practice Vocabulary

Quest FINDINGS

Work with your team to create your comic book. Use the notes you made in your Active Journal.

ASSESSMENT

Vocabulary and Key Ideas

1. **Describe** Why was Henry IV excommunicated by Pope Gregory VII?

2. **Identify** What compromise was achieved by the Concordat of Worms?

3. **Recall** Why did the medieval German kingdom call itself the "Holy Roman Empire?"

4. **Define** What is habeas corpus?

5. **Identify Main Ideas** What effect did the Magna Carta have on the development of English government?

6. **Check Understanding** Why did the pope call for the Crusades?

7. **Identify** Which monarchs completed the Reconquista?

8. **Check Understanding** How did Joan of Arc change the course of the Hundred Years' War?

Critical Thinking and Writing

9. **Draw Conclusions** Why were people afraid of being excommunicated?

10. **Draw Inferences** What role does habeas corpus play in protecting democratic freedom?

11. **Summarize** Why did minorities in Europe suffer during the Crusades?

12. **Cite Evidence** In what ways did the Crusades encourage trade?

13. **Draw Conclusions** What was the connection between international trade and the spread of the plague?

14. **Revisit the Essential Question** In what ways was the Black Death a cause of change in medieval European society?

15. **Writer's Workshop: Write a Research Paper** Using your notes and research, write a brief account of some aspect of Jewish life in medieval Europe.

Analyze Primary Sources

16. The writer of the letter below is describing the effects of the
    A. Crusades.
    B. bubonic plague.
    C. expulsion of Jews from Spain.
    D. Hundred Years' War.

    "I wish, my brother, that I had never been born, or at least had died before these times.
    . . . When has any such thing ever been heard or seen; in what annals has it ever been read that houses were left vacant, cities deserted, the countryside neglected, the fields too small for the dead to be buried, and a fearful and universal solitude over the whole earth?"

Analyze Maps

17. Which letter represents Granada? What happened here in 1492?

18. Which letter represents Caffa? What role did this city play in the spread of the Black Death?

19. Which letter represents Hastings? What important event occurred here?

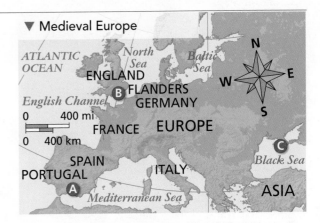
▼ Medieval Europe

The Islamic World and South Asia

(610–1550)

GO ONLINE
to access your
digital course

 VIDEO

 AUDIO

 ETEXT

 INTERACTIVE

 WRITING

 GAMES

 WORKSHEET

 ASSESSMENT

Go back over 1,400 years

to the region where Islam was born. Trade, travel, migration, and conquest spread new ideas throughout Asia and beyond. Islam, Hinduism, and Buddhism grew and spread. Sikhism formed. These religions changed over time.

Explore The Essential Question

How do ideas grow and spread?

The Islamic world and South Asia were ruled by different dynasties and empires. How did the exchange of ideas affect different cultures? How did ideas from one culture change as they merged with those of different cultures? Unlock the Essential Question in your Active Journal.

Watch

NBC LEARN

BOUNCE TO ACTIVATE ▶ VIDEO

Advances in Medicine

Watch the video on scientific and medical achievements to learn about the advancements and key thinkers of this time period.

Read

about the different dynasties, empires, and cultures that converged in the Islamic world and in South Asia.

TOPIC 11

The Islamic World and South Asia (610–1550)

Learn more about the Islamic world and South Asia by making your own map and timeline in your 📙 Active Journal.

 INTERACTIVE

Topic Map

Where was the Islamic world?

The Arab Muslim empire spread from the Arabian Peninsula in Southwest Asia into Spain, North Africa, and Persia. Locate these places on the map.

 INTERACTIVE

Topic Timeline

What happened and when?

Dynasties were building empires . . . new religions and other ideas were forming, being shared, and spreading. Explore the timeline to see some of what was happening in Southwest Asia and South Asia and the rest of the world.

610
According to Islam, Muhammad receives his first revelations.

762
Baghdad founded as capital of Arab Muslim empire.

970
Al-Azhar University, a center of Islamic learning, is founded in Cairo.

TOPIC EVENTS

| 500 | 700 | 900 |

WORLD EVENTS

800
Charlemagne is crowned Holy Roman Emperor.

EUROPE
SPAIN
Rome
Black Sea
Caspian Sea
Aral Sea
Constantinople
ASIA
Strait of Gibraltar
Mediterranean Sea
SYRIA
Damascus
Baghdad
PERSIAN EMPIRE
MOROCCO
Cairo
Jerusalem
Persian Gulf
NORTH AFRICA
EGYPT
Medina
Mecca
ARABIA
Arabian Sea
Red Sea
YEMEN
Gulf of Aden
INDIAN OCEAN

0   1,000 mi
0   1,000 km
Miller Cylindrical projection

KEY
Muslim lands at the death of Muhammad, 632
Muslim world, 1000

Who will you meet?

Ibn Sina made great advancements in medicine and science.

Rumi was a Sufi mystic poet and the founder of the Mawlawiyah order.

Akbar showed religious tolerance and helped build the Mughal empire.

1453
Ottoman Turks conquer Constantinople.

1469
Sikhism founded in South Asia.

c. 1300
The Ottoman Empire is founded by Osman I.

1100   1300   1500   1700

1368
The Ming dynasty is founded in China.

1492
Christopher Columbus reaches the Caribbean Islands.

Quest

Growth of Muslim Empires

▼ Minarets like this are towers used to call Muslims to prayer.

Quest KICK OFF

You have been chosen to select the key events that best show the different Muslim empires that formed and expanded across Southwest Asia, South Asia, and beyond! Don't forget to have your colored pencils ready!

What key Muslim empires formed and expanded during this time?

How did Muslim empires affect other empires and dynasties throughout the region? Explore the Essential Question "How do ideas grow and spread?" in this Quest.

1 Ask Questions

Selecting key Muslim empires to feature on your timeline is part of the challenge, but you must also draw pictures to "show" what they did and whom they affected. Write a list of questions in your 📓 Active Journal to help you determine which Muslim empires to choose.

2 Investigate

As you read the lessons in this Topic, look for **Quest** CONNECTIONS that provide information on key Muslim empires and how they affected other empires and dynasties. Take notes and write ideas for illustrations in your 📓 Active Journal.

3 Conduct Research

Next, research information you need to answer your questions. Write down your notes in your 📓 Active Journal.

Quest FINDINGS

4 Make an Illustrated Timeline

At the end of the Topic, you will create an illustrated timeline of events related to Muslim empires that formed, expanded, and affected other empires and dynasties. Get help for creating your illustrated timeline in your 📓 Active Journal.

Origins of Islam

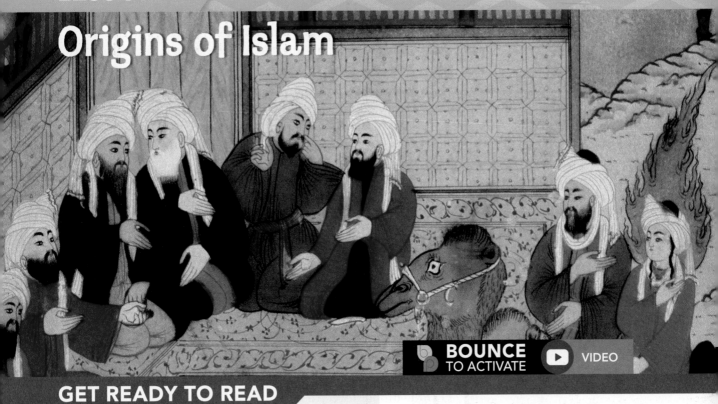

BOUNCE TO ACTIVATE   ▶ VIDEO

GET READY TO READ

START UP

This painting shows a trader arriving in the oasis of Mecca. With him is his nephew, who would become the grandfather of Muhammad. Write down two impressions this image gives you about Mecca.

GUIDING QUESTIONS

- What impact did the environment have on life in Arabia?
- What role did Muhammad play in the development of Islam?
- Why was Muhammad's move from Mecca to Medina important?

TAKE NOTES

Literacy Skills: Identify Main Ideas
Use the graphic organizer in your 📓 Active Journal to take notes as you read the lesson.

PRACTICE VOCABULARY

Use the vocabulary activity in your 📓 Active Journal to practice the vocabulary words.

Vocabulary		Academic Vocabulary
oasis	revelation	oppose
nomad	Hijrah	expand
prophet		

Today, Islam is the world's second-most widely practiced faith, after Christianity. It emerged in the 600s in one of the harshest climate regions in the world.

The Arabian Setting

Arabia is a huge peninsula. It is nearly twice the size of Alaska. It lies south of modern-day Iraq and across the Red Sea from eastern Africa. The geography of Arabia influenced its history and culture.

An Arid Environment Arabia receives little rain and has no permanent rivers. Much of Arabia is covered by desert. Summer temperatures can soar to more than 120 degrees Fahrenheit. The harsh environment helped keep invaders out of Arabia for most of its history.

Arabia's climate limited its population. The people depended on oases (oh AY seez) for water. An **oasis** is a place in a desert where water can be found, usually from a spring. Most early settlement occurred around oases in the Hijaz, a mountainous region along the western coast of Arabia.

Quick Activity

Explore the map of Arabia and then write a travel blog about the climate in your ▢ Active Journal.

As a peninsula, Arabia is surrounded on three sides by water. Arabian sailors crossed the seas around them to trade with East Africa, India, and China. Coasts along the peninsula provide some fertile soil for farming. Date palms thrive here as they are able to withstand the salty soils.

North of the peninsula lies a more fertile area that supported civilizations in Mesopotamia and Persia. In ancient times, farmers in Mesopotamia used irrigation to transport water from the Tigris and Euphrates rivers to their crops.

Life in Arabia Before Islam The Arabs, the people of Arabia, practiced two different ways of life in ancient times. Some were **nomads**. They had no fixed homes. Others were sedentary, or settled. Both nomadic and settled Arabs belonged to tribes. They worshiped many gods and tribal spirits.

Arab nomads, known as Bedouins, lived in rural desert areas. They traveled from oasis to oasis with their flocks of sheep, goats, and camels. Bedouins were skilled warriors. They raided other tribes for animals and goods. Sedentary Arabs lived as farmers and merchants. Merchants set up shops along Arabia's main trade route. Camel caravans stopped at these towns for water, food, and supplies.

Trade brought wealth and attracted settlers. Jews and Christians moved to towns in the Hijaz. The largest town, Mecca, became a trading center. It was there, around 570, that Muhammad (mu HAHM mad) was born. Muhammad was the first person to preach the religion of Islam.

☑ **READING CHECK** **Identify Cause and Effect** How did the geography of the Arabian Peninsula affect settlement patterns?

GEOGRAPHY SKILLS

The Arabian Peninsula is located in the region of Southwest Asia, where arid and semiarid conditions make it challenging to live.

1. **Region** What is the difference in rainfall across the region?

2. **Compare and Contrast** Compare the climates of the Arabian Peninsula and the land north of the peninsula.

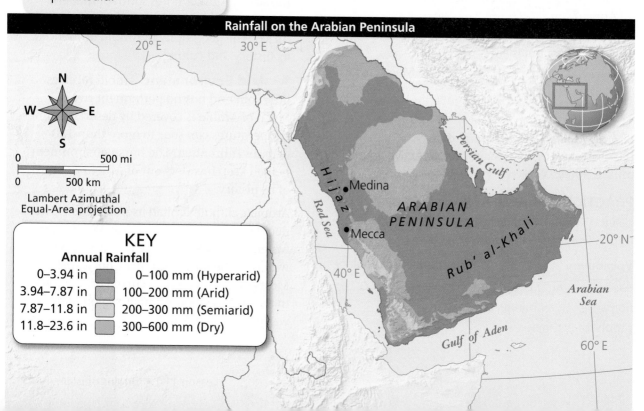

Rainfall on the Arabian Peninsula

N W E S

0 — 500 mi
0 — 500 km
Lambert Azimuthal Equal-Area projection

KEY
Annual Rainfall

0–3.94 in	▢	0–100 mm (Hyperarid)
3.94–7.87 in	▢	100–200 mm (Arid)
7.87–11.8 in	▢	200–300 mm (Semiarid)
11.8–23.6 in	▢	300–600 mm (Dry)

Hijaz
Red Sea
Medina
Mecca
ARABIAN PENINSULA
Persian Gulf
Rub' al-Khali
Arabian Sea
Gulf of Aden
20° E 30° E 40° E 60° E 20° N

The Rise of Islam

Muslims, people who practice Islam, consider Muhammad the prophet of their religion. A **prophet** is a person believed to be chosen by God as a messenger to bring truth to the people.

Mecca Muhammad was born in Mecca, a town in the Hijaz. At the time of Muhammad's birth, Mecca was a religious center. It had an important shrine called the Kaaba where Arabs came to worship their gods. Every year, a religious fair attracted thousands of people.

Muhammad's Early Life Muhammad was orphaned at an early age. He was raised by close relatives. At 25, he married a wealthy, widowed merchant named Khadija. Muhammad prospered in business, but he was critical of Meccan society. All around him, he saw greed, corruption, and violence.

Seeking peace of mind, Muhammad often retreated to a cave outside Mecca to pray and reflect. Muslims believe that one night, in 610, the angel Gabriel appeared before Muhammad in the cave. Gabriel told him to recite, or say out loud, messages from God.

Primary Source

Read: Your Lord is the Most Bountiful One. Who, by the pen, taught man what he did not know.

—Quran 96:1–5

Muslims believe Gabriel brought more messages from God, and Muhammad passed these on to his followers, who memorized them. They were later recorded in the Quran (koo RAHN), Islam's holy book.

Preaching a New Message Muhammad began to preach in the streets of Mecca. He told Arabs to worship only one God and to change many of their behaviors. He said that he had received **revelations**, or revealed truths from God. He said this was the same God who had spoken to Abraham, Jesus, and other figures of Judaism and Christianity. For this reason, Islam is called an Abrahamic religion. Muhammad respected those two religions. But Muslims believe he was the final prophet.

Analyze Images The photo shows a group of Bedouins in the desert. **Synthesize Visual Information** What does the photo tell you about the kinds of challenges people would face living in the Arabian desert?

 INTERACTIVE

Geography of the Arabian Peninsula

▲ Because Islam prohibits the depiction of either humans or animals in religious art, Muhammad is often represented by his name in calligraphy.

Academic Vocabulary

oppose • *v.*, to try to stop or defeat something

Academic Vocabulary

expand • *v.*, to grow, get bigger

Muhammad began to win believers, but many Meccans **opposed** Islam. The Meccans feared that the beliefs preached by Muhammad would reduce their status and wealth as keepers of the Kaaba. They also feared he would anger the gods they worshiped. They began to persecute Muhammad and other Muslims.

The Hijrah In 622, Muhammad and his fellow Muslims fled Mecca. They moved to the town of Medina, about 275 miles to the north. The move to Medina was called the **Hijrah**, which is the Arabic word for migration.

In Medina, Muhammad continued his preaching. He became Medina's political and military leader. The Muslims of Medina fought with the people of Mecca. The Meccans tried to conquer Medina, but Muhammad defeated them. After several key Muslim victories, Mecca's resistance crumbled.

In 630, Muhammad returned to Mecca as its ruler. He banned worship of the old gods and organized the Muslim community. Muhammad destroyed statues of the gods at the Kaaba and rededicated it as an Islamic holy site. The Kaaba became a place for Muslim pilgrims, or people who travel for religious reasons, to visit.

Muhammad led desert tribes to conquer all of the Arabian Peninsula. Quickly, the Muslims united most of Arabia under their rule. Muhammad died, but his death did not halt the spread of his faith. United by Islam, Arabs preached their religion and **expanded** their rule across Southwest Asia and to many other parts of the world.

☑ **READING CHECK** Compare and Contrast According to Islam, how is Muhammad both similar to and different from earlier prophets?

☑ Lesson 1 Check

Practice Vocabulary

1. What is an **oasis**, and how did it affect life on the Arabian Peninsula?

2. How did the climate of the Arabian Peninsula influence the way **nomads** lived?

3. What religion do Muslims practice?

Critical Thinking and Writing

4. **Summarize** Describe Arabia's climate.

5. **Compare and Contrast** How is Islam different from the religion practiced by Arabs in earlier times?

6. **Summarize** Describe what happened to the Muslim community in the years immediately following the Hijrah.

7. **Writing Workshop: Introduce Claims** Write a sentence in your 📕 Active Journal that states your claim about whether you think conquest or trade was the key factor in the growth of Islamic empires. This sentence will become the claim in your argumentative essay that you will write at the end of the Topic.

Beliefs of Islam

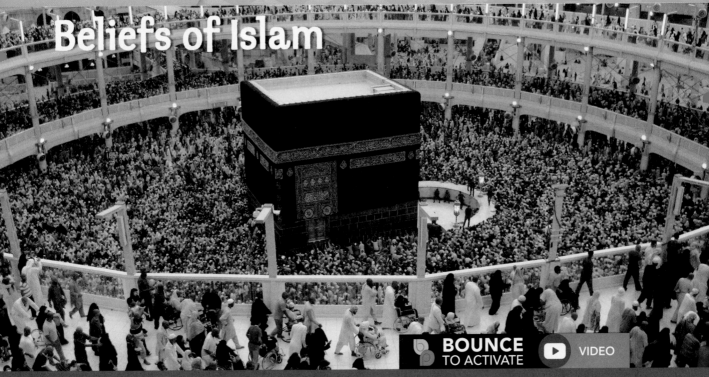

GET READY TO READ

START UP

Examine the photograph of Muslim pilgrims visiting a holy site in the city of Mecca. Why do you think visiting Mecca is seen as a religious duty by Muslims?

GUIDING QUESTIONS

- What are the main sources of Islamic teachings?
- What do Muslims believe about God and the afterlife?
- What are the basic duties and rules all Muslims are expected to follow?

TAKE NOTES

Literacy Skills: Summarize

Use the graphic organizer in your 🗐 Active Journal to take notes as you read the lesson.

PRACTICE VOCABULARY

Use the vocabulary activity in your 🗐 Active Journal to practice the vocabulary words.

Vocabulary		Academic Vocabulary
Quran	mosque	interpret
Sunnah	Sharia	submission
hajj		

If you were visiting any Muslim city in the world, you would likely wake up at dawn hearing the call to prayer chanted from one of the city's houses of worship. In Arabic, you would hear "God is great. I bear witness that there is no God but God. I bear witness that Muhammad is the messenger of God. Come to worship." This call contains the most important beliefs of Islam—belief in one all-powerful God, and belief that Muhammad was God's final messenger to human beings.

What Are the Sources of Islamic Teachings?

The **Quran** is Islam's holy book. It is also the main source of Islamic teaching.

The Quran Muslims believe that the Quran is the record of God's revelations to Muhammad over a period of nearly 23 years. They believe that those revelations began in a cave outside Mecca in the year 610, and continued for the rest of Muhammad's life, until his death in 632.

▲ Copy of the Quran in Arabic

According to Islamic tradition, Muhammad recited the words that had been revealed to him. His followers memorized what Muhammad told them and wrote his messages down. They compiled them into a book called the Quran not long after Muhammad's death. It has remained unchanged since then.

The Quran consists of 114 chapters in verse form. The verses discuss the nature of God, creation, and the human soul. They also address moral, legal, and family issues. Much of the Quran is written in a poetic style that many Arabic speakers find beautiful.

To Muslims, the Quran is the word of God. They recite its passages during daily prayers and on special occasions. They believe that it must be studied in Arabic, the language in which it is written. Muslims throughout the world recite the Quran only in Arabic. Although most Muslims today do not speak Arabic as their home language, the language of the Quran unites all Muslims.

Muslims treat the Quran with great devotion. They take special care of copies of the book. They commit passages to memory. Children often first learn reading and writing from the Quran.

The Sunnah Another key source of Islamic thought is the **Sunnah** (SOON ah), or traditions of Muhammad. The Sunnah refers to the words and actions of Muhammad and his companions. He is considered by Muslims to be the best role model. The Sunnah provides Muslims with guidelines for living a proper life. It also helps believers **interpret** difficult parts of the Quran.

Academic Vocabulary

interpret • v., to explain, give the meaning of

The Sunnah is based on accounts from people who knew Muhammad during his lifetime. They recorded his sayings and actions in a collection of writings called the Hadith. The Hadith is the written record of the Sunnah. Many of its passages deal with Islamic law. Others promote moral or ethical concepts. Here is one example:

Primary Source

He who eats his fill while his neighbor goes without food is not a believer.

—Hadith

✓ **READING CHECK** **Draw Conclusions** Why do you think Muslims study the Quran in the original Arabic?

Islamic Beliefs About God

A number of core beliefs are central to Islam. They are stressed in the Quran and in Islamic tradition.

Monotheism The principal belief of Islam is that there is only one God. He created the universe and all things in it. Muslims believe this is the same God that Jews and Christians worship. Muslims usually refer to God as *Allah*, which is simply the word for "God" in Arabic.

Muslims also believe that Muhammad was a prophet, God's messenger, but that he had no divine, or godlike, power himself. Muslims believe that important Jewish and Christian religious figures like Abraham, Moses, and Jesus were also prophets and that Muhammad is part of this tradition.

Unlike Muslims, Jews and Christians do not believe that Muhammad was a prophet. Unlike Christians, Muslims view Jesus as a human prophet. Most Christians believe Jesus was both God and man.

Submission to God's Will The word *Islam* means "**submission**" in Arabic. A Muslim is one who has submitted to God's will. This means trying to please God by following his teachings.

The Soul and Afterlife Like Christianity, Islam teaches that each person has a soul that keeps living after a person dies and has the freedom to choose between good and evil, which affect what happens to his or her soul after death. The Muslim concept of afterlife also includes the belief that non-believers, or those who do not accept Allah as God, are damned, while the faithful will be rewarded in paradise.

☑ READING CHECK **Identify Main Ideas** Write a sentence explaining how Muslims view Muhammad.

What Are the Five Pillars of Islam?

Muslims have five key religious duties known as the Five Pillars.

- **Belief** The first pillar is stating a belief that "there is no god but God, and Muhammad is the messenger of God."

- **Prayer** It is a religious duty for Muslims to pray five times a day.

- **Charity** Muslims must give charity to the needy. Devout Muslims share 2.5 percent of their wealth or more each year.

- **Fasting** Fasting means not eating or drinking for a period of time. During Ramadan, a month on the Islamic calendar, Muslims fast between daybreak and sunset. Muslims believe that fasting tests their commitment to God and reminds them of the hunger of the poor. The end of Ramadan is marked by an important holiday, Eid al-Fitr (eed al fitter), or Festival of the Breaking of the Fast.

▶ INTERACTIVE

The Five Pillars of Islam

Academic Vocabulary
submission • *n.*, giving control over yourself to someone else

Analyze Images A beggar seeks alms from a wealthy Muslim. **Identify Main Ideas** How does this picture illustrate one of the Five Pillars of Islam?

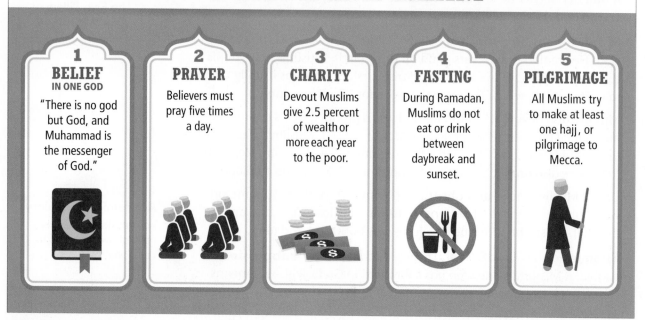

FIVE PILLARS OF ISLAM

1 BELIEF IN ONE GOD
"There is no god but God, and Muhammad is the messenger of God."

2 PRAYER
Believers must pray five times a day.

3 CHARITY
Devout Muslims give 2.5 percent of wealth or more each year to the poor.

4 FASTING
During Ramadan, Muslims do not eat or drink between daybreak and sunset.

5 PILGRIMAGE
All Muslims try to make at least one hajj, or pilgrimage to Mecca.

Analyze Charts Examine the infographic that explains the Five Pillars of Islam. **Identify Main Ideas** Which of these pillars do you think Muslims would consider the most important? Why?

• **Pilgrimage** The Quran instructs every Muslim to make the **hajj**, or pilgrimage to the holy city of Mecca, at least once, if possible. A pilgrimage is a journey to a sacred place or shrine. By bringing Muslims from all parts of the world together every year, the hajj strengthens the global community of Muslims.

☑ READING CHECK **Infer** Why do you think these five duties are called "Pillars" of Islam?

Islamic Prayer, Pilgrimage, and Law

Islam plays a large role in the daily lives of Muslims. It helps shape society in Muslim-majority nations.

Prayer and Worship Prayer and worship are key elements of daily life for Muslims. At five specific times each day, Muslims stop what they are doing to pray. Before praying, Muslims remove their shoes and wash their hands and feet. This is called an ablution. They may bow several times. Then, facing in the direction of Mecca, they kneel and pray.

A Muslim house of worship is called a **mosque**. At a mosque, the community participates in group prayer and other religious activities. Mosques are usually found at the heart of Muslim-majority towns or cities. Their features may differ, but all mosques contain a prayer hall facing in the direction of Mecca. They usually include a special place for the imam, or religious leader, to stand to give sermons. A minaret is attached to most mosques. Minarets are towers from which a man called a muezzin sings the call to prayer. On Fridays, Muslims may gather at a mosque for group worship and to hear a sermon.

Did you know?

Between 3 and 5 million Muslims live in the United States. California has the largest Muslim population of any state.

The Hajj During the hajj, pilgrims take part in many rituals. The most important is walking in a circle around the Kaaba. The Kaaba is a cubelike building in the courtyard of the Grand Mosque in Mecca. Muslims believe that in ancient times, Abraham and his son Ishmael built the Kaaba as a place to worship God. During the hajj, Muslims also visit the place where Muhammad gave his last sermon. The hajj reminds Muslims of Abraham, Ishmael, and Muhammad. It connects Muslims to their religious history.

Islamic Law Muhammad taught that everyday life was no different from religious life. Living a proper life meant following God's laws as revealed in the Quran and the Sunnah. These laws are collected in the Islamic law code known as the **Sharia**. The Arabic word *Sharia* means "the way," as in the right way to act.

The Quran and the Sunnah served as sources for the Sharia. But those sources could not cover every situation that might come up. Religious scholars used their judgment and knowledge of the Quran and Sunnah to apply the Sharia to new situations.

By the 900s, Muslim scholars had established the Sharia as a fixed set of laws. In this form it was used by Muslim societies for centuries. In the 1800s, however, governments in some Muslim-majority lands began replacing parts of Sharia law with law codes based on European models. Other parts of the Sharia were reformed. Today, law codes in some Muslim nations are closely based on Sharia. Others are more secular, or nonreligious.

☑ **READING CHECK** Compare and Contrast How is the Sharia related the Quran?

▼ A Muslim family breaks their Ramadan fast with a special meal known as iftar.

☑ Lesson 2 Check

Practice Vocabulary

1. What is the **Quran**? What do Muslims believe about it?

2. Who must go on the **hajj**, and how often must they go?

Critical Thinking and Writing

3. **Use Evidence** What are the two main sources of Islamic teaching? Use evidence from the text to describe them.

4. **Summarize** What role do the Five Pillars of Islam have in a Muslim's life?

5. **Identify Cause and Effect** How does the hajj help strengthen the community of Muslims around the world?

6. **Writing Workshop: Support Claims** In your 📓 Active Journal, identify two facts in this lesson that you think might help explain why Islam spread. These facts will help you support the claim in your argumentative essay that you will write at the end of the Topic.

The Sunnah

In addition to the Qu'ran, the Islamic holy scripture, Muslims also follow the Sunnah, which is a collection of sayings, practices, and teachings of Muhammad. The practical examples contained in the Sunnah are meant to give guidance to the followers of Islam as they go about their daily lives.

◄ A Muslim woman reads the Sunnah.

Reading and Vocabulary Support

(1) Abu Aiub Al-Ansari was a friend and supporter of Muhammad and also a celebrated military leader.

(2) This represents the phrase, "Peace be upon him."

(3) Why do you think people ask "What is the matter with him?" after the man asks this question?

(4) Something that is obligatory is something you are required or obligated to do.

(5) Your kith are your friends and people you know, and your kin are your family.

Narrated Abu Aiyub Al-Ansari **(1)**:

A man said, "O Allah's Messenger! **(2)** Inform me of a deed which will make me enter Paradise." The people said, "What is the matter with him? What is the matter with him?" **(3)** Allah's Messenger said, "He has something to ask (what he needs greatly)." The Prophet said (to him), (In order to enter Paradise) you should worship Allah and join none in worship with Him: You should offer prayers perfectly, give obligatory **(4)** charity (Zakat), and keep good relations with your Kith and kin." **(5)**

—The Sunnah, Book 78, Hadith 14

Analyzing Primary Sources

1. **Apply Concepts** Connecting what you have already learned about Islam with the excerpt from the *Sunnah*, reread the first sentence of the passage. Who is "Allah's Messenger"?

2. **Paraphrase** According to this passage, what is Allah's message to the man?

3. **Identify Implied Main Ideas** What does the man who speaks to the Prophet believe that he will receive for following this teaching?

Expansion of the Muslim World

GET READY TO READ

START UP

An Ottoman sultan built the Selimiye Mosque in what used to be part of the Byzantine empire. What does this suggest about the spread of Islam?

GUIDING QUESTIONS

- Why was the Muslim empire able to expand so rapidly?
- How did Islam develop and change after the death of Muhammad?
- How did Islam spread to multiple cultures and diverse empires?

TAKE NOTES

Literacy Skills: Sequence

Use the graphic organizer in your 📓 Active Journal to take notes as you read the lesson.

PRACTICE VOCABULARY

Use the vocabulary activity in your 📓 Active Journal to practice the vocabulary words.

Vocabulary		Academic Vocabulary
caliph	dynasty	
Sunni	Sufism	devotion
Shia	sultan	circumstance

At the time of Muhammad's death in 632, many tribes of Bedouin warriors had converted to Islam. United by Islam, these Arab tribes formed a powerful and skilled army. They began an expansion of Arab Muslim rule across three continents.

How Did Islam Spread?

Arab Muslim armies began to conquer new territory in Arabia. After Muhammad's death, some Arab tribes rebelled against Muslim rule, but the Muslims defeated them. After securing Arabia, Arab Muslim soldiers defeated larger rivals in nearby lands.

Conquest of the Persian Sasanian Empire Founded in 224, the Sasanian dynasty was the successor to the ancient Persian empire. The Sasanian Persian empire became the most powerful state in Southwestern Asia. It was a rival to Rome in its final years, as well as a major threat to the Byzantine empire. Most of its people practiced forms of the ancient Persian religion of Zoroastrianism, but the empire was also home to many Jews and Christians.

In 651, Muslim armies conquered the Sasanian empire. Islam replaced Zoroastrianism as the dominant religion. The defeat of the Sasanian Persian empire marked the end of the last major Mesopotamian civilization.

Additional Conquests Arab Muslim armies also took the region of Palestine, as well as Syria, Egypt, and much of the Byzantine empire. Then they moved into western Afghanistan and northern Pakistan. They conquered North Africa and Spain. By 800, Muslims ruled a vast empire.

Islam Spreads As the Arab Muslims built their empire, Islam spread peacefully as well, both inside the empire and to the lands beyond its borders. This happened at different speeds in different regions. For example, most western North Africans were quick to convert to Islam, while most Egyptians remained Christian for centuries. Along with Islam, the Arabic language spread to many parts of the empire.

Merchants traveled outside the empire to many new lands. They carried their faith with them. Missionaries spreading Islam often accompanied traders to preach their faith. Over time, many people in South Asia, Southeast Asia, and Africa turned to Islam.

Reasons for Success Early Arab Muslims built a massive empire in a short period of time. Several factors led to Muslim success. One was the decline of the Persian and the Byzantine empires. Years of warfare had left those large empires weak and vulnerable.

A second factor was the ability and **devotion** of Muslim warriors. They had the fighting skills needed to win battles. Their belief that they were doing God's will may have spurred them to fight especially hard.

Academic Vocabulary
devotion • *n.*, dedication, loyalty

GEOGRAPHY **SKILLS**

The Arab Muslim empire primarily spread north, northwest, and northeast throughout Southwest Asia, North Africa, and Spain.

1. **Location** Which cities were part of the Arab Muslim empire before 632?

2. **Interaction** What were three regions conquered by early Arab Muslims?

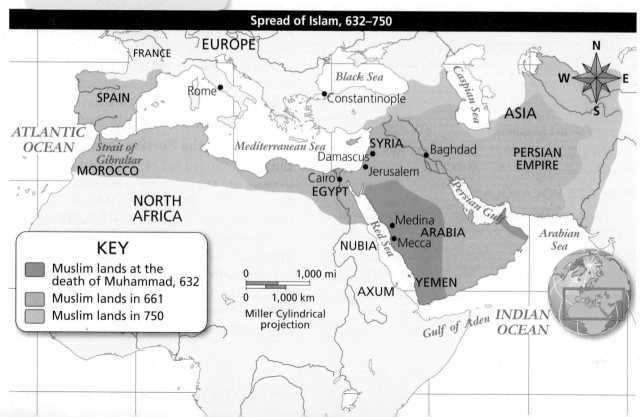

Spread of Islam, 632–750

KEY
- Muslim lands at the death of Muhammad, 632
- Muslim lands in 661
- Muslim lands in 750

0   1,000 mi
0   1,000 km
Miller Cylindrical projection

Religious toleration also helped the Arab Muslim empire expand. Muslims conquered lands where large numbers of Jews and Christians lived. In many areas, Christians remained a majority for centuries, and Jews remained a large presence. After their initial conquests, Muslims did not force their religion on these monotheistic groups, though some later Muslim rulers did. This policy of relative toleration made conquered peoples less likely to rebel. It also set apart areas under Islamic rule from the Byzantine empire, which more often persecuted Jews and non-Orthodox Christians.

Many conquered people converted to Islam to gain political or economic power. Others were attracted to Islam's promise of a direct path to God and salvation. Islam emphasized the equality of all Muslims and justice in human affairs.

☑ **READING CHECK** **Identify Main Ideas** Why did Islam spread and appeal to non-Muslims?

What Was Society Like in the Arab Muslim Empire?

Islam stressed the equality of all Muslim believers. Still, social divisions existed in the Arab Muslim empire.

Distinct Social Divisions In the early days of the Arab Muslim empire, Muslim society was split into four main groups. Arab Muslims were at the top. Next came non-Arab Muslims. The third group consisted of Jews and Christians, although some Jews and Christians rose to high positions in society as the Islamic empire expanded. Slaves were the lowest class.

Slaves were usually non-Muslims captured in war. They did not have all the rights of free people, but Islam required that they should be treated kindly and encouraged freeing slaves. Under some Muslim rulers, many slaves served as soldiers or key government officials. Some slaves even became rulers themselves.

Roles of Men and Women The Quran and the Sharia laid out clear roles for men and women. Men were expected to support their families and to conduct their business in public. Women customarily stayed at home, although some women rose to important positions. In general, however, women had fewer rights than men.

Still, overall, Islam improved conditions for women. Before the development of Islam, Arab women had virtually no rights. They were considered "family property" and were often secluded. Under the Sharia, women and men had religious equality.

▲ These women are wearing two different types of head coverings, a custom that predates the arrival of Islam in the Mediterranean and Persia.

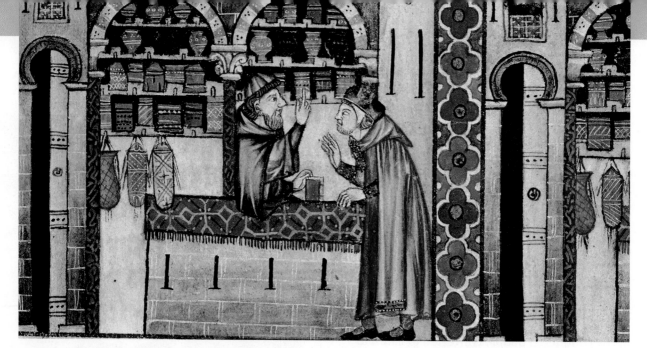

Analyze Images A Jewish apothecary, or pharmacist, sells medicine in a Spanish market. **Draw Conclusions** What does this tell you about life in Muslim regions?

Treatment of Non-Muslims The Arab empire was somewhat tolerant of Jews and Christians. Muslims regarded their scriptures as sacred, so they respected Jews and Christians as "People of the Book." Jews and Christians were allowed to practice their faiths and govern themselves. Still, they had to pay a tax and faced other restrictions. Some Muslim leaders did force non-Muslims to convert to Islam.

Followers of other religions such as Buddhism, Hinduism, and Zoroastrianism were treated much more harshly. Sometimes, their places of worship and holy books were destroyed because they were not considered People of the Book.

☑ **READING CHECK** **Identify Cause and Effect** How was the role of women affected by living under the Arab Muslim empire?

The Caliphs

After Muhammad died, rulers called **caliphs** (KAY lifs) led the Muslim community and empire. In Arabic, *caliph* means "successor," as in successor to Muhammad. A state run by a caliph is a caliphate.

The Succession Question But who was to be the first caliph? Who could follow a man who, for Muslims, was the messenger of God? This difficult issue split Muslims into two competing groups.

Most Muslims believed that the community needed a leader with political skills. They supported Muhammad's main advisor, Abu Bakr, who became the first caliph. Members of this group became known as **Sunnis** (SOO neez) because they hold the Sunnah in high regard.

A minority of Muslims believed that only Muhammad's relatives should become caliph. They were called **Shias** (SHEE uz), or supporters, because they supported Ali, Muhammad's cousin and son-in-law.

The First Caliphs Four caliphs ruled the Arab Muslim empire in its earliest years. Because each had close ties to Muhammad and was guided by Muslim principles, Sunni Muslims referred to them as the "rightly guided caliphs." They ruled the growing empire from Medina.

Quest CONNECTIONS

How did the spread of Islam cause cultural changes within empires? Record your findings in your 📓 Active Journal.

Muhammad's cousin Ali, favored by Shias, finally became the fourth caliph in 656. But by then, he had many enemies. In the fifth year of his reign, he was assassinated. After that, the caliphate passed to the powerful Umayyad family.

The Umayyad Dynasty Begins The Umayyads founded the first Muslim dynasty. A **dynasty** is a family that passes down political power from one relative to another. The Umayyads moved the empire's capital from Medina to Damascus, an ancient city in Syria.

Under the Umayyads, the Arab Muslim empire reached its greatest size, conquering part of the Byzantine Empire and all of the Persian (Sasanian) Empire.

Not all of this expansion came through conquest. Muslim leaders also signed treaties, or written agreements, with foreign lands. People might agree to accept Ummayyad rule in exchange for certain rights. In 688, the caliph and the Byzantine emperor signed a treaty agreeing to joint rule of the island of Cyprus, an agreement that lasted more than 300 years.

Expansion brought Arabs into contact with other cultures. Many non-Arabs adopted Islam and some began to speak Arabic. In turn, non-Arab cultures influenced the Arab conquerors. A distinct Muslim civilization emerged that blended these cultures.

How Did Cultures Change? In some cases, conquered peoples accepted Islam because it offered social, economic, and political advantages. Some converts changed their names and their social status. They befriended and socialized with fellow Muslims.

Analyze Images This gold dinar, dating from 695–696, shows a Umayyad caliph in traditional Arab dress and holding a sword. **Synthesize** What does the caliph's picture on the dinar tell you about his importance in Muslim society?

 INTERACTIVE

The Spread of Islam

Shias and Sunnis

SHIAS

- Believe only descendants of Muhammad should be chosen as caliphs
- Are a minority of Muslims

- Allah as only God
- Quran
- Five Pillars of Islam
- Imams are divinely inspired religious leaders

SUNNIS

- Believe any pious male member of the Muslim community can be chosen as a caliph
- Are the majority of Muslims

Analyze Diagrams The diagram shows how Sunni and Shia beliefs were alike and different. **Compare and Contrast** What beliefs did Sunni and Shia Muslims share? In what ways are they different?

Over time, those who converted to Islam adopted many aspects of Arab culture and changed religious and cultural practices to fit with local traditions. For example, customs such as secluding women to a certain part of the home and only permitting them to go out in public if their hair was covered and much of their bodies were draped was already a local custom in Persia and the Mediterranean. Arabian women did not follow the custom of seclusion in the home until Islam was adopted.

The Abbasid Dynasty Replaces the Umayyads

In 750, rebel Arab forces overthrew the Umayyads and installed a caliph from the Abbasid family. The Abbasids built a new capital called Baghdad, in present-day Iraq. Baghdad was not a prominent village. Under the Abbasids, it held a mix of cultures and became the center of a golden age of art, science, and learning. Baghdad was soon among the leading cities around the world. Its culture was a blend of Arabian, Persian, Indian, Turkish, and other South Asian and Central Asian culture.

But as Islamic civilization flourished, the Abbasids were losing control of their empire. In 756, Spain became an independent Muslim state under its own caliphs. Later, the Shia Fatimid dynasty seized control of Egypt. They founded Al-Azhar university in Cairo. Al-Azhar is still a center of Muslim learning.

Analyze Images The Abbasid built this spiral minaret in Samarra, near their new capital of Baghdad. **Use Visual Information** What purpose did this building serve?

A Change in Power

Power slowly passed from Arabs to non-Arabs. Starting in the 900s, Turks migrated into Muslim lands. The Turks were a nomadic people from Central Asia who became Muslims. The Abbasid caliphs hired Turks as soldiers. Eventually, a group of Turks gained control of Baghdad. They allowed the Abbasid caliphs to remain on the throne, but stripped them of all real power.

In the 1250s, the Mongols invaded Muslim lands. They destroyed the city of Baghdad in 1258. There, they slaughtered tens of thousands of people and killed the Abbasid caliph.

Even though the Abbasid Caliphate had come to an end, Islam continued to spread. Merchants carried Islam across vast trade networks and were highly regarded in Muslim culture. Sufis also spread Islam through their travels. **Sufism** is an Islamic lifestyle that stresses controlling one's desires, giving up worldly attachments, and seeking nearness to God.

✓ READING CHECK **Understand Effects** How did differing views about leadership after Muhammad's death lead to a split in Islam?

Analyze Images This image shows Ottoman invaders breaking through the walls that protected Constantinople. **Draw Conclusions** Based on this image, what were some reasons the Ottomans were able to break through Constantinople's defenses?

Two Non-Arab Muslim Empires

The Mongol invasion ended the caliphate and the golden age of Islamic civilization. But individual Muslim states survived, ruled by non-Arab dynasties. The leaders of many of these states called themselves **sultans**, or rulers of Muslim states.

The Ottoman Empire Begins The largest of these states was the Ottoman empire, which lasted into the 1900s. The Ottoman empire arose in Asia Minor, part of the country now called Turkey. The Ottomans were a Turkish dynasty founded in the early 1300s by Osman I.

Beginning in the 1300s, the Turks had attacked the Byzantine empire in Asia and in Europe, capturing most of Anatolia and taking Constantinople in 1453. This attack was part of the Fourth Crusade. Then, Ottoman armies moved on to conquer an empire that included southeastern Europe, Arabia, and northern Africa.

The Ottoman empire was powered by a strong military, particularly the janissary corps. Janissaries were boys taken from the Christian provinces of southeastern Europe, raised as Muslims, and trained as elite soldiers. A visitor to the empire compared the janissaries favorably with European soldiers of his day.

Primary Source

It is the patience, self-denial and thrift of the Turkish soldier that enable him to face the most trying circumstances and come safely out of the dangers that surround him. What a contrast to our [European] men!

—Ogier Ghiselin de Busbecq

Academic Vocabulary
circumstance • *n.*, condition

▲ This decorative tile from the Safavid dynasty shows a meeting in a Persian garden.

Persia's Safavid Empire In the 1500s, the powerful Safavid empire rose up in Persia and challenged the Ottomans.

Persian culture continued to develop after the Arab conquest of the Sasanian dynasty. Most Persians converted from Zoroastrianism to Islam, but kept the Persian language. Persians remained proud of their ancient heritage.

The Safavid dynasty took power in Persia in the 1500s. They claimed Ali, Muhammad's cousin, as an ancestor. They were Shias and made Shia Islam the official religion of Persia. Today Persia is called Iran, and it remains a majority Shia country.

Under the Safavid dynasty, Persian painting, architecture, carpet weaving, and metalwork all blossomed. So did astronomy and mathematics.

☑READING CHECK **Sequence** How was the Safavid empire similar to and different from the earlier Persian empire?

☑ Lesson 3 Check

Practice Vocabulary

1. What does the word *caliph* mean?

2. Are **Sunnis** or **Shias** a majority in the Muslim world?

Critical Thinking and Writing

3. **Writing Workshop: Identify Supporting Details** Under the early caliphs, what were the main social groups in Muslim society?

4. **Compare and Contrast** How was the early caliphate different from later Muslim states like the Ottoman empire?

5. **Draw Conclusions** In what ways were Muslim rulers tolerant of other religions? In what ways were they not tolerant?

6. **Writing Workshop: Use Credible Sources** Choose one source of information that you would use to research your argumentative essay about the expansion of Islam. Write a paragraph in your 📕 Active Journal that identifies the source and explains why you think the source is credible, or believable.

Construct a Timeline

Follow these steps to construct a timeline about the spread of Islam.

INTERACTIVE

Sequence

1 Identify the time span. To organize information in a timeline, identify the earliest date and the latest date at which key events or periods occurred. For example, in the sample timeline below, the date of the earliest event is 570 and the date of the latest event is 762.

a. Select three additional events from this topic to add to the ones on this timeline. Make sure that at least two of the events took place after 800.

b. Identify the earliest and latest events that will be on your expanded timeline. What was the date of the earliest event?

c. What is the date of the latest event?

Quest CONNECTIONS

How do the events on your timeline show how the spread of Islam affected empires and dynasties? Record your findings in your Active Journal.

2 Identify your timeline's beginning and end points. Begin the timeline at a date just before the oldest date in your list of events or periods. At the end of the timeline, place a date just after the most recent date in your list of events or periods. In the timeline below, the beginning point is 500 and the end point is 800. What will be the beginning and end points of your expanded timeline?

3 Divide the timeline into equal time spans. Calculate the length of your timeline from its beginning point to its end point. Then, divide that time period into equal segments. Mark each segment on the timeline. The sample timeline is divided into 100-year segments. Into what length segments will you divide your expanded timeline?

4 Place items along the timeline. Write down key events and their dates where they fall along the timeline. For time spans, place them at the point they begin. Following the steps above, construct an expanded timeline that includes the additional dates you have selected.

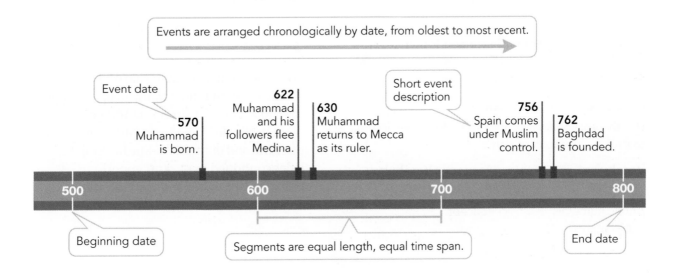

Events are arranged chronologically by date, from oldest to most recent.

Event date

570 Muhammad is born.

622 Muhammad and his followers flee Medina.

630 Muhammad returns to Mecca as its ruler.

Short event description

756 Spain comes under Muslim control.

762 Baghdad is founded.

500   600   700   800

Beginning date

Segments are equal length, equal time span.

End date

Achievements of Islamic Civilization

GET READY TO READ

START UP

Examine this photograph of a modern bazaar, a traditional market in the Muslim world. Why do you think the Muslim world was a center of trade?

GUIDING QUESTIONS

- What impact did trade and the growth of cities have on Islamic civilization?
- What were the main characteristics of Muslim arts and literature?
- How did Muslim rulers encourage learning, science, and mathematics?

TAKE NOTES

Literacy Skills: Identify Cause and Effect
Use the graphic organizer in your 📘 Active Journal to take notes as you read the lesson.

PRACTICE VOCABULARY

Use the vocabulary activity in your 📘 Active Journal to practice vocabulary words.

Vocabulary	Academic Vocabulary
textile	emphasize
Arabic numerals	concept
calligraphy	

As Islam spread to many different lands, a distinctive Muslim culture developed. Muslims in different regions combined Arab culture and Islam with the Persian, Byzantine, Indian, and other cultures that existed before the coming of Muslim rule. Muslim scholars shared ideas and learned from Christian and Jewish scholars. Together, they studied ancient writings from Greece, Persia, and India. This collaboration led to advances in science, mathematics, philosophy, medicine, and the arts.

How Did Cities and Trade Grow?

The expansion of Muslim rule and the spread of Islam united many peoples. Under the protection of a strong central government, trade flourished and cities grew. Even after the end of the Arab Muslim empire, cities continued to play an important role in maintaining a flourishing Islamic civilization.

An Urban Economy By 1000, Muslim culture thrived in Arabian cities such as Mecca, Medina, Damascus, and Baghdad. Other cities under Muslim control, such as Jerusalem, also thrived. Córdoba was the largest city in Muslim Spain. Outside of China, the Muslim empires had the largest, most developed cities in the world.

Cairo, Egypt, was the most important urban center in Africa. Its location made it an important hub for trade goods that traveled to and from the Indian Ocean. It was also situated on a network of inland trade routes. As a result, most trade goods passed through Cairo.

Another major urban center was Baghdad. It was founded by the Abbasid in 762 as their new capital city. Within a few decades, it had become one of the largest cities in the world and a center of learning. Scholars flocked to Baghdad to expand and share their knowledge.

Without a strong economic foundation, Muslim cities could not have grown so rapidly. Farms supplied food, wool, and other basic goods. Traders brought more exotic goods, such as fine silks, from distant lands. Cities produced a wide range of trade goods.

Muslim civilization gained fame for its fine **textiles**, or woven fabric. These valuable goods included cotton cloth from Egypt and beautiful wool carpets from Persia. Artisans also produced finely crafted steel swords in Damascus and beautiful leather goods in Córdoba, Spain.

Trade Expands Geography helped make Muslim lands a center for trade. Muslim lands included parts of Asia, Europe, and Africa. Muslim traders had access to the Mediterranean Sea and the Indian Ocean. Overland routes to and from East and South Asia passed through Muslim territory. As Muslim merchants traveled, they created a network of trade routes that linked three continents.

INTERACTIVE

The Dome of the Rock

Analyze Charts Cairo was a center of sea and land trade routes and an important stopover for pilgrims on their way from Africa to Mecca. **Understand Effects** What do you think were some possible effects of the exchanges at Cairo?

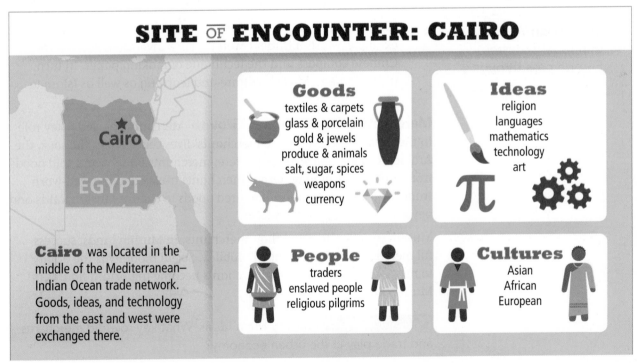

SITE OF ENCOUNTER: CAIRO

Cairo

EGYPT

Cairo was located in the middle of the Mediterranean–Indian Ocean trade network. Goods, ideas, and technology from the east and west were exchanged there.

Goods
textiles & carpets
glass & porcelain
gold & jewels
produce & animals
salt, sugar, spices
weapons
currency

Ideas
religion
languages
mathematics
technology
art

People
traders
enslaved people
religious pilgrims

Cultures
Asian
African
European

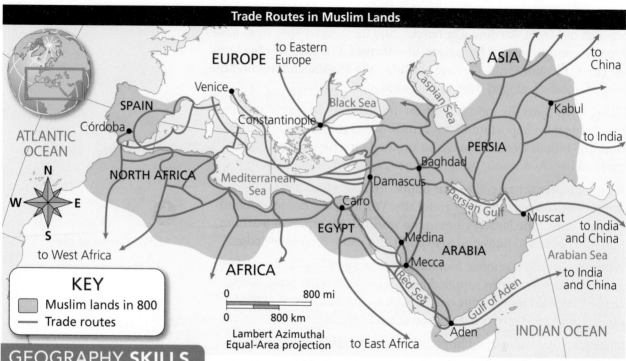

Trade Routes in Muslim Lands

to Eastern Europe

EUROPE

Venice

SPAIN

Córdoba

ATLANTIC OCEAN

N W E S

NORTH AFRICA

Constantinople

Black Sea

Mediterranean Sea

ASIA

to China

Caspian Sea

Kabul

PERSIA

to India

Baghdad

Damascus

Persian Gulf

Muscat

to India and China

Arabian Sea

Cairo

EGYPT

Medina

Mecca

ARABIA

Red Sea

Gulf of Aden

to India and China

to West Africa

AFRICA

0   800 mi

0   800 km

Lambert Azimuthal Equal-Area projection

Aden

INDIAN OCEAN

to East Africa

KEY
- Muslim lands in 800
- Trade routes

GEOGRAPHY SKILLS

Trade routes crisscrossed Southwest Asia, North Africa, Europe, and beyond, which expanded trade and the exchange of ideas.

1. **Region** Where might a merchant traveling to East Africa have left from?

2. **Interaction** Which city did trade to Eastern Europe pass through?

Muslim traders traveled in two main ways. They crossed the seas in small sailing ships called dhows. Dhows sailed from Arabia south to Africa and east to India. On land, merchants traveled by camel caravan. The most famous overland caravan route was the Silk Road. It linked Baghdad to distant China.

As a result of trade, goods flowed into Islamic cities from three continents. From Asia came Chinese silk and dishes as well as Indian spices, gems, coconuts, and tropical woods. Gold and salt came from Africa. Amber and furs arrived from northern Europe.

Ideas and inventions also spread along the trade routes. For example, Muslim traders brought back inventions such as the Chinese compass and the technique of making paper. In turn, traders spread Muslim culture and learning as well as Islam to other lands.

Merchants Bring Economic Growth Merchants played a key role in the urban economy. Some merchants' lives centered on the *souk*, the Arabic word for "marketplace." Here, merchants bought and sold goods from around the empire. Other merchants traveled along well-worn trade routes, carrying manufactured goods to distant Muslim lands and beyond.

Muslim societies honored their merchants. In Muslim lands, successful merchants had great social mobility. Social mobility is the ability to move up in society. Many merchants became important figures in Muslim lands.

☑ **READING CHECK** **Identify Main Ideas** What key role did merchants and trade play in the urban economy?

Achievements in Philosophy and Medicine

Muslim rulers prized learning. They built libraries and academies in Baghdad and other cities where scholars could study and exchange ideas. Muslim scholars collected, translated, and worked closely with Christian and Jewish scholars to study Greek, Persian, and Indian works. They merged ideas from these cultures with their own knowledge. They also created original works.

Philosophy Islamic civilization produced a number of brilliant philosophers. Some of these scholars, such as Ibn Rushd, studied the ideas of Aristotle and other Greeks. They worked to combine Islamic faith with the principles of Greek logic.

Medicine Muslim physicians, too, studied works by ancient Greek scholars. They improved on Greek medical practices. Muslims also made their own contributions to medical science.

The greatest Muslim doctor was Ibn Sina, known in Europe as Avicenna. A Persian physician, he wrote many books on medicine, philosophy, and other topics. His most famous work was a medical encyclopedia that he published in 1025. This book covered every disease and treatment known at that time. It became the standard medical text in Europe for hundreds of years.

✓ READING CHECK **Draw Conclusions** Why did Muslim scholars study and discuss ideas and knowledge with Jewish and Christian scholars?

Did you know?

Words such as *algebra, candy, mattress,* and *rice* all have their origins in the Arabic language.

▼ An eye operation from a Muslim medical textbook

BIOGRAPHY

5 Things to Know About **IBN SINA**
Muslim Physician/Philosopher (980–1037)

- Among his major works was a comprehensive and authoritative book, al-Shifa' ("The Cure"), a scientific and philosophical encyclopedia.

- Some consider Ibn Sina, also known in Europe by the name Avicenna, as the first major Islamic philosopher.

- By the time he was only ten years old, Ibn Sina had memorized the Quran.

- Ibn Sina became a physician to the Persian nobility by the time he was a teenager.

- After he cured a sultan of an unknown illness, the sultan opened a library of science and philosophy to honor Ibn Sina.

Critical Thinking How do you think the opening of the library in his honor affected learning in the Islamic world?

Academic Vocabulary

emphasize • *v.*, stress, mark as important

▼ The poetry of Persian poet Rumi is still read widely today.

How Was Literature Important to Islamic Culture?

As with medicine, Islamic culture put a high value on literature. Literacy, or the ability to read, spread through religion. Many Muslims learned to read in order to study the Quran. Some Muslim writers wrote down folk tales. Others wrote lyrical poetry about love and nature.

History and Geography Muslim scholars wrote about history and geography. The author Ibn Khaldun wrote a famous history of the world that tried to explain the rise and fall of dynasties. Ibn Battuta wrote an account of his travels around many Muslim lands across Asia and Africa.

Folk Tales Muslim folk tales came from a long tradition of storytelling. Some tales featured animals. Others described great heroes and their adventures. Many of these tales appeared in a book titled *The Thousand and One Nights*. This collection includes romantic stories as well as fables that teach lessons. It is popular around the world. These stories have also provided scholars with helpful information about life in early Muslim times, a period described in many of these stories.

Poetry Like folk tales, Muslim poetry began as an oral art form. Arab nomads used spoken verse to praise their tribes and mock their enemies. Poetry was central to early Arab culture. This oral tradition gave rise to many written forms.

The Persians, like the Arabs, also had a long tradition of writing poetry. One of the most famous Muslim poets was a man named Rumi who came from a Persian family. He often wrote about religious themes. Rumi practiced Sufism, which **emphasized** controlling one's desires. He wrote,

Primary Source

"What God said to the Rose

And caused it to laugh in full blown beauty,

He said to my heart

And made it a hundred times more beautiful."

—Rumi, "The Rose"

Poetry served as a way for Sufis to express their connection with God.

☑ READING CHECK **Summarize** Why was literacy important in Islamic culture?

Advances in Mathematics and Astronomy

Muslim scholars made important advances in various fields of science. Some of their main contributions were in mathematics and astronomy.

Mathematics Arab mathematicians used a decimal system based on Indian numerals (sometimes called Hindu numerals). This system included the **concept** of zero.

A book by the Muslim mathematician al-Khwarizmi introduced that number system to Europe. We call the symbols that we use for numbers today (0, 1, 2, 3, . . . 9) **Arabic numerals** because it came to Europe from the Arab world. Previously, Europeans used Roman numerals, but Arabic numerals are easier to work with.

Al-Khwarizmi made groundbreaking advances in the field of algebra. Algebra is a kind of mathematics in which letters are used to stand in for unknown numbers, allowing people to solve complex problems. The word *algebra* comes from Arabic.

Astronomy Muslim astronomers built observatories, buildings for viewing and studying the stars. They created charts that showed the position of stars and planets. They also measured the size of Earth and developed precise calendars.

Analyze Images
Astronomers like these at a Turkish observatory made significant scientific advances that helped change how people thought about and explored the world. **Synthesize Visual Information** What tools are they using?

✓ **READING CHECK** Identify Supporting Details What Muslim mathematician helped advance algebra, and how was algebra important to mathematics?

Islamic Traditions in Art and Architecture

In addition to learning, early Muslims placed a high value on the arts. A hadith says, "God is beautiful and loves beauty." This ideal inspired the creation of beautiful and influential works of art and architecture.

The Art of Design and Calligraphy Before Islam, Arabs worshiped images of their gods. Islam opposed the worship of images and discouraged art that showed humans or animals. In time, some painting of images was allowed, but it never became as important as the decorative arts in Islamic civilization.

Decorative designs appeared on everything from colorful tiles to finely woven carpets to the domes of mosques. One of the most popular designs, the arabesque, consists of a pattern of curved shapes and lines resembling flowers or vines.

Academic Vocabulary
concept • *n.*, idea

In Islamic civilization, calligraphy merged art and religion. **Calligraphy** is the art of decorative writing. Using this art form, artists recreated verses from the Quran. They wrote them in decorated books, carved them on walls, painted them on tiles, and wove them into textiles.

Through trade and travel, the various Muslim decorative styles found their way to Europe. In the 1300s in Italy, a new artistic age began. Artists there applied Muslim styles and techniques to glassware, metalwork, and other forms of art.

Architecture and Influence Muslim architects built striking mosques, fountains, gates, gardens, baths, and palaces. Domes and arches were common features used in Muslim architecture.

Islamic civilization included many cultures that had long histories before the coming of Islam. The influences of these cultures are clearly visible in the buildings designed by Muslims. Byzantine and Roman influences were very strong, especially in western Muslim lands that were once ruled by the Byzantine and Roman emperors. Persian (Iranian) styles were also influential. They spread to many nearby regions including India and East Africa.

✓ READING CHECK **Identify Cause and Effect** What inspired Islamic arabesques, calligraphy, and decorative designs? How are they used?

☑ Lesson 4 Check

Practice Vocabulary

1. What are **textiles**? What is one example of a textile product that was produced in early Islamic civilization?

2. Where did the system of **Arabic numerals** come from originally? To what regions did it spread after al-Khwarizmi wrote his book on the topic?

Critical Thinking and Writing

3. **Identify Main Ideas** How were ideas exchanged between cultures in the Islamic world?

4. **Identify Cause and Effect** How did Ibn Sina use Greek learning? What was the effect of his book in Western Europe?

5. **Infer** What can you infer about Muslim learning considering that the words *algebra* and *chemistry* both come from Arabic?

6. **Writing Workshop: Distinguish Claims from Opposing Claims** Write sentences in your 📕 Active Journal that address opposing claims about whether conquest or trade was a key factor in the growth of Islamic empires. You will use these sentences in your argumentative essay that you will write at the end of the Topic.

📑 Primary Sources

Ibn Khaldun, *The Muqaddimah*

The Muslim historian Ibn Khaldun was born in 1332 in northern Africa. He believed that the study of history should be more than a list of events. He argued that a true study of history must take into account the context in which events occurred. His contributions to the study of history influenced how later scholars viewed history and the study of civilizations.

▶ This statue of Ibn Khaldun is in the North African country of Tunisia.

It should be known that history, in matter of fact, is information about human social organization, which itself is identical with world civilization. It deals with such conditions affecting the nature of civilization as, for instance, savagery and sociability, group feelings, and the different ways by which one group of <u>human beings achieves superiority over another</u> ①. It deals with royal authority and the dynasties that result (in this manner) and with the various ranks that exist within them. (It further deals) with the different kinds of <u>gainful</u> ② occupations and ways of making a living, with the sciences and crafts that human beings pursue as part of their activities and efforts, and with all the other <u>institutions</u> ③ that originate in civilization through its very nature . . .

. . . History is an art of valuable doctrine, numerous in advantages and honorable in purpose; it informs us about <u>bygone</u> ④ nations in the context of their habits, the prophets in the context of their lives and kings in the context of their states and politics, so <u>those who seek the guidance of the past</u> ⑤ in either worldly or religious matters may have that advantage.

—Ibn Khaldun, *The Muqaddimah*

Analyzing Primary Sources

Cite specific evidence from the document to support your answers.

1. **Analyze Information** What do you think the author means by "history . . . is information about human social organization"?

2. **Identify Supporting Details** Name three kinds of information that Khaldun suggests are part of the study of history.

3. **Draw Conclusions** According to Ibn Khaldun, what is the value of studying history?

Reading and Vocabulary Support

① What is a way in which human beings achieve superiority over each other?

② *Gainful* means leading to an increase in income or advantage.

③ An institution in this sense means any practice or organization that is well established.

④ *Bygone* is an adjective that refers to something that no longer exists.

⑤ What do you think Ibn Khaldun means when he writes of "those who seek guidance from the past"?

India After the Fall of the Gupta

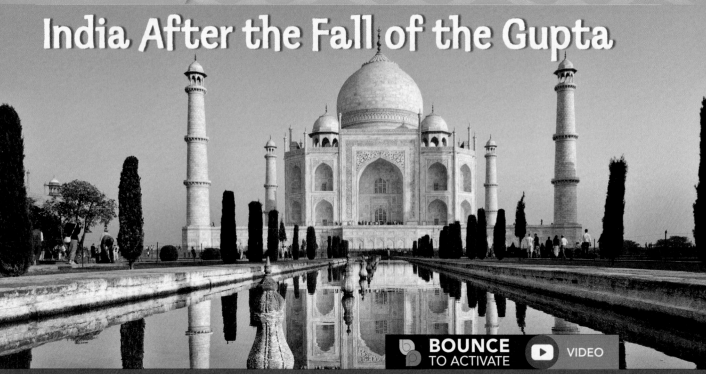

BOUNCE TO ACTIVATE ▶ VIDEO

GET READY TO READ

START UP

A Muslim ruler in India had the Taj Mahal (tahzh muh HAHL) built as a tomb for his wife. What do you think makes the Taj Mahal an enduring symbol of the glory of the Mughal empire and India?

GUIDING QUESTIONS

- What happened to South Asia after the fall of the Gupta empire?
- How did the religions of Hinduism and Buddhism spread and change over time?
- How did the Muslim expansion lead to a new Indian empire and the rise of Sikhism?

TAKE NOTES

Literacy Skills: Use Evidence
Use the graphic organizer in your 📙 Active Journal to take notes as you read the lesson.

PRACTICE VOCABULARY

Use the vocabulary activity in your 📙 Active Journal to practice the vocabulary words.

Vocabulary		Academic Vocabulary
maritime	bodhisattva	adherents
Bhakti		advocated

Today, the subcontinent of India is home to three of the world's most populous nations. India has a majority Hindu population and large Muslim and Sikh minorities. Pakistan and Bangladesh are Muslim nations.

Long before the arrival of Islam, two major religions had emerged in India: Hinduism and Buddhism. From 320 CE, most of South Asia was ruled by the Gupta dynasty. The Gupta period was a golden age of Indian culture. But, like Rome and Persia before it, this powerful empire eventually faced decline.

What Happened After the Fall of the Gupta Empire?

Frequent warfare weakened the Gupta Empire. It began to decline after 467. For centuries, there was no strong empire to keep northern India united.

Divided and Weak After the fall of the Gupta empire, regions of India divided into smaller states and kingdoms, each with its own ruler. Divided and weakened, India was vulnerable to foreigners and rivals. However, sea trade brought some stability and growth to the southern part of the subcontinent.

The Chola Empire In southern India, the Chola dynasty became very powerful in the ninth century. These rulers spoke the Tamil language, not the Sanskrit that was spoken in the north. Over the next four hundred years, the Chola dynasty created an empire that extended beyond India into much of Southeast Asia.

Chola kings used military power to expand their empire. Many supported the arts, architecture, and metallurgy. During this period, great Hindu temples, sculptures, and bronzes were crafted.

Maritime trade routes strengthened the economic and political power of the Chola empire. Key **maritime**, or sea-related, trading networks connected different cultures and empires across the Indian Ocean.

Spread of Ideas and Practices During the Chola period, Indian cultural ideas and practices continued to spread to other lands, where they were adopted and adapted. The main way that ideas spread was through trade networks. The maritime trade network, as well as land routes, served as vehicles for new ideas and cultures.

Trade networks enabled cultures to sell and buy or barter for trade goods, but the merchants were not the only carriers. Travelers and members of religious faiths such as monks and nuns shared ideas. South Asian culture and ideas influenced art, language, and architecture in other parts of Asia such as Srivijaya, Java, and the Khmer.

☑ **READING CHECK** **Understand Effects** How did India change after the fall of the Gupta empire?

How Did Hinduism and Buddhism Change Over Time?

In ancient times, two great world religions developed in South Asia. Hinduism has roots dating back to at least 1500 BCE. Buddhism emerged during the 400s BCE. As new peoples and ideas arrived and spread throughout the region, both religions underwent change.

Bhakti Influences Hinduism In about the seventh century, **Bhakti** movements swept South India in the form of Tamil poetry and prose. Bhakti stressed personal devotion to God in various forms. The forms most commonly worshiped—Vishnu (protector), Siva (transformer), and Devi (Divine Mother) —were viewed as one universal spirit.

Many of the Bhakti movements emphasized equality by allowing males and females and people of all castes to take part in devotional practices. Such practices included daily devotionals, songs, dances, and temple activities. Bhakti also put limits on the power of religious authorities such as priests.

Analyze Images The Brihadeeswarar Temple was built by Chola I, who ruled the Chola dynasty at its height. It was completed in 1010 and dedicated to Shiva. **Use Visual Information** How would you describe the architectural style of this temple?

Bhakti became more popular as ideas traveled and were carried throughout the Indian subcontinent. It spread to northern India through the *Bhagavata-purana*, a Sanskrit text. Bhakti poets and saints such as Meera Bai and Ramananda traveled throughout India to spread the movement's ideas and practices. The Bhakti movement and other Hindu traditions helped create a cultural unity across India at a time of political fragmentation.

Buddhism Changes Over Time Buddhist missionaries and travelers spread Buddhism throughout parts of India and to Central Asia and China. As Buddhism left India, it changed, influenced by the people and cultures it encountered.

The concept of Buddha himself underwent change between 600 BCE and CE 300. The founder of Buddhism, Siddhartha Gautama, was a man who was wise and known to his followers as the "Buddha." Over centuries, many Buddhists began to worship Buddha as a god.

The concept of nirvana also changed over time and as Buddhism spread outside of the Indian subcontinent. Nirvana had originally been seen as a state of blissful peace without desire or suffering. Many later Buddhists, however, came to view nirvana as a form of heaven in the afterlife.

As Buddhism reached Central and East Asia, Mahayana Buddhism developed. This movement followed most of the major Buddhist beliefs, but added the idea that a person could become a bodhisattva. A **bodhisattva** is a person many Buddhists believe to have reached enlightenment, but is reborn again to help others reach nirvana.

Academic Vocabulary
adherent • *n.*, follower; supporter

▼ Xuanzang on his journey through Asia

The Journey of Xuanzang Many **adherents** of Buddhism made pilgrimages to Buddhist holy sites. One of them, Xuanzang, arrived in India from China in the early 630s. He learned Sanskrit at a Buddhist monastery and center of learning. Ten years later, he returned to China, carrying 500 Buddhist texts. He translated these texts into Chinese. Xuanzang's journey helped to spread Buddhist teachings throughout East Asia.

✓ READING CHECK **Compare and Contrast**
How did Hinduism and Buddhism spread and change over time?

Islam Arrives in India

By 712 CE, Arab armies had occupied much of Afghanistan and the lower Indus valley in southern Pakistan. However, Hindu rulers fought off conquest of eastern Afghanistan and northern Pakistan for 250 years. Even after that, Muslim armies could not advance much into northern India for another two centuries. Islam did not begin to spread throughout the subcontinent until after 1000 CE, when Muslim Turks arrived from Central Asia. They conquered the area and expanded their power and control.

5 Things to Know About

AKBAR
Mughal Emperor (c. 1542–1605)

- He was the greatest Mughal emperor and created a strong central government.

- Showing religious tolerance, he opened government jobs to people of all faiths.

- Akbar strengthened the Mughal military and modernized it.

- Even though he was a Muslim ruler, Akbar was interested in other religions and even married a Hindu princess.

- Akbar was not literate and often consulted with advisers of diverse religious faiths.

Identify Main Ideas Why do you think Akbar practiced religious tolerance?

The Delhi Sultanate In the late 1100s, Muslim Turks defeated Hindu armies in northern India and made Delhi the capital of their state. They established a sultanate, or land that is ruled by a sultan, marking the beginning of Muslim rule in India.

Islam dominated northern India under the sultanate, although southern India remained largely Hindu. Muslim traditions of government changed Indian government traditions, and economic ties were strengthened through trade networks. Exports increased, as India became a key producer of cotton, other textiles, and spices.

The sultans allowed Hindu merchants to control most of the trade in their empire and hired some of them to run the administration. But Hindu temples and schools were demolished and Hindu festivals were banned.

The sultanate weakened as Mongols drove into India in the late 1300s. Timur, a Mongol leader, destroyed Delhi. Many Hindu and Muslim states formed as a result of Hindu rebellions and the Mongol invasions.

Sharing Knowledge and Culture As the Mongol raids began in the 1200s in the greater region, many people migrated from Baghdad to Delhi. Some of those who came to Delhi were scholars. Their presence in the capital city stimulated learning, art, and architecture.

Knowledge and ideas traveled in both directions. Many mathematical and astronomical advances were made under the Gupta empire. The base-ten numerical system was applied by Persian mathematician al-Khwarizmi in the 800s.

Founding of the Mughal Empire In 1526, a group of Mongols and Turks overran what remained of the Delhi sultanate. Their leader, Babur, founded the Mughal empire. (*Mughal* is another word for "Mongol.") Mughal emperors expanded Muslim rule over nearly all of India. Scholars, writers, and artists migrated to India from the west, especially Persia, and culture flourished.

 INTERACTIVE

Dynasties and Empires in South Asia

Quest CONNECTIONS

Based on this section, what events can you add to your timeline about how the spread of Islam affected empires and dynasties? List these in your 📓 Active Journal.

▼ A modern Sikh festival in Yuba City

Some Mughal rulers persecuted Hindus, as well as adherents of other non-Muslim faiths such as Sikhism and Jainism. The Mughal emperor Akbar followed a different policy. He treated Hindus with respect and **advocated** religious tolerance.

✓ **READING CHECK** **Summarize** How did warfare affect the religious makeup of South Asia?

The Founding of Sikhism

By 1500, a new religion called Sikhism developed in India. It was influenced by both Hinduism and Islam. Like Islam, Sikhism teaches monotheism. Like Hindus, Sikhs believe in reincarnation.

The founder of Sikhism was a guru, or religious teacher, named Nanak. Guru Nanak declared that "there is neither Hindu nor Muslim." He opposed the caste system, as well as the power of religious elites. He also criticized some Islamic practices and instructed Muslim rulers not to treat their subjects with harshness.

The Sikh holy book, the Guru Granth Sahib, is considered the final teacher of the community. The main teachings of Sikhism are based on three concepts: living truthfully and honestly, helping the needy, and devotion to God and prayer.

Sikhs fought the Mughals after two gurus were murdered by Mughal emperors. In 1801, the Sikhs founded a powerful kingdom in northern India that lasted until 1849. Today, there are about 24 million Sikhs in the world. Most live in India.

✓ **READING CHECK** **Draw Conclusions** How was Sikhism an example of cultural blending?

✓ Lesson 5 Check

Practice Vocabulary

1. How is **maritime** trade conducted?

2. What does a **bodhisattva** seek to do?

Critical Thinking and Writing

3. **Synthesize** Why was there a sharing and blend of cultures and ideas on the Indian subcontinent?

4. **Identify Cause and Effect** How did the passing of time, as well as outside influences, affect the teachings and practices of Hinduism and Buddhism?

5. **Cite Evidence** How did the expansion of the Mughal empire into India influence the rise of Sikhism? Cite evidence from the text in your response.

6. **Writing Workshop: Write a Conclusion** Write a sentence in your 📓 Active Journal that will help you form a strong conclusion for your argumentative essay that you will write at the end of the Topic.

Frame Questions

Follow these steps to frame questions.

 INTERACTIVE

Ask Questions

1 Identify your focus. When reading a primary source, such as this one about a traveling Chinese monk who visits a monastery in India, begin by focusing on what the passage is about and what you are trying to learn. Use the "5WH" technique—ask "Who? What? Where? When? Why? and How?"— to help you.

  a. Who wrote this passage?

  b. When was the passage written?

  c. What can you learn from this passage?

2 Identify the information provided. As you review a source, recognize the questions that your source clearly answers. Ask, "Which of my questions are already answered?" Who are the people described in the passage?

3 Frame remaining questions. Now think about what you still need to learn after having studied your source. Which questions remain to be answered? Remember the 5WH.

  a. What words or ideas are you having trouble understanding?

  b. What questions could help you clarify understanding?

4 Plan your research. With your list of questions, plan how you will seek answers. Ask yourself, "What kinds of sources would help me answer this question?"

  a. What resources will help you to learn more about how Buddhism spread in Asia?

Primary Source

The lord of the country lodged Fa-hien and the others comfortably, and supplied their wants, in a monastery called Gotami, of the mahayana school. Attached to it there are three thousand monks, who are called to their meals by the sound of a bell. When they enter the refectory, their demeanour is marked by a reverent gravity, and they all take their seats in regular order, all maintaining a perfect silence. No sound is heard from their alms-bowls and other utensils. When any of these pure men require food, they are not allowed to call out (to the attendants) for it, but only make signs with their hands.

—Fa Xian, *A Record of Buddhistic Kingdoms, Being an Account by the Chinese Monk of His Travels in India and Ceylon (A.D. 399–414)*

☑ Review and Assessment

VISUAL REVIEW

Muslim and Indian Dynasties and Empires

Dynasty/Empire	Date	Capital
Gupta Empire	280–550	Pataliputra
Muhammad and his first successors	632–661	Mecca
Umayyad Caliphate	661–770	Damascus
Umayyad Caliphate in Spain	756–1031	Cordoba
Abbasid Caliphate	750–1258	Baghdad
Delhi Sultanate	1206–1526	Delhi
Ottoman Empire	Late 1200s–1900s	Constantinople (Istanbul)
Safavid Dynasty	Early 1500s–1700s	Isfahan
Mughal Empire	1526–1800s	Delhi

Key Ideas and Achievements of the Muslim World

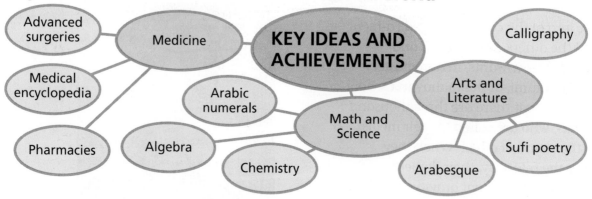

READING REVIEW

Use these resources in your 📖 Active Journal to help you to review your notes and topic vocabulary.

👆 INTERACTIVE

Practice Vocabulary

Quest FINDINGS

Create Your Illustrated Timeline

Get help for creating your timeline in your 📖 Active Journal.

ASSESSMENT

Vocabulary and Key Ideas

1. **Define** Sufism.

2. **Describe** Where was the religion of Sikhism founded? Who was its founding leader?

3. **Identify** What role did Muhammad play in Islam?

4. **Locate** In which modern-day country is the Hijaz located?

5. **Compare and Contrast** How did Sunnis and Shias differ? What did they have in common?

6. **List** What were the main characteristics of Muslim arts and literature?

Critical Thinking and Writing

7. **Sequence** Arrange the following Muslim dynasties, rulers, and empires in the correct order, from earliest to latest and categorize: Abbasid, Muhammad, Mughal, Rightly Guided Caliphs, Umayyad.

8. **Synthesize** Why did the Indian subcontinent serve as a place where many cultural and religious ideas were exchanged?

9. **Compare and Contrast** How did Abbasid rulers support arts and literature?

10. **Revisit the Essential Question** What were the different ways that ideas grew and spread in the Islamic world? Give specific examples of each.

11. **Writing Workshop: Write an Argumentative Essay** Using the outline you created in your Active Journal, answer the following question in a three-paragraph argumentative essay: Was conquest or trade the key factor in the growth of Islamic empires?

Analyze Primary Sources

12. What do these words from a poem written by Ibn Sina illustrate about Islamic culture?
    A. the improved understanding of medicine
    B. the lush environment in the region
    C. the influence of Indian culture
    D. the belief in monotheism

"Insist upon their quiet and rest, for their limbs are weak;

Try to lift their spirit through welcome words and pleasant company;

Give them sweet-scented perfumes and flowers;

Obtain happiness and music for them;

Spare them somber thoughts and fatigue."
—Ibn Sina, "Al-Urjuzah Fi Al-Tibb"

Analyze Maps

Use the map at right to answer the following questions.

13. What is the average rainfall in Mecca?

14. What is the greatest rainfall on the Arabian Peninsula?

15. What does the map tell you about the climate of the Arabian Peninsula?

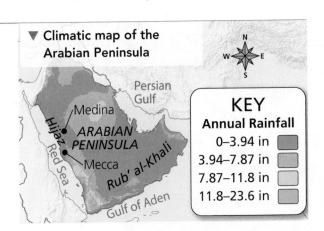

▼ **Climatic map of the Arabian Peninsula**

KEY
Annual Rainfall
0–3.94 in
3.94–7.87 in
7.87–11.8 in
11.8–23.6 in

Civilizations of East Asia and Southeast Asia

(250 BCE–1644 CE)

GO ONLINE
to access your
digital course

- ▶ VIDEO
- 🔊 AUDIO
- 📖 ETEXT
- 👆 INTERACTIVE
- ✍️ WRITING
- 🎮 GAMES
- 📄 WORKSHEET
- ☑️ ASSESSMENT

Travel back in time to nearly 1,400 years ago

to **EAST ASIA**, when China and Japan became two of the most advanced civilizations on the planet. China shared its culture, religious beliefs, and technology with the world, including Japan, Korea, and Southeast Asia. These cultures endured even when the Mongols swept through the region, destroying much in their path.

Explore
The Essential Question

How do ideas grow and spread?

From the 600s through the 1600s, China was ruled by powerful dynasties. Under these rulers, China expanded its economy, its system of government, and its culture. Explore how Chinese ideas grew and spread to mingle with those from the cultures around them.

Unlock the Essential Question in your 📔 Active Journal.

Read

about the culture, economies, religions, and philosophies that shaped culture in East and Southeast Asia.

Watch

NBC LEARN

BOUNCE TO ACTIVATE ▶ VIDEO

Elements of a Culture

Learn about arts and cultural traditions from medieval-era Japan that are still treasured today.

◀ Construction on the Great Wall of China began in the 600s BCE. Most of it was completed during the Ming empire, which began in 1368 CE.

Civilizations of East Asia and Southeast Asia

(250 BCE–1644 CE)

Learn more about China, Japan, Korea, and Southeast Asia by making your own map and timeline in your Active Journal.

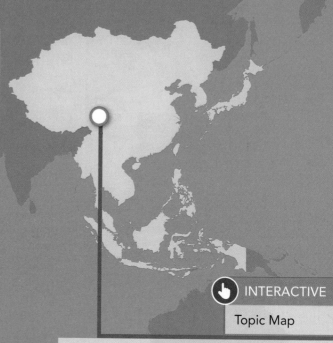

 INTERACTIVE

Topic Timeline

What happened and when?

Mind-changing philosophies . . . innovations that would rock the world . . . Explore the timeline to see what was happening in China, Japan, Korea, and the rest of the world.

 INTERACTIVE

Topic Map

Where were East and Southeast Asia?

China, Japan, and Korea were located in East Asia, near where the countries with the same names are today. Southeast Asia is a region located partly on a peninsula between India and China and partly on thousands of islands.

500s
Buddhism is introduced to Japan.

618
The Tang dynasty begins in China.

794
The Japanese royal court moves to Heian.

TOPIC EVENTS

400   600   800

WORLD EVENTS

527
Justinian becomes ruler of the Byzantine empire.

800
Charlemagne is crowned emperor of the Holy Roman Empire by the pope.

0 | 600 mi
0 | 600 km
Conic projection

N W E S

Altai Mountains
Tian Shan
Taklimakan Desert
Kunlun Shan
HIMALAYAS
Plateau of Tibet
Mongolian Plateau
Gobi Desert
Huang River
Manchurian Plain
Amur River
Sakhalin
Hokkaidō
Sea of Japan (East Sea)
40° N
Honshū
Korean Pen.
Shikoku
Kyūshū
North China Plain
Yellow Sea
30° N
Chang River
East China Sea
Ryukyu Islands
PACIFIC OCEAN
TROPIC OF CANCER
Taiwan
20° N
130° E
Bay of Bengal
90° E
Mekong R.
100° E
South China Sea
110° E
120° E

Who will you meet?

Wu Zhao, China's only empress

Genghis Khan, ruler of the Mongols, who by 1206 would unite warring clans and dominate most of the known world

Prince Shotoku, who sought to unite Japan's warring clans

1279
The Mongol conquest of China is completed.

1392
The Choson dynasty begins its reign in Korea.

960
The Song dynasty is founded in China.

1000

1200

1400

1215
The Magna Carta is signed.

Quest
Document-Based Writing Inquiry

A Strong Influence

Quest KICK OFF

You are a traveler to Japan in the 1300s. During your stay, you notice a temple that looks similar to one that you saw during your travels in China, thousands of miles away. You are intrigued. Are the temples connected? You decide to investigate this Guiding Question:

How did China influence the cultures around it?

What influence did China have on the rest of East Asia and Southeast Asia? Explore the Essential Question "How do ideas grow and spread?" in this Quest.

▼ The Three-Storied pagoda, part of a Buddhist temple complex in Japan

1 Ask Questions
Get started by making a list of questions you have about China's historical, cultural, and political role in the region. Write these questions in your 📓 Active Journal.

2 Investigate
As you read the lessons in this topic, look for **Quest CONNECTIONS** that provide information about China's influence. Write your notes in your 📓 Active Journal.

3 Examine Primary Sources
Next, look at the set of primary sources online that provide clues as to China's influence in the region. Capture your findings in your 📓 Active Journal.

Quest FINDINGS

4 Write an Explanatory Essay
When you think you've learned enough from the sources, put all that you have learned into an essay that explains your observations. Get help writing your essay in your 📓 Active Journal.

LESSON 1

Tang and Song China

VIDEO

GET READY TO READ

START UP
Study the illustration of a city in medieval China. What does this illustration tell you about the economy of China at the time?

GUIDING QUESTIONS
- How did the Tang and Song dynasties gain and maintain power over people and territories?
- How did the civil service system strengthen China's government?
- What were the causes and effects of China's economic revolution?

TAKE NOTES

Literacy Skills: Identify Main Ideas
Use the graphic organizer in your 📓 Active Journal to take notes as you read the lesson.

PRACTICE VOCABULARY
Use the vocabulary activity in your 📓 Active Journal to practice the vocabulary words.

Vocabulary

bureaucracy

scholar-official

merit system

urbanization

money

economy

porcelain

Academic Vocabulary

commercial

device

The Han dynasty made China into a vast empire. The fall of the Han in 220 CE left China divided, only to reunite and experience a golden age under two strong dynasties, the Tang and the Song.

What Was the Tang Dynasty?
For hundreds of years after the fall of the Han dynasty, several kingdoms competed for power. The short-lived Sui (sway) dynasty reunited China between 581 and 618. The next dynasty, the Tang, reigned for nearly 300 years. Tang rulers built a strong central government and conquered new territory.

Tang Rule The military leader Tang Gaozu founded the Tang dynasty. He and his son led the armies that reunited China. His son, Tang Taizong (ty dzoong), became emperor in 626. Other strong rulers followed.

Taizong made the government stable by reviving China's official bureaucracy. A **bureaucracy** is a system of government with many departments and bureaus led by appointed officials. Each official has a rank and fixed responsibilities.

In setting up this bureaucracy, Taizong wanted to create an efficient government. The departments created under Taizong remained the core of Chinese government until the early 1900s.

Under Tang rulers, China grew to its largest size up to that time. The military expanded the borders and protected the growing population. In the late 600s, Wu Zhao (woo jow) became the only woman to rule China on her own. Empress Wu was capable and ruthless. She believed a ruler should care for people as a mother cares for her children.

A Flourishing Capital The Tang capital was Chang'an (chahng ahn), which became the largest city in the world. In 742, more than a million people lived within the city walls, with 700,000 more just outside.

Chang'an may also have been the largest planned city ever built. Its walls formed a rectangle that measured five miles from north to south and six miles from east to west. Great homes, temples, gardens, and the imperial palace stood inside the walls. A wide, tree-lined avenue led to the main gate, impressing visitors.

Sitting at one end of the Silk Road, Chang'an was a thriving cultural and **commercial** center. Turks, Indians, Jews, Koreans, Persians, and other visitors filled its streets and markets. Camels carried goods into and out of the city. Musicians, actors, and other performers provided public entertainment. People practiced many different religions.

Chang'an was welcoming to foreigners, though they lived in their own sections of the city. Chinese nobles used foreign goods, adopted foreign fashions, and borrowed other parts of foreign cultures.

☑ READING CHECK **Identify Supporting Details** What made Chang'an an important cultural and economic center?

Academic Vocabulary

commercial • *adj.,* having to do with trade and business

Analyze Images The Daming Palace was built in Chang'an during the Tang dynasty. **Use Visual Information** How did the planners of Chang'an lay out the streets around the palace?

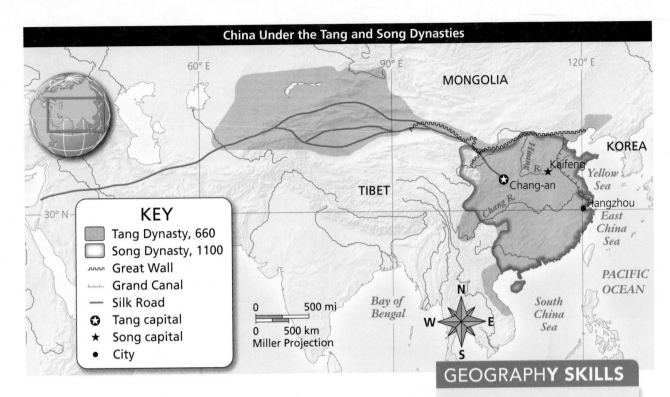

China Under the Tang and Song Dynasties

KEY
- Tang Dynasty, 660
- Song Dynasty, 1100
- Great Wall
- Grand Canal
- Silk Road
- ✪ Tang capital
- ★ Song capital
- • City

0   500 mi
0   500 km
Miller Projection

The Song Dynasty

Eventually, the Tang dynasty fell. After a period of unrest, a new dynasty arose.

Fall of the Tang For much of Tang rule, China was at war with neighboring peoples. This allowed military leaders to gain power. Drought, famine, and high taxes led to problems at home. In the late 700s, several military leaders rebelled.

Although the government survived, it had less control. Military and local leaders took power. Neighboring peoples attacked and often took land. Revolts became more common. In 907, a military leader overthrew the last Tang emperor.

Rise of the Song For more than half a century, China had no clear ruler. Different people ruled parts of China and neighboring peoples took more land.

In 960, a military leader united much of China and began the Song dynasty. It ruled China from 960 to 1279.

To protect the empire, Song rulers kept a huge army. But they did not want the military to have too much power, so they gave control to government officials who were not in the military. Sometimes they tried to buy peace with neighboring peoples who threatened China by making payments to them. At other times, Song rulers made agreements with one outside group to fight another.

✓**READING CHECK** **Identify Supporting Details** How did Song rulers prevent the military from becoming too strong?

GEOGRAPHY SKILLS

The Tang and Song dynasties had some land in common, though the Tang dynasty controlled more territory.

1. **Region** What area did both the Tang and Song dynasties control?

2. **Use Visual Information** What human-made barrier was located north of Chang'an?

Analyze Images Scholars take a civil service examination. **Compare and Contrast** Compare the scholars' test-taking conditions with how students today complete exams.

The Merit System

Civil service examinations are tests required for people to work for the government bureaucracy. The Han dynasty introduced these tests in China. The Tang rulers modeled their government on the Han dynasty, and the Song dynasty expanded the system. At the center of the bureaucracy were the highly educated men who passed the civil service examinations. A man who passed this examination, known as a **scholar-official**, qualified for government jobs.

The examinations were based on teachings of Confucius. They were difficult, and few students passed. Only wealthy men could easily spend years studying. During the Tang, some officials earned positions through the exam system. However, the majority still received positions because of family connections.

During the Song dynasty, the tests became part of a merit system and helped create the world's strongest and most centralized government. In a **merit system**, people are hired and promoted based on talent and skills, rather than wealth or social status. The government opened schools that even poor students could attend. Passing higher-level exams could lead to promotions, but scholar-officials also had to perform their jobs well to move higher in the bureaucracy.

By preventing corruption and promoting the best officials, Song rulers tried to maintain good government. Officials were supposed to act honestly and efficiently.

A later dynasty, the Ming, made new rules for officials. They could not serve in their home district, where they might do favors for family and friends. They also changed jobs every three years so that they could not build up too much power.

☑ **READING CHECK** **Draw Conclusions** How does a merit system promote an effective government?

An Economic Revolution

The Tang and Song eras were times of great prosperity in China. With the support of a stable government, China experienced an economic revolution even greater than the one taking place in medieval Europe around the same time. The revolution started with advances in farming and led to greater trade and **urbanization**, or the growth of cities. By 1100, China had several large cities that were home to hundreds of thousands of people. Many of these cities were in southern China, south of the Chang River, which is also known as the Yangtze or Yangzi.

The Emperor and the Officials A stable and strong government was key to this prosperity. The emperor ruled under the Mandate of Heaven. In theory, this meant that he was all-powerful and had heavenly support. In practice, most early emperors needed the backing of nobles and military leaders to stay in power.

Song rulers changed that. By giving more power to the scholar-official class, emperors developed a base of loyal supporters. Meanwhile, scholar-officials rose in power and influence. They pushed aside the noble families to become the highest-ranking group in Chinese society.

The Song Dynasty Shifts South The Song dynasty became weak over time. The foreign Jin kingdom took control of northern China in 1127. The Song rulers withdrew from the north and established a base in southern China.

This period is called the Southern Song. The port of Hangzhou (hahng joh) became the capital. A European visitor wrote that Hangzhou was "the first, the biggest, the richest, the most populous, and altogether the most marvelous city that exists on the face of the earth."

GEOGRAPHY **SKILLS**

The Song dynasty saw a significant migration in its population.

1. **Movement** In what direction did people move during the Song dynasty?

2. **Use Visual Information** What was the capital of the Jin kingdom?

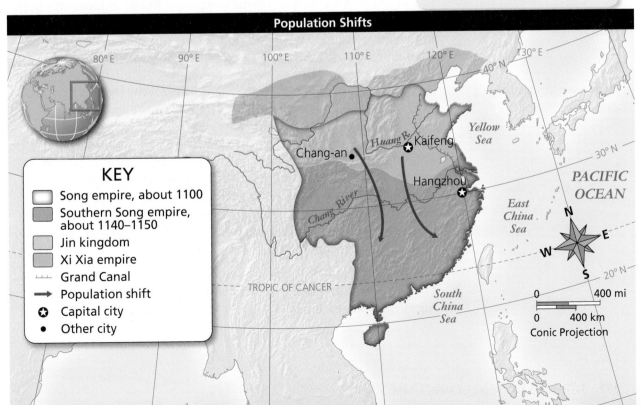

Population Shifts

KEY
- Song empire, about 1100
- Southern Song empire, about 1140–1150
- Jin kingdom
- Xi Xia empire
- Grand Canal
- Population shift
- Capital city
- Other city

Chang-an •   Huang R.   Kaifeng ✪   Yellow Sea

Hangzhou ✪

Chang River

TROPIC OF CANCER

East China Sea

South China Sea

PACIFIC OCEAN

0   400 mi
0   400 km
Conic Projection

Changes in Farming Chinese farming evolved under the Tang and Song. First, patterns of land ownership changed during the Tang dynasty. Since the Han, the Chinese government had owned all farmland. Farmers received equal shares of land. The Tang government changed this system. Under the Tang, rich families bought much of the good farmland. Most peasants worked the land as tenant farmers. Tenant farmers rent the land they farm.

Next, new farming methods and technology allowed farmers to feed more people. In the past, farmers had grown mostly dry-land crops such as wheat and barley. These grew well in the dry north, but not in the humid south. The south, however, was perfect for rice farming. It was warmer and had more rainfall than the north. During this period, rice became China's most important crop.

Analyze Images A nineteenth-century piece of art shows workers in a rice paddy. **Draw Conclusions** How do you think these workers' farming techniques were similar to those of farmers in the Tang and Song dynasties?

Rice grows in flooded fields called paddies. To keep their rice paddies wet, Chinese farmers developed irrigation systems such as pumps and other water-control **devices**. They also developed new strains of fast-ripening rice from Vietnam. With this kind of rice, farmers could harvest two or three crops a year.

Rice provided more food per acre than other grains. With more food available, the population swelled. Between 750 and 1100, the population of China doubled from 50 million people to 100 million. This population growth centered in southern China. Meanwhile, the population in the north shrank. The population boom encouraged the growth of cities and increased the need for more vigorous trade.

Academic Vocabulary

device • *n.,* machine

✓ READING CHECK **Identify Cause and Effect** Why did the population of China double between 750 and 1100?

How Did Trade Fuel Prosperity?

The Tang used the Silk Road as a way to expand their influence westward as far as the eastern border of the Abbasid Caliphate, in what is today Kyrgyzstan and Kazakhstan. The two empires battled one another in Central Asia in 751, and the Abbasid Caliphate won. Even so, the Tang and Song dynasties were able to gain and maintain power by flexing their economic muscle.

During the Song dynasty, many people looked down on merchants. They believed that trade was an unworthy profession. Even so, commerce grew to new levels.

The Grand Canal In the early 600s, the Sui dynasty completed work on the Grand Canal. This canal, which is still in use, is the world's oldest and longest human-built waterway. It connects China's two great rivers, the Huang in the north and the Chang in the south.

The 1,100-mile-long canal quickly filled with barges carrying rice and other goods. The government then built more canals that connected rivers, which increased the flow of trade. The infrastructure was paid for by taxes on trade. By the end of the Song period, China's canals stretched for thousands of miles. These canals cut the cost of transportation and so promoted business.

Currency Another factor that helped fuel growth was the development of a **money economy**. This term refers to an economy in which people use currency rather than bartering to buy and sell goods.

Copper coins were the main currency during the Tang dynasty. But they were heavy and hard to manage in large amounts. During the Song dynasty, the government issued the world's first paper currency, which was easy to use, especially when traveling.

Expanding Industries When farmers grew more food than they needed, they could trade it for craft items such as pottery and cloth. As a result, many industries expanded. For example, the production of silk cloth rose during the Song dynasty. It was usually spun at home by women.

Another important industry was ceramics. During this time, China began to produce **porcelain**, a hard white pottery of extremely fine quality.

One of the biggest industries was iron production. Iron was essential in many industries, such as salt production. It was also used to make weapons, tools, nails, and even Buddhist statues. Improved blast furnaces caused the production of iron and steel to increase greatly. Producing more steel allowed production in other industries to increase as well.

The Growth of Trade With farms and factories producing more goods, trade increased. Canals and the use of money also promoted the growth of trade. A European visitor to China described trade on the Chang River: "In the total volume and value of the traffic on it, it exceeds all the rivers of the Christians put together plus their seas." Like the societies of medieval Europe, which experienced their agricultural revolutions at this same time, China was able to take advantage of trade across Europe, Africa, and Asia.

☑ READING CHECK **Compare and Contrast** Compare the changes in medieval Chinese trade and agriculture to the results of the agricultural revolution in medieval Europe.

Analyze Images Ships still navigate the Grand Canal today. **Main Ideas and Details** What does the present-day use of the canal suggest about it?

China's Golden Age

The Tang and Song eras represent a golden age for Chinese arts and literature. Some of the best-preserved Tang works are pottery figurines of horses, camels, and people. Many of these pieces demonstrate China's knowledge of other cultures. They show that Chinese people enjoyed music and games from Central Asia and India.

The Tang dynasty is also considered the greatest era of Chinese poetry. The famous poet Li Bai wrote in a playful, easygoing style. One of his favorite subjects was the beauty of nature.

Traditional arts were also valued during the Song dynasty. During the Song, architects designed magnificent Buddhist temples filled with statues. Potters turned clay into beautiful ceramic pieces. Artists created fine paintings in soft colors.

During the next dynasty, the Yuan, poets and artists continued to live at the emperor's court. However, the emperor was a Mongol. Many scholars decided to pursue the arts rather than work for the conquerors.

☑ **READING CHECK** **Identify Implied Main Ideas** How did art during China's golden age show the influence of both trade and Chinese history?

▲ This pottery in the shape of a horse was created during the Tang dynasty.

☑ Lesson Check

Practice Vocabulary

1. What is a **bureaucracy**?

2. Describe how a **scholar-official** would qualify for government positions.

3. What term describes the growth of cities?

Critical Thinking and Writing

4. **Identify Cause and Effect** What caused the fall of the Tang dynasty?

5. **Infer** Why was paper money an improvement over coins?

6. **Writing Workshop: Generate Questions to Focus Research** In this topic you will write a research paper about the effect of technology and innovation in this region. As your first step, generate a set of questions in your 📓 Active Journal to ask about each part of the region to focus your research.

Distinguish Fact and Opinion

Follow these steps to distinguish fact from opinion.

INTERACTIVE

Distinguish Between Fact and Opinion

1 Identify the facts. A fact is something that can be proved to be true. A fact often provides information such as *who*, *what*, *where*, *when*, or *how*.

   a. According to the passage, *when* did the civil service examination process became a regular event in China?

   b. What other details answer *who*, *what*, *where*, *when*, or *how* questions?

2 Confirm that the facts can be verified. Use reliable sources to confirm the accuracy of any facts. These include strong online sources, such as edited encyclopedias. Print sources from the library can also confirm facts.

3 Identify the opinions. An opinion is a personal belief or judgment. They are neither true nor false. Statements that make judgments on the events they are describing are usually opinions. What are some examples of opinions from this source?

4 Evaluate opinions. While opinions are not true or false, some are stronger than others. A strong opinion is supported by facts. What are some of the opinions in this source that could be supported by factual information?

Secondary Source

The civil service examination system for those who wanted to become scholar-officials was central to the Chinese state. Many people believed that success on the exam was the only way to achieve success in China during the Song dynasty. They should have expanded their ideas to include other jobs.

Around the start of the 7th century, the civil service exams were administered in various important cities throughout China. This happened once every three years. Before becoming eligible to take one of these "final exams," men had to do well on smaller tests that were given at the local level. Top performers were given government positions. Those with personal influence and high scores got the best jobs.

During this period in China's history, those in the merchant class were looked down upon because of their profession. Chinese culture maintained that working for profit was self-serving and greedy. This attitude was counter-productive because the merchant class helped the economy to grow.

Since most Chinese families did not want to be considered immoral, they pushed their sons to take the tests in order to move up to the official class. This class was believed to be the best in China, in a misguided manner. Most young men, however, were not successful at reaching the top levels of the civil service examination process.

LESSON 2

The Mongol and Ming Empires

BOUNCE TO ACTIVATE ▶ VIDEO

GET READY TO READ

START UP

Invaders called Mongols swept into China. What can you tell about their style of warfare from this artist's depiction?

GUIDING QUESTIONS

- How did the Mongol empire destroy states and increase connections between Europe, Africa, and Asia?
- What steps did Ming emperors take to wipe out Mongol influence and restore Chinese rule?
- Why did Ming rulers choose to reduce contact with the outside world?

TAKE NOTES

Literacy Skills: Sequence
Use the graphic organizer in your 📖 Active Journal to take notes as you read the lesson.

PRACTICE VOCABULARY

Use the vocabulary activity in your 📖 Active Journal to practice the vocabulary words.

Vocabulary		Academic Vocabulary
nomad	despot	expand
steppe	tribute	structure
khan	smuggler	

Throughout its history, China has had to protect its borders from invaders, often tribal nomads. A **nomad** is a person who moves from place to place at different times of the year. These nomads sometimes raided Chinese cities or even formed armies to invade China. In the 1200s, one of these peoples, the Mongols, conquered China and many other lands.

What Were the Mongol Conquests?

The Mongols were nomads who came from the steppes northwest of China. A **steppe** is a large, dry, grass-covered plain. Life on the steppes was difficult. The climate was harsh, and resources were limited. There, the Mongols herded sheep and became great horsemen.

Genghis Khan Mongols lived in clans led by a **khan**, or ruler. By 1206, a warrior had united the Mongol clans under his rule. He was known as Genghis Khan (GEN gis kahn), meaning "ruler of the universe."

After uniting the Mongols, Genghis turned to foreign conquest. He led his armies southeast into China. The Mongols broke through the Great Wall and destroyed many cities. By 1215, they had conquered most of the Jin kingdom that ruled northern China. Later, they swept across Central Asia and into Russia.

Military Victories Genghis was a highly effective military leader. He organized his troops in groups of 10, 100, 1,000, and 10,000 men. An officer chosen for his abilities led each group of fierce warriors. These fighters were expert horsemen who could fire arrows at a full gallop. They moved fast, attacked swiftly, and terrorized enemies.

Genghis also used Chinese weapons. One was the catapult, a device that hurled rocks. The Mongols used it to break down city walls. They also used bombs made with gunpowder.

Genghis was ruthless. He burned the cities of his enemies and left their bones on the ruins as a warning to others. He once said,

Primary Source

"The greatest joy a man can have is victory: to conquer one's enemy's armies, to pursue them, to deprive them of their possessions, to reduce their family to tears, [and] to ride on their horses . . . ."

—Genghis Khan

Finally, Genghis maintained order among the Mongols. He banned theft and feuding. He also dictated harsh punishment, including death, for many crimes.

INTERACTIVE

The Mongol Empire

GEOGRAPHY **SKILLS**

The Mongol empire was one of the largest empires in history.

1. **Region** Describe the greatest extent of the Mongol Empire.

2. **Use Visual Information** What areas did the Mongols conquer after the death of Genghis Khan?

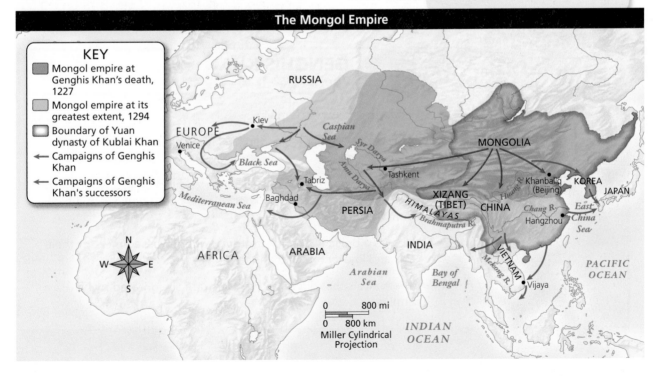

The Mongol Empire

KEY
- Mongol empire at Genghis Khan's death, 1227
- Mongol empire at its greatest extent, 1294
- Boundary of Yuan dynasty of Kublai Khan
- Campaigns of Genghis Khan
- Campaigns of Genghis Khan's successors

Academic Vocabulary

expand • v., to grow, get bigger

Mongols Build an Empire After the death of Genghis Khan in 1227, the Mongol empire continued to **expand**. Its armies conquered what was left of the Jin kingdom in 1234. Then they expanded to the west.

Genghis's grandson, Batu, invaded Russia in 1236. Known as the Golden Horde, this part of the empire ruled Russia for more than 100 years.

Mongol armies also took Persia, Mesopotamia, and Syria. The Mongols under Hulagu, another of Genghis Khan's grandsons, not only captured those regions, but also destroyed the Abbasid Caliphate's capital of Baghdad in 1258. This action ended the symbolic unity of the Muslim world. Many Muslims feared the Mongols would put an end to Islamic culture entirely. However, the Egyptians fought the Mongols and defeated them at the Battle of Ayn Jalut in 1260. Regardless, the Mongols at this time controlled the largest empire the world had ever known.

Ruling the Empire After Genghis Khan died, the Mongols divided the empire into four parts, called khanates. A descendant of Genghis ruled each khanate. One khanate covered southern Central Asia. A second included northern Central Asia and Russia. The third, the land of the Il-Khans, stretched from modern Pakistan to Turkey. The fourth, the Great Khanate, was the largest. It included China and Mongolia.

Outside China, the Mongols ruled through local officials. In Russia, local princes carried out Mongol laws and collected taxes. These princes later became Russia's rulers after the Mongols left.

The Mongols adapted to local culture. For example, the Il-Khans who ruled Muslim lands adopted the religion of Islam.

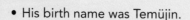 **READING CHECK** **Identify Supporting Details** How did the Mongols conquer northern China?

 **BIOGRAPHY**

5 Things to Know About **GENGHIS KHAN**
Warrior (1162–1227)

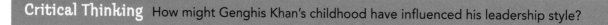

- His birth name was Temüjin.

- A rival Mongol clan poisoned his father when Temüjin was only nine years old.

- He was taken prisoner as a teenager and locked in a wooden collar. He managed to escape by knocking his guard down with a blow from the collar.

- He was a brilliant military strategist who rewarded men for their skill and loyalty rather than their family ties.

- Those rivals that did not surrender were slaughtered by his armies.

Critical Thinking How might Genghis Khan's childhood have influenced his leadership style?

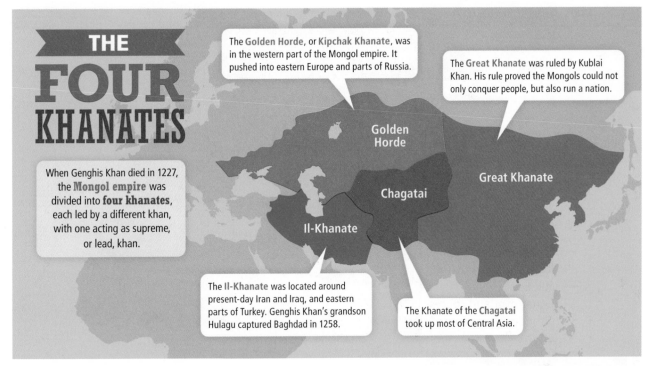

THE FOUR KHANATES

The Golden Horde, or Kipchak Khanate, was in the western part of the Mongol empire. It pushed into eastern Europe and parts of Russia.

The Great Khanate was ruled by Kublai Khan. His rule proved the Mongols could not only conquer people, but also run a nation.

When Genghis Khan died in 1227, the **Mongol empire** was divided into **four khanates**, each led by a different khan, with one acting as supreme, or lead, khan.

Golden Horde

Great Khanate

Chagatai

Il-Khanate

The **Il-Khanate** was located around present-day Iran and Iraq, and eastern parts of Turkey. Genghis Khan's grandson Hulagu captured Baghdad in 1258.

The Khanate of the **Chagatai** took up most of Central Asia.

The Yuan Dynasty

Before they could fully control China, the Mongols had to complete their conquest of the Southern Song. In 1260, Genghis's grandson Kublai (or Kubilai) Khan took over northern China. He began a twenty-year effort to defeat the Song.

Conquering China The many rivers and canals crossing southern China prevented the Mongols from moving quickly on horseback. Kublai Khan solved the problem by building a fleet. With thousands of ships, the Mongols were able to capture cities along southern China's rivers.

In 1279, the Mongols finally gained control of all of China. Kublai had already declared himself the ruler of a new dynasty, the Yuan (yoo-ahn), in 1271. *Yuan* means "the origin," or "beginning."

Mongol Rule in China By declaring a new dynasty, Kublai showed his intention to honor some Chinese traditions. He kept much of the Song bureaucracy. He also adopted rituals of the Chinese court. In these ways, he kept symbols of Chinese royal power.

In other ways, however, Kublai changed China's government. He reduced the power of scholar-officials. He suspended the civil service exams and placed his own followers in office. Kublai also gave more power to regional officials.

How Did Society in Yuan China Change? Perhaps the greatest change under the Mongols was the creation of a new social order. Society was divided into four groups. At the top were the Mongols. Next came other foreigners. Then came the northern Chinese. At the bottom were the recently conquered southern Chinese.

Analyze Diagrams The Mongol empire was divided into four khanates in 1227. **Understand Effects** How would dividing the empire make governing easier?

Did you know?

People in the modern country of Mongolia still value the skills used by Mongol soldiers. Every year, young people from across the country gather at a festival called Naadam to compete in horse races and archery competitions.

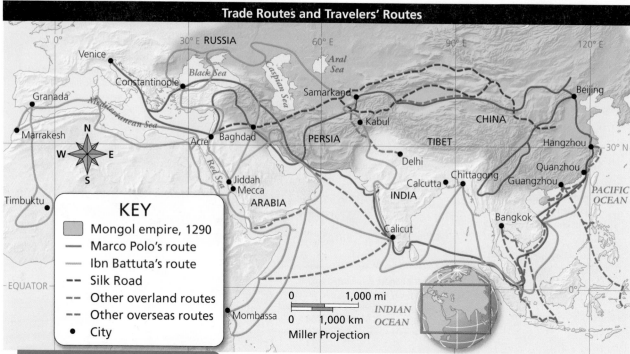

KEY
- Mongol empire, 1290
- Marco Polo's route
- Ibn Battuta's route
- -- Silk Road
- -- Other overland routes
- -- Other overseas routes
- • City

0 — 1,000 mi
0 — 1,000 km
Miller Projection

GEOGRAPHY SKILLS

Marco Polo's journeys to Asia followed trade routes connecting distant lands.

1. **Movement** Where did Marco Polo begin his trip to China along the Silk Road?

2. **Use Visual Information** What part of Polo's trip was within the Mongol empire?

Academic Vocabulary
structure • *n.*, organization

This social **structure** encouraged the Mongols to remain separate from the Chinese. Mongols were the favored group, while the Chinese had few rights or privileges.

To further limit Chinese influence, the Mongols welcomed foreigners in China. Turks and other Muslims were the largest group. They held key positions in the government. Tibetans were encouraged to spread their form of Buddhism across China. The Mongols also allowed Christian missionaries from Europe to preach in China.

✓ READING CHECK **Identify Supporting Details** Why were the Mongols so welcoming to foreigners?

Life in Yuan China

Under Mongol rule, peace and order returned to Asia. In the 1300s, a Muslim traveler named Ibn Battuta wrote of a journey he took to China. He was impressed by how easy it was to travel:

Primary Source

"China is the safest and best regulated country for a traveller. A man may go by himself a nine month's journey, carrying with him large sums of money, without any fear on that account."

—Ibn Battuta, *Travels in Asia and Africa*

Revival of Trade The Mongols encouraged trade and commerce. Merchants held a higher status than they had in earlier times. They were spared certain taxes they had paid under the Song.

The Mongols continued the sea trade begun under the Song. Because of ports on the southeast coast, China had steady contact with the outside world. The port of Quanzhou (chwahn joh) was an especially bustling center of trade. Many of the merchants who carried out this trade were Muslims from southwestern Asia. Maritime, or sea, routes connected China with other parts of Asia, Africa, and Europe.

The Mongols also reopened the ancient Silk Road across Central Asia. As you may recall, the Silk Road was an overland trade route that linked China to Europe. It had been much used during the Han and Tang dynasties, but disorder and warfare in Central Asia had closed this route during the Song dynasty.

Under Mongol rule, traders once again took their caravans across the continent. They carried silk, porcelain, spices, and other luxury goods to southwest Asia and Europe. New crops like tea and cotton also traveled on trade routes. Traders carried ideas and inventions between the different lands as well.

Foreign Visitors The Silk Road and ports such as the one at Quanzhou provided routes for foreign travelers to enter China. The most famous European visitor was Marco Polo, a young man from Venice, Italy.

Polo journeyed to China overland with his father and uncle. He arrived in 1275 and stayed for 17 years. During this time, he was a favored guest of Kublai Khan. The ruler employed Polo as a diplomat and official, sending him on missions around the empire. As a result, Polo got a firsthand look at China.

After his return to Europe, Polo told stories of the places he saw. He described the splendor of Chinese cities and the wonders of Kublai Khan's court. He discussed the use of paper money, which was still unknown in Europe. He told of an amazing kind of stone that burned. Today it is known as coal.

Primary Source

"There is a sort of black stone, which is dug out of veins in the hillsides and burns like logs. . . . I assure you that, if you put them on the fire in the evening . . . they will continue to burn all night."

—*The Travels of Marco Polo*

▲ Kublai Khan's court welcomes Marco Polo in this illustration from the 1800s.

Polo's book gave Europeans their first glimpse of China. Some readers doubted his fantastic tales. On his deathbed, Polo was asked to admit that he had made it all up. He replied that he had described only half of what he had seen.

☑ **READING CHECK** **Identify Supporting Details** How did contact with people in other lands increase under the Mongols?

The Ming Restore Chinese Power

Mongol rule weakened after the death of Kublai Khan in 1294. In the mid-1300s, China suffered through floods, disease, and famine. These hardships led to rebellion against the Mongols. In 1368, Chinese rule was restored under a new dynasty called the Ming.

Ming emperors tried to eliminate all traces of Mongol rule in China because they viewed the Mongols as foreigners. The Ming government lasted until 1644.

Absolute Rule Zhu Yuan Zhang (joo yooahn jahng) joined the rebellion against the Mongols as a young man and became its leader. In 1368, he named himself emperor and took the name Hongwu, which means "vast military."

During his reign, Hongwu took several important steps. He moved the capital to Nanjing. He rejected Mongol trade policies. He also revived the civil service system and Confucian values.

▼ Hongwu restored Chinese power after Mongol rule.

At first, Hongwu tried to rule in the interests of his people. Over time, however, he became a cruel despot. A **despot** is a tyrant or dictator.

Hongwu began to suspect others of plotting against him. He formed a secret police force to seek out his enemies. He had about 100,000 people arrested and executed for treason, or disloyal actions against the state. Hongwu defended his harsh policy:

Primary Source

"In the morning I punish a few; by evening others commit the same crime. I punish these in the evening and by the next morning again there are violations. . . . If I punish these persons, I am regarded as a tyrant. If I am lenient [soft] toward them, the law becomes ineffective, order deteriorates, and people deem me an incapable ruler."

—Hongwu

Analyze Images
Visitors can now tour the Forbidden City in Beijing, but access to the palace complex was limited during the Ming and later Qing dynasties. **Infer** Why do you think that access to the Forbidden City was limited?

Yongle's Rule After Hongwu's death, his son Yongle (yoong luh) took power. Yongle continued his father's pattern of absolute rule. But he decided to move the capital from the southern city of Nanjing to Beijing in the north.

Yongle made this move for two reasons. One was to return the capital to China's northern heartland. The other was to strengthen the country's northern defenses against future Mongol invasion.

The new capital was built to impress visitors with the splendor of the Ming dynasty. At the heart of Beijing lay the Forbidden City, site of the emperor's palace. The design of the city was meant to reinforce the idea of China as the Middle Kingdom, or the center of the world. For many decades, this idea guided Ming rulers in their dealings with other countries.

✓ **READING CHECK** **Identify Supporting Details** Why was the capital of Beijing so magnificent?

What Was the Ming Foreign Policy?

For many years, Ming China acted forcefully on its view that it was the center of the world. Eventually, though, China turned inward and shut itself off from contact with other lands.

The Tributary System Yongle forced foreign countries to recognize China's power. Many countries sent tribute to China. **Tribute** is a payment or gift to a more powerful country. They did this to prevent attacks by China and win favor for their traders.

Ming China traded with other parts of Asia and eastern Africa. Foreign traders brought goods such as horses, spices, and silver from their lands. In return, they received silk, tea, porcelain, and other goods from China.

The system helped both China and the tributary states. China gained peaceful borders. With peace, Ming emperors could spend less money on armies and more on projects such as building canals. Tributary states benefited by getting goods they wanted without going to war.

The Voyages of Zheng He Between 1405 and 1433, Yongle sent an official named Zheng He (jung huh) to lead a series of sea voyages to demonstrate Chinese power and to win more tributary states.

The fleet for the first voyage included more than 60 huge ships and 27,000 men. Zheng He traveled through Southeast Asia to the coast of India on this first trip. Later voyages went as far as the Persian Gulf and the east coast of Africa. Wherever Zheng went, he collected tribute for China.

Primary Source

"The countries beyond the horizon and from the ends of the earth have all becomes subjects. . . . We have crossed immense water spaces . . . and we have set eyes on barbarian regions far away . . ."

— Zheng He

GEOGRAPHY SKILLS

Zheng He traveled nearly as far as Marco Polo.

1. **Place** From which port did Zheng He begin his journey?

2. **Use Visual Information** How far west did Zheng He travel?

China Turns Inward With Yongle's death, the voyages ended and China turned inward. China banned the building of large ships, overseas travel, and contact with most foreigners. Cost was almost certainly one reason. The voyages were very expensive and did not earn enough in trade or tribute to repay their costs.

More important was that scholar-officials believed that China had everything it needed. They saw foreigners as a threat to Chinese culture. They only allowed a few foreign traders to do business in certain cities under strict rules.

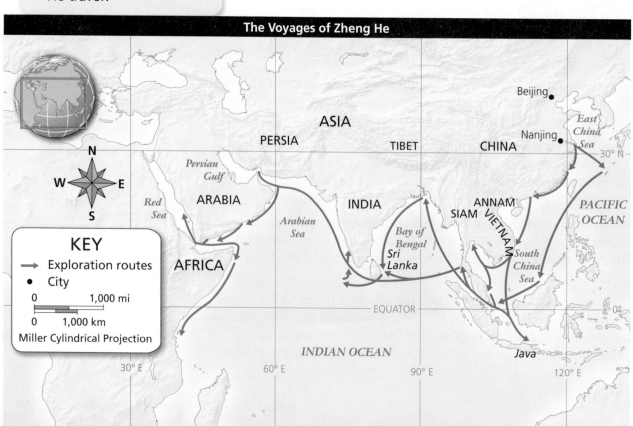

The Voyages of Zheng He

KEY
→ Exploration routes
• City
0   1,000 mi
0   1,000 km
Miller Cylindrical Projection

▲ This artwork depicts the lead ship during one of Zheng He's voyages.

Meanwhile, fewer merchants used the overland Silk Road. After the Mongol empire weakened, the route became dangerous. Despite this, Chinese silk and porcelain remained in great demand.

Decline of the Ming Portuguese sailors arrived in China in 1514. They refused to pay tribute and violated official limits on trade. Chinese officials at first saw Europeans as **smugglers**, or people who trade illegally. However, their silver was hard to resist and trade with Europeans grew.

Meanwhile, the despotism of Ming rulers led to corruption and rebellion. Like the Tang and Song, the Ming also fought invaders along the borders. To repel invasions, especially by Mongols, they rebuilt the Great Wall. But it was not enough. Protests in China and a foreign invasion led to the fall of the dynasty in 1644.

☑ READING CHECK **Identify Supporting Details** How did the Chinese change their attitude toward foreigners?

☑ Lesson Check

Practice Vocabulary

1. What is a **nomad**?

2. What kind of a leader is a **despot**?

3. Describe the role of a **khan**.

Critical Thinking and Writing

4. **Cite Evidence** In what ways might Marco Polo's account of Kublai Khan's court have been biased?

5. **Infer** Why were European traders considered smugglers by the Ming?

6. **Writing Workshop: Support Ideas with Evidence** How did military innovations help the Mongols conquer so much territory? Note evidence from this lesson in your 📕 Active Journal.

LESSON 3
Chinese Thought and Achievements

GET READY TO READ

START UP
Artists during the Song and Tang dynasties created art like the painting shown above. How would you describe the style of this art?

GUIDING QUESTIONS
- What impact did Chinese technology and trade have on the world?
- How did the arts flourish in China under the Tang, Song, and Ming?
- How did Daoism, Confucianism, and Buddhism affect China?

TAKE NOTES
Literacy Skills: Identify Main Ideas
Use the graphic organizer in your 📓 Active Journal to take notes as you read the lesson.

PRACTICE VOCABULARY
Use the vocabulary activity in your 📓 Active Journal to practice the vocabulary words.

Vocabulary		Academic Vocabulary
compass	Buddhism	assemble
block printing	Confucianism	major
Daoism		

During the Tang and Song dynasties, China developed the most advanced civilization in the world. China's technology and culture spread to other regions. Through the Yuan and Ming eras, trade and tribute promoted the flow of goods, technology, and ideas.

Technological Advances
The Chinese pioneered a number of key inventions during the Tang and Song dynasties. These inventions continued to be important to the Ming dynasty and, eventually, to the rest of Asia and Europe.

Shipbuilding and Navigation Chinese shipbuilding technologies were the most advanced in the world through the Ming dynasty. Huge ships, known as "junks," could hold as many as 500 people. These ships had multiple decks, or levels, and masts (tall, vertical posts that carry sails on sailing ships).

Chinese ships also had watertight compartments. If a leak occurred in one place, a section could be sealed off to prevent the ship from sinking.

Marco Polo explained how this worked:

Primary Source

"The sailors promptly find out where the breach is. Cargo is shifted from the damaged compartment into the neighboring ones; for the bulkheads [walls] are so stoutly [strongly] built that the compartments are watertight. The damage is then repaired and the cargo shifted back."

—*The Travels of Marco Polo*

Another important invention was the magnetic compass. A **compass** is a device with a magnetized piece of metal that points to the north. Chinese sailors used the compass to navigate open seas. It allowed them to travel to distant lands without getting lost. As a result, Chinese merchants opened up trade routes to India and Southeast Asia. Zheng He used this technology on his voyages.

Use of the magnetic compass spread through the Muslim lands to Europe. Arab and European sailors used compasses on their voyages by the 1200s.

Paper and Printing A Chinese court official invented paper in 105. Until then, the Chinese wrote on bamboo or silk.

By the 800s, the Chinese were making books using **block printing**, in which workers carved text into blocks of wood. Each block was then covered with ink and pressed on paper to print a page.

Later, Chinese printers crafted movable type. Each piece of type had one character on it. The pieces could be **assembled** to print a page of text and then taken apart to be used again. With this system, printers no longer needed to carve a new block of text for every page of a book.

Printing lowered the cost of books during the Song dynasty. As a result, the number of schools rose. Literacy, or the ability to read and write, also increased. For the first time, common people could hope to become scholar-officials.

Use of paper traveled west to Muslim lands and then to Europe. Printing may have followed a similar path.

Some historians think that printing developed separately in Europe in the 1400s. Others think that Europeans may have gotten the idea from Chinese printed products. Either way, paper and printing made writing and publishing easier. As a result, more people could learn to read and get an education.

Academic Vocabulary

assemble • *v.*, to put together

▲ Wooden Chinese characters used in block printing

CHINESE INNOVATIONS

WE STILL USE MANY CHINESE INNOVATIONS TODAY.

MECHANICAL CLOCK
A Buddhist monk and mathematician invented the first mechanical clock during the Tang Dynasty.

TEA
Legend has it Chinese Emperor Shen Nong first drank tea nearly 4,000 years ago.

SILK
The Chinese harvested fibers from the tiny silkworm to create fabric and paper.

IRON SMELTING
This multi-use metal was first produced during the Zhou dynasty.

PORCELAIN
This high-quality type of ceramic is both useful and beautiful.

THE COMPASS
The Chinese invented this magnetic device key to navigation.

GUNPOWDER
This was originally used for fireworks and then to power weapons.

Analyze Images Chinese inventions and discoveries changed lives around the world. **Understand Effects** How do some of these inventions affect your life?

Gunpowder By the 900s, the Chinese had discovered the mixture of ingredients we know today as gunpowder. They first used gunpowder in fireworks. By the Song era, however, they were using gunpowder to make bombs, rockets, and other weapons.

Like paper, gunpowder spread west to Muslim areas and then to Europe. Gunpowder was the Turks' secret weapon in their conquest of Constantinople. Like Muslims, Europeans were quick to put gunpowder to use in warfare.

Inventions Help Trade The Chinese developed other technologies that improved life and increased trade. In addition to the farming technology you read about, the Chinese developed water pumps for irrigation.

They also crafted a harness to control draft animals. A draft animal is used to pull a load, such as a wagon or a plow. As you have read, extra food from improved farming technology led to more trade.

Other inventions helped industry grow. Weaving and spinning machines allowed workshops to make more and better silk. Methods for making ceramics also improved. These goods were then traded inside and outside China.

Trade led to more creativity. Water pumps and wheelbarrows were used in building projects, such as in canal construction. Canals were used for inland trade. Increased trade led to the greater use of paper money.

☑ **READING CHECK** **Identify Cause and Effect** How did technological innovations help spur trade in China?

Chinese Arts and Culture

China's cultural achievements were also a source of strength and influence. China's artists and craft workers produced work recognized around the world for its quality and beauty.

INTERACTIVE

Arts of Tang China

The Three Perfections From the Tang period through the Ming, scholars valued the "three perfections" of painting, poetry, and calligraphy. Calligraphy is decorative handwriting or lettering. Scholars spent time perfecting their skills in these pursuits. They were also part of the examinations.

The Tang era is known as the peak of Chinese poetry. The Song era is famous for its painters. They created wonderful landscapes, which are images of scenery. Collectors sought out art from the best calligraphers.

Ceramics and Porcelain Ceramics and porcelain were important throughout much of Chinese history. Chinese porcelain became a **major** trade item that was prized around the world. Porcelain was thinner and stronger than other materials used for making plates, bowls, and vases. It was also beautiful, with a smooth white finish. Fancy porcelain plates are still known as "china."

Academic Vocabulary

major • *adj.*, important

The most famous Tang ceramics are figurines, which were often found in tombs. Song ceramics came in many different colors, from greens to blues to browns. Factories in different regions produced items of different colors.

During the Ming era, a town called Jingdezhen made the best porcelain in China. This porcelain, decorated with a blue glaze, was valued around the world.

Other Trade Items Silk was another highly valued trade item. Although silk had been produced since ancient times, it became a more organized industry. Factories improved the quality of silk and improved techniques for dying it.

✓ **READING CHECK Identify Supporting Details** How was porcelain different from other ceramics?

Chinese Belief Systems

Three main belief systems shaped life in China from the Tang period to the Ming period: Daoism, Buddhism, and Confucianism. Each played an important role in Chinese culture.

▲ This ceramic jar from the Tang dynasty could be used to hold household goods.

Look at the map. Where did Buddhism begin, and where did it spread? Record your findings in your 📓 Active Journal.

Daoism **Daoism** is an ancient Chinese philosophy. Its basic teaching is that all things—earth, heaven, and people—should follow the Dao (dow). Dao means "the way," or the flow of nature. A person who follows the way will enjoy peace. For many Daoists, this meant leaving society to live close to nature. By the Tang period, Daoism had priests, temples, and monasteries.

Buddhism **Buddhism** is a religion based on the teachings of the Indian spiritual leader Siddhartha Gautama (sih DAHR tuh GOW tuh muh). He is also known as the Buddha (BOO duh), or "the Enlightened One." Gautama taught that life involves suffering. The way to ease suffering is to give up worldly desires and seek enlightenment, or perfect wisdom. Those who reach enlightenment enter nirvana, which is a state of complete peace. They also escape the endless cycle of suffering, death, and rebirth.

Buddhism reached China during the Han dynasty. It gained strength during the troubled times between the Han and Tang dynasties. Its appeal was based on the hope for an end to suffering.

Over time, Buddhism adapted and absorbed elements of Daoism. By the Tang dynasty, Buddhism had millions of followers in China. Temples and monasteries grew rich from donations.

Attacks on Buddhism Some Chinese thinkers criticized Buddhism as a foreign religion. Because of this, it never became China's official religion. Other critics opposed Buddhists' withdrawal from the world. They believed that people should be

GEOGRAPHY **SKILLS**

Buddhism spread through Asia after its founding by Siddhartha Gautama.

1. **Place** Where did Buddhism originate?

2. **Infer** Which regions do you think Buddhism reached last?

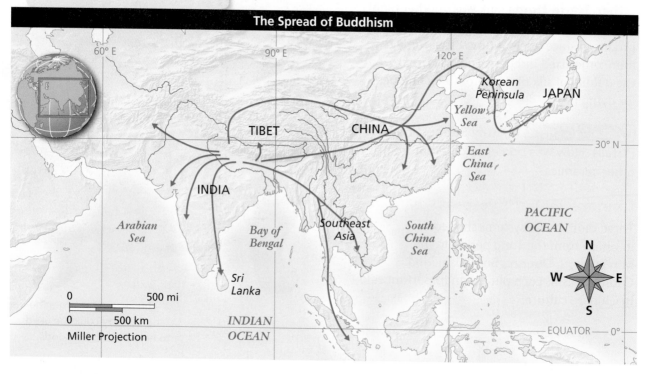

The Spread of Buddhism

involved in society and family life. Still others criticized the wealth and power of the monasteries.

At times, criticism led to persecution. The worst attacks came during the reign of the Tang emperor Wuzong, a Daoist. In 845, Wuzong ordered the destruction of 4,600 Buddhist monasteries and 40,000 temples. Some 250,000 Buddhist monks and nuns were forced to give up religious life. Buddhism never gained support from China's rulers. Still, many Chinese continued to follow Buddhism. Buddhist temples and monasteries still stand in China today.

Confucianism Much of the opposition to Buddhism came from the followers of Confucianism. **Confucianism** is a system of moral behavior, based on the teachings of Confucius. It was an important belief system, especially for scholar-officials.

Confucius lived during a time of warfare and disorder in China. His philosophy was designed to restore peace and stability.

▲ A portrait of Confucius

Confucius stressed the importance of virtue. He said that a wise ruler governed through moral example, not force. He taught that people could gain virtue through education.

Confucianism was also based on respect for family and the social order. Everyone had a role to play in society. As Confucius put it, "Let the prince be a prince, the minister a minister, the father a father, and the son a son." He taught that children should respect their parents. Subjects should respect their rulers. Rulers should respect the nation. By following these roles and respecting social rank, the Chinese would maintain order. Even though Buddhism had lost favor, the Chinese combined some of its teachings with Confucianism and Daoism.

Neo-Confucianism The growth of Buddhism caused Confucian scholars to think about religious questions. By the Song era, a new take on Confucian ideas, later called Neo-Confucianism, arose. The Neo-Confucians found new meanings in the writings of Confucius. In doing so, they answered questions about the meaning and purpose of life.

This form of Confucian thought showed the influence of Buddhism and Daoism. One famous Neo-Confucian, a scholar-official named Zhu Xi (joo shee), said that people should live according to the Dao. But he defined the Dao as a process of self-improvement and education, rather than as a retreat from society. The combination of elements of Confucianism, Buddhism, and Daoism focused on the quest to live a more moral life, emphasizing family and community. The ideas of the Neo-Confucians had a great influence on China from the Song period onward.

Quick Activity

Read the quotes in your 📓 Active Journal and place them under the correct heading—Daoism, Buddhism, or Confucianism.

☑ READING CHECK Compare and Contrast What did Daoism, Buddhism, and Confucianism have in common?

▲ A style of teapot popular since the Song dynasty

How Did Chinese Culture Spread?

Because it was the largest and most powerful country in East Asia, China and its civilization had great effects on smaller countries nearby. In addition, China manufactured more goods than any other country. Through trade, it influenced Central Asia and Europe.

The Impact of Chinese Thought Both Confucianism and Buddhism spread from China to nearby lands. Over time, the governments of Vietnam, Korea, and Japan all adopted practices that reflected Confucian ideas.

For instance, scholar-officials ran their bureaucracies. The influence of Confucian ideas was particularly strong in Korea. Buddhism also spread from China, through Korea, into Japan.

Chinese Culture Vietnam, Korea, and Japan borrowed the Chinese writing system. In time, they adapted it to their needs. They imported Chinese styles of painting, music, and architecture. Both Korea and Japan built capital cities modeled on Chang'an.

Chinese culinary arts also spread throughout East Asia. Culinary arts are styles of cooking and food preparation. Many countries adopted chopsticks as tools for cooking and eating. They borrowed the Chinese wok, a large round-bottomed pan used for frying and steaming foods. These countries also adopted the custom of drinking tea.

Trade and the West The Ming government tried to limit the influence of foreigners, but trade with European merchants brought new goods and technologies to the Chinese. Missionaries brought Western Christianity. In turn, Chinese products and ideas spread to Europe.

☑ **READING CHECK Identify Main Ideas** How did Chinese influence spread?

Did you know?

Today, tea is the second most popular beverage in the world, after water. China and India are the two biggest producers of tea.

☑ Lesson Check

Practice Vocabulary

1. How did the **compass** help sailors?

2. What are the main beliefs of **Buddhism, Confucianism**, and **Daoism**?

Critical Thinking and Writing

3. **Infer** Why might some people believe that the invention of gunpowder is the most important Chinese technological advancement?

4. **Draw Conclusions** How did China influence the countries around it?

5. **Writing Workshop: Develop a Clear Thesis** What effect did Chinese technology have on China and the rest of the world? Use information from this lesson to begin to develop a clear thesis for your research paper in your 📔 Active Journal.

Primary Sources

Zhu Xi, Neo-Confucianist Thought

Confucianism was threatened during the Tang period when Buddhism gained influenced in China, Japan, and Korea. This upset Confucian scholar-officials and Daoist priests. They felt that Buddhism was a foreign influence, and they were threatened by it. In response, Tang emperors began to support a fusion of Confucian, Daoist, and Buddhist beliefs and practices. This formed a new popular religion, emphasizing moral living, daily ritual, and dedication to family and community.

▶ Zhu Xi was a neo-Confucian scholar who lived in China from 1130–1200.

Original nature is an <u>all-pervading</u> ① perfection not contrasted with evil. This is true of what Heaven has <u>endowed</u> ② in the self. But when it operates in human beings, there is the differentiation of good and evil. When humans act in accord with it, there is goodness. When humans act out of accord with it, there is evil ③. How can it be said that the good is not the original nature? It is in its operation in human beings that the distinction of good and evil arises, but conduct in accord with the original nature is due to the original nature. If, as they say, that is the original goodness and there is another goodness contrasted with evil, there must be two natures. Now what is received from Heaven is the same nature as that in accordance with which goodness ensues, except that as soon as good appears, evil, by <u>implication</u>, ④ also appears, so that we necessarily speak of good and evil in contrast. But it is not true that there is originally evil existing out there, waiting for the appearance of good to oppose it. We fall into evil only when our actions are not in accord with the original nature.

Analyzing Primary Sources

Review the passage to find details for your answers. Cite evidence in your answer.

1. **Identify Main Ideas** According to Zhu Xi, what is a person's original nature?

2. **Analyze Information** Explain the existence of evil in neo-Confucian terms.

3. **Write a Summary** Write a summary of the primary source. Stay objective by not allowing any personal feelings to creep in.

Reading and Vocabulary Support

① Something that is all-pervading is spread throughout.

② Endowed is a verb that means "provided" or "given."

③ What is Zhu Xi saying about human beings' actions here?

④ Implication is another word for conclusion.

Emergence of Japan

BOUNCE TO ACTIVATE   ▶ VIDEO

GET READY TO READ

START UP

Study the photograph of Mount Fuji, the largest mountain in Japan. Based on this photograph, how might Japan's landscape have shaped life in that country?

GUIDING QUESTIONS

- How did geography affect the development of Japanese culture?
- What actions did Prince Shotoku take to strengthen Japan as a kingdom?
- How did Chinese culture, ideas, and technologies influence Japan?

TAKE NOTES

Literacy Skills: Sequence

Use the graphic organizer in your 📖 Active Journal to take notes as you read the lesson.

PRACTICE VOCABULARY

Use the vocabulary activity in your 📖 Active Journal to practice the vocabulary words.

Vocabulary		Academic Vocabulary
archipelago	kami	unify
mainland	regent	tradition
clan		

Japan arose in the shadow of its powerful neighbor, China. Early Japanese culture and society often borrowed from China and Japan's other neighbor, Korea. But Chinese and Korean cultures were not the only influences on Japan. Geography also had great effects on the island nation.

How Did Geography Set Japan Apart?

Japan is an **archipelago** (ahr kuh PEL uh goh), or chain of islands. To Japan's west is the continent of Asia. To the east lies the broad Pacific Ocean. In ancient times, the Japanese believed that theirs was the first land to see the sun rise in the morning. They called their country *Nippon*, which means "land of the rising sun." In Japanese tradition, the Sun Goddess was the country's special protector.

What Is Japan's Land and Climate Like? Japan is made up of four large islands and thousands of smaller ones. Its total land area is about the size of the state of California.

The archipelago is very long from north to south. Honshu (HAHN shoo), the main island, is much larger than the others.

A ridge of volcanic mountains runs the length of the island chain. Mount Fuji is the highest peak. It rises more than 12,000 feet above sea level. Because of Mount Fuji's beauty, it has always been an important symbol for the Japanese people.

Japan is so mountainous that less than 15 percent of its land can be farmed. Most people live on plains or along the coastline. The Japanese take much of their food from the ocean.

The Ring of Fire Japan sits at the border between two plates, or sections, of Earth's outer crust. The border forms part of the Ring of Fire. This region of volcanoes and earthquakes circles the Pacific Ocean.

Japan and Its Neighbors Korea and China are Japan's neighbors on the Asian mainland. A **mainland** is an area that is a part of a continent.

About 120 miles of open water separates Korea from Japan. China is farther away. Still, waves of migrants from the mainland settled in Japan. Over time, Japan felt the influence of Korean and Chinese cultures. Many Chinese and Koreans migrated to Japan in search of refuge or opportunity, especially during times of disruption. As the migrants came to Japan, they brought with them knowledge about Buddhism, writing systems, and making metal, paper, and silk.

✓ READING CHECK **Draw Conclusions** Why was Japan's culture able to grow in isolation for so long?

INTERACTIVE

Geography of Japan

GEOGRAPHY **SKILLS**

Japan is an island chain stretching south to north, to the east of China and Korea.

1. **Location** What bodies of water separate Japan from other countries?

2. **Use Visual Information** What route would traded goods and ideas need to take to reach Japan?

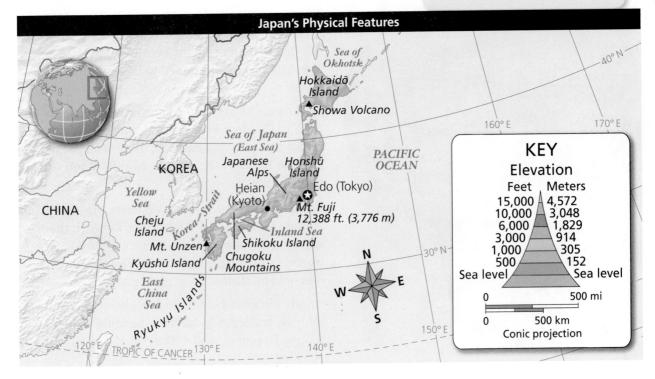

Japan's Physical Features

Sea of Okhotsk

Hokkaidō Island

Showa Volcano

Sea of Japan (East Sea)

PACIFIC OCEAN

40° N

160° E

170° E

KOREA

Japanese Alps

Honshū Island

Heian (Kyoto)

Edo (Tokyo)

Yellow Sea

Mt. Fuji 12,388 ft. (3,776 m)

Korea Strait

Cheju Island

Inland Sea

CHINA

Mt. Unzen

Shikoku Island

Kyūshū Island

Chugoku Mountains

East China Sea

Ryukyu Islands

30° N

KEY

Elevation

Feet	Meters
15,000	4,572
10,000	3,048
6,000	1,829
3,000	914
1,000	305
500	152
Sea level	Sea level

0   500 mi

0   500 km

Conic projection

N / E / W / S

150° E

120° E   TROPIC OF CANCER 130° E   140° E

Japan's Early History

The first groups of humans in Japan arrived many thousands of years ago. Historians have identified one culture group, the Jomon (JOH mun), by their distinctive pottery. The Jomon migrated to Japan some 11,000 years ago. They lived by hunting and fishing.

The Yayoi By 250 BCE a new group had appeared in Japan—the Yayoi (YAH yoy). They probably came from mainland Asia. In time, the Yayoi merged with or pushed out the Jomon. Unlike the Jomon, the Yayoi wove cloth and worked bronze and iron.

Most important, the Yayoi introduced the technique of growing rice in irrigated fields. Rice became Japan's most important crop. A diet based on seafood and rice helped boost the population.

The Yamato Clan Triumphs Local clans ruled Japan by the 200s CE. A **clan** is a group of people with a common ancestor. The head of a clan was also a religious leader. Part of his job was to show respect to the clan's kami so they would have good harvests. A **kami** (KAH mee) is a holy being that represents a spirit of nature, sacred place, ancestor, or clan in Japanese culture. Each clan also had its own land.

From the 200s to the 400s, warlike clans competed for land and power. The winner of this struggle was the Yamato clan from the plains of central Honshu.

Riding horses and fighting with swords and with bows and arrows, the Yamato first gained control over lands to the north and west. They eventually built a small state. Sometimes they went to war against neighboring clans. More often they made alliances through marriage or other ties.

The Yamato applied new technology in their territory. They used iron tools to till the land. They also found better ways to level and flood rice fields. These improvements added to their wealth and power.

Yamato emperors claimed descent from their kami, the Sun Goddess. Even today, Japan's imperial family traces its descent from the Sun Goddess and the Yamato clan. It is the world's oldest ruling royal family.

Yamato Society The most powerful members of Yamato society were clan leaders. Beneath them was a large class of free farmers, with free craft workers ranking below farmers. The lowest rank was held by enslaved Japanese people.

Family life in Yamato times involved different roles for men and women. Males in farming families received a plot of land at the age of 6 to farm the

Analyze Images This piece of pottery dates from the Jomon period. **Use Visual Information** What makes this pottery different from the Chinese pottery pictured in previous lessons?

rest of their lives. Males also had to provide military service to clan leaders. Women had an important role in religion, communicating with kamis. Women were able to hold property, like men. Women could also hold power. There were several female Yamato rulers.

✔ READING CHECK Identify Supporting Details How did the Yamato clan gain control of much of Japan?

How Did Shotoku Strengthen Japan?

Even after the Yamato clan gained power, Japan was not fully united. Clan leaders saw little reason to obey a distant government. In 593, Prince Shotoku took power. He was not an emperor. Instead, he was a regent for the empress, his aunt. A **regent** is someone who governs a country in the name of a ruler who is unable to rule, often because of age.

Support for Buddhism Shotoku began the difficult task of **unifying** Japan. He had to strengthen the central government and reduce the power of clan leaders. One way he did this was by supporting Buddhism, which arrived in Japan from Korea in 538.

Shotoku hoped that the new religion would unite the Japanese people. However, clan leaders opposed the new religion because they were also religious leaders. If people stopped worshiping their kami, clan leaders would lose importance.

Guidelines for Government Japanese leaders also learned about Chinese government and the teachings of Confucius. Shotoku studied these. He believed that Confucianism, like Buddhism, could unify Japan. Shotoku's moral code is laid out in a document known as the Constitution of Seventeen Articles.

This document was not like modern constitutions. It was not a plan for government. Instead, it was a set of guiding principles for people, rulers, and the government itself. It was based on Confucian and Buddhist thought. A section of the first article laid out the Confucian idea of harmony. It read, "Harmony should be valued and quarrels should be avoided."

The second article called for respecting Buddhism. A later article said that clan heads should not be allowed to tax the people. That power, it suggested, belonged only to the central government.

Missions to China In 607, Shotoku sent official representatives to China to study arts and government. This was the first of several official missions to the Chinese mainland. A mission is a group of people sent to represent their country. The mission included scholars, artists, and Buddhist monks.

▲ Prince Shotoku

Academic Vocabulary
unify • v., bring together

Quest CONNECTIONS

How does the quote from the first article of the Constitution of Seventeen Articles show Chinese influence? Record your thoughts in your 📓 Active Journal.

Explore the guidelines for government in your 📓 Active Journal.

When they returned, these experts helped make Japan's government more like that of Tang China. For example, Japanese rulers began using a system of official ranks and duties like those in the Chinese court. Officials could be recognized by the color of their caps.

✓ **READING CHECK** Identify Supporting Details How did Prince Shotoku attempt to unify Japan?

Later Reforms

Prince Shotoku died in 622. Japan was still ruled by clans, but other reformers continued efforts to create a strong government. In 646, they enacted a program known as the Taika Reform. *Taika* means "great change."

The most important new laws said that all land belonged to the emperor and that everyone was his subject. Some clan leaders became local officials. They were responsible for collecting taxes, which were based on the number of people who lived in an area. These changes made Japan more like Tang China.

In 702, a new law code for the entire country made the leader of the Yamato clan the official emperor and said that he should be called "son of Heaven." The new laws also defined crimes and punishments. These criminal laws applied equally to everyone in Japan.

The rulers continued to strengthen their power. In 710 they built a new capital city at Nara.

✓ **READING CHECK** Identify Supporting Details How did Taika Reform increase government's power?

Political Reform in Japan, 646

Land Ownership	Structure of Local Government
• Abolishing all titles held by imperial princes • Abolishing title to lands held directly by the imperial court • Abolishing private titles to lands and works held by ministers and "functionaries" of the court, local nobles, and village chiefs	• Placing the capital under an administrative system • Appointing governors and prefects in other areas of the country • Forming a village out of every 50 households and appointing an alderman for each village who was responsible for assigning the sowing of crops and collecting taxes, among other things

Analyze Charts In 646, Emperor Kōtoku began a set of political reforms. These Taika Reforms were based on Confucianism and other Chinese political philosophies. **Infer** How did these reforms strengthen Japan's government?

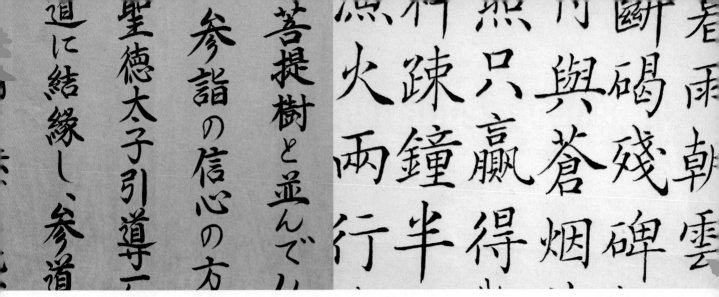

Borrowing From Neighbors

Chinese culture of the Tang dynasty strongly influenced Japan and Korea. As you learned, early Japanese rulers looked to China as a model for government. Japanese scholars organized an official history of Japan, just as Chinese rulers arranged histories of China. Japan also adopted the Chinese calendar.

In the time of the first Yamato emperor, Japanese had only been spoken, not written. Contact with the mainland changed that. Around 500, the Japanese began to adapt China's writing system. They used Chinese characters, with some changes, to write the Japanese language.

Japan and Korea also developed ties. Buddhist monks arrived in Japan from Korea in 538. Most Japanese practiced Shinto, a mix of ancient beliefs and traditions. Over time, Japan's practice of Buddhism would absorb many of the Shinto spirits and **traditions**. You will read more about these religions in Lesson 6.

☑ READING CHECK **Identify Supporting Details** What did most Japanese practice before Buddhism arrived? How did religion in Japan change after Buddhism's arrival?

Analyze Images
Japanese calligraphy is pictured on the left, and Chinese calligraphy on the right. **Synthesize Visual Information** How did Chinese writing affect written Japanese?

Academic Vocabulary

tradition • *n.,* a practice or belief handed down from one generation to another

---

☑ Lesson Check

Practice Vocabulary

1. What is an **archipelago**?

2. What was the role of a **kami** in Japanese culture?

3. What is a **regent**?

Critical Thinking and Writing

4. **Identify Cause and Effect** How did Japanese emperors increase their power?

5. **Infer** Why did Japanese rulers send missions to China?

6. **Writing Workshop: Find and Use Credible Sources** Use tips in your 📓 Active Journal to conduct research to learn more about how technology affected agriculture in Japan under the Yamato.

Japanese Feudalism

BOUNCE TO ACTIVATE   ▶ VIDEO

GET READY TO READ

START UP

Study the picture of the samurai. Samurai had a similar role to knights in medieval Europe. How did knights help to maintain a system of feudalism?

GUIDING QUESTIONS

- Why did Japanese emperors lose power to rival clans?
- How did feudalism structure society in medieval Japan?
- What influence did samurai values have on medieval Japan?

TAKE NOTES

Literacy Skills: Analyze Cause and Effect
Use the graphic organizer in your 📓 Active Journal to take notes as you read the lesson.

PRACTICE VOCABULARY

Use the vocabulary activity in your 📓 Active Journal to practice the vocabulary words.

Vocabulary		Academic Vocabulary
figurehead	daimyo	constantly
shogun	samurai	factor
feudalism	bushido	

Prince Shotoku and other reformers tried to unify Japan. They had only limited success. Over time, the power of the emperor faded and Japan became a violent land ruled by rival warriors. Peace was only restored around 1600.

Power Shifts in Japan

By tradition, each Yamato ruler set up court in his own territory. Then, in 794, the imperial court settled in a new capital city, Heian (HAY ahn). The name meant "capital of peace and tranquility." It later became known as Kyoto. It was modeled after the Chinese city of Chang'an. Emperors lived in Heian for more than a thousand years. But during that time, their power began to shift into other hands.

The Imperial Court The imperial court was divided into different ranks, or levels, of nobles. Privileges and influence depended mainly on one's rank. Unlike China, Japan did not give out government jobs based on merit. Most officials were sons from noble families.

The emperor and nobles of the court appeared to live wonderful lives. Their nights and days were filled with dinner parties, dances, poetry contests, music, and religious rituals. They also produced magnificent art and literature. Among these nobles, the Fujiwara family grew in power.

The Fujiwara Take Over By 860, the emperor was no longer the true ruler. The Fujiwara family was running the country. Behind the scenes, they controlled the government for some 300 years. The emperor was a **figurehead**, which means that he was only a symbolic leader, while someone else was really in control.

The Fujiwara rose to power by having their daughters marry emperors. The sons of these marriages often became emperors. They made sure that members of the Fujiwara clan got high positions in the government.

In the late 800s, the Fujiwara moved closer to taking complete power. They persuaded several emperors to retire. The position of emperor went to the child who was next in line for the throne.

A Fujiwara leader then became regent for the child. He was now the power behind the throne. When the young emperor was finally old enough to rule, the leader became his advisor, thus holding on to power. The Fujiwara repeated this process again and again.

Fortunately for Japan, most of the Fujiwara were able rulers. But their long rule marked a shift in power. Japan remained unified, but the Fujiwara family was in charge, not the emperor. In addition, nobles came to own most of the land.

Japan also began to trade with its neighbors, China and Korea. Merchants from both nations traded luxury goods for Japanese timber, copper, silver, and steel swords. These connections helped China dominate the region economically and culturally by 1300.

✅ **READING CHECK** **Identify Supporting Details** How did social interactions allow the Fujiwara to gain power in Japan's government?

Rival Clans Battle for Power

Outside the capital, other clans envied and resented the Fujiwaras' power. Some clan leaders began to raise their own private armies. Those leaders became warlords. The warriors that they trained were fiercely loyal to their own clans, not to the Fujiwara or the emperor.

Military Leaders Gain Strength The most powerful of these warrior clans were the Taira (TY rah) and the Minamoto (mee nah MOH toh). They worked together just long enough to push the Fujiwara out of power.

▼ Minamoto Yoritomo was a military leader who defied the emperor and the Fujiwaras.

Then they turned against each other. Over long years of war, power moved between the Taira and Minamoto clans. The violence eventually reached Kyoto. In 1159, Minamoto forces stormed into the capital. They burned the emperor's palace and killed many court officials. Japan had entered a long period of warfare and suffering. A poet expressed his sadness this way:

Primary Source

"All hung about with cloud,
The distant mountain meadows
Are in autumn and
All I do recall
Is sadness."

—Saigyo, translated by Thomas McAuley

The First Shogun In 1185, Minamoto warriors defeated Taira forces in a final clash at sea. As a result, Minamoto Yoritomo (yoh ree TOH moh) became the most powerful person in Japan.

Minamoto received the title of **shogun** (SHOH gun), or supreme military commander. The position was supposed to be temporary, but Minamoto wanted to keep the title permanently. In theory, Minamoto served as advisor to the emperor. In reality, he ruled Japan. Shoguns held true power in Japan for hundreds of years.

✓ READING CHECK **Identify Supporting Details** What effect did war between rival clans have on Japan?

Analyze Images A scroll from the 1200s shows Minamoto forces attacking the capital. **Use Visual Information** Based on the details in the picture, how well-equipped do you think the Minamoto were for battle?

Feudalism in Japan

Minamoto's rule marked the beginning of military rule by local lords and their fighters. The central government became weak. Life was often lawless and violent under the shoguns. Local nobles owned much land and fought for power. The result was a new set of social, political, and economic relationships known together as feudalism.

Daimyo, Samurai, and Peasants **Feudalism** was a social system in which landowners granted people land or other rewards in exchange for military service or labor. Landowners, warriors, and peasants served one another's needs. This system spelled out relationships among those different classes of people.

In the Japanese feudal system, people had clearly defined roles. By the 1400s, protecting people had become the responsibility of **daimyo** (DY myoh), or local land-owning lords. Each daimyo relied on peasants to work the land. In exchange for a share of the crop, he promised to protect them.

The daimyo usually had a large wooden castle, surrounded by a strong wall. It offered some safety from attack. The daimyo also provided protection through a small army of **samurai** (SAM uh ry), or highly trained warriors. In Japanese, *samurai* means "those who serve." In exchange for their military service, the daimyo paid his samurai a salary.

The Code of Bushido Two values guided samurai. One was loyalty to one's lord. The other was personal honor. These formed the heart of a set of rules called **bushido** (BOO shee doh)—"the way of the warrior." This strict code of conduct guided samurai behavior. It became an official code in the 1600s and influenced Japan into the 1900s.

The code of bushido governed a samurai's life. He trained hard, fought bravely, and died with honor. "A man born a samurai should live and die sword in hand," one warrior advised.

Under the code of bushido, loyalty to one's lord was more important than loyalty to family, religion, or even the emperor. If a samurai's lord was in danger, he would follow the lord, even if it meant certain death.

An old story relates a conversation between two samurai whose lord is losing a battle. "The general is surrounded by rebels," the first samurai reported. "It is hard to see how he can get away." The second samurai replied:

Primary Source

"If he must die, I intend to share his fate and go with him to the underworld."

—from *Tale of Mutsu*, translated by Helen Craig McCullough

Analyze Images Samurai warriors wore armor like this. **Compare and Contrast** Compare this armor to images you have seen of medieval knights in Europe.

Personal honor was also important. Riding into battle, a samurai shouted out his name and family. He wanted everyone to see his courage and skill. A samurai was also careful about his appearance. His robe, his armor, and even his horse reflected his pride.

Comparing European and Japanese Feudalism

European and Japanese feudalism shared some features. Both began during a time of violence and warfare. Both involved an exchange of land for services. Both knights and samurai were expected to follow codes of conduct that emphasized honor, bravery, and loyalty.

The two forms of feudalism had a major difference: religion. Most Europeans were Christian. Japanese feudalism was influenced by ideas from Buddhism, Shinto, and Confucianism.

☑ READING CHECK **Compare and Contrast** Compare the systems of feudalism in medieval Europe and Japan.

Mongols Threaten Japan

Mongols took over China in the 1200s. Their ruler, Kublai Khan, sent officials to Japan to demand tribute. They said that there would be war if Japan did not pay for the Khan's friendship. The shogun's government sent the officials away.

In November 1274, the Khan sent hundreds of ships across the sea. They carried more than 25,000 troops, along with horses and weapons. This was the first experience Japanese warriors had with gunpowder weapons. Yet the samurai fought bravely and held off the invaders' first attack.

The invaders returned to their ships. That night, a fierce storm shattered the ships. Nearly 13,000 men drowned. Kublai Khan sent more

Analyze Diagrams
Japanese and European feudalism had similar structures. **Infer** Which group shown on the diagram had the most people for both societies?

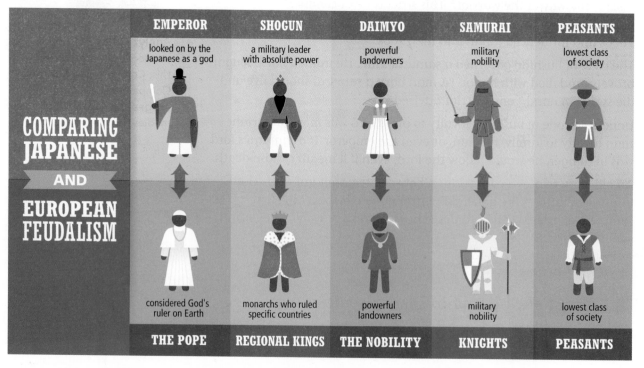

COMPARING JAPANESE AND EUROPEAN FEUDALISM

EMPEROR	SHOGUN	DAIMYO	SAMURAI	PEASANTS
looked on by the Japanese as a god	a military leader with absolute power	powerful landowners	military nobility	lowest class of society
considered God's ruler on Earth	monarchs who ruled specific countries	powerful landowners	military nobility	lowest class of society
THE POPE	REGIONAL KINGS	THE NOBILITY	KNIGHTS	PEASANTS

officials to Japan to demand tribute. This time, the shogun had them beheaded on the beach. In 1281, Kublai Khan tried again, with almost 140,000 soldiers. The samurai held off the invaders for nearly two months.

The Japanese prayed to their gods, the kami, for help. A typhoon, a violent tropical storm, came roaring across the sea. Thousands of Mongol and Chinese soldiers drowned. More were stranded on shore, where Japanese warriors killed them. The Japanese believed that the kami had sent the typhoon to save them. They called it *kamikaze* (kah mee KAH zay), or the "wind of the gods."

READING CHECK Identify Supporting Details Why is the *kamikaze* remembered?

Japan's Reunification

The end of the Mongol threat did not bring peace to Japan. With weak shoguns, the clans continued to fight among themselves. Hundreds of years passed before Japan was unified again.

Strong Leaders Emerge During the 1400s and 1500s, Japan was controlled by daimyo who **constantly** fought for land and power. Historians call this violent period the "Era of the Warring States."

Finally, in the 1500s, three ambitious leaders managed to end the constant warfare. The first, Oda Nobunaga, worked all his life to bring Japan "under a single sword." Nobunaga did not fully succeed, but he reduced the power of the warlords.

The second great leader, Toyotomi Hideyoshi, unified Japan in 1590. He achieved peace only because the daimyo pledged loyalty to him. When Hideyoshi died, clans began to quarrel once more.

Analyze Images This artwork depicts the typhoon that helped the Japanese defeat a Mongol and Chinese invasion. **Identify Supporting Details** Why did the Japanese call this typhoon *kamikaze*?

Academic Vocabulary
constantly • *adv.*, again and again

▲ A Japanese artist created this woodblock of Matthew Perry (center), an American naval officer who arrived in Japan in 1852, and two of his men.

Tokugawa Ieyasu Brings Peace The third leader, Tokugawa Ieyasu (toh koo GAH wah ee YAY ah soo), united the country again in 1600. He took the title of shogun, then founded a new capital at Edo (present-day Tokyo). Ieyasu made laws that finally brought peace to Japan.

He ordered the daimyo to destroy their castles and spend much of the year in Edo, where he could watch them. When they left, they had to leave their families behind. Edo grew to be a huge city.

Ieyasu officially divided society into four classes, ranked from top to bottom: samurai, farmers, artisans, and merchants. Only samurai were allowed to own weapons. Farmers produced food. Artisans made the goods people needed, such as cloth, pottery, and weapons. Merchants traded goods.

Ieyasu's measures ended the violence at last. The Tokugawa family ruled a peaceful, unified Japan until 1868.

Life in Peacetime Once Japan was at peace, Japanese life changed. Merchants became wealthy as the country's population began to grow.

The new economic forces caused the daimyo, samurai, and peasants to become less prosperous. Many samurai took government jobs, but others could not support themselves. Meanwhile, famines hurt peasants. Unrest among these groups led, in part, to the end of the Tokugawa shoguns.

Another **factor** was the arrival of Western traders. Since the 1500s, Japanese leaders had tried to limit the influence of Europeans and other outsiders. In 1853, however, American warships arrived and forced Japan to accept trade. In 1868, the last shogun-led government fell.

Academic Vocabulary

factor • *n.*, cause

☑ READING CHECK **Identify Supporting Details** How did the Tokugawa shoguns bring peace to Japan?

☑ Lesson Check

Practice Vocabulary

1. Who were the **daimyo**?

2. What was the code of **bushido**?

3. What were the duties of the **samurai**?

Critical Thinking and Writing

4. **Identify Cause and Effect** How did the rise of the Fujiwara lead to feudalism?

5. **Infer** Why did Tokugawa Ieyasu force the daimyo to leave their families in Edo?

6. **Writing Workshop: Cite Sources** As you continue to research the effects of technology and innovation on Japan, be sure to properly keep track of the sources you will cite in your final essay.

Primary Sources

The Tale of the Heike

The Tale of the Heike is a classic of medieval Japanese literature that describes in the warrior culture of that time and place. This passage tells the story of Kumagai Naozane, an older warrior from the Heike clan who must decide whether or not to slay a younger warrior he encounters. It highlights Japanese military values, the importance of samurai ethics, and the role of religion.

▶ Samurai were celebrated in art, both through paintings such as this one and stories like *The Tale of the Heike*.

Quickly hurling the warrior to the ground, Kumagi sprang upon the warrior and tore off his helmet to cut off his head, when he beheld the face of a youth sixteen or seventeen. . . .

"Though he is one of their leaders," mused Kumagai, "if I slay him it will not turn victory into defeat, and if I spare him, it will not turn defeat into victory. When my son Kojirû was but slightly wounded at Ichi no tani this morning, did it not pain me? How this young man's father would grieve to hear that he had been killed! I will spare him." ①

Just then, looking behind him, he saw Doi and Kajiwara coming up with fifty horsemen. "Alas! Look there," he exclaimed, the tears running down his face, "though I would spare your life, the whole countryside swarms with our men, and you cannot escape them. If you must die, let it be by my hand, and I will see that prayers are said for your rebirth in Paradise." . . .

Kumagi's eyes swam and he hardly knew what he did, but <u>there was no help for it</u> ②. . . . He pressed his face to the sleeve of his armor and wept bitterly. Then, he was stripping off the young man's armor when he discovered a flute in a <u>brocade</u> ③ bag. "Ah," he exclaimed, "it was this youth and his friends who were amusing themselves with music within the walls this morning. Among all our men of the Eastern Provinces I doubt if there is any who has brought a flute with him."

—*The Tale of the Heike*, from *Anthology of Japanese Literature from the Earliest Era to the Mid-Nineteenth Century*, edited by Donald Keene

Reading and Vocabulary Support

① What conflict does Kumagai experience when about to kill the soldier?

② What do you think the phrase *there was no help for it* means?

③ A brocade bag is made of heavily embroidered cloth

Analyzing Primary Sources

Review the passage to find details for your answers.

1. **Infer** Why did Kumagi still kill the young warrior?

2. **Analyze Author's Purpose** What point does the author make by including Kumagai finding the flute?

Recognize the Role of Chance, Error, and Oversight

Follow these steps using the sources below to recognize the role of chance, oversight, and error.

INTERACTIVE

Anayze Cause and Effect

1 Identify the topic. Begin by identifying the topic you are studying.

   a. Is the second passage about a military campaign or the rise of a new leader?

   b. Where did the event happen?

   c. Who were the key figures?

2 Identify the goal or expected outcome. In the second passage, two leaders are mentioned, Kublai Khan, the leader of the Mongols, and the shogun of Japan. What is each leader trying to accomplish? What is likely to happen if everything goes as planned?

3 Identify any unexpected outcomes. As you consider the event or time period, ask: Did events happen as you expected? Did something go wrong? Did key people achieve their original goals? Did the goals of the key individuals change as the circumstances changed?

4 Analyze the cause of the unexpected outcomes. Look for explanations for unexpected outcomes.

   a. Did something that nobody could have predicted go wrong—a storm or illness, for example?

   b. Did a person make a key mistake?

   c. Was the unexpected outcome the cause of chance, oversight, or error?

Secondary Source

The Unexpected Ancient peoples often blamed the gods when bad things happened. Historians, however, look for human causes of unexpected events. Many things go wrong because of oversight or error. An oversight is a mistake people make by not paying attention to something. An error is an action that people intend to do but that turns out to be a mistake.

Some events are caused by things that happen by chance. The sudden death of a leader due to an accident is an example of a chance event. No one can plan for such events, but they do change history.

Secondary Source

The Mongol Invasions Mongol invaders took over China in the 1200s. The Mongol ruler, Kublai Khan, soon ruled all of East Asia—except Japan.

In 1268, Kublai Khan sent official representatives to demand tribute from Japan. They promised war if Japan did not pay for Kubilai Khan's friendship. However, the shogun's government refused. This so angered the Great Khan that he began to build a fleet of ships to invade Japan. This effort was a spectacular failure, in part because terrible storms disrupted the Great Khan's invasion plans.

Japanese Society and Culture

BOUNCE TO ACTIVATE · ▶ VIDEO

GET READY TO READ

START UP
Look at the photo of a modern Kabuki play. List several ways the performing arts can enrich a culture.

GUIDING QUESTIONS
- What forms of literature, drama, and art flourished at the Heian Court?
- What values shaped Japanese culture?
- How did Shinto and Buddhism influence Japan?

TAKE NOTES
Literacy Skills: Identify Main Ideas
Use the graphic organizer in your 📕 Active Journal to take notes as you read the lesson.

PRACTICE VOCABULARY
Use the vocabulary activity in your 📕 Active Journal to practice the vocabulary words.

Vocabulary		Academic Vocabulary
Noh	Shinto	despite
Kabuki	shrine	exclude
consensus	mantra	

China had a strong influence on Japan. But the Japanese added their own ideas and values to whatever they borrowed from China. The result was a country that shared much with its mainland neighbor, but still had its own unique culture and society.

Japan's Golden Age

Many historians call the Heian period Japan's golden age. Lasting from 794 to 1185, it was a time of great cultural flowering in Japan. Japanese culture today still reflects developments from this period.

Literature Nobles of the Heian court wrote journals, poems, and stories. They wrote in a script called *kana*, adapted from Chinese characters. Each symbol represented a sound in Japanese. In the past, Japanese writers had written in Chinese.

One lengthy story, *The Tale of Genji*, still entertains readers today. The story describes the romantic adventures of a prince named Genji. Murasaki Shikibu, the story's author, joined the Heian court around 1005.

Quest CONNECTIONS

Look at the two photos of the Japanese and Chinese buildings. Describe their similarities and differences in your Active Journal.

While serving the emperor's wife, she wrote her tale, which is now praised as a great masterpiece of Japanese literature.

Many regard this work as the world's first novel. A novel is a long fictional story, often with a complex plot and many chapters. Murasaki's work, though fiction, has provided scholars with many details about life in the Heian court.

Art and Architecture Japanese artists and architects added their own ideas to styles borrowed from China. Heian artists admired Chinese scroll painting, but they developed scrolls with a distinctively Japanese style.

Homes of nobles looked similar in Japan and China. They included several buildings around a garden. But facing the garden, Japanese homes had sliding doors instead of fixed walls. In warm weather the doors were removed and the rooms became part of the garden.

The art of gardening also came from China. The Japanese garden usually had flowering trees and a small stream or pond. It might also have a teahouse. A practice borrowed from China, the formal tea ceremony was designed to calm the mind and heart.

Drama In the 1300s in Japan, well after the Heian period, a new kind of drama developed. **Noh** was drama that appealed to the nobles and samurai. It is serious and intense. A Noh play takes place on a simple, almost bare stage. The players wear colorful costumes and masks. They dance and chant to the music of flutes and drums. Through movement and words, they tell a story.

The early 1600s saw the rise of a new form of drama, Kabuki. Like Noh, it uses music and dance to tell a story. Unlike Noh, **Kabuki** was aimed at farmers, merchants, and other common folk. Its stunning sets and flashy costumes excite the senses. During performances, viewers even yell out the names of favorite actors.

✓ **READING CHECK** **Identify Supporting Details** What influences did China have on Japanese architecture, art, and literature?

▼ Both of the buildings shown here are temples. The one on the left is in Japan, while the one on the right is in China.

Japanese Society

The nobles at the Heian court enjoyed a life of luxury and leisure. Most other people in Japan did not. Yet as the economy grew, the lives of most Japanese improved. One thing that did not change was the society's shared values.

Family Loyalty and Harmony In Japan, family loyalty was a basic value. Following Shinto tradition, people honored their ancestors. The head of a family or clan put the welfare of the group ahead of other concerns. Individuals put family interests above personal interests.

This devotion to family remained strong through the feudal age and beyond. A modern historian wrote,

▲ An illustration from a Japanese legend shows samurai who were so loyal to their leader that they plotted for two years to kill the official who caused his death. Whether in battle or at home, the concept of loyalty was highly valued in Japanese culture.

Primary Source

"The keys to the continuity and toughness of Japanese society have been the family and traditional religion. The clan was the enlarged family, and the nation the most enlarged family of all."

—J. M. Roberts, *History of the World*

Confucianism also introduced the value of harmony to Japanese society. Concern for harmony led to the practice of seeking consensus. **Consensus** is agreement among the members of a group.

Economic Life Most people lived in rural areas, away from cities. Local daimyo kept order. Most rural people worked the land as tenant farmers. They paid rent with crops. As long as they kept up with the rent, the daimyo usually let them run their own affairs. A village assembly made most local decisions.

Despite the violence of the feudal age, Japan's economy grew. Farmers produced more crops, thanks to improved tools and techniques. Craftworkers made more goods to meet the demands of farmers, warriors, and wealthy daimyo. A merchant class arose to carry on the increased trade in goods. Merchants often set up markets near temples and within castle walls. Towns sprang up from these sites and along important travel routes.

Trade with China expanded as well. At first, Japan exported raw materials such as copper, pearls, and wood. In exchange for these items, Japan acquired books, silk, coins, and other manufactured goods. Then the Japanese began to make goods for export, including the world's finest swords. One shipment to China included 37,000 shiny samurai swords.

Academic Vocabulary

despite • *prep.,* even with or in spite of

- Murasaki Shikibu's real name is not known. She may have adopted the name *Murasaki* from a character in her novel.

- Her father insisted that she receive an education, and she learned Chinese, usually forbidden to women.

- She started to write *The Tale of Genji* after her husband died. It may have taken her as many as nine years to complete.

- Her Buddhist faith is reflected in the novel, as she wrote about the dark side of vanity.

- In addition to *The Tale of Genji,* she kept a detailed diary that reveals important information about Japanese life at the time.

Critical Thinking Why are Murasaki Shikibu's writings important to modern scholars?

Status of Women Early in Japanese history, women headed clans and ruled as empresses. That changed, however, as Confucianism took root. Men dominated Confucian relationships. A woman was expected to obey first her father and then her husband.

Some forms of Buddhism held a similar view of women. According to one Buddhist scripture, or sacred writing, "no women are to be found" in paradise. Women were **excluded** from some temples. As Murasaki Shikibu wrote in *The Tale of Genji*, ". . . [W]omen are bound to have a hard lot, not only in this life but in the world to come."

Academic Vocabulary
exclude • *v.,* to keep out

✓ READING CHECK **Identify Supporting Details** What forms of inequality existed during the Heian era?

Shinto

Shinto is the traditional religion of Japan. It means "the way of the gods." After Buddhism entered Japan, many elements of Shinto merged into that new religion. Shinto lost many followers, especially in the cities. But it remained strong in rural areas. Today, Shinto and Buddhism exist side by side in Japan. Many Japanese think of themselves as followers of both religions.

Shinto had no known founder. It had no scripture. It had no permanent set of gods. For centuries, it didn't even have a name. Yet it was a vital force in everyone's life.

Creation Myths Traditional Shinto stories describe how various aspects of Japanese life came to be. The Sun Goddess plays a central role in these creation stories.

One story explains how Japan came to be ruled by an emperor. It explains how the Sun Goddess and her brother, the Storm God, often quarreled. Each supported different clans who were fighting to rule Japan. The Sun Goddess won the conflict. She sent her grandson Ninigi to rule Japan.

The Sun Goddess gave Ninigi three treasures. The first, a bronze mirror, symbolized truth. The second, an iron sword, stood for wisdom. The third, a string of jewels, represented kindness.

Ninigi passed down all three treasures to his great-grandson, Jimmu. According to myth, Jimmu became Japan's first emperor in 660 BCE. As a result, all Japanese emperors came to be thought of as living gods on Earth.

Honoring Local Spirits Under Shinto, each clan worshiped its own local kami, a spirit that the Japanese believed could be found in mountains, trees, rivers, and other natural objects. Through the kami, they learned proper behavior and values.

The Japanese built Shinto **shrines**, or places of worship, wherever they felt the power of kami. Thousands of such shrines still exist throughout Japan. Many people visit them each year. Shinto has grown and changed, but it still influences how the Japanese think and act.

✓ READING CHECK **Identify Supporting Details** How did Shinto and Buddhism coexist in Japan?

Japanese Buddhism

Buddhism originated in India. It attracted a large following in China and Korea before it appeared in Japan. As it spread, this religion changed to meet the needs of different peoples.

Spread of Buddhism When Buddhism arrived in Japan, some people opposed it. They feared that the new faith would offend the Shinto gods. Over time, more and more Japanese accepted the Buddha's teachings. Yet even as the Japanese turned to Buddhism, they did not completely give up their Shinto beliefs. Buddhism was able to adapt to Japanese needs, in part, because it adopted Shinto gods.

Analyze Images A Shinto shrine is still in use in Kyoto, Japan. **Compare and Contrast** How does the architecture of this shrine compare to that of the Chinese-influenced buildings pictured earlier in the lesson?

Analyze Images This artwork shows people enjoying a stroll among blossoming cherry trees. **Infer** How does this scene reflect both Chinese influence and Japan's unique culture?

New Sects Emerge Long before it appeared in Japan, Buddhism had split into different schools of thought. The most popular in Japan, the Mahayana school, teaches that all living beings have the potential to be enlightened. No one is too bad or lowly to be saved.

Within the Mahayana school, Buddhist monks in Japan founded different sects, or forms, of Buddhism. Each sect taught its own way to enlightenment.

One monk started the Shingon, or "true word," form of Buddhism in the 800s. Followers of the Shingon sect recited "true words" in the form of mantras. A **mantra** is a sacred word, chant, or sound that is repeated over and over to advance one's spiritual growth.

Another sect, Pure Land Buddhism, centered on the concept of the bodhisattva (boh di SAHT vah), a merciful being who has gained enlightenment but chooses to remain on Earth to help others.

Zen Buddhism Probably the most famous Buddhist sect is Zen. Known in China as *Chan*, this sect came to Japan in the 1100s. The central practice of Zen Buddhism is meditation. For Zen followers, meditation means the emptying of the mind of thoughts in order to aid spiritual growth.

To find enlightenment through Zen Buddhism, individual efforts, not prayers or rituals, are required. That focus on self-control and discipline had great appeal among samurai. Samurai used Zen meditation to help them drive all fear of danger and death from their minds. Its popularity among samurai helped shape Japanese Zen.

☑️ **READING CHECK** **Draw Conclusions** Why might Buddhism have appealed to people from different parts of Japanese society?

☑️ Lesson Check

Practice Vocabulary

1. How is **Noh** drama different from **Kabuki**?

2. What is a **consensus**?

3. Describe the role of a **mantra** in Buddhism.

Critical Thinking and Writing

4. **Use Evidence** Explain why people can follow both Buddhism and Shinto.

5. **Draw Conclusions** Why did Zen Buddhism appeal to samurai?

6. **Writing Workshop: Organize Your Essay** Now that you've gathered evidence to support your thesis, choose an organizing strategy and outline your essay in your 📓 Active Journal.

Distinguish Cause and Effect

Follow these steps to distinguish cause and effect in the chart.

INTERACTIVE

Analyze Cause and Effect

1 **Understand the relationship between causes and effects.** Causes are events that lead to other things happening. Effects are the things that happen as a result of a cause. Knowing the cause or causes of an event enables you to understand why it happened. It helps you make connections between things that occur in history. Sometimes, you will have to pick out causes and effects from what you read. In other cases, tables such as the one below present causes and effects for you.

2 **Identify the key event.** Choose one event or condition in the table below as a starting point. Once you know the starting point, you can look for possible causes and effects of that event. The chart is about the effect of Buddhism on Japan. What is the starting point of Buddhism's influence on Japan?

3 **Study later events or conditions as possible effects.** Effects must follow the key event. They may include short-term effects or longer-lasting ones. To find later events, ask, "What did the key event lead to?" or "What was a result of the key event?" You may also find clue words or phrases, such as *brought about, led to, as a result,* or *therefore.*

a. What is one example of an effect of the key event in this source?

b. What are some other examples of effects of the key event in this chart?

The Effect of Buddhism on Japan

Buddhism came to Japan in the 500s CE from Korea. Buddhism went through a series of changes, each having a lasting effect on the country.	
Cause	**Effect**
• Government support of Buddhism	• The government builds temples called *kokubunji*.
• Increase in the number of monks	• Six schools of Buddhism emerge; beliefs brought to Japan from China.
• Introduction of Tendai Buddhism	• Two new schools of Buddhist thought are introduced, overshadowing the six previous schools.
• Introduction of Shingon Buddhism	• Buddhist thought is now classified into two parts, one for highly trained and learned people and one for everyday worshippers.
• Development of Popular Buddhism	• Buddhism becomes popular with the common people, not just the elites.

LESSON 7

Korea and Southeast Asia

BOUNCE TO ACTIVATE ▶ VIDEO

GET READY TO READ

START UP

Look at the image of the Buddhist temple in Korea. What details of this building's design remind you of Chinese architecture in this topic?

GUIDING QUESTIONS

- How did powerful neighbors influence the cultures of Korea and Southeast Asia?
- What dynasties developed in Korea?
- What unique cultures emerged in Southeast Asia?

TAKE NOTES

Literacy Skills: Analyze Text Structure

Use the graphic organizer in your 📓 Active Journal to take notes as you read the lesson.

PRACTICE VOCABULARY

Use the vocabulary activity in your 📓 Active Journal to practice the vocabulary words.

Vocabulary	Academic Vocabulary
Hangul	descendant
celadon	conglomeration
monsoon	
stupa	

For most of its history, Korea has been influenced by its larger neighbor to the west—China. Still, the Koreans created their own distinct and separate culture. China, along with India, also had a profound impact on the many cultures of Southeast Asia.

Korea's Geography

Korea is located on a peninsula extending from the Asian mainland into the Sea of Japan (also called the East Sea). The Yalu River and mountains located in the north separate Korea from China.

Among the Sea and Mountains Most of Korea, nearly 70 percent, is covered by low and steep mountains. The T'aebaek (ta bak) mountain range runs along the eastern seaboard. Smaller mountain chains extend throughout the rest of the country. Farming has always been difficult in the mountains. As a result, most people settled along the western coastal plains, Korea's rich farming region.

With 5,400 miles of coastline, Koreans have always turned to the sea for food and commerce. Fish and other seafood are still staples of the Korean diet, and South Korea's fishing industry is still among the world's largest. South Korea is also a leader in shipping.

A Cultural Bridge Because of China's closeness, the Chinese have for centuries played a critical role in Korean politics, culture, and technology. As a result, Korea acted as a bridge through which culture and technology passed from China to Japan. For their part, the Koreans adapted Chinese traditions to forge their own unique culture. Korea's own culture also influenced Japan.

China's second imperial dynasty, the Han, were the first to take note of Korea because of its strategic location. The most famous Han emperor, Wudi (woo dee), expanded China's borders by invading Manchuria, Korea, northern Vietnam, Tibet, and Central Asia. Chinese soldiers, traders, and settlers moved into these conquered regions, bringing with them ideas about government, writing, and farming.

☑ **READING CHECK** Identify Supporting Details How has Korea's geography affected its history?

The Silla Unite Korea

Three ancient kingdoms ruled Korea from 100 BCE to 676 CE. The Koguryo ruled the north, the Paekche the southwest, and the Silla the southeast. Each expanded its borders by conquering neighbors. Each also had an organized military and a king who passed on his rule to a **descendant**. Aristocracies, made up of tribal chiefs, developed in each kingdom, dividing society into distinct social classes. Although the three kingdoms had many things in common, they often fought one another.

Academic Vocabulary
descendant • *n.*, a person related by birth to another, such as a child or grandchild

Analyze Images Most of Korea is covered in mountains like these. **Draw Conclusions** How might this kind of landscape have affected life in Korea?

▲ Pottery from the Silla period

How Did Buddhist Monks Spread Ideas? During this period, Chinese culture spread into the Korean kingdoms, partly through the travels of Buddhist monks. These Chinese monks arrived on the peninsula, hoping to share the teachings of Buddhism. The religion appealed to Koreans, especially to people of the elite and ruling classes. Korean monks, influenced by China's brand of Buddhism, then traveled to both China and India to learn more. When they returned, they brought with them Chinese learning.

The Silla Take Control By the late 600s, the Silla, with the help of China's Tang emperor, were able to conquer and defeat the Paekche and the Koguryo. Silla's conquests helped unify the peninsula under one government and social structure. The Silla were so closely connected to the Tang dynasty that Korean elites used Chinese as their written language.

Economic and Cultural Powerhouse The Silla turned Korea into an economic and cultural center, one of the most advanced civilizations in the world at the time. The Silla established trade networks between Japan, China, and India. The rich and powerful who lived in Silla's capital were learned in Buddhist teachings and high culture. Medicine, astronomy, metal casting, and textile manufacturing also flourished.

Politics in Silla The Silla also instituted a series of policies to govern Korea. Aristocrats in the government were given a salary and land. However, they had to turn over their property to the government once they left office. The measure was a way to reduce aristocratic control over land and people. It also made the monarchy stronger.

The Silla set up an academy to train government officials based on the philosophy of Confucianism. They offered a civil service test based on a similar Chinese test. Only aristocrats were eligible.

☑ **READING CHECK** Identify Main Ideas What role did religion play in China's influence on Korea?

Koryo Culture

In 918, the Koryo dynasty replaced the Silla. The modern name "Korea" comes from the Koryo. Under the Koryo, Buddhism and Confucianism were powerful forces. Civil service examinations and official jobs were opened to all Koreans. Koreans used the Chinese method of block printing to produce Buddhist texts. At first, Koreans used the Chinese alphabet, but by 1443, they had established their own system of writing—**Hangul**. The Koreans also learned to make porcelain, a staple of

Chinese culture. The Koreans even developed their own secret technique of making **celadon**, a blue-green glaze, or coating, for porcelain.

While the Koryo enjoyed good relations with the Chinese, the Mongols invaded in 1231. The invaders destroyed parts of cities and town in Korea, including the celadon factories. The Koreans fought for more than 25 years, but eventually made peace with the Mongols. By 1392, a lack of tax revenue had weakened the Koryo. The Choson dynasty, led by General Yi Song-gye (yee sung gyeh), came to power. It would rule Korea for more than 500 years.

☑ READING CHECK **Identify Supporting Details** How did the Koreans put their own mark on Chinese influences?

Southeast Asia as a Crossroads

Southeast Asia is a **conglomeration** of several peninsulas located between China and India and more than 20,000 islands between the Indian Ocean and South China Sea. Today, the nations of Myanmar, Thailand, Cambodia, Laos, Vietnam, and part of Malaysia are part of mainland Southeast Asia. The modern-day nations of Indonesia, Singapore, Brunei, and the Philippines are also part of Southeast Asia, located on archipelagos. An archipelago is an island chain.

Although the Southeast Asian mainland is separated from the rest of Asia by high mountains and plateaus, traders, invaders, and monks were able to travel overland into the region. Each group influenced the region's culture.

Trade routes across the southern seas were even more important to the region's development. Ships sailing between China

Academic Vocabulary

conglomeration • *n.*, grouping of different parts

GEOGRAPHY **SKILLS**

The empires and kingdoms of Southeast Asia were located on peninsulas and islands.

1. **Location** What bodies of water separated the islands of Southeast Asia from China and India?

2. **Draw Conclusions** Which empires and kingdoms would you expect to be most heavily influenced by China?

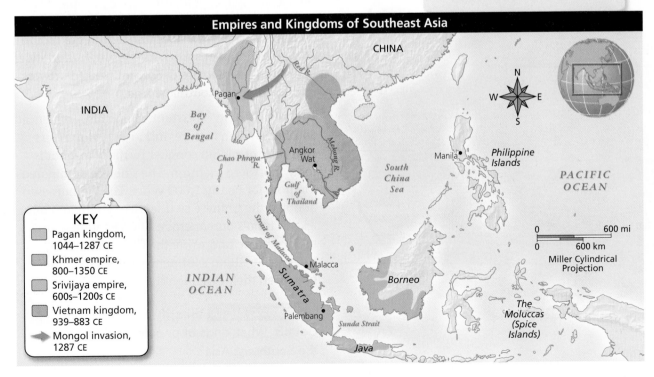

Empires and Kingdoms of Southeast Asia

CHINA

INDIA

Pagan

Bay of Bengal

Chao Phraya R.

Angkor Wat

Mekong R.

Red R.

Gulf of Thailand

Strait of Malacca

Sumatra

Malacca

Palembang

Sunda Strait

Java

South China Sea

Manila

Philippine Islands

Borneo

The Moluccas (Spice Islands)

PACIFIC OCEAN

INDIAN OCEAN

KEY

- Pagan kingdom, 1044–1287 CE
- Khmer empire, 800–1350 CE
- Srivijaya empire, 600s–1200s CE
- Vietnam kingdom, 939–883 CE
- Mongol invasion, 1287 CE

0   600 mi
0   600 km
Miller Cylindrical Projection

INTERACTIVE

Angkor Wat

and India had to pass through either the Strait of Malacca or the Sunda Strait. Whatever power commanded these waterways controlled rich trade routes. Trade routes also developed depending on the **monsoon**, or rainy, season. Ships traveled depending on the direction of these seasonal winds.

Merchants docked their vessels in port cities between monsoons, turning these ports into important centers of trade and culture. Trade networks throughout Southeast Asia linked India, China, East Africa, and the Middle East.

☑ **READING CHECK** **Draw Conclusions** Why was control of the sea so important to the region of Southeast Asia?

How Did Indian and Chinese Culture Spread?

Traveling along these trade routes, Indian merchants and Hindu priests fanned out across Southeast Asia, especially during the Gupta empire, which ruled India from the 300s through the 500s. As the priests and traders moved across the region, they spread Indian culture. Buddhist monks and nuns soon followed, spreading Buddhism to such places as Srivijaya (modern-day Indonesia), Java, and the Khmer Empire (modern-day Cambodia and Thailand). Scholars also traveled the trade routes, bringing with them new ideas. As elsewhere, the local people blended these ideas with their own traditions and beliefs.

▼ These Hindu temple ruins are in what is today Vietnam.

Indian Influences As more and more Indian traders settled in the port cities of Southeast Asia, India's influence spread. The Indians formed close ties with local leaders. Trade with India meant prosperity. Goods such as cotton cloth, jewels, and other commodities were traded for raw materials such as spices, gold, and timber. People traveled to India to study, bringing back ideas. Some Southeast Asians saw adopting features of Indian culture as a sign of status. As a result, Indian styles of art and architecture deeply influenced artwork and buildings in Southeast Asia.

China's Role in Vietnam China also influenced Southeast Asian culture. In 111 BCE, Han rulers sent their armies to conquer territory in what is today northern Vietnam. The Chinese dominated Vietnam for nearly 1,000 years. The Vietnamese adopted the Chinese civil service system and mimicked China's bureaucracy. The Vietnamese aristocracy spoke and wrote the Chinese language. Yet, despite China's influence, the Vietnamese preserved their own identity.

☑ **READING CHECK** **Identify Supporting Details** What kinds of people spread ideas into the Southeast Asia?

The Kingdoms of Southeast Asia

The kingdoms of Southeast Asia were as diverse as the region was large. The kingdom of Pagan, for example, prospered in the Irrawaddy Valley, in what is today Myanmar. By 1050, Buddhism had spread across the kingdom, making Pagan one of the world's largest Buddhist centers. Pagan's King Anawrahta (uh NAW yuh tah), a devout Buddhist, built magnificent dome-shaped shrines called **stupas**. The Mongols would conquer Pagan in 1287.

Analyze Images This stupa was built in what is today Myanmar. **Compare and Contrast** How does this stupa differ in appearance from the Japanese shrine pictured in the previous lesson?

The Khmer Empire The Khmer empire reached its peak in the 1300s, when it stretched from modern-day Cambodia into Thailand and Vietnam. Heavily influenced by India, the Khmer adapted Indian systems of writing, architecture, and mathematics. Many Khmer rulers became Hindus and saw themselves as god-kings. Suryavarman II built the great temple Angkor Wat in the early 1100s to honor the Hindu god Vishnu. Most of the common people, however, continued to practice Buddhism.

The Srivijaya Empire Beginning in the 600s and lasting to the 1200s, the Srivijaya empire flourished in what is today Indonesia. The empire controlled the all-important Strait of Malacca, creating a wealthy and culturally diverse region. Although India's influence was evident, the local people, as they did elsewhere, blended their own beliefs with Hinduism and Buddhism from India.

☑ READING CHECK **Identify Cause and Effect** How did Indian culture influence rulers of the Khmer empire?

☑ Lesson Check

Practice Vocabulary

1. What did the Koreans use **celadon** for?

2. What was the purpose of **Hangul**?

Critical Thinking and Writing

3. **Revisit the Essential Question** What motivated the movement of people who spread ideas into Korea and Southeast Asia?

4. **Draw Conclusions** Why did Korea's location have strategic importance to both China and Japan?

5. **Writing Workshop: Draft Your Essay** Revisit your thesis one more time in light of the new information in this lesson. Then begin writing! Remember to support your key points with evidence and cite your sources properly.

TOPIC 12 ☑ Review and Assessment

VISUAL REVIEW

COMPARING BUDDHISM, DAOISM, CONFUCIANISM

Buddhism
- Founded by Siddhartha Gautama
- Originated in India
- Goal is to attain spiritual enlightenment from within
- Most popular during Tang dynasty

Daoism
- Founded by Laozi
- Emphasized spiritual growth and harmony with nature
- Popular, but did not enjoy government support

Confucianism
- Founded by Confucius
- Valued order, harmonious relationships, and respect for authority
- Viewed as both a philosophy and religion
- Neo-Confucianism rose in the later part of the Tang era, incorporating ideas from Buddhism and Daoism
- Backed by most dynasties

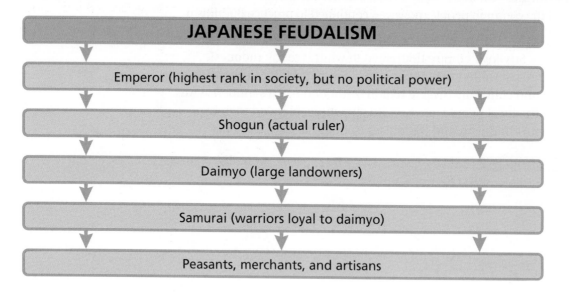

JAPANESE FEUDALISM

Emperor (highest rank in society, but no political power)

Shogun (actual ruler)

Daimyo (large landowners)

Samurai (warriors loyal to daimyo)

Peasants, merchants, and artisans

READING REVIEW

Use the Take Notes and Practice Vocabulary activities in your 📓 Active Journal to review the topic.

 **INTERACTIVE**

Practice vocabulary using the Topic Mini-Games.

Quest FINDINGS

Write Your Explanatory Essay
Get help for writing your essay in your 📓 Active Journal.

ASSESSMENT

Vocabulary and Key Ideas

1. **Define** What is a bureaucracy?

2. **Explain** How did the Silk Road help the Tang dynasty capital, Chang'an, flourish?

3. **Draw Conclusions** How did the merit system contribute to good government in the Song dynasty?

4. **Identify Cause and Effect** Why is so little of Japan's land suitable for farming?

5. **Identify Cause and Effect** Why did Prince Shotoku encourage the spread of Buddhism?

6. **Draw Conclusions** What role did Korea play in spreading Chinese culture throughout Southeast Asia and Japan?

Critical Thinking and Writing

7. **Compare and Contrast** How was the Chinese government during the Yuan physically different than it was during the Tang, Song, and Ming dynasties?

8. **Compare and Contrast** How did physical features affect the development of China, Japan, and Korea in similar ways? What were the key differences?

9. **Identify Main Ideas** How did the people of medieval Japan borrow parts of other cultures and then change them?

10. **Classify and Categorize** What features of feudalism existed in both Japan and Europe in the Middle Ages?

11. **Revisit the Essential Question** Trace the movement of one cultural influence between the countries of China, Japan, and Korea.

12. **Writing Workshop: Write a Research Paper** Using the thesis statement and details you recorded in your 📓 Active Journal, complete your research paper on this question: How did new technology and innovations affect China, Japan, Korea, and Southeast Asia?

Analyze Primary Sources

13. Read this excerpt from the Constitution of Prince Shotoku. What is the prince's general attitude about vassals?
    A. They are inferior.
    B. They are wise.
    C. They are the backbone of society.
    D. They should be treated with respect.

    "Do not fail to obey the commands of your Sovereign. He is like Heaven, which is above the Earth, and the vassal is like the Earth, which bears up Heaven. When Heaven and Earth are properly in place, the four seasons follow their course and all is well in Nature. But if the Earth attempts to take the place of Heaven, Heaven would simply fall in ruin."
    —*Constitution of Prince Shotoku*

Analyze Maps

Use the map at the right to answer the following questions.

14. Which letter is on part of China on this map?

15. What letter represents the Khmer empire?

16. Which body of water separated the kingdoms of Southeast Asia from India?

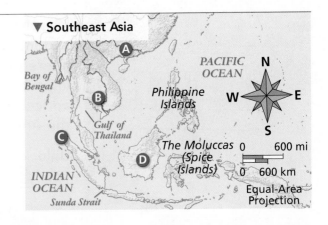

▼ **Southeast Asia**

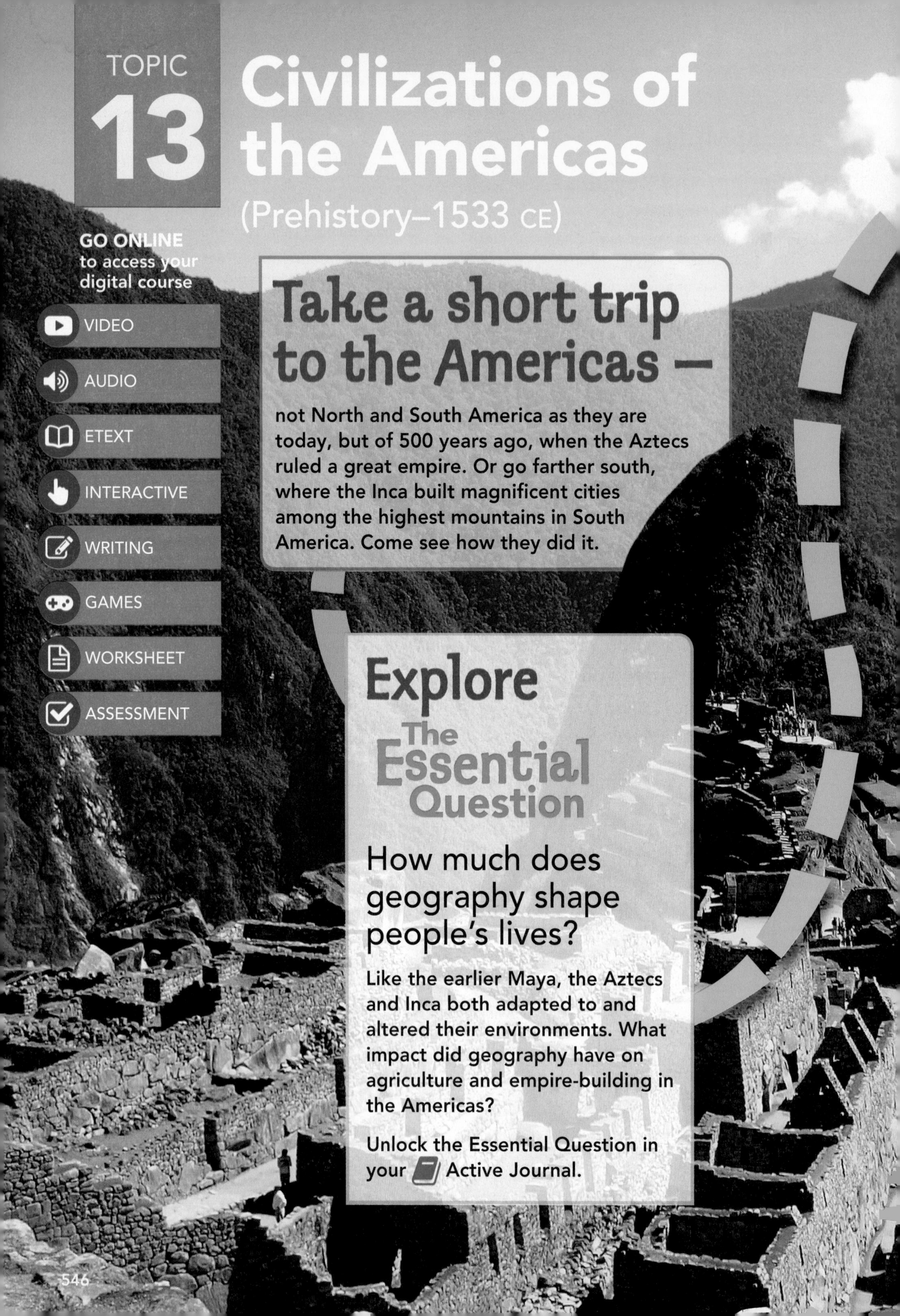

Civilizations of the Americas

(Prehistory–1533 CE)

GO ONLINE
to access your
digital course

- ▶ VIDEO
- 🔊 AUDIO
- 📖 ETEXT
- 👆 INTERACTIVE
- ✏️ WRITING
- 🎮 GAMES
- 📄 WORKSHEET
- ☑️ ASSESSMENT

Take a short trip to the Americas —

not North and South America as they are today, but of 500 years ago, when the Aztecs ruled a great empire. Or go farther south, where the Inca built magnificent cities among the highest mountains in South America. Come see how they did it.

Explore The Essential Question

How much does geography shape people's lives?

Like the earlier Maya, the Aztecs and Inca both adapted to and altered their environments. What impact did geography have on agriculture and empire-building in the Americas?

Unlock the Essential Question in your 📔 Active Journal.

Watch

NBC LEARN

BOUNCE TO ACTIVATE ▶ VIDEO

Farming in Ancient Empires

Learn about methods of farming, such as terracing and vertical farming, first used centuries ago—and still in use today.

◁ The Inca people built the fortress of Machu Picchu, high in the Andes Mountains, in the 15th century.

Read

about how geography influenced various early American civilizations.

Civilizations of the Americas (Prehistory–1533 CE)

Learn more about migrations and civilizations in the Americas by making your own map and timeline in your 📕 Active Journal.

 INTERACTIVE

Topic Map

Where did the first Americans come from?

They came from Asia. Some may have come by water; others probably crossed a frozen land bridge from modern-day Siberia to Alaska.

🖐 INTERACTIVE

Topic Timeline

What happened and when?

Descendants of the first settlers from Asia migrated southward and westward. Some settled in frigid regions, while others made their homes in warmer climes. Explore the timeline to see the development of ancient civilizations in North and South America.

1200 BCE
Olmec civilization develops.

TOPIC EVENTS

| 1200 BCE | 1000 BCE | 800 CE | 1000 |

WORLD EVENTS

Around 1000 BCE
The kingdom of Israel is founded.

1054 CE
Great Schism divides Eastern Orthodox and Roman Catholic churches.

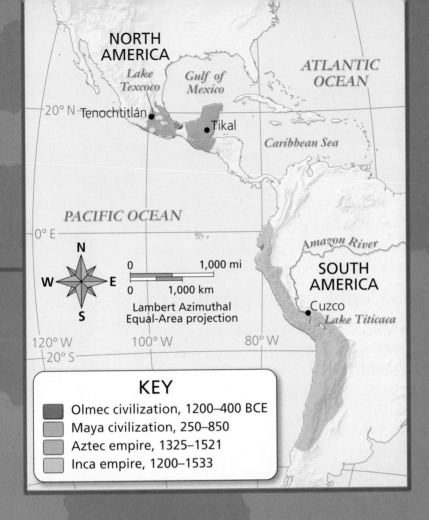

NORTH
AMERICA

*Lake
Texcoco*

*Gulf of
Mexico*

ATLANTIC
OCEAN

20° N Tenochtitlán

Tikal

Caribbean Sea

PACIFIC OCEAN

0° E

N
W E
S

0   1,000 mi
0   1,000 km
Lambert Azimuthal
Equal-Area projection

Amazon River

SOUTH
AMERICA

Cuzco
Lake Titicaca

120° W   100° W   80° W

20° S

KEY

- Olmec civilization, 1200–400 BCE
- Maya civilization, 250–850
- Aztec empire, 1325–1521
- Inca empire, 1200–1533

Who will you meet?

The Maya, who built an early civilization in Mexico and Central America

The Aztec god Huitzilopochtli, whom the Aztecs believed ensured success in battle and made the sun rise

Huayna Capac, one of the last emperors of the Incan empire

1150
Ancestral Pueblo peoples live in large complexes of stone dwellings.

1200
The Inca settle in the Cuzco Valley.

1325
Aztecs found the city of Tenochtitlan and begin to gain power.

1533
The Incan empire falls to Spanish invaders.

1200   1400   1600

1215
The Magna Carta is signed.

1492
Columbus arrives in the Caribbean.

Quest
Project-Based Learning Inquiry

Be a Map-Maker

For decades, scientists have been discovering settlements of America's earliest people. Your quest is to create a variety of illustrated maps.

How much does geography shape people's lives?

Why did certain groups of Americans settle where they did? Why did major civilizations arise in certain regions? Explore the Essential Question "How much does geography shape people's lives?" in this Quest.

1 Ask Questions

Read the map assignment given to you by your teacher. Begin by making a list of questions you will need in order to create your map. Write these questions in your 📖 Active Journal.

▼ This map of North and South America was created by a Spanish mapmaker in 1562.

2 Investigate

As you read the lessons in the Topic, look for **Quest** CONNECTIONS that provide information related to your map. Write down your notes in your 📖 Active Journal.

3 Conduct Research

Next, research information you need to answer your questions. Write down your notes in your 📖 Active Journal.

Quest FINDINGS

4 Create Your Atlas

Once you have your information, create maps that fulfill your mapmaker assignment. Check maps throughout the topic and make sure to include features such as a title, map key, relevant labels, and physical landforms such as rivers and lakes. Once you have completed your map, write down your conclusions about how geography shaped the lives of people in that area in your 📖 Active Journal.

The Maya

BOUNCE TO ACTIVATE **VIDEO**

GET READY TO READ

START UP

What does photo of a pyramid built by the Maya more than 900 years ago tell you about Mayan technology?

GUIDING QUESTIONS

- How did the environment affect the expansion of agriculture, population, cities, and empires in Mesoamerica?
- How were religion and government related in the Mayan civilization?
- What advances did the Maya make in writing, mathematics, science, and architecture?

TAKE NOTES

Literacy Skills: Sequence
Use this graphic organizer in your ▤ Active Journal to take notes as you read the lesson.

PRACTICE VOCABULARY

Use the vocabulary activity in your ▤ Active Journal to practice the vocabulary words.

Vocabulary

slash-and-burn   hieroglyphic
drought   observatory

Academic Vocabulary

dense
economy

The oldest civilizations in the Americas formed in an area called Mesoamerica. Mesoamerica extends south from central Mexico into northern Central America.

Settlement and Geography of the Americas

The first people to settle in the Americas came from Asia. They arrived between about 40,000 and 15,000 years ago.

Some of these people probably came by land. Thousands of years ago, Earth's climate was very cold. Much of Earth's water was frozen into ice on land. As a result, sea levels were lower than they are now. Lower sea levels exposed the Bering Land Bridge. This was a strip of land connecting Asia to North America where Alaska is today. People may have crossed that land bridge into the Americas in search of food.

Early settlers of the Americas may also have come from Asia by boat. These people would have paddled or sailed from place to place south of the ice sheets along the Pacific coast of the Americas.

Environmental Diversity The first Americans found a variety of environments in which to settle. Great mountain chains, such as the Rockies, the eastern and western Sierra Madre, and the Andes, dominated the western Americas. Farther east were two of the world's longest rivers—the Mississippi in North America and the Amazon in South America. In the far northern and southern parts of the hemisphere, people learned to live in cold regions with little vegetation. Closer to the equator, groups settled in the hot tropical forests of the Amazon. Elsewhere, these early hunter-gatherers adapted to desert regions, such as in Chile and the American Southwest. They also learned to live in the woodlands of North America and the fertile plains of both continents.

Slowly people learned to adapt in these environments. They built villages and learned to domesticate and cultivate a range of crops such as beans, sweet potatoes, peppers and maize–the food called "corn" in English. Populations slowly expanded, and some villages eventually grew into great cities, especially in Mesoamerica.

Geographic Features In the part of Mesoamerica that gave rise to the first civilizations in the region, highlands cover the south, and lowlands lie to the north. The highlands have warm temperatures year-round and rain from April to October. The lowlands have a hot, wet climate.

Ash from volcanoes in the highlands has produced rich soils. Volcanoes have also produced obsidian, or natural volcanic glass, a rock used in the past to make very sharp blades for spears and arrows.

Heavy rainfall in parts of the hot lowlands supports a **dense** tropical forest. The forest produced plant foods and supported abundant wildlife hunted for their meat, skin, or feathers.

✓ READING CHECK **Draw Conclusions** Why might have early Mesoamerican civilizations thrived in the highlands?

Academic Vocabulary
dense • *adj.*, thickly clustered

Analyze Images Olmec stone heads like this one range from 5 to 11 feet tall and weigh from 6 to 50 tons each. **Infer** What can you infer about the people who may have been the models for these heads?

The Olmec and Maya Civilizations

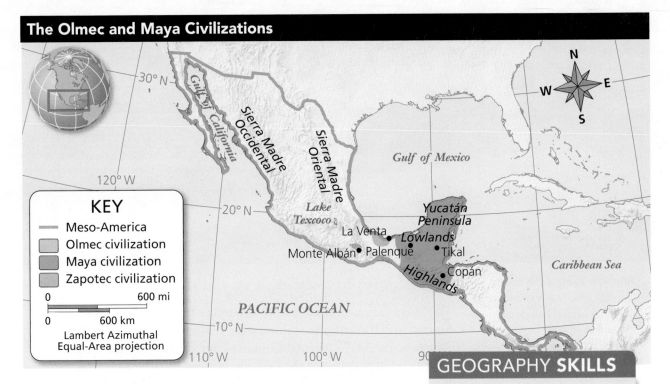

KEY
— Meso-America
Olmec civilization
Maya civilization
Zapotec civilization

0 — 600 mi
0 — 600 km
Lambert Azimuthal
Equal-Area projection

Who Were the Olmecs and Zapotecs?

The Olmec (OHL mek) people lived in the tropical forest. They used **slash-and-burn** agriculture, a farming method in which trees and other plants on a plot of land are cut down and burned. The ash fertilizes the soil. After a few years, when the soil would wear out, farmers let the old fields rest and grow trees before clearing them again. While such methods allow populations to grow, they also tend to wear out the soil over time.

Olmec farmers grew corn and beans. They also planted tomatoes, squash, sweet potatoes, cotton, and peppers. As Olmec farmers learned to produce more food, the population grew. The Olmecs found that they had a surplus of food that they could trade for obsidian, jade, feathers, and other commodities. As trade increased, Olmec influence began to spread over a wider area. The Olmecs set a pattern for future Mesoamerican civilizations.

The Olmecs are known for their art, including the huge heads they carved out of stone. These heads may portray Olmec rulers.

Olmec civilization lasted from about 1200 BCE to about 400 BCE. Although their civilization ended, Olmec beliefs and practices helped shape the cultures of other Mesoamerican peoples.

One of those groups was the Zapotecs (ZAH poh teks). They lived in the highlands southwest of the Olmecs. The Zapotecs developed what may have been the first system of writing in the Americas around 600 BCE.

✓ **READING CHECK** Understand Effects What is the environmental impact of farming methods like that of the Olmecs?

GEOGRAPHY SKILLS

Early Mesoamerican civilizations rose in what is today southern Mexico and northern Central America.

1. **Region** Which Mayan city was in the highlands?

2. **Use Visual Information** Using the scale bar, find how far this city is from the Caribbean coast.

Quest CONNECTIONS

Look at the map of the Olmec and Mayan civilizations. If you were a Mayan trader from Tikal, how difficult would it be to trade goods across the Mayan region? Record your thoughts in your 📓 Active Journal.

Analyze Images On courts like this one, Maya athletes played a sacred ball game. Players used their hips, thighs, or upper arms to hit a small ball through a stone hoop. Sometimes the losers sacrificed their lives.
Analyze Visual Information Based on this photo, how skilled did a Maya ballplayer have to be?

Quick Activity

What details would you include in a monument to the Maya? Follow the directions in your 📙 Active Journal to complete a Human Monument activity.

Academic Vocabulary

economy • *n.,* the system by which a country's people make a living

The Civilization of the Maya

The Maya (MY uh) lived in what are today the Yucatán Peninsula of Mexico and the nations of Honduras, Guatemala, and Belize. Like the Zapotecs, the Maya learned from the Olmecs. The earliest Mayan cities developed at the time of the Olmecs. Most of the great Maya cities were built during the Classic Maya period, between 250 and 850 CE.

Mayan Cities Archaeologists have learned much about the Maya by studying cities such as Tikal, Calakmul, and Copán. Mayan cities were widely scattered and tended to grow in environments that were favorable to food production.

These cities resembled huge royal courts or households. They had hundreds of buildings, including stone pyramids, temples, and palaces. Raised roads connected large, paved plazas.

Most Mayan people, however, did not live in the center of a city. Instead, most lived in farming villages surrounding a city.

Mayan Society The Maya had complex societies. The three main groups were nobles, a middle class, and commoners. Slaves occupied the lowers level of society. The nobles were people born into powerful families. They included the king, high officials, and priests.

Most Maya were commoners who raised crops. Men worked in the fields and on the village buildings. Women raised children, tended gardens and farm animals, and cooked food. They also wove cloth and made pottery.

Lower-ranking lords and higher-ranking commoners formed a kind of middle class. Some were minor officials, warriors, and scribes. Others were skilled craftworkers who served the nobles.

The basic social unit was the extended family. Families often included an older couple, their children, and their grandchildren.

Farming Nobles controlled large plots where corn was grown. Most families also had small plots of their own, where they grew fruit, beans, and other vegetables, and raised turkeys and ducks. The production of food on farms was at the center of the Mayan **economy**.

During the Classic period, the Maya farmed different regions using a variety of techniques. Farmers used slash-and-burn agriculture in the heavily forested lowlands. Near their cities, they also fertilized fields so that they could use them year after year. In wetlands, they farmed in the swamps. On the Yucatán Peninsula there are few rivers, so the Maya got their water from sinkholes, or deep pits in the ground. They also built cisterns, or tanks, to hold rainwater.

Trade Traveling merchants linked Mayan cities in a large trade network. Merchants traveled on footpaths or by canoe along the coast.

Merchants traded the natural resources of different Mayan regions. Traders from farming villages traded food, cotton, and cacao beans, used to make chocolate. Those from the highlands traded obsidian, jade, and feathers from the quetzal, a colorful tropical bird. Traders from the coast brought salt, dried fish, and pearls. In fact, salt was used as currency, like money, in Tikal and other Mayan cities.

Mayan Government The Mayan region contained dozens of independent city-states. Each Mayan city-state had its own ruler. Usually, kingship passed from a father to his son. Nobles helped run the government. Mayan rulers increased their power through warfare. Mayan cities went to war to take or to control trade routes and land.

Mayan Religion The Maya worshiped many gods. Most of these gods represented forces of nature, such as rain and lightning. The following description came from a creation myth, which was handed down orally, or by repetition, through the generations:

Primary Source

Thus let it be done! Let the emptiness be filled! Let the water recede and make a void, let the earth appear and become solid; let it be done. Thus they spoke. Let there be light, let there be dawn in the sky and on the earth! There shall be neither glory nor grandeur in our creation and formation until the human being is made, man is formed.

—From *Popol Vuh: Sacred Book of the Ancient Quiché Maya*, translated by Delia Goetz and Sylvanus G. Morley

The Maya believed that their priests and kings could communicate with the gods through religious rituals. Priests and kings performed many of these rituals in temples atop pyramids. Temples were built on pyramids so that they could be closer to the gods in heaven. Also, the towering pyramids were meant to show the power of the priests and kings.

▲ The Quetzal can still be found in Mexico and parts of the southern United States.

▼ Carving of a Mayan sun god

Many Mayan nobles were priests, and it is thought that many kings served as priests before becoming king. Mayan commoners feared displeasing priests or kings because they believed that their leaders could call on the gods to punish them.

Some rituals involved human sacrifice and bloodletting. People killed included prisoners of war, slaves, and even children. Many Maya also cut themselves and sacrificed their own blood. To the Maya, these sacrifices were part of the natural cycle of death and rebirth. They saw it as a way to keep the gods satisfied and the universe in balance.

The Fall of the Maya Between 800 and 1000 CE, many great Mayan cities fell into ruin. Warfare was one cause. Drought may also have caused food shortages. **Drought** is a prolonged period of little or no rainfall.

Smaller Mayan cities lasted another 600 years in the northern Yucatán Peninsula. These Mayan cities traded with peoples such as the Aztecs. The Spanish conquered the Maya in the early 1500s, but the Mayan people and language survive to this day.

INTERACTIVE

Mayan Learning

✓ READING CHECK **Identify Supporting Details** Give two examples that show religion was central to Mayan culture and society.

What were Some Mayan Achievements?

The Maya made many great achievements, often built on those of earlier cultures. They developed a complex writing system, created impressive works of art, and made key discoveries in astronomy and mathematics. Many of these achievements influenced other civilizations of Mesoamerica and had a lasting influence on the cultures of Mexico and Central America.

▼ Not until the late 1900s could modern scholars decipher the meaning of most Mayan glyphs like these.

Writing The Maya developed the most advanced writing system in the ancient Americas. This system used hieroglyphics. A **hieroglyphic**—also known as a glyph—is a symbol that stands for a word, idea, or sound. The Maya could combine 800 individual glyphs to form any word in their language.

Mayan books recorded Mayan learning and beliefs. The Spanish destroyed most of them, but scholars have learned much from the few that survive. Carved glyphs have also been preserved on stone monuments called stelae. These carvings celebrate rulers and their deeds.

Astronomy The Maya were excellent astronomers. Although they had no telescopes, they plotted the movements of the sun, moon, and planets. They used this information to predict events such as eclipses.

Mayan astronomers developed a complex system of calendars. They used a 260-day religious calendar and a 365-day solar calendar. The Maya used these calendars to plan religious festivals and seasonal farming tasks. They also used a 394-year calendar for historical dates.

Mathematics The Maya also developed an advanced system of numerals. This system, unlike that of Europeans at the time, included a numeral for zero. Zeros made calculation easier.

Architecture and Art The Maya created impressive architecture and art. All Mayan cities contained pyramids, temples, and palaces. Pyramids, the largest buildings, rose hundreds of feet into the air. All had temples at the top. A Mayan city might also contain **observatories**, or buildings for observing the sky. Mayan astronomers used observatories to follow the paths of the sun, moon, and other objects in the sky.

Almost all the bulk of a big Mayan building like a temple, palace, or observatory consisted of small stones, rubble, and earth that was carried in baskets or by hand. This core material was then covered by a thin skin of well-shaped stone.

Today, most Mayan buildings are just plain, gray stone structures. But when they were built, they had elaborate decorations. Sculptures of kings, gods, jaguars, and other figures lined the walls. The buildings were also painted bright blue, green, yellow, and red.

Mayan artists painted colorful murals on the walls of temples and palaces. Artists also created fine pottery. They crafted jewelry and masks from jade and pearls. Historians appreciate the art of the Mayan stelae. These stone slabs are carved with writing about Mayan history. They are monuments to the glory of Mayan civilization.

▲ Like many modern observatories, Mayan observatories had domed roofs for viewing the heavens.

☑ **READING CHECK** **Identify Supporting Details** Why were calendars important to the life of the Maya?

☑ Lesson Check

Practice Vocabulary

1. Describe **slash-and-burn agriculture**.

2. How might **drought** have affected the Maya?

3. How did the Maya use **observatories?**

Critical Thinking and Writing

4. **Summarize** How did the environment of the Maya affect their culture?

5. **Draw Inferences** How did Mayan architecture reflect Mayan religious beliefs?

6. **Compare and Contrast** How were the Olmec, Zapotec, and Mayan cultures similar and different?

7. **Writing Workshop: Develop a Clear Thesis** Write an explanatory essay comparing the impact of geography on Mayan, Aztec, and Incan agriculture. Write a thesis statement about the importance of agriculture in Mesoamerica in your 📄 Active Journal. Add details from this lesson.

The *Popol Vuh*

The *Popol Vuh* was the sacred text of the Quiché Mayan people. *Popol* could be translated as "woven mat," and *vuh* meant "book." This book wove together different Mayan myths. In 1700, a Spanish Dominican priest named Francisco Ximénez recorded the myths told to him, preserving them in print. The following is part of the text's creation myth.

◀ Quetzal Serpent, an important god in Mayan beliefs, was thought to have feathers like the quetzl bird.

Reading and Vocabulary Support

① The word *them* refers to the creator spirits, or spirit forefathers, of the Maya.

② The god Quetzalcoatl, translated as "Quetzal Serpent," combined characteristics of birds and serpents, representing the air and the earth.

③ These gods represented different elements of storms. The word *hurricane* may have evolved from a form of the name *Huracan*.

④ *Fruitful* means "productive."

Then the earth was created by them. ① So it was, in truth, that they created the earth. Earth! they said, and instantly it was made.

Like the mist, like a cloud, and like a cloud of dust was the creation, when the mountains appeared from the water, and instantly the mountains grew.

Only by a miracle, only by magic art were the mountains and valleys formed; and instantly the groves of cypresses and pines put forth shoots together on the surface of the earth.

And thus Gucumatz [Quetzal Serpent] ② was filled with joy, and exclaimed: "Your coming has been fruitful, Heart of Heaven, and you, Huracan, and you Chipi-Calculha, Raxa-Calculha!" ③

"Our work, our creation shall be finished," they answered.

First the earth was formed, the mountains and the valleys; the currents of water were divided, the rivulets were running freely between the hills, and the water was separated when the high mountains appeared.

Thus was the earth created, when it was formed by the Heart of Heaven, the Heart of Earth, as they are called who first made it fruitful, ④ when the sky was in suspense, and the earth was submerged in the water.

Analyzing Primary Sources

Cite specific evidence from the document to support your answers.

1. **Identify Supporting Details** What did the spirits have to do to create the earth? What does this tell you about them?

2. **Draw Conclusions** How did the Mayas' ideas about their gods reflect their relationship with nature?

Update an Interpretation

Follow these steps to learn ways to update interpretations of history as new information is uncovered.

INTERACTIVE

Make Decisions

1 Identify the interpretation that may need to change. Historians use evidence to create a picture of life in the past. However, if the evidence is incomplete, the interpretation may be faulty.

a. Read the excerpt below. According to the first paragraph, what evidence did earlier scholars have of early Mayan culture?

b. What was their interpretation of this evidence?

2 Study new information about the subject. Thanks to the work of archaeologists, historians, and other scholars, new evidence about the past may be uncovered. What details in the passage tell what new information about the Maya became available?

3 Revise the interpretation, if needed, to reflect the new information. Often, new evidence confirms what historians believe about the past or gives a more complete picture. In some cases, however, new evidence may force historians to reinterpret their view of the past.

a. Compare the new findings to the original interpretation of Mayan society. Does the new evidence confirm the previous interpretation?

b. If not, how would scholars need to change their interpretation?

Secondary Source

Until the 1970s, scholars could not read most Mayan writing. They had translated Mayan calendars and recognized numbers and dates. However, they did not realize that Mayan writings also recorded history. Scholars pictured the Maya as a peaceful people who studied the stars so that they could mark the passage of time.

Today, scholars can read most Mayan writing. Archaeologists have uncovered more Mayan cities and artifacts. Three of their discoveries are listed below.

- Ruins at Yaxuna show burned buildings, broken pottery, and other signs of violent conflict.

- Hieroglyphs in Copán say a ruler known as 18 Rabbit was captured and beheaded by Copán's enemies.

- Paintings discovered at Bonampak show scenes of fierce fighting.

LESSON 2

The Aztecs

BOUNCE TO ACTIVATE ▶ VIDEO

GET READY TO READ

START UP

Study the photo of the Aztec capital city. What factors help a society grow large enough to build a city like this?

GUIDING QUESTIONS

- Why did the Aztec empire gain power over people and territories?
- How did the Aztecs develop a highly organized government and advanced achievements in engineering and architecture?
- How did Mesoamerican religion change over time?

TAKE NOTES

Literacy Skills: Summarize

Use this graphic organizer in your 📓 Active Journal to take notes as you read the lesson.

PRACTICE VOCABULARY

Use the vocabulary activity in your 📓 Active Journal to practice the vocabulary words.

Vocabulary		Academic Vocabulary
basin	absolute	rigid
chinampa	monarchy	purchase
dike	aqueduct	

A few hundred years after Mayan civilization flourished, a new power emerged in central Mexico. In this section, you will learn about the Aztec empire and its civilization.

Where Did the Aztecs Live?

The Aztec empire developed in the highlands of central Mexico. The highlands' geography was different from that of the Mayan lowlands.

The Valley of Mexico A broad, high plateau stretches across the central highlands. Because of its high elevation, this plateau has cooler temperatures than the hot Mayan lowlands. Volcanoes rise above the plateau. Some of the best farmland in this plateau is located in highland basins below volcanoes. A **basin** is a bowl-shaped area.

One of these basins—the Valley of Mexico— was the center of the Aztec empire. Fertile volcanic soils and water flowing from the mountains around it made the valley a good place to settle. At the center of the Valley of Mexico was a large lake, Lake Texcoco (tesh KOH koh).

The Great Capital, Tenochtitlan The Aztecs came to the Valley of Mexico from the north during the 1200s. They first settled on a hill called Chapultepec, but later moved to a small island in Lake Texcoco. There they built the city of Tenochtitlan (tay nawch TEE tlahn). They built causeways to connect the island city to the lakeshore.

This setting had several advantages. Although other city-states surrounded the island, the Aztecs could easily defend it from attack. The water in the lake and the canals the Aztecs built made it easy to move goods and people. The lake was rich with fish and ducks. The land around the lake was ideal for farming.

The Aztecs could add to their farmland by building a **chinampa**, or an artificial island. Farming the chinampas helped the Aztecs feed a growing population.

Because the water of Lake Texcoco was at the bottom of a basin, it had no outlet that drained it. Over hundreds of years, it had become brackish, or partly salty. The Aztecs built a **dike**—a wall to hold back water—across the middle of the lake. Mountain streams brought fresh water to Tenochtitlan's side of the dike, which kept the brackish water away from the city.

Conquering an Empire Fierce warriors, the Aztecs began to take on their enemies in the early 1400s. The powerful Aztec army rarely suffered defeat. Soldiers swung heavy wooden clubs spiked with sharp obsidian blades. By 1440, the Aztecs ruled an empire that extended beyond the Valley of Mexico.

During the late 1400s, the Aztec empire continued to grow. By the early 1500s, the empire extended from central Mexico to Guatemala. Around ten million people lived within its borders.

Quest CONNECTIONS

Compare the map of the Aztec empire with the text description of the development of the empire. Record your thoughts in your 📓 Active Journal.

GEOGRAPHY SKILLS

By the early 1500s, the Aztecs had established a vast empire.

1. **Location** What geographic feature determined the location of the Aztec capital?

2. **Use Visual Information** How far did the Aztec empire extend from north to south?

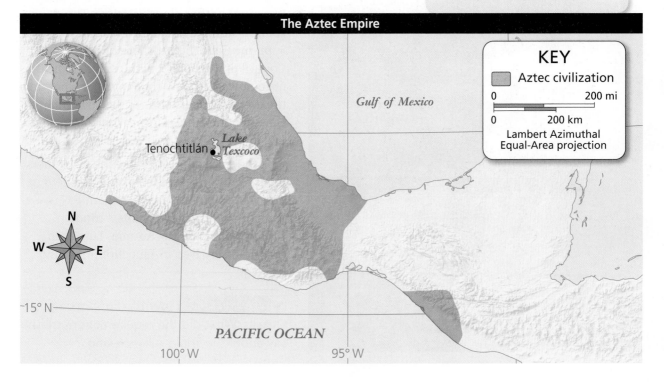

The Aztec Empire

KEY

▨ Aztec civilization

0 — 200 mi
0 — 200 km
Lambert Azimuthal
Equal-Area projection

Gulf of Mexico

Tenochtitlán • Lake Texcoco

N W E S

15° N

PACIFIC OCEAN

100° W   95° W

By this time, the Valley of Mexico had become a great urban area of about one million people on and around Lake Texcoco. In the center of Lake Texcoco stood the rich island city of Tenochtitlan, with its magnificent pyramids and glittering palaces. Goods and people from around the empire flowed into Tenochtitlan.

☑ READING CHECK Identify Supporting Details List two ways the environment influenced the growth and expansion of the Aztec empire.

INTERACTIVE

Aztec Temple

How Was the Aztec Empire Ruled?

The Aztec king, or the king of Tenochtitlan, was part of a Triple Alliance that included the the kings of Tlacopan and Texcoco. They agreed to support each other with troops and to share control of the Aztec empire. After 1428, the Aztec king was the most important ruler in the Triple Alliance. The Aztec king made all decisions having to do with war.

The three kings of the Triple Alliance demanded tribute, or regular payments of valuable goods, from the kings of the lands they conquered. Tribute goods ranged from clothing, food, and military supplies to jewelry, chocolate, quetzal feathers, and building materials. A Spanish visitor in the early 1500s wrote that "vast quantities" of tribute flowed into Tenochtitlan every day. As long as conquered kings paid the tribute, the Triple Alliance largely allowed them to control their own lands.

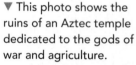

▼ This photo shows the ruins of an Aztec temple dedicated to the gods of war and agriculture.

The Aztec king had total power over the people of Tenochtitlan. The Aztecs had an **absolute monarchy**, a system in which one person from a ruling family has unlimited powers.

When an Aztec king died, a Supreme Council of nobles chose a member of the ruling family as the new king. Sometimes kingship passed from father to son, but sometimes it passed to other blood relatives. Three councils advised the king. These included the Supreme Council that chose him and a War Council of warriors. The third, the Council of Four, was led by a chief minister who ran the everyday operations of the government. However, the king made all major decisions.

The final king in this line, Moctezuma II, took the throne in 1502. Like the other men in his family, he presided over a prosperous and vast empire, which he expanded through warfare to its greatest range. Unfortunately for Moctezuma, European conquerers arrived in Tenochtitlan during his reign.

☑ READING CHECK Identify Supporting Details What did the requirement of tribute say about the Triple Alliance kings?

AZTEC SOCIAL STRUCTURE

Aztec social structure differed from the hierarchies in other Meso-American societies. Unlike the Maya, for example, the Aztec had a single ruler.

EMPEROR
The leader of the Aztecs came from the noble class. Unlike other kingdoms, Aztec leadership did not pass down through the generations.

NOBILITY AND PRIESTS
Aztec nobles, priests, and military leaders were just below the ruler. Nobles served as officials, judges, and governors of conquered territory.

MIDDLE CLASS
Traders and farmers were part of the largest Aztec group, the middle class.

SLAVES
Slaves and serfs, including prisoners of war, made up the bottom of Aztec society. Slaves could still own land and buy their freedom.

Aztec Society

Aztec society revolved around farming, warfare, and religion. It also had a **rigid** class structure that shaped people's lives.

Religion The Aztecs worshiped many gods. They believed that the gods gave them life and controlled everything on Earth. The most important Aztec gods were Huitzilopochtli and Tlaloc. Aztecs believed that Huitzilopochtli brought success in battle and made the sun rise. Without human blood, they believed, Huitzilopochtli would grow weak, and the sun would disappear.

The Aztecs sacrificed thousands of victims every year, cutting out their hearts and offering them to Huitzilopochtli. Like the Maya, the Aztecs often used prisoners of war in their sacrificial rituals. This practice was more central to Aztec culture than it had been to the Maya, however. Part of the Aztec religion was the belief that the universe would collapse if they did not continually sacrifice human hearts and blood to the god of the sun. Finding humans to sacrifice was of extreme importance to their way of life.

The Aztecs waged war partly to capture prisoners for sacrifice. The Aztecs also hoped to terrify conquered peoples, making them easier to control.

Nobles and Commoners Like the Maya, the Aztecs had two classes: nobles and commoners. Nobles belonged to families descended from the first Aztec king. Many were government officials.

Nobles owned slaves. Some were commoners who had sold themselves into slavery to escape poverty. Other slaves were war captives. Slaves could marry and could buy their own freedom. The children of slaves were born free.

Analyze Visual Information By the mid-1400s, the Aztec empire was an absolute monarchy. **Infer** How does this diagram show the importance of warfare to Aztec society?

Academic Vocabulary
rigid • *adj.,* inflexible, unchanging

Most Aztecs were commoners. Commoners lived simply. Extended families lived in small houses around a shared courtyard. Commoners ate mainly corn, beans, and chili peppers.

Agriculture and Economy For most commoners, life centered around farming or household duties. Men tended the fields, while women cooked, cleaned, and raised children. Aztec farmers planted corn and beans together, since they helped each other grow. Farmers also grew tomatoes, chili peppers, and squash, and they raised dogs and turkeys.

Some commoners worked as artisans. Artisans made fine craft goods for noble families, including jewelry and feather-decorated capes and headdresses.

The wealthiest commoners traveled the empire as traders. They traded Aztec craft goods for exotic feathers and precious stones. Trade let each town specialize in a particular craft. In each town, traders would **purchase** goods made in that town and sell goods made in other towns.

Academic Vocabulary
purchase • *v.*, to buy

☑ READING CHECK **Identify Main Ideas** How were religion and warfare linked in Aztec culture?

Aztec Achievements

You have read about the dike the Aztecs built across Lake Texcoco. The Aztecs made other achievements in engineering, urban planning, and the arts.

Engineering and Architecture The Aztecs designed and built an extraordinary capital city. Canals within the city and causeways across Lake Texcoco helped people move goods. To carry fresh water, the Aztecs could build an **aqueduct**—a canal or pipe—across Lake Texcoco from the hills surrounding the lake.

▼ The Aztec Calendar Stone depicts the sun god at its center. Historians are not sure of its exact purpose or how it was used.

At the heart of Tenochtitlan was a large walled plaza. Palaces and temples surrounded the plaza. The largest structure was the Templo Mayor, or Great Temple.

Arts Jewelry was a specialty of Aztec craftsmen. Jewelers used gold, silver, and semiprecious stones.

One of the finest forms of Aztec art was feather work. Specialists made fans, headdresses, capes, and shields from the brightly colored feathers of tropical birds.

The Aztecs also carved beautiful stone sculptures. One of the best-known examples is the great Aztec Calendar Stone.

The Oral Tradition Unlike the Maya, the Aztecs did not have a well-developed writing system. They had symbols to represent some ideas, but not an actual written language. Oral, or spoken, language was more important to the Aztecs than writing.

The Aztecs were skilled orators, or public speakers. One of the titles of the Aztec king was "great speaker." Orators told stories from the past and legends of the gods. In this way they passed down Aztec history and religion from one generation to the next.

Poets were highly respected in Aztec society. Even kings composed poetry. The most famous of the poet kings was Nezahualcoyotl (nay sah wahl KOH yohtl). In one of his poems, he reflects on the passing nature of life:

Primary Source

"Not forever on earth, only a little while. Though jade it may be, it breaks; though gold it may be, it is crushed; though it be quetzal plumes, it shall not last. Not forever on earth, only a little while."

—Nezahualcoyotl

Analyze Visual Information Featherwork was one of the most important Aztec crafts. **Identify Supporting Details** How does this headdress reflect the physical environment of the Aztec empire?

Lasting Impact on Mexico and Beyond The Aztec empire fell in the 1500s to an alliance of European conquerors, led by the Spanish, and native peoples who resented Aztec rule. Still, the Aztecs had a lasting impact. Tenochtitlan became Mexico City, the capital of Mexico. To this day, Mexicans cook with corn, beans, and chili. Words such as *chocolate, tomato,* and *avocado* passed from the Aztec language, Nahuatl, through Spanish and into English.

☑ READING CHECK **Identify Supporting Details** What are some lasting influences of the Aztecs on Mexico?

☑ Lesson Check

Practice Vocabulary

1. Explain the importance of **chinampas** to the Aztecs.

2. What is an **absolute monarchy**?

3. Use the word **aqueduct** in a sentence about Tenochtitlan.

Critical Thinking and Writing

4. **Analyze Cause and Effect** Explain how tribute could have strengthened the Aztec empire and led to more conquests.

5. **Draw Conclusions** How did the Aztecs' location and environment help them conquer an empire?

6. **Compare and Contrast** How did Mesoamerican religious practices change from the time of the Maya to the time of the Aztecs?

7. **Writing Workshop: Support Ideas with Evidence** List the differences and similarities between Maya and Aztec agriculture using what you have read in Lesson 1 and Lesson 2. Take notes in your 📓 Active Journal.

Primary Sources

The *Florentine Codex*

In 1529, a Franciscan missionary, Fray Bernardino de Sahagún, arrived in Mexico. Over the next several decades, he gathered information about the people and cultures of the land Spain had recently conquered. He carried out interviews with people and recorded their beliefs and stories. Sahagún finally collected his research in a multi-volume work that came to be known as the *Florentine Codex*. The passage here describes the Aztec system of raising young boys to fill the important roles of warrior or priest.

◀ The *Florentine Codex* contains many pictures created by the people of Mexico.

Reading and Vocabulary Support

① Penances are punishments one gives oneself after admitting to doing wrong.

② To consort with other people means to spend time with them.

③ *Perchance* is an outdated word that means "maybe."

④ This describes a mature boy who had good judgment—prudence—and was careful in what he said.

⑤ A valiant person shows courage.

And when he entered the young men's house, then [the leaders] charged him with sweeping [of the house] and with the laying of fires. And then they had him begin the penances. ① When there was singing at night (which was called song with dance), there he consorted ② with the others, he danced with the others. With the others there was conversation; songs were composed.

And when [he was] yet an untried youth, then they took him into the forest. They had him bear upon his back what they called logs of —perchance ③ now only one, or, then, two. Thus they tested whether perhaps he might do well in war when, still an untried youth, they took him into battle. He only went to carry a shield upon his back.

And when [he was] already a youth, if mature and prudent, if he was discreet in his talking, ④ and especially if [he was] of good heart, then he was made a master of youths; he was named tiachcauh. And if he became valiant, ⑤ if he reached manhood, then he was named ruler of youths (telpochtlato). He governed them all; he spoke for all the youths. If one [of them] sinned, this one judged him; he sentenced [the youths] and corrected them. He dealt justice.

—Appendix to the Third Book of the *Florentine Codex*

Analyzing Primary Sources

Cite specific evidence from the document to support your answers

1. **Summarize** What kind of character would a boy have to demonstrate in order to be named a tiachcauh or telpochtlato? What responsibilities would he then take on?

2. **Draw Conclusions** How could it benefit a society to have a set system for putting young people through tests and training?

LESSON 3
The Incas

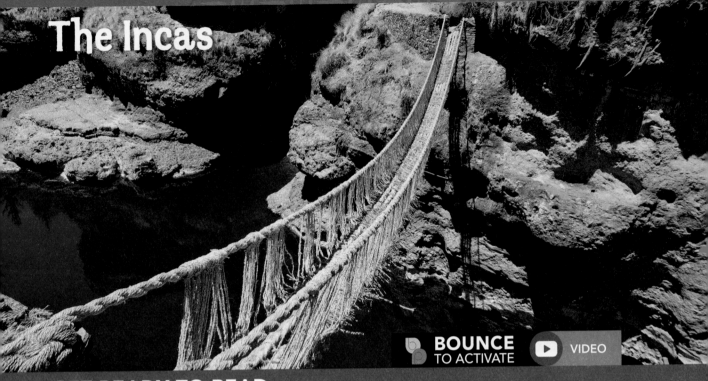

BOUNCE TO ACTIVATE   ▶ VIDEO

GET READY TO READ

START UP
Rope bridges like this were built throughout the Incan empire. How does this show one way the Incas adapted to their environment?

GUIDING QUESTIONS
- How did the environment affect the expansion of agriculture, population, cities, and empires in the Andean region?
- How did the Incan Empire gain and maintain power over people and territories?
- What were the chief Incan achievements in engineering and the arts?

TAKE NOTES
Literacy Skills: Analyze Text Structure
Use this graphic organizer in your 📖 Active Journal to take notes as you read the lesson.

PRACTICE VOCABULARY
Use the vocabulary activity in your 📖 Active Journal to practice the vocabulary words.

Vocabulary		Academic Vocabulary
terrace	ayllu	distribute
quipu	mita system	mortar
hierarchy		

Advanced civilizations arose throughout South America long before Europeans arrived in the 1500s. The greatest of these was the Incan empire. At its peak, it stretched 2,500 miles.

How Did the Geography of the Andes Shape Life?

The Andes (AN deez) are a mountain range along the western edge of South America. These huge mountains are a hard place for people to live. The slopes are rocky and steep. The climate is cold. Breathing is difficult because the air is thin at high elevations. The Incas and others before them adapted to these harsh conditions.

A narrow desert lies between the Andes and the Pacific Ocean. The world's largest rain forest, the Amazon, lies to the east of the Andes. These provided resources for Andean people.

The Chavín Many peoples lived in the Andes region before the Incas arrived. High mountains shaped the way of life for them and the Incas. Unlike the first civilizations

 CONNECTIONS

Imagine you were an early American migrating to the region. How might the geography of the region impact your travel plans? Write your thoughts down in your 📓 Active Journal.

INTERACTIVE

Growth of the Incan Empire

GEOGRAPHY SKILLS

The Incan empire developed in the Andes.

(a) **Region** How far did the Incan empire extend?

(b) **Draw Conclusions** What challenges might the geography and size of the empire cause?

of Mesopotamia and China, the civilizations of the central Andes did not grow along great rivers. Thousands of years ago, people settled in fishing villages along the desert coast of Peru and Chile. Farmers began to cultivate the river valleys and move into the highland plateaus.

The Chavín were one of the first civilizations to appear in the region. Modern archaeologists named them for the ruins at Chavín de Huantar. The Chavín built great temples. Although experts are not sure how the Chavín were organized politically, they believe that religion united the people throughout northern and central Peru. The Chavín were able to trade crops and other products to export their culture, which extended across the high Andes to the lowlands on either side of the mountains.

Andean Agriculture In the Andes, as in other places, agriculture led to the growth of civilization. Andean peoples farmed lands along rivers. They also farmed the hillsides by cutting **terraces**, or strips of level land that are planted with crops. Irrigation canals carried water to terraces. With this technology, people grew more food, including corn, chili peppers, squash, beans, cotton, peanuts, and hundreds of types of potato.

Andean people hunted game on the mountain slopes and fished in the nearby ocean. Farmers raised llamas and alpacas, which are related to the camel. Andean people used llamas for meat and to carry large loads. Alpacas provided soft wool.

☑ READING CHECK **Identify Supporting Details** How did altering the environment help Andean agriculture expand?

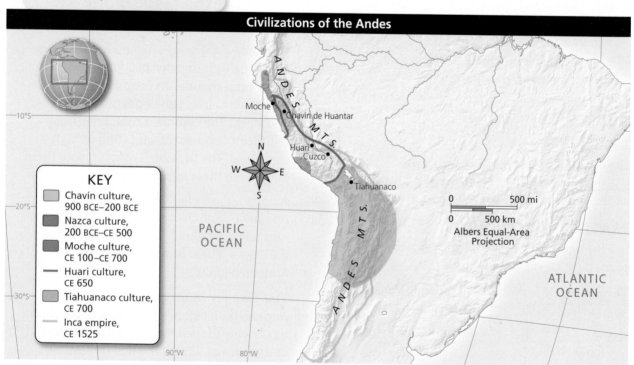

Civilizations of the Andes

KEY
- Chavín culture, 900 BCE–200 BCE
- Nazca culture, 200 BCE–CE 500
- Moche culture, CE 100–CE 700
- Huari culture, CE 650
- Tiahuanaco culture, CE 700
- Inca empire, CE 1525

Moche
Chavín de Huantar
Huari
Cuzco
Tiahuanaco

PACIFIC OCEAN

ATLANTIC OCEAN

ANDES MTS.

0   500 mi
0   500 km
Albers Equal-Area Projection

10°S
20°S
30°S
90°W   80°W

How Did the Incan Empire Expand?

The Incas built an empire in the 1400s and 1500s by taking over the lands of other peoples. Their success was partly due to their well-organized society.

The Incan Empire Grows Historians believe the Incas settled in the valley of Cuzco (KOOS koh), in present-day Peru, around 1200. Over the next 300 years they built a great empire, led by a series of warrior-kings called Sapa Incas.

The greatest Sapa Inca was Pachacuti (pahch ah KOO tee), who took power in 1438. Under Pachacuti, the Incas built a powerful army. Marching into battle, soldiers often sang bloodthirsty songs to terrify their enemy. One such song began:

Primary Source

We'll drink . . . from your skull, From your teeth we'll make a necklace, from your bones, flutes.

—Incan victory song

A strong army helped the Incas expand, but they preferred not to use it. Pachacuti offered peace and protection to those who agreed to join the empire. They kept their local rulers and customs. In return, they paid taxes in the form of labor and accepted Incan authority. Pachacuti ruled for more than 30 years.

A Strong Government Incan government was centered in Cuzco. Below the Sapa Inca, four governors each ruled a province. Below them, the administration was based on multiples of ten. Each village was divided into groups of ten families. Those were organized into larger groups of 100, 1,000, and 10,000 families. A government official was responsible for each group.

Interpret Visual Evidence
With flat land scarce, Incan farmers built terraces into the mountainside. **Draw Conclusions** Based on this photograph, what skills would Incan farmers have needed to build terraces?

Quick Activity

Write a song praising something else about the Incan empire. Record the lyrics to your song in your Active Journal.

HUAYNA CAPAC
Incan emperor (1493–1525)

- He was named emperor when he was still a child, so he was appointed a regent, or an adult who helps to rule until a child is old enough to do so.

- His regent attempted to make his own son the emperor instead. Huayna Capac's supporters had the regent assassinated.

- Once he became emperor, Huayna Capac was a mostly peaceful leader. He expanded roads and built food storehouses.

- He expanded the northern boundary of the Incan Empire to what is now the border between Ecuador and Colombia.

- He died in an epidemic, possibly smallpox or measles, both of which had been brought to the Americas by the Spanish.

Critical Thinking **Draw Conclusions** How do you think Huayna Capac's death affected the Incan empire?

Academic Vocabulary
distribute • *v.,* to divide and give out

The Incan government took responsibility for the well-being of its people. In times of crisis, such as a crop failure or natural disaster, officials **distributed** food and clothing. These goods came from storehouses spread out across the empire. But these benefits came at a price. People had little freedom.

Unifying the Empire The Incas forced their language, Quechua (KECH wuh), on conquered peoples. This helped to unify the empire. It was only spoken, however. As was the case with other Andean cultures, the Incas did not have a written language. They passed their history down orally.

Official messengers sped reports across the empire. They often carried a **quipu** (KEE poo), a record-keeping device made of knotted strings. The Incas used quipus to keep records of people or goods.

The messengers traveled quickly along a system of roads built throughout the empire. Soldiers could also be sent along the roads to put down rebellions.

The End of the Empire The last great Sapa Inca, Huayna Capac (WY nuh kah PAHK), took power in 1493. By this time, the Incan empire stretched 2,500 miles from north to south. It may have included as many as ten million people who lived mostly in peace.

This time of peace did not last long. Huayna Capac died between 1525 and 1530 and his chosen heir died soon afterward.

Two of Huayna Capac's sons fought to decide who would take his place. Their brutal civil war shattered the Incan world. The war had barely ended when Spanish soldiers invaded. The weakened empire fell to the invaders, called conquistadors.

✓ READING CHECK Identify Supporting Details How did the Incan government respond to environmental disasters?

Incan Achievements

The Incas achieved great feats in architecture, astronomy, and metalwork.

Architecture The Incas were great architects. They built with huge stone blocks. They cut the blocks with great precision using only stone tools. Each stone fit in place perfectly. No **mortar** was needed to hold the blocks together. Many Incan buildings still stand after hundreds of years.

Incan cities were marvels of stone architecture. The Incan capital of Cuzco was filled with great palaces and temples. "Cuzco was grand and stately," wrote an early Spanish visitor. "It had fine streets . . . and the homes were built of solid stones, beautifully joined."

The Incas' greatest engineering feat was their road system. Incan roads stretched more than 15,000 miles across the empire. They crossed deserts, mountains, and jungles. They also spanned rivers on bridges that swung from cables. In some places, floating bridges rested on pontoons. Incan roads, often paved with stone, were very durable. Today, they can still be seen in parts of the Andes.

▼ Surrounded by more modern roads and bridges, this leather suspension bridge still carries foot traffic.

Arts and Crafts The Incas called gold the "sweat of the sun" and silver the "tears of the moon." With these metals, they crafted jewelry, dishes, statues, and wall decorations. Here is how a Spaniard described the Temple of the Sun in Cuzco:

Primary Source

The . . . doors were covered with sheets of [gold]. There was an image of the sun, of great size made of gold, beautifully wrought and set with precious stones.

—Pedro de Cieza de León

▲ Although some Incan goldwork survives, much more of it was melted down by Spanish conquerors.

The Incas valued textiles even more than gold. They wove richly colored and patterned cloth out of cotton, alpaca, and vicuña. Vicuña is an animal similar to the llama and the alpaca. Like the alpaca, it has rich, soft fur. Today, descendants of the Incas still produce beautiful textiles using ancient techniques and designs.

Science Like other ancient peoples, the Incas were skilled in astronomy. Astronomy is the study of stars, planets, and other heavenly bodies. The Incas made careful observations of the locations of different groups of stars. Many of the stars and planets were linked to gods and myths of their religion.

The Incas also studied movements of the sun and moon to develop calendars. These were used to decide when to plant crops or celebrate festivals. They knew which days of the year had the most and fewest hours of daylight and on which days daylight and night were equal.

☑ **READING CHECK** **Identify Supporting Details** Why are the Incas known for their building?

What was the Makeup of Incan Society?

Incan society was marked by strong government, religion, and a class system.

Social Order Incan society was divided into two large classes: nobles and commoners. Each class had its own hierarchy. A **hierarchy** is a system for ranking members of a group according to their importance.

The highest ranking nobles were close relatives of the ruling family. They lived in the finest houses, enjoyed the best food and clothes, and held the highest positions in government. The lower ranks of nobles held lower government positions. These included non-Incan local leaders.

Most non-Incan peoples were commoners. They were divided into categories based on age and gender. Each category had its own work and duties. For example, boys between the ages of 12 and 18 herded llamas and alpacas. Girls aged 9 to 12 gathered wild plants for dyes and medicines. Men aged 25 to 50 raised crops and served as soldiers.

Economy Incan society was organized into ayllus. The **ayllu** was a group of related families that pooled resources to meet people's needs. It owned and distributed land. The leader distributed food and materials to make sure that everyone received the goods they needed.

The Inca did not formally practice slavery. Still, because there was no money, people paid taxes with labor. This was called the **mita system**. Under the Incas, the ayllu's land was divided into three parts: one for the government, one for the priests and gods, and one for the people.

Members of the ayllu farmed government and religious lands to pay the mita. The government saved the crops for the army, times of famine, and ceremonies.

Incan Religion The Incas worshiped many gods. The most important was Inti, the sun god. The Incas believed they were descended from Inti. The Sapa Inca was honored as Inti's descendant and a living god. As long as they honored the Sapa Inca, conquered people were allowed to worship their own deities as well.

READING CHECK Identify Supporting Details How was land divided in the Incan empire?

Use Visual Information
Llamas were the only pack animals available to the Inca. Today, Andean farmers continue to breed llamas. **Infer** What uses might farmers have for domesticated llamas?

☑ Lesson Check

Practice Vocabulary

1. What was the purpose of a **quipu**?
2. What was an **ayllu**?
3. Why was the **mita** paid with labor?

Critical Thinking and Writing

4. **Compare Viewpoints** How do you think conquered people felt about joining the Incan empire? Why?

5. **Make Decisions** What was the Incas' greatest achievement? Explain.

6. **Identify Cause and Effect** In what ways were the Incas shaped by their environment?

7. **Writing Workshop: Support Thesis with Details** Find details from this lesson that can support your thesis statement. Take notes in your 📖 Active Journal.

Interpret Thematic Maps

Follow these steps to interpret thematic maps.

INTERACTIVE

Read Special-Purpose Maps

1 Identify the type and general topic of the thematic map. Often the map title indicates both the general type of map and its specific topic. Also helpful is any text that accompanies the map.

a. What does the key of the map shown here suggest about the general topic of the map?

b. What information about the map topic can you get from the secondary source below?

2 Determine the place shown on the map. Again, map titles often indicate the place or region shown. Based on the title of this map and the text accompanying it, what area is covered?

3 Determine the time shown on the map. The map title and key may contain this information. If it does not, the map may be showing features from the present day. Or, there may be clues about the time period under study from the content of the map. When did the Incan empire reach its greatest extent?

4 Explain what the map shows. Use all the information you have gathered from the title, contents, and key of the map to analyze the information it contains.

a. What information about the Incan road system can you get from the map that you cannot get from the text?

b. What other uses might this road system have?

Secondary Source

Incan Roads At its peak, which lasted from the mid-1400s to the 1530s, the empire of the Inca covered a vast area in the Andes Mountains of South America. The empire featured a system of roads that allowed for the easy movement of people and goods over long distances. Over these roads traveled trade goods, including gold and silver. These flowed into the capital at Cuzco, enriching the empire and its ruler, the Sapa Inca.

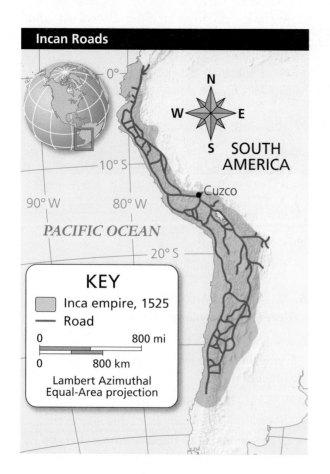

Incan Roads

KEY

Inca empire, 1525
Road

0 — 800 mi
0 — 800 km

Lambert Azimuthal Equal-Area projection

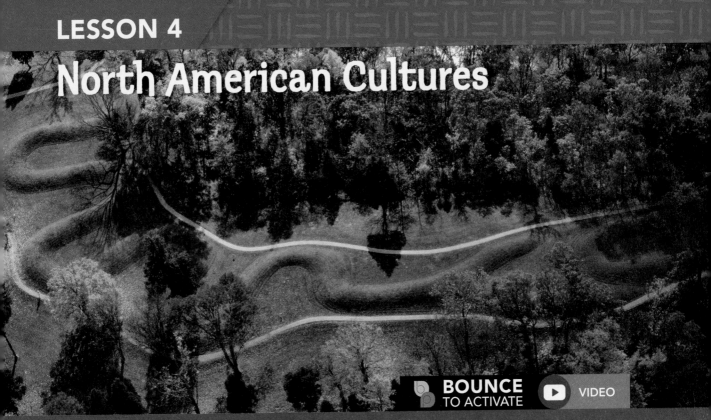

LESSON 4
North American Cultures

BOUNCE TO ACTIVATE VIDEO

GET READY TO READ

START UP
Study this aerial photograph of an ancient Native American mound in Ohio. Write three questions you would ask about the mound and the people who built it.

GUIDING QUESTIONS
- What does archaeological evidence reveal about early North American cultures?
- How were Native American cultures shaped by a variety of geographic conditions?
- What diverse cultures arose in North America?

TAKE NOTES
Literacy Skills: Compare and Contrast
Use this graphic organizer in your 📓 Active Journal to take notes as you read the lesson.

PRACTICE VOCABULARY
Use the vocabulary activity in your 📓 Active Journal to practice the vocabulary words.

Vocabulary		Academic Vocabulary
artifact	tepee	complex
drought	igloo	distinct
wigwam	potlatch	
longhouse		

Native North Americans lived in places with very different landforms, weather, and vegetation. Each group developed a way of life that matched its resources, including unique beliefs, languages, and traditions. Historians divide later groups into ten culture areas. These are described in this section and shown on the map at the end.

What Early Cultures Inhabited North America?

The first people to settle in the Americas came from Asia more than 15,000 years ago. Over time, people settled all over the Americas. Native North Americans did not leave written records. Even so, scientists have learned a lot about these peoples by studying artifacts. An **artifact** is an object that people make, such as tools, pottery, or jewelry. Scientists study them to figure out what crops Native Americans grew, what they hunted, what they wore, and what their homes were like.

The Ancestral Pueblo Several groups of people settled in the region that became the southwestern United States. They are

▲ The Ancestral Pueblo built complex housing like this in the desert Southwest.

Academic Vocabulary

complex • *adj.*, having many related parts; not simple

called Ancestral Pueblo because they are the ancestors of people the Spanish later called the Pueblo peoples. Archaeologists also call them the Anasazi. They flourished for hundreds of years and built complex cultures.

At first, they dug houses into the ground. By 1150 CE, they were building connected stone homes similar to apartment buildings. They had up to four stories and were sometimes built into the sides of cliffs.

Little rain fell in the Southwest, so the Ancestral Pueblo people had to use water wisely. For example, they dug ditches to carry water from streams to fields where they grew corn, beans, and squash.

Long droughts around 1300 made farming difficult. A **drought** (drowt) is a period of little or no rain. In response, Ancestral Pueblo groups left their villages and moved south. Some settled near rivers, where it was easier to farm. Others returned to hunting and gathering.

The Mississippians Another **complex** culture arose in the Mississippi River valley. It is known as Mississippian culture. Like the Ancestral Pueblo, the Mississippians lived in large communities and corn was their most important crop, but there were also big differences between these cultures.

The Mississippians are called mound builders because they made hills of earth near their villages for religious reasons. They respected the sun and their ancestors. Some mounds rose as high as 100 feet and covered many acres. Temples and priest-leaders' homes sat on the mounds.

Mississippian villages grew because of advances in farming. For example, they used tools such as hoes to help grow maize, another name for corn. The largest Mississippian town was Cahokia (kuh HOH kee uh), in today's state of Illinois. More than 10,000 people lived there.

As with the Ancestral Pueblo, a drought made it difficult for the Mississippians to grow their corn, beans, and squash. This led to violence between groups, so villagers surrounded their towns with thick walls made of logs and made alliances with other groups.

✓ READING CHECK Identify Supporting Details What facts show that early American farmers learned to adapt to their environments?

Who Were the People of the Eastern Woodlands?

By the 1500s, the Northeast and Southeast were home to groups called Eastern Woodlands peoples.

The Iroquois League The Northeast woodlands were mostly covered with forests. The climate was warm in the summer and cold in the winter. The women usually farmed. They grew "the three sisters" of corn, squash, and beans. The men hunted forest animals such as deer and wild turkey. Some fished from canoes made from tree trunks or birch bark.

Most people lived in a longhouse or a wigwam. A **wigwam** was a home formed by bending the trunks of young trees and tying them together to make a round frame. It was covered with bark or reed mats. A **longhouse** was similar, but rectangular.

In the 1500s, five groups in today's New York State formed the Iroquois League to end frequent wars among them. Each nation governed itself, but a joint council decided important matters. They agreed upon a constitution for the League:

Primary Source

"Thus shall all Great Peace be established and hostilities shall no longer be known between the Five Nations but only peace to a united people."

—The Constitution of the Five Nations

The Southeast Winters were milder in the Southeast, so the growing season was longer than in the Northeast. In addition to the three sisters, Southeastern peoples grew tobacco and sunflowers. They lived in houses on stilts or made with sticks covered in clay or mud.

Some peoples of this region, such as the Natchez, followed Mississippian traditions. They lived in villages, built mounds, worshiped the sun, and had social classes.

Other groups lived in the forest, hunting and gathering. Social classes were less important for these groups.

☑ READING CHECK **Identify Implied Main Ideas** What fact implies that Native American groups did not always live at peace with one another?

GEOGRAPHY SKILLS

Analyze Maps Native Americans' culture regions were defined by climate and other environmental factors.

1. **Region** Use the map to identify the culture region in which your state was located.

2. **Compare and Contrast** What is one way that life in the Arctic region would differ from life in the Southwest?

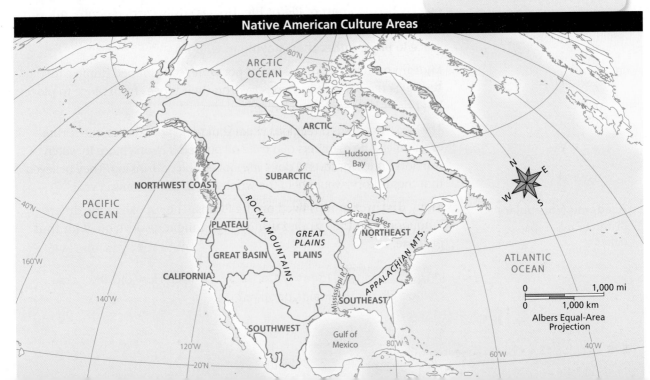

Native American Culture Areas

Analyze Images Many Native Americans of the Great Plains used every part of the bison as a source of food, clothing, shelter, and even weapons. **Cite Evidence** How can you tell that this painting depicts a time after the arrival of Europeans in North America?

People of the Great Plains

Many Native American groups lived on a vast grassland called the Great Plains. It stretches across central North America. In 1500, the Plains were home to huge herds of bison. These animals were very important to the Native Americans who lived on the Plains.

Before the arrival of Europeans, many Plains peoples were farmers. Their homes were large, round, and made from dirt and grass. They grew corn, beans, squash, sunflowers, and tobacco.

Bison hunts took place outside the planting and harvesting seasons. Men followed the bison on foot, shooting them with bows and arrows.

When the hunt was over, women prepared the animal skin, called the hide, to make leather. They made tools from bones and cooking pots from the stomachs. They used most other parts of the animal for food.

Europeans brought horses to North America. Hunting from horseback quickly became part of Plains life. Horses easily carried goods, allowing more groups to become migrants. That means that they moved from place to place rather than staying in villages.

Migrant groups lived in a kind of portable, coneshaped home called a **tepee**. Some people used dogs to drag their tepees from place to place, but horses later took their place.

The Sun Dance was a religious ritual that took place during the spring or summer. The members of a tribe all gathered in one place to watch warriors dance for several days without eating or drinking. They believed that these efforts would help the whole group in the coming year.

Academic Vocabulary

distinct • *adj.*, separate, different

Many **distinct** groups lived on the Plains. They spoke many different languages, but they traded using a sign language developed for that purpose.

☑ **READING CHECK** **Identify Cause and Effect** How did the horse change life for the Plains peoples?

Which Cultures Lived in the North and Northwest?

Northern North America includes three culture areas. They are the Arctic, the Subarctic, and the Pacific Northwest.

Native Americans of the Northwest Peoples of the Northwest cultures lived along the coast of the Pacific Ocean. They had a rich and varied environment. The climate was neither very hot nor very cold. Forests provided plenty of game and plant foods.

Northwestern people cut down the large trees in these forests to make huge canoes. They took these canoes onto the nearby ocean to hunt seals, sea otters, and whales. They also caught fish, like salmon, and harvested shellfish.

Food was so plentiful in the Northwest that people did not need to farm. They also spent less time gathering, hunting, and storing food than other Native Americans. They were also able to settle in permanent communities.

Abundant food and permanent communities led to complex societies with social ranks. This means that some people and families had higher status, or social value, than others.

Dozens of related people may have lived in each large wooden family house. Set out in front of the family home was a totem (TOHT um) pole. This tall structure, made from a tree, was carved and painted to relate important events and individuals in a family's history.

Wealthy families hosted potlatches to mark important events. A **potlatch** was a ceremony in which a wealthy and high-ranking family had a feast and gave gifts to their guests. The ceremonies were also a time for telling stories about a family's history. In this way, a family's heritage was passed down from one generation to the next.

Arctic Cultures Arctic peoples live in a harsh environment. Winters are long, cold, snowy, and dark. The sun appears for only a few hours each day. In southern Arctic areas, herds of caribou came to feed on summer plants. Arctic peoples used long summer days to gather as much food as possible. They hunted these caribou and moose.

Arctic people also hunted sea mammals such as seals, walrus, and whales. Hunters waited at seals' air holes or chased them in kayaks. They hunted whales using larger boats. From these animals, Arctic people gained meat and materials for clothing and tools. They even used whale and seal oil to heat their homes.

Arctic people lived in several different types of homes. Some lived in igloos during the winter. An **igloo** is a domed house made from blocks of snow. Those people usually lived in tents or underground homes during the summer.

▼ Unlike many Native American artifacts, totem poles like this one did not serve a religious purpose.

Subarctic Cultures Subarctic cultures covered much of modern Canada and Alaska. Winters there are cold and summers short. Food was scarce, but more easily available than in the Arctic.

The peoples of this region, like the Ojibwa, lived in small groups. They hunted animals like moose and elk. They also caught beaver and waterfowl, such as ducks. In the warmer months, they collected berries and other plant foods.

Some people lived in tents during the summer. In winter, people dug homes into the ground for protection from the wind. To stay warm, they wore fur clothing. They also used snowshoes and toboggans to move goods in the snow.

✓ READING CHECK **Compare and Contrast** How did arctic and subarctic cultures differ?

Western and Southwestern Cultures

Western North America included several Native American culture areas. The many environments led to diverse ways of life.

Which Cultures Lived in the Southwest? The descendants of the Ancestral Pueblo settled in New Mexico. There, they built homes out of adobe, or dried mud. These homes had several stories. When Spaniards arrived in the region, they called the large structures *pueblos*, from the Spanish word for "town." Today, these peoples are called the Pueblos.

Like many native groups, the Pueblo peoples grew corn, beans, and squash. Some also grew cotton. Other Southwestern Native Americans lived as hunter-gatherers. Peoples who lived near water built homes from logs. Other groups lived in wigwams or tepees.

Analyze Diagrams Identify two types of dwelling that would allow for the growth of permanent communities.

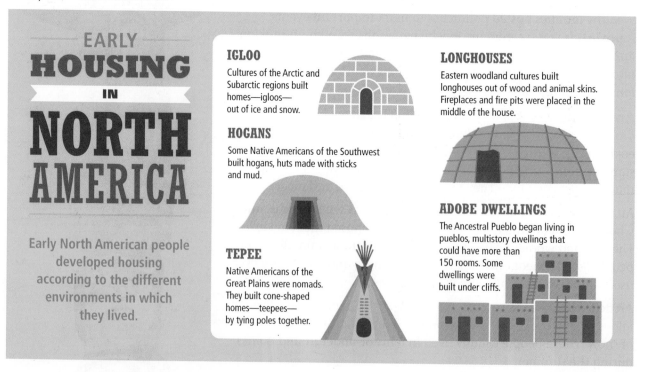

EARLY HOUSING IN NORTH AMERICA

Early North American people developed housing according to the different environments in which they lived.

IGLOO
Cultures of the Arctic and Subarctic regions built homes—igloos—out of ice and snow.

HOGANS
Some Native Americans of the Southwest built hogans, huts made with sticks and mud.

TEPEE
Native Americans of the Great Plains were nomads. They built cone-shaped homes—teepees—by tying poles together.

LONGHOUSES
Eastern woodland cultures built longhouses out of wood and animal skins. Fireplaces and fire pits were placed in the middle of the house.

ADOBE DWELLINGS
The Ancestral Pueblo began living in pueblos, multistory dwellings that could have more than 150 rooms. Some dwellings were built under cliffs.

Later, European settlers introduced sheep to the region. Some people, like the Navajo, began herding sheep. They used the wool to make blankets.

The Plateau and Great Basin The Plateau region was surrounded by mountains and had little rainfall. Most people in this area lived in permanent villages. After horses came to North America, many shifted their way of life. The Nez Percé (nez purse), for example, began to live nomadically, following bison herds.

Some peoples lived in the region called the Great Basin. This desert area sits between the Rocky Mountains and the Sierra Nevada. Food was scarce in this hot, dry region.

People lived in small groups and moved often to find food. They ate mostly plants, though they also hunted small animals. In the 1600s, some groups began using horses and became more like the Plains peoples, hunting buffalo and living in tepees.

California Native American Groups As in the Plateau area, the California Native American groups were very diverse. Most people were hunter-gatherers, though a few groups farmed. Many peoples who lived in California relied on acorns that they ground into flour.

Those living near water usually fished and lived in villages, while those in deserts moved around. Groups in California were also known for oral stories and poems.

▲ Baskets of this style were produced by one of the Native American groups of California.

✓ READING CHECK Compare and Contrast In what way did people of the Plateau live differently from the people of the Great Plains? What made some of them change their way of life?

☑ Lesson Check

Practice Vocabulary

1. How does a historian use an **artifact**?

2. Describe a **longhouse**.

3. What happened at a **potlatch**?

Critical Thinking and Writing

4. **Identify Cause and Effect** How did agriculture affect the Mississippian societies?

5. **Draw Conclusions** Why did some Native Americans develop farming while others did not?

6. **Compare and Contrast** Choose two Native American culture regions. Compare how geography affects the housing available there.

7. **Writing Workshop: Clarify Relationships with Transition Words** Reread the thesis statement and supporting details that you recorded in your 📓 Active Journal. Think of ways to clarify your writing, using words and phrases to create smooth transitions between the different ideas.

VISUAL REVIEW

Comparing the Maya, Aztec, and Inca

	Maya	Aztec	Inca
Economy	Based on agriculture, craft production, and trade	Based on trade of raw materials and finished products, as well as agriculture	Based on farming, mining, and tribute from conquered areas
Government	Ruled by kings and priests	Ruled by one emperor	Ruled by emperor with unlimited power
Religion	Worshiped more than 150 gods, each with clearly defined purposes; practiced human sacrifice	Believed in many gods, most related to agriculture; practiced human sacrifice on greater scale than Maya	Worshipped many gods, including Inti, the sun god, considered the most important one

Comparing Eastern and Southwest Cultures of North America

EASTERN CULTURES
- Mississippi and Ohio river valleys
- Giant earthworks and mounds
- Homes made of wood

- Ancestors came to North America from Asia
- Adapted to specific environments

DESERT SOUTHWEST/GREAT BASIN
- Farming settlements
- Cliff dwellers
- Complex irrigation systems

READING REVIEW

Use the Take Notes and Practice Vocabulary activities in your 📓 Active Journal to review the topic.

👆 INTERACTIVE

Practice vocabulary using the Topic Mini-Games.

Quest FINDINGS

Present Atlas

Get help for presenting your maps in your 📓 Active Journal.

ASSESSMENT

Vocabulary and Key Ideas

1. **Define** What is **slash-and-burn agriculture**?

2. **Describe** How does **drought** affect a society?

3. **Cause and Effect** How did the location in the Valley of Mexico help the Aztecs build an empire?

4. **Define** What is a **basin**?

5. **Summarize** What was the Triple Alliance?

6. **Identify Details** Who were the highest-ranking nobles in Incan society?

7. **Categorize** Which groups of early peoples settled in what is now the southwestern United States?

Critical Thinking and Writing

8. **Identify Evidence** What evidence indicates the Inca were master builders?

9. **Compare and Contrast** How did the Mayan, Aztec, and Incan empires have similar structures of social order?

10. **Explain** Give an example of how a group of early Americans adapted to their environment, and one example of how a group changed their environment to fit their needs.

11. **Synthesize** How did geography lead to such major differences among North American cultures?

12. **Writing Workshop: Write an Explanatory Essay** Write an explanatory essay comparing the impact of geography on Mayan, Aztec, and Incan agriculture.

Analyze Primary Sources

13. Which of these statements best describes why the Iroquois used a tree as a symbol in the Iroquois Constitution?

    Roots have spread out from the Tree of the Great Peace, one to the north, one to the east, one to the south and one to the west. The name of these roots is The Great White Roots and their nature is Peace and Strength. If any man or any nation outside the Five Nations shall obey the laws of the Great Peace and make known their disposition to the Lords of

    the... they shall be welcomed to take shelter beneath the Tree of the Long Leaves.

    —*The Iroquois Constitution*

    a. Trees, like peace treaties, are sometimes weak and cannot weather storms.
    b. Trees have many branches, as do peace alliances.
    c. Trees, like peace treaties, can stand up to any storm.
    d. Trees have strong roots and can provide protection for all those who are part of the alliance.

Analyze Maps

14. Which shaded area represents the Mayan civilization?

15. Along which coast did the Olmecs live?

16. The Yucatán Peninsula borders which two bodies of water?

17. Which civilization is indicated by the region shaded in purple?

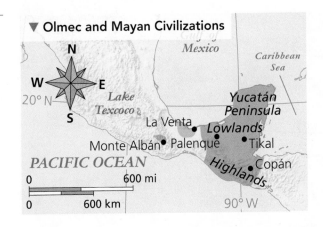

▼ **Olmec and Mayan Civilizations**

GO ONLINE
to access your
digital course

 VIDEO

 AUDIO

 ETEXT

 INTERACTIVE

 WRITING

 GAMES

WORKSHEET

ASSESSMENT

Go back over 1,700 years

when great trading kingdoms and rulers rose in **WEST AND EAST AFRICA**. Using the region's natural resources and connections to other regions, these empires grew wealthy and powerful.

Explore
The Essential Question

What makes cultures endure?

Even long ago, Africa was a land of many cultures. How did written and oral traditions allow those cultures to endure? What role did trade play?

Explore the Essential Question in your 📖 Active Journal.

Watch

NBC LEARN

BOUNCE TO ACTIVATE ▶ VIDEO

A Keeper of History

Learn how modern griots, or storytellers, keep African culture alive.

Read

about the way location, environment, and trade transformed the medieval-era civilizations of West and East Africa.

This mosque, part of the University of Sankore in Timbuktu, Mali, has been a center of learning since the mid-1300s.

African Civilizations
(300–1591)

Learn more about the geography and trading patterns of West and East Africa by making your own map and timeline in your Active Journal.

 INTERACTIVE

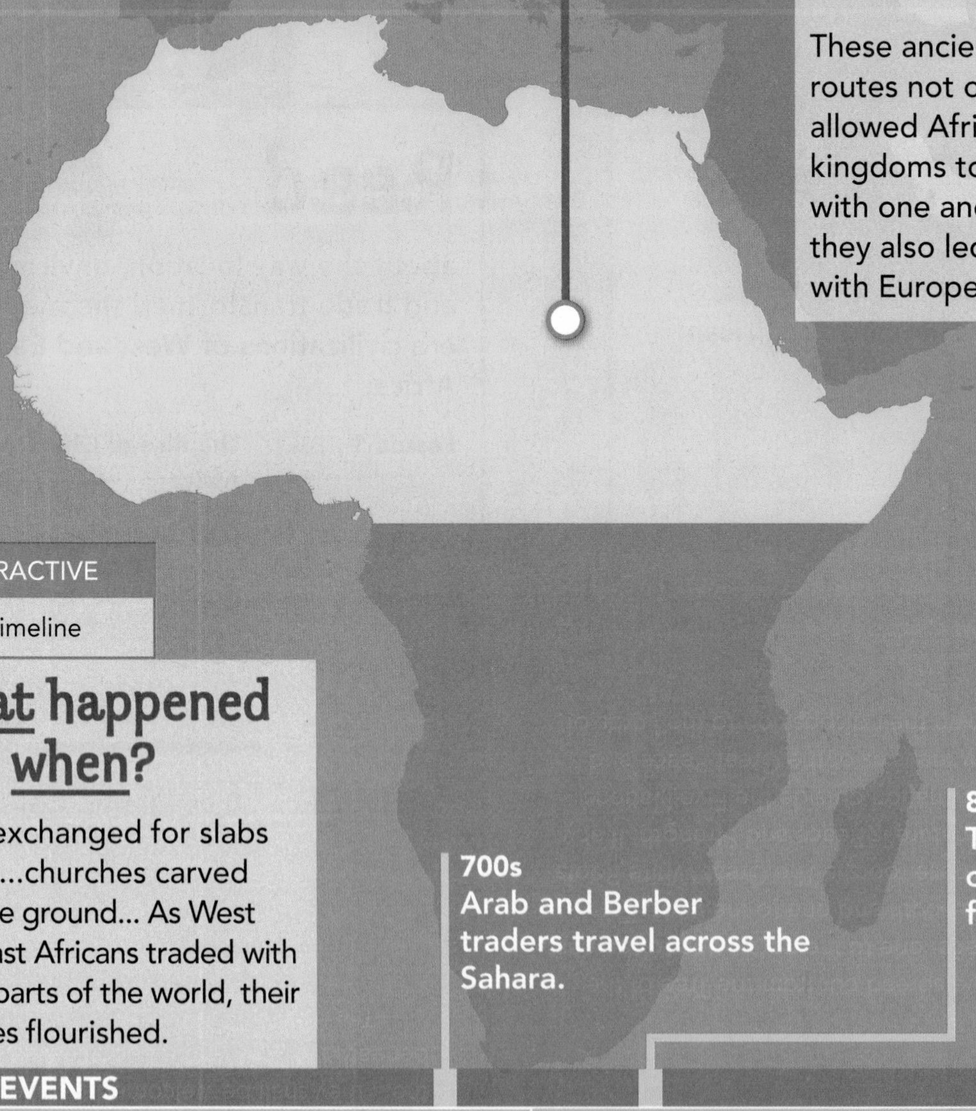

Topic Map

Where did these trade routes exist?

These ancient trade routes not only allowed African kingdoms to trade with one another, but they also led to trade with Europe and Asia.

INTERACTIVE

Topic Timeline

What happened and when?

Gold exchanged for slabs of salt...churches carved into the ground... As West and East Africans traded with other parts of the world, their empires flourished.

700s
Arab and Berber traders travel across the Sahara.

800
The Kingdom of Ghana flourishes.

TOPIC EVENTS

500

750

WORLD EVENTS

800
Charlemagne is crowned first Holy Roman Emperor.

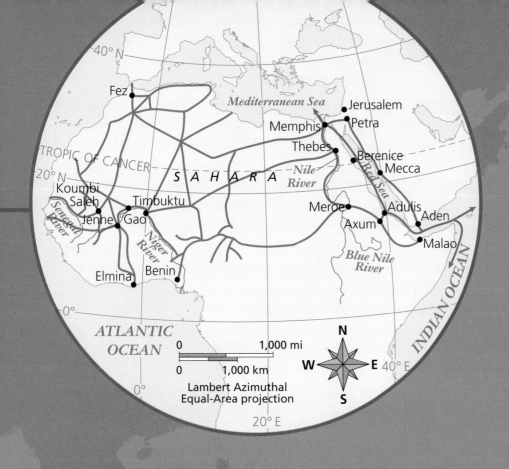

Fez

Mediterranean Sea

Jerusalem
Memphis
Petra
Thebes
Berenice
Mecca

TROPIC OF CANCER

S A H A R A
Nile River

Koumbi Saleh
Timbuktu

Meroe
Adulis
Aden

Jenne
Gao

Axum
Malao

Niger River

Senegal River

Elmina
Benin

Blue Nile River

ATLANTIC OCEAN

0   1,000 mi
0   1,000 km

Lambert Azimuthal
Equal-Area projection

N
W   E   40° E
S

INDIAN OCEAN

40° N
20° N
0°
20° E

1100
The empire of Mali is formed.

1324
Mansa Musa makes the hajj to Mecca.

1000

1250

1500

1162
Genghis Khan is born in present-day Mongolia.

1325
The Aztec establish their capital at Tenochtitlán.

Quest
Project-Based Learning Inquiry

Create an Oral History

Quest KICK OFF

Griots, West Africa's oral historians, are masters of words and music. They tell tales from long ago, about real events and parts of their culture, such as folktales. Now it's your turn to preserve African culture by acting as a griot. Consider this Guiding Question:

How has oral tradition helped to preserve African history?

As societies changed, so did the griots. Their work helped to preserve African culture and history. Explore this topic's Essential Question "What makes a culture endure?" through this Quest.

1 Ask Questions

Griots have important jobs. Get started now by making a list of questions you would want to ask about being a griot. Write the questions in your 🗐 Active Journal.

▼ Griots in present-day West Africa

2 Investigate

As you read the lessons in this topic, look for **Quest** CONNECTIONS that provide information about communicating information orally and about the history and culture of Africa during this period. Write your notes in your 🗐 Active Journal.

3 Conduct Research

Next, research and explore a set of African folktales or information about an important historical event that griots might have passed down. Capture your notes in your 🗐 Active Journal.

Quest FINDINGS

4 Retell a Piece of African History

Today's griots perform on television, radio, and the Internet. Some are very popular. Pick a method in which to deliver your story. It can be a video, a digital recording, or standing in front of the class. Prepare for your performance using your 🗐 Active Journal.

LESSON 1

The Rise of Ghana in West Africa

BOUNCE TO ACTIVATE   ▶ VIDEO

GET READY TO READ

START UP
Study the photograph of the people riding camels, and list several ways modern traders can cross the Sahara today.

GUIDING QUESTIONS
- What are Africa's chief geographical regions and natural resources?
- What impact did ironworking and the gold-salt trade have on West Africa?
- How did the environment affect the development and expansion of Ghana?
- How did Ghana create a powerful empire?

TAKE NOTES

Literacy Skills: Summarize
Use the graphic organizer in your 📓 Active Journal to take notes as you read the lesson.

PRACTICE VOCABULARY
Use the vocabulary activity in your 📓 Active Journal to practice the vocabulary words.

Vocabulary

plateau   labor

savanna   specialization

natural   caravan
  resource   trans-Saharan

Academic Vocabulary

conquest

prosperity

Africa's unique geography shaped the growth of African civilizations. Early kingdoms earned great wealth and power by adapting to a rich but challenging environment.

The African Landscape
The interior of Africa is like a plate turned upside down. This raised but flat region is called a **plateau**. The rivers flowing across the plateau fall as waterfalls at the edge. Here, the plateau meets a thin strip of coastal plain. Africa's coastline, with its lack of natural harbors and many waterfalls, discouraged seagoing trade.

Africa is the world's second-largest continent. It has many climates, types of vegetation, and types of land. Its geography encouraged trade. As a result, goods and ideas moved throughout Africa, Europe, and Asia. Several great West African empires, including Mali and Ghana, developed.

Rain is critical to life in Africa. People tend to live where rain falls the most. Africa consists of several vegetation zones, or bands of plant

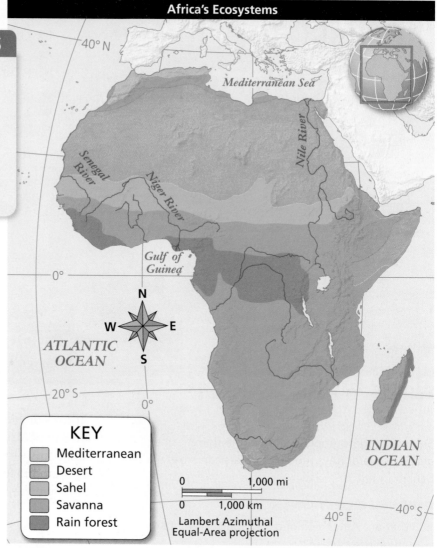

GEOGRAPHY **SKILLS**

Several ecosystems span the continent of Africa.

1. **Region** What are Africa's five ecosystems?

2. **Compare and Contrast** How are the ecosystems different?

KEY
- Mediterranean
- Desert
- Sahel
- Savanna
- Rain forest

0   1,000 mi
0   1,000 km
Lambert Azimuthal
Equal-Area projection

life. Each zone has its own climate. At the northern tip of Africa is the Mediterranean zone. Here summers are warm and dry, and winters are rainy.

The Sahara The world's largest desert, the Sahara, covers most of northern Africa. Today, the Sahara measures about 3.5 million square miles. In ancient times, however, the desert was not so large. Thousands of years ago, rivers, trees, and grasslands covered much of the region. Then, about 6,000 years ago, the climate began to get drier. Travel across the Sahara grew more difficult as the years passed. About 2,000 years ago traders began to use camels, rather than horses, for the long, dry trip. Camels made it possible for trade to occur between West Africa and the Mediterranean world. Camels can travel much farther than horses on much less water. They can also cross sandy areas more easily.

The Sahel and Savanna Just south of the Sahara is the Sahel zone, a slightly dry region that extends from the Atlantic Ocean through northern Senegal well into East Africa. The Sahel separates the very dry climate of the desert from the **savanna**, a zone of trees, grasses and moderate rain. Farmers and cattle and camel herders did well in the Sahel. The rainfall in the savanna supported crops such as rice, sorghum, and millet. People were able to keep herds of animals, such as cattle, sheep, and horses. Agriculture and herding, and the transportation provided by the Niger River, led to the growth of trade.

The Rain Forest Rain in Africa is most common along the equator. This is the rain forest zone. It is hot and wet year round. Thousands of different insects, plants, and animals live here. Some of the rain forest has been cut down to make way for towns and cities. In other places, the land has been cleared for farming. In this vegetation zone, life has often depended on the cultivation of root crops and fruits.

Some variations can be found within these seemingly similar zones. The oceans affect local climates, as do cooler highland regions.

The Niger and Senegal Rivers The two largest rivers of West Africa are the Niger (ny jur) and the Senegal. Early civilizations formed near these rivers. Rivers provided people with a reliable source of water in a dry region. They let farmers grow crops even in years with little rainfall. Boats could travel rivers most of the year. People used both the Niger and the Senegal rivers to travel and trade across West Africa.

Natural Resources A natural material that people can use to meet their needs is called a **natural resource**. Some of these materials include land used for farming or grazing; trees that provide fuel or building material; and minerals such as gold, copper, and salt.

Some natural resources made valuable trade items. Prized items like gold, along with agricultural wealth, gave rise to powerful trading empires. Trade brought Africans into contact with one another and with people and ideas from other parts of the world.

✓ **READING CHECK** Identify Cause and Effect How did climate and vegetation affect settlement in Africa?

What Led to the Rise of Ghana?

Learning to work with metals was an important step in the development of West African civilizations and empires. Metal tools and weapons were stronger than those made of stone, wood, or bone. People with metalworking skills had an advantage over their neighbors.

▼ The Niger River flows along the shores of Bamako, in the present-day country of Mali.

Quick Activity

Think of the items you would need to travel across the Sahara in a caravan. Record your checklist in your 📓 Active Journal.

Ironworking Technology By 350 BCE, West Africans began making iron tools in a place called Nok in present-day Nigeria. Iron was much harder than other materials used. With the help of iron tools, the people of West Africa could grow more food. As food supplies increased, so did the population. Ironworking technology then spread throughout West and Central Africa. In the 200s BCE, people established a settlement at Jenne-Jeno (also spelled Djenné-Jeno) in present-day Mali. By 800 CE, the city had become a thriving metropolis where artisans produced iron tools, gold jewelry, and fine painted pottery.

Ancient Ghana As the population of West Africa grew, governments were formed to keep order. Around 300 CE, the Soninke people founded the kingdom of Ghana between the Niger and Senegal rivers. (The modern African nation of Ghana is named after this ancient empire, but it is in a different part of West Africa.) As food supplies grew, not everyone had to grow food. Some could become experts in things like government or crafts. The division of jobs and skills in a society is called **labor specialization**.

Academic Vocabulary

conquest • *n.,* capturing something, especially in war

Families were very important in Ghana. Each clan, or group of related families, specialized in a craft or trade. The Sisse clan, for example, formed the ruling class. Its members became Ghana's kings and officials. Other clans specialized in trades such as fishing, cloth making, or cattle raising.

The Soninke benefited from the use of iron. They had iron swords and spears, while their enemies still used wooden clubs. Over time, they used their superior weapons to control others. The kingdom grew into an empire. Like many ancient empires—including Greece and Rome—Ghana enslaved people in its wars of **conquest**. Ghana sold gold, slaves, and other goods, while they imported horses, salt, and luxury items.

☑ **READING CHECK** **Analyze Interactions** How did technology and labor specialization lead to the growth of Ghana?

The Growth of the Ghana Empire

By the 700s, Arab and Berber traders of northern Africa regularly traveled across the Sahara. Traders would walk and ride their camels in a **caravan**, which is a group that travels together. They traded salt, horses, cloth, swords, and books for gold and ivory. Ghana was located across trade routes. It acted as a go-between for the North African traders and the producers of gold and ivory in the south.

▲ In addition to ironworking, the Nok culture is known for its terracotta sculptures, like the one shown here.

Gold–Salt Trade **Trans-Saharan** trade (trade across the Sahara) relied heavily on gold and salt. North Africans wanted gold to make into coins, since most states in the area based their currency on gold. This gold flowed into Europe and Asia, as well, in smaller quantities. West Africans were rich in gold, but they needed salt—a mineral necessary for good health. Miners removed slabs of salt from ancient sea beds in the Sahara. North African traders loaded salt onto camels and crossed the desert to West Africa to trade the salt for gold.

Wealthy Rulers Emperors of Ghana grew rich from the gold–salt trade. They taxed gold producers and every load of goods that entered or left Ghana. Ghana's rulers also controlled the gold supply. They knew that if the supply grew too large, its price would fall. Gold taken from the ground became the emperor's property. This law removed much gold from the market, keeping the price high. It also made the emperors rich. It was said that one emperor had a gold nugget weighing 30 pounds!

In 1067, a Spanish Muslim scholar described an emperor's court:

▲ Salt is still sold in West African marketplaces like this one in Ghana.

INTERACTIVE

Africa's Vegetation Regions

Primary Source

"He sits in a pavilion around which stand ten horses with gold-embroidered trappings. Behind the king stand ten pages holding shields and gold-mounted swords; on his right are the sons of princes of his empire, splendidly clad and with gold plaited [braided] in their hair. . . . The door of the pavilion is guarded by dogs of an excellent breed . . . who wear collars of gold and silver. . . . The king of Ghana, when he calls up his army, can put 200,000 men into the field, more than 40,000 of them archers."

—Al-Bakri, from *African Kingdoms* by Basil Davidson, 1966

Quest CONNECTIONS

How does Al-Bakri's story preserve part of the history of Ghana? Look for another piece of information about Ghana in this lesson. How would you tell a friend this information? Record your ideas in your 📓 Active Journal.

▲ This city from the Ghana empire survives in ruins. **Use Visual Information** What details in the ruins above give information about how people used to live?

Academic Vocabulary

prosperity • *n.,* the condition of being successful

Why Did Ghana Decline? For centuries Ghana prospered. Its rulers welcomed North African traders, who brought Islam to West Africa. Ghana kept its traditional religions. However, Ghana was known for its religious tolerance and welcomed Muslims. Ghana's leaders borrowed and used Islamic administrative and legal practices to run the government.

However, Ghana eventually began to decline. Among the reasons are overpopulation, food shortages, and an over-dependence on trade. To make matters worse, around 1060 the Almoravids, a group of Berbers from northwest Africa, expanded their empire into Ghana. They were religious reformers who wanted to purify the Islamic practices of Muslims in Ghana and spread their own interpretation of Islam. They also wanted to control the gold-salt trade.

Although the Almoravid invasion failed in the end, it disrupted trade and weakened the monarchy. The Almoravids brought with them large flocks of animals that took over much farmland. Soon, Ghana had trouble supporting its population. Ghana never returned to its **prosperity** after the Almoravid invasion.

☑ READING CHECK **Identify Supporting Details** What two goods were most important to trans-Saharan trade?

☑ Lesson Check

Practice Vocabulary

1. How is a **plateau** described in this lesson?

2. What is a **savanna**?

3. How does **labor specialization** help a society?

Critical Thinking and Writing

4. **Summarize** Explain how ancient Ghana became powerful and then declined.

5. **Identify Main Ideas and Details** Describe how the Sahara and regions south of the Sahara differ from each other.

6. **Writing Workshop: Develop a Clear Thesis** Write a sentence in your 📕 Active Journal about how the environment affected African empires such as Ghana and the development of trading networks. This sentence will become the thesis statement for an essay you will write at the end of the topic.

Mali and Songhai

BOUNCE TO ACTIVATE ▶ VIDEO

GET READY TO READ

START UP

The building in the photograph is a mosque that still stands in the country of Mali. What does that tell you about religion in the region?

GUIDING QUESTIONS

- How did the Mali empire rise?
- What made Mali a site of encounter?
- What were the effects of cultural exchange in Mali?
- How did the Songhai empire encourage the spread of Islam?

TAKE NOTES

Literacy Skills: Sequence

Use the graphic organizer in your 📓 Active Journal to take notes as your read the lesson.

PRACTICE VOCABULARY

Use the vocabulary activity in your 📓 Active Journal to practice the vocabulary words.

Vocabulary	Academic Vocabulary
scholarship	commercial
griot	legacy

After the fall of Ghana, even larger empires rose in West Africa. With people's movements along trade routes, news of these wealthy West African empires spread to distant places.

Rise of Mali

After Ghana fell, the small kingdoms it once ruled competed for power. In about 1203, a ruler named Sumanguru took over what was left of the old empire. He ruled over many small kingdoms that had been under the control of Ghana. One of these was the home of the Malinke people.

Triumph of Sundiata According to oral history, the Malinke tired of Sumanguru's cruel rule. They asked Sundiata (soon JAH tah), the son of a Malinke ruler, to free their kingdom. In 1230 Sundiata led a rebellion with the help of Malinke kings. By 1235 he ruled over a new empire, Mali. It took over all the former territory of Ghana, and added more. Sundiata became Mali's national hero and remains honored by the Malinke.

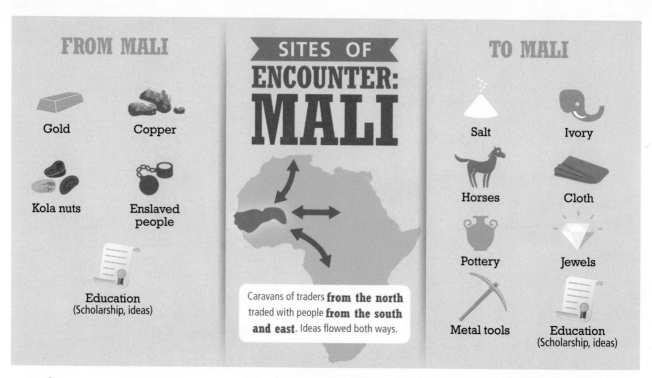

FROM MALI

Gold

Copper

Kola nuts

Enslaved people

Education
(Scholarship, ideas)

SITES OF ENCOUNTER: MALI

Caravans of traders **from the north** traded with people **from the south and east**. Ideas flowed both ways.

TO MALI

Salt

Ivory

Horses

Cloth

Pottery

Jewels

Metal tools

Education
(Scholarship, ideas)

Analyze Diagrams As a center of trade, Mali was a site for commercial and cultural exchanges. **Categorize** What cultural exchanges took place?

Exchanges at Mali Sundiata proved to be a wise ruler. The people called him mansa, or emperor. He ruled with an assembly of kings. At their first meeting, the assembly put forth a set of laws. The laws dealt with the social classes, property rights, the environment, and personal conduct. Passed by word of mouth, they became the law of the land. The rules divided responsibilities and privileges among the clans. The laws allowed women to serve in government on rare occasions. Mali's kings grew wealthy by collecting tribute from farmers and taxing trade.

Under Sundiata, Mali gained control of the gold-producing regions and trade routes and grew wealthy from trade. It traded items like gold, salt, cloth, books, and copper with places in North Africa, Arabia, and Europe. Because of Mali's location, the empire became the center of trans-Saharan trade, a site of encounter where cultures and commerce intersected. In addition to salt from the Sahara, southbound caravans brought copper, books, and horses to Mali. Northbound caravans brought in gold (the most important) plus ivory, ostrich feathers, and enslaved people. Merchants sold these captives, which included many women, along the Mediterranean Sea and in the Middle East. Many of these enslaved people were servants in Muslim households in Mediterranean and Middle Eastern communities.

READING CHECK **Draw Conclusions** Why do people in Mali still revere Sundiata?

What Was Mali LIke at its Peak?

Mansa Musa, emperor from 1312 to 1337, ruled Mali during its most prosperous period. He made the empire larger. By embracing Islam, he changed the empire into a center of Muslim learning and art.

Mansa Musa's Hajj A hajj, or religious journey to the holy city of Mecca, is one of the duties of a faithful Muslim. In 1324 Mansa Musa made a great hajj. He set off from Mali with a caravan of twelve thousand officials and slaves and more than 80 camels loaded with bags of gold dust. Arab writers at the time were amazed by Mansa Musa's great wealth. It was reported that he spent so much gold in Cairo that he upset the economy of Egypt for years. His great hajj brought world attention to the empire. North Africans, Arabs, and Europeans began to understand just how wealthy and advanced the empire had become. The Arab historian Ibn Khaldun wrote:

Primary Source

"The authority of the people of Mali became mighty. All the nations of the Sudan stood in awe of them, and the merchants of North Africa traveled to their country."

—Ibn Khaldun, quoted in *West Africa before the Colonial Era: A History to 1850* by Basil Davidson

Muslim Culture in Mali Mansa Musa returned home from his hajj with Muslim scholars, artists, and teachers. One such person was a famous poet, scholar, and architect called As-Saheli. Mansa Musa had As-Saheli build great mosques in the cities of Gao and Timbuktu (also spelled Tombouctou). Timbuktu became a center for Islamic **scholarship**, or formal study and learning. Students and teachers from North Africa and the Middle East traveled to Timbuktu to study.

A great traveler of the time was Ibn Battuta (IB un bat TOO tah) of Morocco. He wrote about his 1352 visit to Mali.

Did you know?

"Timbuktu" has long been used in the English language as a term to refer to faraway and mysterious places.

BIOGRAPHY
5 Things to Know About

MANSA MUSA
Ruler of Mali (late 1200s–circa 1337)

- Records are unclear, but Mansa Musa may have been related to Mali's great ruler, Sundiata.

- At the time of his reign, his empire was one of the largest and richest in the world.

- During his pilgrimage to Mecca, he spent so much gold that the economy of Cairo still had not recovered 12 years later.

- By building centers of learning, including universities, he helped foster Islamic education.

- He changed Mali's system of government to conform to Islamic law.

Critical Thinking How did Mansa Musa leave a lasting legacy?

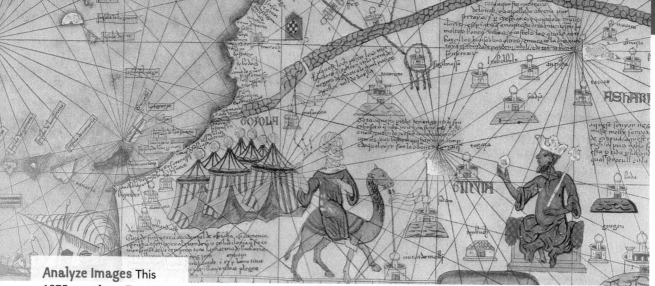

Analyze Images This 1375 map from Europe shows Mansa Musa holding a scepter and gold nugget. **Infer** What does this image tell you about the impression Mansa Musa made on Europeans?

Primary Source

"Amongst their good qualities is the small amount of injustice amongst them, for of all people they are the furthest from it. Their sultan leader does not forgive anyone in any matter to do with injustice. Among these qualities there is also the prevalence of peace in their country, the traveller is not afraid in it nor is he who lives there in fear of the thief or of the robber by violence."

—Ibn Battuta, quoted in *Ibn Battuta in Black Africa* by Said Hamdun and Noël King, 1995

Expansion of Mali During Mansa Musa's long rule, he extended Mali's territory westward to the Atlantic Ocean and northward, creating one of the largest empires of its time. At its height Mali covered an area about the size of Western Europe. It supported a population of roughly 50 million. Some think that the people of Mali may have explored the ocean at this time, but there is no evidence to support this claim.

✓ **READING CHECK Identify Main Ideas** What influence did Mansa Musa's religion have on the empire of Mali?

How Did the Songhai Empire Overtake Mali?

In the 1300s, Mali controlled trading cities along the Niger River. One of these cities was Gao, the capital of the Muslim kingdom of Songhai. Rulers of Mali following Mansa Musa began losing control of the empire in the 1400s. When they lost control of Gao, Songhai grew in power. Under a Muslim leader named Ali, it became the center of a new empire.

Conquests of Ali In 1464, Ali Ber became king of Songhai, taking the title *sunni*. (*Ali Ber* means "Ali the Great.") Sunni Ali was a great military leader. He kept mounted warriors to protect the land. He also had a fleet of war canoes patrolling the Niger River. This extended Songhai's empire along the great bend of the Niger River.

Once in power, Ali wanted to gain control of Timbuktu, still a center of the gold-salt trade. At that time a nomadic people called the Tuareg controlled the city. In 1468, Ali's well-equipped army drove the Tuareg out of Timbuktu. Ali next captured Jenne (also spelled Djenné), another wealthy trading city founded near the site of the ancient city of Jenne-jeno. With the successful capture of Jenne, Songhai controlled the trans-Saharan trading routes.

The Largest Empire Later rulers conquered still more territory, making Songhai the largest of West Africa's trading empires. The greatest of these rulers was Askia Muhammad. A successful military leader, he used a well-trained army to control the empire. He was an even better administrator. The government system he set up brought the region together. Business ran smoothly with the help of highly trained administrators. The system of weights and measures Muhammad established helped ensure the wealth of the empire.

Islamic Law and Scholarship Askia Muhammad strengthened the influence of Islam within the empire. He appointed Muslim judges to enforce laws, which were based on Islamic values. Since the Quran was written in Arabic, Songhai's laws were written in Arabic also.

Muhammad further promoted scholarship as well. Songhai's scholars learned to read and write Arabic to study the Quran. They copied old manuscripts and wrote new books in Arabic. These books focused on advanced topics, such as biology, medicine, law, ethics, agriculture, mathematics, and astronomy. The books, which were sold at great expense, demonstrate the advanced society of Timbuktu at the time.

Arabic also assisted in leadership and trade. No matter where members of the court were born, they could use Arabic as the official language of the government. It provided a common language for traders in West Africa and traders from Arab regions to set up deals and keep records. As a result, Timbuktu's **commercial** success soared to new heights.

Decline of Songhai When Askia Muhammad could no longer rule due to his health, his sons competed to take over their father's lands. The empire slowly began to weaken.

Songhai's era came to a close in 1591. In that year, soldiers from Morocco invaded Songhai. Armed with guns, the Moroccan forces overpowered the Songhai warriors and captured Timbuktu and other cities of the proud empire.

⬤ **INTERACTIVE**

Comparing Mali, Ghana, and Songhai

Academic Vocabulary
commercial • *adj.,* having to do with trade and business

GEOGRAPHY **SKILLS**

Three major empires dominated medieval-era West Africa.

1. **Interaction** How do you think the people of these empires made use of the Niger River?

2. **Synthesize Visual Information** How does this map show movement over time?

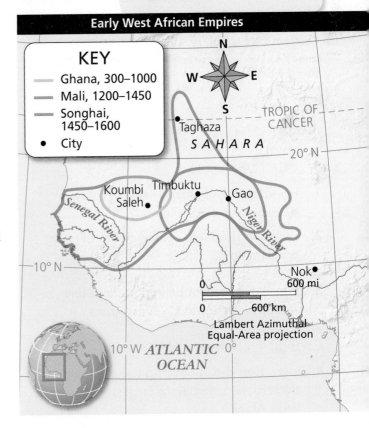

Early West African Empires

KEY
— Ghana, 300–1000
═ Mali, 1200–1450
▬ Songhai, 1450–1600
• City

N
W E
S

TROPIC OF CANCER
Taghaza
S A H A R A
20° N

Koumbi Saleh • Timbuktu • Gao
Senegal River
Niger River

10° N

Nok •
0   600 mi
0   600 km

Lambert Azimuthal Equal-Area projection

10° W *ATLANTIC* 0°
OCEAN

▲ Many valuable Islamic manuscripts are stored in Timbuktu.

A historian from Timbuktu described the effects of the invasion on Songhai:

Primary Source

"From that moment on, everything changed. Danger took the place of security; poverty of wealth. Peace gave way to distress, disasters, and violence."

—Abd al-Rahman al-Sadi

The invasion caused the Songhai empire to collapse. Its once-thriving cities came under Moroccan control.

☑ **READING CHECK** **Identify Supporting Details** Why were Songhai's laws written in Arabic?

Legacy of Empires

The powerful empires of Ghana, Mali, and Songhai are long gone, but their **legacy** remains. Millions of Africans speak modern forms of the languages of Mali and Songhai. Today, a **griot**, a professional storyteller and oral historian who is a keeper of West African history, might still sing about the achievements of great kings like Sundiata.

Families form the basis of modern African society, as you will learn in the last lesson. Likewise, markets and farming remain key parts of the economy. Islam continues to be a major influence in West African life, along with many traditional religions.

Academic Vocabulary

legacy • *n.*, an influence from the past

☑ Lesson Check

Practice Vocabulary

1. How did Mansa Musa's hajj and caravan show he was a great leader?

2. Why was Timbuktu a great center of **scholarship**?

3. Why would a **griot** be important before writing was adopted in West Africa?

Critical Thinking and Writing

4. **Infer** How did controlling the gold-salt trade make Songhai the largest empire in West Africa?

5. **Compare and Contrast** How did Sundiata, Mansa Musa, and Askia Muhammad compare as rulers?

6. **Revisit the Essential Question** How have the cultures of the Ghana, Mali, and Songhai empires endured in Africa?

7. **Writing Workshop: Support Thesis with Details** Add details from the lesson to support the thesis statement you wrote in your 📓 Active Journal in the previous lesson.

Primary Sources

Ibn Battuta, Travels in Asia and Africa, 1325–1354

Ibn Battuta was a Moroccan of Muslim faith. At the age of 21, he decided to make the hajj, or Muslim pilgrimage, to Mecca. His journey, beginning in the 1320s, turned into one of history's greatest treks. In the 1350s, Battuta traveled across the Sahara to Mali. He met the sultan, or king, of Mali at the time, as described in these accounts.

▶ Ibn Battuta, the great traveler

"On certain days the sultan holds audiences in the palace yard, where there is a platform under a tree, with three steps; this they call the "pempi." It is carpeted with silk and has cushions placed on it. [Over it] is raised the umbrella, which is a sort of pavilion ① made of silk, surmounted by a bird in gold, about the size of a falcon. The sultan comes out of a door in a corner of the palace, carrying a bow in his hand and a quiver ② on his back. On his head he has a golden skull-cap, bound with a gold band which has narrow ends shaped like knives, more than a span in length. His usual dress is a velvety red tunic, made of the European fabrics called "mutanfas." The sultan is preceded by his musicians, who carry gold and silver guimbris ③, and behind him come three hundred armed slaves. He walks in a leisurely fashion, affecting a very slow movement, and even stops from time to time. On reaching the pempi he stops and looks round the assembly, then ascends it in the sedate ④ manner of a preacher ascending a mosque-pulpit. As he takes his seat the drums, trumpets, and bugles are sounded...."

—From Ibn Battuta's *Travels in Asia and Africa, 1325–1354*

Reading and Vocabulary Support

① A pavilion is a structure that has open sides.

② Archers, who carry bows, also wear quivers for their arrows. What do you think a quiver is?

③ A *guimbri* is a two-stringed guitar.

④ To be sedate is to be calm and relaxed.

Analyzing Primary Sources

Cite specific evidence from the document to support your answers.

1. **Summarize** What impression of the ruler of Mali do you get from Battuta's description?

2. **Draw Conclusions** Based on Battuta's description, how had the trans-Saharan trade benefited Mali at this point in history?

Distinguish Verifiable From Unverifiable Information

Follow these steps to distinguish verifiable from unverifiable information in the primary source.

1 **Identify statements that could be verified.** Historical sources may contain facts, or statements that can be proved true. In the excerpt below, an Arab historian, al-Umari, records the observations of Egyptians who had been present for Mansa Musa's visit to the country. This account is from a local leader named Abu. What details in al-Umari's writing do you think you could double-check with reference materials?

2 **Determine how you might verify these statements.** Find ways to verify each statement. For example, you could check in a book about West African kingdoms. What would you look for in a book's index to find information to verify that Mansa Musa traveled through Cairo?

3 **Identify statements that cannot be verified.** It is not possible to verify something like a person's opinion. It is also not possible to prove true tall tales or myths about events from an ancient time.

a. Notice that al-Umari's friend, the emir Abu, realizes that Mansa Musa refuses to meet the sultan. Why does he think Mansa Musa refuses?

b. Why is it impossible to verify this thought?

Primary Source

"From the beginning of my coming to stay in Egypt I heard talk of the arrival of this sultan Musa on his Pilgrimage. . . . I asked the emir Abu . . . and he told me of the opulence [great wealth], manly virtues, and piety of his sultan. 'When I went out to meet him [Abu said]. . .he did me extreme honour and treated me with the greatest courtesy. He addressed me, however, only through an interpreter despite his perfect ability to speak in the Arabic tongue. Then he forwarded to the royal treasury many loads of unworked native gold and other valuables. I tried to persuade him to go up to the Citadel to meet the sultan, but he refused persistently saying: 'I came for the Pilgrimage and nothing else. I do not wish to mix anything else with my Pilgrimage.' He had begun to use this argument but I realized that the audience was repugnant [offensive] to him because he would be obliged to kiss the ground and the sultan's hand. I continue to cajole [persuade] him and he continued to make excuses but the sultan's protocol demanded that I should bring him into the royal presence, so I kept on at him till he agreed.'"

— Al-Umari, Arab historian, writing about Mansa Musa's 1324 visit from the Corpus of Early Arabic Sources for West African History.

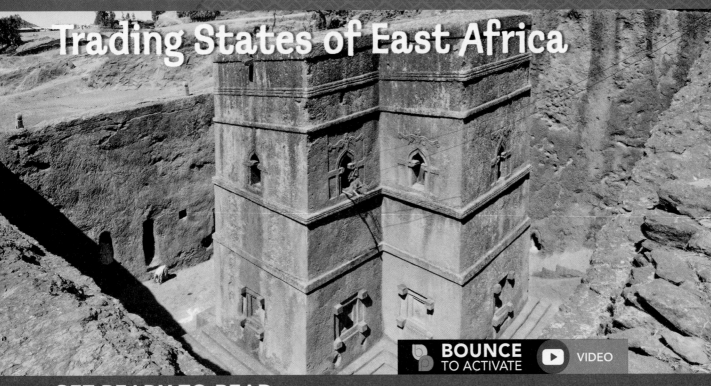

Trading States of East Africa

BOUNCE TO ACTIVATE ▶ VIDEO

GET READY TO READ

START UP

This massive Ethiopian church, Beta Ghiorgis (Church of Saint George), was carved into the ground. What do you think it shows about Christianity in Ethiopia?

GUIDING QUESTIONS

- How did Axum become an important trading kingdom?
- What kingdom became a center of Christianity in East Africa?
- What role did East Africa play in ocean trade?

TAKE NOTES

Literacy Skills: Identify Cause and Effect
Use the graphic organizer in your 📓 Active Journal to take notes as you read the lesson.

PRACTICE VOCABULARY

Use the vocabulary activity in your 📓 Active Journal to practice the vocabulary words.

Vocabulary		Academic Vocabulary
stele	dynasty	influence
Greco-Roman	stonetown	tradition
monk		

Early civilizations often formed near rivers or larger bodies of water. The East African civilizations were no different. The Nile River and the Red Sea made East Africa an ideal location for settlement.

The Kingdoms of Kush and Axum

The area along the Nile River south of the Egyptian empire was called Kush (sometimes also called Nubia). Desert covered much of the region. The Nile, however, created fertile land along its banks. The civilization of Kush formed there around 2000 BCE. The people of Kush tapped into the trade routes of the Red Sea and the Nile River. By the late 1400s BCE, however, Egypt took direct control of Kush.

Decline of Kush Over the years, Egypt lost its hold over Kush. By the 1000s BCE, Kushite kings again ruled. After many generations, however, the kingdom began to fail. By 150 CE, Kush was too weak to defend itself from invaders from the highlands.

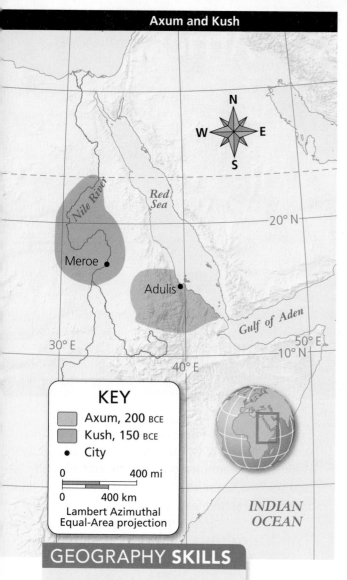

Axum and Kush

KEY

- Axum, 200 BCE
- Kush, 150 BCE
- City

0 ——— 400 mi
0 ——— 400 km

Lambert Azimuthal Equal-Area projection

Meroe
Adulis
Nile River
Red Sea
Gulf of Aden

20° N
30° E
40° E
50° E
10° N

INDIAN OCEAN

GEOGRAPHY **SKILLS**

Two wealthy kingdoms grew along and near the Nile River in East Africa.

1. **Interaction** What might have made Axum a place of high interaction?

2. **Compare and Contrast** How do you think East Africa differed from West Africa?

Axum: A Great Trading Kingdom In the year 325, King Ezana of Axum took over Kush. Axum (also spelled Aksum) replaced Kush as the commercial center of northeast Africa. Axum now controlled the trade routes to Roman Egypt, southern Arabia, and India.

Axum's wealth and power can be seen in its huge monuments. Great stairways led to altars honoring Axum's gods. A kind of grand stone pillar, called a **stele**, marked each grave of Axum's rulers. Each stele looked like a skyscraper. It had false doors and windows carved into the stone. Beneath the stele lay royal burial tombs and chambers.

☑ READING CHECK Why was Axum a major commercial center?

How Did Christianity Grow in East Africa?

In the 300s, the Red Sea was bustling with trading activity. **Greco-Roman** (Greek and Roman) trading settlements dotted the region. Christianity had been spreading in this region. Christian merchants and traders interacted daily with the people of Axum. They introduced Axum to a type of Christianity from the eastern shores of the Mediterranean. Before long, Christian churches began to appear alongside the stelae along the coast of East Africa. The Church of Saint Mary, built in the 300s, was probably the earliest. A member of the Portuguese embassy, Francisco Alvarez, visited the church in the 1520s. He described this grand church:

Primary Source

"This church is very large. . . . It has seven chapels, all with their backs to the east, and their altars well placed. . . . This church has a large enclosure, and it is also surrounded by another larger enclosure, like the wall of a large town or city. . . . Inside this large enclosure there are two palaces, one on the right hand and the other on the left, which belong to two rectors [directors] of the church."

—Francisco Alvarez

- In the early 300s, King Ezana was the ruler of Axum, which was located in present-day Ethiopia and Eritrea.

- King Ezana made Christianity Axum's official religion.

- He conquered the city of Meroë in 350.

- He ruled over a prosperous trading kingdom with wide contacts in the Mediterranean world.

- He ordered the minting of coins bearing the Christian cross as a means of spreading the religion among his people.

Critical Thinking How does the coin photographed reflect King Ezana's accomplishments and beliefs?

Christianity in Axum Christianity grew significantly after 340. Around this time, two Syrian brothers on their way to India were shipwrecked in Axum. They were captured and put to work in the king's court. One brother, Frumentius, became a trusted civil servant. Frumentius was a Christian. Under his **influence**, King Ezana became a Christian. Monks continued to establish Christianity throughout the kingdom. A **monk** is a man who dedicates himself to worshiping God.

Ethiopia, a Christian Kingdom Axum slowly began to weaken in the 600s due to economic problems. Another factor was the spread of Islam to the area. Eventually a new **dynasty** (ruling family), called the Zagwe, emerged in what is now Ethiopia. The Zagwe rose to power in the mid-1000s, and continued the Christian **tradition**. They replaced officials with those who were Christian. They also traded successfully with the Muslim world.

Zagwe rulers saw Ethiopia as a Christian holy land. They carved huge churches out of solid rock. The religious literature and music produced during the Zagwe period are still used in the Ethiopian Christian church.

Academic Vocabulary
influence • *n.,* the power to cause change

tradition • *n.,* an established or customary pattern

☑ **READING CHECK** **Identify Supporting Details** What did the Zagwe do with Christianity in Ethiopia?

East African City-States

Trade between cultures created unique societies along the East African coast. Between the 800s and the 1400s, Arab and Persian immigrants blended with the local communities. They formed more than three dozen city-states along the coast of present-day Somalia, Kenya, Tanzania, Mozambique, and Madagascar.

Indian Ocean Trade Routes The peoples of East Africa, the Mediterranean, and India traded with each other as early as the year 100. Traders sailed to western India for cotton cloth, grain, oil, sugar, and ghee (strained butter). Others sailed down the coast of the

Analyze Images Stone ruins of a mosque remain in present-day Kenya. **Synthesize** What do long-standing stone structures like this and the picture of Beta Ghiorgis earlier this lesson help us understand about people's past beliefs?

INTERACTIVE

Architecture of the African Kingdoms

Indian Ocean in search of cloaks, tunics, copper, and tin. They traded gold, tortoiseshell, ivory, timber, and slaves in return. From about 700, Arab traders exchanged metal weapons and iron tools for raw materials such as tortoiseshell, rhinoceros horn, ivory, and coconut oil.

The Swahili Culture Over time a new culture, Swahili, formed in trading towns along the coast of East Africa. This African culture was primarily Muslim. The Swahili imported ceramics, glassware, silver and copper jewelry from the Middle East, and Chinese silk. They adopted Islam by the 700s, which had been brought to the area by Muslim traders, immigrants, and teachers of Islam.

Blending of Cultures By the 1000s, Swahili settlements had grown into city-states, called stonetowns. A **stonetown** received its name for the multistoried stone houses built there. Through trade, cultural contact spread among the East Indies, China, India, Arab lands, Persia, and East Africa.

The Swahili imported trade goods from the interior of East Africa to be traded for goods from distant lands. In the interior, wealth was based on control of resources. Some kingdoms grew wealthy from their control of copper and gold mines or grazing land.

Contact through trade brought a multicultural mix to the East African coast. Swahili, for example, became a language that includes words from trade languages spoken on the coast of the Indian Ocean. Islam was the shared religion, but the East African version of Islam included parts of folk religions from the region.

READING CHECK **Identify Main Ideas** What was the Swahili culture?

☑ Lesson Check

Practice Vocabulary

1. What could a **stele** from a monument represent about the kingdom of Axum?

2. What did **monks** of the Zagwe help do?

3. What gave Swahili **stonetowns** their names?

Critical Thinking and Writing

4. **Draw Conclusions** Why are port cities important for trade?

5. **Compare and Contrast** How were Kush and Axum alike and different?

6. **Writing Workshop: Pick an Organizing Strategy** Look at your thesis statement and the details you recorded to support it in your 📓 Active Journal. Add details from this lesson. Then, think about a way to organize the details into an essay. Write an outline for your essay.

LESSON 4
African Traditions

BOUNCE TO ACTIVATE   ▶ VIDEO

GET READY TO READ

START UP

Look at the traditional dance being performed by members of the Dogon ethnic group in modern-day Mali. What are some ways that art, culture, and tradition can be preserved through the years?

GUIDING QUESTIONS

- How did kinship and caste shape African society?
- How were African religions similar and different from one another?
- Why were written and oral traditions important in African culture?

TAKE NOTES

Literacy Skills: Synthesize Visual Information

Use the graphic organizer in your ▤ Active Journal to take notes as you read the lesson.

PRACTICE VOCABULARY

Use the vocabulary activity in your ▤ Active Journal to practice the vocabulary words.

Vocabulary

caste
kinship
lineage
ethnic group

oral tradition
proverb
polyrhythmic
drumming

Academic Vocabulary

diversity
transmission

In the last lesson, you read about East African societies and cultures. The West African empires of Ghana, Mali, and Songhai had organized societies with unique cultures of their own. There were large empires, but also cities, towns, and villages. Throughout the empires, societies had complex, family-based relationships. "Kings may come and go," observed a popular saying from Mali, "but the family endures."

Society in West African Empires

A few cultural qualities were widespread across West Africa. Throughout the West African empires, most positions of leadership were reserved for men. Men also took part in warfare and Islamic learning. In later African societies, women farmed and took care of the family. Early West African society was organized by a ranking of social classes. In West Africa a person's social class, or **caste**, determined that individual's place in the social structure. A person's caste was established by the family he or she was born into.

Social Structure The emperor ruled each empire. He had the most power and the highest status, or social rank.

The nobility and kings formed the next-highest caste. Nobles helped the emperor govern the various parts of the empire and lead its armies. They paid tribute to the emperor.

Below the noble families were traders and free people of the towns. They ran the businesses and farms. Next down the rung of the social ladder were the skilled workers. Each trade formed a different caste. For example, members of one caste might specialize in ironworking, but members of another might work as musicians.

Slavery in West Africa Enslaved people made up the lowest level of society. People were enslaved for different reasons. Some people were born into slavery. Often, however, war captives, political prisoners, and kidnap victims were enslaved. Slaves performed many tasks. In the Songhai empire they served as soldiers, farm workers, and servants. In Mali, slaves served in the royal court and in the government.

Some slaves had rights in West African society. Some could marry, and families could not be separated. Slaves were also protected from harsh punishment. They could earn money and buy their freedom. One enslaved person even became an emperor of Mali.

Importance of Kinship In West Africa, family members shared a strong sense of **kinship**, or connection based on family relationships. Families included grandparents, aunts, uncles, and cousins. These large families formed lineages. A **lineage** is a group of people descended from a common ancestor. Often the head of a lineage controlled the family members and property.

Analyze Diagrams West African villages consisted of several clans, or larger groups of related families. **Use Visual Information** What two things connect every person in the diagram?

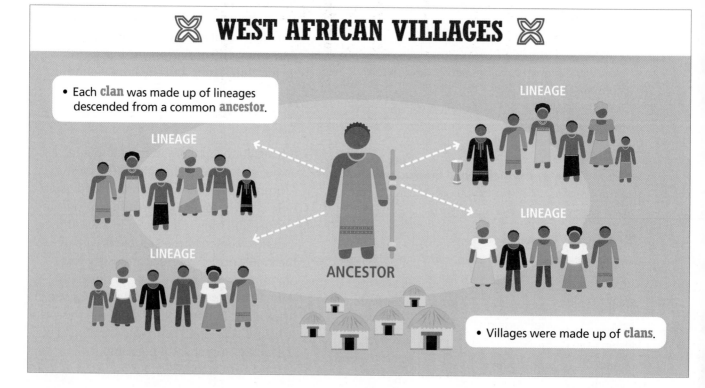

✖ WEST AFRICAN VILLAGES ✖

- Each **clan** was made up of lineages descended from a common **ancestor**.

LINEAGE

LINEAGE

LINEAGE

LINEAGE

ANCESTOR

- Villages were made up of **clans**.

Lineages were the building blocks of West African society. Each lineage was part of a clan, or larger group of related families. In turn, West African clans formed even larger groupings. Several closely related clans lived together in a village. A region consisting of many villages shared a distinct culture, language, and identity. Such a social unit is called an **ethnic group**. The West African empires included many ethnic groups, each with its own customs and traditions.

City and Village Life In many urban areas, Arabic was the main language of trade and Islamic worship and teaching. In rural villages, families spoke the languages of their ancestors. Some worshiped ancient gods.

Village economies were based on producing food. Farmers grew crops such as rice, yams, and beans. Herders raised animals such as cattle for meat, milk, and skins. Villagers traded in markets.

City economies were based on trade. Markets offered goods brought on the caravan routes. City dwellers could count on a varied and steady supply of food. They could also buy finely crafted goods. Thousands lived in large cities such as Jenne, Gao, and Timbuktu.

▲ Ancient West African village economies were based on producing food, a tradition that still exists in parts of Africa.

☑ **READING CHECK** Analyze Interactions How were lineages, clans, villages, and ethnic groups related in West African society?

African Religions

A great **diversity** of ethnic groups populated West Africa. Although Islam and Christianity were practiced to a great extent during this era, some people followed traditional religions. These traditional religions shared some common characteristics. Many African religions had religious leaders to guide prayers, and followers prayed on a daily basis. Most traditional religions also involved religious rituals, and promoted the honoring of ancestors. Many Muslims also practiced rituals and honored ancestors.

Religious Rituals People engaged the gods on a daily basis. They attended shrines to pray, get advice, and make offerings. Religious officials helped people communicate with the gods. Rituals reinforced the social and moral values represented by the gods. Following religious teachings helped keep society functioning smoothly.

Honoring Ancestors Africans also honored their ancestors. Upon death, they believed a person became a spirit and joined the spirits of ancestors. Some families created shrines to their ancestors, so that they could remain in touch with them. Rituals and spiritual mediums helped some people seek ancestors' help with their problems, much like they sought help from the gods.

☑ **READING CHECK** Identify Main Ideas How did West Africans treat their ancestors?

Academic Vocabulary
diversity • *n.,* variety

▶ **INTERACTIVE**

Religious Traditions of Africa

What Are Key Features of Africa's Cultural Legacy?

The Arabic language allowed for more learning and teaching within the African empires. Writings in Arabic allowed for faster exchange of ideas and preserved the area's history. Many African cultures also had a strong **oral tradition**; that is, Africans used oral history, poetry, folk tales, and sayings both to teach and to entertain. The societies of West Africa were also rich with music, dance, and art. These artistic traditions helped to pass on each group's history and culture.

A Rich Oral Tradition Storytelling was a part of daily life. Families shared folk tales at home. A popular fable, still shared today, told how Ananse the Spider gave people wisdom.

Primary Source

". . . Ananse did indeed finish collecting the world's wisdom. He packed all this in a gourd and began to climb a tall palm. Halfway to the top he got into difficulties. He had tied on the gourd in front of him, and it hampered his climbing. At this point his son, Ntikuma . . . called in a shrill young voice: 'Father, if you really had all the wisdom in the world up there with you, you would have tied that gourd on your back.' This was too much even for Ananse, who was tired from long labor. He untied the gourd in a fit of temper and threw it down. It broke and the wisdom was scattered far and wide. After a while people who had learned their lesson came and gathered in their own gourds whatever each could find; it is this that explains why a few people have much wisdom, some have a little, but many have none at all."

—African folk tale

A **proverb**, or wise saying, provided a quicker way to share wisdom. For example, the proverb "Every time an old man dies, it is as if a library has burnt down" reminds us to value our elders. Such sayings were passed down through countless generations.

Professional storytellers and oral historians, the griots served West African leaders and people. Griots memorized and told stories of famous events and people.

▲ A religious artifact from Ghana

Quest CONNECTIONS

Read the story. How could you retell it to an audience, using only your voice and body movements? What could a griot rely on to express emotion and meaning to an audience? Record your findings in your 📓 Active Journal.

Griots' main job was the **transmission** of their people's history and culture. "Without us the names of kings would vanish," explains a modern-day griot.

The tradition of griots and griottes (female storytellers) remains today. Their role has changed with time and circumstance. It will continue to change as griots accompany West Africans wherever they live.

Music, Dance, and Art   West Africans' lives were filled with dance and music. Dance and music marked many important stages in people's lives. Dancers celebrated births and marriages and performed at funerals.

West Africans created many musical instruments, including stringed instruments, horns, and drums. African drummers created polyrhythmic music. **Polyrhythmic drumming** combines two or more different rhythms at the same time. Dancers performed complex movements to match the drummers' polyrhythms. Dancers' feet might follow one rhythm, while their hands or hips moved to another.

Dancers wore masks of gods and spirits carved by skilled artists. West African artists created art for many purposes. Art was used in everyday life to express people's beliefs. For example, people honored the dead with carved wooden images of their ancestors. In the kingdom of Benin, sculptors made metal plaques and figures to record important events and people. In Mali, artists crafted clay soldiers in fine detail.

☑ READING CHECK **Identify Main Ideas** Why were both the written and oral traditions important to West African culture?

Academic Vocabulary
transmission • *n.*, the passing on of something, such as stories or history

▼ Drummers in Ghana carry on musical traditions from long ago.

☑ Lesson Check

Practice Vocabulary

1. How does a **lineage** show **kinship**?

2. How is a **proverb** an example of an **oral tradition**?

3. What three things does an **ethnic group** share?

Critical Thinking and Writing

4. **Compare and Contrast** How did slavery function in West African societies?

5. **Infer** Why do you think the story about Ananse is included in this lesson?

6. **Writing Workshop: Consider Your Purpose and Audience** Look back at your outline in your 📓 Active Journal. Check your thesis statement. Does it address the writing prompt? Do the sections of your outline all work toward the purpose of answering the writing prompt? Make adjustments as needed.

Primary Sources

Djibril Tamsir Niane, Sundiata: An Epic of Old Mali

Sundiata was a boy who overcame great hardship to found the Mali empire in West Africa during the 1200s. His story was retold by griots. It is an epic tale, based on an actual figure, Sundiata. It is part history and part legend. It tells how an awkward boy became king and united the twelve kingdoms of Mali into a powerful empire.

◀ West African griots still tell stories about the leader Sundiata.

Reading and Vocabulary Support

① Sundiata's other names include "Manding Diara," or "gift of the Mande people." "Sogolon Djata" was Sundiata's childhood name, meaning "son of Sogolon." Sogolon was his mother.

② Why do you think the storyteller added this line about a person's inability to change his or her own destiny?

③ *Taciturn* describes someone who speaks very little.

④ Calabashes are white-flowered gourds. They can be used to store water or food.

Quest CONNECTIONS

What do you think an audience might be thinking about Mali's history as they heard this story? Record your thoughts in your 📓 Active Journal.

Listen, then, sons of Mali, . . . I am going to talk of Sundiata, . . . Manding Diara, Lion of Mali, Sogolon Djata, son of Sogolon. ①

God has his mysteries which none can fathom. You, perhaps, will be a king. You can do nothing about it. You, on the other hand will be unlucky, but you can do nothing about that either. Each man finds his way already marked out for him and he can change nothing of it. ②

Sogolon's son (Sundiata) had a slow and difficult childhood. At the age of three he still crawled along on all fours while children of the same age were already walking. He had nothing of the great beauty of his father Naré Maghan. He had a head so big that he seemed unable to support it; he also had large eyes which would open wide whenever anyone entered his mother's house. He was taciturn ③ and used to spend the whole day just sitting in the middle of the house. Whenever his mother went out he would crawl on all fours to rummage about in the calabashes ④ in search of food, for he was greedy.

Malicious tongues began to blab. What three-year-old has not yet taken his first steps? What three-year-old is not the despair of his parents through his whims and shifts of mood? What three-year-old is not the joy of his circle through his backwardness in talking? . . . Sogolon Djata, then, was very different from others of his own age. He spoke little and his severe face never relaxed into a smile. You would have thought that he was already thinking, and what amused children of his age bored him.

—From *Sundiata: An Epic of Old Mali* by Djibril Tamsir Niane (translated by G. D. Pickett)

Analyzing Primary Sources

Cite specific evidence from the document to support your answers.

1. **Determine Author's Purpose** Why do you think the teller of the epic goes into such great detail about Sundiata's physical appearance and problems when he was a child?

2. **Draw Conclusions** Why do you think the storyteller included the last two lines in this excerpt?

Identify Sources of Continuity

INTERACTIVE

Identify Trends

Follow these steps to learn to identify the sources of continuity in a society.

1 Gather information about the society. Look at a variety of resources to learn about life in the society that you are studying. Below is a source that describes African traditions.

2 Identify possible sources of continuity in the society. Look for information about the society's government, values, family life, economy, religion, philosophy, and culture. Which of these help the society preserve information or values from the past and help pass it on to people today?

3 Determine which sources of continuity are important in the society. List the sources of continuity shown in the source below, and take notes about each one.

4 Summarize what you discover. Use the information you have learned to make a general statement.

a. What parts of African society and culture have lasted over time?

b. How did African societies preserve these traditions from one generation to the next?

Secondary Source

African Traditions

Although Islam and Christianity were practiced in early Africa, some people followed traditional religions. These traditional religions shared some common characteristics. Many promoted the honoring of ancestors.

Also important was the oral tradition. Storytelling was a part of daily life. Proverbs, or wise sayings, were passed down through countless generations. Families shared folk tales at home. Griots memorized and told stories of famous events and people, helping to transmit people's history and culture.

Many African societies were also rich with music, dance, and art. These artistic traditions helped to pass on each group's history and culture.

▲ This clay sculpture, created in the 1300s, was found in a burial mound in modern-day Mali.

☑ Review and Assessment

VISUAL REVIEW

Trade in West and East African Kingdoms

West Africa	East Africa
• Trade throughout ecosystems (Sahara, Sahel, savannah, Mediterranean, rain forest) • Dominated by salt and gold • Spread Islamic learning • Helped to create centers of education	• Trade with Arabia, Persia, and China brought wealth • Dominated by trade in ivory, enslaved people, animal skins, and iron • Rise in Christianity • Strong coastal trading cities

West African Empires

Empire	Key Accomplishments	How Empire Ended
Ghana	People of Ghana worked with iron and prospered from the gold-salt trade.	Almoravids from northwest Africa invaded, disrupting the empire.
Mali	Mali created a code of laws, made Timbuktu the center of Islamic scholarship, expanded its empire to 50 million people, and prospered from trade.	Poor leadership resulted in loss of control of Gao, and then the rest of the empire.
Songhai	Songhai maintained a strong military, established a government system, and became the largest of the West African empires.	Soldiers from Morocco invaded and overpowered Songhai.

READING REVIEW

Use the Take Notes and Practice Vocabulary activities in your 📓 Active Journal to review the topic.

INTERACTIVE

Practice vocabulary using the Topic Mini-Games.

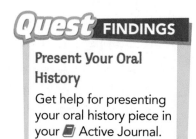

Quest FINDINGS

Present Your Oral History

Get help for presenting your oral history piece in your 📓 Active Journal.

ASSESSMENT

Vocabulary and Key Ideas

1. **Describe** What impact did **griots** have on West African society?

2. **Describe** How did ecosystem zones impact African culture and history?

3. **Define** What is a **savannah** and where is it found on the African continent?

4. **Explain** What is the importance of **hajj**?

5. **Describe** How was culture spread through the Arabic written word?

6. **Explain** What were **stonetowns**, and why were they important to trade in East Africa?

Critical Thinking and Writing

7. **Compare and Contrast** How did Islam spread in both West and East Africa?

8. **Make Inferences** What did Mansa Musa's caravan during his hajj show about him?

9. **Compare and Contrast** What effect did the gold trade have on both Ghana and Mali?

10. **Draw Conclusions** Why do you think West and East Africa saw a series of kingdoms develop within the same general areas?

11. **Revisit the Essential Question** What factors in West and East Africa allowed their cultures to endure?

12. **Writing Workshop: Write an Explanatory Essay** Using the thesis statement and details you recorded in your ▪ Active Journal, write a three-paragraph explanatory essay answering this question: How did the environment affect the development of African empires and the trade networks that connected them to other lands, including Europe and Asia?

Analyze Primary Sources

13. After reading the source below, why do you think the merchants of the port city used this method of conducting business?
    A. to create a bond between merchant and host
    B. to influence domestic trading
    C. to create a system of trading alliances
    D. to forge a sense of community for the port city

"When a vessel reaches the port it is met by *sumbuqs*, which are small boats, in each of which are a number of young men, each carrying a covered dish containing food. He presents this to one of the merchants. . . . Each merchant . . . goes only to the house of the young man who is his host. . . . The host then sells his goods for him and buys for him."

—Ibn Battuta, *Travels in Asia and Africa, 1325-1354*

Analyze Maps

Use the map at the right to answer the following questions.

14. What is the name of the West African empire labeled with letter C?

15. What are the names of the other two empires shown?

16. What landform is represented by letter E?

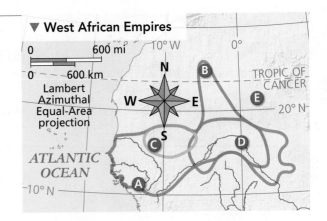

▼ **West African Empires**

The Renaissance and Reformation
(1300–1648)

GO ONLINE
to access your
digital course

▶ VIDEO

◀)) AUDIO

📖 ETEXT

👆 INTERACTIVE

✎ WRITING

🎮 GAMES

📄 WORKSHEET

✅ ASSESSMENT

It's the early 1500s.

EUROPE is in the midst of two major movements—the Renaissance and the Protestant Reformation. The Renaissance, which means "rebirth," was the dawn of a new age that gave rise to great artists and remarkable thinkers. Meanwhile, the Protestant Reformation was a time of religious upheaval that affected Christians at all levels of society. At the same time, a Scientific Revolution changed how people understood the world.

Explore
The Essential Question

How do ideas grow and spread?

The quest for knowledge brought about changes in the arts, science, politics, and religion. What caused these changes, and why did they spread across Europe?

Unlock the Essential Question in your 📕 Active Journal.

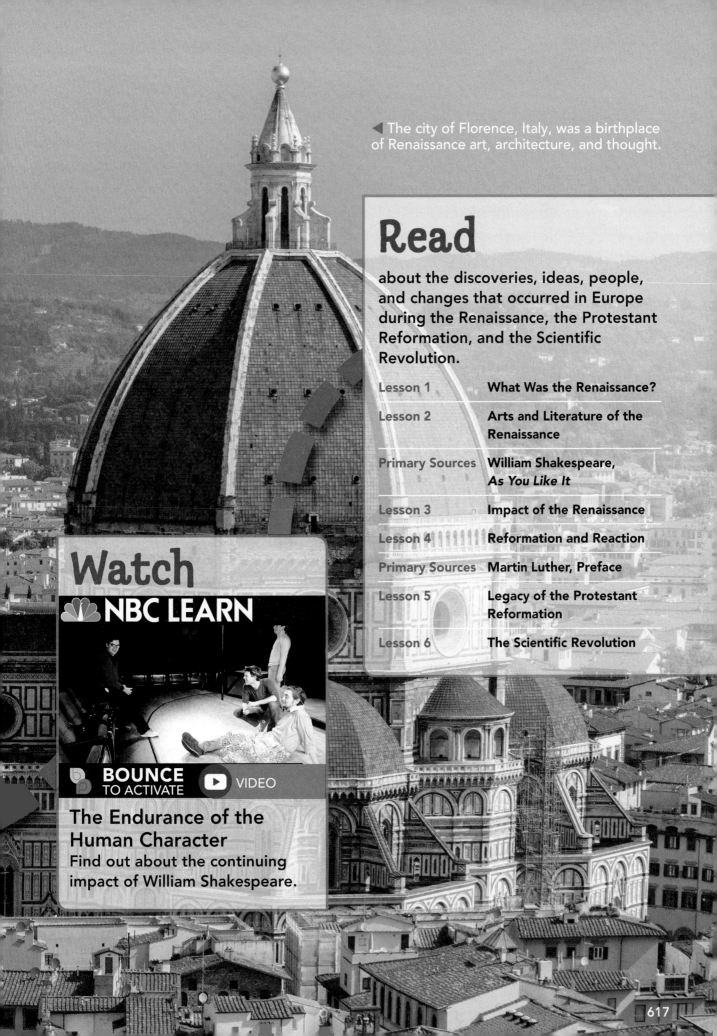

◀ The city of Florence, Italy, was a birthplace of Renaissance art, architecture, and thought.

Read

about the discoveries, ideas, people, and changes that occurred in Europe during the Renaissance, the Protestant Reformation, and the Scientific Revolution.

Watch

NBC LEARN

BOUNCE TO ACTIVATE ▶ VIDEO

The Endurance of the Human Character
Find out about the continuing impact of William Shakespeare.

The Renaissance and Reformation (1300–1648)

Learn More about the Renaissance and the Protestant Reformation by making your own timeline in your 📓 Active Journal.

 INTERACTIVE

Topic Map

Where did the Renaissance and Protestant Reformation begin?

The Renaissance began in the city-states of Italy, notably Florence, and spread outward, while the Protestant Reformation began in Germany.

👆 INTERACTIVE

Topic Timeline

What happened and when?

In Western Europe in 1300s, a new way of thinking took hold. It began in Italy and spread quickly across the continent, giving voice to writers, artists, political leaders, and scientists. By 1500, the ideas of the Renaissance would help spark the Protestant Reformation.

1434–1494
Medici family rules Florence.

1454
The Gutenberg Bible is published.

1508–1512
Michelangelo paints the Sistine Chapel.

1517
Martin Luth issues 95 Theses.

TOPIC EVENTS

1400

1500

WORLD EVENTS

1492
Explorer Christopher Columbus sails to the Americas.

1521
The Aztec empire falls at the hands of Spanish conquistador Hernán Cortés.

Warburg

Wittenberg

Nuremberg

Augsburg

Venice

Florence

Rome

Naples

Mediterranean Sea

Adriatic Sea

N W E S

Who will you meet?

Leonardo da Vinci, an artist, scientist, and inventor who had endless curiosity

Martin Luther, a Catholic monk who ignited the Protestant Reformation

Isaac Newton, who formulated the theory of gravity

1529
England's Parliament begins passing laws to make Henry VIII head of the Church of England.

1543
Nicolaus Copernicus publishes his theory that the planets revolve around the sun.

1572
St. Bartholomew's Day Massacre occurs.

1600

1591
Soldiers from Morocco invade the great African empire of Songhai.

1620
Pilgrims found the Plymouth Colony in Massachusetts.

Quest
Document-Based Writing Inquiry

Learning Through the Ages

Quest KICK OFF

You're a historian investigating the impact the ideas of the Renaissance have had on what students learn today.

How do the ideas of the Renaissance impact today's students?

What are students currently learning as a direct result of the ideas explored by Renaissance figures? Explore the Essential Question "What is the goal of learning?" in this Quest.

▼ The invention of the printing press had a huge impact on education and the spread of ideas.

1 Ask Questions

Historians have to sniff out the facts so they can draw a complete picture of the issue they are studying. Get started now by making a list of questions you have about the connections between your schoolwork and the Renaissance. Write these questions in your 📙 Active Journal.

2 Investigate

As you read the lessons in this topic, look for **Quest CONNECTIONS** that provide information on some of the ideas of the Renaissance. Write your notes in your 📙 Active Journal.

3 Examine Primary Sources

Next, look at the primary sources in this topic that provide clues to connections in education. Capture your findings in your 📙 Active Journal.

Quest FINDINGS

4 Create a Chart

Once you have finished your research, do what historians do best—tie all the information together. Create a three-column chart that explores the relationship between the **Ideas of the Renaissance**; **What Students Are Learning in School**; and the **Benefits of Each Subject**. What can you conclude? Write down your answer in your 📙 Active Journal.

What Was the Renaissance?

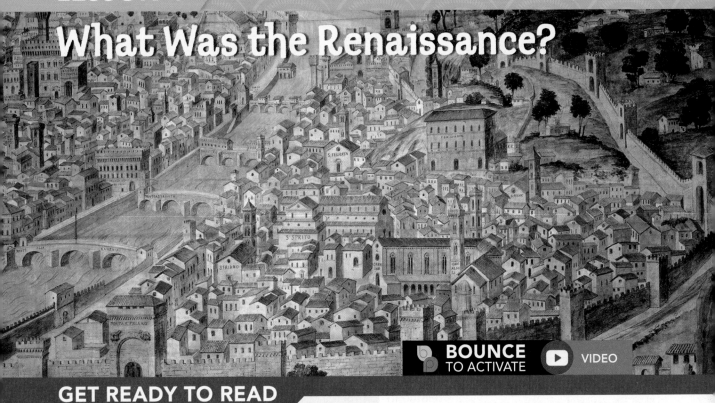

BOUNCE TO ACTIVATE ▶ VIDEO

GET READY TO READ

START UP

Look at the image of Florence, Italy, painted about 1490. How can you tell that this was an important population center at the time?

GUIDING QUESTIONS

- Why did the Renaissance begin in Italy?
- How did classical thought inspire the new learning and humanism?
- How did Renaissance ideas influence northern Europe?

TAKE NOTES

Literacy Skills: Identify Cause and Effect
Use the graphic organizer in your 📕 Active Journal to take notes as you read the lesson.

PRACTICE VOCABULARY

Use the vocabulary activity in your 📕 Active Journal to practice the vocabulary words.

Vocabulary		Academic Vocabulary
mercantile	vernacular	civic
Renaissance	individualism	prestige
patron	utopia	
humanism	satire	
secularism		

During the Middle Ages, life for most Europeans revolved around the manor and the Church. By the 1300s, however, new forces were at work that would bring considerable changes to Europe.

The Feudal Order Breaks Down

As trade and industry grew, feudalism and manorialism weakened. A wealthy merchant in Scotland could now drink French wine, buy clothing made of Asian silk, and flavor his food with spices from Africa or India. In one Italian textile factory, there were 30,000 workers.

Urban Growth The labor force for this economic expansion came from migrants who moved from manors to towns. Peasants were drawn to towns by the promise of wages. Nobles were also attracted to towns for economic reasons. They saw opportunities to make money by buying property and holding public office.

In Italian cities, the rural nobility married into the mercantile middle class to form a new urban aristocracy. **Mercantile** means

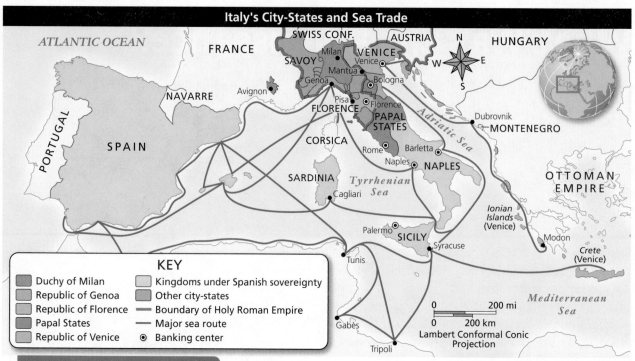

Italy's City-States and Sea Trade

ATLANTIC OCEAN

FRANCE
SWISS CONF.
AUSTRIA
HUNGARY
SAVOY
Milan
VENICE
Venice
Mantua
Genoa
Bologna
Avignon
Pisa
Florence
FLORENCE
PAPAL STATES
Dubrovnik
MONTENEGRO
Adriatic Sea

NAVARRE

PORTUGAL

SPAIN

CORSICA
Rome
Barletta
Naples
NAPLES
OTTOMAN EMPIRE

SARDINIA
Tyrrhenian Sea
Cagliari

Ionian Islands (Venice)
Modon
Crete (Venice)

Palermo
SICILY
Syracuse
Tunis

Mediterranean Sea

KEY
- Duchy of Milan
- Republic of Genoa
- Republic of Florence
- Papal States
- Republic of Venice
- Kingdoms under Spanish sovereignty
- Other city-states
- — Boundary of Holy Roman Empire
- — Major sea route
- ◉ Banking center

Gabès

0   200 mi
0   200 km
Lambert Conformal Conic Projection

Tripoli

GEOGRAPHY SKILLS

The city-states of Italy were important centers of trade and cultural exchange.

1. **Place** Which city-state controlled the city of Florence?

2. **Draw Conclusions** Why was Venice a key trading partner with eastern lands?

related to commerce or trade. This urban upper class kept its ties to the land, but lived mainly in town. Instead of spending money on rural castles, the new nobility used its wealth to build beautiful homes in the city.

A Diversity of Knowledge For centuries, learning had been based in the Church. Even after universities sprang up in European cities, theology, the study of religions—remained the most important course of study. In time, interest grew in non-religious subjects such as law, medicine, philosophy, engineering, and science.

Italian professor Petrus Paulus Vergerius wrote about the trend toward studying subjects other than theology.

Primary Source

"We call those studies liberal which are worthy of a free man; those studies by which we attain and practise virtue and wisdom; . . . that education which calls forth, trains and develops those highest gifts of body and of mind which ennoble men. . . ."

—Petrus Paulus Vergerius, *De Ingenuis Moribus*

The Great "Rebirth" Around 1300, these different trends came together to begin the Renaissance. The **Renaissance** was a great cultural revival that swept through Europe from the 1300s through the 1500s. *Renaissance* is French for "rebirth."

Through trade, European countries had contact with ideas flowing from the east and south. Through this exchange of ideas, Renaissance thinkers of Europe rediscovered the literature, art, and learning of ancient Greece and Rome preserved by Byzantine and Islamic scholars. European thinkers now looked to these classical cultures for models of how to live.

✓ **READING CHECK** **Identify Cause and Effect** What role did economic change play in urban growth in the 1300s?

Where Did the Renaissance Begin?

In England, France, and Spain, the feudal order defined the structure of life. In Italy, however, feudalism had never developed in the same way. This may help explain why Italy was the birthplace of the Renaissance.

Italian City-States By the 1300s, Italy was divided into several city-states. Because they were located near the Mediterranean Sea, the Italian city-states served as a natural crossroads between northern Europe and the lands of the Middle East and Africa. Merchants traveling on land and sea made the Italian peninsula a trading center. For this reason, Italy led medieval Europe in commercial growth.

Many Italian city-states became thriving centers of economic activity. In Venice and Genoa, merchants bought and sold Indian spices, Scandinavian furs, Chinese silk, and English wool. Venetian shipyards employed thousands of workers.

The growth of trade and commerce in Italy also promoted a free flow of ideas. People began to open their minds to new ways of thinking and doing things. For example, contact through trade gave Italy access to the Muslim world's knowledge of science, math, and classical Greek and Roman scholarship.

Patrons of the Arts In the Italian city-states, the old aristocrats competed for power and status with wealthy merchants and bankers. The newly rich gained status by becoming patrons of art and learning. A **patron** is someone who gives money or other support to a person or group.

Members of the nobility and the mercantile class used their wealth to support artists and to elevate their own status in society. Some patrons commissioned artists to paint portraits of them wearing jewels from India and their best clothing made from Chinese silk. Other patrons awarded architects commissions for designing grand palaces, filled with frescoes and marble sculptures.

✓ **READING CHECK** **Identify Main Ideas** What were the benefits of becoming a patron on the arts?

Analyze Images Money changers, like this Dutch couple, played a key role in Renaissance trade. They exchanged the coins issued by a foreign nation or city-state for local money. **Use Visual Information** Based on this painting, do you think money changing was a profitable business?

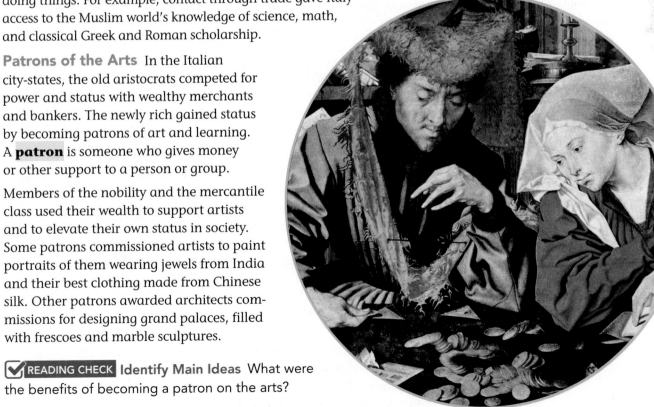

Analyze Images This fresco, or wall painting, shows a group of young artists presenting Lorenzo de Medici with a statue. **Use Visual Information** How does this fresco show the importance of the patron in Renaissance Florence?

Florence: Heart of the Early Renaissance

Several Italian cities became important centers during the Renaissance. Shipping through its port made Venice rich and cosmopolitan. Rome was the home of the powerful Catholic Church. However, it was the city of Florence that became the artistic center of the Renaissance.

Since ancient Roman times, Florence had been a major stop on trade routes. It was accessible from the Arno River or through passes in the Tuscan Apennines mountains. In addition to developing as a commerce center, Florence became known for its banking activity—even the pope kept his money there. Banking encouraged many other types of businesses such as silk manufacturing, the wool trade, and silver and gold crafts. Many of these groups established guilds.

One of the most powerful banking families in the city was the Medici (med EE chee) family. For several generations, the Medici ruled Florence. They were also patrons of the arts. Much of the art and architecture they commissioned was influenced by the grandeur they had seen while visiting aristocratic courts in France. Painters, sculptors, and other craftsmen had a chance to practice their arts working on the grand palaces and public buildings requested and paid for by the Medici. The Medici built many new churches in Florence and hired artists to decorate them.

Florentine merchants, too, spent money on artistic projects. Artists were also sought after by guilds and **civic** groups. In this way, painters and sculptors worked alongside gold artists or stone carvers on larger projects such as cathedrals. As a result, Florence became a showcase of Renaissance art and architecture.

☑ READING CHECK **Summarize** How did the role of the Medici family link trade, politics, and the arts?

New Viewpoints

The new learning of the Renaissance suggested that human beings and the world deserved contemplation and study as much as matters of God and faith. This led to new ways of seeing the world and the role of humans in it. These new viewpoints include the three key Renaissance ideas: humanism, secularism, and individualism.

Humanism Knowledge of classical Greek and Roman thought did not suddenly come to light in the 1400s. Thinkers such as Petrarch (PEA trahrk) did much during the Renaissance to revive interest in classical learning. They applied what they learned about classical Greece and Rome to their own world. This new focus was called humanism, from the Latin word *humanitas*. **Humanism** was a cultural movement of the Renaissance based on the study of classical works. To humanists, learning led to a better earthly life rather than serving solely as preparation for eternity. Medieval thinkers had focused on spirituality and faith rather than self-worth.

Humanists studied many subjects, including philosophy and poetry. Like medieval artists, Renaissance artists often focused on religious themes, but they set religious figures such as Jesus and his mother against classical Greek or Roman backgrounds.

Secularism The Renaissance also marked a growing trend toward **secularism**, or the view that religion need not be the center of human affairs. People began to view life as an opportunity for enjoyment and pleasure. This contrasted with the medieval attitude of life as little more than a painful pilgrimage striving toward heaven. The growth of secularism was clear in writings that were intended to entertain or inform rather than to promote spirituality. One example was *The Decameron*, by Giovanni Boccaccio (bo CAH chee oh). This collection of tales, written in the mid-1300s, reflected the worldly views of Florentine society. It was written in the **vernacular**, or everyday spoken language of the people.

Quest CONNECTIONS

Look at the graphic. How were a Renaissance scholar's interests similar to what you study during a typical day? Record your thoughts in your 📖 Active Journal.

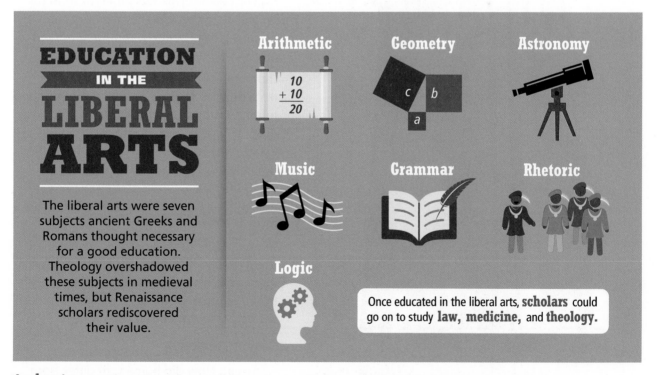

EDUCATION IN THE LIBERAL ARTS

The liberal arts were seven subjects ancient Greeks and Romans thought necessary for a good education. Theology overshadowed these subjects in medieval times, but Renaissance scholars rediscovered their value.

Arithmetic
10
+ 10
20

Geometry
c b
a

Astronomy

Music

Grammar

Rhetoric

Logic

Once educated in the liberal arts, **scholars** could go on to study **law, medicine,** and **theology.**

Analyze Images Rhetoric, or the art of persuasive speaking, was considered one of the seven liberal arts. **Draw Conclusions** What subjects would you add to this list today? Why?

INTERACTIVE

Renaissance Italy's City-States

Academic Vocabulary

prestige • *n.,* respect and admiration from others

NICCOLÒ MACCHIAVELLI

▲ Machiavelli

Another secular book was *The Prince* (1513) by Niccolò Machiavelli (mahk ee uh VEL ee). *The Prince was* a highly influential work of political thought in which Machiavelli described how leaders gain power, keep power, and lose power. He chose "to represent things as they are in real truth, rather than as they are imagined." Today, the word *Machiavellian* is used to describe someone who tries to achieve something by manipulating, or controlling the actions of, others. But Machiavelli was simply describing the realities of Renaissance politics.

Individualism The third idea that defined Renaissance thought was **individualism**, the belief that the individual was more important than the larger community. During the medieval period, the individual's needs had been less significant than the needs of larger groups such as the residents of a manor. This concern for the worth of the individual was rooted in classical philosophy and reappeared in Renaissance thinking.

Protagoras (pro TA guh rus), the ancient Greek philosopher, voiced humanist ideas when he wrote, "Man is the measure of all things." Renaissance thinkers took this to mean that the individual is the ultimate judge of what is good or important for him or herself. This was different from the typical attitude of medieval artists and architects who believed that they worked to glorify God rather than themselves.

Individualism freed Renaissance artists from an emphasis on sin and human imperfection. These painters, sculptors, architects, authors, poets, and composers began to explore the imagination and human potential instead. They came to value creativity for its own sake. Proud of their achievements, they signed their works and left records of their lives.

In turn, these artists' patrons encouraged them to take risks that expanded creative ideas even more. These risks led to exceptional efforts that brought **prestige** to both the artists and their patrons.

READING CHECK **Compare and Contrast** How did humanism differ from medieval values?

Renaissance Ideas Spread

Scholars traveled to Italy from all parts of Europe and took the new learning back to their home countries. Inspired by renewed interest in ancient languages, northern scholars produced new Greek and Latin versions of the New Testament. Some also began to translate the Bible into other languages. The new translations helped a wider range of people understand the text of the Bible.

As Renaissance ideas spread, northern European cities became important centers of humanist scholarship. Many northern scholars looked to the new learning to bring about reforms in the Church and in society.

More's *Utopia* One such reformer was Sir Thomas More, an English church leader and scholar. His best-known work is the book *Utopia* (1516). More coined the word *utopia* from the Greek words meaning "no place." It was the name he gave to his ideal society. Today, we use **utopia** to mean an imaginary, ideal place.

▲ Thomas More's Utopia

In More's book, Utopia is an island community governed entirely by reason. Everyone is equal and there is no private property. Everyone receives a free education. This imaginary place offered a sharp contrast to corruption common in the Church and the government of the day. More wanted to suggest a better way to organize human affairs.

Erasmus and Satire Another important reformer was Desiderius Erasmus (ih RAZ mus), a Dutch scholar and lifelong friend of Thomas More. Erasmus believed that the life and lessons of Jesus should be the model for Church doctrine. But he claimed that the Church had abandoned Christian morality for empty rituals and ceremonies. Erasmus' most famous book, *In Praise of Folly,* used satire to criticize Church leaders and practices. **Satire** is a kind of writing that uses ridicule or sarcasm to criticize vice or folly. Erasmus wrote in the book's preface,

Primary Source

"[H]e that spares no sort of men cannot be said to be angry with anyone in particular, but the vices of all."

—Desiderius Erasmus, *In Praise of Folly*

▲ This illustration from the 1800s shows a scene in which the giant Gargantua eats a salad made up of religious pilgrims.

The book's wit and wisdom made it popular. Historians credit Erasmus with making humanism an international movement.

François Rabelais The French humanist François Rabelais (rab uh LAY) was a monk, a doctor, a scholar, and an author. In the books *Gargantua* and *Pantagruel*, he used humor and exaggeration to criticize traditions in religion, education, and politics. On the surface, these are comic tales of the giant Gargantua and his son Pantagruel. (The term *gargantuan*, meaning huge, comes from Rabelais' writings.) The character of Gargantua, for example, acts in disgusting ways while learning from a scholar, doing things like blowing his nose and spitting instead of paying attention. This was also a commentary on the differences between medieval scholars—represented by the giant—and the most advanced scholars of the Renaissance. Rabelais' characters show the social upheaval that was occurring during the transition from feudalism to mercantilism.

✓ **READING CHECK Compare and Contrast** What attitude toward society was shared by More, Erasmus, and Rabelais?

✓ Lesson Check

Practice Vocabulary

1. Define each of the following key terms in a complete sentence: *mercantile, Renaissance, patron.*

Critical Thinking and Writing

2. **Analyze Cause and Effect** During the Renaissance, how did trade promote new ideas and learning?

3. **Synthesize** What characteristics helped Italy to become the birthplace of the Renaissance?

4. **Compare and Contrast** In what ways did Renaissance thinkers move away from medieval philosophies?

5. **Writing Workshop: Generate Questions to Focus Research** You will be writing a research paper describing the work of a selected figure of the Renaissance, Reformation, or Scientific Revolution, such as Michaelangelo, Martin Luther, or Leonardo da Vinci. Start thinking about the person you want to write about. Scan this lesson for ideas and look for possible topics in the following lessons. Write questions you have about these historic figures in your 📓 Active Journal.

Arts and Literature of the Renaissance

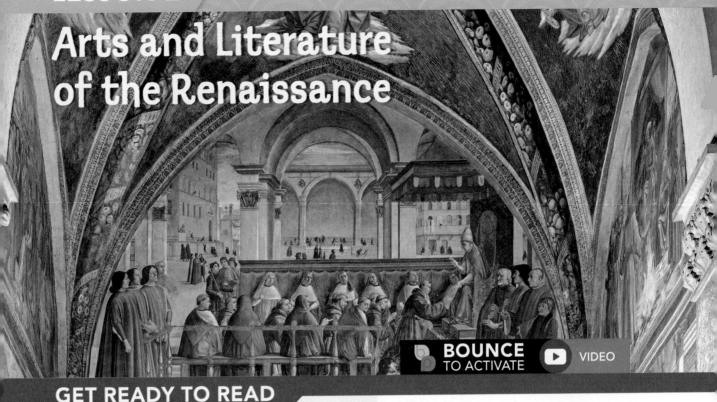

BOUNCE TO ACTIVATE ▶ VIDEO

GET READY TO READ

START UP

How does this painting by Italian artist Pietro Perugino, called *Giving of the Keys to St. Peter*, compare to works of medieval art that you saw in earlier topics?

GUIDING QUESTIONS

- What changes in style and subject made Renaissance art differ from medieval art?
- How did Renaissance art and architecture shape Western standards of beauty?
- What major writers emerged during the Renaissance?

TAKE NOTES

Literary Skills: Synthesize Visual Information
Use the graphic organizer in your 📓 Active Journal to take notes as you read the lesson.

PRACTICE VOCABULARY

Use the vocabulary activity in your 📓 Active Journal to practice the vocabulary words.

Vocabulary

linear perspective   sonnet
engraving   picaresque
proportion

Academic Vocabulary

artificial
melancholy

During the Middle Ages, interest in the cultures of the ancient Greek and Roman civilizations had declined. During the Renaissance, however, scholars considered this ancient heritage a foundation for a cultural revival.

An Artistic Revolution

Classical influences helped to shape Renaissance art. Art began to reflect a change in focus from religious devotion to worldly concerns.

Secular Themes Medieval art generally had religious themes. Renaissance art often did as well, but with a twist. For example, Italian artist Benozzo Gozzoli (beh NOH tzoh goh TZOH lee) was commissioned by the Medici family to paint *The Journey of the Magi*, depicting the procession to visit the baby Jesus in Bethlehem. Gozzoli's work includes portraits of Medici family members dressed in rich garments as if they had attended the actual event.

Analyze Images Portraits of the infant Jesus with his mother Mary were common in both medieval and Renaissance art. The example on the left is a medieval painting. On the right is a painting by the Renaissance painter Bernadino Luini. **Compare and Contrast** What differences in style can you see between these two paintings?

Increasingly, the subjects of Renaissance art were not religious at all. Greek and Roman mythology provided popular themes. The painting *The Birth of Venus* by Botticelli (boh tee CHEH lee) portrays an event in Greek mythology. In addition, individual portraits, usually of wealthy people, became popular, as did artists' self-portraits. Landscapes and scenes of daily life were also common.

Realism Medieval painters and sculptors had celebrated the glory of God—not the human figure, as did ancient Greek and Roman artists. Just as Renaissance thinkers revived the wisdom of the ancient world, so Renaissance artists examined again classical art.

Renaissance art centered on realism and the living world. Artists used live models to draw or sculpt the human form—whether it was beautiful or grotesque. They depicted emotions ranging from bliss to grief. They were fascinated with nature and portrayed every detail of it.

Renaissance artists took inspiration from classical ideas and added harmony, proportion, and a new realism. Renaissance art, ranging from architecture to furniture, celebrates these qualities.

Perspective: A New Tool for Realism In their quest for greater realism, Renaissance artists experimented with a new technique. They developed the rules of **linear perspective**, a mathematical system for representing three-dimensional space on a flat surface. When transferred to art forms such as painting, this discovery introduced true realism in art on flat surfaces. The painting on the first page of this lesson is an example of linear perspective.

☑ READING CHECK **Compare and Contrast** How did Renaissance and medieval artists differ in their treatment of religious themes?

Quick Activity

Test your Renaissance art skills. Follow the instructions in your 📓 Active Journal to practice drawing three-dimensional figures.

Great Artists of the Renaissance

The phrases "Renaissance man" and "Renaissance woman" describe people who have many different kinds of talents. The phrase originated as a description for Leonardo da Vinci.

Leonardo da Vinci Leonardo was one of the most versatile artists of the Renaissance. He was talented at almost everything he tried—painting, drawing, engineering, architecture, and music. He wrote theories about painting, the flight of birds, and the human body. His ideas and curiosity seemed endless.

Leonardo's best-known painting is the famous *Mona Lisa*. The woman in the portrait has a smile that has intrigued art lovers for centuries. For this painting, Leonardo invented a technique called sfumato (sfoo MAH toh), or "smoky" in Italian. This technique softens outlines and shadows to produce an effect of distance.

However, Leonardo wanted to master more than painting techniques. He was curious about almost every aspect of the natural world. He performed dissections of horses and human cadavers to learn how bones and muscles work. He experimented endlessly to discover how birds fly, how the eye works, and how rivers flow. To Leonardo, true wisdom resulted only from constant, careful observation: "All our knowledge has its origins in our perceptions."

Leonardo's studies of human anatomy were striking in their thoroughness and clarity. Not all of his conclusions were correct, but his research was centuries ahead of its time.

BIOGRAPHY

5 Things to Know About

LEONARDO DA VINCI
Scientist, Artist, Inventor 1452–1519

- Leonardo created a clockwork-motion piece in which each planet—only five were known at the time—revolved in its orbit along with the signs of the zodiac.

- Leonardo drew up the first plans for a mechanized military-style tank and helicopter.

- In 1503, Leonardo began painting Mona Lisa, the wife of a Florentine banker.

- Leonardo wanted to see how the human body worked from the inside, so he began dissecting dead bodies. He had to do this work secretly at night by candlelight.

- When he painted the *Last Supper*, he was so absorbed in his ideas that worked for days without eating.

Critical Thinking Why is Leonardo considered a good example of the Renaissance values?

Michelangelo Another renowned Renaissance artist was Michelangelo Buonarroti, known as Michelangelo. He was a painter, sculptor, and architect as well as a poet. His works possess great energy and never seem **artificial**. The reality of his figures comes from his mastery of anatomy and drawing.

In the early 1500s, Pope Julius II, a patron of the arts, asked Michelangelo to paint the huge ceiling of the Sistine Chapel in the Vatican. His series of frescoes shows the biblical history of the world. It took four and a half years to complete and left Michelangelo partially crippled. On the rear wall of the chapel, Michelangelo painted *The Last Judgment.* This monumental work includes the artist's self-portrait in which, true to his nickname the "**melancholy** genius," Michelangelo looks sad and resigned. Today, millions of people travel to Italy each year to marvel at Michelangelo's works.

Analyze Images The *Pietà* is one of Michelangelo's most famous sculptures. It shows Mary cradling the body of Jesus after his death. **Use Visual Information** Identify two qualities of Renaissance art shown in this statue.

Northern Renaissance Painters At the beginning of the Renaissance, much of northern Europe was still recovering from the Black Death. Gradually, the prosperous cities of Flanders, France, Germany, Belgium, and England joined the cultural rebirth.

The Flemish painter Jan van Eyck (yahn van YK) dazzled the eye with his realistic scenes. In *The Arnolfini Portrait*, a mirror on the wall reflects the couple in the painting. Below the mirror, the artist noted "Jan van Eyck has been here. 1434."

Peter Paul Rubens—humanist, artist, and diplomat—blended northern Renaissance realism with the classical influences of the Italian Renaissance artists. His paintings show his wide knowledge of mythology, the Bible, and classical history.

Northern European artists like Pieter Bruegel (BROY gul) painted complex and realistic scenes of peasant life. Bruegel and many of his fellow artists found the new medium of oil paints perfect for trying to achieve realism in their works.

👆 **INTERACTIVE**

Realism in Northern European Renaissance Art

Albrecht Dürer German artist Albrecht Dürer (DYOOR ur) is sometimes called the "Leonardo of the North" for his wide-ranging interests and great artistic skill. Following a trip to Italy in 1494, Dürer brought back many new painting and engraving techniques. **Engraving** is an art form in which the artist etches a design on a metal plate with a needle and acid. The image is then inked and the plate pressed on paper. Dürer's work helped spread Renaissance ideas to northern Europe.

Academic Vocabulary

artificial • *adj.,* unnatural or human-made

melancholy • *adj.,* depressed or sad

✓ READING CHECK **Identify Supporting Details** How did northern Renaissance painters combine modern and classical ideas?

Architecture Advances

Renaissance architect Leon Alberti called architecture "a social art," meaning that it should blend beauty and usefulness for the improvement of society. Renaissance architects sought to adapt classical ideas to new needs.

Renaissance architects modeled their works on the elements of classical Greek and Roman architecture—the column, the round arch, and the dome. They designed structures that were beautiful because of their harmony and proportion. **Proportion** is a way of balancing the parts of a design to make a pleasing whole.

Renaissance artists understood that classical architecture relied on simple geometric forms such as the circle and the square. They were also influenced by the works of the ancient builders of Egypt, Mesopotamia, Greece, and Rome.

Renaissance architects like Filippo Brunelleschi (broo nel LES kee) studied the proportions of ancient buildings. With what he learned he built the Duomo, or dome, of the Cathedral of Santa Maria del Fiore, a masterpiece of simple forms.

Following principles of classical mathematics, Renaissance architects and engineers developed new kinds of structures and machines. Renaissance engineers also pioneered the craft of technical drawing.

☑ READING CHECK **Identify Supporting Details** How did Renaissance architecture reflect the idea of "rebirth"?

▼ The Duomo, designed by Brunelleschi

Renaissance Literature

The Renaissance gave the world many great writers who all continue to influence literature hundreds of years later.

Dante and Petrarch Dante Alighieri was born in Italy in the late 1200s. Although he wrote during the late Middle Ages, his ideas looked forward to those of the Renaissance. He is best known for *The Divine Comedy*, a long poem about an imaginary journey through hell and ending in heaven. Dante wrote the poem in Italian rather than in Latin. By writing in the vernacular, he helped shape Italian as a written language. In these lines, Dante describes an inscription on the Gate of Hell:

Primary Source

"Through me the way is to the city dolent [sorrowful]; Through me the way is to eternal dole; Through me the way among the people lost."

—Dante Alighieri, *The Divine Comedy*

The Italian poet Francesco Petrarch is perhaps best known for his love poems to Laura, a woman who has never been identified. Petrarch sought to bring together the ideas of pagan classical culture and Christianity. For this reason, scholars consider him the founder of Renaissance humanism.

Shakespeare William Shakespeare was born in 1564 in the English town of Stratford-upon-Avon. Shakespeare wrote 37 plays—comedies, histories, and tragedies.

▲ Modern actors perform a scene from Shakespeare's play *Richard II*. The theatre is a recreation of the Globe Theatre in London, where Shakespeare's plays were originally performed.

Shakespeare also wrote poems, most notably sonnets. A **sonnet** is a poem of 14 lines with a fixed rhyming pattern. His work had a profound impact on the development of the English language.

Shakespeare is even more well known for his examination of the many shades of human character. In the midst of the tragic play *Hamlet*, Shakespeare uses satire to mock human weakness:

Primary Source

"What a piece of work is a man! how noble in reason! how infinite in faculty! in form and moving how express and admirable! in action how like an angel! in apprehension how like a god! the beauty of the world! the paragon [model of excellence] of animals!"

—*Hamlet*, Act II, Scene 2

Other popular plays by Shakespeare include *Romeo and Juliet, Julius Caesar,* and *Macbeth.*

The Mad Knight *Don Quixote* Spanish author Miguel de Cervantes (sur VAHN teez) lived around the same time as Shakespeare. His 1605 novel *Don Quixote* follows the journey of a bumbling landowner (a "don," or Spanish nobleman) who believes it is his duty to become a knight and right every wrong.

Cervantes' novel combines the chivalric tale of honor with satire of Spain's empire-building. The novel's style is known as picaresque. **Picaresque** refers to a series of comic episodes usually involving a mischievous character.

As the idealistic Don Quixote and his companion Sancho Panza travel around the countryside, they encounter many people and adventures. In one comic scene, Don Quixote tries to battle a windmill, thinking it is a gigantic enemy. The word *quixotic* commonly refers to any idealistic, but hopeless, endeavor.

Don Quixote was one of the first novels to portray many characters with different perspectives. Cervantes also shows in the novel that he is aware of the power of the printed word. *Don Quixote* continues to influence literature and arts of all kinds, from ballet to opera and film.

✓ **READING CHECK** **Make Connections** Why do you think Shakespeare continues to be so important?

▼ Statues of Don Quixote (left) and Sancho Panza

☑ Lesson Check

Practice Vocabulary

1. How did the concepts of **proportion** and **linear perspective** combine ideas about math and art?

2. How would you know if you were reading a **picaresque** novel?

Critical Thinking and Writing

3. **Draw Conclusions** Why did Renaissance artists favor realism in their work?

4. **Identify Supporting Details** How did Renaissance artists and architects use mathematical principles in their work?

5. **Identify Evidence** How did Dante, Shakespeare, and Cervantes demonstrate the new trend toward secularism?

6. **Writing Workshop: Generate Questions to Focus Research** Revisit the questions you recorded in your 📔 Active Journal. What additional questions do you need to ask? Revise your questions and make a decision about which person you want to write about.

Primary Sources

William Shakespeare, *As You Like it*

Like many of Shakespeare's comedies, *As You Like It* is a love story about young aristocrats. The play contains one of Shakespeare's most famous speeches, known as "the seven ages of man." It is spoken by Jaques, a sad nobleman who comments on the romantic action going on around him.

◄ William Shakespeare

Reading and Vocabulary Support

① To mewl is to cry.

② The lover writes poems praising everything about his lady, even her eyebrows. Why do you think Shakespeare compares him to a furnace?

③ A pard is a mythical beast related to the leopard.

④ Why does Shakespeare compare reputation, or fame, to a bubble?

⑤ A saw is an old saying or proverb. An instance is an example, such as in the phrase "for instance."

⑥ In Italian comedies, Pantaloon was foolish old miser.

All the world's a stage,
And all the men and women merely players;
They have their exits and their entrances;
And one man in his time plays many parts,
His acts being seven ages. At first the infant,
Mewling ① and puking in the nurse's arms;
And then the whining school-boy, with his satchel
And shining morning face, creeping like a snail
Unwillingly to school. And then the lover,
Sighing like furnace, with a woeful ballad
Made to his mistress' eyebrow. ② Then a soldier,
Full of strange oaths, and bearded like the <u>pard</u>, ③
Jealous in honor, sudden and quick in quarrel,
Seeking the bubble reputation ④
Even in the cannon's mouth. And then the justice....
Full of wise <u>saws</u> ⑤ and modern instances;
And so he plays his part. The sixth age shifts
Into the lean and slipper'd <u>pantaloon</u>, ⑥
With spectacles on nose and pouch on side....
Last scene of all,
That ends this strange eventful history,
Is second childishness and mere oblivion....

—*As You Like It*, Act II, William Shakespeare

Analyzing Primary Sources

Cite specific evidence from the document to support your answers.

1. **Paraphrase** How does Jacques describe the schoolboy and the soldier?

2. **Determine Author's Point of View** What does this speech suggest about Jacques' view of the human race?

3. **Draw Conclusions** Does this passage support the idea that Shakespeare's writing still applies to people today? Explain.

LESSON 3

Impact of the Renaissance

BOUNCE TO ACTIVATE • VIDEO

GET READY TO READ

START UP

Look at this picture of the first printing press. What impact do you think this invention might have on European society? Write down your thoughts in your ▤ Active Journal.

GUIDING QUESTIONS

- What were the effects of the Renaissance?
- How did the printing press spread new ideas?
- How did the Renaissance change daily life?

TAKE NOTES

Literacy Skills: Identify Main Ideas

Use the graphic organizer in your ▤ Active Journal to take notes as you read the lesson.

PRACTICE VOCABULARY

Use the vocabulary activity in your ▤ Active Journal to practice the vocabulary words.

Vocabulary	Academic Vocabulary
movable type	linen
censor	doctrine
recant	

The Renaissance was not just a time for thinkers and scholars to make great advances in their fields. New ways of looking at the world also meant changes in the way people lived their daily lives.

How Did the Renaissance Change Daily Life?

During the Renaissance, literature and the written word were not just for men involved in scholarship. More people from different walks of life learned to read and write. Additionally, a new calendar appeared, changing how people thought about the concept of time itself.

Learning in the Vernacular In the Middle Ages, educated people spoke Latin. These people were generally men who had attended universities—women were excluded—to become physicians, lawyers, or priests. Ordinary people spoke in vernacular, or everyday languages, such as Italian or French.

By the time of the Renaissance, more books written in the vernacular were available. Literacy increased among ordinary people.

In some homes, family members or tutors used printed books in the vernacular to teach children how to read and write.

Although there were learned women during the Middle Ages and the Renaissance, most young girls did not receive a formal education. Most of their education consisted of learning the skills needed to run a home and raise a family. A few boys could expect to learn to read and write. Some went on to university educations or to apprenticeships to acquire a craft.

Renaissance Women Another part of the Renaissance legacy was the increasing number of women visible in politics and the arts. Queens such as Elizabeth I of England and Catherine de Médici of France ruled with tolerance and courage.

The poet Laura Battiferri wrote verse in Italian. Painters like Artemisia Gentileschi and Sofonisba Anguissola introduced influential styles. Diana Mantuana, the first female Italian printmaker to sign her work, made engravings in order to support her architect husband.

☑ READING CHECK **Draw Conclusions** What effects would the use of vernacular have on the separations between social classes?

How Did the Printing Press Revolutionize Society?

New developments promoted the spread of humanism. These included advances in the technology of printing.

New Tools for Printing In the 1200s, block printing traveled from China to Europe by way of Muslim traders. In block printing, the text of a book page was carved into a block of wood. Block printing, however, was time-consuming and expensive. Wood blocks could only be used a few times.

In the 1300s, Europeans learned to make paper out of **linen** rags. In the 1400s, they learned how to make oils for use in painting and then for printing inks. These improvements led to a communications revolution.

Gutenberg's Metal Type Around 1450, a German printer named Johann Gutenberg (YOH hahn GOOT un burg) invented movable metal type. With **movable type**, individual letters formed in metal could be used again and again to form words, lines, and pages of text.

In 1455 Gutenberg published the Bible, an event that increased literacy as never before. Printed Bibles were less expensive than handwritten ones, and many people

Academic Vocabulary

linen • *n.*, cloth made from the flax plant

Analyze Images In this painting from the 1500s, two women look on as a third woman plays music from a printed book. **Draw Conclusions** To what social class do you think these women belonged? Explain.

THE REVOLUTION IN PRINTING

Around **1455**, Johann Gutenberg printed the Bible using the moveable type of the printing press. Before this, books were copied by hand, generally by monks.

Before 1455

- It took months to produce a single book.
- Most books were written on expensive parchment, made from animal skin.
- A scribe could use **80** quills a day.
- There were only about **30,000** books in all of Europe in 1455.

1455

- It took one day to print **600** pages.
- Most Gutenberg Bibles were printed on paper, developed in China.
- By 1500, there were **10** to **12** million books in Europe.

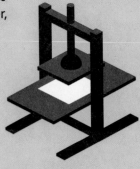

Source: Harry Ransom Center at the University of Texas at Austin

learned to read using Bibles they had at home. By 1490, printing presses were in use from London to Constantinople. By 1500, between 8 million and 20 million books had been printed in Europe.

✓ READING CHECK Identify Cause and Effect What impact did movable type have on the spread of information?

Literacy and Censorship

More reading materials encouraged more people to learn to read and write. However, the Catholic Church had strong ideas about what people should read.

Spread of Literacy Historians believe that literacy rates in medieval Europe were extremely low. Perhaps fewer than half of all men could read and maybe only one woman out of ten was literate. With the invention of mass printing, however, the literacy rate began to rise.

In addition to the Bible, people had other kinds of reading material. Printers published medical manuals and accounts of travelers. Governments used print to communicate with their subjects. People began to circulate broadsheets, or large printed sheets that often included woodcut illustrations. These broadsheets were the earliest form of newspapers.

Rise of Censorship As the number of books increased, so did efforts to censor what people read. To **censor** means to remove material from published works or to prevent its publication. The idea of censorship goes back to ancient Rome when an official called a censor regulated public morals. Until modern times, people did not associate censorship with limits on individual freedom.

Analyze Images The invention of the printing press led to an information revolution. **Compare and Contrast** How was the impact of the printing press on Renaissance society similar to the impact of the Internet on today's society?

INTERACTIVE

The Printing Press

▲ Title page from an 1841 edition of the *Index of Forbidden Books*

Academic Vocabulary
doctrine • *n.*, a set of principles or system of belief

It was during the Renaissance that self-expression became associated with the freedom to form one's own opinion. For centuries, the Church had formed people's ideas. But with self-expression in books and broadsheets, people began to criticize institutions such as the Church.

The Church Reacts The Church took steps to stop such criticism. In 1557, the Inquisition published the *Index of Forbidden Books*, a list of works that Catholics were forbidden to read. Censorship was seen as a way to reduce bad influences on people's morality. The list included Bible translations and interpretations, novels, and works of theology, philosophy, and science. It also included traditional Jewish works like the Talmud, copies of which the Church burned. Some authors decided to prevent the risk of appearing on the list by changing their works before they were published. In this way, these authors acted as self-censors.

One of the most famous incidents of Church censorship involved the Italian astronomer Galileo. When he stated that the sun, not Earth, was the center of the solar system, Galileo violated church **doctrine**. In 1638, he was forced to **recant**, or withdraw his statements, and he spent the rest of his life under house arrest.

☑ READING CHECK **Identify Main Ideas** How did the printing press set the stage for conflict?

☑ Lesson Check

Practice Vocabulary

Use the key term *censor* in a complete sentence.

Critical Thinking and Writing

1. **Synthesize** What developments in technology paved the way for Gutenberg's printing press?

2. **Draw Conclusions** Why did the Catholic Church try to censor books?

3. **Identify Evidence** How did printing by machine revolutionize daily life?

4. **Writing Workshop: Find and Use Credible Sources** As you narrow down the topic of your paper, find locations in this book with relevant information. Then, start to look for credible sources with information about important people from the Renaissance and Reformation. Write down your notes in your 📓 Active Journal.

Reformation and Reaction

BOUNCE TO ACTIVATE ▶ VIDEO

GET READY TO READ

START UP

In the picture above, a monk named Martin Luther nails arguments against the Church to a church. What does this show about his intentions?

GUIDING QUESTIONS

- How did the Reformation divide the Christian Church?
- How did Protestantism spread and lead to the formation of different churches?
- How did the Jesuit movement and the Council of Trent shape the Counter-Reformation?

TAKE NOTES

Literacy Skills: Summarize

Use the graphic organizer in your 📓 Active Journal to take notes as you read the lesson.

PRACTICE VOCABULARY

Use the vocabulary activity in your 📓 Active Journal to practice the vocabulary words.

Vocabulary

Reformation
indulgence
sacrament
sect

predestination
theocracy
ghetto

Academic Vocabulary

temperament
isolation

The northern European humanists laid the foundation for the **Reformation**, a religious movement that gained momentum in the 1500s with the aim to reform the Catholic Church. Reformation thinkers changed European society in ways that are still felt today.

How Did Martin Luther Challenge the Church?

An important leader of the Reformation was Martin Luther, a German monk. Luther was born in 1483, at a time of uneven prosperity and change in Germany. New universities were spreading the ideas of the northern European humanists. These thinkers had urged reform in the Church, but Luther offered a stronger challenge.

As a young man, Luther was caught one day in a thunderstorm. He vowed that if he lived through the storm, he would become a monk. Luther survived and, keeping his promise, entered a monastery.

Church Corruption In 1510, Luther visited Rome, the center of the Catholic Church.

Academic Vocabulary
temperament • *n.*, a specific person's way of behaving and thinking

He was shocked by the corruption of the Roman clergy. The pope and high-ranking Church officials had become increasingly involved in politics. They also spent a great deal of time trying to raise money to complete construction of St. Peter's Basilica, the center of the Catholic Church. Luther thought that they seemed more concerned with secular matters than with saving souls.

Luther noted other problems as well. Many priests were poorly trained. Church leaders rose to power through wealth or political influence rather than because of their moral qualities.

The Catholic Church also imposed taxes on its members. This money financed the construction of fine churches such as St. Peter's Basilica in Rome, as well as a rich lifestyle for the pope. The Church also raised money by selling indulgences. An **indulgence** is a kind of cancellation of punishment for sins that had been confessed and forgiven by God. Some priests promised that followers who contributed money or did good works would ensure that both they and their relatives would go to heaven.

Luther began to criticize what he saw as the Church's abuses. Like other Renaissance rulers, popes lived lavish lifestyles. The Church increased fees for services such as marriage and baptisms.

Analyze Images Luther was outraged when friar Johann Tetzel came to Wittenberg to sell indulgences. This nineteenth-century illustration shows Tetzel speaking to a crowd. **Identify Main Ideas** How does this picture support Luther's objection to selling indulgences?

Luther also rejected five of the seven sacraments. A **sacrament** is a sacred ritual in Christianity. The church believed only a priest could perform the seven sacraments. Luther, however, believed that only baptism and communion were necessary, and that the rest of the sacraments, such as confession, should not be required. He also believed marriage, although important, was not one of the sacraments and that any Christian could perform duties such as leading church services. The services of a priest, he insisted, were not required.

Luther's 95 Theses Luther especially opposed the idea of indulgences. He reasoned that if people could buy indulgences, they might think they could buy God's forgiveness. Luther did not believe that salvation—given freely by God—should depend on a complex system of indulgences and good works. To Luther, faith, or trust, in God was all that was needed to gain salvation.

When a priest appeared in Wittenberg selling indulgences, an outraged Luther decided to act. "I am hotblooded by **temperament**," Luther said, "and my pen gets irritated easily." He wrote a list of theses, or arguments, against the sale of indulgences. In 1517, he posted the list on a church door in Wittenberg.

- Luther was 37 years old when he appeared at the Diet of Worms.
- After riding home from the Diet of Worms, Luther was kidnapped by Frederick the Wise, a friend who wanted to keep Luther safe from his enemies.
- Luther hid for months in a well-fortified castle.
- He translated the New Testament into German and wrote the popular hymn "A Mighty Fortress Is Our God."
- Luther married a former Catholic nun, Katherine of Bora.

Critical Thinking Why do you think Frederick was worried for Luther's safety?

The 95 Theses, as they became known, challenged the Church's authority and stressed the spiritual, inward character of the Christian faith. Thesis 37 targeted letters of indulgence, or pardon. "Every true Christian," Luther wrote, "whether living or dead, has part in all the blessings of Christ . . . and this is granted him by God, even without letters of pardon." In other words, God gave every true Christian salvation as a gift that did not need to be earned or bought.

The 95 Theses were soon translated into German and other languages. Due to the growing number of printing presses, copies quickly spread across Europe.

Many Church leaders saw the 95 Theses as an attack on the Church itself. In 1521, the pope excommunicated, or expelled, Luther from the Church.

The Diet of Worms Later that year, the Holy Roman emperor summoned Luther before a diet, or a meeting, in the city of Worms (vohrms). There, he was put on trial and had to defend his writings. Luther was ordered to recant, or withdraw his words, but he declared,

 INTERACTIVE

The Reformation and Counter-Reformation

Primary Source

"Unless I am convinced by the testimony of the Holy Scriptures or by evident reason—for I can believe neither pope nor councils alone . . . I consider myself convicted by the testimony of Holy Scripture, which is my basis; my conscience is captive to the Word of God. Thus I cannot and will not recant, because acting against one's conscience is neither safe nor sound. God help me. Amen."

—Martin Luther

The diet branded Luther an outlaw. However, throughout Germany, thousands hailed Luther as a hero for his stand against corrupt Church practices and teachings. At the same time, his actions and writings directed against Jews are considered to have influenced later German anti-Semitism.

☑ READING CHECK **Identify Supporting Details** Why did Church leaders look with disdain on the 95 Theses?

How Did the Reformation Grow?

As Luther's ideas, or Lutheranism, spread, Protestant sects sprang up all over Europe. A **sect** is a subgroup of a major religious group. Protestants were people who protested against the authority of the Catholic Church. A French scholar named John Calvin was one of the most influential of the new Protestant leaders.

Calvin and Salvation John Calvin was born in France in 1509. Calvin had studied to be a priest in the Roman Catholic Church, but in the early 1530s, he declared himself a Protestant.

In 1536, Calvin published the *Institutes of Christian Religion* in which he set out the basic ideas of the Protestant faith. One of Calvin's most influential teachings focused on the question of salvation. Like Luther, Calvin believed that salvation was gained through faith alone. Calvin also regarded the Bible as the sole source of religious truth.

Catholicism, Lutheranism, and Calvinism

Structure and Beliefs	Catholicism	Lutheranism	Calvinism
Salvation	Salvation is achieved through faith and good works.	Salvation is achieved through faith alone.	God alone predetermines who will be saved.
Sacraments	Priests perform seven sacraments, or rituals—baptism, confirmation, marriage, ordination, communion, anointing of the sick, and repentance.	Accepts some sacraments but rejects others because of belief that only God can erase sin.	Accepts some sacraments but rejects others because of belief that only God can erase sin.
Head of Church	Pope	Elected councils	Council of elders
Importance of the Christian Bible	Bible and Church tradition are sources of truth.	Bible alone is source of truth.	Bible alone is source of truth.
How Belief is Revealed	Priests interpret the Bible and Church teachings for people.	People read and interpret the Bible for themselves.	People read and interpret the Bible for themselves.

Analyze Charts What is one thing on which Luther and Calvin disagreed? What is one thing Catholicism, Lutheranism, and Calvinism had in common?

In addition, Calvin supported the concept of **predestination**, the idea that God had long ago determined who would gain salvation. At that time, the Catholic Church and some other Protestant churches taught that people had free will to choose or reject the path to salvation.

Calvin taught that salvation was not a human choice, but a decision made by God. No one, however, knows who God has chosen for salvation. Therefore, he preached, all people should lead God-fearing, religious lives. Calvin called this the "doctrine of election."

Calvin's "City of God" Calvin also applied his ideas to government. Many of the Protestant reformers had been accused of lawlessness, and Calvin came to their defense. He said that people were subject to both civil law and to the law of God. At the same time, rulers should not act as tyrants, but keep in mind the law of God. In this way, people who obeyed an earthly government were also following God's laws.

In the 1530s, Protestants in Geneva, Switzerland, invited Calvin to help them rule their city and reform their church. Calvin set up a theocracy in Geneva. A **theocracy** is a government ruled by religious leaders.

Calvin's goal was to found a "city of God." He stressed hard work, honesty, and morality. He imposed strict laws on behavior. He also set up schools for the education of children. Calvin wrote:

Primary Source

"Since it is impossible to profit by such instruction without first knowing languages and the humanities, and also since it is necessary to prepare for the future in order that the church may not be neglected by the young, it will be necessary to establish a school to instruct the youth, to prepare them not only for the ministry but for government."

—John Calvin, *Institutes of the Christian Religion*

Analyze Images This woodcut from the 17th century shows a service at a Calvinist church in Nuremberg, Germany. **Compare and Contrast** How does the appearance of the church compare to images of Catholic cathedrals from the medieval period?

Quest CONNECTIONS

Read this quotation. Did Calvin's reasons for favoring education differ from those of Renaissance humanists? Record your thoughts in your Active Journal.

Translating the Bible By the early 1500s, the Bible's New Testament had appeared in French, Spanish, Italian, and Dutch. Luther's German translation appeared in 1534. It was now easier for most Europeans—not just scholars who read Latin—to read the Bible and think about its meaning.

John Wycliffe, an English preacher and reformer, had translated parts of the Bible from Latin into English as early as 1382. In the 1520s, the Protestant reformer William Tyndale translated the Greek New Testament into English.

After years of working in defiance of Catholic authorities, Tyndale had become an enemy of the Church. In 1536, he was working on a translation of the Old Testament in Antwerp (in present-day Belgium) when he was turned over to the authorities. Tyndale was convicted as a heretic, strangled, and burned at the stake.

☑ READING CHECK **Identify Supporting Details** How did Calvin view the relationship between religion and government?

The Counter-Reformation

As Protestantism spread, the Catholic Church began its own reform movement. The movement to strengthen the teachings and structure of the Catholic Church was called the Counter-Reformation. During the Counter-Reformation, also known as the Catholic Reformation, reformers founded new religious orders, or groups with their own particular structure and purpose. They won respect by helping the poor, teaching, and leading spiritual lives. One of the most influential reformers was Ignatius of Loyola who founded the Society of Jesus, or the Jesuits.

Ignatius of Loyola In 1491, Ignatius of Loyola was born in northern Spain. As a young man, he entered military service and was seriously injured in battle. While recovering, Ignatius read about the lives of Jesus and the saints. Inspired, he vowed to lead a religious life.

Ignatius studied in Paris. There, with a small group of followers, he founded the Society of Jesus in 1534. Its goal was to defend and spread the Catholic faith throughout the world. The Society was organized like a military troop, with strict discipline. Ignatius was elected a "general" of the order, and members were organized into "companies." Recruits trained for years before joining the order.

The Jesuits' Influence The Jesuits helped end some of the corruption within the Church. Priests received stricter training. Jesuits served the poor and helped the sick in hospitals. The Jesuits also

Analyze Images This stained glass window from a French church shows Ignatius of Loyola (top left) next to his friend and fellow Jesuit Francis Xavier. **Cite Evidence** What details show that the builders of this church honored the Society of Jesus?

expanded the membership of the Church. Jesuit missionaries spread the Catholic faith to Africa, Asia, and the Americas. In Asia, the Jesuit Francis Xavier was said to have converted thousands of people to Catholicism.

The Jesuits also made important contributions to education. They founded schools and universities and wrote books on religion and secular topics like medicine. Their students included an emperor, dukes, and cardinals. The Jesuits also served as advisors to kings and popes.

Teresa of Avila During the Counter-Reformation, many Catholics experienced renewed feelings of faith. One of these was Teresa of Avila, a Spanish nun. Born into a wealthy family, Teresa entered the Carmelite convent at Avila in 1535 without her father's consent. Teresa lived an intensely spiritual life, often seeing visions she said were sent from God. She felt that convent life was not strict enough, so she founded her own order of nuns. They lived in **isolation**, completely dedicated to prayer and meditation. Teresa was widely honored for her efforts to reform Spanish convents and monasteries.

▲ Teresa of Avila

✓ **READING CHECK** **Identify Supporting Details** How did the Jesuits try to restore the authority of the Catholic Church?

The Council of Trent and the Inquisition

In 1545, Pope Paul III began a series of meetings known as the Council of Trent. During these meetings, Catholic leaders sought ways to revive the moral authority of the Catholic Church and to stop the spread of Protestantism. The Council of Trent took place at various times over the course of about 20 years.

Upholding Tradition At its meetings, the Council reaffirmed traditional Catholic doctrines that had been challenged by the Protestants. It rejected Luther's view of the Bible as the only source of truth. The Bible *and* church tradition, declared the Council, were equal sources of knowledge. While Luther said that faith is all that is needed for salvation, the Council said faith *plus* good works and receiving the sacraments are needed as well. Finally, the Council affirmed that people had free will. The Council of Trent also made sweeping reforms of Catholic practices and called for the education and training of priests.

The Inquisition The Church enforced the Council's decisions through the Inquisition. This institution was set up in the Middle Ages to combat heresy, or beliefs that clashed with Church teachings.

Many of the Inquisition's policies came from Pope Innocent IV's papal order of 1252, which stated that heretics, or people accused of heresy, should be "forced" to confess. This statement encouraged torture and unjust imprisonment. This brutal policy had continued for centuries,

Academic Vocabulary

isolation • *n.*, the condition of being alone

Quick Activity

Match the quotations from the Reformation and Counter-Reformation to the speaker. Explain your answers in your 📖 Active Journal.

with judges seizing property, torturing, and condemning to death thousands of victims.

By the 1500s, Inquisitions existed in Portugal, Italy, and Spain. Protestants living in Catholic lands were frequently the target of the Inquisition. However, even Church leaders and important nobles could be accused of heresy. The Spanish Inquisition went on to target Jews and Muslims. Conversos, or Jews who had converted to Christianity, often by force, were accused of secretly practicing Judaism. Moriscos, or Muslim converts, faced similar charges. In 1492, Spain forced Jews to leave the country. In 1509, the Moriscos were expelled as well.

Intolerance Grows Both Catholics and Protestants were intolerant of each other. Catholics launched attacks against Protestants. Protestants destroyed Catholic churches and attacked priests.

Religious anxiety also brought a fear of witches, or people believed to be evil spirits. Between 1450 and 1750, tens of thousands of people, frequently women, died in witch hunts in Europe.

Analyze Images The Jewish ghetto in Rome, shown here, was established by the Pope in 1555. **Infer** Based on this image, what do you think life in the ghetto was like?

Another group that suffered during this period were Jews. After being driven from Spain, many Jews went to Italy where they had prospered. However, by 1516, Jews in Venice were restricted to living and working in a separate quarter called a **ghetto**. This practice of keeping Jews separate from the population within walled areas spread to other parts of Europe. In some places, Jews were required to wear yellow identification badges if they traveled outside the ghetto.

☑ **READING CHECK** **Identify Main Ideas** Why was religious anxiety so high in Europe during the years following the Reformation?

☑ Lesson Check

Practice Vocabulary

1. Define each of the following key terms in a complete sentence: *Reformation, indulgence, sect, predestination, theocracy.*

Critical Thinking and Writing

2. **Draw Conclusions** Why did John Calvin believe that people should lead God-fearing, religious lives?

3. **Compare and Contrast** In what ways were the ideas of Luther and Calvin similar?

4. **Compare and Contrast** How did the religious views of the Council of Trent differ from those of Martin Luther?

5. **Support Ideas with Evidence** In what ways did intolerance grow around the time of the Reformation?

6. **Writing Workshop: Develop a Clear Thesis** Finalize the topic for your research paper and work on a thesis, based on your initial research. Work on a draft of your thesis in your 📓 Active Journal.

Martin Luther, Preface

One of the most famous debates of this period was the debate over free will. Martin Luther, a German priest, maintained that humans are saved by God's grace, and that human action does not contribute toward their salvation. He wrote about how he experienced this awakening as he struggled with a passage in the Bible about the "justice of God."

▶ Martin Luther

I meditated night and day on those words until at last, by the mercy of God, I paid attention to their context: "The justice of God is revealed in it, as it is written: 'The just person lives by faith.'" I began to understand that in this verse the justice of God is that by which the just person lives by a gift of God, that is by faith ①. I began to understand that this verse means that the justice of God is revealed through the Gospel, but it is a passive justice ②, i.e. that by which the merciful God justifies us by faith, as it is written: "The just person lives by faith." All at once I felt that I had been born again and entered into paradise itself through open gates. . . . I exalted ③ this sweetest word of mine, "the justice of God," with as much love as before I had hated it with hate.

Martin Luther, "Preface to the Complete Edition of Luther's Latin Works 1545", trans. by Bro. Andrew.

Reading and Vocabulary Support

① In other words, "God's gift of faith makes it possible for humans to lead just and good lives."

② By calling it a passive justice, Luther means that this justice is given to people by God without them needing to do something to receive it.

③ *Exalted* means to think very highly of something. How does Luther's exaltation of the phrase "the justice of God" show a shift in his viewpoint?

Analyzing Primary Sources

Cite specific evidence from the document to support your answers.

1. **Vocabulary: Use Context Clues** Using your background knowledge of Martin Luther and context clues from the text, explain the meaning of the word *verse* as it is used in the passage.

2. **Cite Evidence** Identify textual evidence that supports the idea that Luther's revelation has changed how he understands his relationship with God.

3. **Identify Implied Main Ideas** Based on this passage, how would Luther answer the question of whether a person can gain salvation by doing good works?

Analyze Sequence, Causation, and Correlation

INTERACTIVE

Analyze Cause and Effect

Follow these steps to help you identify sequence and to distinguish between causation and correlation.

1 **Choose an event or a condition as a starting point.** Sequence, causation, and correlation are different ideas. However, they all involve understanding the order of events. To begin, identify the starting point, or earliest event.

2 **Identify sequence.** "Sequence" refers to the order in which events or developments occurred in time. Use clue words and phrases such as *meanwhile* and *at the same time* to help determine when an event occurred in relation to other events.

   a. Identify the individual events or developments described in the passage below.

   b. Organize these events on a timeline to help you visualize the sequence.

3 **Identify cause-and-effect relationships.** Just because one event occurred before another event, that does not mean that the first event caused the second event. To identify cause-and-effect relationships, look for clue words or phrases like *because, as a result,* and *led to.* Identify one clear cause-and-effect relationship in the passage below.

4 **Look at other events or conditions for possible correlations.** Look for clue words or phrases like *meanwhile, at the same time,* and *also.* Terms like these suggest that there may be a correlation between two events. While they may be related in some way, such as having the same cause, one event has not caused the other. Identify two events in the passage below that may be correlated.

5 **Summarize the cause-and-effect relationships and correlations.** Once you have distinguished between causation and correlation, you can better understand a sequence of events. Make a table or chart showing the different relationships among the events described in this passage.

Secondary Source

The fifteenth and sixteenth centuries were a time of great change in Europe. The invention of the printing press about 1450 led to the production of more books and written materials than ever before. As a result, words and ideas raced across Europe. During the Reformation, the printing press brought Martin Luther's teachings into homes and cities across the continent. Meanwhile, Europe was changing in other ways. New universities were founded. More and more people learned to read. Conflicts and the wars of religion led to national governments. At the same time, explorers set sail for new lands across the sea.

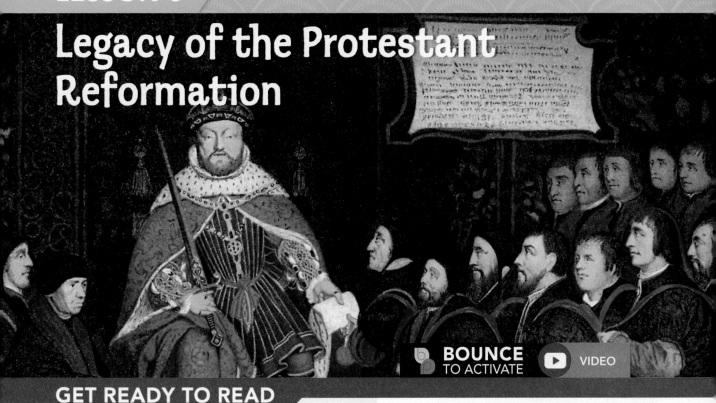

Legacy of the Protestant Reformation

BOUNCE TO ACTIVATE ▶ VIDEO

GET READY TO READ

START UP

Europe's rulers, including Henry VIII of England shown here, reacted to the Protestant Reformation in different ways. Why might some of the rulers have joined the Reformation while others did not?

GUIDING QUESTIONS

- How did the Reformation divide European states?
- What conflicts arose from the division of Protestant Europe and Catholic Europe?
- What were the long-term effects of the Reformation?

TAKE NOTES

Literacy Skills: Summarize
Use the graphic organizer in your 📙 Active Journal to take notes as you read the lesson.

PRACTICE VOCABULARY

Use the vocabulary activity in your 📙 Active Journal to practice the vocabulary words.

Vocabulary	Academic Vocabulary
annulment	controversial
edict	invalid
armada	
federalism	

As the Reformation spread, the differences between the Catholic Church and the evolving Protestant sects became more striking. Many Protestants rejected the rituals of the Catholic Church. "Communion" in the Catholic Church was often called "The Lord's Supper" by Protestants. Catholics believed the pope in Rome was the final earthly authority on matters of faith, while Protestants believed God's word as expressed in the Bible was the final authority.

The Protestant Reformation destroyed the religious unity that had held together medieval Europe. Ordinary people and rulers took sides, leading to a new era of religious conflct and warfare.

Protestantism Dominates Northern Europe

Germany was the birthplace of the Protestant faith. From northern Germany, Luther's followers took the faith to Sweden, Denmark, Norway, and Poland. John Calvin's ideas spread to Switzerland, Scotland, and the Netherlands. In some

Major European Religions, About 1600

KEY
- Catholic
- Anglican
- Lutheran
- Calvinist
- Areas of Muslim minorities
- Mainly Orthodox Christian
- — Boundary of Holy Roman Empire

ATLANTIC OCEAN

0   300 mi
0   300 km
Lambert Conformal
Conic Projection

NORWAY
SWEDEN
RUSSIA
Moscow
SCOTLAND
IRELAND
DENMARK
ENGLAND Neth.
PRUSSIA LITHUANIA
London
Munster
Wittenberg POLAND
Canterbury
Wartburg
Worms
Bohemia
Paris
Swiss Conf.
Augsburg
FRANCE
AUSTRIA
Geneva
Trent Venice
HUNGARY
Avignon Savoy
PAPAL STATES
Black Sea
PORTUGAL Madrid
Rome ITALY
OTTOMAN EMPIRE
Constantinople
SPAIN
Mediterranean Sea

GEOGRAPHY SKILLS

The Reformation shattered the religious unity of Europe.

1. **Region** Name three countries or regions west of the Holy Roman Empire that were mainly Roman Catholic.

2. **Synthesize Visual Information** Based on your reading and the information shown on the map, why do you think Lutheranism became the dominate religion in the areas shown?

Academic Vocabulary

controversial • adj., tending to cause dispute or disagreement

places, the ideas of Martin Luther and Calvin took hold peacefully. In other areas, religious conflict erupted.

The Reformation in England and Scotland In England, Luther's ideas were at first met with opposition. Henry VIII, the Catholic king of England, wrote a book criticizing Luther's beliefs. He was declared by the Church a "defender of the faith" for his words. Protestant reformers were burned at the stake or forced out of England.

In 1529, however, Henry VIII came into conflict with the pope. Henry wanted the pope to annul his marriage to Catherine of Aragon, as she had yet to give birth to a surviving male heir. An **annulment** is an official action canceling a marriage. The pope refused.

Henry decided to take the control of the English church away from the pope. Henry called Parliament into session and urged its members to pass a series of laws. These laws formed the Church of England, or the Anglican Church, and declared it to be independent of the Catholic Church. The archbishop of the Anglican Church annulled the king's marriage to Catherine, and Henry married Anne Boleyn in 1533. Parliament passed the Act of Supremacy in 1534, making the monarch the leader of the Church of England.

In Scotland, a **controversial** preacher named John Knox spread Calvin's ideas. Protestants there established the Church of Scotland, or Presbyterian Church, and the Scottish Episcopal Church.

Religious War in Germany Luther's ideas took hold in northern Germany, but not in the south. In southern Germany, the Holy Roman emperor was Catholic and wanted his empire to be Catholic as well.

In 1547, the emperor initiated a crackdown against Protestants in Germany that resulted in religious war. The war ended in 1555 with the Peace of Augsburg. This treaty allowed each German ruler to decide which religion his realm would follow—Catholic or Lutheran.

Instead of a unified Catholic empire, Germany was now a group of independent regions with different religious traditions. Northern Germany was mostly Protestant, while most of southern Germany was Catholic.

✓ READING CHECK **Identify Supporting Details** How did politics influence the spread of Protestantism?

Catholicism Dominates Southern Europe

Although Protestantism spread, the nations of southern Europe remained largely Catholic. The city-states of Italy retained their Catholic faith. The powerful Catholic rulers of Spain became the main defenders of the Catholic Church in Europe. France remained Catholic, though not without friction from a growing number of French Protestants.

Religious Conflict in France At first, the Catholic king of France allowed Huguenots, or French Protestants, to worship freely. In 1534, however, the situation changed. Huguenots put up posters all over Paris—even on the king's bedroom door—denouncing the Catholic Church. The king ordered the arrest of hundreds of Protestants. Some were burned alive for their views.

By 1559, the French queen Catherine de Médici arranged a marriage between her daughter Margaret and Henry of Navarre, the leader of the Huguenots. The marriage that was to have brought peace to the nation resulted in disaster.

In 1572, outraged anti-Protestants in Paris killed some 3,000 Huguenots in the St. Bartholomew's Day Massacre. Afterward, a French Protestant general said,

Primary Source

"It was our wars of religion that made us forget our religion."

—General François de La Noue

INTERACTIVE

Major European Religions About 1600

Analyze Images
This painting of the St. Bartholomew's Day Massacre is the only surviving work of artist Francois Dubois, a French Huguenot. **Infer** What effect do you think the artist's background had on his depiction of this event.

Still, French Catholics refused to accept a Protestant king. Finally, in 1593, Henry converted to Catholicism and became King Henry IV the following year. The civil war ended.

In 1598, Henry IV proclaimed the Edict of Nantes. An **edict** is an official public order made by a king or another authority. It made the Catholic Church the official church of France, but it also gave Huguenots the freedom to practice their own religion.

Spain Defends Catholicism Unlike France, Spain did not allow Protestants to worship freely. Philip II, Spain's Catholic king, championed the Counter-Reformation as a way to force Catholicism on his people. He used the religious tribunal known as the Inquisition to bring suspects to trial for heresy. Although inquisitions had been known since medieval times, the Spanish Inquisition founded in 1478 was more feared than any previous church court. Among those tried and tortured were Protestants, Jews, and Muslim converts to Christianity.

In 1555, Philip inherited control of the Netherlands. Many of the Dutch had converted to Calvinism. Philip set up the Inquisition in the Netherlands to combat this Protestantism. The Dutch people rebelled, and Philip went to war. The fighting lasted more than 75 years. The mainly Calvinist Netherlands gained independence.

When Henry VIII's daughter, Queen Elizabeth I, sent troops to aid the Dutch rebels, Philip responded with a sea attack on England. In 1588, King Philip sent an **armada**, or fleet of ships, to attack England. The English navy fought back and won. The Battle of the Spanish Armada ended Spain's domination of the seas.

Christianity in the United States

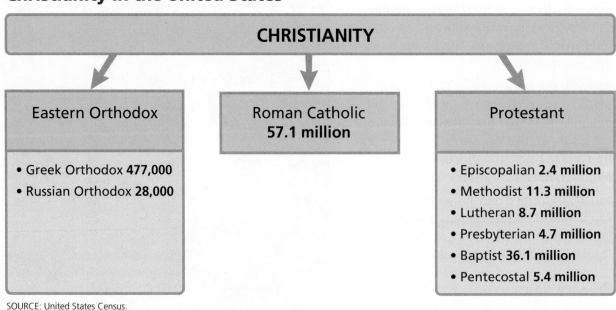

CHRISTIANITY

Eastern Orthodox
- Greek Orthodox **477,000**
- Russian Orthodox **28,000**

Roman Catholic
57.1 million

Protestant
- Episcopalian **2.4 million**
- Methodist **11.3 million**
- Lutheran **8.7 million**
- Presbyterian **4.7 million**
- Baptist **36.1 million**
- Pentecostal **5.4 million**

SOURCE: United States Census.

Analyze Charts There are three major branches of Christianity in the world today. This chart shows several of the larger Christian denominations in the United States. The numbers shown provide recent data about membership in the groups. What two events led to the division of Christianity?

The Thirty Years' War In spite of this loss, Philip was determined to restore Catholicism to other parts of Europe. His aggressiveness resulted in Spain joining in the Thirty Years' War.

This war, fought between 1618 and 1648, involved most of the major European powers. It began as a religious conflict between Protestants and Catholics. As time went on, however, the war developed into a political clash. Soldiers from many nations roamed northern Europe, stealing and burning towns and farms.

Analyze Images Spanish artist Francisco Goya painted this Inquisition in the 1810s. The accused wear pointed caps and clothing that lists their offenses. **Use Visual Information** Why do you think the accused were forced to dress this way?

The Peace of Westphalia ended the war in 1648. It allowed people to practice their own religion in private, even if it differed from the king's religion. But religious warfare had taken its toll. Some Europeans began calling for religious tolerance to end the violence.

Religious Divisions Spread Spain was at the forefront of European countries that began to export religion to other regions of the world. Spain spread Catholicism to its new colonies in the Americas and in the Pacific, specifically the Philippines. Later, Protestant countries began to form their own colonies. Spanish and Portuguese colonies in Mesoamerica and South America were dominated by the Catholic Church. French Canada became largely Catholic, while English and Dutch colonies in North America became largely Protestant.

☑ READING CHECK **Identify Main Ideas** What was the guiding principle behind the Inquisition?

What Was the Impact of the Reformation?

Under feudalism, Europe had consisted of a few large kingdoms. By the late 1600s, it was a patchwork of hundreds of smaller, separate states.

In addition, the Reformation had ended the supremacy of the pope and the Catholic Church. Leaders needed new forms of government to meet the challenges of their developing nations.

Rulers Grow Stronger The wars of religion increased the authority of rulers outside the Church. Some of this authority included some control over religious affairs. The Peace of Westphalia, for example, had given rulers the right to determine their country's religion. Catholicism, Lutheranism, and Calvinism all became recognized religions. Sensing the treaty's threat to his authority, the pope declared it "null, void, **invalid**." However, it was a turning point in political and religious life in Europe.

Academic Vocabulary
invalid • *adj.*, without truth or unlawful

Experiments in Self-Government During this time, some Protestant nations moved toward self-government. In Geneva, Calvinist churches elected their own leaders, some of the earliest elected leaders in Europe. Protestants also promoted civic participation, or regular people having a voice in government.

The German Calvinist Johannes Althusius (al THOO sih us) was influenced by Calvin's idea that churches should be subject to God's law alone, not to those of a government. Althusius developed the idea of **federalism**, a form of government in which power is shared between local and national levels. Federalist ideas would later influence the framers of the Constitution of the United States.

◀ One long-term effect of the Protestant Reformation is that many churches now have female ministers, such as this Anglican priest.

Economic and Social Effects Some scholars believe that Protestant ideas about self-government led to economic trends like free market capitalism. Scholars also observe that Calvin's teachings about the value of hard work also had economic impacts. Protestant ideas also contributed to social changes such as greater access to education and increased literacy.

Women and the Reformation The Reformation had some impact on the status of women. Catholic priests and nuns were required to remain unmarried. Only men were allowed to be priests. Many Protestant churches allowed their clergy to get married, as Martin Luther himself did. In some sects, women even became church leaders. Women and men were seen as equal in the eyes of God.

Still, women remained in an inferior position to men. Catholic and Protestant thought agreed that women should obey their fathers or husbands in matters of religion.

☑ READING CHECK **Identify Cause and Effect** What impact did the Reformation later have on the United States?

☑ Lesson Check

Practice Vocabulary

1. Define each of the following key terms in a complete sentence: *annulment, armada, federalism.*

Critical Writing and Thinking

2. **Sequence** List in chronological order the main legal decisions and treaties that contributed to the spread of Protestantism in northern Europe.

3. **Analyze Cause and Effect** How did the Reformation affect the distribution of religions in the Americas?

4. **Explain an Argument** Why do many people argue that the Reformation encouraged democratic values?

5. **Writing Workshop: Find and Use Credible Sources** Begin your research about the figure that you have chosen to write about. Use the questions that you recorded earlier to start your search for information. Record your findings in your 📓 Active Journal.

The Scientific Revolution

BOUNCE TO ACTIVATE

▶ VIDEO

GET READY TO READ

START UP

Based on the image above, what was one area of knowledge Renaissance scientists explored?

GUIDING QUESTIONS

- What were the causes and effects of the Scientific Revolution?
- How did the discoveries about the universe challenge ancient and medieval ideas?
- How did the scientific method encourage new discoveries?

TAKE NOTES

Literacy Skills: Identify Main Ideas
Use the graphic organizer in your 📓 Active Journal to take notes as you read the lesson.

PRACTICE VOCABULARY

Use the vocabulary activity in your 📓 Active Journal to practice the vocabulary words.

Vocabulary		Academic Vocabulary
rationalism	empiricism	text
heliocentric theory	inductive reasoning	conclude
heresy	scientific method	

Scientific research has given us lifesaving medicines and new technologies. Scientists use observation, experiments, and reasoning to learn about the world. Thinkers began to develop this way of learning in the 1500s and 1600s. During this time, a revolution of new ideas, the Scientific Revolution, swept Europe.

What Were the Origins of the Scientific Revolution?

The roots of the Scientific Revolution reach back to ancient and medieval times. The ancient Greeks used reason to try to discover laws that control the universe. Thinkers who followed the Greeks built on their ideas. This body of knowledge was the foundation of the Scientific Revolution.

Greek Rationalism People have always wondered how the universe works. Ancient Greek religion explained the natural world in terms of gods who controlled important events and natural forces, such as the weather. By the 500s BCE, some Greeks began to look for explanations of the natural

Analyze Images Muslim scholars studied ancient Greek thinkers, preserving and advancing Greek knowledge. **Cite Evidence** How does this illustration show that these scientists used technology to study the universe?

Academic Vocabulary

text • *n.,* a written source, such as a book

world that went beyond stories about gods. They thought the universe must follow certain rules, and they turned to reason to try to discover these rules. This approach is called **rationalism**, the belief that knowledge is gained by using reason.

Medieval Scholars With the fall of the Roman empire, most Europeans lost interest in Greek rationalism. In places such as Baghdad and Spain, however, Muslim and Jewish scholars studied Greek learning. They translated Greek writings into Arabic, Latin, and Hebrew. These scholars also developed new ideas. A Muslim mathematician contributed to the branch of mathematics known today as algebra.

In the 1200s, European scholars began to study ideas from Muslim and Jewish thinkers as well as those from the ancient Greeks. The scholar Thomas Aquinas read translations of the Greek philosopher Aristotle. Aquinas blended Greek ideas with Christian teachings. He believed faith and reason worked hand in hand. Christian thinkers took many ideas from the Greeks, such as the idea that Earth is at the center of the universe. Christian thinkers believed Earth was at the center because it is home to God's most important creation—humankind.

Developments During the Renaissance Discoveries during the Renaissance also contributed to knowledge about the natural world. Renaissance thinkers rediscovered work created by ancient philosophers. They found they could read an old **text** or historical account and build on the knowledge to arrive at new ideas. In addition, Renaissance thinkers made careful observations of the world. What they saw did not always match what was accepted at the time. They were willing to challenge long-held beliefs.

Europeans also began exploring unfamiliar lands in the Americas, Africa, and Asia. They returned home with plants and animals never before seen in Europe. These discoveries showed the limitations of ancient and medieval science.

✓ **READING CHECK** **Identify Cause and Effect** What impact did Greek Rationalism on have scientific thought during medieval times?

New Views of the Universe

Scientists in the 1500s and 1600s built on the ideas of the thinkers who came before them. They found new answers to questions that generations of thinkers had asked about the universe. New theories about the universe marked the beginning of the Scientific Revolution.

Copernicus In the early 1500s, Polish astronomer Nicolaus Copernicus spent 25 years tracking the movements of the sun, moon, and planets. His observations did not fit with the commonly held idea that Earth was at the center of the universe. Copernicus was able to **conclude** that Earth and the other planets revolve around the sun. The idea that the sun is at the center of the solar system is called the **heliocentric theory**. Most people ridiculed his conclusion. They thought Earth was too heavy to move. Later scientists would confirm Copernicus' ideas.

Kepler and Galileo The German astronomer Johannes Kepler used mathematics to prove that Earth revolves around the sun. Kepler also discovered the laws that describe the movement of planets in the solar system.

The Italian mathematician Galileo Galilei (gal uh LAY oh gal uh LAY ee) also supported Copernicus' heliocentric theory. Galileo built his own telescope. He saw, among other things, that moons revolve around the planet Jupiter. The medieval view was that all heavenly objects circle Earth. Galileo's observations showed this was not correct.

Galileo published his findings in 1610. His ideas created great controversy. The Catholic Church said the heliocentric theory was **heresy**—a belief that goes against Church teachings. The Church put Galileo under house arrest for continuing to argue for the theory. Galileo's writings were taken out of Italy and published in the Netherlands. His ideas influenced many other scientists.

Galileo was also one of the first scientists to use experiments to discover laws of nature. According to legend, Galileo dropped a large stone and a small stone from the top of the Tower of Pisa. Both hit the ground at the same instant. The Greek thinker Aristotle had said that heavier objects fall faster than lighter ones. Galileo showed that objects of different weights fall at the same speed.

Newton The work of Copernicus, Kepler, and Galileo gave a new view of the universe, but many questions remained. What makes

Academic Vocabulary
conclude • *v.*, to decide; to bring something to an end

> INTERACTIVE

The Heliocentric Universe

▼ A monument to Copernicus in Warsaw, Poland

5 Things to Know About **ISAAC NEWTON**
English Physicist and Mathematician (1643-1727)

- Newton is often called the father of modern physics.

- Newton formulated the theory of gravity, the force of attraction between two objects with mass.

- Many believe his book *Philosophae Naturalis Principia Mathematica* is one of history's most important science books.

- His three laws of motion include the idea that an object in motion tends to stay in motion until acted upon by an outside force.

- He once said, "If I have seen further, it is by standing on the shoulders of giants."

Critical Thinking What do you think Newton meant by "standing on the shoulders of giants"?

planets circle the sun? Why do objects fall to Earth? The English mathematician Isaac Newton set out to answer these questions.

Newton thought that some force must hold the moon in its orbit around Earth. Legend says that one day as Newton sat under an apple tree, he saw an apple fall to the ground. He realized that the same force that pulled the apple to the ground kept the moon in its orbit. He called this force *gravity*. More massive objects pull with greater gravitational force than less massive ones. Newton also made important advances in the study of light, mathematics, and motion.

✓**READING CHECK** **Draw Conclusions** Why did people feel threatened by Copernicus' and Galileo's ideas?

How Did Bacon and Descartes Support Inductive Reasoning?

Galileo's experiments pointed the way to modern science. Like Galileo, scientists today use observation and experiments to explore nature. Modern scientists rely on **empiricism**, the theory that all knowledge is gained through experience and making observations using the senses. Two thinkers, Francis Bacon and René Descartes (ruh NAY day KAHRT), supported this way of developing new knowledge.

Francis Bacon The English philosopher Francis Bacon was an early supporter of the new science. Bacon argued against reaching conclusions based on ancient learning. He thought that scientists should rely on their own observations to explain nature.

Bacon developed the use of inductive reasoning. **Inductive reasoning** is the process of looking at specific facts and making a rule or general principle based on those facts. A scientist guided by inductive reasoning first uses observations and experiments to gather facts. Then the scientist uses reason to think of a general conclusion based on these facts. Bacon put a high priority on knowledge:

Primary Source

"Seek first the virtues of the mind; and other things either will come, or will not be wanted."

—*The Advancement of Learning*, Francis Bacon

René Descartes The French philosopher René Descartes thought it was necessary to question everything except ideas that were certain beyond doubt. For Descartes, the most basic certainty was his own existence. He wrote, "I think, therefore I am." Descartes knew he existed because he was questioning his own existence. From that point, he went on to reason that God and the physical world must also exist.

Descartes also put forth the idea that the universe could be explained entirely by mechanical laws. Some believed that mysterious forces directed the physical world. Descartes, on the other hand, saw the universe as a machine guided by predictable physical laws.

The Scientific Method The work of Bacon and Descartes helped establish what we know today as the **scientific method**. This is a method of using observation, experiments, and careful reasoning.

The scientific method involves several steps. First, a question is identified for research. Information is gathered through observations and research.

Quest CONNECTIONS

Look at the diagram of the scientific method. How have you followed similar steps when learning something in school? Record your thoughts in your 📓 Active Journal.

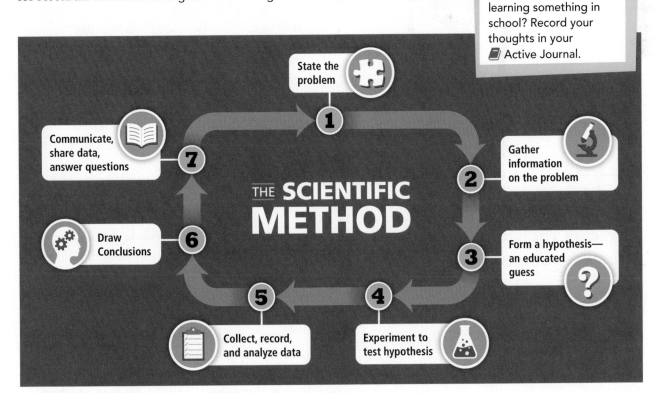

THE SCIENTIFIC METHOD

1. State the problem
2. Gather information on the problem
3. Form a hypothesis—an educated guess
4. Experiment to test hypothesis
5. Collect, record, and analyze data
6. Draw Conclusions
7. Communicate, share data, answer questions

Analyze Diagrams The scientific method gave scientists a rational way to test new ideas. Why do you think the last step leads back to the first step?

This information is the basis of a hypothesis, or possible answer. This hypothesis is then tested through more observations and experiments.

☑ READING CHECK **Identify Supporting Details** How did Bacon and Descartes approach the new scientific method?

New Inventions Support Scientific Discovery

During the Scientific Revolution, scientists developed tools that helped them make new discoveries. One such tool was the telescope. It increased a person's ability to see distant objects. With the telescope, scientists were able to see the planets, the stars, and much more. They learned, for example, that the moon's surface was covered with craters and not smooth as it appeared to the naked eye.

▼ Though this telescope from the 1600s is much less powerful than modern telescopes, it works on many of the same scientific principles.

The microscope was another important invention. A microscope is a device that uses a lens to magnify objects. Using this tool, scientists could see the details of small objects such as insects and even blood cells. Both the microscope and the telescope uncovered new worlds.

The thermometer, which scientists could use to measure the temperature of objects, was also a major discovery. Scientists would now understand how materials changed as they became hotter and colder. The barometer was another important invention. It measured changes in air pressure that were related to changes in weather.

☑ READING CHECK **Make Connections** How did new forms of technology allow Renaissance scientists to practice inductive reasoning?

☑ Lesson Check

Practice Vocabulary

1. What is **rationalism**?

2. Use the term **heliocentric theory** to describe the work of Copernicus.

Critical Writing and Thinking

3. **Synthesize** How is inductive reasoning part of the scientific method?

4. **Cause and Effect** What was Galileo's purpose when he dropped two stones from the Tower of Pisa? How is it an example of the new methods developed during the Scientific Revolution?

5. **Writing Workshop: Pick an Organizing Strategy** Use the information you have recorded in your 📒 Active Journal to start organizing your research. Will you put the information about your subject in chronological order, or does another strategy make sense? Draft an outline to help you plan.

Distinguish Relevant from Irrelevant Information

INTERACTIVE

Identify Main Ideas and Details

When writing about a topic, you want to make sure that all the information you include is relevant, or related, to that topic. For example, knowing Martin Luther's favorite food is irrelevant to a discussion of his religious ideas. Follow these steps to learn how to distinguish relevant from irrelevant information.

1 Identify your focus or topic. By clearly defining your topic, you can better determine which pieces of information will be relevant or irrelevant. What kind of information would you be looking for if you were writing about (a) Galileo's childhood, (b) his contributions to astronomy?

2 Locate sources and read about the topic. Based on the topic you identified, select and read a number of sources that will likely offer information on this topic. You may find sources online or in your school's media center. The bulleted list provided here serves as a source. What other sources could you turn to?

3 Identify the information that is relevant to your topic. Once you have gathered information, decide which facts are related to the topic you want to discuss. Identify three facts on the list below that are relevant to the topic of Galileo's contributions to the development of astronomy.

4 Identify the information that is irrelevant to your topic. Irrelevant information, such as anecdotes or personal details, may be interesting, but not central to the topic. Identify two facts from the list that you could disregard when putting together information about the development of astronomy.

Secondary Source

Facts about Galileo Galilei

- Galileo was born in Pisa, Italy, but moved with his family to Florence, Italy, when he was still a young boy.

- Galileo worked as a professor of mathematics at the University of Padua.

- Galileo's discoveries proved the Copernican system: that the Earth and other planets revolve around the sun.

- Galileo invented the telescope in 1609.

- Galileo observed both the moon and Jupiter's four moons with his telescope.

- Galileo invented a compass used by surveyors.

- Galileo was one of the first scientists to use experiments to discover a law of nature.

- Galileo had three children: two girls and one boy.

- Galileo was put under house arrest for stating that Earth and other planets revolve around the sun, rather than the sun and planets revolve around Earth.

- Galileo's ideas could not be published in Italy, but they were published in the Netherlands, where they influenced the work of other scientists.

☑ Review and Assessment

VISUAL REVIEW

Thinkers of the Scientific Revolution

Thinker	Achievement
Nicolaus Copernicus	Advanced idea of sun-centered solar system
Francis Bacon	Developed the scientific method
Isaac Newton	Developed the theory of gravity
Johannes Kepler	Calculated the orbits of the planets revolving around the sun
Galileo Galilei	Developed the telescope; proved Copernicus' heliocentric theory

GENERAL ADVANCES DURING THE RENAISSANCE

Art and Literature
- New artistic techniques
- Realism
- Influence of humanism and secularism

Science
- Changing views of the universe
- Development of scientific method
- Dramatic changes in medicine and chemistry

Architecture
- Rejection of Gothic style
- Use of ancient Greek and Roman models
- Blending of beauty with functionality

READING REVIEW

Use the Take Notes and Practice Vocabulary activities in your Active Journal to review the topic.

 **FINDINGS**

Create Your Chart
Get help with finalizing your chart in your 📘 Active Journal.

👆 **INTERACTIVE**

Practice Vocabulary

ASSESSMENT

Vocabulary and Key Ideas

1. **Define** What is the meaning of *mercantile*?

2. **Explain** the importance of Florence in the early stages of the Renaissance.

3. **Identify Main Ideas** Who were the Medici? What role did they play in the development of the Renaissance?

4. **Describe** What factors set the stage for the Protestant Reformation?

5. **Define** What is humanism? How is it related to secularism?

Critical Thinking and Writing

6. **Compare Points of View** How did Martin Luther's ideas differ from those expressed by the Catholic Church?

7. **Analyze Information** What was the impact of the printing press on the Reformation? On the Scientific Revolution?

8. **Synthesize Information** In what ways was the Renaissance a break with medieval times?

9. **Explain** What was the goal of many northern humanists?

10. **Identify Main Ideas** How did increased contact with the world outside Europe encourage both the Renaissance and the Scientific Revolution?

11. **Writing Workshop: Write an Explanatory Essay** Using details you recorded in your 📖 Active Journal, write a research paper describing the work of a selected figure of the Renaissance, Reformation, or Scientific Revolution.

Analyze Primary Sources

12. Which person wrote the quote below?

    A. Leonardo da Vinci
    B. Nicolaus Copernicus
    C. Martin Luther
    D. Niccolò Machiavelli

    "How praiseworthy it is for a prince to keep his word and to live with integrity and not by cunning, everyone knows. Nevertheless, one sees from experience in our times that the princes who have accomplished great deeds are those who have thought little about keeping faith and who have known how cunningly to manipulate men's minds; and in the end they have surpassed those who laid their foundations upon sincerity."

Analyze Maps

Use the map on the right to answer the following questions:

13. Which letter represents the location where Martin Luther presented his 95 Theses?

14. Which letter represents the Duchy of Milan?

15. Which letter represents the Papal States?

▼ **Reformation-Era Italy and Germany**

Global Convergence

(1415–1763)

GO ONLINE
to access your
digital course

▶ VIDEO

◀)) AUDIO

📖 ETEXT

👆 INTERACTIVE

✏️ WRITING

🎮 GAMES

📄 WORKSHEET

☑️ ASSESSMENT

Go back over 500 years

to **THE ERA OF EXPLORATION AND COLONIALIZATION**. Learn about how the great voyages of discovery and the spread of European and African peoples and cultures laid the foundation for the world we live in today.

Explore
The
Essential
Question

What are the costs and benefits of human expansion?

It was not only people who traveled to faraway parts of the globe. What ideas, technologies, diseases, plants, and animals also made a historic voyage?

Unlock the Essential Question in your 📓 Active Journal.

◀ Spanish explorer Hernán Cortés receives submission from the conquered Aztec rulers.

Read

Watch

NBC LEARN

BOUNCE TO ACTIVATE ▶ VIDEO

The Conquest of a Golden City

Watch as the great Aztec ruler surrenders to his Spanish conqueror.

Global Convergence (1415–1763)

Learn more about the age of global convergence by making your own map and timeline in your 📓 Active Journal.

INTERACTIVE

Topic Map

Where did European powers explore and found colonies?

Europeans traveled to India, Africa, and South, Central, and North America. Locate South and Central America on the larger map.

 INTERACTIVE

Topic Timeline

What happened and when?

Awesome voyages into the unknown. . . the intermingling of civilizations and cultures. . . Explore the timeline to see some of what was happening during the ages of exploration and colonization.

1520s–1530s
Spanish conquer Aztec and Incan empires.

1492
Columbus reaches the Caribbean.

1522
Magellan's expedition circumnavigates the globe.

1400
Portuguese explore the coast of Africa.

TOPIC EVENTS

1400	1500

WORLD EVENTS

early 1400s
Chinese Admiral Zheng He explores Asia and Africa.

1526 Babur
founds the Mughal dynasty in India.

NORTH AMERICA

Santa Fe

NEW SPAIN

St. Augustine

Gulf of Mexico

Cuba

Hispaniola

Puerto Rico

20° N

Mexico City

Caribbean Sea

Gulf of California

ATLANTIC OCEAN

NEW GRANADA

Bogotá

Quito

0°

Amazon River

PACIFIC OCEAN

SOUTH AMERICA

PERU

Lima

0   1,500 mi

0   1,500 km

Lambert Azimuthal Equal-Area projection

Santiago

CHILE

Asunción

Buenos Aires

Rio de la Plata

120° W   100° W   80° W   60° W   40° W   20° W

ANDES MTS.

KEY

Areas colonized by Spanish

Who will you meet?

The explorer Christopher Columbus, who reached the Caribbean in 1492

Atahualpa, ruler of the Incan empire in South America

Queen Nzinga, who led her southern African nation in war and peace

1763
The Treaty of Paris ends the French and Indian War.

1607
English colonists found Jamestown.

1619
First enslaved Africans arrive in Virginia.

1600

1700

1600s
Europe adopts capitalism and mercantilism.

late 1600s
Osei Tutu unifies the Asante kingdom in West Africa.

Quest

Discussion Inquiry

Colonizing Planets

Quest KICK OFF

In the late **1400s** and **1500s**, European monarchs and merchants supported global voyages of discovery. Some Europeans began to think about setting up overseas trading posts and colonies.

Your quest is first to understand the costs and benefits of establishing colonies in Africa, Asia, and the Americas. Then recall these costs and benefits as you discuss the question:

Should the United States invest in colonizing other planets?

What parallels can you draw based on decisions made during the age of exploration? Consider the Essential Question "What are the costs and benefits of human expansion?" in this Quest.

1 Ask Questions
Begin by remembering what you know or have learned about the voyages of exploration and the colonies European countries set up. Write down in your 📘 Active Journal a list of questions that you want to answer about the costs and benefits of creating those colonies.

2 Investigate
As you read in the topic, watch for **Quest** CONNECTIONS about decisions Europeans made to develop colonies.

▲ A Portuguese caravel of the 1400s

3 Examine Primary Sources
Carefully review primary sources provided to you. Record your notes in your 📘 Active Journal.

Quest FINDINGS

4 Prepare Your Position
State whether you think the United States should invest in colonizing other planets. Write a sentence presenting your position. Now gather and list details that support your position from Quest Connections and your research findings. Get help in your 📘 Active Journal.

LESSON 1
Voyages of Discovery

BOUNCE TO ACTIVATE ▶ VIDEO

GET READY TO READ

START UP
In this illustration from the 1400s, a French trader samples pepper harvested by workers. Write a short letter from this trader to his family back in France.

GUIDING QUESTIONS
- How did trade and competition lead to voyages of exploration?
- What new technology made long ocean voyages possible?
- How did the voyages of Columbus and other explorers change European views of the world?

TAKE NOTES
Literacy Skills: Identify Cause and Effect
Use the graphic organizer in your 📖 Active Journal to take notes as you read the lesson.

PRACTICE VOCABULARY
Use the vocabulary activity in your 📖 Active Journal to practice the vocabulary words.

Vocabulary	Academic Vocabulary
missionary	ivory
circumnavigate	treacherous
cartography	
caravel	

European merchants had traded with Asia since ancient times. During the Crusades, Europeans brought back silks and jewels from Asia. For a time, the Black Death and the Mongol invasions had interrupted this trade. By the 1500s, traders were eager to return to Asia. At the same time, strong European states were emerging. Rulers of centralized states such as Spain, Portugal, England, and France saw world trade as the key to increasing their own power and prosperity.

What Motivated Europeans to Explore the Seas?
During the Middle Ages, Europe's economy lagged behind those of China and many other parts of Afroeurasia. However, the European market for foreign goods was growing fast, especially after the Crusades.

Europe in the World Economy
European rulers and nobles wanted silk and porcelain from China, spices from South and Southeast Asia, cotton cloth from India and Egypt, and gold from West Africa.

▲ Colorful spices lure shoppers at an Egyptian spice market.

Europeans, however, offered few products that people in Asia and Africa wanted to buy. To pay for the goods they wanted, Europeans had to export silver and gold.

By the time of the Renaissance, commerce between Europe and Asia was largely under the control of Italian city-states. Ships and merchants from Venice and Genoa had strong ties with Cairo and other Muslim trading cities. Renaissance merchants had grown wealthy trading goods imported from Asia. Other European nations wanted access to this trade without going through the Italians. They sought a sea route to Asia that bypassed Italian trade routes in the Mediterranean Sea.

The Search for Spices Renaissance traders were particularly interested in the spice trade. Valuable spices were to be found in India, China, and the Spice Islands, or the Moluccas, a chain of islands in present-day Indonesia. There, traders could purchase spices such as pepper, clove, nutmeg, and cinnamon—all in demand in Europe.

Winning Converts to Christianity Another reason for exploring new lands was to win converts for Christianity. Ships' crews often included Christian **missionaries**. Missionaries are members of a religious order who encourage people to convert to a particular religion. Missionaries remained in these new lands to set up communities and schools.

☑ **READING CHECK** **Compare and Contrast** What different reasons did merchants and missionaries have for exploring overseas lands?

Portugal Takes the Lead

Portugal led the world in global exploration. It was the first European nation to acquire an overseas empire.

How Did Prince Henry the Navigator Encourage Exploration? Portuguese expansion began with the invasion of North Africa and the conquest of Ceuta in 1415. One of the most distinguished soldiers in that battle was Prince Henry, third son of King John I of Portugal. Around 1432, Prince Henry claimed for Portugal the rich islands of Madeira and the Azores. Known as Prince Henry the Navigator, he also sought to gain direct access to the rich African trade in **ivory**, gold, and slaves. Prince Henry is credited as well with sponsoring many explorers and training them in mapmaking, ship design, and navigation.

Part of Henry's mission in Africa was to drive out Muslims from North Africa and the Holy Land. As a devout Catholic, Henry wanted to recover Christian lands in the Mediterranean that had been taken

Academic Vocabulary

ivory • *n.*, a hard white substance from the tusk of an animal such as an elephant by the Muslims. The Portuguese also hoped to convert Africans—most of whom practiced Islam or traditional religions—to Christianity. In addition, the Portuguese were looking for a faster sea route to Asia by sailing around Africa.

Dias Rounds the Cape In 1488, Bartolomeu Dias (bahr too loo MEE oo DEE us), a Portuguese captain, made a great discovery. Dias and his crew became the first Europeans to sail around the Cape of Good Hope at the southern tip of Africa. They proved that it was possible to reach the Indian Ocean by sea.

Da Gama's Round-Trip Route In 1497, Captain Vasco da Gama also sailed south from Portugal. In three months, his ships rounded the Cape of Good Hope and then sailed on to India. Da Gama returned with a cargo of spices that he sold at a huge profit. With the money, he outfitted a new fleet of cargo ships. He returned to India to seek more profit from the spice trade. Eventually, the Portuguese seized key ports in the Indian Ocean and established a vast trading empire. Da Gama confirmed Portugal's status as a world power.

☑ READING CHECK **Draw Conclusions** How did Vasco da Gama improve on Dias's accomplishment?

Explorers Find New Routes

Portugal's sea captains left Europe and headed southward in their search for sea routes to Asia. Christopher Columbus, an Italian navigator, took a different route.

Analyze Images This statue of Prince Henry stands near the harbor in Sagres, Portugal. **Synthesize Visual Information** Why would the sculptor show Henry pointing to the sea and holding a map?

BIOGRAPHY
5 Things to Know About ▶ VASCO DA GAMA
Portuguese Explorer (c. 1460–1524)

- He was born into a noble family in Sines, southwestern Portugal. His father commanded the fortress there.

- In the navy he gained a reputation as a fearless navigator. Following King John II's orders, he seized French ships in response to French interference with Portuguese shipping.

- In 1497, da Gama led the Portuguese expedition to find a sea route to India from Europe.

- His expedition, stopping often in Africa along the way, successfully reached Calicut in India in May 1498.

- He returned to Portugal a hero and made a second voyage to India in 1502. Much later, he became the Portuguese viceroy of India.

Draw Conclusions How did Vasco da Gama help fulfill Prince Henry's goals for Portuguese exploration?

Quest CONNECTIONS

What do you think Ferdinand and Isabella considered to be the costs of supporting Columbus's voyages of discovery? The benefits? Record your findings in your 📔 Active Journal.

Columbus Sails West Like most well-educated Europeans, Columbus knew that Earth was a sphere. He reasoned that, by sailing west, he could reach the East Indies, a group of islands in Southeast Asia. But he made some errors. First, Columbus underestimated the distance from Europe west to Asia. Also, no European knew at the time that two huge landforms—North America and South America—barred the way.

With backing from Spain's monarchs, Columbus sailed in August 1492. His three ships made swift progress across the Atlantic and landed on an island in what are known today as the Bahamas. Columbus believed that he had reached lands just off the coast of China. He made three return voyages, hoping to find gold and other riches. He also captured and enslaved native peoples. Columbus died believing he had found the gateway to Asia.

Other Explorers Follow Inspired by Columbus and the Portuguese explorers, other nations sought new lands for trade. From its location on the North Sea, the Netherlands had long had access to European markets. Dutch merchants soon reached Asia, where they were especially successful in the East Indies spice trade. Dutch trading colonies sprang up in Suriname, South Africa, and in the Dutch East Indies (present-day Indonesia).

In 1500, Pedro Álvares Cabral, a Portuguese sea captain, led a fleet to the Indian Ocean. He sailed too far west and landed on the east coast of South America. He came upon the land that we now know as Brazil.

Analyze Images This illustration from the 1500s shows King Ferdinand and Queen Isabella saying farewell to Columbus as he sets off on his voyage. **Infer** What are some reasons the king and queen would have agreed to sponsor Columbus's voyage?

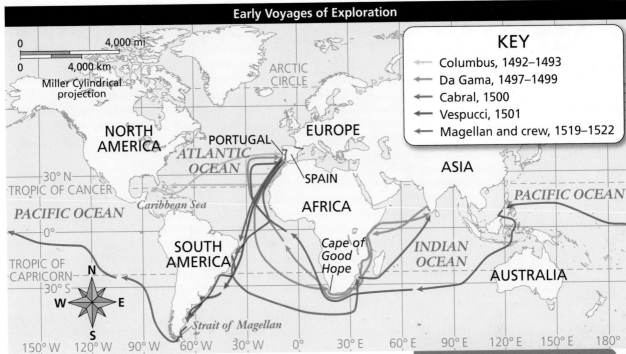

Early Voyages of Exploration

0 — 4,000 mi
0 — 4,000 km
Miller Cylindrical projection

KEY
← Columbus, 1492–1493
← Da Gama, 1497–1499
← Cabral, 1500
← Vespucci, 1501
← Magellan and crew, 1519–1522

NORTH AMERICA
PORTUGAL
EUROPE
ATLANTIC OCEAN
SPAIN
ASIA
ARCTIC CIRCLE
30° N
TROPIC OF CANCER
Caribbean Sea
AFRICA
PACIFIC OCEAN
PACIFIC OCEAN
0°
SOUTH AMERICA
Cape of Good Hope
INDIAN OCEAN
TROPIC OF CAPRICORN
30° S
AUSTRALIA
N W E S
Strait of Magellan
150° W   120° W   90° W   60° W   30° W   0°   30° E   60° E   90° E   120° E   150° E   180°

In 1500, he reached India and loaded six ships with precious spices for a return voyage to Portugal.

Between 1497 and 1504, Amerigo Vespucci, an Italian navigator, made four voyages of exploration. He concluded that the lands Columbus called "the Indies" were, in fact, part of a "New World."

Vespucci's report was very popular in Europe. A German mapmaker named the newly encountered lands "America," a Latin version of Vespucci's first name.

What Was Magellan's Feat? In 1519, Ferdinand Magellan launched the most ambitious voyage of discovery. He set out from Spain to cross the Atlantic with five ships and a crew of more than 250. He hoped to find a western route to Asia.

Unlike Columbus, Magellan knew that a continent stood in his way. His fleet sailed south along the uncharted continent. For 38 days, Magellan and his weary crew navigated the **treacherous** waters. Finally, they threaded their way through a strait, or narrow channel, that led them to the Pacific Ocean. This channel was named the Strait of Magellan. The continent was South America, and Magellan's feat had confirmed that there was a southwest passage to Asia.

Magellan continued north and sailed west across the Pacific Ocean. The journey used up all of the ships' food supplies. Many crew members died from a lack of certain nutrients such as vitamins in their diets.

GEOGRAPHY Skills

European explorers went on long journeys in different directions to find a sea route to Asia.

1. **Movement** Which explorers followed the coast of Africa to Asia?

2. **Draw Conclusions** Why do you think many explorers sailed along coasts when they could?

Academic Vocabulary
treacherous • *adj.,* dangerous or hazardous

Analyze Maps This map of the Mediterranean is known as a portolan chart. Their accuracy made them extremely valuable to seafaring nations. **Draw Conclusions** What advantages would accurate maps provide to both ship captains and nations?

Crew member Antonio Pigafetta described the hardships of the voyage:

Primary Source

We ate biscuit . . . swarming with worms, for they had eaten the better part (it stank strongly of rat urine); and we drank yellow water that had been putrid for many days, and we also ate some ox hides . . . which had become hard because of the sun, rain, and wind.

—Antonio Pigafetta, *The First Voyage Around the World*

INTERACTIVE

Explorer's Ship

Magellan next reached the Philippine Islands, claiming them for Spain. In 1521, he died in a battle with the islanders. In September 1522, three years after departing, the sole surviving ship of the fleet returned to Spain. Only 18 crew members survived. They had achieved the most difficult navigational feat of the age. They had **circumnavigated**, or sailed completely around, the world.

READING CHECK Identify Main Ideas What is the significance of the Strait of Magellan?

What New Tools Aided Exploration?

The voyages of exploration could not have been made without advances in sailing technology. These included improvements in mapmaking, navigation, and shipbuilding.

More Accurate Maps For 1,300 years, explorers had been guided by the works of the ancient Egyptian geographer Ptolemy. Crusaders and medieval traders also made maps. Catalans, Genoese, Iberian Jews, Iberian Muslims (Moors), and Portuguese created maps, such as the Catalan Atlas (1375). Though valuable, these early maps were inaccurate or incomplete.

During the Renaissance, mapmakers developed the science of making maps and globes, known as **cartography**. Those who made more accurate maps, atlases, and globes were called cartographers.

In 1569, Gerardus Mercator (juh RAHR dus mur KAY tur) discovered how to project the curved surface of the globe onto a flat page. His world map distorted the extreme northern and southern regions, but left the most traveled areas of the globe undistorted. Mercator projections, as these maps are called, continue to be used today.

Advances in Navigation The most commonly used navigational tool was the magnetic compass, used to show direction. This device was invented in China and came to Europe via the Silk Road traders. Navigators also used the astrolabe, which determined the ship's north-south position based on measurements of the stars. With these tools, sailors could navigate without being close to land.

Quick Activity

Discover the art and craft of mapmaking in your Active Journal.

Analyze Diagrams Technological advances such as those shown helped Europeans explore the world. **Use Visual Information** Which improvements show that Europeans were in contact with other regions of the world?

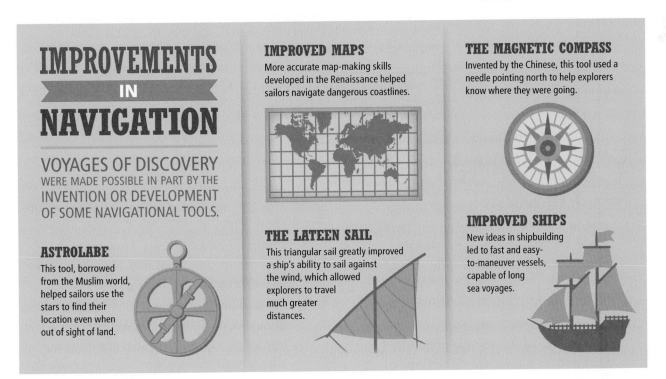

IMPROVEMENTS IN NAVIGATION

VOYAGES OF DISCOVERY WERE MADE POSSIBLE IN PART BY THE INVENTION OR DEVELOPMENT OF SOME NAVIGATIONAL TOOLS.

IMPROVED MAPS More accurate map-making skills developed in the Renaissance helped sailors navigate dangerous coastlines.

THE MAGNETIC COMPASS Invented by the Chinese, this tool used a needle pointing north to help explorers know where they were going.

ASTROLABE This tool, borrowed from the Muslim world, helped sailors use the stars to find their location even when out of sight of land.

THE LATEEN SAIL This triangular sail greatly improved a ship's ability to sail against the wind, which allowed explorers to travel much greater distances.

IMPROVED SHIPS New ideas in shipbuilding led to fast and easy-to-maneuver vessels, capable of long sea voyages.

Understanding Winds Understanding ocean winds was vital to European explorers. After much trial and error, mariners learned that winds were divided into zones and that these zones changed with the seasons. With this knowledge, they could map travel routes to catch the best winds. Explorers could also determine the best time of year to catch the winds for their voyages.

The Shipbuilding Revolution The Renaissance also launched a revolution in shipbuilding. Until the Middle Ages, rowers worked to move ships. These slow and heavy ships needed large crews with many rowers. They were difficult to steer and best suited for calm seas.

European craftworkers developed new oceangoing ships. They modified a ship called a **caravel**, a small, narrow vessel with two or three masts and triangular sails. It was fast and easier to maneuver in different wind and sea conditions.

Analyze Images
Magellan's ships pass the stormy southern tip of South America. **Use Visual Information** Which navigational improvements shown on the previous page would have aided Magellan and his crew?

Europeans View a Wider World The voyages of discovery revealed wonders and created excitement about the natural world. Explorers discovered the vastness of the African continent and the existence of North America and South America. "The hidden half of the globe is brought to light," rejoiced a scholar in 1493.

Suddenly, even ordinary Europeans wanted to know about world geography. Printers made cheap, portable atlases to meet the demand. Illustrated travel books became popular for those who wanted to read first-hand accounts of exploration on sea and land. An account of Magellan's voyage was published as early as 1523 and included interviews with the expedition's survivors.

☑ **READING CHECK** **Identify Supporting Details** What technologies allowed navigators to plot an accurate course?

☑ Lesson Check

Practice Vocabulary

1. Define each of the following key terms in a complete sentence: **missionary, circumnavigate, cartography,** and **caravel**.

Critical Thinking and Writing

2. **Identify Evidence** What was the significance of the voyage of Bartolomeu Dias and his crew around the Cape of Good Hope?

3. **Categorize** What inventions helped sailors determine their location at sea?

4. **Compare and Contrast** How were the voyages of Columbus and Magellan similar and different?

5. **Writing Workshop: Introduce Claims** Think about what you have learned about the impact produced by global convergence. Was it mostly positive or mostly negative? Write a sentence in your 📓 Active Journal that makes a claim on this issue.

Vasco da Gama, Journal

In his journey of discovery, Portuguese explorer Vasco da Gama sailed into treacherous waters. This excerpt from his journal describes the experiences of his crew and the difficulty of sailing around the Cape of Good Hope.

▶ Vasco da Gama's ships faced treacherous seas.

At daybreak of Thursday the 16th of November, having careened our ships ① and taken in woods we set sail. At that time we did not know how far we might be abaft ② the Cape of Good Hope. Pero d'Alenquer thought the distance about thirty leagues ③, but he was not certain, for on his return voyage (when with B. Dias) he had left the Cape in the morning and had gone past this bay with the wind astern, whilst on the outward voyage he had kept at sea, and was therefore unable to identify the locality where we now were. We therefore stood out towards S.S.W. ④, and late on Saturday (November 18) we beheld the Cape. On that same day we again stood out to sea, returning to the land in the course of the night. On Sunday morning, November 19, we once more made for the Cape, but were again unable to round it, for the wind blew from the S.S.W., whilst the Cape juts out towards S.W. We then again stood out to sea, returning to the land on Monday night. At last, on Wednesday (November 22), at noon, having the wind astern ⑤, we succeeded in doubling the Cape, and then ran along the coast. To the south of this Cape of Good Hope, and close to it, a vast bay, six leagues broad at its mouth, enters about six leagues into the land.

—*The Library of Original Sources*, Oliver J. Thatcher, editor

Analyzing Primary Sources

Use specific evidence from the excerpt to answer the questions.

1. **Understand Effects** How did the crew's knowledge of previous explorers help them navigate past the Cape of Good Hope?

2. **Identify Supporting Details** What kept da Gama and his crew from sailing around the Cape of Good Hope on November 19?

3. **Identify Supporting Details** What details from this passage suggest that the passage of the Cape of Good Hope was a difficult one?

Reading and Vocabulary Support

① To career a ship is to clean the underside.

② *Abaft* is "in or behind the stern [back] of a ship."

③ If the distance of a league is about three miles, about how many miles is *thirty leagues*?

④ When da Gama writes he "stood out to sea," he means that he sailed out to sea, away from shore. *S.S.W.* stands for the direction south-southwest.

⑤ What do you think *astern* means? Use context to determine its meaning.

Quest CONNECTIONS

Vasco da Gama's expedition faced many dangers. What dangers would colonizers of space face? How might they address these dangers? Record your findings in your 📓 Active Journal.

The Conquest of the Aztec and Incan Empires

GET READY TO READ

START UP

Examine the mural by twentieth-century Mexican artist Diego Rivera. Tell a partner what your life might be like if you lived in this Aztec city. What do you think your daily life would be like in this place? Based on the illustration, write three statements that describe your everyday experiences in this place.

GUIDING QUESTIONS

- Why was Spain able to conquer the Aztec and Incan empires?
- How did conquests in the Americas benefit Spain?
- What impact did Spanish conquest have on the peoples of Mesoamerica and the Andes?

TAKE NOTES

Literacy Skills: Sequence

Use the graphic organizer in your 📓 Active Journal to take notes as you read the lesson.

PRACTICE VOCABULARY

Use the vocabulary activity in your 📓 Active Journal to practice the vocabulary words.

Vocabulary		Academic Vocabulary
conquistador	bullion	devastate
colonization	immunity	pagan

At the time the Spanish explorers arrived, the Aztec leader Moctezuma ruled an empire that extended throughout Mexico. In South America, the Incan emperor Atahualpa (ah tuh WAHL puh) ruled more than 10 million people. These two empires were large and complex, but they were no match for the Spanish forces.

How Did the Spanish Conquer Two Empires?

The Spanish explorers and soldiers who conquered territory were known as **conquistadors**. Spain quickly began **colonization**, or the process of establishing settlements called colonies. Towns were settled and new governments were established. Spain's Caribbean colonies served as bases for conquering the mainland.

Cortés Defeats the Aztecs In 1519, Hernán Cortés sailed to Mexico to conquer the rich Aztec empire. He had fewer than 600 soldiers to counter Moctezuma's strong army.

One of Cortés's advantages was his native interpreter, an Aztec woman named Malinche. Through her and a Spanish interpreter, the conquistador learned vital details about the Aztecs and their army.

This information helped Cortés form alliances with the Aztecs' enemies. Thousands of native warriors joined the Spaniards as they marched to Tenochtitlan, the Aztec capital. These local groups, including the Tlaxcalans, opposed the Aztecs and wanted freedom from their harsh rule.

Moctezuma and Cortés met on the outskirts of the grand imperial capital. Though Moctezuma welcomed Cortés at first, tension mounted between the Aztecs and the Spaniards. A battle broke out, and Moctezuma was killed. By August 1521, the Aztecs had surrendered Tenochtitlan. A poem in the Aztec language of Nahuatl described the defeat:

Analyze Images Cortés takes Moctezuma prisoner. **Identify Main Ideas** What key advantage did the Spanish have over the Aztecs?

Primary Source

Nothing but flowers and songs of sorrow / are left in Mexico /. . . . We are crushed to the ground; / we lie in ruins.

—unknown Aztec poet from *The Broken Spears*, by Miguel León-Portilla

Pizarro Defeats the Inca Rumors of another golden empire drew Francisco Pizarro and a group of conquistadors to South America in the 1530s. It was a time of chaos for the Inca. The vast empire had split into factions and civil war erupted. Smallpox had arrived from Central America, killing thousands of Inca. Finally, a new emperor, Atahualpa, took the Incan throne.

Spanish Conquest in the Americas

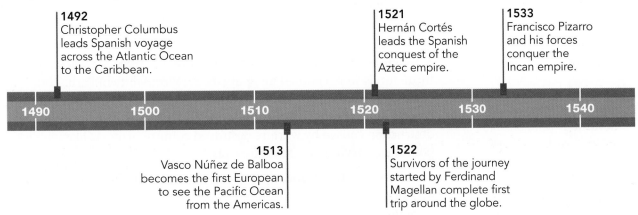

1492 Christopher Columbus leads Spanish voyage across the Atlantic Ocean to the Caribbean.

1521 Hernán Cortés leads the Spanish conquest of the Aztec empire.

1533 Francisco Pizarro and his forces conquer the Incan empire.

1490   1500   1510   1520   1530   1540

1513 Vasco Núñez de Balboa becomes the first European to see the Pacific Ocean from the Americas.

1522 Survivors of the journey started by Ferdinand Magellan complete first trip around the globe.

Analyze Images The timeline shows key dates in the Spanish exploration of the Americas. **Use Visual Information** Which Spanish explorer died during his exploration?

▲ This engraving from the late 1500s shows Pizarro meeting the Incan emperor Atahualpa. **Infer** How would you have felt if you were an Inca seeing the Spanish for the first time?

Pizarro took advantage of the instability. He invited Atahualpa to a meeting and then threw him in prison. Atahualpa arranged for a ransom of almost 20 tons of gold and silver. This astonishing sum was said to be the largest ransom in history. Pizarro rejected Atahualpa's ransom and ordered the emperor killed.

Pizarro appointed a new Incan emperor who agreed to cooperate with the Spanish. Pizarro then marched to the Incan capital of Cuzco. In November 1533, his army took control of the city. The Incan empire was now in Spanish hands.

✓ **READING CHECK** **Identify Cause and Effect** How did Atahualpa's death affect the Incan empire?

What Was the Impact of the Conquest?

Aztec lands then became part of New Spain and were renamed Mexico. Incan lands were claimed for Spain as the Viceroyalty of Peru. Both colonies brought great wealth to Spain. By contrast, the Aztecs and the Inca were **devastated**. Disease had wiped out millions of people. The destruction caused by warfare destroyed cultural artifacts like temples, paintings, carvings, and manuscripts.

Academic Vocabulary
devastate • v., to bring to chaos, disorder, or ruin

Treasure for the Spanish Crown The Spanish monarch took one fifth of all the treasures taken by the conquistadors from these new colonies.

The Incan writer Felipe Guamán Poma de Ayala described the conquistadors' search for treasure:

Primary Source

Every day they did nothing but think about the gold and silver and riches. They were like desperate men, foolish, crazy, their judgment lost with the greed for gold and silver.

—Felipe Guamán Poma de Ayala, *The First New Chronicle and Good Government*

Every year, ships filled with treasure sailed from the Americas to Europe. These ships carried mostly gold and silver bullion from the colonies' mines. **Bullion** is precious metals melted into bars. By 1660, 200 tons of gold and 18,000 tons of silver had gone to Spain.

In addition to bullion, Spanish fleets took back tons of dried insects valued for the red dye they produced. This insect, the cochineal (KAH chuh neel), feeds on cactus plants and produces a vibrant red dye. The Spanish had seen the red dye in woven garments in Mexico and Peru. It was a brighter red than that produced by European dyes. Cochineal red transformed the European textile industry.

However, not all these treasures reached Spain and Portugal. Some ships sank in storms or were raided by pirates. Attracted by New World wealth, other European nations also competed with Spain and Portugal and sent their own explorers to map and conquer colonies.

The Loss of People and Cultures Aztec and Incan gold and silver enriched the Spanish and Portuguese treasuries. The conquistadors melted down carved gold ornaments, statues, and wall decorations.

INTERACTIVE

Spanish Exploration and Conquest of the Americas

Analyze Graphs This line graph shows the population of Native Americans in central Mexico in the 1500s. **Synthesize Visual Information** What is the estimated population decline between 1519 and 1540? How does it compare with the change in population between 1540 and 1580? Why?

Native American Population of Central Mexico

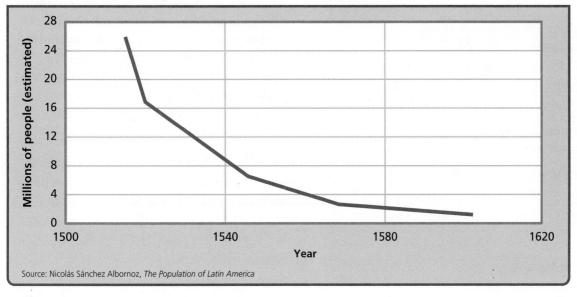

Source: Nicolás Sánchez Albornoz, *The Population of Latin America*

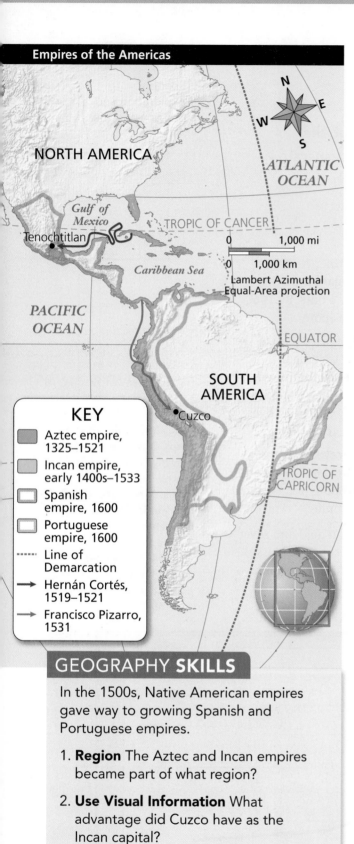

Empires of the Americas

NORTH AMERICA

ATLANTIC OCEAN

Gulf of Mexico

TROPIC OF CANCER

0   1,000 mi

0   1,000 km

Lambert Azimuthal Equal-Area projection

Caribbean Sea

Tenochtitlan

PACIFIC OCEAN

EQUATOR

SOUTH AMERICA

Cuzco

TROPIC OF CAPRICORN

KEY

- Aztec empire, 1325–1521
- Incan empire, early 1400s–1533
- Spanish empire, 1600
- Portuguese empire, 1600
- Line of Demarcation
- → Hernán Cortés, 1519–1521
- → Francisco Pizarro, 1531

GEOGRAPHY SKILLS

In the 1500s, Native American empires gave way to growing Spanish and Portuguese empires.

1. **Region** The Aztec and Incan empires became part of what region?

2. **Use Visual Information** What advantage did Cuzco have as the Incan capital?

Academic Vocabulary

pagan • *adj.,* related to a religion with many gods

The cultures of the Aztecs and the Inca—as well as the collapsed culture of the Maya—had all produced manuscripts recording religious or political aspects of their civilizations. The Spanish burned most of these manuscripts, considering them to be worthless, **pagan** scraps. At the same time, some Spaniards, such as Fray (Father) Bernardino de Sahagún, helped preserve native cultures and language in priceless documents like the *General History of the Things of New Spain.*

The conquistadors also wrecked Native American cities. In Tenochtitlan, the Spanish tore down the Templo Mayor and other Aztec buildings. On the ruins, the Spanish built their own capital, Mexico City. In Peru, Pizarro stripped all the riches from Incan cities such as Cuzco.

Eager to convert the natives to Catholicism, the Spaniards destroyed religious artifacts and temples related to the native religions. They also killed native priests.

In Peru, the Spanish encountered the quipu, the Incan recordkeeping tool made up of knotted strings. The Spanish viewed the quipu with suspicion and destroyed many of them. However, they also found them surprisingly accurate and useful for dividing up their own empire.

The presence of the Spanish also resulted in loss of life due to disease. Millions of natives died from smallpox or influenza. The natives died because they lacked **immunity**, or the ability of the body to fight a disease. The Spanish, by contrast, had built up resistance to smallpox, a disease that was common in Europe. Later epidemics killed even more, further weakening Aztec and Incan cultures.

✓ READING CHECK **Compare and Contrast** Why did the Aztecs and the Inca suffer more from smallpox than the Spanish did?

Cultural Blending in the Spanish Empire

In Spanish America, the mix of diverse people gave rise to a new social structure.

The blending of Native Americans, European peoples, and imported African slaves resulted in a culture unique to the Americas.

Native Influences Native culture that outlasted the Spanish conquest influenced colonial life. Incan architecture impressed the Spanish. Native artisans and workers blended their own painting or carving styles with those of the Europeans. Colonists also learned to eat foods indigenous to the Americas or traveled in Indian-style canoes.

European Influences At the same time, European customs dominated the newly conquered territories. The Spanish brought in their language, laws, and religion. They remade cities with buildings and homes in the Spanish style. Their Catholic churches were often built on top of Aztec or Incan temples.

Animals brought to the Americas, such as sheep, pigs, goats, and cows, changed eating habits. Animal husbandry, or raising livestock, continues to be an important occupation in the Americas. The Spanish also introduced horses, which transformed life by offering new means of transportation and new hunting options. Horses migrated northward, where they became important to many Native American cultures.

African Influences Other influences came with enslaved Africans imported to work the plantations. They contributed African farming methods, cooking styles, and crops. African drama, dance, and songs became part of some Christian services. In Cuba, Haiti, and Brazil, Africans forged new religions that blended African and Christian beliefs.

▲ Students in Rio de Janeiro show the ethnic diversity of modern-day Brazil, a former Portuguese colony.

☑ READING CHECK **Identify Cause and Effect** How did new animals change life in the Americas?

☑ Lesson Check

Practice Vocabulary

1. For each of the key terms, write a complete sentence that explains its relationship to the Age of Exploration: **conquistador**, **colonization**, **bullion**, **immunity**.

Critical Thinking and Writing

2. **Infer** How did the way the Aztec ruled their empire contribute to their own defeat?

3. **Compare Points of View** Reread the quotation by Felipe Guamán Poma de Ayala. How did his viewpoint differ from that of the Spaniards he described?

4. **Identify Bias** Why did the Spanish destroy the temples, statues, and books of the people they conquered?

5. **Writing Workshop: Support Claims** What evidence supports your claim about the impact of global convergence? Write down ideas, facts, and examples that support your claim in your 📙 Active Journal.

Distinguish Relevant from Irrelevant Information

Follow these steps to learn to distinguish relevant from irrelevant information.

1 **Identify your focus or topic.** By clearly defining your topic, you can better determine which pieces of information will be relevant or irrelevant.

   a. Are you focusing on the experiences of the conquistadors? Perhaps your focus is on Native American groups after they encountered Spanish explorers.

   b. Make sure you clearly define the topic before beginning.

2 **Locate sources and read about the topic.** Based on the topic you identified, select a number of sources that will likely offer information on this topic. You may find sources online or in your school's media center. This source has been provided for you.

3 **Identify the information that is relevant to your topic.** Scan your source to find passages that may relate to your topic.

   a. Which of the paragraphs below seem like it could relate to the Spanish conquistadors?

   b. Once you have identified key passages, read them closely to determine whether or not they provide relevant information.

4 **Identify the information that is irrelevant to your topic.** Irrelevant information—such as anecdotes, or stories about individuals— may be interesting, but not central to the topic. Make sure to focus on your specific topic to determine which information is relevant. If your topic is the conquistadors and their motivation, which information below is relevant? Which is irrelevant?

Secondary Source

The Spanish explorers, or conquistadors, traveled throughout the southern and southwestern region of North America. Conquistadors occupied this area for over 300 years, from the fifteenth to seventeenth centuries. These explorers and colonists came to present-day Mexico and the southwestern United States in search of wealth and power and to earn new lands for the Spanish crown.

Conquistadors were often on a quest to find riches, and many believed a story that circulated at the time about the Seven Cities of Cibola, which were said to be full of riches and made of gold. Many explorers, including Francisco Vasquez de Coronado, discovered many landmarks in the Southwest. Coronado is credited with discovering the Grand Canyon.

Conquistadors encountered native peoples, too. These encounters exposed native people to new diseases, and a great many died. In other cases, explorers killed or displaced Native Americans.

Missionaries who traveled with the conquistadors wanted to spread Christianity. Although some native people converted willingly, others were forced into roles as servants or slaves.

LESSON 3
The Spanish Empire

BOUNCE TO ACTIVATE ▶ VIDEO

GET READY TO READ

START UP

Study the photograph of Castillo de San Marcos, begun by the Spanish in 1672 at St. Augustine, Florida. Why do you think the Spanish built forts like these throughout the Americas?

GUIDING QUESTIONS

- What were the causes and effects of colonialism?
- How did Spain keep control of the government and economy of its colonies?
- How did missions and plantations affect traditional Native American culture?

TAKE NOTES

Literacy Skills: Identify Main Ideas and Details
Use the graphic organizer in your 📓 Active Journal to take notes as you read the lesson.

PRACTICE VOCABULARY

Use the vocabulary activity in your 📓 Active Journal to practice the vocabulary words.

Vocabulary		Academic Vocabulary
viceroy	mestizo	carpentry
encomienda	mulatto	accomplished
peninsulare	mission	
creole		

A flood of Spanish settlers and missionaries followed Cortés and the conquistadors to Spain's new empire. In time, a new culture emerged that reflected a mix of European, Native American, and African traditions.

Expanding the Spanish Empire

After the fall of the Aztec empire, the Spanish expanded into areas of Central America. The Spanish government sent explorers and colonists to conquer new lands in the Americas.

Further Explorations Even before the conquest of Mexico, news of Columbus's voyage in 1492 had electrified Western Europe. In the next few years, Spain and other European countries raced westward, hoping for adventure and riches.

In 1513, the Spanish explorer Juan Ponce de León reached the North American continent during the Easter season, or the feast of flowers (*flores* in Spanish), so he named the region La Florida. Some years later, Hernando de Soto landed in Florida. De Soto

Analyze Images Santa Barbara in California is one of many Spanish missions in the Americas. **Identify Main Ideas** What was the primary purpose of missions like Santa Barbara?

traveled as far as the Appalachian Mountains into what is now Georgia and the Carolinas before turning west toward Tennessee, Alabama, and Mississippi.

In early 1540, Francisco Vásquez de Coronado explored the American Southwest in search of the "seven cities of gold." He encountered the Zuni and the Pueblo people, but he never discovered these mythical cities of riches.

How Did Spain Rule its Empire? With their rich natural resources of gold, silver, and tin, Mexico and Peru attracted large numbers of explorers and settlers. Following closely behind were government officials. They settled in the colonies to make sure the crown received its share of the wealth from the New World.

Spain appointed local governors, but they frequently clashed with the conquistadors as well as with the Catholic missionaries. To govern more efficiently, Spain's king Charles V appointed **viceroys**, or officers who ruled in the name of the king in the Spanish Americas.

By the end of the 1500s, Spain had expanded its territory to the Philippines, a group of islands off the coast of Southeast Asia. By 1570, the viceroy of New Spain ruled territory in the Philippines, Mexico, and the Caribbean.

Christianity in the Americas For many in Spain, winning souls for Christianity was as important as empire building. The Catholic Church converted thousands of Native Americans in New Spain to Christianity. Church leaders also served as royal officials and helped regulate the activities of Spanish settlers. As the Spanish empire expanded, Church authority grew as well.

⏺ **INTERACTIVE**

Causes and Effects of Spanish Colonization

In the frontier communities, Franciscans, Jesuits, and other missionaries built churches and schools. They introduced crafts such as **carpentry** and metalworking. To communicate, many missionaries learned native languages and translated the Bible. One such priest, Bernardino de Sahagún, learned Nahuatl and preserved many aspects of Aztec culture in a valuable book called *General History of the Things of New Spain*.

However, not all missionaries valued the cultures of the Native Americans. Some sought to eliminate native culture and forcibly replace it with European culture, which they felt was superior. Missionaries also destroyed artifacts and writings of native people, losing forever valuable records of life in the Americas before the arrival of Columbus.

Wealth from the Americas To make the empire profitable, Spain closely controlled trade in the colonies. Colonists could ship raw materials only to Spain and could buy only goods manufactured in Spain. Laws forbade colonists from trading with any other European nations or other Spanish colonies.

With the introduction of sugar cane, the colonies added another important source of profit. Sugar cane is native to South Asia and was cultivated in southern Spain by Muslims in the Middle Ages. Spanish and Portuguese merchants first brought it to the New World.

Sugar cane could be refined into sugar, molasses, and rum, all in demand in Europe. It was grown on plantations that required large numbers of workers, but finding such workers was a problem. At first, the colonists used the encomienda (en koh mee EN dah) system granted by the Spanish crown. In the **encomienda** system, colonists had the right to demand labor or tribute from nearby Native Americans. This led to forced labor abuses and the enslavement of Native Americans. Eventually, disease and cruel treatment led to massive declines in the native population.

▲ Spanish priest and historian Bartolomé de las Casas (c. 1484–1566) spoke out against the mistreatment of native peoples.

Academic Vocabulary

carpentry • *n.*, the art or trade of woodworking

Analyze Images These Caribbean natives suffered cruel punishments on a sugar encomienda on the island of Santo Domingo. **Compare and Contrast** How are the two images on this page similar? How are they different?

Analyze Images This Mexican painting from the 1700s shows a Spanish man with his Native American wife and their mestizo child. **Infer** What does this painting suggest about the social and economic status of this mestizo child?

To meet the labor shortage, Spanish officials turned to enslaved workers from Africa. As the European demand for sugar rose, millions of Africans were brought to plantations in the Caribbean and Brazil. Most worked as field hands and servants.

As you have read, other sources of wealth in the Americas were gold, silver, and tin. Many enslaved Africans were sent to work in colonial mines. Within a few generations, these Africans and their American-born descendants outnumbered Europeans in the Americas.

✓ READING CHECK Draw Conclusions Why did Spain forbid its colonists from trading with other countries?

Colonial Society and Culture

During the 1500s, hundreds of ships arrived in American ports. The many passengers they carried eventually made up a society unique to the Americas.

Social Classes Spanish colonial society was made up of distinct social classes. At the top were the **peninsulares**, people born in Spain, on the Iberian Peninsula. Peninsulares filled the highest positions in government and the Catholic Church. Next came **creoles**, American-born descendants of Spanish settlers. Creoles owned plantations, ranches, and mines.

Lower social groups included **mestizos**, people of Native American and European descent. In addition, there were **mulattoes**, people of African and European descent. Native Americans and people of African descent occupied the lowest classes in society.

Spanish Influences Colonists built hundreds of new cities and towns in the Spanish Americas. These cities reflected many urban elements from the home country. Churches and government and commercial buildings typically bordered large plazas, or squares. Around the square, residential streets were laid out in a grid pattern.

To educate priests, the Church established colonial universities. By 1551, there were universities in the Dominican Republic, Mexico, and Peru. Many young men in the Spanish Americas were receiving university educations long before Harvard was founded in 1636 as the first college in North America.

The options for education among the women in the Spanish Americas were few. Often women who wanted an education entered a convent. One such woman was Sor Juana Inés de la Cruz (sawr HWANuh eeNEZ deh lah krooz). She entered a convent at age 18 and devoted herself to study and writing poetry and plays. She also defended the right of women to study and write. She became one of the most **accomplished** women writers in the Spanish language.

✔️ READING CHECK **Compare and Contrast** What did Malinche and Sor Juana have in common?

Effects on Native Americans

Native Americans were affected in several ways by the arrival of the Spanish. One of the greatest effects of the encounter with the Spanish was the exposure to Old World diseases. Because they lacked immunity to these diseases, millions of natives died from diseases such as smallpox and measles.

What Was Life on the Missions Like? When they arrived in the Spanish colonies, Jesuit and Franciscan priests began **missions**, or communities dedicated to spreading the faith or to educating and protecting people. Their main aim was to convert Native Americans to Christianity and to educate them. These communities were also set up to be self-supporting. The missions grew their own food and made clothing. Native people on the missions learned skills, and some missions even had small industries to generate profits.

Living on the missions could be difficult for native people as they adjusted to new beliefs and a new lifestyle. Missionaries encouraged them to adopt European culture and customs. They had to learn a new language. They were also strictly supervised by the priests, and discipline could be harsh. Because everyone on the missions lived so close together, diseases and illness spread quickly.

Outside the missions, colonists were trying to establish plantations. They wanted to use the native population as laborers, but the missionaries believed it was more important for the natives to remain on the mission. Clashes erupted between the missionaries and planters.

Academic Vocabulary
accomplished • *adj.,* highly skilled

Analyze Images Sor Juana Inés de la Cruz defended women's right to learn and was recognized as an important writer. **Infer** Why might a nun have been more likely to become an accomplished writer than a secular woman?

Analyze Images These Caribbean natives were forced to work washing gold for their Spanish conquerors. **Identify Main Ideas** As native workers began to die, what solution did the Spanish find to the labor shortage?

What Was Life on Plantations Like? Plantation work was generally much more difficult than mission life. Sugar cane and coffee were the main plantation crops, and each required a great deal of physical labor. Unlike the missions, plantations were run by colonists primarily to make a profit for the owners and investors back home.

Gradually, exposure to tropical heat, injuries, and disease all led to a population decline among the native workers. This created a labor shortage. By the early 1500s, plantation owners were bringing in African slave labor.

The majority of enslaved Africans labored on large sugar cane plantations in Spanish colonies like Santo Domingo (present-day Dominican Republic and Haiti). For decades, Santo Domingo was a vital colony for Spain, exporting sugar and coffee. However, by 1600, the sugar cane industry there had collapsed due to increasing competition from the Portuguese colony of Brazil.

☑ READING CHECK **Identify Cause and Effect** Why was plantation life harsher than mission life?

☑ Lesson Check

Practice Vocabulary

1. What was the **encomienda** system?

2. Use the terms *viceroy*, *creole*, *mestizo*, *peninsulare*, and *mulatto* to describe colonial society.

3. What was a **mission**?

Critical Thinking and Writing

4. **Compare and Contrast** How was life on plantations similar to and different from life on missions?

5. **Synthesize** How was land ownership related to social class in the Spanish colonies?

6. **Writing Workshop: Distinguish Claims from Opposing Claims** Write a few sentences in your 📓 Active Journal explaining how your claim about global convergence's impact differs from possible opposing claims.

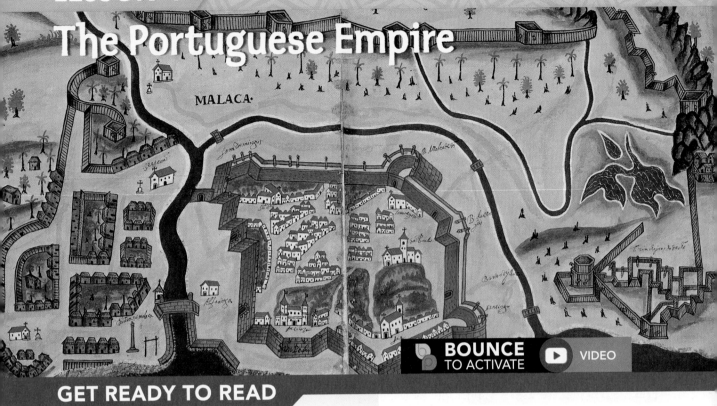

LESSON 4
The Portuguese Empire

MALACA.

BOUNCE TO ACTIVATE ▶ VIDEO

GET READY TO READ

START UP
Look at the map of the Portuguese settlement of Malacca in the East Indies. Describe the fort's defenses. Why was defense such an important factor in settlements like this one?

GUIDING QUESTIONS
- How did Portugal benefit from its colony in Brazil?
- How did Portugal build a trade empire in Asia?
- Why did Portugal's Asian empire decline?

TAKE NOTES
Literacy Skills: Analyze Text Structure
Use the graphic organizer in your 📖 Active Journal to take notes as you read the lesson.

PRACTICE VOCABULARY
Use the vocabulary activity in your 📖 Active Journal to practice the vocabulary words.

Vocabulary	Academic Vocabulary
Line of Demarcation	ruthless
Treaty of Tordesillas	lucrative
brazilwood	
spice trade	
privateer	

Portugal led the way in worldwide exploration. With its advanced navigational tools and maps, Portugal eagerly sought to expand its global empire just as its neighbor Spain had begun to do.

How Did the Portuguese Colonize Brazil?

Portugal began exploring and colonizing the Americas in the early 1500s. The center of the Portuguese empire would be South America's largest colony, Brazil.

Dividing the Globe in Half In the 1400s, Portugal began establishing fortresses along the African coast and claiming African lands for the Portuguese crown. Spain feared that Portugal would soon compete for land and riches in the Americas.

In 1493, Spain's monarchs appealed to the Spanish-born pope to support their claim for lands in the new world. The pope set a **Line of Demarcation**, dividing the non-European world into two zones. Spain had claims to all land to the west of the line.

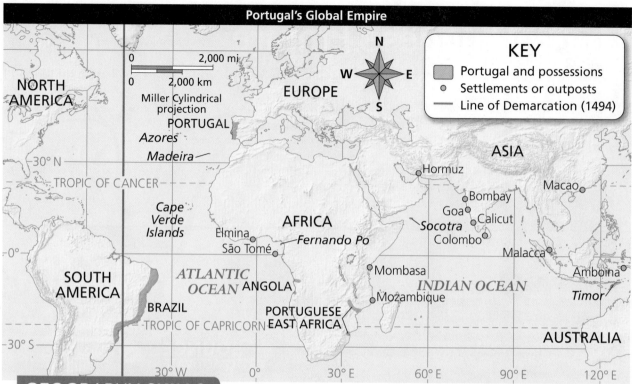

Portugal's Global Empire

KEY
- Portugal and possessions
- Settlements or outposts
- Line of Demarcation (1494)

NORTH AMERICA
EUROPE
ASIA
PORTUGAL
Azores
Madeira
30° N
TROPIC OF CANCER
Cape Verde Islands
AFRICA
Elmina
São Tomé
Fernando Po
Hormuz
Bombay
Macao
Goa
Calicut
Socotra
Colombo
Malacca
Amboina
Mombasa
INDIAN OCEAN
Timor
SOUTH AMERICA
ATLANTIC OCEAN
ANGOLA
Mozambique
BRAZIL
TROPIC OF CAPRICORN
PORTUGUESE EAST AFRICA
AUSTRALIA
30° S
0
2,000 mi
0
2,000 km
Miller Cylindrical projection
30° W
0°
30° E
60° E
90° E
120° E

GEOGRAPHY **SKILLS**

The Line of Demarcation divided the world, as it was known in 1494, into Spanish and Portuguese areas of influence.

1. **Location** What part of the Western Hemisphere was mistakenly assigned to Portugal?

2. **Understand Effects** How do you think countries such as England and France felt about the Treaty of Tordesillas?

Portugal had the same rights to the east of the line. In 1494, the **Treaty of Tordesillas** (tawr day SEE yahs) established specific terms about the Line of Demarcation. Since neither the Spanish nor the Portuguese had yet reached South America, neither knew that part of the continent lay east of the Line of Demarcation. In 1500, Portuguese navigator Pedro Álvares Cabral sighted the coast of South America and immediately claimed it for Portugal. This land, soon named Brazil, became vital to Portuguese colonization.

The Settlement of Brazil Unlike the Spanish Americas, Brazil offered no instant wealth from silver or gold. Early settlers did discover an important export—the **brazilwood** tree. The Portuguese named the colony after this tree whose wood produced a valuable reddish-purple dye.

The pace of settlement was slow until the French began to trespass on Portuguese claims in South America. The Portuguese king responded by dividing Brazil into 15 parcels of land. This land was given to favored Portuguese nobles called captains. They agreed to develop the land and share the profits with the crown. Landowners sent settlers to build towns, plantations, and churches in the new territory.

Settlers soon established sugar cane plantations and began raising cattle. About four million enslaved Africans were eventually sent to Brazil to work on the large plantations. A new culture began to emerge, one that blended European, Native American, and African influences.

Politics and Wealth For most of the colonial period, Brazil was ruled by a series of royal governors. During the 1500s and 1600s, the French and the Dutch attempted to gain a foothold in Brazil, but they were defeated.

Portugal wanted to secure the wealth of Brazil without interference. It aimed to challenge Spain's position as the most powerful country in Europe. The discovery of gold and diamonds in Brazil financed further colonial expansion.

How Did Portuguese Colonization Affect Native Americans?

The initial encounter between the Portuguese and the Native Americans of Brazil, the Tupi, was similar to what happened when the Spanish arrived in Mexico and Central America. The Tupi had little immunity to European diseases, and illness and death were widespread.

Like the Spanish, the Portuguese aimed to convert native people to Christianity. Jesuit missionaries traveled to Brazil and set up villages with schools, housing, and churches. The Jesuits learned the Tupi language so they could communicate. Some, like António Vieira, worked tirelessly to protect both Native Americans and African slaves from brutal treatment.

The Jesuits came into conflict with the Portuguese colonists who believed that all Native Americans should be available to work on the plantations. The Jesuits sought to protect Native Americans by encouraging them to live on the missions. Those who remained outside the missions were usually slave laborers on rural estates. Over time, the colonists became resentful of what they saw as Jesuit control of a valuable labor source. The Portuguese king supported the Jesuits,

Analyze Images Over the last 500 years, Brazil has experienced numerous economic booms. **Infer** How do you think the different booms affected Brazil's European population?

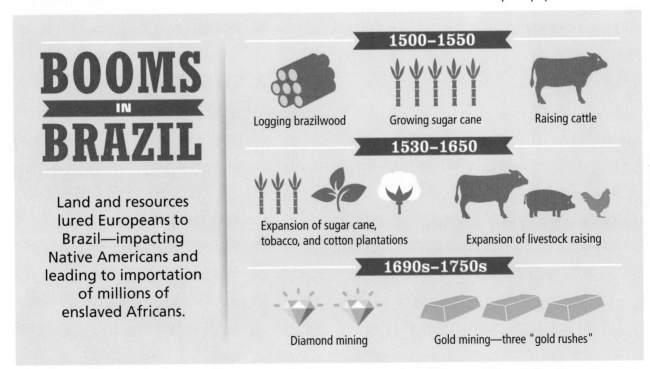

BOOMS IN BRAZIL

Land and resources lured Europeans to Brazil—impacting Native Americans and leading to importation of millions of enslaved Africans.

1500–1550
Logging brazilwood   Growing sugar cane   Raising cattle

1530–1650
Expansion of sugar cane, tobacco, and cotton plantations   Expansion of livestock raising

1690s–1750s
Diamond mining   Gold mining—three "gold rushes"

INTERACTIVE

Brazil: Portuguese Exploration and Colonization

but the colonists still needed workers. They filled the shortage by importing more African slaves. Eventually, as many as 41 percent of the African slaves imported to the Americas came to Brazil.

The Jesuits contributed in other ways as well. They elevated the moral level of colonial society, making the frontier safer for women and children. Unfortunately, as elsewhere in the Americas, they also enslaved Africans and spread deadly European diseases to the native people.

☑ READING CHECK Identify Cause and Effect Why did Portugal want to keep other countries out of Brazil?

Portugal's Trade Empire in Asia

By the 1500s, Portugal was a small but powerful nation. In addition to a string of fortified trading cities along the coast of Africa and growing colonies in the Americas, Portugal had developed a thriving sea trade with Asia.

Da Gama Reaches India One of Portugal's most celebrated seafarers was actually a sailor with almost no experience. In 1497, Vasco da Gama, the son of a Portuguese nobleman, led the first European expedition to India. The king sent him to break the strong Muslim control of Indian trade routes.

On the way to India, da Gama proved that he was **ruthless** and cunning. In Mozambique, he and his crew pretended to be Muslims in order to gain the trust of the local sultan, or ruler. Some historical accounts claim that da Gama's crew then looted some Arab and Indian ships along the African coast.

Academic Vocabulary

ruthless • *adj.,* having no pity, cruel

Analyze Images Vasco da Gama meets with the ruler of the Indian state of Calicut in 1498. **Identify Main Ideas** Why did the Portuguese want to reach India?

Trade Among Europe, Africa, and Asia

KEY

Ports controlled by:
- ○ England
- ● France
- ○ Netherlands
- ○ Portugal
- ○ Spain
- — Trade routes

On May 20, 1498, da Gama's ships arrived at Calicut, India. Located on India's southwestern coast, Calicut had long been a major center of the Indian Ocean trading network. It was one of many southern and southeast Asian sites of encounter—places where people from different cultures exchanged goods, technologies, and ideas. Ships from many states came to Calicut, including the Ming fleets commanded by Admiral Zheng He. Merchants from different cultures met together peacefully to trade spices and goods profitably. Sailing with favorable monsoon winds, trading ships brought Chinese, Hindu, Buddhist, and Muslim cultural and religious ideas along with their trade goods.

Portugal Joins the Spice Trade Da Gama's voyage to India brought Portugal into the **lucrative** spice trade. The **spice trade** brought seasonings such as cinnamon, cardamom, cloves, ginger, and pepper by sea and land from Africa and Asia to European markets.

Da Gama returned to India in 1502. At Goa, some accounts say that da Gama seized an Arab ship loaded with cargo and passengers. He took the ship's cargo, locked up its passengers as hostages, and set the ship on fire. In 1524, he returned to India as the king's viceroy.

Another nobleman who furthered Portugal's ambitions was Afonso de Albuquerque (ah FAHN so day AL bur kur kee). A man of great military experience, Albuquerque ousted Goa's Muslim rulers to secure the city as a Portuguese trading center. Albuquerque then conquered Malacca in 1511 and the Persian trading center of Hormuz in 1515. With armed

GEOGRAPHY **SKILLS**

Merchants and traders soon followed European explorers to Africa and Asia.

1. **Movement** What was the farthest east traders reached? Which country's merchants reached this location?

2. **Draw Conclusions** Why do you think the Portuguese established so many outposts on the southeastern coast of Africa?

Academic Vocabulary
lucrative • *adj.,* profitable

Quest CONNECTIONS

Portugal's colonies faced many enemies and other obstacles. What enemies and obstacles might people of Earth face in colonizing other planets? Record your findings in your Active Journal.

Analyze Images
The Dutch East India Company, which operated this shipyard in what is now Indonesia, was the world's first multinational corporation. **Classify and Categorize** For what activities do you think the Dutch used this outpost?

trading posts in India, Persia, and Southeast Asia, Portugal became an important spice trader.

☑ **READING CHECK Draw Conclusions** Why did Portugal want armed fortresses along its trading routes?

How Did the Portuguese Empire Decline?

By the early 1600s, Portugal had secured a global empire. It also had many enemies. Intense competition from the Netherlands and other European nations began to weaken Portugal's hold on its Asian trading empire.

The Dutch took advantage of the great distance that separated Portuguese trading posts in India and the Far East from the home country. This distance meant that Portuguese control would be weaker. Dutch attacks resulted in the loss of much Asian territory for the Portuguese.

Like Spain, Portugal attempted to maintain strict control over colonial trade. As a result, illegal smuggling was frequent in the colonies. In the Caribbean and elsewhere, Dutch, French, and English pirates preyed on royal cargo ships coming from the Americas. Some pirates, called **privateers**, even operated with the approval of European governments. Piracy proved to be quite troublesome to both Spain and Portugal. These empires lost much treasure—gold, silver, and spices—when their ships were captured.

The Dutch eventually eroded other Portuguese strongholds in Persia and Southeast Asia. The English became the dominant power in India. In places such as Macao in China, Portugal had a thriving trade relationship, but it never succeeded in dominating the Chinese authorities. Until the nineteenth century, Europeans were unable to conquer China, India, Africa, and most of Asia. The major Afroeurasian centers—China, India, and the Islamic World—remained too powerful for Europeans to take over.

Portugal also suffered setbacks following the 1755 earthquake, one of the early modern world's worst natural disasters. The quake destroyed the capital of Lisbon, killing about 90,000 people. Tsunamis and fires followed. Tremors were felt as far away as Finland and Barbados. Portugal's empire had indeed reached around the world, but it did not endure.

☑ READING CHECK Identify Cause and Effect Why would the governments of England, France, and the Netherlands give their approval to the actions of privateers?

Analyze Images An earthquake and a tsunami destroyed much of Lisbon, Portugal, in 1755. **Understand Effects** Based on this picture and your reading, how do you think this earthquake affected the Portuguese?

☑ Lesson Check

Practice Vocabulary

1. How did **brazilwood** and the spice trade affect Portugal's economy?

2. How were the **Line of Demarcation** and the **Treaty of Tordesillas** related?

3. Who were **privateers**?

Critical Thinking and Writing

4. **Solve Problems** Did the Treaty of Tordesillas fix the problem it was intended to solve? Explain.

5. **Summarize** How would you describe the actions that enabled Portugal to become an important spice trader?

6. **Classify and Categorize** Which of Portugal's colonies depended on plantation agriculture as well as trade?

7. **Writing Workshop: Use Credible Sources** Consider what are credible sources on the impact of global convergence. Write a list of these sources and the evidence they provide in your ▤ Active Journal.

Impact of Global Trade

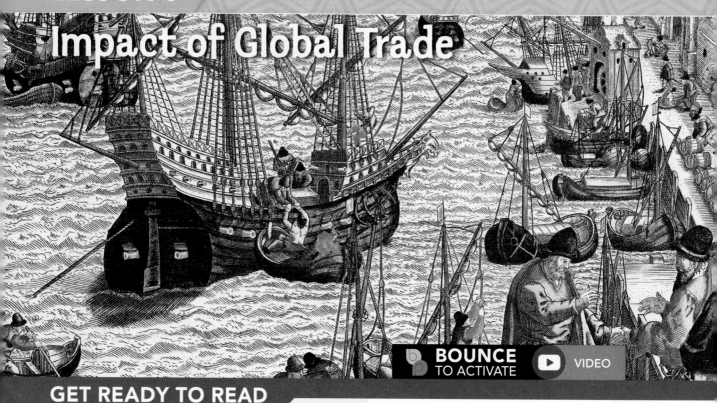

BOUNCE TO ACTIVATE ▶ VIDEO

GET READY TO READ

START UP

Look at the illustration of ships preparing to leave Lisbon, Portugal, bound for Asia and the Americas. What might these ships be carrying? What will they bring back to Portugal?

GUIDING QUESTIONS

- How did exploration affect the environment, trade and global interconnection?
- What economic changes led to the development of mercantilism and capitalism?
- What role did Asia play in global trade?

TAKE NOTES

Literacy Skills: Summarize

Use the graphic organizer in your 📖 Active Journal to take notes as you read the lesson.

PRACTICE VOCABULARY

Use the vocabulary activity in your 📖 Active Journal to practice the vocabulary words.

Vocabulary		Academic Vocabulary
Columbian Exchange	inflation	staple
mercantilism	cottage industry	enormous
capitalism	traditional economy	incentive
	market economy	

The voyages of exploration linked the hemispheres. By the mid-1500s, the Atlantic Ocean had become a busy sea highway, populated with ships bearing explorers and settlers. It was also part of the global exchange network.

What Was the Columbian Exchange?

Columbus's voyages linked the Americas to the rest of the world. People, plants, animals, diseases, and ideas from the Eastern Hemisphere, or the continents east of the Atlantic Ocean, changed the Americas. Plants, animals, and diseases from the Western Hemisphere, or the Americas, transformed the Eastern Hemisphere. The exchange of people, other living things, and ideas between the Eastern and Western hemispheres is called the **Columbian Exchange.** The Columbian Exchange primarily took place across the Atlantic Ocean between the Americas, Europe, and Africa. However, exchanges also took place across the Pacific Ocean in Asia.

Settlers Cross the Oceans Soon after the first wave of European settlers came enslaved Africans. These first migrations, or movements of people, were like waves on the ocean. A larger migration in the 1800s was more like a flood. More than 50 million people from all across Europe eventually settled in the Americas. People from Asia came to the Americas by the thousands, too, starting in the 1800s. The Americas continue to attract immigrants today. As a result, North America and South America have extremely diverse societies.

Important New Crops and Foods Plants from the Americas altered worldwide eating habits and helped increase global population. One of the most important of these plants was maize, or corn. Corn harvests led to a population explosion in Africa and Asia. Peanuts became a **staple** crop in Africa, adding protein to soups or being pressed to make cooking oil. Other important food crops were potatoes, manioc, beans, and tomatoes. Other major transplanted American crops included corn, potatoes, and sweet potatoes in China and chili pepper in Southeast Asia.

Plants from the Eastern Hemisphere also changed life in the Americas. Once introduced in the Caribbean and Brazil, sugar cane, the plant that makes sugar, became a major profit source. As the raising of livestock increased, ranchers in the Americas depended on grains such as barley and oats. The Western Hemisphere was also transformed by new crops like rye, rice, grapes, bananas, and coffee.

Exchanges of Animals and People On his second voyage, Columbus introduced horses, cows, pigs, goats, and chickens to the Americas. Horses and cows thrived on the pampas, or grassy plains, of South America. They also adapted to the scrublands of northern Mexico and the Great Plains of North America.

Academic Vocabulary

staple • *adj.,* used or needed regularly

Analyze Charts The Columbian Exchange affected people around the world. **Use Visual Information** What livestock were introduced to the Americas by the Columbian Exchange?

THE COLUMBIAN EXCHANGE

Famines and starvation were common events in Europe during the Middle Ages. Famine affected native peoples of the Americas as well. As a result of the Columbian Exchange, newly arrived species made the food supply more abundant and diverse on both sides of the ocean.

— CORN OR MAIZE —
Previously unknown, corn became a dietary staple in Mediterranean, African, and Asian countries.

— WHEAT AND RICE —
Brought by Spaniards, wheat and rice grew well in the Americas. Rice was sometimes used as a substitute for corn.

— FROM THE AMERICAS TO EUROPE, AFRICA, AND ASIA —
- maize
- potatoes
- sweet potatoes
- beans
- peanuts
- squash
- pumpkins
- peppers
- pineapples
- tomatoes
- cocoa

— FROM EUROPE, AFRICA, AND ASIA TO THE AMERICAS —
- wheat
- sugar
- bananas
- rice
- grapes
- olive oil
- dandelions
- horses
- pigs
- cows
- goats
- chickens

— SUGAR —
Europeans brought both sugar cane and enslaved Africans to grow it to the Americas.

— COWS AND PIGS —
Cows and pigs were unknown in the Americas before Europeans brought them. Over time, Native Americans added beef and pork to their diets.

Analyze Images Native Americans meet English settlers at Massachusetts Bay Colony. **Identify Main Ideas** How does this picture illustrate part of the Columbian Exchange?

The horse became a central part of Native American cultures. Many native groups from the North American Great Plains stopped farming and began hunting buffalo from horseback. They also began to use horses and European guns in warfare.

The first cowboys in the New World were South American gauchos and North American vaqueros. They started livestock practices still used in the Americas. The words *rodeo, lariat, buckaroo,* and *bronco* are all Spanish ranching words.

Diseases and Other Exchanges Some exchanges happened by accident. As you have read, European diseases had a deadly effect on the people of the Americas. Sailors returning from tropical regions in the New World also brought back new diseases to Europe.

The Columbian Exchange also led to shared technologies. Before the arrival of the Spanish, civilizations in the Americas did not have the wheel, iron tools, firearms, or large work animals like horses or oxen.

Yet the Spanish admired the stone buildings the Aztec and the Inca built without metal tools. Incan buildings could even withstand earthquakes due to advanced stone-carving methods.

✅ **READING CHECK** **Identify Main Ideas** Identify two exchanges that had a great impact on the Americas.

What Was Mercantilism?

Changes in global trade led to a new economic system known as mercantilism. **Mercantilism** is an economic policy that promotes strengthening a nation by expanding its trade. The goal is to bring wealth into the country and make it powerful.

Trade and Wealth Mercantilists believed that the main goal of trade is to make a nation more powerful. Traders pursued this goal by selling goods in exchange for gold and silver. Money made from trading these precious metals paid for a powerful army and navy.

Mercantilists supported policies to increase a nation's wealth by regulating trade and boosting production. One English merchant explained:

Primary Source

We must ever observe this rule: to sell more . . . yearly than we consume . . . in value.

—Thomas Mun, *England's Treasure by Foreign Trade*

Impact of Mercantilism Most European nations practiced mercantilism by the 1600s and the 1700s. They taxed imports to keep foreign goods out and to increase the market for domestic goods.

They also founded colonies. Colonies provided the raw materials that the home country made into products to sell to other countries. Colonies bought the home country's goods, but were not allowed to trade with other nations. In this way, the home country kept profits circulating within its own economy.

By buying and selling with other nations, mercantilist nations ensured that they would have access to growing markets and increasing revenue. When traders sold goods, buyers in other nations paid with gold and silver. This payment made the sellers' country richer and the buyers' country poorer—unless, they, too, did business in a mercantilist manner.

☑ READING CHECK **Draw Conclusions** Would mercantilism increase or decrease competition among nations? Explain.

A Commercial Revolution in Europe

Expanded trade, an increased money supply, and overseas empire-building spurred the growth of capitalism. **Capitalism** is an economic system in which business is privately owned and operated for profit. Capitalism is also called the free market or free enterprise system.

What Was the Price Revolution? A free market is one in which sellers compete to supply goods to buyers who demand them. The interplay of supply and demand determines prices. In the 1500s, prices for food and other goods went up. At the same time, there was a sharp increase in the amount of money in circulation. A rise in prices and an increase in available cash leads to a situation called **inflation.** This historical

INTERACTIVE

Trade Among Europe, Africa, and Asia

Analyze Diagrams The diagram shows some of the important characteristics of capitalism. **Use Visual Information** Where does the term *capitalism* come from?

KEY FEATURES OF CAPITALISM

Private Ownership	Supply and Demand	Responsive Prices
• People take the risk to buy businesses and farms. They hope to earn profits. • Business owners decide what to make and how to make it. • Investors invest money—called *capital*—with businesses hoping for a share of the profits.	**Supply** • *Supply* is how much of a product businesses will make at a certain price. • Supply can be affected by scarcity of resources needed to make the product. **Demand** • *Demand* is how much of a product consumers will buy at a certain price. • Demand can be affected by how necessary or how popular a product is.	• If demand is much greater than supply, prices rise. • If supply is much greater than demand, prices fall. • Changes in price, in turn, affect supply and demand. Prices tend to settle when supply and demand are in balance.

Analyze Images These Irish women are boiling flax and spinning yarn to make linen cloth. Enterprising capitalists employed peasant cottagers like these in the "putting-out" system. **Infer** Why might rural workers like these women have liked the "putting-out" system?

Academic Vocabulary

enormous • *adj.*, very large

period of runaway inflation in Europe is known as the price revolution.

There were two causes of this price revolution. One was rapid population growth. More people led to a demand for more food. However, farmers could not supply enough to keep up with the demand. As a result, food prices increased. For example, food was four to six times more expensive in England in 1640 than in 1500.

The second cause was the **enormous** flow of gold and silver from the Americas into Europe. These precious metals added to the money supply in Europe. People had more money, but there were fewer things, such as food, to buy. This worked to drive up prices.

Higher prices meant greater profits for landowners and merchants. They used the profits to invest in their businesses. Using capital, or money, to increase profits is a key part of capitalism.

Land, Crops, and Prices Under Capitalism Another aspect of capitalism is the private ownership of land. In a capitalist economy, individuals rather than the government own the land and tools needed to grow crops. Individuals thus benefit not only from their crops and profitable harvests, but they may also buy and sell land for gain.

Under capitalism, farmers benefit by working for landowners and making wages that enable them to buy goods such as food and clothing. Some farmers saved money, purchased land, and became landowners themselves.

The price revolution benefited landowners the most. Higher prices for crops meant higher profits. Because excess harvests from larger farms could bring in more profits, some landowners in Holland and England forced peasants off their land. They could then use all of these lands to raise sheep for the profitable wool trade.

These economic changes ended what remained of the feudal system in the Netherlands and in England. Peasants no longer farmed the lord's land in exchange for part of the crop. Many moved to cities to find new ways to make a living.

Goods and Profits The price revolution also drove up prices for widely used goods, such as cloth. Like landowners, cloth merchants wanted to produce more and make larger profits.

In England, cloth merchants devised a clever system for making and selling cloth. They bought raw wool from sheep farmers at the cheapest prices they could find and took it to nearby villages. There, they paid families to spin and then weave the wool into cloth. When the cloth was ready, the merchants picked it up and took it to another location to be finished and dyed. Merchants then sold this cloth wherever prices were the highest. In this way, they produced cloth as cheaply as possible and then sold it for the greatest profit.

The people who wove this cloth worked in their own homes, called cottages, in a system known as **cottage industry**. They used their own equipment, and they often worked long hours.

For the first time, capital and labor became separated. This idea would be greatly expanded later in the huge capitalist-owned factories of the Industrial Revolution in the 1800s.

Gradually, capitalists also invested money in other developing industries. In England, they operated coal mines, ironworks, breweries, and shipyards. Dutch capitalists founded printing, diamond cutting, sugar-refining, and even chocolate industries.

How Does a Market Economy Work? Over time, these changes in industry and agriculture transformed the English and Dutch economies. The Netherlands and England were the first European nations to move away from a traditional economy. A **traditional economy** is an economy in which the exchange of goods is based on custom or tradition. These practices are usually handed down from generation to generation without much change.

By contrast, a **market economy** is one in which prices and the distribution of goods are based on competition in a market. In a market economy, prices are not fixed by guilds, by the government, or by custom. Instead, forces of supply and demand set prices. A market economy requires private property ownership, a free market, and profit-making **incentives**.

The Middle Class Grows In Europe's growing cities, merchants and skilled workers became prosperous. This group became known as the middle class and included merchants, traders, and artisans. In contrast, hired laborers and servants in upper- and middle-class households often lived in poor, crowded conditions. These economic changes took generations, even centuries, to reach all levels of European society. This was because so many people lived in rural areas.

✓READING CHECK **Classify and Categorize** If a blacksmith trades horseshoes for a side of beef, is that an example of a traditional economy or a market economy?

Academic Vocabulary

incentive • *n.*, something that leads to action

Analyze Images New economic ideas led to the growth of a prosperous middle class. **Use Visual Information** What signs of prosperity can you see in the painting of the Dutch family?

Asia Leads the World

Europe's economy was growing rapidly. Still, through much of this period, Asia continued to lead the world in agriculture and manufacturing. During China's Ming dynasty (1368–1644), the Hongwu Emperor acted to stimulate agricultural production. The state repaired or extended agricultural canals, roads, and bridges, and steeply cut taxes. Ming farmers introduced important innovations, including water-powered plows and crop rotation. Vast agricultural plantations were established, producing corn and other new crops from the Columbian Exchange. The resulting huge agricultural surplus became the foundation of a market economy. The Ming population boomed to an estimated 160 to 200 million.

Chinese products, especially silk and porcelain, were in extremely high demand in Europe. Europeans attempted to trade with their European goods, but China practiced a form of mercantilism. The Chinese required European merchants to pay for trade goods in gold or silver. A large part of the silver mined in the New World went to China to pay for Chinese products shipped to Europe. Chinese merchants made great fortunes. An estimated 300 million taels—about $190 billion in today's money—flowed to the Ming dynasty.

READING CHECK Compare and Contrast How was China's trade policy similar to mercantilism?

Analyze Images Chinese porcelain was much desired by both European and African elites. **Summarize** What did Europeans trade to the Chinese for luxury goods like this vase?

☑ Lesson Check

Pratice Vocabulary

1. Define each of the following key terms in a complete sentence: **Columbian Exchange, mercantilism, capitalism, cottage industry, traditional economy, market economy.**

Critical Thinking and Writing

2. **Analyze Cause and Effect** How did the Columbian Exchange alter the way Native Americans of the Great Plains lived?

3. **Draw Conclusions** In a mercantilist system, would all nations be able to prosper? Explain.

4. **Synthesize** Who benefited more from mercantilism, European nations or their colonies? Explain. How did the rise in land prices cause benefits for some people and losses for others?

5. **Writing Workshop: Clarify Relationships with Transition Words** Write several sentences in your 📓 Active Journal that offer supporting evidence for your claim about the impact of global convergence. Add or adjust transition words to clarify the connections between the evidence and your claim.

Interpret Economic Performance

Follow these steps to learn how to interpret economic performance.

INTERACTIVE

Analyze Data and Models

1 **Identify the type of economic information being presented.** Economists often refer to different statistics or theories to explain economic performance. For example, they use a graph showing the rate of unemployment, tables about the standard of living, or statements about levels of income inequality.

   a. In this passage, what kind of economic information is presented?

   b. Could any of the information be presented in a chart, graph, or diagram?

2 **Summarize the main points of your source.** Try to identify the key economic points that the source is presenting. If there are graphs or tables, you can often find key information there.

   a. In discussions like the one below, pay close attention to the first and last sentences of the paragraphs.

   b. What do you consider the key points in this passage?

3 **Interpret the information presented in your source.** Using your source, formulate a conclusion about the economic information presented.

   a. Is the author noting positive or negative economic performance?

   b. In this passage, what conclusions can you draw about the theory of mercantilism?

Secondary Source

Mercantilism

Mercantilism was a popular economic theory in Europe in the 1600s. The theory holds that the economic success of a country depends on the amount of gold the country has. A country can get more gold by exporting more goods to other countries than it imports. So, the theory goes, a country should take steps that encourage exports, such as giving all kinds of support to chosen producers. In addition, mercantilism held, a country should act to discourage imports—for example, by charging high tariffs on imported goods.

Mercantilists believed that the volume of global trade was fixed at a set level. Under this view, every transaction had a winner and a loser. Mercantilists failed to understand that trade could benefit both parties or improve conditions for everyone. They did not see that all countries would be better off if they focused on producing goods they could produce most efficiently and at the lowest cost—and traded with other countries that did the same.

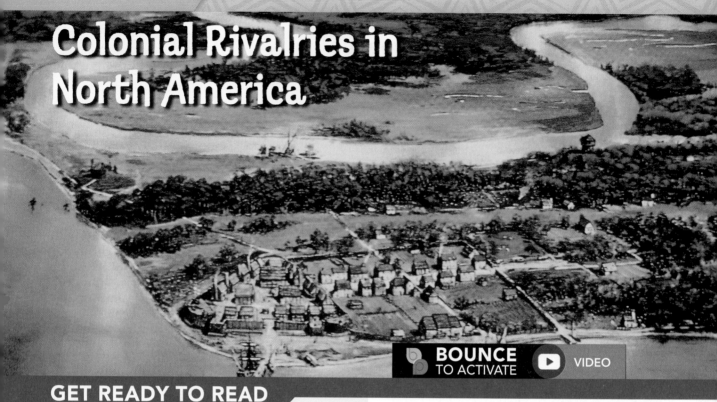

LESSON 6
Colonial Rivalries in North America

GET READY TO READ

START UP
Examine this illustration of the Jamestown colony. Write a few sentences describing the colony's most important geographic features.

GUIDING QUESTIONS
- What motivated England, France, and the Netherlands to establish colonies in North America?
- What culture did the English colonies develop?
- How did colonial rivalries in North America and Asia lead to war?

TAKE NOTES
Literacy Skills: Compare and Contrast
Use the graphic organizer in your 📙 Active Journal to take notes as you read the lesson.

PRACTICE VOCABULARY
Use the vocabulary activity in your 📙 Active Journal to practice the vocabulary words.

Vocabulary	Academic Vocabulary
northwest passage	stagnant
push-pull factor	dissenter
indentured servant	
Treaty of Paris	

The French, the Dutch, the Swedish, and the English focused on exploring and settling North America's east coast. Over time, it became clear that North America would yield neither vast treasure nor a **northwest passage**, a water route to Asia through present-day Canada. Still, North America proved to be a land of opportunity.

England's First American Colonies

In the early 1600s, the English developed two clusters of settlements along the Atlantic coast. The British Southern colonies consisted of Maryland, Virginia, the Carolinas, and Georgia. To the north were the New England colonies.

How Did Jamestown Succeed? After two failed attempts, the English finally succeeded with Jamestown, a colony established in Virginia in 1607. The area was already heavily populated by Native Americans who shared the Algonquian language. They were ruled by a powerful chief named Powhatan.

Life in the colony was difficult, and tensions grew between the colonists and their neighbors. In 1613, the English captured Powhatan's daughter, Pocahontas. As a captive, she converted to Christianity and married a colonist named John Rolfe. Rolfe later transformed the colony by introducing tobacco as a commercial crop. It was a success and drew other settlers to the colony.

The Pilgrims Arrive Another group of English settlers arrived in 1620 to found the Plymouth colony in present-day Massachusetts. These settlers were Puritans who had separated from the Church of England. Although the Church of England was Protestant, the Puritans wanted to "purify" it because they believed it kept too many ceremonies from the Catholic Church.

The first Puritans who came to North America, also known as Pilgrims, wanted to worship God in their own way as well as to govern themselves. Before they left their ship, the *Mayflower*, they made an agreement called the Mayflower Compact. They agreed to form a government and obey its laws. The idea of self-government later became a founding principle, or belief, of the United States.

As at Jamestown, the Pilgrims learned from Native Americans about crops and farming. They survived thanks to this help.

☑ READING CHECK **Compare and Contrast** Identify one similarity and one difference between the Jamestown colonists and the Pilgrims.

Other Nations Start Colonies

Other European countries also sent explorers and settlers to North America. France sent some of the earliest explorers.

What Was New France? During the 1500s, France sponsored explorers like Giovanni da Verrazano and Jacques Cartier who came to North America looking for a northwest passage. Cartier explored eastern Canada in the 1530s and 1540s, finding sources of valuable beaver fur. This area became known as New France.

Analyze Images
Frenchman Jacques Cartier explores the St. Lawrence River. **Draw Conclusions** Why would Native American guides like those shown here prove useful to European explorers?

Analyze Images Ships arrive at the Dutch colony of New Amsterdam.
Synthesize Visual Information Which building in the illustration is a hint that this is a Dutch colony?

In 1608, Samuel de Champlain founded Quebec, the first permanent European settlement in Canada. He also traded with the Native Americans for fur and animal hides. Unlike the Spanish in Mexico, the French generally did not threaten or enslave the natives. Rather, they cooperated with willing Native American trappers and fur suppliers. The French were also less of a threat because they came in smaller numbers and took little land.

New France grew slowly compared to other colonies. Immigrants were unwilling to brave the long, cold Canadian winter, and they feared attacks from the Iroquois.

Many who did come to New France were Jesuit missionaries. They made many converts among the Huron people who lived beside Lake Huron. The Jesuits' actions angered Iroquois warriors, who wrecked several Huron villages and left hundreds dead. The Jesuit missions survived only in the St. Lawrence River Valley near Montreal and Quebec.

In 1682, Robert de La Salle traveled south on the Mississippi River searching for a route to the Pacific Ocean. What he found was the Gulf of Mexico. He named the area he explored Louisiana in honor of the French king, Louis XIV.

The Settlement of New Netherland In 1609, the Dutch East India Company sent Henry Hudson to North America to find a water route to Asia. Instead, he discovered a major river in New York and named it the Hudson. A permanent settlement followed in 1624, called New Netherland.

In 1625, the Dutch built New Amsterdam at the mouth of the Hudson River to protect their fur trade routes. The city (later New York City) had the finest harbor on the Atlantic coast, and the settlement grew quickly. It became the seat of colonial government. Unlike the French or the Spanish, the Dutch made almost no effort to convert the natives to Christianity.

People of many different nationalities, classes, and religions were attracted to the new colony, including a large number of Jewish settlers, yet New Netherland failed to thrive.

Academic Vocabulary
stagnant • *adj.*, not advancing or developing

The colony's failure was the result of **push-pull factors**. Push factors motivate people to leave their homes. Pull factors attract people to move to new locations. In England, the **stagnant** economy and religious intolerance pushed groups like the Puritans to leave home. In contrast, fewer people were dissatisfied with life in the Netherlands, where the economy was booming and the standard of living high. Thus, fewer Dutch immigrants found New Netherland attractive.

The Founding of New Sweden In 1638, traders founded New Sweden in present-day Delaware. New Sweden's economy was a mix of fur trading and grain farming. Most colonists came from Sweden and Finland and were experts at pioneer farming in the forests of Scandinavia. New Sweden surrendered to Dutch control in 1655.

Impacts on Native Americans As you have read, the encounter between Europeans and Native Americans had several positive and negative aspects. Europeans had built up immunity to many diseases, but the Native Americans with whom they traded had not. Europeans introduced useful items such as new tools and crops as well as less positive ones like firearms and alcohol. A brisk fur trade benefited both Europeans and native trappers. One of the most far-reaching changes to Native American culture was the introduction of Christianity.

There were also clashes between colonists and Native Americans. The Puritans were fur traders with the Pequot. However, the Pequot grew unhappy about English intrusions on their land. In the Pequot War of 1637, the Puritans, along with native groups who were enemies of the Pequot, attacked Pequot villages and took all their land.

✓ READING CHECK **Identify Cause and Effect** Why were the Pequot angry with the English?

How the English Colonies Grew

English settlers came to North America for many reasons. Their motives were both personal and political.

Reasons for Settlement Some colonists came to North America for profit, some for greater freedom. Early colonies such as Virginia were established by British companies seeking to increase profits for shareholders. In New England, colonies were sometimes supported by British companies, but their settlers often sought religious freedom as well as prosperity.

Forms of Colonial Government In the 1600s, the English developed two types of colonial government. Royal colonies, such as Virginia, belonged to the crown and were run by royal governors. Colonies such as Maryland were proprietary colonies, in which individuals owned the land and had the authority to govern.

Some proprietors were also religious **dissenters**. George Calvert (Lord Baltimore) established Maryland as a refuge for Catholics who were

Did you know?

Historians believe Swedes and Finns in New Sweden invented our log cabin. They were skilled in building with logs in their home countries.

Analyze Images This reconstruction of the first capitol building in Williamsburg, Virginia, was finished in 1934. **Classify and Categorize** Which type of colony was Virginia?

Academic Vocabulary
dissenter • *n.,* one who refuses to follow accepted law or practices

Analyze Images Enslaved African Americans lived throughout the English colonies. **Draw Conclusions** Do you think this is a realistic picture of slavery? Why or why not?

persecuted in England. William Penn founded Pennsylvania as a haven for Quakers, a religious sect that believed in equality and religious freedom. Penn signed a treaty with the Native Americans of Delaware, agreeing to respect their land rights.

Forms of government differed within the colonies themselves. North and South Carolina, New York, Virginia, and Georgia were directly ruled by a governor and a council appointed by the British government.

Pennsylvania, Delaware, New Jersey, and Maryland were ruled by governors and legislatures. But the real power lay with the proprietor.

Massachusetts, Rhode Island, and Connecticut governed themselves under royal charters. They had governors and legislatures appointed by those who were granted the charter, or license, to govern.

How Did Colonial Economies Work? Virginia became the first economic success story in the colonies. Its rich soil proved to be perfect for crops like tobacco, sugar cane, and rice—all in demand in British and European markets.

By the 1600s, most of the settlers came from England. Of these, many were **indentured servants**, poor immigrants who paid for passage to the colonies by agreeing to work for four to seven years. They received no wages, but were supplied with basic food, clothing, and shelter.

African workers were also in demand, especially on the tobacco and rice plantations in the southern colonies of Virginia and South Carolina. At first, these workers were treated like indentured servants who later lived as freed blacks. However, by the mid-1600s, most colonies had passed laws supporting the permanent enslavement of Africans.

In the New England colonies, fishing, shipbuilding, and trade became important. Farming was difficult due to the rocky soil and cold climate.

The Middle Atlantic colonies had richer soil, plenty of water, and a gentle climate. Agriculture was successful here and, when combined with lumber, shipbuilding, and trade, led to rapid growth. In addition to tobacco and rice, the Southern colonies grew indigo and, later, cotton.

☑ **READING CHECK** **Compare and Contrast** How was William Penn different from other colonial leaders?

Rivalries Among Colonial Powers

By the 1600s, Spain, France, England, and the Netherlands all had colonies in North America. They began to fight to protect and expand their interests.

European Interests Compete Spain's vast land claims in the New World spurred competition among European powers. The extensive missions and trade network drew the attention, in particular, of England. The British sent sea captains like Sir Francis Drake to challenge these Spanish settlements.

The European powers often fought one another to control shipping routes, trade cities, and access to valuable resources, Merchant ships were armed with cannons and sometimes engaged in armed combat with other ships.

Relations between the Dutch and the English grew increasingly tense by the mid-1600s. The British and the Dutch had become violent rivals in global commerce, and this conflict spilled over into the colonies. By the late 1600s, the Middle Colonies—New York, New Jersey, Delaware, and Pennsylvania—were all completely under British control.

GEOGRAPHY SKILLS

European nations competed to acquire North American lands for their colonies.

1. **Region** Which nation gained vast western territory after the Seven Years' War?

2. **Synthesize Visual Information** Which nation was Britain's main rival in 1750? How was that rivalry different in 1763?

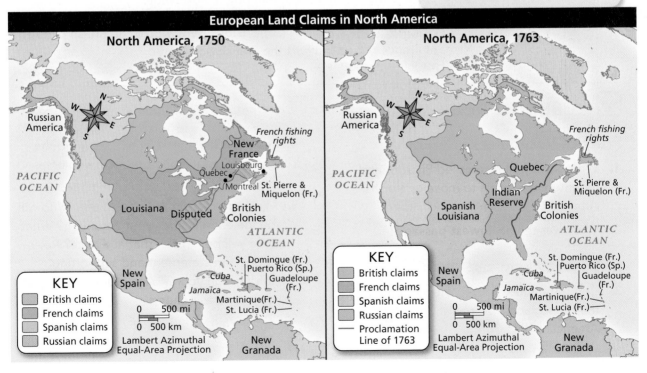

European Land Claims in North America

North America, 1750

Russian America

French fishing rights

New France

Louisbourg

Québec

Montreal · St. Pierre & Miquelon (Fr.)

PACIFIC OCEAN

Louisiana   Disputed   British Colonies

ATLANTIC OCEAN

New Spain

St. Domingue (Fr.)
Puerto Rico (Sp.)
Cuba   Guadeloupe (Fr.)
Jamaica
Martinique(Fr.)
St. Lucia (Fr.)

KEY
☐ British claims
☐ French claims
☐ Spanish claims
☐ Russian claims

0   500 mi
0   500 km

Lambert Azimuthal Equal-Area Projection

New Granada

North America, 1763

Russian America

French fishing rights

Québec

St. Pierre & Miquelon (Fr.)

PACIFIC OCEAN

Indian Reserve

Spanish Louisiana   British Colonies

ATLANTIC OCEAN

KEY
☐ British claims
☐ French claims
☐ Spanish claims
☐ Russian claims
— Proclamation Line of 1763

New Spain

St. Domingue (Fr.)
Puerto Rico (Sp.)
Cuba   Guadeloupe (Fr.)
Jamaica
Martinique(Fr.)
St. Lucia (Fr.)

0   500 mi
0   500 km

Lambert Azimuthal Equal-Area Projection

New Granada

The Seven Years' War During the 1700s, Britain clashed with France in Europe, Africa, and Asia. In North America, the British wanted a share of the fur trade as well as use of the rich fishing grounds off the coast of eastern Canada. The British became allies of the Iroquois Confederacy, a league of six Native American groups opposed to the French and their allies, the Huron.

By 1750, British colonists had reached territory claimed by the French, such as the Ohio River valley. The French built a fort in the region, angering the British governor of Virginia. He sent a young officer named George Washington to attack the fort. Washington surrendered but the conflict was not over.

The clash, known as the French and Indian War, lasted from 1754 to 1763. Eventually, the British defeated the French. This war touched off the Seven Years' War in Europe, India, and Africa.

How Did the Treaty of Paris Change North America? During the Seven Years' War, Britain blockaded France's coastline and harmed the French economy. This act of aggression also meant that France could not ship supplies and troops to its North American colonies. In June 1759, the British marched on Quebec City, the capital of New France. After a siege that lasted three months, the British took the city. By the end of the year, the British seemed to be in position to control most of North America.

Talks began in 1762 for the **Treaty of Paris**, the agreement among England, France, Spain, and Portugal that ended the Seven Years' War. The British gained all French territories east of the Mississippi River. France also gave up its lands west of the Mississippi to Spain.

The balance of power in North America changed. In addition to gaining new territory in North America, the Caribbean, and India, England became the dominant colonial power worldwide.

✓ READING CHECK **Draw Conclusions** Why would the British blockade of France's coastline hurt the French economy?

✓ Lesson Check

Practice Vocabulary

1. What **push-pull factors** led Pilgrims and indentured servants to move to North America?

2. What was the **northwest passage**?

Critical Thinking and Writing

3. **Compare and Contrast** How did the way the French and the Spanish treat Native Americans differ?

4. **Identify Cause and Effect** How did the growing population of Britain's colonies help start the French and Indian War?

5. **Writing Workshop: Shape Tone** Who will be the audience for your argument? What tone will best reach that audience? Review your claim statement and supporting evidence in your 📓 Active Journal. Adjust their tone as needed.

The Atlantic Slave Trade

BOUNCE
TO ACTIVATE

VIDEO

GET READY TO READ

START UP

Study this illustration of enslaved workers on a plantation in the Americas. Based on the illustration, write a paragraph describing the role played by enslaved labor in the colonial Americas' economy and what you think life was like for these enslaved workers.

GUIDING QUESTIONS

- How did the transatlantic slave trade begin?
- What impact did the Middle Passage have on African captives?
- How did enslaved Africans try to preserve their culture?

TAKE NOTES

Literacy Skills: Integrate Visual Information
Use the graphic organizer in your 📓 Active Journal to take notes as you read the lesson.

PRACTICE VOCABULARY

Use the vocabulary activity in your 📓 Active Journal to practice the vocabulary words.

Vocabulary		Academic Vocabulary
triangular trade	mutiny	perilous
Middle Passage	chattel	arbitrary

Enslaved Africans formed part of the trade network that arose during the 1500s.

The Long History of Slavery

There were slaves in Mesopotamia, Egypt, and China. Slavery existed in ancient Greece and Rome, in the Maya and Aztec cultures, and through much of Africa. They belonged to all ethnic groups. In the medieval Mediterranean, Christians and Muslims made slaves of captives who did not belong to their own religions. In fact, the English word 'slave' comes from 'Slav.' The Slavs were an Eastern Europe ethnic group who were sold as slaves in Muslim Spain.

In the ancient world, slaves were usually war captives, although some were enslaved as punishment and others sold themselves into slavery to get out of debt. People were not always enslaved for life and children of slaves did not always become slaves. A very different form of slavery developed in the Americas.

✅ READING CHECK **Summarize** What kinds of people became slaves in ancient civilizations?

INTERACTIVE

Triangular Trade
Routes

Origins of the Atlantic Slave Trade

The Atlantic slave trade formed one part of an international trade network known as **triangular trade**. This triangular-shaped group of Atlantic trade routes linked Europe, Africa, and the Americas. Between 1500 and 1870, about 9 million to 11 million Africans were enslaved and transported to the Americas.

A New Source of Labor As the Spanish settlements grew, land-owners and mine owners found that they did not have enough labor-ers. Native workers living on the Jesuit missions were protected from enslavement. The Spanish needed to find a new source of labor.

The practice of using slave labor was not new to upper-class people from Spain or Portugal. It was not uncommon for the wealthy in Spain and Portugal to have African slaves working on farms or in homes. So, in 1518, the year before he was crowned king, Spain's Charles V licensed the import of 4,000 African slaves to the New World. As the native population declined in the Americas, more African laborers were imported. Slave labor became vital to the economy of the New World, especially for its sugar plantations.

There was fierce competition among European slave traders, but the Portuguese had an advantage. Since the 1400s, they had set up trading posts along the West African coast. There, they bought and sold enslaved Africans destined for the New World. When the Spanish and Portuguese monarchs united in 1580, the Portuguese monopoly on the slave trade became even stronger.

How Did the Slave Trade Grow? Merchants shipped African slaves into the Americas through Spanish colonial ports

GEOGRAPHY SKILLS

During the 1500s, a series of Atlantic trade routes formed a triangle.

1. **Location** What four continents were involved in the Triangular Trade?

2. **Draw Conclusions** How did enslaved labor make the trade with Europe possible?

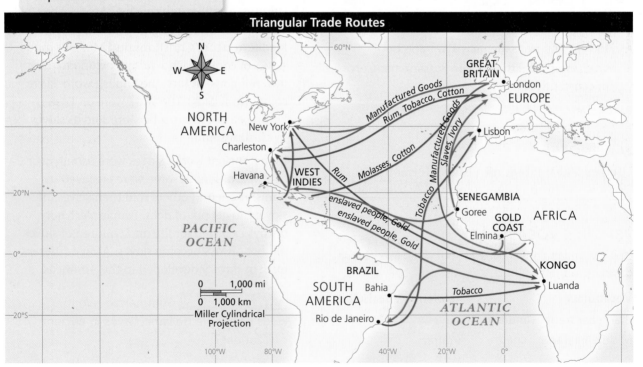

Triangular Trade Routes

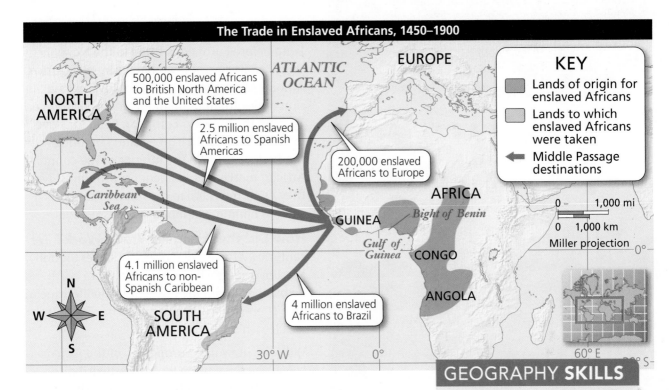

The Trade in Enslaved Africans, 1450–1900

500,000 enslaved Africans to British North America and the United States

2.5 million enslaved Africans to Spanish Americas

200,000 enslaved Africans to Europe

4.1 million enslaved Africans to non-Spanish Caribbean

4 million enslaved Africans to Brazil

ATLANTIC OCEAN

EUROPE

NORTH AMERICA

Caribbean Sea

AFRICA

GUINEA

Bight of Benin

Gulf of Guinea

CONGO

ANGOLA

SOUTH AMERICA

N W E S

30° W   0°   60° E

KEY

Lands of origin for enslaved Africans

Lands to which enslaved Africans were taken

Middle Passage destinations

0 ___ 1,000 mi
0 ___ 1,000 km
Miller projection

in Cuba, Santo Domingo, Mexico, and New Granada (now Colombia). Slaves worked on plantations and in the tin, copper, or silver mines. Some worked as servants or artisans in towns. Over time, the slave population outnumbered Europeans in cities such as Quito, Ecuador, and Santo Domingo, Dominican Republic.

The Spanish already had experience growing sugar cane on a large scale with slave labor in the Canary Islands off the coast of Africa. They brought this expertise to the plantations in the Caribbean where the climate was similar. Experts came from the Canary Islands to set up both the plots for cultivation and the equipment for processing the harvested cane. The plantations grew quickly and exported sugar became a staple of the New World economy.

In the mid-1500s, enslaved African laborers helped Brazil become a leading sugar producer. Its climate was ideal, labor was plentiful, and settlers had the support of the Portuguese crown. During the 300-year period of the slave trade, 41 percent of slaves arriving in the New World—perhaps as many as five million Africans—came to Brazil.

The British and Dutch were attracted to the profits that the Spanish and Portuguese were making by growing sugar. When they set up colonies in Barbados and Virginia, British and Dutch colonists copied their rivals' techniques to produce sugar and tobacco using slave labor.

✔ **READING CHECK** **Identify Main Ideas** What crop became most important to the New World economy? What effect did its importance have on the slave trade?

GEOGRAPHY SKILLS

The Middle Passage was the name given to the enslaved Africans' journey across the Atlantic to the Americas.

1. **Place** How did the new homes of the enslaved Africans differ from their former homes?

2. **Infer** Why do you think the slaves' journey to the Americas was called the Middle Passage?

An Atlantic Trade Network

Long before Europeans came to the New World, slavery had been big business in Africa. Among African states, owning slaves was a sign of wealth and an important labor source. To meet the growing European need for slave labor, dominant African coastal kingdoms made slave raids in the interior of the country. African merchants and leaders brought slaves they captured there to coastal trading posts such as Elmina, Ghana, or Gorée, Senegal.

How Did the Triangular Trade Work? For centuries, Africans had also sold slaves to Arab Muslim traders who transported them north across the Sahara to ports on the Mediterranean Sea. There, they were purchased by Christian and Jewish slave traders.

With the arrival of Europeans off the African coast, the slave trade took a westward direction. At this point, it became part of the triangular trade. On the first leg, merchants shipped European goods—guns, cloth, and alcohol—to Africa. In Africa, merchants traded these goods for slaves. On the second leg, known as the **Middle Passage**, the slaves were transported to the Americas. Sugar, molasses, and other colonial products were sent back for sale in Europe on the third leg of the triangular trade.

As the need for labor grew in the colonies, Europeans demanded more workers than African traders could supply. In order to meet the needs of the colonial plantations, the Europeans searched for other sources of workers. They made agreements with African slave traders who would kidnap anyone they could find to sell as slaves.

After being captured, slaves—men, women, and children—were marched to coastal forts where they were shut into cells. There, they waited to be transported to the Americas. After being purchased by merchants, several hundred captives at a time were put aboard slave ships. The men were chained together to prevent escapes. Chaining the men together also prevented **mutinies**, or revolts.

Once the ships arrived in Caribbean ports, buyers purchased slaves on board or at public auctions. There was no concern for the dignity of the enslaved Africans. Their bodies were inspected thoroughly to ensure that they were in good health. Auctioneers then sold these slaves to the highest bidder. There was little or no consideration about keeping families together.

Analyze Images Forts like this one in Ghana housed kidnapped Africans before their voyage to the Americas. **Sequence** How did the soon-to-be-enslaved Africans get to forts like this one?

Quick Activity

Analyze accounts of the Middle Passage in your Active Journal to learn what the journey must have been like for enslaved Africans.

Horrors of the Middle Passage The Middle Passage voyage might take three weeks or three months, depending on ocean winds. The journey was long and **perilous**. Ships faced threats from storms, pirate raids, or mutinies.

Academic Vocabulary
perilous • *adj.*, dangerous

Most slave ship captains had only one goal: to pack as many slaves as possible onto the ship to maximize profits. Disease was the greatest threat to the captives and to the merchants' profits. Many slaves died of dysentery, an intestinal ailment. Many contracted smallpox, cholera, or yellow fever. In the confined quarters of the slave ship—a "floating coffin"—any contagious disease quickly became a deadly epidemic. Historians find it difficult to estimate just how many Africans died on the Middle Passage. Most guess that between 1 and 2 million died on the journey.

Olaudah Equiano wrote one of the best known accounts of the Middle Passage and life under slavery. His story is one of the first slave narratives. In this passage, he relates the despair of an African captive aboard a slave ship bound for Barbados.

Primary Source

I became so sick and low that I was not able to eat. I now wished for the last friend, death, to relieve me.

—Olaudah Equiano, *The Interesting Narrative of the Life of Olaudah Equiano, or Gustavus Vassa, the African*

✓ READING CHECK **Sequence** What occurred on the first leg of the triangular trade?

What Was Life Like Under Slavery?

By treating them as property, slave owners denied Africans rights and freedom. Slavery became associated with race. Europeans slave traders and owners came to see Africans as an inferior people meant by nature to be enslaved. Even after the abolition of slavery in the 1800s, these racist ideas continued in societies that had participated in the slave trade.

A Life of Hardship Enslaved Africans in the Americas had to adjust to life in unfamiliar surroundings and harsh living conditions. They could not understand the language of their masters and were often beaten for failing to follow orders. Families that had been separated were seldom reunited. In order

Analyze Images This diagram shows how enslaved people were packed into a slave ship for transportation from Africa. **Understand Effects** How would the close quarters on the slave ship put people's lives at risk?

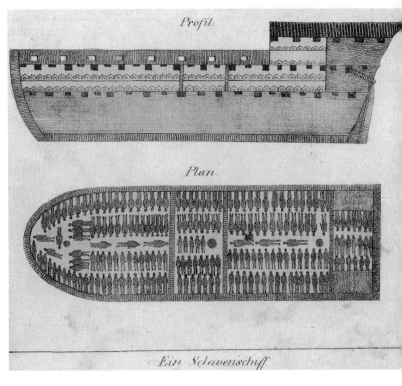

Profil.

Plan.

Ein Sclavenschiff.

to prevent uprisings, slaves were not allowed to live among their own ethnic or tribal groups.

Slaves were also given new names. Those who resisted their duties or tried to run away were beaten or branded. Work began at dawn and continued to sundown. Food was meager and housing was uncomfortable and primitive.

Some slaves worked in the homes of their owners. Those deemed trustworthy were given more responsibility. Whatever their position, slaves were considered **chattel**, or property, and subject to the **arbitrary** whims of their owners. Furthermore, their children were also considered the property of the slave owner and could be sold without regard to their parents.

Maintaining a Culture Over time, enslaved Africans found ways to gain a measure of control over some parts of their lives. Some maintained a garden for their own food or sold items at markets. They also maintained African styles of cloth weaving and basketmaking.

For later generations, family life was one way to lessen the harshness of slavery. Women played a large role in keeping families together. They kept house and told stories from their African heritage. Africans also introduced new foods and cooking methods to the Americas.

Many slaves adopted Christianity. Some combined its practices with elements of African music or dance. Africans also introduced musical instruments such as the banjo and drums.

☑ READING CHECK **Summarize** How did slave owners keep control over their slaves?

Academic Vocabulary
arbitrary • *adj.*, random or by chance

BIOGRAPHY
5 Things to Know About

QUEEN NZINGA
Queen of Ndongo and Matamba (1583–1663)

- In 1624 she inherited leadership of the kingdom of Ndongo in today's Angola.

- To survive attacks by both Portuguese and local African states, she allied with Portugal.

- Her alliance ended Portuguese slave raiding in Ndongo and helped fend off African enemies.

- Betrayed by the Portuguese, she founded a new state at Matamba, allied with the Dutch, and brilliantly led anti-Portuguese rebels.

- She made Matamba into a powerful trading state. A major street in Luanda, Angola's capital, is named after her.

Critical Thinking How did Queen Nzinga protect Ndongo and Matamba?

Slave Trading Impacts Africa

African coastal kingdoms such as Dahomey (present-day Benin) and Asante had grown wealthy capturing and selling their fellow Africans into slavery.

They soon found that trading slaves in greater numbers was more profitable and easier than mining gold. Asante leaders actively partnered with European merchants to build coastal fortresses that served as focal points for the shipping of goods and slaves. The Asante gained power by conquering smaller kingdoms along the coast and bringing their war captives to these slave trading centers. Many captives made desperate efforts to escape or overpower their captors. Revolts might take place before slave groups reached the coast or while they awaited transport in coastal fortresses.

The forced removal of millions of people to be sold as slaves had a major impact on the economies and populations of Africa. Some African slave-trading states became powerful and wealthy. Some states were destroyed by rivals. Africans also became enslaved in Africa or were killed in slaving wars. Families were torn apart and many settlements were depopulated. Because many more men were taken than women, women were left to rebuild their damaged communities.

▲ Many West Africans honor ancient customs and traditions today, such as these people in Burkina Faso.

✓READING CHECK **Identify Cause and Effect** How did slaving wars in Africa affect family and community life?

☑ Lesson Check

Practice Vocabulary

1. How was the **Middle Passage** related to the triangular trade?

2. What are **mutinies**, and why did they occur aboard slave ships?

3. Rephrase in your own words how **chattel** is used in the text.

Critical Thinking

4. **Analyze Cause and Effect** Why did some African kingdoms help Europeans capture slaves?

5. **Infer** Why do you think slave owners prevented slaves from living with people from their own ethnic group?

6. How did chattel slavery as practiced in the Americas differ from slavery as practiced in most ancient civilizations?

7. **Compare and Contrast** How did the Africans' reason for moving to the Americas differ from the Europeans' reasons?

8. **Writing Workshop: Write a Conclusion** Review your claim and evidence about the impact of global convergence. Write a strong conclusion in your 📓 Active Journal, briefly summing up your argument.

VISUAL REVIEW

The French and English in North America

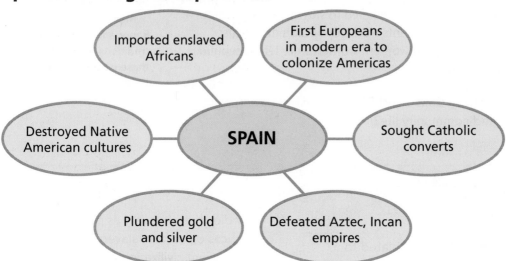

FRANCE
- Settled in the north and west
- Focused on fur trapping
- Had relatively little conflict with Native Americans
- Had relatively few settlers
- Missionaries sought conversion of Native Americans

- Fought to protect their interests
- Had Native American allies

ENGLAND
- Settled on East Coast
- Planted first colonies
- Settlers sought commercial success
- Some settlers sought religious freedom
- Many conflicts with Native Americans
- Slavery widespread in Southern colonies

Spain in the Age of Exploration

- Imported enslaved Africans
- First Europeans in modern era to colonize Americas
- Destroyed Native American cultures
- **SPAIN**
- Sought Catholic converts
- Plundered gold and silver
- Defeated Aztec, Incan empires

READING REVIEW

Use the Take Notes and Practice Vocabulary activities in your Active Journal to review topic vocabulary.

👆 **INTERACTIVE**

Practice Vocabulary

Quest FINDINGS

Hold your discussion on whether the United States should invest in colonizing other planets. Be sure to consider the question, "What are the costs and benefits of colonization?" Use the notes you made in your 📓 Active Journal.

ASSESSMENT

Vocabulary and Key Ideas

1. **Describe** Why did European nations embark on voyages of exploration?

2. **Define** Use the key term **immunity** in a sentence that explains its relationship to the era of exploration.

3. **Check Understanding** What was the **encomienda** system in the Spanish colonies?

4. **Identify Main Ideas** What was the **Columbian Exchange**?

5. **Describe** According to mercantilists, what was the main goal of trade?

6. **Describe** How was **mission** life both positive and negative for Native Americans?

7. **Check Understanding** What were the various **push-pull factors** that caused English and French settlers to move to North America?

8. **Recall** What goods were carried on the first leg of the **triangular trade**?

Critical Thinking and Writing

9. **Compare and Contrast** How was the Portuguese approach to exploration different from the Spanish approach to exploration?

10. **Draw Conclusions** Do you think the Spanish leaders treated the Incan and Aztec leaders fairly? Explain.

11. **Understand Effects** How did the price revolution demonstrate the law of supply and demand?

12. **Revisit the Essential Question** What did the people of the Americas gain or lose from their dealings with the Spanish? Is it possible to have fair trade between a group of conquerors and the people they conquered? Explain.

13. **Writer's Workshop: Write an Argument** Using your notes and research, write an argument about whether or not the impact of global convergence was mostly positive or mostly negative.

Analyze Primary Sources

14. According to Equiano's account below, why did many slaves die?
    A. They were beaten to death.
    B. They were starved to death.
    C. They were killed in mutiny attempts.
    D. They could not breathe due to overcrowding.

    "The closeness of the place, and the heat of the climate, added to the number in the ship, which was so crowded that each had scarcely room to turn himself, almost suffocated us. This produced copious perspirations, so that the air soon became unfit for respiration, from a variety of loathsome smells, and brought on a sickness among the slaves, of which many died."

    —Olaudah Equiano, *The Interesting Narrative of the Life of Olaudah Equiano, or Gustavus Vassa, the African, 1789*

Analyze Maps

15. Which letter represents the Line of Demarcation? Which two countries were involved in the treaty that created it?

16. Which letter represents the Strait of Magellan? What achievement did Magellan's crew accomplish?

17. Which letter represents the Cape of Good Hope? What did sailing by this point allow da Gama to do?

▼ **The Atlantic Region**

US: Political

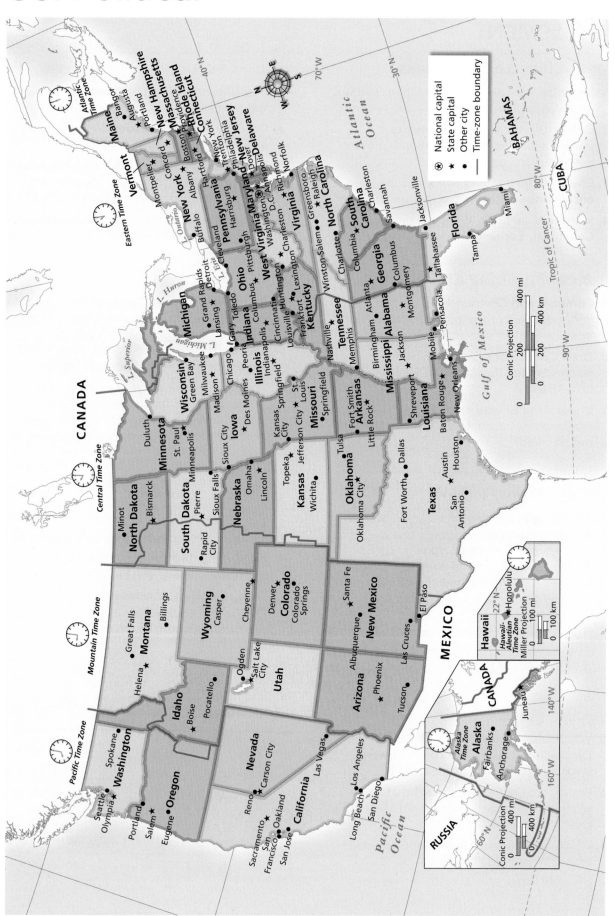

US: Physical

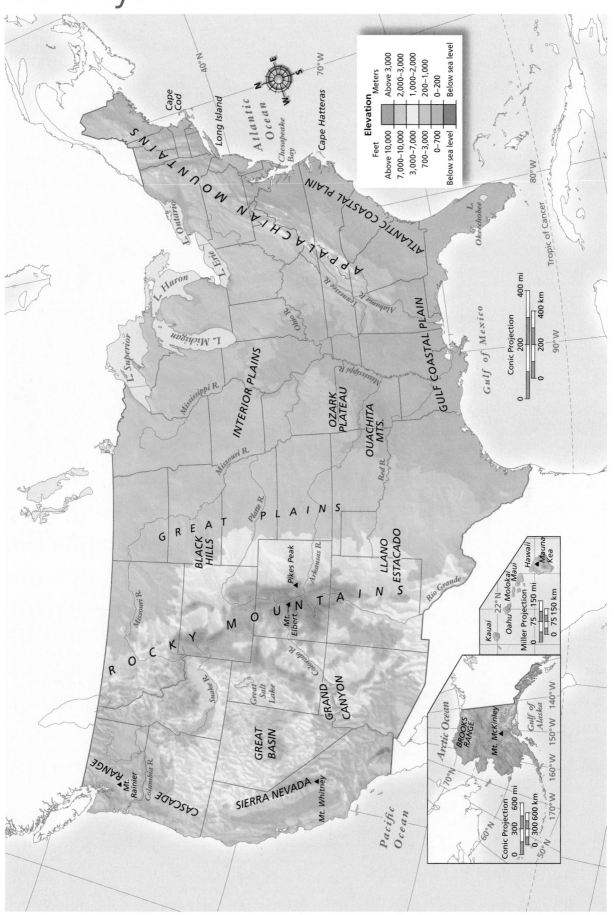

Elevation

Meters	Feet
Above 3,000	Above 10,000
2,000–3,000	7,000–10,000
1,000–2,000	3,000–7,000
200–1,000	700–3,000
0–200	0–700
Below sea level	Below sea level

Cape Cod

Long Island

Chesapeake Bay

Cape Hatteras

Atlantic Ocean

40° N

70° W

80° W

90° W

Tropic of Cancer

APPALACHIAN MOUNTAINS

ATLANTIC COASTAL PLAIN

L. Ontario

L. Erie

L. Huron

L. Michigan

L. Superior

Tennessee R.

Alabama R.

Ohio R.

Mississippi R.

INTERIOR PLAINS

Mississippi R.

Missouri R.

Platte R.

GREAT PLAINS

BLACK HILLS

OZARK PLATEAU

OUACHITA MTS.

Red R.

GULF COASTAL PLAIN

Gulf of Mexico

L. Okeechobee

400 mi

400 km

200

200

0

0

Conic Projection

Pikes Peak

Arkansas R.

Mt. Elbert

ROCKY MOUNTAINS

Colorado R.

LLANO ESTACADO

Rio Grande

Hawaii

Mauna Kea

Molokai

Maui

Oahu

Kauai

22° N

150 mi

75 150 km

75

0

0

Miller Projection

Missouri R.

Snake R.

Great Salt Lake

GREAT BASIN

GRAND CANYON

Columbia R.

CASCADE RANGE

Mt. Rainier

SIERRA NEVADA

Mt. Whitney

Pacific Ocean

Arctic Ocean

BROOKS RANGE

Mt. McKinley

Gulf of Alaska

140° W

150° W

160° W

170° W

70° N

60° N

50° N

600 mi

300 600 km

300

0

0

Conic Projection

The World: Political

Legend
- ⊛ Capital
- ● Other city

Conic Projection
0   200   400 mi
0   200   400 km

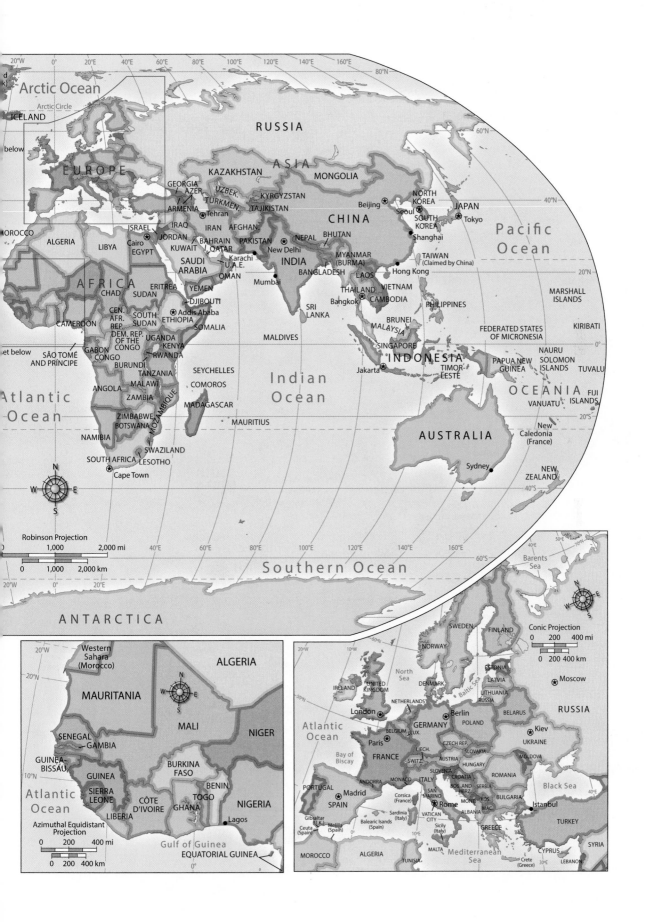

Arctic Ocean
Arctic Circle
ICELAND
below
EUROPE
MOROCCO
ALGERIA
LIBYA
AFRICA
CHAD
SUDAN
CAMEROON
CEN. AFR. REP.
SOUTH SUDAN
ERITREA
YEMEN
DJIBOUTI
DEM. REP. OF THE CONGO
UGANDA
ETHIOPIA
SOMALIA
Addis Ababa
et below
SÃO TOMÉ AND PRÍNCIPE
GABON
CONGO
RWANDA
KENYA
BURUNDI
TANZANIA
SEYCHELLES
ANGOLA
MALAWI
COMOROS
ZAMBIA
MADAGASCAR
ZIMBABWE
BOTSWANA
MOZAMBIQUE
MAURITIUS
NAMIBIA
SWAZILAND
SOUTH AFRICA
LESOTHO
Cape Town

Atlantic Ocean

RUSSIA
ASIA
KAZAKHSTAN
MONGOLIA
GEORGIA
AZER.
UZBEK.
KYRGYZSTAN
ARMENIA
TURKMEN.
TAJIKISTAN
Beijing
NORTH KOREA
Seoul
JAPAN
IRAQ
IRAN
AFGHAN.
CHINA
SOUTH KOREA
Tokyo
Tehran
JORDAN
BAHRAIN
NEPAL
BHUTAN
Shanghai
ISRAEL
Cairo
KUWAIT
PAKISTAN
New Delhi
TAIWAN
(Claimed by China)
EGYPT
QATAR
Karachi
SAUDI ARABIA
U.A.E.
INDIA
MYANMAR (BURMA)
Hong Kong
OMAN
BANGLADESH
LAOS
MARSHALL ISLANDS
Mumbai
THAILAND
VIETNAM
SRI LANKA
Bangkok
CAMBODIA
PHILIPPINES
MALDIVES
BRUNEI
FEDERATED STATES OF MICRONESIA
KIRIBATI
MALAYSIA
SINGAPORE
NAURU
SOLOMON ISLANDS
Jakarta
INDONESIA
PAPUA NEW GUINEA
TUVALU
TIMOR-LESTE
OCEANIA
FIJI
Indian Ocean
VANUATU
ISLANDS
New Caledonia (France)
AUSTRALIA
NEW ZEALAND
Sydney

Pacific Ocean

Robinson Projection
1,000   2,000 mi
0   1,000   2,000 km

Southern Ocean

ANTARCTICA

Western Sahara (Morocco)
ALGERIA
MAURITANIA
MALI
NIGER
SENEGAL
GAMBIA
GUINEA-BISSAU
BURKINA FASO
GUINEA
BENIN
SIERRA LEONE
CÔTE D'IVOIRE
TOGO
NIGERIA
LIBERIA
GHANA
Lagos
Atlantic Ocean
Gulf of Guinea
EQUATORIAL GUINEA

Azimuthal Equidistant Projection
0   200   400 mi
0   200 400 km

Barents Sea

SWEDEN
FINLAND
Conic Projection
0   200   400 mi
0   200 400 km
NORWAY
Moscow
North Sea
ESTONIA
LATVIA
IRELAND
UNITED KINGDOM
DENMARK
LITHUANIA
RUSSIA
London
NETHERLANDS
Baltic Sea
BELARUS
Berlin
RUSSIA
Atlantic Ocean
BELGIUM
GERMANY
POLAND
Kiev
LUX.
Paris
UKRAINE
Bay of Biscay
FRANCE
LIECH.
CZECH REP.
SLOVAKIA
MOLDOVA
SWITZ.
AUSTRIA
HUNGARY
SLOVENIA
ROMANIA
PORTUGAL
ANDORRA
CROATIA
SERBIA
Black Sea
MONACO
ITALY
BOS. AND HERZ.
Madrid
SAN MARINO
MONT.
BULGARIA
Istanbul
SPAIN
Rome
KOS.
Corsica (France)
VATICAN CITY
ALBANIA
MAC.
TURKEY
Gibraltar (U.K.)
Sardinia (Italy)
GREECE
Ceuta (Spain)
Melilla (Spain)
Balearic Isands (Spain)
Sicily (Italy)
CYPRUS
SYRIA
MOROCCO
ALGERIA
MALTA
LEBANON
TUNISIA
Crete (Greece)
Mediterranean Sea

Africa: Political

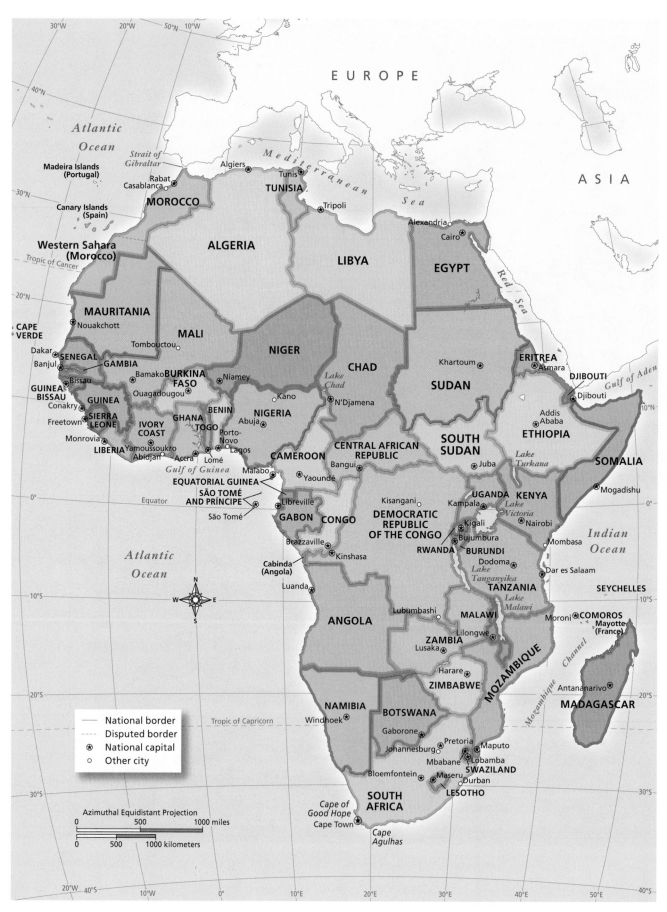

EUROPE

ASIA

Atlantic Ocean

Strait of Gibraltar

M e d i t e r r a n e a n

S e a

Algiers ⊛
Tunis ⊛

Madeira Islands
(Portugal)

Rabat
Casablanca ○
MOROCCO

TUNISIA

Tripoli ⊛

Canary Islands
(Spain)

Alexandria ○
Cairo ⊛

EGYPT

**Western Sahara
(Morocco)**

Tropic of Cancer

ALGERIA

LIBYA

Red Sea

MAURITANIA

Nouakchott ⊛

MALI

Tombouctou ○

NIGER

CHAD

Khartoum ⊛

ERITREA

Asmara ⊛

DJIBOUTI

**CAPE
VERDE**

Dakar ⊛
Banjul ⊛ **SENEGAL**
GAMBIA

Bamako ○ **BURKINA
FASO**

Niamey ⊛

SUDAN

Djibouti ⊛ *Gulf of Aden*

**GUINEA
BISSAU**

Bissau ⊛
GUINEA

Ouagadougou ⊛

Kano ○

N'Djamena ⊛

*Lake
Chad*

Addis
Ababa ⊛

ETHIOPIA

Conakry ⊛

**SIERRA
LEONE**

Freetown ⊛

GHANA
**IVORY
COAST**

BENIN
TOGO

NIGERIA

Abuja ⊛

**CENTRAL AFRICAN
REPUBLIC**

**SOUTH
SUDAN**

*Lake
Turkana*

SOMALIA

Mogadishu ⊛

Monrovia ⊛
LIBERIA

Yamoussoukro ○

Abidjan ○

Accra ⊛
Lomé ⊛

Porto-
Novo ⊛
Lagos ○

Bangui ⊛

Juba ⊛

Kisangani ○

UGANDA
Kampala ⊛

KENYA

*Lake
Victoria*

Nairobi ⊛

Equator

Gulf of Guinea

Malabo ⊛

CAMEROON

Yaoundé ⊛

EQUATORIAL GUINEA

**SÃO TOMÉ
AND PRÍNCIPE**

Libreville ⊛

São Tomé ⊛

GABON
CONGO

**DEMOCRATIC
REPUBLIC
OF THE CONGO**

Kigali ⊛
Bujumbura ⊛

RWANDA
BURUNDI

Dodoma ⊛

Mombasa ○

*Indian
Ocean*

Dar es Salaam ○

Brazzaville ⊛

Kinshasa ⊛

*Lake
Tanganyika*

TANZANIA

*Atlantic
Ocean*

Cabinda
(Angola)

Luanda ⊛

Lubumbashi ○

MALAWI

Lilongwe ⊛

*Lake
Malawi*

SEYCHELLES

Moroni ⊛ **COMOROS**
Mayotte
(France)

ANGOLA

ZAMBIA

Lusaka ⊛

Harare ⊛

MOZAMBIQUE

Antananarivo ⊛

MADAGASCAR

NAMIBIA

Tropic of Capricorn

Windhoek ⊛

BOTSWANA

ZIMBABWE

Mozambique Channel

Gaborone ⊛

Pretoria ⊛
Johannesburg ○

Maputo ⊛

Mbabane ⊛
Lobamba ⊛

SWAZILAND

Bloemfontein ⊛

Maseru ⊛
Durban ○

*Cape of
Good Hope*

**SOUTH
AFRICA**

LESOTHO

Cape Town ⊛

*Cape
Agulhas*

N
W E
S

— National border
--- Disputed border
⊛ National capital
○ Other city

Azimuthal Equidistant Projection

0   500   1000 miles

0   500   1000 kilometers

Africa: Physical

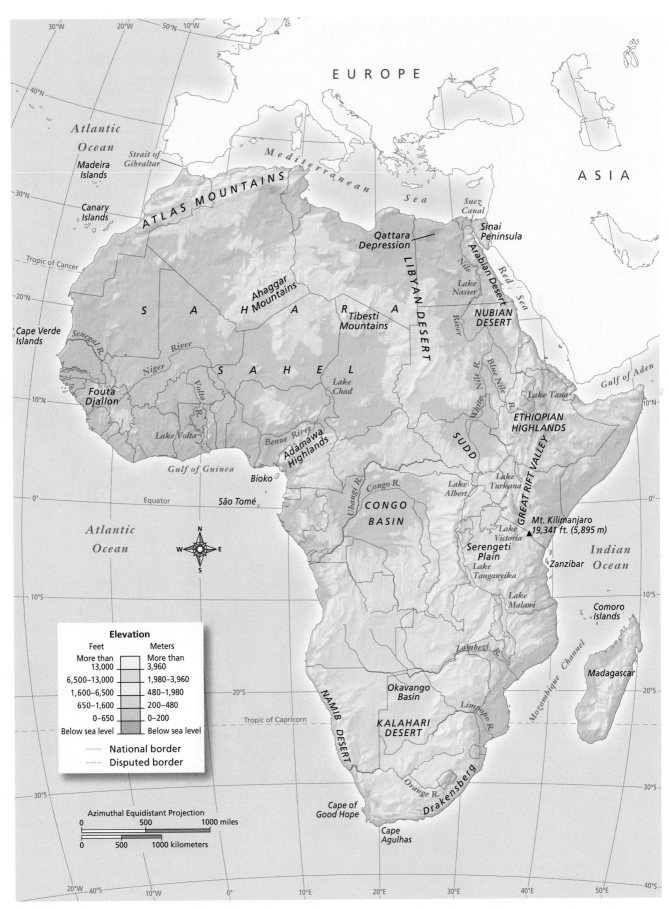

EUROPE

ASIA

Atlantic Ocean

Madeira Islands

Strait of Gibraltar

Mediterranean Sea

Suez Canal

Sinai Peninsula

Canary Islands

Tropic of Cancer

ATLAS MOUNTAINS

Qattara Depression

LIBYAN DESERT

Nile

Lake Nasser

Arabian Desert

Red Sea

Ahaggar Mountains

Tibesti Mountains

NUBIAN DESERT

Cape Verde Islands

S A H A R A

Senegal R.

River

Niger

S A H E L

Volta R.

Lake Chad

Benue River

White Nile R.

Blue Nile R.

Lake Tana

Gulf of Aden

ETHIOPIAN HIGHLANDS

10°N

Fouta Djallon

Lake Volta

Adamawa Highlands

SUDD

Gulf of Guinea

Bioko

Ubangi R.

Congo R.

Lake Albert

Lake Turkana

GREAT RIFT VALLEY

Equator

São Tomé

CONGO BASIN

Mt. Kilimanjaro 19,341 ft. (5,895 m)

Atlantic Ocean

N
W   E
S

Lake Victoria

Serengeti Plain

Lake Tanganyika

Indian Ocean

Zanzibar

Lake Malawi

Comoro Islands

Zambezi R.

Mozambique Channel

Madagascar

Elevation

Feet	Meters
More than 13,000	More than 3,960
6,500–13,000	1,980–3,960
1,600–6,500	480–1,980
650–1,600	200–480
0–650	0–200
Below sea level	Below sea level

—— National border
----- Disputed border

Okavango Basin

Limpopo R.

NAMIB DESERT

KALAHARI DESERT

Tropic of Capricorn

Azimuthal Equidistant Projection

0   500   1000 miles

0   500   1000 kilometers

Orange R.

Drakensberg

Cape of Good Hope

Cape Agulhas

Asia: Political

Asia: Physical

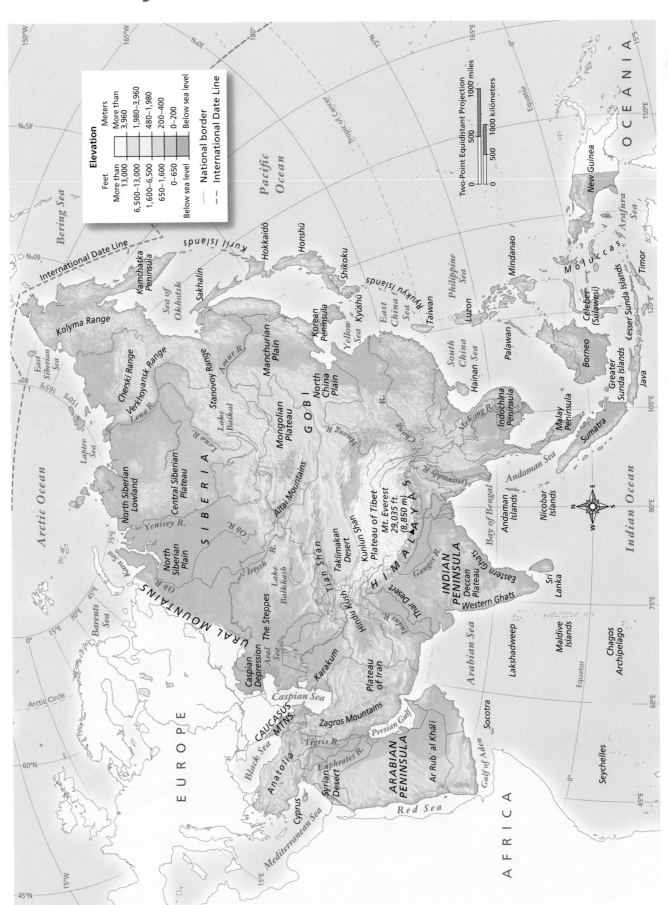

Elevation

Feet	Meters
More than 13,000	More than 3,960
6,500–13,000	1,980–3,960
1,600–6,500	480–1,980
650–1,600	200–400
0–650	0–200
Below sea level	Below sea level

—— National border
- - - International Date Line

Two-Point Equidistant Projection

1000 miles
1000 kilometers

OCEANIA

New Guinea

Moluccas

Arafura Sea

Mindanao

Celebes (Sulawesi)

Timor

Philippine Sea

Luzon

Lesser Sunda Islands

South China Sea

Palawan

Borneo

Greater Sunda Islands

Java

Hainan Sea

Taiwan

Indochina Peninsula

Malay Peninsula

Sumatra

East China Sea

Ryukyu Islands

Yellow Sea

Korean Peninsula

Kyūshū

Shikoku

Honshū

Hokkaidō

Kuril Islands

Sakhalin

Sea of Okhotsk

Kamchatka Peninsula

Pacific Ocean

Tropic of Cancer

Bering Sea

Kolyma Range

Cherski Range

Verkhoyansk Range

Stanovoy Range

Amur R.

Manchurian Plain

North China Plain

Huang R.

GOBI

Mongolian Plateau

Lake Baikal

Lena R.

SIBERIA

Central Siberian Plateau

North Siberian Lowland

East Siberian Sea

Laptev Sea

Arctic Ocean

Yenisey R.

Ob R.

North Siberian Plain

Irtysh R.

Lake Balkhash

Altai Mountains

Tian Shan

Taklimakan Desert

Kunlun Shan

Plateau of Tibet

Mt. Everest 29,035 ft. (8,850 m)

HIMALAYAS

Chang R.

Mekong R.

Irrawaddy R.

Andaman Sea

Bay of Bengal

Ganges R.

INDIAN PENINSULA

Deccan Plateau

Eastern Ghats

Western Ghats

Sri Lanka

Andaman Islands

Nicobar Islands

Indian Ocean

Thar Desert

Indus R.

Hindu Kush

Karakum

Plateau of Iran

The Steppes

Aral Sea

Caspian Depression

Caspian Sea

URAL MOUNTAINS

Kara Sea

Barents Sea

Ob R.

EUROPE

Arctic Circle

CAUCASUS MTNS.

Black Sea

Zagros Mountains

Tigris R.

Euphrates R.

Anatolia

Cyprus

Syrian Desert

Mediterranean Sea

ARABIAN PENINSULA

Ar Rub' al Khālī

Persian Gulf

Red Sea

Gulf of Aden

Socotra

Arabian Sea

Lakshadweep

Maldive Islands

Chagos Archipelago

Seychelles

Equator

AFRICA

International Date Line

Europe: Political

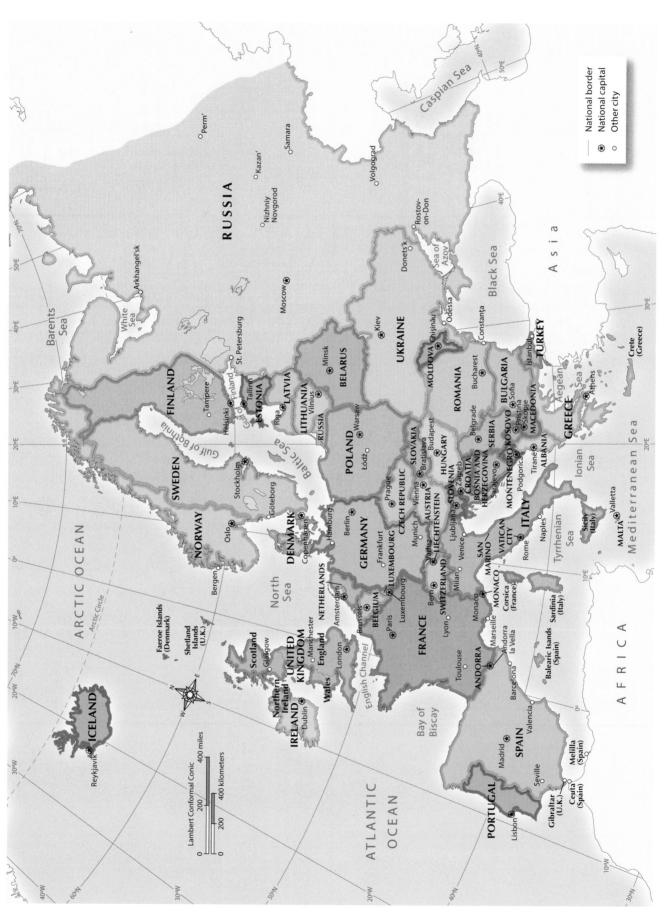

Europe: Physical

Elevation

Feet	Meters
More than 13,000	More than 3,960
6,500–13,000	1,980–3,960
1,600–6,500	480–1,980
650–1,600	200–400
0–650	0–200
Below sea level	Below sea level

—— National border

URAL MOUNTAINS

Pechora R.
Kama R.
Ural R.
Caspian Sea
40°N
50°E
Volga R.
Caspian Depression
Volga Upland
Don R.
CAUCASUS MTS.
Mt. Elbrus 18,510 ft. (5,642 m)
40°E
Sea of Azov
Black Sea
Bosporus
Sea of Marmara
Dardanelles
A s i a
30°E

N. Dvina R.
Lake Onega
Lake Ladoga
Central Russian Upland
Dnieper R.
Dniester R.
Danube R.
Aegean Sea
Crete

Barents Sea
Kola Peninsula
White Sea
N O R T H E U R O P E A N P L A I N
Carpathian Mountains
Transylvanian Alps
Balkan Mountains
BALKAN PENINSULA
Pindus Mts.

50°E
40°E
30°E
Gulf of Finland
Gulf of Bothnia
Baltic Sea
Gotland
Vistula R.
Oder R.
Great Hungarian Plain
Dinaric Alps
Adriatic Sea
Ionian Sea
Mediterranean Sea
20°E

SCANDINAVIAN PENINSULA
Kjølen Mountains
Lake Vänern
Lake Vättern
Sjælland
Elbe R.
A L P S
Apennines
ITALIAN PENINSULA
Tyrrhenian Sea
Sicily
Maltese Isands
20°E

ARCTIC OCEAN
Arctic Circle
Norwegian Sea
Jutland
North Sea
Rhine R.
Danube R.
Po R.
Lake Geneva
Mt. Blanc 15,775 ft. (4,808 m)
Corsica
Sardinia
Balearic Isands
10°E

Jan Mayen
10°W
Faeroe Islands
Shetland Islands
N E W S
Great Britain
Thames R.
English Channel
Seine R.
Loire R.
Massif Central
Garonne R.
Pyrenees
Ebro R.

Iceland
20°W
British Isles
Ireland
Bay of Biscay
Douro R.
Meseta
Tagus R.
IBERIAN PENINSULA
Guadalquivir R.
Strait of Gibraltar

ATLANTIC OCEAN

A F R I C A

Denmark Strait
40°N

Lambert Conformal Conic
0   200   400 miles
0   200   400 kilometers

North & South America: Political

ASIA

Arctic Ocean

EUROPE

Bering Strait

180°

International Date Line

Bering Sea

Beaufort Sea

Baffin Bay

Greenland (Denmark)

Arctic Circle

60°N

0°

Alaska (United States)

Nuuk

Gulf of Alaska

Great Bear Lake

Great Slave Lake

Hudson Bay

Davis Strait

Labrador Sea

45°N

45°N

CANADA

Lake Winnipeg

Vancouver

Great Lakes

Ottawa

Toronto

Atlantic Ocean

Chicago

New York
Washington, D.C.

UNITED STATES

30°N

30°N

Los Angeles

Houston

Tropic of Cancer

MEXICO

Gulf of Mexico

Nassau

Mexico City

Havana

BAHAMAS

DOMINICAN REPUBLIC

CUBA

HAITI

Puerto Rico (United States)

15°N

JAMAICA

Belmopan

BELIZE

Kingston

Port-au-Prince

Santo Domingo

U.S. Virgin Islands (United States)

Guadeloupe (France)

Guatemala City

HONDURAS

Martinique (France)

15°N

GUATEMALA

San Salvador

Tegucigalpa

NICARAGUA

Caribbean Sea

DOMINICA

BARBADOS

EL SALVADOR

Managua

Caracas

TRINIDAD AND TOBAGO

San José

Panama

GUYANA

COSTA RICA

VENEZUELA

Georgetown

Paramaribo

PANAMA

Bogotá

French Guiana (France)

Cayenne

N

W   E

S

Equator

0°

Galápagos Islands (Ecuador)

COLOMBIA

Quito

ECUADOR

SURINAME

0°

Pacific Ocean

PERU

BRAZIL

Lima

15°S

Lake Titicaca

La Paz

Brasília

15°S

BOLIVIA

Sucre

Tropic of Capricorn

PARAGUAY

Rio de Janiero

CHILE

Asunción

São Paulo

ARGENTINA

National border

International Date Line

National capital

Other city

Santiago

URUGUAY

30°S

Buenos Aires

Montevideo

30°S

Río de la Plata

Atlantic Ocean

Lambert Azimuthal Equal-Area Projection

0   1000   2000 miles

0   1000   2000 kilometers

Falkland Islands (U.K.)

45°S

45°S

165°W   150°W   135°W   120°W   105°W   90°W   75°W   60°W   45°W   30°W   15°W

North & South America: Physical

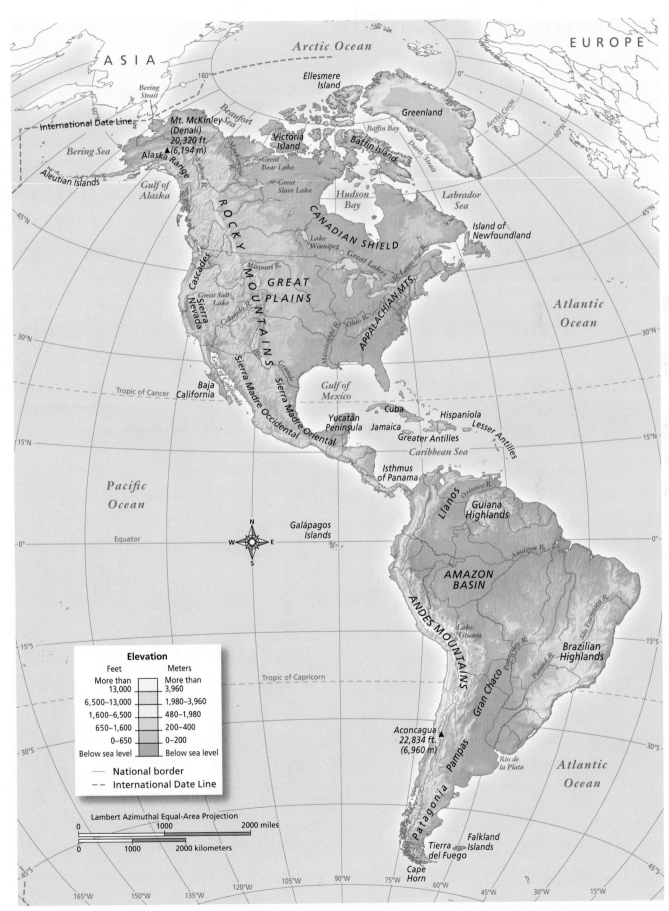

ASIA

Arctic Ocean

EUROPE

Bering Strait

International Date Line

Beaufort Sea

Ellesmere Island

Greenland

Arctic Circle

Mt. McKinley (Denali) 20,320 ft. (6,194 m)

Bering Sea

Alaska Range

Victoria Island

Baffin Bay

Baffin Island

Davis Strait

Aleutian Islands

Gulf of Alaska

Mackenzie R.

Yukon R.

Great Bear Lake

Great Slave Lake

Hudson Bay

Labrador Sea

Island of Newfoundland

R O C K Y

Cascades

Sierra Nevada

Great Salt Lake

Missouri R.

Lake Winnipeg

CANADIAN SHIELD

Great Lakes

St. Lawrence R.

Atlantic Ocean

M O U N T A I N S

GREAT PLAINS

Colorado R.

Ohio R.

Mississippi R.

APPALACHIAN MTS.

Sierra Madre Occidental

Baja California

Gulf of California

Sierra Madre Oriental

Rio Grande

Tropic of Cancer

Gulf of Mexico

Cuba

Hispaniola

Lesser Antilles

Yucatán Peninsula

Jamaica

Greater Antilles

Caribbean Sea

Isthmus of Panama

Pacific Ocean

Galápagos Islands

Equator

Llanos

Orinoco R.

Guiana Highlands

Amazon R.

AMAZON BASIN

ANDES MOUNTAINS

Lake Titicaca

Gran Chaco

Pilcomayo R.

Paraguay R.

Paraná R.

São Francisco R.

Brazilian Highlands

Aconcagua 22,834 ft. (6,960 m)

Pampas

Rio de la Plata

Patagonia

Atlantic Ocean

Tierra del Fuego

Falkland Islands

Cape Horn

Elevation

Feet	Meters
More than 13,000	More than 3,960
6,500–13,000	1,980–3,960
1,600–6,500	480–1,980
650–1,600	200–400
0–650	0–200
Below sea level	Below sea level

— National border
- - - International Date Line

Lambert Azimuthal Equal-Area Projection

0   1000   2000 miles

0   1000   2000 kilometers

Australia, New Zealand & Oceania: Political-Physical

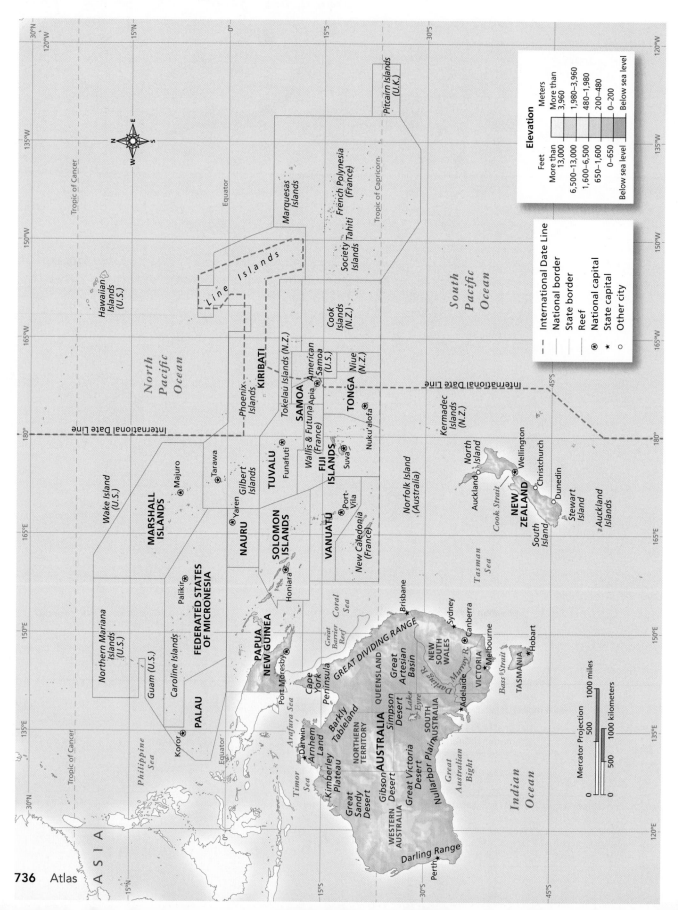

Elevation

Feet	Meters
More than 13,000	More than 3,960
6,500–13,000	1,980–3,960
1,600–6,500	480–1,980
650–1,600	200–480
0–650	0–200
Below sea level	Below sea level

- – – International Date Line
- —— National border
- —— State border
- ·········· Reef
- ⊛ National capital
- ★ State capital
- ○ Other city

Tropic of Cancer

Equator

Marquesas Islands

French Polynesia (France)

Society Islands Tahiti

Tropic of Capricorn

Pitcairn Islands (U.K.)

South Pacific Ocean

Cook Islands (N.Z.)

North Pacific Ocean

Hawaiian Islands (U.S.)

Line Islands

Phoenix Islands

International Date Line

KIRIBATI

Tokelau Islands (N.Z.)

American Samoa (U.S.)

Niue (N.Z.)

SAMOA Apia ⊛

TONGA Nuku'alofa ⊛

International Date Line

Wake Island (U.S.)

Tarawa ★

Majuro ★

MARSHALL ISLANDS

Gilbert Islands

Yaren ⊛

NAURU

TUVALU Funafuti ⊛

Wallis & Futuna (France)

FIJI ISLANDS Suva ⊛

Kermadec Islands (N.Z.)

NEW ZEALAND

North Island

Wellington ⊛
Christchurch ○
Dunedin ○

Auckland ○

Cook Strait

South Island

Stewart Island

Auckland Islands

Norfolk Island (Australia)

Northern Mariana Islands (U.S.)

Guam (U.S.)

Caroline Islands

FEDERATED STATES OF MICRONESIA

Palikir ⊛

PALAU Koror ⊛

SOLOMON ISLANDS Honiara ⊛

VANUATU Port-Vila ⊛

New Caledonia (France)

PAPUA NEW GUINEA Port Moresby ⊛

Philippine Sea

Coral Sea

Tasman Sea

Bass Strait

Great Barrier Reef

Cape York Peninsula

GREAT DIVIDING RANGE

Brisbane ○

Sydney ○

Canberra ⊛

Melbourne ○

Hobart ○

QUEENSLAND

Great Artesian Basin

NEW SOUTH WALES

VICTORIA

TASMANIA

Arafura Sea

Darwin ★

Arnhem Land

Kimberley Plateau

NORTHERN TERRITORY

Barkly Tableland

Simpson Desert

Lake Eyre

SOUTH AUSTRALIA

Adelaide ★

Murray R.

Darling

Timor Sea

Gibson Desert

Great Sandy Desert

Great Victoria Desert

Nullarbor Plain

WESTERN AUSTRALIA

AUSTRALIA

Great Australian Bight

Indian Ocean

Darling Range

Perth ★

ASIA

Mercator Projection

0 500 1000 miles

0 500 1000 kilometers

The Arctic: Physical

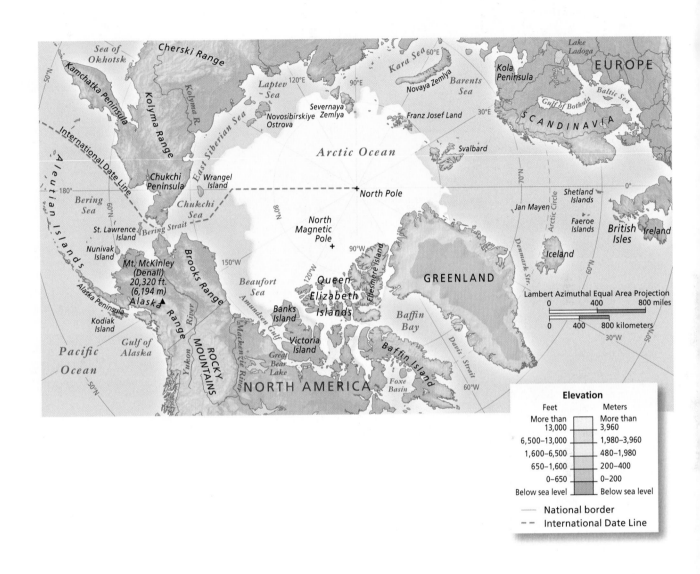

Elevation

Feet	Meters
More than 13,000	More than 3,960
6,500–13,000	1,980–3,960
1,600–6,500	480–1,980
650–1,600	200–400
0–650	0–200
Below sea level	Below sea level

— National border
- - - International Date Line

Lambert Azimuthal Equal Area Projection

Antarctica: Physical

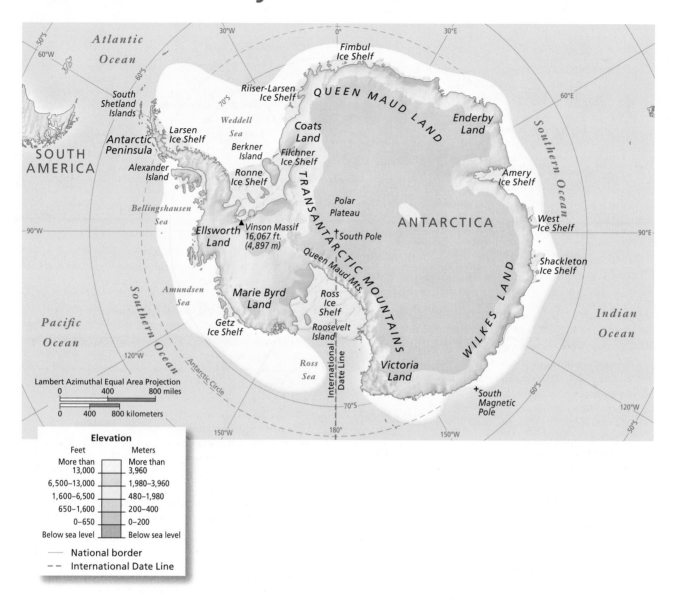

Elevation

Feet		Meters
More than 13,000		More than 3,960
6,500–13,000		1,980–3,960
1,600–6,500		480–1,980
650–1,600		200–400
0–650		0–200
Below sea level		Below sea level

— National border
-- International Date Line

Glossary

A

absolute monarchy system of government in which the monarch has unlimited power over the government

abundant *adj.*, existing in a large amount

Academy school of philosophy founded by Plato

accomplished *adj.*, highly skilled

accumulate *v.*, collect or attain a large amount of something

achievement *n.*, accomplishment that requires effort or skill

acquire *v.*, to get hold of; obtain

acropolis "high city" in Greek; the upper part of an ancient Greek city, where public buildings and the city's defenses were located

acupuncture therapy that uses needles to cure sickness and stop pain

adapt change

adherent *n.*, follower; supporter

advocate *v.*, support; speak out in favor of

ahimsa avoiding doing harm to any living thing

ally independent state that works with other states to achieve a shared military or political goal

alphabet small set of letters or symbols, each of which stands for a single sound

anatomy study of the structure of the body and its organs

animism belief that the natural world is full of spirits

annulment an official act ending a marriage

anthropology study of humankind in all aspects, especially development and culture

aqueduct channel that moves water over a long distance

Arabic numerals the system of writing numbers we use today

arbitrary *adj.*, random or by chance

archaeologist scientist who studies human life in the past by examining the things that people left behind

archipelago group of islands

aristocracy hereditary class of rulers, Greek for "rule by the best people"

armada a fleet of warships

artifact object made by a human being

artificial *adj.*, unnatural or human-made

artisan skilled worker who practices a handicraft

assemble *v.*, to put together

assembly *n.*, a company of persons gathered for deliberation and legislation, worship, or entertainment

assign *v.*, to give as a job or task

Augustus title used by Roman emperors meaning venerable or greatly honored person

authority *n.*, people in power

authority *n.*, the power to make decisions and rules

ayllu in Incan society, a group of related families that pooled its resources to meet people's needs

B

baptism ritual cleansing by plunging into water

barbarian word used by Greeks and Romans for all people who did not share their cultures

barracks military housing

barter trading system in which people exchange goods directly without using money

basin bowl-shaped area

Battle of Marathon Greek victory over the Persian army that ended the First Persian War

Battle of Salamis Greek victory over the Persian navy during the Second Persian War

benefit *n.*, gain; favorable result

Bhakti devotion to a deity, constituting a way to salvation in Hinduism

Black Death epidemic of the bubonic plague that killed as many as one third of all Europeans between 1347 and 1352

block printing early form of printing invented in China in which text was carved into a block of wood

bodhisattva a person many Buddhists believe to have reached enlightenment, but who is reborn again to help others on earth reach nirvana

Brahman in Hinduism, the supreme cosmic consciousness, spiritual force, or God

brazilwood a tree found in tropical regions whose wood is valuable for the production of purple or red dye

bubonic plague a deadly infection spread by fleas that live on rats

Buddhism religion that developed out of the teachings of Siddhartha Gautama, the Buddha

bullion precious metals melted into bars

bureaucracy system of many government officials who carry out government rules and regulations

bushido "the way of the warrior," a strict code of conduct that guided samurai behavior

Byzantine word used by historians to describe the eastern Roman empire after the fall of the western Roman empire

C

caliph title meaning "successor" in Arabic, used by leaders of the Muslim community who followed Muhammad

calligraphy art of beautiful writing

capitalism economy based on the private ownership of property and the use of property to compete for profits or gains in a market

caravan group of people traveling together

caravel a small, light ship developed by the Portuguese that performed well on long voyages

carpentry *n.*, the art or trade of woodworking

cartography the science of making maps and globes

caste fixed social class into which a person is born

cataract group of rocky rapids

cavalry soldiers who fight while riding horses

cease *v.*, to stop

celadon a ceramic glaze originated in China that is greenish in color

censor to ban dangerous or offensive ideas, or remove material from published works or prevent its publication

challenge *n.,* something that is difficult or demanding to do

chaos total disorder and confusion

chattel property

chinampa artificial island built by the Aztecs

chivalry code of conduct in medieval Europe that required knights to be brave, loyal, and honest

chorus in ancient Greek drama, a group of people who commented on the action of a play and advised the characters

Christendom large community of Christians spread across the world

circumnavigate to sail completely around

circumstance *n.,* condition

citadel fortified area

citizen legal member of a country or city-state

citizenship membership in a state or community which gives a person civil and political rights and obligations

city-state independent state consisting of a city and its surrounding territory

civic having to do with city or town life

civil service the people who work for a government

civil war war between groups from the same country

civilization complex society that has cities, a well-organized government, and workers with specialized job skills

clan group of families with a common ancestor

classical civilization the civilization of the ancient Greeks and Romans

clearly *adv.,* in a clear manner, without doubt or question

clergy people who are trained and ordained for religious services

collapse *v.,* to break down or fall down

colonization establishment of new settlers and their culture in other territories

colony group of people living in a new territory with ties to a distant state

Columbian Exchange exchange of people, plants and animals, and ideas between the Eastern Hemiphere and Western Hemisphere

commandment an order to do something

commentary *n.,* a set of comments or a recorded discussion about something

commerce buying and selling of goods and services

commercial *adj.,* having to do with trade and business

commission *v.,* order the creation of

common law a body of law that has developed from custom and from judges' decisions rather than from laws passed by a lawmaking assembly

communication *n.,* way of passing on information

compass device with a magnetized piece of metal that points to the north, used for navigation

compel *v.,* force

complex *adj.,* having many related parts; not simple

concept *n.,* idea

conclude *v.,* to decide as a result of thinking or reasoning

concrete building material made by mixing small stones and sand with limestone, clay, and water

Confucianism a belief system based on the ideas of the Chinese thinker Confucius

conglomeration *n.,* grouping of different parts

conquest *n.,* capturing something, especially in war

conquistador Spanish soldier-explorer

consensus agreement among the members of a group

consequence *n.,* result of an action, effect

constantly *adv.,* again and again without end

constitution system of basic rules and principles by which a government is organized

construct *v.,* to build or put together

consul one of two top officials and military leaders in the Roman republic

controversial *adj.,* tending to cause dispute or disagreement

convent religious community for women known as nuns

conversion heartfelt change in one's opinions or beliefs, especially in religion

convert *v.,* to switch from one belief system to another

core *n.,* center, most important part

cottage industry business that uses people who work at home with their own equipment

covenant binding agreement

creed statement of beliefs

creole person in Spain's colonies in the Americas who was an American-born descendant of Spanish settlers

crop rotation practice of changing the use of fields over time

crucifixion Roman method of execution by nailing a person to a wooden cross

Crusades a series of military campaigns to establish Christian control over the Holy Land

cuisine style of food

cultural diffusion spread of cultural traits from one culture to another

cultural trait idea or way of doing things that is common in a certain culture

culture beliefs, customs, practices, and behavior of a particular nation or group of people

cuneiform Mesopotamian system of writing that uses triangular-shaped symbols to stand for ideas or things

currency money that is used as a medium of exchange, usually bills or coins

Cyrillic alphabet alphabet used mostly for Slavic languages such as Russian and Bulgarian, as well as for other languages

D

daimyo local landowning lord in feudal Japan

Daoism a philosophy of following the Dao, that is, the natural way of the universe

decimal system counting system based on units of ten

deify officially declare a person to be a god

Delian League military alliance led by Athens

delta a flat plain formed on the seabed where a river deposits material over many years

democracy form of government in which citizens hold political power

denomination religious group

dense *adj.,* thickly clustered

descendant a person related by birth to another, such as a child or grandchild

despite *prep.*, even with or in spite of

despot a tyrant or dictator

determined *adj.*, to have a strong feeling about doing something

devastate *v.*, to bring to chaos, disorder, or ruin

device *n.*, machine

devote *v.*, to set aside for a purpose

devotion *n.*, dedication, loyalty

dharma a person's duty or what is right for him or her

Diaspora Jewish communities outside the ancient Jewish homeland, from a Greek word meaning dispersion, or scattering

dike wall to hold back water

diplomacy *n.*, the ability to handle relationships without increasing hostility

direct democracy government in which citizens take part directly in the day-to-day affairs of government

discriminate *v.*, treat some people differently or worse

dissenter *n.*, one who refuses to follow accepted law or practices

distinct *adj.*, separate, different

distribute *v.*, to divide and give out

diversity *n.*, variety

doctrine *n.*, a set of principles or system of belief

domesticate change the growth of plants or behavior of animals in ways that are useful for humans

draft *adj.*, drawing or pulling, as of a load

drama *n.*, plays or performances that tell stories

dramatically *adv.*, greatly

drought long period of extremely dry weather

dynasty a series of rulers from the same family

E

ebony black wood from West Africa

economy *n.*, the system by which a country's people make a living

edict an official public order made by a king or other authority

element *n.*, part

elite *adj.*, representing the best

emphasize *v.*, stress, mark as important

empire state containing several countries or territories

empiricism theory that all knowledge is gained through experience and observing with the senses

encomienda right granted by the Spanish government to its American colonists to demand labor or tribute from Native Americans

engraving an art form in which an artist etches a design on a metal plate with a needle and acid

enlightenment in Buddhism, a state of perfect wisdom

enormous *adj.*, very large

environment surroundings

environmental *adj.*, having to do with natural surroundings

envoy representative of a government sent to another country

ephor man responsible for the day-to-day operation of the government in Sparta

epistle formal letter, several of which form part of the New Testament

equipment *n.*, things used for a specific purpose

establish *v.*, to set up

established religion official religion supported by the government

ethics beliefs about what is right and wrong

ethnic group group of people who share a distinct culture, language, and identity

eventual *adj.*, final

eventually *adv.*, after a time

evidence *n.*, information used to prove something

exclude *v.*, to shut out, keep from participating

excommunicate to exclude a person from a church or a religious community

exempt *adj.*, to be free from a punishment or duty

exile separation from one's homeland

Exodus escape of the Israelites from slavery in Egypt

expand *v.*, to grow, get bigger

export good or service produced within a country and sold outside the country's borders

extract *v.*, remove, draw out

F

factor *n.*, cause

fallow unplanted

famine an extreme scarcity of food

federalism a form of government in which power is shared between local and national levels

Fertile Crescent a region with good conditions for growing crops that stretches from the Mediterranean coast east through Mesopotamia (modern Iraq) to the Persian Gulf

feudalism a strict social system in which landowners grant people land or other rewards in exchange for military service or labor

fief estate granted by a lord to a vassal

figurehead person who appears to be in charge when someone else is really in control

filial piety devotion of children to their parents

forum open area in a Roman city filled with public buildings, temples, and markets

fossil preserved remains of ancient human, animal, or plant

G

generally *adv.*, on the whole, as a rule

generate *v.*, to produce, create

geologist scientist who studies the physical materials of the Earth itself, such as soil and rocks

ghetto separate section of a city where members of a minority group are forced to live

gladiator man who fought as part of public entertainment in ancient Rome

Gospel one of the first four books of the New Testament that describe the life and teachings of Jesus

govern *v.*, to control or strongly influence

granary special building used to hold grain

Great Schism split between the Eastern Orthodox and Roman Catholic churches in 1054

Great Wall long wall running east and west along the Chinese empire's northern border

Greco-Roman something that combines elements of Greek and Roman culture and traditions

Greek fire a chemical mixture that burned in water which was used by the Byzantine empire against enemy ships

griot African musician-storyteller who uses music and stories to track heritage and record history as well as entertain

guild association of people who have a common interest

guru thinker or teacher

H

habeas corpus a court order to bring an arrested person before a judge or court

hajj pilgrimage made by Muslims to their holy city of Mecca

Hammurabi's Code a set of laws that governed life in the Babylonian empire

Hangul the alphabetic script in which Korean is written

heliocentric theory the theory that places the sun at the center of the universe

Hellenistic the form of Greek culture that emerged after Alexander's conquests

helot Messenian person forced to work as a lowly farmer by Sparta

heresy a belief that is rejected by official Church doctrine

hierarchy system for ranking members of a group according to their importance

hieroglyphic symbol that stands for a word, idea, or sound

Hijrah Muhammad's migration with his followers from Mecca to Medina

Hippocratic oath oath taken by medical students swearing to practice medicine in an ethical way

humanism a cultural movement of the Renaissance based on the study of classical works

Hundred Years' War destructive war between France and England that lasted from 1337 to 1453

hunter-gatherer person who lives by hunting animals and gathering plants

hypothesis logical guess

I

Iberian Peninsula the peninsula where present-day Spain and Portugal are located

icon a holy image, usually a portrait of Jesus or a saint

iconoclast "image-breaker," person who opposed the use of icons in Christian worship

identify v., consider or treat as the same

igloo domed house made from blocks of snow by Native Americans who lived in the Arctic

immunity natural defense against disease

impact n., to have a strong and often bad effect on (something or someone)

import good or service sold within a country that is produced in another country

incentive n., something that leads to action

income n., payments of money

indentured servant a poor immigrant who paid for passage to the colonies by agreeing to work for four to seven years

individual adj., having to do with a single person or thing

individualism the belief in the importance of the individual as opposed to the larger community

inductive reasoning the process of looking at specific facts and making general principles or rules based on those facts

indulgence a kind of cancellation of punishment for sin

inflation general increase in prices

influence n., the power to cause change

innovation n., new ways of doing things

Inquisition a series of investigations designed to find and judge heretics

interdependence dependence by each country or group on the other

interpret v., to explain, give the meaning of

invalid adj., without truth or unlawful

invisible adj., not visible

irrigate to supply water to

isolated adj., set away from other people or places

isolation n., the condition of being alone

issue n., problem or subject to be discussed or decided

ivory n., a hard white substance from the tusk of an animal such as an elephant

J

jati occupation-based caste

judge in the Hebrew Bible, a leader who could rally the Israelites to defend their land

judiciary a system of law courts outside the control of other branches of government

justice fairness or fair treatment

Justinian's Code a law code published by the Byzantine emperor Justinian

K

Kabuki Japanese drama aimed at farmers, merchants, and other common folk

kami god or spirit who represents a force of nature in the Japanese religion

karma in Hinduism, the effect of a person's actions in this and in previous lives

khan Mongol ruler

kinship connection based on family relationships

knight warrior mounted on horseback

L

labor specialization division of jobs and skills in a society

lacquer a protective coating made from the sap of a special tree

lecturer n., person who gives an informative talk to students

legacy n., an influence from the past

legal adj., having to do with the law

Legalism an ancient Chinese philosophy stating that a strong leader and a strong legal system, not moral values, are needed to create social order

legion basic unit of the Roman army, consisting of 4,500 to 5,000 heavily armed soldiers

Line of Demarcation line set by the Treaty of Tordesillas dividing the non-European world into two zones, one controlled by Spain and one controlled by Portugal

lineage group of people descended from a common ancestor

linear perspective a mathematical system for representing three-dimensional space on a flat surface

linen *n.,* cloth made from the flax plant

loess a dustlike material that can form soil

logograph *n.,* a symbol that represents a word or group of words

longhouse rectangular type of home built by northeastern Native Americans, made from wood and bark or mats made of reeds

loyalty *n.,* the state of being faithful

lucrative *adj.,* profitable

lyric poetry poetic songs

M

magistrate government official who enforces the law

Magna Carta a document that promised barons certain rights

Mahayana Buddhism Buddhist sect that focuses on the compassion of the Buddha

mainland area that is a part of a continent

maintain *v.,* to keep and support

major *adj.,* important

manage *v.,* to direct; have control over

Mandate of Heaven in ancient China, the presumed right to rule given to a dynasty by heaven, the highest force of nature

maniple unit of 60 to 120 soldiers within a Roman legion that could act independently in battle

manor self-sufficient estate of a medieval lord

mantra sacred word, chant, or sound that is repeated over and over to advance one's spiritual growth

maritime having to do with the sea

market economy economy in which individual consumers and producers make all economic decisions

martyr person who dies for his or her beliefs

medieval from the Latin for "middle age," relating to the Middle Ages

meditate calm or clear the mind, often by focusing on a single object

melancholy *adj.,* depressed or sad

mendicant order order founded to fight heresy and to preach to ordinary people

mercantile related to commerce or trade

mercantilism economic policy in which a nation gains strength by controlling its trade, agriculture, industry, and money

mercenary soldier who fights for pay rather than for his or her country

merit system system in which people are hired and promoted based on talent and skills, rather than wealth or social status

Meroitic script one of the world's first alphabets, invented in ancient Nubia

Mesopotamia wide, flat plain in between the Tigris and Euphrates rivers in present-day Iraq

mestizo person in Spain's colonies in the Americas who was of Native American and European descent

metallurgy science that deals with extracting metal from ore and using it to create useful objects

metic foreigner in a Greek city-state, often a merchant or artisan

Middle Ages period between ancient times and modern times, roughly from 500 to 1500 CE

Middle Passage the leg of the triangular trade route on which slaves were transported from Africa to the Americas

migrate *v.,* to move from one region to another in order to live there

migration movement of people from one place to another

military state society organized for the purpose of waging war

minor *adj.,* not serious, not important

minority *n.,* a group that is less than half of a population

mission a community dedicated to spreading the faith or to educating and protecting people

missionary someone who tries to convert others to a particular religion

mita system Incan system of payment of taxes with labor

moat trench filled with water as part of a fortification

moksha liberation from reincarnation

monastery secluded religious community

money economy economic system in which people use currency rather than bartering to buy and sell goods

monk man who dedicates himself to worshiping God

monopoly single person or group who controls the production of a good or service

monotheism belief in a single God

monsoon seasonal wind that brings rain to the Indian subcontinent during parts of the year

Moors the Muslims in Spain

mortar *n.,* a cement mixture used to hold bricks together

mosaic design formed with small tiles of glass, stone, or pottery

mosque Islamic house of worship

movable type a format of printmaking, in which individual letters formed in metal could be used again and again

mulatto in Spain's colonies in the Americas, person who was of African and European descent

mummy a body that has been preserved so it will not decompose

mutiny revolt especially of soldiers or sailors against their officers

mythology collection of myths or stories that people tell about their gods and heroes

N

natural law idea that there are laws in nature that are basic to both the natural world and human affairs

natural resource useful material found in the environment

navigation art of steering a ship from place to place

network *n.,* a closely interconnected group of people or things

New Testament writings that form part of the Christian Bible which tell the story of Jesus and his early followers

nirvana a state of blissful peace without desire or suffering

Noh Japanese drama that appealed to the nobles and samurai

nomad *n.,* person who moves from place to place without a permanent home

northwest passage a water route to Asia through present-day Canada

numeral symbol used to represent a number

O

oasis place in the desert where water can be found

observatory building for observing the sky

obtain *v.,* to get or to receive something

official person who holds a government job

oligarchy government in which a small group of people rule

Olympic games in ancient Greece, an athletic competition held every four years in honor of Zeus

oppose *v.,* to try to stop or defeat something

oracle bone animal bone or shell carved with written characters that was used to predict the future in ancient China

oral tradition community's cultural and historical background, passed down in spoken stories and songs

oratory art of giving speeches

orthodoxy traditional or established religious beliefs

P

pagan *adj.,* related to a religion with many gods

pagan follower of a polytheistic religion

papyrus a writing surface similar to paper named after the papyrus reed that grew along the Nile River in ancient Egypt

parable story with a religious moral

parliament an assembly of representatives who make laws

paterfamilias oldest man in a Roman family who had absolute power over his family

patriarchal society society in which men rule their families, and people trace their origins through male ancestors

patron someone who gives money or other support to a person or group

Pax Romana period of stability in the Roman empire

Peasants' Revolt unsuccessful revolt by peasants against feudal lords in England in 1381

Peloponnesian League military alliance led by Sparta

peninsular member of the highest class in Spain's colonies in the Americas

perilous *adj.,* dangerous

period *n.,* a span of time

phalanx Greek military formation of heavily armed foot soldiers who moved together as a unit

pharaoh king of ancient Egypt

philosophy general study of knowledge and the world; Greek for "love of wisdom"

picaresque a series of comic episodes usually involving a mischievous character

pictograph a picture that represents a word or idea

pilgrimage journey undertaken to worship at a religious place

plateau large, mostly flat area that rises above the surrounding land

policy *n.,* course of action taken by a government

polis Greek city-state

politics art and practice of government

polyrhythmic drumming type of drumming that combines two or more different rhythms at the same time

polytheism worship of many gods or deities

pope leader of the Roman Catholic Church

populate to become an inhabitant of a place

porcelain a hard white pottery of extremely fine quality

potential *n.,* possibility to grow or change in the future

potlatch feasting and gift-giving ceremony in northwestern Native American culture

predestination the idea that God had long ago determined who would gain salvation

prehistory time before humans invented writing

prestige *n.,* respect and admiration from others

privateer privately owned ship commissioned by a government to attack and capture enemy ships, especially merchants' ships

professional *adj.,* trained, expert

profit *v.,* to make a gain

prophet person believed to be chosen by God to bring truth to the people

proportion using balanced or symmetric elements to form a pleasing design

prosper *v.,* gain in wealth

prosperity *n,* the condition of being successful

proverb wise saying

province territory that is under the control of a larger country

purchase *v.,* to buy

pursue *v.,* to chase

push-pull factors push factors motivate people to leave their homes, while pull factors attract people to move to new locations

pyramid structure with triangular sides

Q

quipu record-keeping device made of knotted strings, used by the Incas

Quran holy book of Islam

R

rabbi Jewish religious teacher

rationalism the belief that knowledge is gained by thinking things through using reason

reason *n.,* the power to think clearly

recant to withdraw or take back

Reconquista the movement to drive the Muslims from Spain

reform *v.,* to improve

Reformation a religious movement that began in the 1500s to reform the Catholic Church

regent someone who governs a country in the name of a ruler who is unable to rule, often because of age

region area with at least one unifying physical or human feature such as climate, landforms, population, or history

reincarnation rebirth of a soul in a new body

reject v., decide against, turn away

reliable adj., dependable; steady; not risky

religion people's beliefs and practices about the existence, nature, and worship of a god or gods

rely v., to depend, trust

Renaissance French for "rebirth"; refers to a period of cultural revival in Europe from the 1300s to the 1500s

representative democracy democracy in which people elect representatives to make the nation's laws

republic form of government in which citizens have the right to vote and elect officials

resource supply of something that can be used as needed

resurrection coming back to life

revelation n., message, usually one believed to come from God

revolution a complete change in ways of thinking, working, or living

righteousness acting or living in a way that is ethically right and obeys God's laws

rigid adj., inflexible, unchanging

river system main river and all of the other rivers and streams that drain into it

Romance language language that developed from Latin, such as French, Spanish, Portuguese, or Italian

rule of law idea that all members of a society—even the rich and powerful—must obey the law

ruthless adj., having no pity, cruel

S

Sabbath weekly day of rest

sacrament sacred rites of Christianity, such as baptism and communion

saint person believed to be especially holy

samurai highly trained Japanese warrior in feudal Japan

sarissa 18-foot-long Macedonian pike

satire work of literature that makes fun of its subject, often mocking vice or folly

savanna parklike landscape of grasslands with scattered trees that can survive dry spells, found in tropical areas with dry seasons

scholar-official highly educated person who passed civil service examinations and worked in the government

scholarship formal study and learning

scientific method a method of using observation, experiments, and careful reasoning to gain new knowledge

sculpture statue or other free-standing piece of art made of clay, stone, or other materials

sect a subgroup of a major religious group

secular nonreligious

secularism the view that religion need not be the center of human affairs

seismometer a tool to measure earthquakes

serf a peasant who is legally bound to live and work on land owned by a lord

Sharia Islamic law

Shia member of an Islamic religious group that supported Ali as the first caliph and now forms a minority of the world's Muslims

Shinto traditional religion that originated in Japan

shogun powerful Japanese military leader who often had more power than the emperor

shrine place of worship

Silk Road series of trade routes that crossed Asia

site of encounter place where people from different cultures meet and exchange products, ideas, and technologies

slavery ownership and control of other people as property

smuggler person who trades illegally

social class group of people living in similar economic conditions

Socratic method form of teaching in which the teacher asks students question after question to force them to think more clearly

sonnet a poem of 14 lines with a fixed rhyming pattern

specialization act of concentrating on a limited number of goods or activities

spice trade sea route and overland trade routes from Africa and Asia that brought spices and seasonings to the European markets

stable adj., able to last, not likely to fall apart

stagnant adj., not advancing or developing

standardize to set rules to make things more similar

standardized adj., the same everywhere

standing army a permanent army of professional soldiers

staple adj., used or needed regularly

status position or rank in relation to others

stele grand stone pillar

steppe vast area of grasslands

stonetown word used to describe Swahili city–states and their multistoried stone houses

strait narrow body of water that cuts through land, connecting two larger bodies of water

strategy a long-term plan for achieving a goal

structure n., building

structure n., organization

stupa Buddhist commemorative burial mound

subcontinent a large landmass that is set apart from the rest of the continent

subject person under the rule of a monarch

submission n., giving control over yourself to someone else

succession n., one person or thing following another

successor n., person who follows another in an office or role

Sufism an Islamic lifestyle that emphasizes controlling one's desires, giving up worldly attachments, and seeking nearness to God

sultan title for a ruler of a Muslim country

Sunnah traditions believed by many Muslims to come from their prophet Muhammad

Sunni member of an Islamic religious group that supported Abu Bakr as the first caliph and now forms a majority of the world's Muslims

surplus extra

survive v., to last, to continue to live

symbolize v., to represent

synagogue Jewish house of worship

T

Talmud collection of oral teachings and commentaries about the Hebrew Bible and Jewish law

temperament *n.,* a specific person's way of behaving and thinking

tenant *n.,* person who rents land or a home

tenant farmer person who pays rent, either in money or crops, to grow crops on another person's land

tepee portable, cone-shaped home made by Native Americans who lived on the Plains

terrace strip of level land cut into a slope that is planted with crops

text *n.,* a written source, such as a book

textile woven fabric

theocracy a government run by religious power

Theravada Buddhism Buddhist sect that focuses on the wisdom of the Buddha

three-field system system of planting invented in the High Middle Ages which increased the amount of land that could be planted each year

toga garment that adult men wore wrapped around their bodies as a symbol of Roman citizenship

tolerance willingness to respect different beliefs and customs

topography physical features of a place

Torah first five books of the Hebrew Bible

tradition *n.,* a practice or belief handed down from one generation to another

traditional economy economy in which people make economic decisions based on their customs and habits

trans-Saharan across the Sahara

transform *v.,* to change

transmission *n.,* the passing on of something, such as stories or history

treacherous *adj.,* dangerous or hazardous

Treaty of Paris treaty of 1763 that ended the Seven Years' War and resulted in British domination of the Americas

Treaty of Tordesillas treaty signed between Spain and Portugal in 1494 which divided the non-European world between them

triangular trade colonial trade routes among Europe and its colonies, the West Indies, and Africa in which goods were exchanged for slaves

tribute payment or gift to a stronger power

Trinity the three persons, or forms, of God according to Christian belief: God the Father, Jesus the Son, and the Holy Spirit

tyranny unjust use of power, or in ancient Greece a government run by a strong ruler

U

unified *adj.,* joined together as a single whole

uniform *adj.,* unchanging; fixed

unify *v.,* bring together

unite *v.,* to bring together

university school, or group of schools, that trains scholars at the highest levels

urbanization movement of people from rural to urban areas

utopia an imaginary, ideal place

V

varna grouping based on one's skill

vassal in medieval Europe, a nobleman who received land from other noblemen in return for his service

Veda collection of hundreds of sacred hymns composed by the Aryans of ancient India

vernacular everyday spoken language

veto stop or cancel the action of a government official or body

viceroy representative who ruled one of Spain's provinces in the Americas in the king's name

villa large country home

violate *v.,* break a rule or agreement

W

warlord military ruler

welfare *n.,* well-being, comfort, prosperity

widespread *adj.,* common, spread across a large area

wigwam a home made by Northeastern Native Americans, formed by bending the trunks of young trees and tying them together to make a round frame covered with bark or reed mats

writ a court order

Z

ziggurat brick, pyramid-shaped Mesopotamian temple

Glosario

A

absolute monarchy > monarquía absoluta sistema de gobierno en el que el poder del monarca es ilimitado

abundant > abundante que existe en gran cantidad

Academy > Academia escuela de filosofía fundada por Platón

accomplished > experto con mucha habilidad

accumulate > acumular *v.* reunir u obtener una gran cantidad de algo

achievement > logro resultado que requiere esfuerzo o habilidad

acquire > adquirir conseguir algo; obtener

acropolis > acrópolis "ciudad alta" en griego; la parte elevada de una ciudad griega de la antigüedad, donde se ubicaban los edificios públicos y las defensas

acupuncture > acupuntura terapia que utiliza agujas para curar enfermedades y aliviar el dolor

adapt > adaptarse cambiar

adherent > partidario seguidor; defensor

advocate > defender apoyar; hablar a favor de algo

ahimsa > ahimsa evitar hacerle daño a un ser viviente

ally > aliado estado independiente que colabora con otros estados para lograr un objetivo militar o político común

alphabet > alfabeto conjunto limitado de letras o símbolos, cada uno de los cuales representa un sonido

anatomy > anatomía estudio de la estructura del cuerpo y sus órganos

animism > animismo la creencia de que la naturaleza está llena de espíritus

annulment > anulación decreto oficial de la terminación de un matrimonio

anthropology > antropología estudio de todos los aspectos de la humanidad, especialmente el desarrollo y la cultura

aqueduct > acueducto canal que transporta agua a grandes distancias

Arabic numerals > números arábigos sistema de escritura de números que usamos hoy en día

arbitrary > arbitrario por azar o casualidad

archaeologist > arqueólogo científico que estudia la vida humana del pasado mediante el estudio de los objetos que las personas dejaron

archipelago > archipiélago grupo de islas

aristocracy > aristocracia clase hereditaria de gobernantes, "gobierno ejercido por los mejores" en griego

armada > armada flota de barcos de guerra

artifact > artefacto objeto hecho por un ser humano

artificial > artificial no natural o hecho por el hombre

artisan > artesano trabajador especializado que ejerce un oficio manual

assemble > montar armar

assembly > asamblea grupo de personas que se reúnen para deliberar, legislar, practicar una religión o entretenerse

assign > asignar dar una tarea o trabajo

Augustus > Augusto título usado por los emperadores romanos, significa persona venerable o con muchos honores

authority > autoridad personas que están en el poder

authority > autoridad poder de tomar decisiones y crear reglas

ayllu > ayllu en la sociedad inca, conjunto de familias emparentadas que juntaban sus recursos para satisfacer sus necesidades

B

baptism > bautismo limpieza ritual que se realiza sumergiéndose en agua

barbarian > bárbaro término usado por los griegos y romanos para referirse a los pueblos que no compartían sus culturas

barracks > barracas alojamientos militares

barter > trueque sistema de comercio en el cual las personas intercambian bienes directamente, sin usar dinero

basin > cuenca área en forma de cuenco o vasija

Battle of Marathon > Batalla de Maratón victoria griega sobre el ejército persa que terminó la Primera Guerra Médica

Battle of Salamis > Batalla de Salamina victoria griega sobre la armada persa durante la Segunda Guerra Médica

benefit > beneficio ganancia, resultado favorable

Bhakti > Bhakti Devoción a una deidad, que constituía un camino a la salvación en el hinduismo

Black Death > Peste Negra epidemia de peste bubónica que causó la muerte de cerca de un tercio de la población europea entre 1347 y 1352

block printing > impresión con bloques forma temprana de impresión inventada en China, en la que el texto se tallaba en un bloque de madera

bodhisattva > bodhisattva person que, según creen muchos budistas, alcanzó la iluminación pero volvió a nacer para ayuday a otros en la tierra a alcanzar el nirvana

Brahman > Brahman en la religión hindú, la conciencia cósmica suprema, fuerza espiritual, o Dios

brazilwood > palo brasil árbol que se encuentra en las regiones tropicales, cuya madera es valiosa para la producción de una tintura púrpura o roja

bubonic plague > peste bubónica infección mortal propagada por las pulgas que habitan en las ratas

Buddhism > budismo religión que se desarrolló a partir de las enseñanzas de Siddhartha Gautama, el Buda

bullion > lingotes metales preciosos fundidos en forma de barra

bureaucracy > burocracia sistema de numerosos funcionarios que ejecutan las normas y reglamentos del gobierno

bushido > bushido término japonés que significa "el camino del guerrero", código estricto de conducta que guiaba las acciones de los samuráis

Byzantine > bizantino término usado por los historiadores para describir el Imperio Romano oriental después de la caída del Imperio Romano occidental

C

caliph > califa significa "sucesor" en árabe; título utilizado por los líderes de la comunidad musulmana, seguidores de Mahoma

calligraphy > caligrafía arte de escribir con letra bella

capitalism > capitalismo economía que se basa en la propiedad privada y en el uso de la propiedad para competir por beneficios o ganancias en un mercado

caravan > caravana grupo de personas que viajan juntas

caravel > carabela nave pequeña y ligera diseñada por los portugueses, especialmente efectiva en viajes largos

carpentry > carpintería el arte u oficio de trabajar con madera

cartography > cartografía técnica de trazar mapas y globos terráqueos

caste > casta clase social fija en la que nace una persona

cataract > catarata formación de rápidos rocosos

cavalry > caballería soldados que combaten montados a caballo

cease > cesar parar

celadon > celadón esmalte de cerámica de origen chino de color verdoso

censor > censurar prohibir ideas peligrosas u ofensivas, o retirar materiales de obras publicadas o impedir su publicación

challenge > desafío algo que es difícil de hacer o exigente

chaos > caos desorden y confusión totales

chattel > bien mueble propiedad

chinampa > chinampa isla artificial construida por los aztecas

chivalry > Código de Caballería normas de conducta en la Europa medieval que requería que los caballeros fueran valerosos, leales y honestos

chorus > coro en el teatro griego de la antigüedad, grupo de personas que comentaban sobre la acción de la obra y aconsejaban a los personajes

Christendom > cristiandad la gran comunidad de cristianos extendida en el mundo entero

circumnavigate > circunnavegar dar una vuelta completa en barco alrededor de un lugar

circumstance > circunstancia condición

citadel > ciudadela área fortificada

citizen > ciudadano miembro legal de un país o ciudad estado

citizenship > ciudadanía membresía en un estado o una comunidad que confiere derechos y obligaciones civiles y políticos a las personas

city-state > ciudad-estado estado independiente que consiste en una ciudad y el territorio aledaño

civic > cívico relacionado con la vida de una ciudad o un pueblo

civil service > servicio civil las personas que trabajan para un gobierno

civil war > guerra civil guerra entre grupos de un mismo país

civilization > civilización sociedad compleja con ciudades, un gobierno organizado y trabajadores con destrezas especializadas

clan > clan grupo de familias con un ancestro común

classical civilization > civilización clásica la civilización de los griegos y romanos antiguos

clearly > claramente de manera clara, sin dudas ni interrogantes

clergy > clero personas entrenadas y ordenadas para el servicio religioso

collapse > colapsar desmoronarse o caer

colonization > colonización establecimiento de nuevos pobladores y su cultura en otros territorios

colony > colonia grupo de personas que viven en un nuevo territorio que tiene vínculos con un estado distante

Columbian Exchange > intercambio colombino intercambio de personas, plantas, animales e ideas entre los hemisferios oriental y occidental

commandment > mandamiento una orden de hacer algo

commentary > comentarios una serie de explicaciones o el registro de una discusión sobre algo

commerce > comercio compra y venta de bienes y servicios

commercial > comercial relacionado con el comercio y los negocios

commission > encargar ordenar la creación de algo

common law > derecho consuetudinario conjunto de leyes basadas en costumbres y decisiones judiciales, en lugar de leyes aprobadas por una asamblea legislativa

communication > comunicación manera de transmitir información

compass > brújula instrumento con una pieza de metal imantada que señala el norte, usado en la navegación

compel > obligar forzar

complex > complejo que tiene muchas partes relacionadas; que no es simple

concept > concepto idea

conclude > concluir decidir algo como resultado de pensar o razonar

concrete > concreto material de construcción fabricado mediante la mezcla de piedras pequeñas y arena con piedra caliza, arcilla y agua

Confucianism > confucianismo sistema de creencias basado en la ideología del filósofo chino Confucio

conglomeration > conglomeración agrupación de diferentes partes

conquest > conquistar capturar algo, especialmente en la guerra

conquistador > conquistador soldado explorador de origen español

consensus > consenso acuerdo entre los miembros de un grupo

consequence > consecuencia resultado de una acción, efecto

constantly > constantemente una y otra vez sin fin

constitution > constitución sistema de reglas y principios básicos que establece la organización de un gobierno

construct > construir fabricar o armar

consul > cónsul uno de los dos altos funcionarios y líderes militares en la República romana

controversial > controvertido que tiende a causar disputa o desacuerdo

convent > convento comunidad religiosa para mujeres conocidas como monjas

conversion > conversión cambio sincero de opiniones o creencias, especialmente en el campo religioso

convert > convertirse pasar de un sistema de creencias a otro

core > núcleo centro, parte más importante

cottage industry > industria artesanal negocio que utiliza gente que trabaja en casa con su propio equipo

covenant > alianza pacto vinculante

creed > credo afirmación de creencias

creole > criollo en las colonias españolas de las Américas, una persona nacida en las Américas y descendiente de colonos españoles

crop rotation > rotación de cultivos práctica de alternar el uso que se le da a un campo de cultivo

crucifixion > crucifixión método romano de ejecución clavando a una persona a una cruz de madera

Crusades > Cruzadas serie de campañas militares para establecer el control cristiano de la Tierra Santa

cuisine > cocina estilo de comida

cultural diffusion > difusión cultural propagación de los rasgos culturales de una cultura a otra

cultural trait > rasgo cultural idea o manera de hacer las cosas que es común en una cultura determinada

culture > cultura creencias, costumbres, prácticas y comportamientos de una nación o un grupo de personas determinado

cuneiform > cuneiforme sistema de escritura usado en Mesopotamia que emplea símbolos de forma triangular para representar ideas y objetos

currency > moneda corriente dinero que se usa como medio de intercambio, usualmente en forma de billetes y monedas

Cyrillic alphabet > alfabeto cirílico alfabeto utilizado sobre todo para las lenguas eslavas, como el ruso, el búlgaro y otras

D

daimyo > daimyo señor terrateniente local en el Japón feudal

Daoism > taoísmo filosofía que sigue el Tao, es decir, el orden natural del universo

decimal system > sistema decimal sistema para contar basado en unidades de diez

deify > deificar declarar oficialmente dios a una persona

Delian League > Liga de Delos alianza militar liderada por Atenas

delta > delta llanura plana que se forma en el lecho marino donde un río deposita sedimento a través de los años

democracy > democracia tipo de gobierno en el que los ciudadanos tienen el poder político

denomination > denominación grupo religioso

dense > denso agrupado en forma compacta

descendant > descendiente persona vinculada por nacimiento con otra persona, como un hijo o un nieto

despite > a pesar por más que, aunque

despot > déspota un tirano o dictador

determined > decidido estar convencido de hacer algo

devastate > devastar traer caos, desorden o ruina

device > aparato máquina

devote > dedicar reservar para un propósito

devotion > devoción dedicación, lealtad

dharma > dharma el deber de una persona o lo que es correcto para él o ella

Diaspora > Diáspora conjunto de comunidades judías que viven fuera de la antigua patria judía; viene de una palabra griega que significa dispersión

dike > dique muro construido para contener el agua

diplomacy > diplomacia la capacidad de manejar relaciones sin aumentar la hostilidad

direct democracy > democracia directa tipo de gobierno en el que los ciudadanos participan directamente en los asuntos diarios del gobierno

discriminate > discriminar tratar peor o de forma diferente a ciertas personas

dissenter > disidente alguien que se niega a seguir leyes o prácticas aceptadas

distinct > distinto separado, diferente

distribute > distribuir dividir y repartir

diversity > diversidad variedad

doctrine > doctrina grupo de principios o sistema de creencias

domesticate > domesticar cambiar el crecimiento de las plantas o la conducta de los animales de maneras que sean útiles para los seres humanos

draft > de tiro que jala o empuja una carga

drama > drama obras o representaciones que cuentan historias

dramatically > dramáticamente enormemente

drought > sequía largo período de tiempo extremadamente seco

dynasty > dinastía serie de monarcas pertenecientes a la misma familia

E

ebony > ébano madera negra del África occidental

economy > economía sistema con el que las personas de un país se ganan la vida

edict > edicto orden pública oficial dada por un rey u otra autoridad

element > elemento parte

elite > élite que representa lo mejor

emphasize > enfatizar destacar, señalar como importante

empire > imperio estado que incluye a varios países o territorios

empiricism > empirismo teoría según la cual todo conocimiento se adquiere por medio de la experiencia y la observación con los sentidos

encomienda > encomienda derecho que el gobierno español cedía a sus colonos en América para que éstos percibieran el tributo o trabajo que debían pagar los indígenas americanos

engraving > grabado forma artística en la que se graba un diseño en una placa de metal usando una aguja y ácido

enlightenment > iluminación en el budismo, un estado de sabiduría perfecta

enormous > enorme muy grande

environment > medio ambiente lo que hay en los alrededores

environmental > medioambiental relacionado con los entornos naturales

envoy > enviado representante de un gobierno ante otro gobierno

ephor > éforo hombre encargado de las operaciones cotidianas del gobierno en Esparta

epistle > epístola carta formal; escritos que forman parte del Nuevo Testamento

equipment > equipo cosas usadas con un propósito específico

establish > fundar crear

established religion > religión establecida religión oficial apoyada por el gobierno

ethics > ética creencias sobre el bien y el mal

ethnic group > grupo étnico grupo de personas que comparten una cultura, un idioma y una identidad

eventual > eventual final

eventually > con el tiempo después de un tiempo

evidence > evidencia información que se usa para probar algo

exclude > excluir apartar, evitar la participación de alguien

excommunicate > excomulgar excluir a una persona de una iglesia o comunidad religiosa

exempt > exento libre de un castigo o una obligación

exile > exilio separación de la patria

Exodus > Éxodo huida de los israelitas de la esclavitud en Egipto

expand > expandirse crecer, aumentar de tamaño

export > exportación bien o servicio que se produce en un país y se vende fuera de los límites del país

extract > extraer quitar, sacar

F

factor > ser un factor causar

fallow > barbecho tierra que se deja sin sembrar

famine > hambruna escasez extrema de alimentos

federalism > federalismo forma de gobierno en la que el poder es compartido entre el nivel local y el nacional

Fertile Crescent > Creciente Fértil región con buenas condiciones para cultivos que se extiende desde las áreas de la costa del Mediterráneo, hacia el este por Mesopotamia (que hoy se conoce como Iraq) hasta el golfo Pérsico

feudalism > feudalismo un sistema social estricto en el que los terratenientes dan a las personas tierras u otras recompensas a cambio de servicios militares o de trabajo

fief > feudo propiedades otorgadas por un señor feudal a un vasallo

figurehead > testaferro persona que aparenta estar a cargo cuando en realidad otra persona tiene el control

filial piety > amor filial devoción de los hijos hacia sus padres

forum > foro área abierta en una ciudad romana llena de edificios públicos, templos y mercados

fossil > fósil restos conservados de personas, animales o plantas de la antigüedad

G

generally *adv.*, **> generalmente** en conjunto, comúnmente

generate > generar producir, crear

geologist > geólogo científico que estudia los materiales físicos de la Tierra, como el suelo y las rocas

ghetto > gueto área separada de una ciudad donde se fuerza a vivir a los miembros de una minoría

gladiator > gladiador hombre que combatía en espectáculos públicos en la antigua Roma

Gospel > Evangelio cada uno de los primeros cuatro libros del Nuevo Testamento, que describen la vida y las enseñanzas de Jesús

govern > gobernar controlar o influir fuertemente

granary > granero edificio especial usado para almacenar granos

Great Schism > Gran Cisma separación de la Iglesia ortodoxa oriental y la Iglesia católica romana en 1054

Great Wall > Gran Muralla China largo muro que recorre lo que fue la frontera norte del imperio Chino en dirección este-oeste

Greco-Roman > greco-romano que combina elementos de las culturas y tradiciones griega y romana

Greek fire > fuego griego una mezcla química que ardía en el agua y era usada por el Imperio Bizantino contra los barcos enemigos

griot > griot músico y narrador africano que usa canciones y cuentos para registrar la historia y la herencia cultural, además de entretener

guild > gremio asociación de personas que comparten un interés común

guru > gurú pensador o maestro

H

habeas corpus > hábeas corpus orden judicial de llevar a una persona arrestada ante un juez o una corte

hajj > hajj peregrinación que realizan los musulmanes a la ciudad santa de La Meca

Hammurabi's Code > Código de Hammurabi conjunto de leyes que regían la vida en Babilonia

Hangul > hangul alfabeto coreano

heliocentric theory > teoría heliocéntrica teoría que afirma que el Sol está en el centro del universo

Hellenistic > helenística la forma de cultura griega que surgió después de las conquistas de Alejandro

helot > ilota persona originaria de Mesenia forzada a trabajar como siervo agrícola en Esparta

heresy > herejía creencia rechazada por la doctrina oficial de la Iglesia

hierarchy > jerarquía sistema de rangos asignados a los miembros de un grupo según su importancia

hieroglyphic > jeroglífico símbolo usado para representar una palabra, idea o sonido

Hijrah > hégira emigración de Mahoma con sus seguidores de La Meca a Medina

Hippocratic oath > juramento hipocrático juramento hecho por los estudiantes de medicina en el que prometen practicar su profesión de una manera ética

humanism > humanismo movimiento cultural en el Renacimiento basado en el estudio de obras clásicas

Hundred Years' War > Guerra de los Cien años guerra cruenta entre Francia e Inglaterra que duró desde 1337 hasta 1453

hunter-gatherer > cazador-recolector persona que vive de la caza de animales y la recolección de plantas

hypothesis > hipótesis suposición lógica

I

Iberian Peninsula > península Ibérica península en la que se ubican España y Portugal hoy en día

icon > ícono imagen sagrada, usualmente un retrato de Jesús o de un santo

iconoclast > iconoclasta "destructor de imágenes", persona que se oponía al uso de íconos en el rito cristiano

identify > identificar considerar o tratar como una misma cosa

igloo > iglú vivienda en forma de cúpula construida con bloques de nieve por los indígenas norteamericanos que habitan en el Ártico

immunity > inmunidad defensa natural contra las enfermedades

impact > impacto tener un efecto fuerte y a menudo malo sobre algo o alguien

import > importación bien o servicio que se vende en un país pero se produce en otro

incentive > incentivo algo que lleva a la acción

income > ingreso pagos de dinero

indentured servant > siervo por contrato inmigrante pobre que aceptaba trabajar de cuatro a siete años a cambio de su pasaje a las colonias

individual > individual relacionado con una sola persona o cosa

individualism > individualismo creencia en la importancia del individuo en lugar de la comunidad

inductive reasoning > razonamiento inductivo proceso de observar hechos específicos y basarse en ellos para establecer principios generales o normas

indulgence > indulgencia una especie de anulación del castigo por los pecados cometidos

inflation > inflación alza general de los precios

influence > influencia el poder de causar cambios

innovation > innovación nuevas formas de hacer las cosas

Inquisition > Inquisición una serie de investigaciones diseñadas para encontrar y juzgar herejes

interdependence > interdependencia dependencia de cada país o grupo respecto de otro

interpret > interpretar explicar, dar un significado

invalid > no válido que no es verdadero o no cumple con la ley

invisible > invisible no visible

irrigate > irrigar suministrar agua

isolated > aislado alejado de otras personas o lugares

isolation > aislamiento la condición de estar solo

issue > cuestión problema o tema que debe ser discutido o decidido

ivory > marfil sustancia blanca dura que proviene del colmillo de un animal como el elefante

J

jati > jati casta definida por la ocupación

judge > juez en la Biblia hebrea, se refiere a un líder que podía organizar a los israelitas para defender su tierra

judiciary > magistratura sistema de cortes que está fuera del control de otros poderes del gobierno

justice > justicia equidad o trato equitativo

Justinian's Code > Código de Justiniano un código de leyes publicado por el emperador bizantino Justiniano

K

Kabuki > Kabuki tipo de teatro japonés dirigido a agricultores, comerciantes y a las personas comunes

kami > kami divinidad o espíritu que representa una fuerza de la naturaleza en la religión japonesa

karma > karma en el hinduismo, el efecto de las acciones de una persona en su vida actual y en las anteriores

khan > kan gobernante mongol

kinship > parentesco conexión basada en relaciones de familia

knight > caballero guerrero montado a caballo

L

labor specialization > especialización laboral división de trabajos y destrezas en la sociedad

lacquer > barniz capa protectora hecha de la savia de un árbol especial

lecturer > profesor disertante persona que da una charla informativa a estudiantes

legacy > legado influencia del pasado

legal > legal relacionado con la ley

Legalism > legismo antigua filosofía china según la cual se requiere de un líder y de un sistema legal fuertes, y no de valores morales, para mantener el orden social

legion > legión unidad básica del ejército romano, formada por 4,500 a 5,000 soldados fuertemente armados

Line of Demarcation > Línea de demarcación línea imaginaria establecida por el Tratado de Tordesillas, que dividía el mundo fuera de Europa en dos zonas, una controlada por España y otra por Portugal

lineage > linaje grupo de personas que descienden de un ancestro común

linear perspective > perspectiva lineal sistema matemático para representar el espacio tridimensional en una superficie plana

linen > lino tela hecha a partir de la planta de lino

loess > loes material en forma de polvo que puede formar tierra

logograph > logograma símbolo que representa una palabra o un grupo de palabras

longhouse > vivienda comunal casa de tipo rectangular construida por los indígenas norteamericanos del Noreste y hecha de madera y corteza o caña

loyalty > lealtad la condición de ser fiel

lucrative > lucrativo rentable

lyric poetry > poesía lírica canciones poéticas

M

magistrate > magistrado funcionario de gobierno encargado de hacer cumplir las leyes

Magna Carta > Carta Magna documento que prometía a los barones ciertos derechos

Mahayana Buddhism > budismo mahayana secta budista que se concentra en la compasión de Buda

mainland > tierra firme área que forma parte de un continente

maintain > mantener sostener y apoyar

major > mayor importante

manage > administrar dirigir; tener control sobre algo

Mandate of Heaven > Mandato Celestial en la antigua China, el supuesto derecho a gobernar concedido a una dinastía por el Cielo, la más alta fuerza de la naturaleza

maniple > manípulo unidad de 60 a 120 soldados en una legión romana que podía actuar con independencia en la batalla

manor > señorío propiedad autosuficiente de un señor medieval

mantra > mantra palabra, canto o sonido sagrado que se repite numerosas veces para ayudar al crecimiento espiritual

maritime > marítimo relacionado con el mar

market economy > economía de mercado economía en la que los consumidores y los productores toman todas las decisiones económicas

martyr > mártir persona que muere por sus creencias

medieval > medieval en latín significa "edad media", relacionado con la Edad Media

meditate > meditar calmar o aclarar la mente, generalmente mediante la concentración en un único objeto

melancholy > melancólico deprimido o triste

mendicant order > orden mendicante orden fundada para combatir la herejía y para predicar a la gente corriente

mercantile > mercantil referente al comercio o los negocios

mercantilism > mercantilismo política económica según la cual una nación se fortalece por medio del control de su comercio, agricultura, industria y moneda

mercenary > mercenario soldado que combate a cambio de dinero, en lugar de hacerlo por su país

merit system > sistema de mérito sistema en el que las personas son contratadas y ascendidas por su talento y destrezas, en lugar de por su riqueza o estatus social

Meroitic script > escritura meroítica uno de los alfabetos más antiguos del mundo, inventado en la antigua Nubia

Mesopotamia > Mesopotamia planicie ancha situada entre los ríos Tigris y Éufrates en el Iraq actual

mestizo > mestizo persona de las colonias españolas de las Américas descendiente de indígenas y europeos

metallurgy > metalurgia ciencia que se ocupa de la extracción de metales y su uso en la creación de objetos útiles

metic > meteco extranjero en una ciudad estado griega, con frecuencia un mercader o artesano

Middle Ages > Edad Media período entre la antigüedad clásica y los tiempos modernos, aproximadamente de 500 a 1500 D.C.

Middle Passage > Travesía intermedia parte de la ruta del comercio triangular en la que los esclavos eran transportados desde África a las Américas

migrate > migrar pasar de una región a otra para vivir allí

migration > migración desplazamiento de personas de un lugar a otro

military state > estado militarista sociedad organizada con el propósito de hacer la guerra

minor > menor no serio, no importante

minority > minoría grupo que representa menos de la mitad de una población

mission > misión comunidad dedicada a la difusión de la fe o a educar y proteger a las personas

missionary > misionero alguien que intenta convertir a otras personas a una religión en particular

mita system > mita en el Imperio Inca, sistema de pago de impuestos por medio del trabajo

moat > foso trinchera llena de agua usada como parte de una fortificación

moksha > moksha liberación de la reencarnación

monastery > monasterio comunidad religiosa retirada

money economy > economía monetaria sistema económico en el que las personas usan moneda corriente en lugar de trueque para comprar y vender bienes

monk > monje hombre que dedica su vida a la adoración de Dios

monopoly > monopolio control de la producción de un bien o servicio por parte de una sola persona o grupo

monotheism > monoteísmo creencia en un solo Dios

monsoon > monzón viento de estación que trae lluvia al subcontinente índico durante partes del año

Moors > moros musulmanes de España

mortar > mortero mezcla de cemento usada para unir ladrillos

mosaic > mosaico diseño formado usando pequeñas tejas de vidrio, piedra o cerámica

mosque > mezquita lugar de culto islámico

movable type > tipo móvil formato de grabado en el que letras individuales hechas de metal pueden usarse una y otra vez

mulatto > mulato en las colonias españolas de las Américas, persona que tenía ascendencia africana y europea

mummy > momia cadáver preservado para evitar su descomposición

mutiny > motín revuelta, especialmente de soldados y marineros contra sus oficiales

mythology > mitología colección de mitos o historias que la gente cuenta sobre sus dioses o héroes

N

natural law > ley natural idea de que hay leyes en la naturaleza que son esenciales tanto para el mundo natural como para los seres humanos

natural resource > recurso natural material útil que se encuentra en el medio ambiente

navigation > navegación arte de conducir un barco de un lugar a otro

network > red un grupo de personas o cosas conectadas entre sí

New Testament > Nuevo Testamento escritos incluidos en la Biblia cristiana que cuentan la historia de Jesús y sus primeros seguidores

nirvana > nirvana estado de paz beatífica sin deseo ni sufrimiento

Noh > Noh tipo de teatro japonés que gustaba a los nobles y los samuráis

nomad > nómada persona que se desplaza de un lugar a otro sin un hogar permanente

northwest passage > paso del noroeste ruta marítima hacia Asia a través de lo que hoy es Canadá

numeral > número símbolo usado para representar una cantidad

O

oasis > oasis lugar del desierto donde se puede encontrar agua

observatory > observatorio edificio usado para observar el cielo

obtain > obtener conseguir o recibir algo

official > funcionario persona que trabaja para el gobierno

oligarchy > oligarquía tipo de gobierno en el que un grupo pequeño de personas tienen el poder

Olympic games > Juegos Olímpicos en la antigua Grecia, competición atlética celebrada cada cuatro años en honor a Zeus

oppose > oponerse intentar detener o derrotar algo

oracle bone > hueso oracular hueso animal o caparazón tallado con caracteres escritos que se usaba para predecir el futuro en la antigua China

oral tradition > tradición oral antecedentes culturales e históricos de una comunidad, transmitidos por cuentos hablados y canciones

oratory > oratoria arte de dar discursos

orthodoxy > ortodoxia creencias religiosas establecidas o tradicionales

P

pagan > pagano relacionado con una religión con muchos dioses

pagan > pagano seguidor de una religión politeísta

papyrus > papiro superficie para escribir similar al papel, nombrada así por los papiros, juncos que crecían en la ribera del río Nilo en el antiguo Egipto

parable > parábola historia con una moraleja religiosa

parliament > parlamento asamblea de representantes encargados de hacer leyes

paterfamilias > paterfamilias el hombre de más edad en una familia romana, que tenía poder absoluto sobre su familia

patriarchal society > sociedad patriarcal sociedad en la cual los hombres rigen las familias y las personas establecen sus orígenes a través de ancestros masculinos

patron > mecenas alguien que da dinero u otro tipo de apoyo a una persona o grupo

Pax Romana > Paz Romana período de estabilidad del Imperio Romano

Peasants' Revolt > Rebelión de los campesinos fracasada revuelta de campesinos contra los señores feudales en Inglaterra en 1381

Peloponnesian League > Liga del Peloponeso alianza militar liderada por Esparta

peninsular > peninsular miembro de la clase más alta en las colonias españolas de las Américas

perilous > riesgoso peligroso

period > período un lapso de tiempo

phalanx > falange formación militar griega compuesta por soldados a pie fuertemente armados que se movían juntos como una unidad

pharaoh > faraón rey del antiguo Egipto

philosophy > filosofía estudio general sobre el conocimiento y el mundo; en griego significa "amor por la sabiduría"

picaresque > picaresca serie de episodios cómicos que suelen incluir un personaje tramposo y desvergonzado

pictograph > pictografía imagen que representa una palabra o idea

pilgrimage > peregrinaje viaje por devoción a un lugar sagrado

plateau > meseta gran extensión de terreno, generalmente plano, que se eleva sobre la tierra circundante

policy > política curso de acción que toma un gobierno

polis > polis ciudad estado en Grecia

politics > política arte y práctica de gobernar

polyrhythmic drumming > percusión polirrítmica tipo de percusión que combina dos o más ritmos diferentes al mismo tiempo

polytheism > politeísmo adoración de muchos dioses o deidades

pope > papa líder de la Iglesia católica romana

populate > poblar habitar un lugar

porcelain > porcelana cerámica blanca y dura de muy alta calidad

potential > potencial posibilidad de crecimiento o cambio en el futuro

potlatch > potlatch ceremonia con comidas y entrega de obsequios en la cultura indígena norteamericana del noroeste

predestination > predestinación idea de que Dios determinó hace mucho tiempo quién obtendrá la salvación

prehistory > prehistoria época anterior a la invención de la escritura

prestige > prestigio respecto y admiración por parte de otros

privateer > corsario barco privado comisionado por un gobierno para atacar y capturar barcos enemigos, especialmente los barcos mercantes

professional > profesional entrenado, experto

profit > obtener ganancias obtener un beneficio económico

prophet > profeta persona de quien se cree que ha sido elegida por Dios para enseñar la verdad a la gente

proportion > proporción uso de elementos equilibrados o simétricos para formar un diseño agradable

prosper > prosperar mejorar en lo económico

prosperity > prosperidad la situación de tener éxito

proverb > proverbio dicho que contiene sabiduría

province > provincia territorio que se encuentra bajo la administración de un país más grande

purchase > adquirir comprar

pursue > perseguir seguir

push-pull factors > factores de expulsión y de atracción los factores de expulsión obligan a la gente a dejar su casa, mientras que los factores de atracción animan a la gente a mudarse a nuevos lugares

pyramid > pirámide estructura con lados triangulares

Q

quipu > quipu aparato para registrar datos utilizado por los incas formado por cuerdas con nudos

Quran > Corán libro sagrado del islam

R

rabbi > rabino maestro espiritual de la religión judía

rationalism > racionalismo creencia de que el conocimiento se adquiere pensando las cosas por medio de la razón

reason > razón capacidad de pensar claramente

recant > abjurar retractarse de algo

Reconquista > Reconquista movimiento para expulsar a los musulmanes de España

reform > reformar mejorar

Reformation > Reforma movimiento religioso iniciado en el siglo XVI para la reforma de la Iglesia católica

regent > regente alguien que gobierna un país cuando el gobernante no puede hacerlo, con frecuencia debido a su edad

region > región área con al menos una característica física o humana que es unificadora, como el clima, los accidentes geográficos, la población o la historia

reincarnation > reencarnación renacimiento del alma en un nuevo cuerpo

reject > rechazar negarse, alejar algo

reliable > confiable digno de confianza, estable, no riesgoso

religion > religión creencias y prácticas de los seres humanos acerca de la existencia, la naturaleza y la adoración de un dios o dioses

rely > confiar depender de algo, tener confianza

Renaissance > Renacimiento del francés "renacer"; se refiere a un período de revitalización cultural en Europa entre los siglos XIV y XVI

representative democracy > democracia representativa democracia en la que el pueblo elige representantes que redactan las leyes de la nación

republic > república forma de gobierno en la que los ciudadanos tienen el derecho a votar y elegir funcionarios

resource > recurso existencia de algo que puede usarse según se necesite

resurrection > resurrección retorno a la vida

revelation > revelación mensaje, generalmente uno que se cree que proviene de Dios

revolution > revolución cambio completo en la forma de pensar, trabajar o vivir

righteousness > rectitud cualidad de comportarse o vivir de una forma éticamente correcta y obedecer la ley de Dios

rigid > rígido inflexible, invariable

river system > sistema fluvial río principal y los ríos y arroyos que desembocan en él

Romance language > lengua romance idioma que derivó del latín, como el francés, el español, el portugués o el italiano

rule of law > imperio de la ley la idea de que todos los miembros de una sociedad, incluso los ricos y poderosos, deben obedecer la ley

ruthless > despiadado que no tiene piedad, cruel

S

Sabbath > sabbat día de la semana establecido para el descanso

sacrament > sacramento rito sagrado en el cristianismo, como el bautismo o la comunión

saint > santo persona reconocida como especialmente sagrada

samurai > samurái guerrero altamente entrenado en el Japón feudal

sarissa > sarissa pica macedonia de 18 pies de largo

satire > sátira obra literaria que se burla de su tema, con frecuencia los vicios o los absurdos de la vida

savanna > sabana pradera con árboles dispersos que pueden sobrevivir periodos de sequía; se encuentra en las áreas tropicales que tienen estaciones secas

scholar-official > mandarín persona con alto grado de educación que pasaba los exámenes del servicio civil y trabajaba para el gobierno

scholarship > erudición estudio y aprendizaje formales

scientific method > método científico método que consiste en el uso de la observación, la experimentación y un razonamiento riguroso para obtener nuevos conocimientos

sculpture > escultura estatua u otra pieza de arte hecha de arcilla, piedra o materiales similares

sect > secta subgrupo de un grupo religioso mayor

secular > laico no religioso

secularism > laicismo la idea de que la religión no debe ser el centro de los asuntos humanos

seismometer > sismómetro instrumento para medir terremotos

serf > siervo persona que está legalmente forzada a vivir y trabajar en la tierra de su señor

Sharia > sharia la ley islámica

Shia > chií miembro de un grupo religioso islámico que apoyaba a Alí como primer califa y que ahora constituye una minoría de los musulmanes

Shinto > sintoísmo religión tradicional que se originó en el Japón

shogun > shogún poderoso líder militar japonés que a veces tenía más poder que el emperador

shrine > santuario lugar de veneración religiosa

Silk Road > Ruta de la Seda red de rutas comerciales que atravesaban Asia

site of encounter > lugar de encuentro lugar donde las personas de diferentes culturas se encuentran e intercambian producos, ideas, y tecnologías

slavery > esclavitud control y propiedad de algunas personas por otras

smuggler > contrabandista persona que comercia de forma ilegal

social class > clase social grupo de personas que tienen una condición económica similar

Socratic method > método socrático forma de enseñanza en la que el maestro hace preguntas a los estudiantes continuamente para hacerlos pensar con más claridad

sonnet > soneto poema de catorce versos con un patrón de rima fijo

specialization > especialización concentración en una cantidad limitada de bienes o actividades

spice trade > comercio de las especias rutas de comercio marítimo y terrestre por las que se llevaban especias y condimentos de África y Asia a los mercados europeos

stable > estable capaz de durar, con pocas posibilidades de deteriorarse

stagnant > estancado que no avanza o no se desarrolla

standardize > estandarizar establecer normas para hacer las cosas más similares

standardized > estandarizado que es igual en todas partes

standing army > ejército regular un ejército permanente compuesto por soldados profesionales

staple > básico algo que es usado o es necesario a menudo

status > estatus posición o rango en relación con otros

stele > estela gran pilar de piedra

steppe > estepa territorio extenso de llanuras

stonetown > stonetown palabra usada para describir ciudades-estado suajilis y sus casas de piedra de varios pisos

strait > estrecho masa de agua angosta que atraviesa la tierra y conecta dos masas de agua mayores

strategy > estrategia plan de largo plazo para obtener un objetivo

structure > estructura edificio

structure > estructura organización

stupa > estupa montículo funerario conmemorativo de la religión budista

subcontinent > subcontinente masa continental separada del resto del continente

subject > súbdito persona gobernada por un monarca

submission > sumisión darle a otra persona el control sobre uno mismo

succession > sucesión una persona o cosa que sigue a otra

successor > sucesor persona que sigue a otra en un puesto o función

Sufism > sufismo estilo de vida islámico que enfatiza el control de los propios deseos, la renuncia a los lazos con el mundo y la búsqueda de cercanía con Dios

sultan > sultán título de un gobernante de un país musulmán

Sunnah > sunna tradiciones y enseñanzas que muchos musulmanes atribuyen al profeta Mahoma

Sunni > suní miembro de un grupo religioso islámico que apoyaba a Abu Bakr como el primer califa y que ahora constituye la mayoría de musulmanes del mundo

surplus > superávit excedente

survive > sobrevivir persistir, seguir viviendo

symbolize > simbolizar representar

synagogue > sinagoga casa de reunión y culto de las comunidades judías

T

Talmud > Talmud colección de enseñanzas orales y comentarios sobre la Biblia hebrea y la ley judía

temperament > temperamento la manera de comportarse y pensar de una persona en particular

tenant > arrendatario persona que alquila tierra o un hogar

tenant farmer > granjero arrendatario persona que paga renta, ya sea en dinero o cosecha, para poder cultivar en la tierra de otra persona

tepee > tipi vivienda portátil de forma cónica usada por los indígenas norteamericanos que vivían en las Llanuras

terrace > terraza parcela de tierra nivelada que se corta en una colina y se cultiva

text > texto fuente escrita, como un libro

textile > textil tejido

theocracy > teocracia gobierno en el que rige el poder religioso

Theravada Buddhism > budismo teravada secta budista que se concentra en la sabiduría de Buda

three-field system > rotación trienal sistema de siembra inventado en la Alta Edad Media, que incrementó la cantidad de tierras que podrían ser cultivadas cada año

toga > toga vestimenta que los hombres adultos usaban, envolviéndose en ella, como símbolo de ciudadanía romana

tolerance > tolerancia voluntad de respetar costumbres y creencias diferentes

topography > topografía características físicas de un lugar

Torah > Torá primeros cinco libros de la Biblia hebrea

tradition > tradición práctica o creencia transmitida de una generación a otra

traditional economy > economía tradicional economía en la que la gente toma decisiones económicas de acuerdo a sus costumbres y hábitos

trans-Saharan > transahariano a través del Sahara

transform > transformar cambiar

transmission > transmisión la acción de transferir algo, como relatos o la historia

treacherous > traicionero peligroso o riesgoso

Treaty of Paris > Tratado de París tratado de 1763 que puso fin a la Guerra de los Siete Años y que dio por resultado el dominio británico de las Américas

Treaty of Tordesillas > Tratado de Tordesillas tratado firmado por España y Portugal en 1494 por el que se dividían entre ellos el mundo fuera de Europa

triangular trade > comercio triangular ruta colonial de comercio entre Europa y sus colonias en las Indias Occidentales y África, donde las mercancías se cambiaban por esclavos

tribute > tributo pago u obsequio a un poder mayor

Trinity > Trinidad las tres personas o formas de Dios según las creencias cristianas: Dios padre, Dios hijo y Espíritu Santo

tyranny > tiranía uso injusto del poder; en la antigua Grecia, el gobierno controlado por un gobernante firme

U

unified > unificado unido de modo que forma una totalidad

uniform > uniforme invariable; constante

unify > unificar unir

unite > unir juntar

university > universidad escuela o grupo de escuelas que imparte enseñanza académica a los niveles más altos

urbanization > urbanización desplazamiento de personas de las áreas rurales a las áreas urbanas

utopia > utopía lugar imaginario e ideal

V

varna > varna forma de agrupar a los personas según sus habilidades

vassal > vasallo en la Europa medieval, señor noble que recibía tierras de otros señores nobles a cambio de sus servicios

Veda > Vedas colección de cientos de himnos sagrados compuestos por los arios de la antigua India

vernacular > lengua vernácula idioma hablado en la vida cotidiana

veto > vetar detener o cancelar las acciones de un funcionario o agencia de gobierno

viceroy > virrey representante que en nombre del rey gobernaba una de las provincias de España en las Américas

villa > villa casa de campo grande

violate > violar no cumplir una regla o acuerdo

W

warlord > señor de la guerra gobernante militar

welfare > bienestar buena situación, comodidad, prosperidad

widespread > extendido común, difundido a través de una gran área

wigwam > wigwam vivienda de los indígenas norteamericanos del noreste fabricada con troncos de árboles jóvenes curvados y amarrados entre sí para formar una estructura redonda cubierta con corteza de árboles o esteras de caña

writ > mandato judicial la orden de una corte de justicia

Z

ziggurat > zigurat templo de Mesopotamia de forma piramidal, hecho de ladrillo

Index

The letters after some page numbers refer to the following: *c* = chart; *g* = graph; *m* = map; *p* = picture; *q* = quotation.

Arab Muslim traders, 718
Arabs, 332, 446, 592, 597, 606
Arachne (mythical figure), 251
archaeological sites, 5m, 8–9
archaeologists, 7, 131
archaeology, 117
Archimedean screw, 271, 271p
Archimedes, 262, 271
archipelagos, 516, 541
architecture
    Aztec, 564
    Byzantine, 355
    Chinese, 496
    as civilization feature, 37
    Egyptian, 109p, 111
    Greek, 254, 255p
    Inca, 571
    Indian, 171
    Islamic, 474, 474p
    Mayan, 557
    religion and, 392–393, 393p
    Roman, 312–313
Arctic, 737m
Arctic cultures, 579
Ardi (hominin), 10
Areopagus, 230
Ares (Greek god), 253
argument, evaluating, xli
argument, writing, lii
aristocracy, 226, 227, 228, 239, 282, 539
Aristophanes (Greek author), 256
Aristotle, 261, 262, 262p, 268, 273q, 395, 471
armada, 655
Arnolfini Portrait, The, 632
Arno River, 624
arrowheads, North American, 11p
art, 21–23, 37, 151p. *See also* term art *under name of country; type of art, e.g.* cave paintings
    African, 611
    Aztec, 564
    Islamic, 473–474
    Mayan, 557
    medieval painting, 630p
    Middle Ages, 396
    Renaissance, 629
Arthashastra, 162q, 165
artifacts, 9, 11p, 575
artisans, Egyptian, 101
The Art of War (Sun Tzu), 189q
Aryabhata (Indian astronomer), 172
Aryans, 126p, 135–140
Asante leaders, 721
ascetics, 152, 154
Ashurbanipal, Assyrian ruler, 60
Asia
    Central, 204, 207, 539
    geography, 129, 173m
    goods, 621
    physical map, 731m
    political map, 730m
    South, 28, 34, 124, 129–130
    Southeast, 168

    Southwestern, 28, 34
    trade routes, 205–207, 205m
Asia minor, 224
Asoka, 127p, 164–167, 164p, 169
As-Saheli, 597
assemblies, Roman, 287, 288, 337
assembly (defined), 67
Assyria
    art, 59p, 64, 64p
    Fertile Crescent conquered by, 118
    geography, 61
    Israel conquered by, 85, 91
    as military state, 59–60
    palaces, 64p
Assyrian empire, 59–60, 61m, 92c
astronomy
    Chinese, 211
    defined, 113
    Egyptian, 113
    Indian, 172
    Sumerian, 51
Atahualpa, 680, 682, 682p
Atharva Veda, 137
Athena (Greek goddess), 220p, 231p, 247p
    as Athens guardian, 253
    myths about, 251
    Roman goddess similar to, 282
    statues, 254
Athens, Greece, 225, 225p
    alliance, 247
    coins, 243, 243p
    democracy in, 227–231, 230p, 236, 261, 282
    golden age, 247
    government in, 237c
    guardian of, 253
    Persian war victory, 246
    siege of, 248–249, 249p
    Sparta compared to, 234–235, 236–237, 238, 272p
Atlantic Ocean, 598
Atlantic slave trade, 715–721
atoms, 262
auctioneers, 718
Augustus, Emperor of Rome, 300, 309–310, 310p, 316q
Australia, 18, 736m
authorities (defined), 320
authority, respect for, 213
autobiography, first known, 261
Avela (sacred text), 63
Averroës (Ibn Rushd), 429
Axum kingdom, 120, 603–604, 604m, 605
ayllus, 573
Ayn Jalut, Battle of, 500
Ayurveda, 172
Azores, 672
Aztec calendar stone, 564, 564p
Aztec civilization, 560–565, 562p, 563p, 565p
Aztec empire, 549m, 560–562, 561m, 565, 680–685, 715
Aztec gods, 563
Aztecs, 403, 563–564, 702

Babylon (city-state), 43, 54p, 56, 85
Babylonian Empire, 56–58, 58p, 61
Babylonian Exile, 86
Bacon, Francis, 660
Baghdad, 446, 469, 500
Bai, Meera, 478
Bali, 148
banking, 624
    system, 386
Ban Zhao, 209, 209q
baptism, 319, 374
barbarians, 341
barley, 28
barons, 414, 416
barter (defined), 47
baths, ancient, 2p–3p
Battiferri, Laura, 638
battle. *See under name of battle, e.g.:* Hastings, Battle of
battle formations, Greek, 228, 228p
battle gear
    Greek, 236p, 247p
    Macedonian, 267p
    Roman, 283p
Batu, 500
Becket, Thomas, 403, 415, 415p
Bedouins, 450, 451p, 459
Belize, 554
Benedict, 372–373, 373p
Benedictine Rule, 372, 373p
Ber, Ali, 598–599
Berbers, 592
Bering Land Bridge, 551
Bhagavad-Gita (Hindu sacred text), 144, 145, 146, 146q
Bhagavatapurana, 478
Bhakti movements, 477–478
Bhutan, 157
Bible, 75, 325–326. *See also* Hebrew Bible
Bills of exchange, 386
Bindusara, 164–165
Birth of Venus, The, 630p
bishops, 352, 407–408
bison hunting, 578, 578p
Black Death, 436–439, 437g, 440, 440p, 441q, 671
block printing, 638
Blue Nile, 99
boats, 18, 238p, 244p
Boccaccio, Giovanni, 440q
bodhisattva, 478
Bodhi Tree (Tree of Knowledge), 153, 154
Bologna, 386p
book burning, 202q
Book of History, 186, 190q
Book of Revelation, 326
Bosporus Strait, 344
Brahman (Hindu concept), 145, 146, 147
Brahmins, 139, 140, 147
brahmins, 480

F

fable (defined), 256
fables, 170, 256, 256p
fact, distinguishing from opinion, 190, 497
fallow (defined), 384
family
    China, 188
    Greek, 238–239, 253
    Roman, 291, 292
famine, 434–435
farmers as social class, 36–37, 208
farming, 27–29
    in Africa, 685
    agricultural revolution, 25
    Aztec society, 564
    beginning of, 6, 14, 24, 25, 27–28, 38
    Bible references to, 76
    China, 494, 495, 706
    in China, 28, 183, 188, 208, 210, 210q
    Cistercians and, 384
    costs and benefits of, 28–29
    culture and, 29–31
    early, 24p
    economy based on, 32
    in Egypt, 27p, 101
    Europe, 383–384, 384p
    in Greece, 235, 240, 241
    in India, 130, 137
    in Mesopotamia, 45–47, 58
    Phoenician, 67
    in Rome, 292, 315
    slash-and-burn, 553, 555
    spread of, 27–28
    Sumerian, 51
    supply of grains with, 384
    three-field system, 384
    tools, 26, 26p
farming villages
    in China, 183
    cities compared to, 31–32
    development and growth of, 29, 30
    in Turkey, 5p
Fa Xian (Buddhist monk), 169
Ferdinand of Aragon, King of Spain, 403, 431, 432p, 674p
Fertile Crescent, 40p–41p, 45, 46m, 93m
    civilizations and peoples of, 42–43
    Egypt compared to, 99
    geography, 73
    location and description of, 42, 43m
feudalism, 362, 377–382, 379c, 381p, 621, 623
    end of, 439
    in England, 414
    Europe and Japan compared, 526, 526p
    in Japan, 522–528
feudal life, xli
fiefs, 379

filial piety, 193, 209
Finland, 699
fire, use of, 11, 12q
fir trees, 24
fishing, 24, 222, 592
flax, 30
floating coffin, 719
floods, 100, 101p, 102, 134
Florence, 440, 440p, 624, 626
folk tales, 472, 610
food
    sources, 14, 24, 25–26, 27
    surpluses, 30–31, 33, 101, 131
Forbidden City in Beijing, 505m
foreigners (in Greece), 226, 231
Forum, 281
fossils, 7, 8, 17
Four Noble Truths (Buddhism), 154, 156
France, 11p, 21–22, 338, 623
    coastline, 714
    Joan of Arc, 436, 436p
    monarchy in, 409–410
    religions in, 653
Franciscan order, 361, 392
Francis of Assisi. St., 391–392, 391p
Francis Xavier, 646
Franks, 365, 368q
freedom, individual, 90
freedom vs. security, 362
free enterprise, 703
free market, 703
French and Indian War, 714
French wine, 621
Frumentius, 605
Fujiwara, 523
funeral orations, 232q, 237

G

Gabriel, angel, 451
Galen, Claudius, 336
Galilei, Galileo, 640, 659
Gama, Vasco da, 673, 673p, 679, 696, 696p, 697
Gandhi, Mohandas, 157
Ganges Basin, 168
Ganges Plain, 130, 138
Ganges River, 130, 149
Gao, 597
garden design, Chinese, 208p, 211
Gargantua, 628, 628p
Gaul, 365
Gautama, Siddhartha, 478
gender roles, 239q, 291–292. *See also* women
General History of the Things of New Spain, 684, 689
Genesis, 72, 72q
Geneva, 645
Genghis Khan, 487p, 498–499, 499q, 500, 500p
Genoa, 623, 672
Gentileschi, Artemisia, 638

geography, 2, 61. *See also under location, e.g.: Asia: geography*
geography skills
    agriculture, 29
    Alexander the Great's empire, 269m
    Arabian peninsula, 450m
    Arab Muslim empire, 460m
    archaeological discoveries, 8
    Assyrian empire, 29
    Black Death, 437m
    China, 182p, 491m, 493m, 502m
    Christianity, spread of, 321m, 372m
    Constantinople, 345
    Crusades, 422m
    Egyptian and Kush trade routes, 116m
    Egyptian civilization, 100m
    Greek civilization, ancient, 222m
    Greek trade, 242m
    Holy Roman Empire, 406m
    human migration, 17
    Israelites, Fertile Crescent and Mesopotamia, 73
    Kingdom of Israel, 85
    medieval civilization, 364
    medieval Europe, 385m, 395m
    Mesopotamia, 46
    Messenia and Sparta, 235m
    Mongolian Empire, 499m
    Norman conquest, 413m
    Peloponnesian War (431-404 BCE), 248m
    Persian wars, 246m
    Phoenicia, 67
    Reconquista, 430m
    Roman civilization, 280m
    Roman empire, 312m
    Roman republic, 297
    Roman trade network, 314m
    Silk Road, 205m
    Vikings, 378m
    Zheng He, voyages of, 506m
geologists (defined), 8
Georgia, 688
Germanic tribes, 341, 365, 412–413
Germans, 341, 342–343, 347
Germany, 651
    castles, 358p–359p
    kings and emperors, 405–406
    religious war in, 652–653
Ghana, 610p, 611p
Ghana, ancient, 590–594
Ghana empire, 591–594, 594p, 600
ghetto, 648
Gilgamesh (Gish), 13q
glaciers, 19
gladiators, 336–337
glass, 113
glassware, 315p
global commerce, 714
global convergence, 668–669
Globe Theatre, 634p

Goa, 697
goals of Hinduism, 146
Gobi desert, 182
God
    in Christianity, 327, 328
    common beliefs about, 90
    communicating with, 82
    in Hinduism, 145, 147, 148
    in Islam, 455
    Israelites, covenants with, 77
    nature of, 80
    relationship with, 76
gods and goddesses
    Egyptian, 243
    Greek, 251, 252–253, 252c, 254, 255q, 282, 294
    Roman, 282, 294, 294q, 323
Goetz, Delia, 555q
gold, 593, 597, 704, 721
golden age, 496, 531
Golden Rule, 194, 328
gold-mounted swords, 593
Gospels, 319, 326
Gothic cathedrals, 392–393, 393p
Goths, 342–343
government
    Ancient Ghana, 592
    centralized, 199, 204
    China, 489, 494
    city versus village, 32
    England, 413
    English colonies, 711–712
    forms of, 216, 227–228, 261, 274, 278, 282, 302p
    Japan, 519
    organized as civilization feature, 35
Gozzoli, Benozzo, 629
grains, 24
Granada, 403, 431, 432p
granary, 131
Grand Canal, 495
Grand Mosque, 457
Great Basin, 581
Great Britain
    migration to, 149
Great Famine, 435
Great Library of Alexandria, 270–271
Great Plains, 578, 701
Great Pyramid of Ghiza, 111p
Great Pyramid of Khufu, 111
Great Schism, 353–354
Great Wall, 499, 507
Great Wall of China, 197p, 198
Greco-Roman (classical) civilization, 271
Greco-Roman culture, 332–333
Greco-Roman trading settlements, 604
Greece, 623, 633
    empire, 592
    mathematics and medicine, 471
Greece, ancient, 216p–217p, 273m
    achievements, 272c
    architecture, 254, 255p

art, 251p, 254–256, 334
civilization, origin of, 34
conquest of, 249
courts, 230
defenses, 228
documents, preserving, 355
early years, 221–226
economy, 238–243, 238p
education and learning, 229, 236, 258–264, 270–271
family life, 238–239, 253
farming in, 235, 240, 241
geography, 218m–219m, 221–223, 221p, 222p, 225
golden age, 247, 249
history, study of, 260–261
influence of, 220
influences on, 223
literature, 224, 254–256, 334
Macedonia, 249, 266–268
mathematics and medicine, 263–264
mythology, 243, 251–253, 251p, 282
politics and government, 225–226, 227–228, 237c, 261, 282 (see also form of government under city-state, e.g.: Athens, Greece: democracy in)
science and technology, 261–262
social classes and divisions in, 236, 239–241, 240p
trade, 222, 223, 237, 238, 243
trade routes, 242m
warfare in, 228, 234, 235, 236, 237, 241, 244–249
writing and alphabet, 70, 243, 349
Greece, modern, 347
Greek culture, spread and influence of, 69, 171, 255p, 267, 269, 270–271, 282
Greek Egypt, 120
Greek empire, fall of, 270
Greek fire, 347
Greek language, 271, 322, 326, 354
Greek Rationalism, 657–658
Greek rule, Jews under, 87
Greeks, Phoenician influence on, 69, 70
Greeks as slaves, 293
Gregory I, Pope, 371
Gregory IX, Pope, 426
Gregory VII, Pope, 403p, 407p
    conflict with Henry IV, 407–409, 408p, 409p
    listed principles, 411q
griots, 600, 610–611, 612
griottes, 611
Guamán Poma de Ayala, Felipe, 682, 683q
Guatemala, 554
guilds, 387, 387p, 394
gunpowder, 187p, 510
guns, 702

Gupta Empire, 168–172, 169m, 169q, 464–465, 476, 479
Guru Granth Sahib, 480
Guru Nanak, 480
gurus, 143, 152
Gutenberg, Johann, 638

H

habeas corpus, 417
Hades (Greek god), 252
Hadith, 454, 454q
Hadrian, Emperor of Rome, 311
Hadrian's walls, 311, 311p
Hagia Sophia (Byzantine church), 346, 354p, 355
hajj, 456, 457
Hamlet, 634
Hammurabi, King of Babylon, 43p, 56, 59, 60, 64
Hammurabi's Code, 56–57, 57p, 58, 64
Han dynasty, 203–212, 214c, 489, 492
Han Feizi, 200, 200q
Hanging Gardens of Babylon, 60
Hannibal, 277p, 296–297, 301q
Hanukkah, 87
Harappa, India, 131, 141
harness, 384, 384p
Harold, king of England, 412–413
Harvard, 691
Hastings, Battle of, 414
Hatshepsut, pharaoh of Egypt, 97p, 98p, 105, 106, 106p
Hebrew Bible, 77–82
    Christianity and, 72, 318, 321, 325, 329
    lands of, 73m
    legacy of, 90
    Psalms, 76q
    translations of, 271
Heian artists, 536
Heian period, 531
Hellenistic learning, 270–271
Hellenistic period, 269, 270, 271
helots, 235
Helu, Chinese king, 189
Henry II, King of England, 415, 418
Henry IV, King of France, 653–654, 653p, 654
    conflict with Pope Gregory VII, 407–409, 408p, 409p, 411q
Henry of Navarre, 653
Henry the Navigator, Prince, 672, 673p
Hera (Greek goddess), 252, 282
Hercules (mythical figure), 252
herders, 137
herding metaphor, 76q
heresy, 426
heretics, 426–427
Hermonthis, Egypt, 107
Herodotus, 63q, 65q, 246q, 250q, 260

as social class, 37
trading and sale of, 120
smugglers, 507
social classes, 36–37, 48, 596
social differences, 31, 58
social divisions, 461
social justice, 88–89
social mobility, 470
social order (Confucianism), 193, 194, 208–209
social organization
Chinese, 193
farming and, 31
Sumerian, 48
social structure, Mongolian, 501–502
societal change, forces causing, 304
Socrates, 219p, 259, 259p, 259q, 260, 260p
Socratic method, 259
Solomon, King of Israel, 85, 91
Solon (leader of Athens), 229, 229p
Song dynasty, 491, 491m, 492, 493, 493m, 494, 496, 503
Songhai empire, 598–600
Soninke, 592
Son of God (Christianity), 327
Son of Heaven (Chinese ruler title), 186
Sophocles, 255, 255q
Soto, Hernando de, 687
souk, 470
soul
in Buddhism, 154
in Christianity, 327
in Hinduism, 144, 145, 147
soul in Islam, 455
sources
assess credibility of, 441
assessing credibility of, 163
Buddhism, spread of, 173
Chinese civil service examination system, 497
Constantine, Emperor of Rome, 350
drawing sound conclusions from, 202
South America, 674, 678, 680
farming in, 28
physical map, 735m
political map, 734m
South Asia, 124, 129–130
Islam in, 460
Southeast Asia, 168, 538, 541–543
geography, 399, 486, 541g
goods from, 671
Islam in, 460
Southern Europe Catholicism, 653
Southern Song, 495, 501
Southwestern Asia, 446, 450m
southwestern Asia, 28, 34
Spain, 22, 338, 441c, 623, 671, 676, 687–692, 693
Caribbean natives, 689p, 690
Catholicism and, 654

Catholic missionaries, 688
in coast of Southeast Asia, 688
colonial society, 690
conquest of Mexico, 687
cultures, 689–690
explorations, 687
goods manufactured in, 689
Islam/Muslims in, 428–429, 431, 446, 464, 689
local governors, 688
Mexican painting, 690p
monarchy in, 693
Native Americans and, 688–689, 691
Old World diseases, 691
in Philippines, 688
plantations, 692
Portuguese merchants and, 689
Santo Domingo, 692
social classes, 690
source of wealth, 690
in Western Europe, 687
Spanish Americas, 684, 685, 690, 694
Spanish Armada, Battle of, 655
Spanish exploration, 681m
Spanish Inquisition, 647
Spanish language, 691
Spanish settlements, 713, 716
Sparta, Greece, 227, 235m, 272p
alliance, 247–248
battle gear, 236p, 238
government in, 237c
military conquests by, 234, 237, 241
oligarchy in, 234–237
women in, 239
Spartacus, 293
spears, 267
specialization (defined), 31
Spice Islands, 672
spice trade, 672, 672p, 697–698
spinning yarn, 30, 30p
spoken Chinese, 184
Sri Lanka, 157, 165, 166, 173
Srivijaya empire, 543
stable currency (defined), 315
staff (defined), 76
standing army (defined), 61
staple crop, 701
state, church and, 415
statues
Chinese, 198p
Egyptian, 106p, 112p
examples of, 37
Greek, 253p, 254
in Iraq, 34p
Roman, 278p, 333–334
steam power, 262
steel, 495
stelae, 64, 556, 604
steppe, 498
St. Lawrence River Valley, 710
Stoicism, 335

Stoics, 260
Stone Age
art, 21–23
burials, 5p, 23, 23p
peoples, 15–16
religion, 23
tools in, 26
Stone Age, New, 24
Stone Age, Old, 11
stone architecture, 571
stone-carving methods, 702
stone homes, 576
stone pillars (Asoka's), 166
stone pyramids, 554
stone tools, 11, 26
stonetowns, 606
storytelling, African, 610
St. Patrick, 371p
St. Peter's Basilica, 642
strait (defined), 344
strangers, care for, 89
strategy (defined), 160
structures (defined), 313
study (Judaism), 82
stupas, 165, 166, 543, 543p
Subarctic cultures, 580
subcontinent (defined), 129
submission (defined), 255q
Sudan, 99, 115
Sudras, 139
suffering
in Buddhism, 154, 155
in Greek mythology, 252
Sufism, 464
Sui dynasty, 495
suit of armor, 380p
Sulla (dictator), 298–299
sultans, 465
Sumanguru, 595
Sumer, 45, 92c
achievements, 51
art, 51p, 64
city-states in, 53
conquest of, 54–56
Egypt compared to, 102, 109
geography, 46
government, 50–51
Indus Valley, trade with people from, 132
legacy, 58
religion in, 36, 48
social classes, 48
social hierarchy, 48p
Sun Dance, 578
Sundiata, 612p
Sung dynasties, 491, 491m
Sun Goddess, 534
Sunnah, 454, 457, 458q
Sunnis, 462, 463p
Sun Tzu, 189q
supply and demand, 703
surplus (defined), 30
Swahili culture, 606
Switzerland, 645
swords, 593
synagogues, Jewish, 77p

Acknowledgments

Photography

ELA 0 Hero Images Inc./Alamy Stock Photo; **ELA 9** Chassenet/BSIP SA/Alamy Stock Photo; **002–003** Ursula Gahwiler/Robertharding/ Alamy Stock Photo; **005T** John Reader/Science Source; **005C** Marion Bull/Alamy Stock Photo; **005BL** Ann Ronan Picture Library Heritage Images/Newscom; **005BR** Interfoto/Fine Arts/Alamy Stock Photo; **006** E&E Image Library Heritage Images/Newscom; **007** Eric Cabanis/ Staff/AFP/Getty Images; **009** John Reader/Science Source; **010** Julian Stratenschulte/Dpa picture alliance/Alamy Stock Photo; **011T** World History Archive/Alamy Stock Photo; **011B** Werner Forman Archive/ Heritage Image Partnership Ltd/Alamy Stock Photo; **012** Eyal Bartov/ Alamy Stock Photo; **013** Zev Radovan/BibleLandPictures/Alamy Stock Photo; **015** Clement Philippe/Arterra Picture Library/Alamy Stock Photo; **016** John Reader/Science Source; **019** Steppenwolf/Alamy Stock Photo; **021** Pierre Andrieu/Staff/AFP/Getty Images; **022** lorenzo rossi/ Alamy Stock Photo; **023** Marion Bull/Alamy Stock Photo; **024** The Irish Image Collection/Design Pics Inc/Alamy Stock Photo; **025L** Critterbiz/ Shutterstock; **025R** Mikkel Bigandt/Shutterstock; **026** Zev Radovan/ BibleLandPictures/Alamy Stock Photo; **027** Ancient Art & Architecture Collection Ltd/Alamy Stock Photo; **030** Will Steeley/Alamy Stock Photo; **031** Ann Ronan Picture Library Heritage Images/Newscom; **032** Debu55y/Fotolia; **033** Essam Al-Sudani/Stringer/AFP/Getty Images; **034** Interfoto/Fine Arts/Alamy Stock Photo; **036** Werner Forman Archive/Heritage Image Partnership Ltd/Alamy Stock Photo; **037** Werner Forman/Universal Images Group/Getty Images; **040–041** Peter Horree/Alamy Stock Photo; **042** Interfoto/Personalities/Alamy Stock Photo; **043T** Image Asset Management/World History Archive/ AGE Fotostock; **043C** Pictures From History/The Image Works; **043B** Fine Art Images/Heritage Image Partnership Ltd/Alamy Stock Photo; **044** Image Asset Management/World History Archive/AGE Fotostock; **045** CM Dixon Heritage Images/Newscom; **047** Mediacolor's/Alamy Stock Photo; **049** ZUMA Press, Inc./Alamy Stock Photo; **051** M. Seemuller/DEA/Getty Images; **052** Photo Researchers, Inc/Alamy Stock Photo; **054** View of Ancient Babylon showing the Hanging Gardens and the Temple of Jupiter Belus, plate 3 from 'Entwurf einer historischen Architektur', engraved by Johann Adam Delsenbach (1687–1765) 1721 (engraving) (later colouration), Fischer von Erlach, Johann Bernhard (1656–1723) (after)/Private Collection/The Stapleton Collection/Bridgeman Art Library; **055** Interfoto/Personalities/Alamy Stock Photo; **056** Josse Christophel/Alamy Stock Photo; **058** Peter Horree/Alamy Stock Photo; **059** ZevRadovan/www.BibleLandPictures. com/Alamy Stock Photo; **060** Adam Eastland Art + Architecture/Alamy Stock Photo; **062** Pictures From History/The Image Works; **063** W. BUSS/De Agostini/DEA/Getty Images; **064** Pictures From History/ Newscom; **066** Fabian von Poser/ImageBROKER/AGE Fotostock; **068** Nicholas Pitt/Alamy Stock Photo; **070** Goir/Shutterstock; **071** Eddie Gerald/Alamy Stock Photo; **072** ArtPix/Alamy; **075** Lawrence Migdale/Science Source; **076** www.BibleLandPictures.com/Alamy Stock Photo; **077** Ira Berger/Alamy Stock Photo; **078** Israel Images/ Alamy Stock Photo; **079** Prisma Archivo/Alamy Stock Photo; **081** Dpa picture alliance archive/Alamy Stock Photo; **082** Nir Elias/Reuters; **083** Corey Weiner/Alamy Stock Photo; **084** Fine Art Images/Heritage Image Partnership Ltd/Alamy Stock Photo; **087** Sebastian Scheiner/AP Images; **088** Flik47/iStock/Getty Images; **090** Jack Guz/Staff/AFP/ Getty Images. **094–095** Sylvain Grandadam/Age Fotostock; **096** Fatih Kocyildir/Shutterstock; **097T** Peter Horree/Alamy Stock Photo; **097C** David Keith Jones/Images of Africa Photobank/Alamy Stock Photo; **097B** Prisma Archivo/Alamy Stock Photo; **098** Efesenko/Fotolia; **099** The Print Collector/Alamy Stock Photo; **102** David Keith Jones/Images of Africa Photobank/Alamy Stock Photo; **104** DEA/S. VANNINI/De Agostin/Getty Images; **105** Epa european pressphoto agency b.v./ Alamy Stock Photo; **106** Peter Horree/Alamy Stock Photo; **107** Akg Images/Franois Gunet/Newscom; **108** Kostin SS/Shutterstock; **109** Brian_Kinney/Fotolia; **110** Michael DeFreitas Middle East/Alamy Stock Photo; **111T** H.M. Herget/National Geographic Creative/Alamy Stock Photo; **111B** Fatih Kocyildir/Shutterstock; **112** CULTNAT, Dist. RMN-GP/Art Resource,New York; **113** Tor Eigeland/Alamy Stock Photo; **114** Mickael David/Invictus SARL/Alamy Stock Photo; **115** Fabian von Poser/imageBROKER/Alamy Stock Photo; **117** Mary Evans Picture Library/Alamy Stock Photo; **118** INTERFOTO/Fine Arts/Alamy Stock

Photo; **119L** Kokhanchikov/Shutterstock; **119C** Peter Horree/Alamy Stock Photo; **119R** Jim Batty/Alamy Stock Photo; **120** Werner Forman Archive/Heritage Image Partnership Ltd/Alamy Stock Photo; **121** Natasha Owen/Fotolia; **124–125** Ephotocorp/Alamy Stock Photo; **126** De Agostini/G. Dagli Orti/UIG Universal Images Group/Newscom; **127T** Godong/Alamy Stock Photo; **127C** Coins depicting the King Chandragupta and Queen Durdhara, Mauyra Dynasty (gold), Indian School/Dinodia/Bridgeman Art Library; **127B** Mary Evans Picture Library/Alamy Stock Photo; **128** Pjhpix/Alamy Stock Photo; **129** Arnim Schulz/Moment Open/Getty Images; **131T** Peter Horree/Alamy Stock Photo; **131B** G NIMATALLAH/DEA/De Agostini Editore/AGE Fotostock; **133** Robert Harding Productions/Alamy Stock Photo; **134** Twinsterphoto/Fotolia; **135** Anders Blomqvist/Lonely Planet Images/ Getty Images; **137** DEA PICTURE LIBRARY/De Agostini Editore/AGE Fotostock; **138** Yasir Nisar/Getty Images; **140** STR/EPA/Newscom; **142** Dbrnjhrj/Fotolia; **143** De Agostini/G. Dagli Orti/UIG Universal Images Group/Newscom; **144T** Dinodia Photos/Alamy Stock Photo; **144B** Bl/ Robana/Robana Picture Library/AGE Fotostock; **145** Fedyaeva Maria/ Shutterstock; **146** K.Decha/Shutterstock; **147** Michael Runkel/ robertharding/Alamy Stock Photo; **149** Gunnar Kullenberg/RGB Ventures/SuperStock/Alamy Stock Photo; **150** Bl/Robana/Robana Picture Library/AGE Fotostock; **151** Davidevison/Fotolia; **152** Godong/ Alamy Stock Photo; **153** Godong/Alamy Stock Photo; **154** Marc Bruxelle/Alamy Stock Photo; **156** Kaitune/Fotolia; **157** Roger Bacon/ Reuters/Alamy Stock Photo; **158** Peter Horree/Alamy Stock Photo; **159** Ashish Bhatnagar; **161** Coins depicting the King Chandragupta and Queen Durdhara, Mauyra Dynasty (gold), Indian School/Dinodia/ Bridgeman Art Library; **162** Chandragupta (w/c on paper)/Indian School/Dinodia/Bridgeman Art Library; **164** Mary Evans Picture Library/Alamy Stock Photo; **165** Saiko3p/iStock/Getty Images; **166** M.A. PUSHPA KUMARA/EPA/Newscom; **167** Rafal Cichawa/Fotolia; **168** Roger Bacon/Reuters/Alamy Stock Photo; **170** Paul Kim/ DBImages/Alamy Stock Photo; **172** Angelo Giampiccolo/Shutterstock; **176–177** Jean-Pierre De Mann/Robertharding/Alamy Stock Photo; **178** V&A Images, London/Art Resource, New York; **179T** Pictures From History/Newscom; **179C** BnF, Dist. RMN-Grand Palais/Art Resource, New York; **179B** Robana/BL/Robana Picture Library/AGE Fotostock; **180** 360b/Alamy Stock Photo; **181** Paul Springett 10/Alamy Stock Photo; **183** Zens photo/Moment Open/Getty Images; **184** V&A Images, London/Art Resource, New York; **185** The Emperor Mu Wang (c.985–c.907 BC) of the Chou Dynasty in his chariot, from a history of Chinese emperors (colour on silk), Chinese School, (17th century)/ Bibliotheque Nationale, Paris, France/Bridgeman Art Library; **187** Chronicle/Alamy Stock Photo; **188** SSPL/The Image Works; **189** Pictures From History/Newscom; **191** Christopher Pillitz/Corbis Historical/Getty Images; **192** Ivy Close Images/Alamy Stock Photo; **194** BnF, Dist. RMN-Grand Palais/Art Resource, New York; **195** Weerapong Pumpradit/Shutterstock; **196** Zhuhe2343603/Shutterstock; **197** Danita Delimont/Gallo Images/Getty Images; **198** Hung Chung Chih/Shutterstock; **200** Robana/BL/Robana Picture Library/AGE Fotostock; **201** Snark/Art Resource, New York; **203** Transporting ceramics (painted silk), Chinese School, (15th century)/Topkapi Palace Museum, Istanbul, Turkey/Bridgeman Art Library; **204** Emperor Wu Ti (156–87, r.141–87 BC), leaving his palace, from a history of Chinese emperors (colour on silk), Chinese School, (17th century)/Bibliotheque Nationale, Paris, France/Archives Charmet/Bridgeman Art Library; **207** Dorling Kindersley ltd/Alamy Stock Photo; **208** Manfred Gottschalk/Lonely Planet Images/Getty Images; **209** Burt Silverman/ National Geographic Creative/Alamy Stock Photo; **210** Prisma Bildagentur AG/Snyder Collection/Alamy Stock Photo; **211** Martha Avery/Corbis Historical/Getty Images; **212** SSPL/The Image Works; **216–217** Lambros Kazan/Shutterstock; **218** The Print Collector/Alamy Stock Photo; **219T** Martin Beddall/Alamy Stock Photo; **219CL** Akg Images/Newscom; **219CR** Stefanos Kyriazis/Fotolia; **219B** Ancient Art & Architecture Collection Ltd/Alamy Stock Photo; **220** Dimitrios/ Shutterstock; **221** Andrei Nekrassov/Fotolia; **223** Leonid Serebrennikov/Alamy Stock Photo; **224** AF archive/Alamy Stock Photo; **225** Starush/Fotolia; **226** John Hios/akg-images/Newscom; **227** North Wind Picture Archives/Alamy Stock Photo; **228** Chigi vase, 650–640 BC (ceramic),Greek, (7th century BC)/Museo Nazionale Etrusco di Villa

Giulia, Rome, Italy/De Agostini Picture Library/Bridgeman Images; **229** Lanmas/Alamy Stock Photo; **231** Erich Lessing/Art Resource, New York; **232** Martin Beddall/Alamy Stock Photo; **234** Tatiana Popova/Shutterstock; **236** Illustration Art/Alamy Stock Photo; **238** H.M. Herget/National Geographic Creative/Alamy Stock Photo; **239** World History Archive/Alamy Stock Photo; **241** Stefano Bianchetti/Corbis Historical/Getty Images; **243** Glevalex/Fotolia; **244** Mike Andrews/Ancient Art & Architecture Collection Ltd/Alamy Stock Photo; **245** Akg Images/Newscom; **247** Anatoly Vartanov/Fotolia; **249** Classic Image/Alamy Stock Photo; **251** AF Fotografie/Alamy Stock Photo; **253** Vvasiliki/E+/Getty Images; **254** George Papapostolou/Moment Open/Getty Images; **255L** Olga Drabovich/Shutterstock; **255R** Zack Frank/Fotolia; **256** Ivy Close Images/Alamy Stock Photo; **257** Kpzfoto/Alamy Stock Photo; **258** Fine Art Images/Heritage Image Partnership Ltd/Alamy Stock Photo; **259** Tomas Abad/Alamy Stock Photo; **260** Stefanos Kyriazis/Fotolia; **261** North Wind Picture Archives/Alamy Stock Photo; **262** Richard Osbourne/Alamy Stock Photo; **263** Ancient Art & Architecture Collection Ltd/Alamy Stock Photo; **264** Ancient Art & Architecture Collection Ltd/Alamy Stock Photo; **266** Peter Horree/Alamy Stock Photo; **267** Ivy Close Images/Alamy Stock Photo; **268** M.Coudert/Fotolia; **270** Antiqua Print Gallery/Alamy Stock Photo; **271** World History Archive/Alamy Stock Photo; **274–275** Dmitry Naumov/123RF.com; **277T** Heritage Image Partnership Ltd/Alamy Stock Photo; **277C** Rabatti-Domingie/Akg-Images/Newscom; **277BL** Niday Picture Library/Alamy Stock Photo; **277BR** Caesar Dictating his Commentaries (oil on canvas), Palagi, Pelagio (1775–1860)/Palazzo del Quirinale, Rome, Italy/Bridgeman Art Library; **278** alessandro0770/123RF.com; **279** Laura Zulian Photography/Getty Images; **281** Nito/Shutterstock; **283** Album/Prisma/Newscom; **284** Heritage Image Partnership Ltd/Alamy Stock Photo; **285** Atlaspix/Alamy Stock Photo; **287T** Yullishi/Shutterstock; **287B** De Agostini Picture Library Universal Images Group/Newscom; **289** Le Pictorium/Active Museum/Alamy Stock Photo; **290** Cliff Owen/AP Images; **291** Christine Osborne Pictures/Alamy Stock Photo; **292** Paco Gómez García/Age Fotostock/Alamy Stock Photo; **293** Fine Art/Getty Images; **294** World History Archive/Alamy Stock Photo; **296** Niday Picture Library/Alamy Stock Photo; **298** Caesar Dictating his Commentaries (oil on canvas), Palagi, Pelagio (1775–1860)/Palazzo del Quirinale, Rome, Italy/Bridgeman Art Library; **299** Rabatti-Domingie/Akg Images/Newscom; **300** The Turmoils in Rome after the Death of Caesar (oil on panel), Roore, Jacques Ignatius de (1686–1747)/Private Collection/Photo Christie's Images/Bridgeman Art Library; **304–305** David Soanes Photography/Moment Open/Getty Images; **307T** FineArt/Alamy Stock Photo; **307C** Vicspacewalker/Fotolia; **307BL** Bible Land Pictures/akg-images; **307BR** JT Vintage/Glasshouse Images/Alamy Stock Photo; **308** C M Dixon/AAA Collection/Ancient Art & Architecture Collection Ltd/Alamy Stock Photo; **309** RMN-Grand Palais/Art Resource, New York; **310** Peter Horree/Alamy Stock Photo; **312** David Ball/Alamy Stock Photo; **315** Ilan Amihai/PhotoStock-Israel/Alamy Stock Photo; **316** Interfoto/Personalities/Alamy Stock Photo; **318** Mattes Rene/Hemis/Alamy Stock Photo; **319** The Artchives/Alamy Stock Photo; **320** PjrTravel/Alamy Stock Photo; **322** Niday Picture Library/Alamy Stock Photo; **323** Prisma Archivo/Alamy Stock Photo; **325** Melvyn Longhurst/Alamy Stock Photo; **326** FineArt/Alamy Stock Photo; **327** Walker Art Library/Alamy Stock Photo; **329** EPA/EPA European Pressphoto Agency b.v./Alamy Stock Photo; **330** Zvonimir Atletić/Alamy Stock Photo; **331** Vasily Kovalev/Alamy Stock Photo; **332** Peter Horree/Alamy Stock Photo; **333** Adam Eastland Art + Architecture/Alamy Stock Photo; **334** Gabriel Jules Thomas/Getty Images; **335** Ann Ronan Picture Library Heritage Images/Newscom; **336** Reconstruction of the Colosseum, Rome (w/c on paper), French School, (20th century)/Archives Larousse, Paris, France/Bridgeman Art Library; **337** Chariot race at the Circus Maximus, Baraldi, Severino (b.1930)/Private Collection/Look and Learn/Bridgeman Images; **338** Ivy Close Images/Alamy Stock Photo; **339** Viacheslav Lopatin/Shutterstock; **340** Akg Images/Newscom; **341** Erich Lessing/Art Resource, New York; **343** Universal Images Group/Superstock; **344** Realy Easy Star/Alamy Stock Photo; **346** Hackenberg/F1online digitale Bildagentur GmbH/Alamy Stock Photo; **347** Sadikgulec/IStock/Getty Images; **348** Popovariel/Shutterstock; **349** Verkhovynets Taras/Shutterstock; **351** Ig0rZh/Fotolia; **352** Erich Lessing/Art Resource, New York; **354** EpicStockMedia/Fotolia; **355** Interfoto/History/Alamy Stock Photo; **358–359** Harald Lueder/Shutterstock; **360** David Lomax/robertharding/Alamy Stock Photo; **361T** Interfoto/Personalities/Alamy

Stock Photo; **361C** Mary Evans Picture Library/Alamy Stock Photo; **361B** INTERFOTO/Personalities/Alamy Stock Photo; **362** Prisma Archivo/Alamy Stock Photo; **363** Fine Art Images/Heritage Image Partnership Ltd/Alamy Stock Photo; **365T** Lic0001/Fotolia; **365B** North Wind Picture Archives/Alamy Stock Photo; **366** Pictures From History/Akg Images; **367** JT Vintage/Glasshouse Images/Alamy Stock Photo; **368** Charlemagne and his paladins in battle against the Saracens, miniature from 'Charlemagne and his paladins' (vellum), French School, (13th century)/Private Collection/Index/Bridgeman Images; **370** Constantinos Iliopoulos/Alamy Stock Photo; **371** St. Patrick and a King, miniature from a manuscript (vellum), Irish school (13th century)/Huntington Library and Art Gallery, San Marino, CA, USA/Bridgeman Images; **373** Kim Petersen/Alamy Stock Photo; **374** Akg Images; **375** Akg Images; **377** Investiture of a Knight, from the 'Metz Codex', 1290 (vellum), French School, (13th century)/Private Collection/Index/Bridgeman Art Library; **378** David Lomax/robertharding/Alamy Stock Photo; **380** Jeff Greenberg/The Image Works; **382** Andrey_Popov/Shutterstock; **383** RMN-Grand Palais/Art Resource, New York; **384** North Wind Picture Archives/The Image Works; **386** View of the Market in Bologna (vellum) (detail of 125859), Italian School, (14th century)/Museo Civico, Bologna, Italy/Roger-Viollet, Paris/Bridgeman Art library; **388** Life at Wartburg in Thuringen at the time of the legendary minstrels' contest under Landgrave Hermann in the year 1207, from the Tannhauser Saga, King's Dining Room and Study (oil on canvas), German School, (19th century)/Schloss Neuschwanstein, Bavaria, Germany/De Agostini Picture Library/A. Dagli Orti/Bridgeman Art library; **389** Shock/Fotolia; **390** North Wind Picture Archives/Alamy Stock Photo; **391** St. Francis of Assisi preaching to the birds (oil on panel), Giotto di Bondone (c.1266–1337)/Louvre, Paris, France/Bridgeman Art library; **392T** David C. Phillips/Garden Photo World/Alamy Stock Photo; **392B** Grenville Collins Postcard Collection/Chronicle/Alamy Stock Photo; **393** Dakid/Fotolia; **394** bpk Bildagentur/Art Resource, New York; **396** Prisma Archivo/Alamy Stock Photo; **397** Interfoto/Personalities/Alamy Stock Photo; **400–401** Fine Art Images/Heritage Image Partnership Ltd/Alamy Stock Photo; **402** North Wind Picture Archives/Alamy Stock Photo; **403T** INTERFOTO/Personalities/Alamy Stock Photo; **403CL** Pictures From History/Akg Images; **403CR** Prisma Archivo/Alamy Stock Photo; **403B** GL Archive/Alamy Stock Photo; **404** Fine Art Images/Heritage Image Partnership Ltd/Alamy Stock Photo; **405** The Print Collector/Alamy Stock Photo; **407** INTERFOTO/Personalities/Alamy Stock Photo; **408** Stapleton Historical Collection/Heritage Image Partnership Ltd/Alamy Stock Photo; **409** INTERFOTO/Personalities/Alamy Stock Photo; **410** Photo12/Archives Snark/Alamy Stock Photo; **412** Jorisvo/Fotolia; **414** Rafael Ben-Ari/Fotolia; **415** North Wind Picture Archives/Alamy Stock Photo; **416** SuperStock/Alamy Stock Photo; **417** Brandon Bourdages/Shutterstock; **418** Jayne Fincher/Photo Int/Alamy Stock Photo; **419** Julian Elliott/Robertharding/Alamy Stock Photo; **420** Matthaeus Merian, The Younger/Akg Images; **421** Bettmann/Getty Images; **423** Chronicle/Alamy Stock Photo; **424T** Fine Art Images/Heritage Image Partnership Ltd/Alamy Stock Photo; **424B** Geoffroi de Villehardouin, illustration from 'Le Plutarque Francais' by E. Mennechet, engraved by Delaistre, 1835 (coloured engraving), Jacquand, Claude (1804–78) (after)/Bibliotheque des Arts Decoratifs, Paris, France/Archives Charmet/Bridgeman Art Library; **425** Joseph Martin/Akg Images; **426** Lanmas/Alamy Stock Photo; **427** Loading Goods on to a Ship, from the manuscript 'Justiniano Institutiones Feodorum et Alia', c.1300 (vellum), Bolognese School, (14th century)/Biblioteca Nazionale, Turin, Italy/Index/Bridgeman Art Library; **428** Spain/Maghreb From the 13th-century 'Book of Chants', an Arab (left) and a Christian play the oud together./Pictures from History/Bridgeman Art Library; **429** M.V. Photography/Fotolia; **432** Pictures From History/Akg Images; **433** Photo Researchers, Inc/Alamy Stock Photo; **434** Stuart Black/Robertharding/Alamy Stock Photo; **435** Fototeca Gilardi/Akg Images; **436** GL Archive/Alamy Stock Photo; **439** World History Archive/Alamy Stock Photo; **440** De Agostini Picture Library/Akg Images; **444–445** Ahmad Faizal Yahy/Fotolia; **446** Heritage Image Partnership Ltd/Fine Art Images/Alamy Stock Photo; **447T** Pictures From History/Newscom; **447C** G.Dagli Orti/Dea/Getty Images; **447BL** PRISMA ARCHIVO/Alamy Stock Photo; **447BR** Roland and Sabrina Michaud/Akg Images; **448** Raga Jose Fuste/Prisma Bildagentur AG/Alamy Stock Photo; **449** Universal Images Group/Art Resource, New York; **451** Stefan Auth/

imageBROKER/Alamy Stock Photo; **452** Philippe Lissac/Photononstop/ Getty Images; **453** Roger Bacon/REUTERS/Alamy Stock Photo; **454** Melvyn Longhurst/Alamy Stock Photo; **455** Roland and Sabrina Michaud/Akg Images; **456** MichaeRM RunkeRM/Robertharding/ Alamy Stock Photo; **457** Louise Batalla Duran/Alamy Stock Photo; **459** Bora/Alamy Stock Photo; **461** AMR NABIL/AP Images; **462** Album/ Oronoz/Superstock; **463** The Trustees of the British Museum/Art Resource, New York; **464** Mediacolor's/Alamy Stock Photo; **465** Yolanda Perera Sánchez/Historimages Collection/Alamy Stock Photo; **466** Lanmas/Alamy Stock Photo; **468** Neil Farrin/robertharding/Getty Images; **471T** Photo Researchers, Inc/Alamy Stock Photo; **471B** Pictures From History/Newscom; **472** G.Dagli Orti/Dea/Getty Images; **473** Sonia Halliday Photo Library/Alamy Stock Photo; **474** Zurijeta/ Shutterstock; **475** Jeremy Graham/dbimages/Alamy Stock Photo; **476** Jorg Hackemann/Shutterstock/Asset Library; **477** Alisa/Fotolia; **478** Pictures From History/Newscom; **479** Roland and Sabrina Michaud/ Akg Images; **480** ZUMA Press Inc/Alamy Stock Photo; **481** Pictures From History/Newscom; **484–485** Hung Chung Chih/Shutterstock; **487T** Pictures From History/Newscom; **487C** GL Archive/Alamy Stock Photo; **487BL** Pictures From History/Newscom; **487BR** Peter Horree/ Alamy Stock Photo; **488** JTB Media Creation, Inc./Alamy Stock Photo; **489** Pictures From History/Akg Images; **490** Jaturunp/iStock/Getty Images; **492** Pictures From History/Newscom; **494** World History Archive/Alamy Stock Photo; **495** Ma Hongjie/TAO Images Limited/ Alamy Stock Photo; **496** Li Xuejun/123RF.com; **498** Images & Stories/ Alamy Stock Photo; **500** GL Archive/Alamy Stock Photo; **503** North Wind Picture Archives/Alamy Stock Photo; **504** GL Archive/Alamy Stock Photo; **505** Superjoseph/Fotolia; **507** Chris Hellier/Alamy Stock Photo; **508** The Garden of Wang Chuan's Residence, after the Painting Style and Poetry of Wang Wei (701–761) (ink and colour on silk) (see also 105926), Qiu Ying (c.1495–1552)/Private Collection/Photo © Christie's Images/Bridgeman Art Library; **509** AGE Fotostock; **511** Guo Zhonghua/123RF.com; **513T** Mary Evans Picture Library/Alamy Stock Photo; **513B** Sanchai Loongroong/123RF.com; **514** ZUMA Press Inc/ Alamy Stock Photo; **515** Hiroshi Higuchi/Photographer's Choice/Getty Images; **516** Raga/Photolibrary/Getty Images; **518** Peter Horree/ Alamy Stock Photo; **519** Peter Horree/Alamy Stock Photo; **521L** Fike2308/Fotolia; **521R** Swisshippo/Fotolia; **522** Pictures From History/Newscom; **523** World History Archive/Alamy Stock Photo; **524** Fine Art Images Heritage Images/Newscom; **525** Peter Horree/Alamy Stock Photo; **527** Nichiren summoning the divine Shinpu wind to destroy the Mongol-Chinese fleet attacking Japan in 13th century (engraving), Kuniyoshi, Utagawa (1798–1861)/Private Collection/ Ancient Art and Architecture Collection Ltd./Bridgeman Art Library; **528** Pictures From History/Akg Images; **529** Pictures From History/ Newscom; **531** Wenn/Wenn Ltd/Alamy Stock Photo; **532L** Orpheus26/ Fotolia; **532R** Feiyuwzhangjie/123RF.com; **533** Pictures From History/ Newscom; **534** Pictures From History/Newscom; **535** SeanPavonePhoto/Fotolia; **536** Universal Images Group/Universal History Archive/Akg-Images; **538** Dallas and John Heaton/Travel Pictures/Alamy Stock Photo; **539** Maxim Tupikov/Shutterstock; **540** World History Archive/Alamy Stock Photo; **542** Cristaltran/Fotolia; **543** Siraanamwong/Fotolia. 546–547 Pyty/Shutterstock; **548** Zbiq/ Shutterstock; **549T** Gary718/Shutterstock; **549B** Album/Prisma/ Newscom; **549C** Werner Forman/Art Resource, New York; **550** Photo Researchers Inc/Alamy Stock Photo; **551** Gary718/Shutterstock; **552** Zbiq/Shutterstock; **554** Robert Wyatt/Alamy Stock Photo; **555T** AGE Fotostock; **555B** Werner Forman/Art Resource, New York; **556** Peter Horree/Alamy Stock Photo; **557** Jo Ann Snover/Shutterstock; **558** Peter Horree/Alamy Stock Photo; **560** DeAgostini/Superstock; **562** Universal Images Group North America LLC/Alamy Stock Photo; **564** Felix Lipov/Alamy Stock Photo; **565** Headdress (feather), Aztec/Museo Nacional de Antropologia, Mexico City, Mexico/Jean-Pierre Courau/ Bridgeman Images; **566** De Agostini Picture Library/Akg Images; **567** Wigbert Röth/imageBroker/Getty Images; **569** Emil von Maltitz/ Alamy Stock Photo; **570** Album/Prisma/Newscom; **571** Takepicsforfun/Fotolia; **572** Deco/Alamy Stock Photo; **573** Peter Groenendijk/Publisher Mix/Getty Images; **575** Tom Till/Alamy Stock Photo; **576** Pedrosala/Shutterstock; **578** Lebrecht Music and Arts Photo Library/Alamy Stock Photo; **579** Gunter Marx/Alamy Stock Photo; **581** Print Collector/Hulton Archive/Getty Images; **584–585** Ivern Photo/Age Fotostock/Alamy Stock Photo; **586** André Held/Akg Images; **587T** Abraham Cresques/Getty Images; **587C** Lanmas/Alamy Stock Photo; **587BL** Piccaya/Fotolia; **587BR** J.D. Dallet/age fotostock/

Alamy Stock Photo; **588** Bruno Morandi/robertharding/Alamy Stock Photo; **589** Jan Wlodarczyk/Alamy Stock Photo; **591** Bruno Morandi/ robertharding/Alamy Stock Photo; **592** Werner Forman Archive/ Heritage Image Partnership Ltd/Alamy Stock Photo; **593** Greenshoots Communications/Alamy Stock Photo; **594** Archivio World 1/Alamy Stock Photo; **595** Piccaya/Fotolia; **597** Abraham Cresques/Getty Images; **598** Abraham Cresques/Getty Images; **600** Sébastien Cailleux Corbis Historical/Getty Images; **601** Lanmas/Alamy Stock Photo; **603** Paul Springett B/Alamy Stock Photo; **605** J.D. Dallet/Age Fotostock/ Alamy Stock Photo; **606** Jeremy Graham/dbimages/Alamy Stock Photo; **607** DEGAS Jean-Pierre/hemis.fr/Alamy Stock Photo; **609** Rachel Carbonell/Alamy Stock Photo; **610** André Held/Akg Images; **611** Michael Macintyre/Eye Ubiquitous/Alamy Stock Photo; **612** Bruno Morandi/Robertharding/Alamy Stock Photo; **613** Werner Forman Archive/Heritage Image Partnership Ltd/Alamy Stock Photo; **616–617** KavalenkavaVolha/Fotolia; **619T** B.A.E. Inc./Alamy Stock Photo; **619C** Prisma Archivo/Alamy Stock Photo; **619BL** Sheila Terry/Science Source; **619BR** Age Fotostock/Pixtal/Alamy Stock Photo; **620** Dja65/ Shutterstock; **621** Rabatti-Domingie/AKG Images; **623** World History Archive/Alamy Stock Photo; **624** Adam Eastland/Alamy Stock Photo; **626** Wjarek/Shutterstock; **627** Photos 12/Alamy Stock Photo; **628** Prisma Archivo/Alamy Stock Photo; **629** Mondadori Portfolio/Hulton Fine Art Collection/Getty Images; **630TL** Scala/Art Resource, New York; **630TR** Active Museum/Alamy Stock Photo; **630B** Mondadori Portfolio/Hulton Fine Art Collection/Getty Images; **631** B.A.E. Inc./ Alamy Stock Photo; **632** Pandapaw/Shutterstock; **633** Jonathan Littlejohn/Alamy Stock Photo; **634** Franz Marc Frei/LOOK Die Bildagentur der Fotografen GmbH/Alamy Stock Photo; **635** Ken Welsh/Getty Images; **636** Fine Art Images/Heritage Image/AGE Fotostock; **637** Prisma/UIG/Getty Images; **638** Prisma Archivo/Alamy Stock Photo; **640** Three Suns and Book Burning, published in the Nuremberg Chronicle, 1493 (woodcut), German School, (15th century)/Private Collection/Prismatic Pictures/Bridgeman Art Library; **641** Akg Images/The Image Works; **642** Dominican Friar Johann Tetzel handing out indulgences for money (Luther preached against him) (chromolitho), German School, (19th century)/Private Collection/© Look and Learn/Bridgeman Art Library; **643** Prisma Archivo/Alamy Stock Photo; **644L** Pictorial Press Ltd/Alamy Stock Photo; **644C** Prisma Archivo/Alamy Stock Photo; **644R** Akg Images; **645** Album/Prisma/Superstock; **646** GODONG/Fred de Noyelle/ Universal Images Group/Akg Images; **647** Akg Images/Newscom; **648** 2d Alan King/Alamy Stock Photo; **649** North Wind Picture Archives/ Alamy Stock Photo; **651** Lebrecht/Lebrecht Music and Arts Photo Library/Alamy Stock Photo; **653** Science Source; **655** Fine Art Images/ Heritage Image Partnership Ltd/Alamy Stock Photo; **656** Godong/ Alamy Stock Photo; **657** Jean-Leon Huens/National Geographic Creative/Alamy Stock Photo; **658** Erich Lessing/Art Resource, New York; **659** Dario photography/Alamy Stock Photo; **660** Age Fotostock/ Alamy Stock Photo; **662** World History Archive/Alamy Stock Photo. 666–667 Fototeca Gilardi/Akg Images; **668** Deborahatl/Fotolia; **669T** Bpk Bildagentur/Art Resource, New York; **669C** Interfoto/Travel/ Alamy Stock Photo; **669BL** JT Vintage/Glasshouse Images/Alamy Stock Photo; **669BR** Chronicle/Alamy Stock Photo; **670** Zoonar/ Michael Rosskothen/Zoonar GmbH/Alamy Stock Photo; **671** Ms Fr 2810 f.84v, Pepper Harvest in Coilum, Southern India, illustration from the 'Livre des Merveilles du Monde', c.1410–12 (tempera on vellum), Boucicaut Master, (fl.1390–1430) (and workshop)/ Bibliotheque Nationale, Paris, France/Archives Charmet/Bridgeman Art Library; **672** Onfilm/E+/Getty Images; **673T** Cro Magnon/Alamy Stock Photo; **673B** Akg Images/Newscom; **674** Bpk Bildagentur/Art Resource, New York; **676** Paris Pierce/Alamy Stock Photo; **678** North Wind Picture Archives/Alamy Stock Photo; **679** Vasco da Gama's Ships Rounding the Cape (gouache on paper), English School, (20th century)/Private Collection/Look and Learn/Bridgeman Art Library; **680** Bildarchiv Steffens/Henri Stierlin/Diego Rivera/akg-images; **681** Prisma Archivo/Alamy Stock Photo; **682** Interfoto/Travel/Alamy Stock Photo; **685** Jag Images/Cultura Creative (RF)/Alamy Stock Photo; **687** James Schwabel/Alamy Stock Photo; **688** Nik wheeler/Alamy Stock Photo; **689T** Classic Vision/Age Fotostock/SuperStock; **689B** North Wind Picture Archives/Alamy Stock Photo; **690** Scala/Art Resource, New York; **691** Tono Labra/Age Fotostock/Alamy Stock Photo; **692** North Wind Picture Archives/Alamy Stock Photo; **693** DEA/A. C. COOPER/Getty Images; **696** Stock Montage, Inc./Alamy Stock Photo; **698** Indonesia/Netherlands The East India Company shipyard on

Onrust Island near Batavia (Jakarta), attributed to Adam Storck, 1699, Storck, Abraham (1644–1708) (attr. to)/Pictures from History/Woodbury & Page/Bridgeman Art Library; **699** North Wind Picture Archives/Alamy Stock Photo; **700** Theodore De Bry/Getty Images; **702** North Wind Picture Archives/Alamy Stock Photo; **704** Universal History Archive/Getty Images; **705** Prisma Archivo/Alamy Stock Photo; **706** Insyszg/Fotolia; **708** JT Vintage/Glasshouse Images/Alamy Stock Photo; **709** DeAgostini/Superstock; **710** North Wind Picture Archives/Alamy Stock Photo; **711** Matt Purciel/Alamy Stock Photo; **712** Scala/White Images/Art Resource, New York; **714** Marmaduke St. John/Alamy Stock Photo; **715** Florilegius/Akg Images; **718** David Wall/Alamy Stock Photo; **719** Chronicle/Alamy Stock Photo; **720** Chronicle/Alamy Stock Photo; **721** Rupert Sagar-Musgrave/Alamy Stock Photo.

Text

Academy of Achievement Donald Johanson Interview, January 25, 1991. Copyright © Academy of Achievement. **Archaeological Institute of America** Was There a Trojan War, Vol 57, No. 03 by Manfred Korfmann. Copyright © 2004 by Archaeological Institute of America. **Archaeology Online** Harappan Horse: Polemics and Propaganda by Michael Witzel. Copyright © by Archaeology online. **Archaeology Online** The Horse and the Aryan Debate by Michel Danino. Copyright © by Archaeology online. **BBC** Death's Men by Dennis Winter. BBC. Copyright © 2014. **Beacon Press** The Broken Spears by Miguel Leon-Portilla. Copyright © 1962, 1990 by Miguel Leon-Portilla Expanded and Updated Edition © 1992 by Miguel Leon-Portilla. Reprinted by permission of Beacon Press, Boston. **C.A. Watts & Co., Ltd.** Man Makes Himself: Found in: The Human Venture: Readings in World History, Vol. 01 by V Gordon Childe. Published by C.A. Watts & Co, Copyright © 1951. **Cambridge University Press** Account of visit in 1324 to Cairo by the king of Mali, Mansa Musa. Published by Cambridge University Press. **Cambridge University Press** History of England, Volume 2 by Thomas Babington Macaulay. Published by Cambridge University Press, © 1953. **Cambridge University Press** African Civilizations by Abd al-Rahman al-Sadi and Graham Connah. Copyright © Cambridge University Press. **Cambridge University Press** Corpus of Early Arabic Sources for West African History Edited by Nehemia Levtzion and JFP Hopkins. Copyright © Cambridge University Press. **Cambrigde University Press** African Civilizations by Abd al-Rahman al-Sadi and Graham Connah. Copyright © Cambridge University Press. **Christian Liberty Press** Streams of Civilizations, Volume 2 by Garry J Moes. Published by Christian Liberty Press, Copyright © 1953. **Columbia University Press** Sources of Chinese Tradition, compiled by Wm. Theodore de Bary and Irene Bloom, 2nd ed., vol. 1 (New York: Columbia University Press, 1999), 704–705. Copyright © 1999 Columbia University Press. Reproduced with the permission of the publisher. All rights reserved. **France 24** France 24 by Leela Jacinto. Copyright © 2016 by France 24. Reprinted by permission. **Futurism, LLC** Astronauts May Face Long-Term Brain Damage as a Result of Space Travel by Jelor Gallego. Courtesy of Futurism.com. Reprinted by permission. **Harper Collins Publishers** Empire: How Spain Became a World Power by Henry Kamen. Copyright © by Harper Collins. **Harvard University Press** Xenophon in Seven Volumes by E. C. Marchant and G. W. Bowersock. Copyright © by Harvard University Press, 1925. **Institute of Islamic Knowledge** Quran 96:1–3. Copyright © The Institute for Islamic Knowledge. Used by permission. **Jewish Publication Society** Genesis 17:7. Reproduced from the Tanakh: The Holy Scriptures by Permission of the University of Nebraska Press. Copyright 1985 by The Jewish Publication Society. Reprinted by permission. **Jewish Publication Society** Psalms 43:1, 4 from Tanakh. The Holy Scriptures. Philadelphia: Jewish Publication Society. The Holy Scriptures. Copyright © 1985 by The Jewish Publication Society. Reprinted by permission. **Jewish Publication Society** Proverbs 3:31 from Tanakh. The Holy Scriptures. Philadelphia: Jewish Publication Society. The Holy Scriptures. Copyright © 1985 by The Jewish Publication Society. Reprinted by permission. **Jewish Publication Society** Jeremiah 23:23–24 from Tanakh. The Holy Scriptures. Philadelphia: Jewish Publication Society. The Holy Scriptures. Copyright © 1985 by The Jewish Publication Society. Reprinted by permission. **Jewish Publication Society** Psalms 43:1, 4 from Tanakh. The Holy Scriptures. Philadelphia: Jewish Publication Society. The Holy Scriptures. Copyright © 1985 by The Jewish Publication Society. Reprinted by permission. **Jewish Publication Society** Bible Hub, from Tanakh. The Holy Scriptures. Philadelphia: Jewish Publication Society. The Holy Scriptures. Copyright © 1985 by The Jewish Publication Society. Reprinted by permission. **Kreis, Steven** Steven Kreis From Chronicle by Jean de Venette. Copyright © by Steven Kreis. **Lockman Foundation** Matthew 5:1–12 Scripture quotations taken from the New American Standard Bible®, Copyright © 1960, 1962, 1963, 1968, 1971, 1972, 1973, 1975, 1977, 1995 by The Lockman Foundation (www.Lockman.org). **Lockman Foundation** Matthew 6: 25–34 Scripture quotations taken from the New American Standard Bible®, © 1960, 1962, 1963, 1968, 1971, 1972, 1973, 1975, 1977, 1995 by The Lockman Foundation Used by permission. (www.Lockman.org) **Marcus Wiener Publishers** Ibn Battuta in Black Africa by S Hamdun and N King. Published by Marcus Wiener Publishers, © 1998. **Medieval Academy of America** The Russian Primary Chronicle translated by Samuel Hazzard Cross and Olgred P. Sherbowitz-Wetzor. Copyright © Medieval Academy of America. **Ministry of Culture and Communication** The Cave of Chauvet-Point-D'Arc by Robert Begouen. Published by Ministry of Culture and Communication. **Munshiram Manoharlal Publishers** The Travels of Ibn Battuta by Ibn Battuta. Published by Munshiram Manoharlal Publishers, A.D. 1325–1354. **Natural History Magazine** This Old House by Ian Hodder. Published by Natural History Magazine. **Nature Publishing Group** Evolution, consequences and future of plant and animal domestication by Jared Diamond, August 8, 2002. Copyright © Nature Publishing. **New Advent** The Summa Theologica of St. Thomas Aquinas, Second and Revised Edition, 1920 Literally translated by Fathers of the English Dominican Province. Online Edition Copyright © 2016 by Kevin Knight. Reprinted by permission. **NRSV** Matthew 22:37–39. Copyright © NRSV Bible. **NRSV** Matthew 7:12. Copyright © NRSV Bible. **NRSV** Matthew 16:18–19. Copyright © NRSV Bible. **Office of the United Nations High Commissioner for Human Rights (OHCHR)** Press Release "UN rights experts urge France to protect fundamental freedoms while countering terrorism" from ohchr.org. January 19, 2016. Copyright © 2016 by The Office of the High Commissioner for Human Rights. **Oxford University Press** The Oxford History of Ancient Egypt Betsy M. Bryan. Copyright © Oxford University Press. **Oxford University Press** The Tale of Sinuhe and Other Ancient Egyptian Poems, 1940–1640 B.C Translated by R B Parkinson. Copyright © 1997 by Oxford University Press. **Pearson Education, UK** Pearson Education, UK Sundiata: An Epic of Old Mali by D.T. Niane. Copyright © 1965 fourth reprint 1970 by Pearson Education Ltd. Used with permission of Pearson Education. All rights reserved. **Presence Africaine** Sundiata: An Epic Of Old Mali by D.T. Niane. Copyright © Presence Africaine Editions. Reprinted with Permission. **Psychology Press & Routledge** Travels in Asia and Africa, 1325–1354 by Ibn Battuta. Published by Psychology Press, Copyright © 2004. **Random House, Inc.** Bhagavad-Gita - Barbara Stoler. Copyright © by Random House, Inc. **Routledge** Travels in Asia and Africa, 1325–1354 by Ibn Battuta. Translated by Sir Hamilton Alexander Rosskeen Gibb. Copyright © Routledge Publishing. **Square Fish Publishers** The Cow-Tail Switch and other West African Stories by Harold Courlander and George Herzog. Published by Square Fish Publishers Copyright © 2008. **The Chinese University of Hong Kong** The Records of the Grand Historian by Sima Qian. Published by The Chinese University of Hong Kong. **The Economist** Opposition's Opening Remarks by Jim Harper. Copyright © by The Economist. **The Heritage Foundation** The Heritage Foundation by Evan Bernick. Copyright © 2010 by The Heritage Foundation. **The Mars Society** The Founding Declaration by the Mars Society. Copyright © 1998 by The Mars Society. Reprinted by permission. **University of Iowa Press** The Book of Korean Poetry: Songs of Shilla and Koryo Translated by Kevin O'Rourke. Copyright © 2006 by University of Iowa Press. Reprinted by permission. **University of Oklahoma Press** Popol Vuh: Sacred Book of the Ancient Quiché Maya by Delia Goetz and Sylvanus G Morley translated by Adrián Recinos. Published by University of Oklahoma Press © 1991. **University of Pennsylvania Press** Description of Sicily, in Medieval Italy by Ibn Jubayr translated by Katherine L Jansen, Joanna Drell and Frances Andrews. Copyright © University of Pennsylvania Press.